COMPUTATIONAL ECONOMETRICS: ITS IMPACT ON THE DEVELOPMENT OF QUANTITATIVE ECONOMICS

Computational Econometrics: Its Impact on the Development of Quantitative Economics

Edited by

Charles G. Renfro

New York, USA

IOS Press

Amsterdam • Berlin • Oxford • Tokyo • Washington, DC

ISBN 1 58603 426 X
Library of Congress Control Number: 2004107151

Publisher
IOS Press
Nieuwe Hemweg 6B
1013 BG Amsterdam
The Netherlands
fax: +31 20 620 3419
e-mail: order@iospress.nl

Distributor in the UK and Ireland
IOS Press/Lavis Marketing
73 Lime Walk
Headington
Oxford OX3 7AD
England
fax: +44 1865 75 0079

Distributor in the USA and Canada
IOS Press, Inc.
5795-G Burke Centre Parkway
Burke, VA 22015
USA
fax: +1 703 323 3668
e-mail: iosbooks@iospress.com

PRINTED IN THE NETHERLANDS

Contents

Journal of Economic and Social Measurement 29 (2004) 1–7
IOS Press

Preface

Charles G. Renfro
601 West 113th Street, #12G, New York, NY 10025, USA
E-mail: cgrenfro@modler.com

This is the second preface that has been written for this special volume on econometric software and its evaluation. The first also started out in the same way to be a short introductory piece, intended to describe the various articles that appear in order to provide you, the reader, with some indication of where each fits into the overall scheme of things. As an opening gambit, it seemed reasonable to begin that introduction by making a few remarks on the early history of the development of this type of software, which has commonly been thought to have been rooted in the efforts of a small band of people sometime in the mid-1960s, although it has long been known that Houthakker, Klein, and Leontief began to use the computer in some way in the late 1940s and early 1950s – but apart from such vague notions, there were mists swirling about. Therefore, having pieced together two or three paragraphs essentially based on personal recollection and some gleanings from articles by Klein, Leontief and others, I sent these out to a dozen or so econometricians, using of course email. Almost immediately, I was startled to find in my inbox something on the order of 25 responses, for of course nearly everyone who has ever created an econometric software package is still alive and the bush telegraph quickly spread the word.

That original introduction in expanded form is now the first article in this volume [10]. It contains a substantial amount of detail about the broad history of the development of econometric software based on the personal recollections of many people. Although I take responsibility for all errors made and all opinions stated that are not enclosed in quotation marks, the article as it stands is the direct result of the patience and cooperation of these people, most of whom have been kind enough to read multiple versions, as the article has steadily grown in size, and to provide a steady stream of information, comments, and suggestions. Moreover, it now represents a diligent effort on the part of all these people to track down information on the history of econometric software development worldwide. Although no doubt still incomplete, for not everyone who has played a part could be tracked down and interrogated under a bare light bulb, the article nevertheless provides, both in its text and its references, enough information that a later generation might be able to make use of it, together with other materials, to actually write a history that puts all this into the proper perspective.

Of course, you may be saying to yourself, why a history of econometric software? And why now? The short answer to these questions is that for economists the computer has increasingly become the primary applied research tool, and it is software that makes the computer work. Moreover, it matters that this software should be the best that it can be, for not only does it permit necessary calculations to be performed but it also determines, for better or worse over time, how easy or how difficult the applied research process will be for each succeeding generation of economists. This assertion assumes of course the availability of the necessary data, and that observations can be obtained relatively easily – but in the day of the Internet, data distribution is also a matter of software. And, in addition, there is the consideration that both the quality and the amount of possible research, as a matter of time spent, may be crucially dependent on just how good that software is, both in its computational properties and as a time saver. All these considerations argue for greater attention being paid to the process of the development of such software, particularly inasmuch as – unlike disciplines such as physics, which have been able over the years to attract substantial funding for the development of research tools – economics is a shoestring activity. We are not blest with major research centers supporting research software development, economists are relatively few in number, and, at the same time, we all wish to obtain software cheaply. These are not circumstances that on their own will naturally lead to the development of more and better software.

In any case, once the word got out about this special volume, the information streaming in from around the world began to fill a sizeable portion of a backup CD-Rom. Furthermore, it soon became clear that there was no point in simply citing quantities of unpublished material. There were too many good stories to tell, not only amusing ones about card decks being run over by delivery trucks or eggs being cooked on the top of the central processing unit of the first operative stored-program computer, but also revealing descriptions of computer-based research that illustrate the role of the computer in the progress of econometric theory and economic research. Consequently, it seemed a very good idea to encourage a number of people to expand their emails into short pieces that describe some of this work. As the second "article," you will find what is in fact a group of short articles, under the rubric *Some Milestones in Econometric Computing*, that together describe aspects of the development of econometric software, starting from the hand calculation era and continuing to relatively modern times. Complementing these, at the end of this issue is a piece entitled *A Compendium of existing econometric software packages*, which brings together descriptions of currently available econometric software packages, in order to provide a statement of where we are now. In almost all cases, these descriptions have been provided by the developers of the individual packages. The exception to this rule is the description of certain software packages that have an historical importance but are no longer supported.

The articles following the Milestones section essentially consist of two types, the first being those that consider characteristics of the computing environment and the second a group focused on the evaluation of econometric software. In the first category, the article by Houston Stokes [12] considers in some detail a number of aspects of the design of econometric software. As Stokes points out, at the beginning of its use by economists the computer was seen simply as an enhancement of hand methods of computing – of the electromechanical desktop calculator in particular – with the then-prevailing sense of the computer being simply that it was a faster way to do what had been done before. However, in recent years especially, with the development of the Internet, the computer has taken on a persona quite different than that of just being fast.

In fact, the Internet is only part of the story. For example, consider word processing: the capability to edit a printed document once it has been created and then simply reprint it is another order of ease of use – as compared to the need, as recently as the late 1970s, to retype entire documents repeatedly as successive changes were made, including (memorably for many people) doctoral dissertations. Other such examples come easily to mind: whereas once an economists might "program the computer," implying essentially making the computer perform a specific set of calculations, today increasingly programs are *designed*, with consideration equally given to the user interface and the process of managing the data used internally, making a variety of the calculations, and then providing an intelligible display of the final results. A number of the facilities that now exist to support software design, as well as the improvement in operating systems and architectural issues associated with various design configurations, are considered in the Stokes paper.

Marc Nerlove [8], in contrast, focuses on the characteristics of programming languages, as these have developed since the early 1950s. The native language of a computer – namely, machine language – is a set of primitive operations that may, for example, simply copy a number from one memory location to another or perform a specific, simple arithmetic operation that today is normally built into the hardware of the central processing unit. The order in which these primitive operations are performed is what determines the work done, inasmuch as complex procedures can be created by combining simple operations in a specific order. Originally, computers needed to be programmed at this primitive level. However, since 1956, with the development of Fortran and subsequently other higher level programming languages, it has increasingly become possible for people to program computers in a way that, although still formalized in style, is nonetheless closer to a "natural" language, each of the statements of which are more content-rich from a human perspective. This evolution of programming languages has in turn set the stage for the development of a generally free-format human-computer interface that has permitted the development of econometric modeling languages, in the 1970s, and econometric programming languages during the 1980s and 1990s, in addition to providing the modern Graphical User Interface (GUI).

In contrast to the papers just mentioned, the next four are much more directly focused on the evaluation of the characteristics of specific econometric software packages. Since 1997, when papers by Bruce McCullough [3] and Charles Renfro [9] separately appeared that each noted and deplored the general absence of the numeric evaluation of econometric software – as opposed to scores of reviews that simply described the offerings and other surface characteristics of such software – there has been a series of papers, beginning with one in this journal in 1998 [4] and another by McCullough and Vinod [5] in the *Journal of Economic Literature* in 1999, that have begun to redress the balance. The latest is to be found in the June 2003 issue of the *American Economic Review* [7]. McCullough has been particularly prominent in both advocating the need for numeric evaluation and leading the charge. In this issue, McCullough [6] in this leading role considers a set of tests originally developed by Leland Wilkinson in the context of more general statistical packages and applies these to number of econometric software packages. The McCullough paper presents important results that need to be carefully considered by econometric software developers, but this paper also raises some general issues concerning both program design and the scope of evaluative tests. In particular, given the inherent imprecision of most economic data, there is, for example, a question whether memory space should be devoted to high precision storage (as opposed to calculation in high precision) simply to insure that a package pass a particular set of tests. It is also open for debate whether tests should be created specifically for econometric software packages, or if it is useful to import them from other, albeit closely related, disciplines.

The next paper by Giuseppe Bruno and Riccardo De Bonis [1] considers existing packages that permit the estimation of panel data. Beyond its specific findings, this paper raises a number of general evaluative issues that need further consideration. From the outset, Bruno and De Bonis encountered a common evaluative problem, which is the absence of a readily available benchmark. One of the effects of this problem is that it prevents a tester from determining more than that the same results can, or cannot, be obtained for two or more packages. Obviously, if the same results can be obtained, the finding would appear to create confidence in the packages' accuracy. If they cannot be, such findings at least flag a need to discover why. But, of course, in the first case, the inference crucially depends upon a presumption that the packages are independently developed, a presumption that itself needs to be examined, inasmuch as a number of econometric software packages contain essentially similar, if not identical code. It may or may not be widely known, but a number of the programs that date from the late 1970s or before involve some sharing of code, usually Fortran code. More recently, as packages have been written or re-written in C, C++ and other languages, the degree of development independence may have increased, but even this is not certain, for there are a number of published listings that are available, dating from even the 1990s, that have no doubt been used to create ostensibly different packages – not to mention the widespread existence of various machine-language code libraries.

There is in fact a general need for the much wider development of benchmark results, and not only to support independent evaluation. The benefit of the development of benchmarks also extends to the support provided to developers during software development. In the absence of the availability of such benchmarks, a developer not only needs to create the code, but also various numeric tests of that code, thus extending the required development time. In addition, it is also true that any test by a developer may be too closely related to the code developed, and thus not necessarily provide the equivalent of a well-founded independent test. Ideally, upon first public release of a software package, it already should have been tested intensively. Independent testing should simply confirm numeric accuracy, not expose inaccuracies. Such an ideal is ideal, but it is too much to expect its achievement in practice. However, if there were to be an increase in the number of available benchmarks, it is likely that both developers and evaluators would take advantage of this, leading to at least closer conformity between reality and the ideal.

The next paper, another by Houston Stokes [11], sheds additional light upon the several matters just discussed. This paper also considers the evaluation of two or more programs together, but from the point of view of a developer. A particularly interesting aspect of this paper is that it demonstrates, among other things, that as a developer it pays to look carefully at results, as well as to approach any particular estimation problem from more than one direction, as the title of his paper implies. The most significant finding is that the properties of estimators can critically depend upon the context in which they are applied, and that routine applications may be as likely to involve inherent computational problems as those of greater ostensible complexity. This paper furthermore demonstrates the importance, after the fact, of a full reporting of computational details as a part of any description of applied research – at least to the degree of identifying at the absolute minimum the software used, including also the platform and version used. Moreover, the paper additionally demonstrates that the careful documentation of a developer's own package can be self-educational.

The final evaluative paper of this volume is that by Ric Herbert, which considers the use of the widely used MATLAB package in a somewhat broader setting than econometrics as normally defined. The Herbert paper does not evaluate the numeric characteristics of this program, particularly issues of numeric accuracy, so much as consider aspects of the applicability of packages like this to economic modeling, to include the use of control theoretic techniques. MATLAB is an example of a specialized programming language that, as Herbert points out, fits "between the conventional programming languages (such as C++ and Java) and the higher level applications packages." As described in the Renfro paper [10], during the past 15 years or so, several programs have appeared that have the characteristics of high level programming languages. These in principle permit their users to exercise greater control over the results obtained, at the cost of taking on more of a programmers role. MATLAB is a member of a class of these packages, which generally do not support parameter estimation – particularly the variety of econometric methods, yet permit the construction and use of models. Inasmuch as parameters can be estimated in one package and the estimated equations then transferred to a package such as MATLAB, there is clearly a use overlap between this program and econometric software.

Apart of the software compendium mentioned earlier, the last paper in this volume is one by Tim Harrison and Charles Renfro [2], which considers data transfer protocols, both those that have been used widely for many years and two that are now proposed as extensions in order to meet future needs. In the early 1980s, Harrison, Renfro and others developed the TSD (Time Series Data) transfer format, originally in order to transfer time series data and associated documentation between the AREMOS and MODLER packages, but also between the mainframe and microcomputer versions of AREMOS. The underlying concept was that economic data series consist not only of observations, but also certain properties that include some sort of identifying name, an observational frequency and a particular date range of availability, at minimum. In addition, ideally, in order for a potential or actual user to understand exactly what the numbers refer to in particular case, additional information is needed, including a short written description, an indication of the original source, the units of measurement, and other such associated documentation. The TSD protocol permits the rapid and efficient transfer of documented time series data and slowly its use has become progressively more widespread. The format is now supported by such data vendors as Economy.Com, Global Insight (the merger of Chase Econometric Associates, Data Resources, and Wharton Econometric Forecasting Associates, all of which previously used it) and Haver Analytics, among others. It is also supported by a number of econometric software packages, as can be seen from the software Compendium. However, the Harrison-Renfro paper now proposes certain extensions to this protocol, including an XML version that permits the extended protocol to be better utilized in the context of the Internet.

This special volume has steadily grown in size during the past six to eight months, to the point that it now forms an entire volume. Notwithstanding, it is not intended to be, in any sense, the final word on the subject of econometric software and its evaluation, but rather only a first contribution to what could be a steadily wider and deeper investigation of this topic over time. The *Journal of Economic and Social Measurement* stands ready to consider for publication additional scholarly articles of the types just described. It stands ready to consider unreservedly articles that take issue with opinions expressed in the articles in this special volume, or that seek to provide a more accurate or more comprehensive historical statement concerning the design or development of econometric software, or the impact of that development on econometric theory or practice. Moreover, such contributions need not be restricted to econometric software as defined in this special volume. This journal today, as it has been the past 30 years, is dedicated to the investigation of all aspects of social and economic measurement and generally seeks to complement and broaden the subject focus of the disciplinary journals in order to encourage and support empirical research.

References

[1] G. Bruno and R. De Bonis, A comparative study of alternative econometric packages with an application to Italian deposit interest rates, *Journal of Economic and Social Measurement* **29** (2004), 271–295, this volume.

[2] T. Harrison and C.G. Renfro, TSX and TSE: A proposal for an extended time series data interchange and transfer format, *Journal of Economic and Social Measurement* **29** (2004), 339–358, this volume.

[3] B.D. McCullough, A review of RATS v4.2: Benchmarking numeric accuracy, *Journal of Applied Econometrics* **12** (1997), 181–190.

[4] B.D. McCullough and C.G. Renfro, Benchmarks and software standards: a case study of GARCH procedures, *Journal of Economic and Social Measurement* **25** (1998), 59–71.
[5] B.D. McCullough and H.D. Vinod, The numerical reliability of econometric software, *Journal of Economic Literature* **37**(2) (1999), 633–665.
[6] B.D. McCullough, Wilkinson's tests and econometric software, *Journal of Economic and Social Measurement* **29** (2004), 261–270, this volume.
[7] B.D. McCullough and H.D. Vinod, Verifying the solution from a nonlinear solver: a case study, *American Economic Review* **93**(3) (2003), 873–892.
[8] M. Nerlove, Programming languages: A short history for economists, *Journal of Economic and Social Measurement* **29** (2004), 189–203, this volume.
[9] C.G. Renfro, Normative Considerations in the development of a software package for econometric estimation, *Journal of Economic and Social Measurement* **23**(4) (1997), 277–330.
[10] C.G. Renfro, Econometric software: The first fifty years in perspective, *Journal of Economic and Social Measurement* **29** (2004), 9–107, this volume.
[11] H.H. Stokes, On the advantage of using two or more econometric software systems to solve the same problem, *Journal of Economic and Social Measurement* **29** (2004), 307–320, this volume.
[12] H.H. Stokes, The evolution of econometric software design: A developer's view, *Journal of Economic and Social Measurement* **29** (2004), 205–259, this volume.

Journal of Economic and Social Measurement 29 (2004) 9–107
IOS Press

Econometric software: The first fifty years in perspective*

Charles G. Renfro
601 West 113th Street, #12G, New York, NY 10025, USA
E-mail: cgrenfro@modler.com

This paper introduces a special volume of the Journal of Economic and Social Measurement on the development and evaluation of computer software for econometric applications. It describes at least certain aspects of the history of the development of this software during the past approximately 50 years, beginning with the first use of the programmable electronic computer by economists in the early 1950s. It considers the various types of software developed, ranging from packages that permit the user to select from a particular set of options, to those that form essentially an econometric modeling language, to those that offer econometric programming capabilities, potentially allowing the individual specification of the characteristics and properties of the operations performed. This paper provides a relatively extensive list of references and is supplemented by a separate compendium of existing econometric software packages.

1. Introduction

When we look at an acorn, it is difficult to imagine the tree that it might become. In 1933, in his introduction to the first issue of Econometrica, Ragnar Frisch famously characterized econometrics as

> by no means the same as economic statistics. Nor is it identical with what we call general economic theory, although a considerable portion of this theory has a definitely quantitative character. Nor should econometrics be taken as

*The historical development of econometric software occurred sufficiently recently in the past that most of the developers are still alive. This article benefits both from correspondence with a number of them and from having been circulated widely and from the comments received. I am particularly grateful to Gerry Adams, Terry Barker, David Belsley, Jon Breslaw, Allin Cottrell, Clint Cummins, Kenneth Berk, Tom Doan, Jurgen Doornik, James Davidson, Mark Eisner, Ray Fair, Bruno Giuseppe, Arthur Goldberger, Richard Goldstein, William Greene, Bronwyn Hall, Robert Hall, Stephen Hall, Tim Harrison, David Hendry, Peter Hollinger, Charles C. Holt, Howard Howe, Lawrence Klein, Robert Lacey, Cynthia Latta, Edward Leamer, David Lilien, James MacKinnon, Keith May, the late Michael McCarthy, Michael McCracken, Bruce McCullough, Marc Nerlove, Ray O'Brien, William Peterson, Peter Phillips, Richard Pierse, Robert Pindyck, David Reilly, Colin Rose, George Schink, Ronald Schoenberg, Lucy Slater, Richard Startz, Houston Stokes, Daniel Suits, William Teeters, Kenneth White, Mike Wickens, Vince Wiggins, Mark Wiley, Clifford Wymer, Michael Young, and Arnold Zellner for their patient willingness to assist me. This account should nonetheless be regarded as a memoir, rather than history, both because it is written by an actor in the process, and because there are no doubt others who have developed such software and whose contributions are not recognized here. I am wholly responsible for all errors of fact and omissions, and for the opinions stated.

> synonymous with the application of mathematics to economics. Experience has shown that each of these three view-points, that of statistics, economic theory, and mathematics, is a necessary, but not by itself sufficient, condition for a real understanding of the quantitative relations in modern economic life. It is the unification of all three that is powerful. And it is this unification that constitutes econometrics.

This depiction does not provide an accurate prediction of the subsequent development of this subject. In particular, whereas there has been intensive focus over the years on the properties of parameter estimators and much work done to frame parameter-related hypotheses tests, there has not been nearly the same degree of attention paid to "this unification." Quantitative economics, as the broader area is often termed today, includes a number of topics, such as index numbers, activity analysis, and economic measurement generally, that are seldom addressed in any modern econometrics textbook. The techniques of experimental economics are similarly ignored, and the orientation of econometrics implicitly remains the estimation of parameters using time series data, even if there is nowadays increasingly consideration of panel data and related statistical techniques. On a purely nominal level, it can of course be argued that to call the broader range of topics Quantitative Economics and the narrower issue of parameter estimation Econometrics is simply semantics, but it is hard to argue that during the next 70 years econometrics should not further evolve.

To a degree, the present state of econometrics reflects the research tools historically at the disposal of economists, including both the availability of data and the computer. However, the issue is not just when the computer began to be used in applied economic research, but rather when it became ubiquitous. Although "born" in the 1940s and used first by economists during the early 1950s [174], as a general phenomenon the programmable electronic computer became an economic research tool only during the 1960s.[1] A major part of this use was to support the creation of macroeconometric models, obviously reflecting the scope and funding of such projects. Computing

[1] There are a variety of reasons that 1960 is more or less the date at which the mainframe computer began to be used widely, but not the least of them is the fact that the first "transistorized" computers, the so-called second generation, such as the IBM 7090/7094, were only then becoming generally available, followed by other machines that began to be used later during this decade, such as the Atlas, the CDC 1604, the IBM 1620, and the IBM 1130. A number of technical developments also occurred at this point. For example, initially in late 1959, the 7090 incorporated an oil-cooled memory system, which was somewhat unreliable, and was replaced by air-cooled memory in 1960. In addition, in 1962–1963, IBM introduced the 7040 and 7044 computers, similar to the 7090, but offering somewhat less performance at a much lower price. In the UK, the development of the Atlas introduced so-called "single level storage," which today is usually called "virtual" storage and conceptually permitted the "virtual machine," allowing each programmer to treat the whole of RAM as if available to him or her alone. In short, 1960 essentially marks the point at which mainframe computers began to be both reliable and affordable (for universities and other organizations, that is) and to provide features that supported progressively more interesting software development, leading to greater adoption. For details of the various hardware innovations at this time, in the context of an historical survey, see for instance Rosen [291].

required first the creation of software, and even more generally involved a steep learning curve, not to mention access to a computer. Robert Hall remembers that when he arrived at MIT in 1964, "there was an IBM 1620 in the basement of the Sloan Building, but no usable econometric software" [142]. To Hall, who by the spring of 1965 had developed his first program, this lack was a challenge. Similarly, in the early 1960s at the University of Wisconsin, Arnold Zellner and Arthur Stroud created programs to implement Seemingly Unrelated Regression Estimates and Two and Three Stage Least Squares as a by product of the development of these concepts [354–356].[2] At the London School of Economics, Mike Wickens submitted as his M.Sc. thesis in 1964 a Fortran program based on James Durbin's FIML algorithm [83] that, among other things, utilized Newton-Raphson convergence and demonstrated that the second iteration of the process generated Three Stage Least Squares estimates [346].[3] In April 1965, Michael McCracken's DATABANK system was in operation on a CDC 1604 at Southern Methodist University [216]. At about this time, in Auckland, New Zealand, a succession of Rex Bergstrom's graduate students began to create linear and nonlinear, single-equation and system estimator regression programs on another IBM 1620 and later an IBM 1130 [265,266]. But these are exceptional cases. Large research projects were best able to incorporate and support such activity, inasmuch as even until the mid to late 1980s any project with computational complexity involved considerable time and effort, apart from conceptual design issues. Contemporaneous descriptions of model building projects undertaken during the 1960s and well into the 1970s commonly presented this process as necessarily involving 10 to 15 economists and research assistants for time periods of as much as a year or more, in order to construct a model of 100 to 200 or more equations [188,219]. In the 1960s and 1970s, the reasons for such resource requirements included the lack of easily accessible data as well as adequate computing facilities. Even in the case of the Brookings Model, a major National Science Foundation-funded project, at Brookings it was only in 1969–1970 that a regression program was created that combined an online database with a regression package in such a way as to permit time series to be retrieved, transformed if necessary, and then included in a regression as an integrated process [277,289]. At that time, almost universally, large card decks, combining both code and data, were fed into often temperamental card reader machines hardwired to the computer in its air conditioned "glass house" [28,215], although in some cases paper tapes and paper tape readers were used instead, most notably in the UK.

Particularly in retrospect, the impediments are obvious and only slowly dissipated. In the late 1970s, shortly after the birth of the microcomputer, users of mainframe

[2] Art Stroud and others also created other programs at Wisconsin during this period, such as RGR, a regression program [125,327]. These, however, did not introduce new econometric methods, but were interesting for other aspects, as is described later.

[3] Prior to the submission of this thesis, Wickens and Durbin jointly gave a seminar at the LSE to present the theory and results. The program was subsequently used to estimate Rex Bergstrom's model. See also Hausman [145], which this work in part anticipates.

computers normally had access to less than 640K of Random Access Memory (RAM). And throughout those years, more often than not, it continued to be necessary to keypunch the data from printed documents. Whereas by late 1982 or early 1983 the microcomputer potentially provided the individual user a full 640K of RAM, drawing abreast of if not surpassing many mainframes in this respect, it is only much more recently, during the past ten years, that economic data have become widely available in machine-readable form and, in particular, easily downloaded from the Internet. It is only since the mid 1980s that it has been generally possible for someone working alone, with a personal computer and a data base, to construct and solve a large-scale econometric model within a short time period [284].[4] Milton Friedman has described the process of computing regression parameters for a single equation as taking essentially an entire day in the late 1940s [112]. Writing in 1960, Klein provided a similar time estimate, when he said, "Ten or fifteen years ago, the greatest single obstacle to the application of the newly proposed methods of estimation was the heavy computational burden. Single equation methods of correlation analysis had been developed to the point where an individual human computer could cope with practically any problem arising in econometrics. In a matter of weeks, allowing for much experimental calculation, a large system of 10, 20, or even more equations could be estimated by single-equation methods. Many such systems have, in fact, been estimated" [174, p. 868]. Ronald Bodkin [28] more recently describes the early 1960s as the beginning of the time that one could look forward to estimating an equation's parameters in less than hour, taking into account related variable transformations. But the issue is actually not the time of computation: by 1968, it took less than a minute in many if not most cases to make this calculation, but the circumstance that mainframes were then shared facilities meant that it might take as much as 1–8 hours or more for the results to be distributed by the computer operator to the individual user. As a consistent experience, it was not until 1985, or even later, that the average user of a computer could expect to run a regression and obtain the results in less than a minute. Today, in contrast, with certain specific exceptions [75], few tasks performed by an econometrician need take more than a few seconds, even the solution of econometric models numbering in the hundreds of equations.

However, this description does not entirely convey the essential characteristic of the microcomputer revolution of the past 25 years, which is the degree of replication it permits. Prior to 1980, mainframe computers were located in many places around the world and some of these could be accessed from a dial-up telephone link from virtually anywhere, providing in principle worldwide use – but in practice comparatively

[4] The issue here of course is the general possibility and the amount of time and skills required. There are a number of examples of econometricians essentially working alone to build and solve large econometric models earlier than this, taking on the roles of model builder, programmer, and data key puncher, among the various activities, but this work was akin to that of the early trans-Appalachian pioneers, alone chopping trees, clearing fields of stones and stumps, and only then planting the first crop. See, for example, the several books by Fair for glimpses of one of these pioneers at work [94,97].

restricted access. The significance of the advent of the personal computer is that for the first time it became commonplace to transfer copies of software, data sets, and even multi-equation models from one computer to another, thus allowing the creation of a true worldwide community of users. As early as 1970, or even before, it was possible to move a model from one machine to another, but not easily; often this involved considerable additional programming and was a rare event. The truth is, other than Klein Model I, very few econometric models were ever mounted on more than a single computer prior to 1984 [284]. The modern ability to share easily both large and small data sets and large and small models across many machines constitutes a major breakthrough, yet one that so far has been only partially realized.

Surprising as it sometimes seems to those who have spent years working with computers, we are still in the early days of econometric computing. The first development of software was essentially an outgrowth of the local needs of particular research projects. During the period prior to 1985, there was in any case little scope to develop for a numerous user population, so that such development as occurred reflected largely own-consumption interests. Sophisticated programs were created that can be regarded as intellectual contributions in their own right, and in particular cases the development of software can be seen as embodying specific econometric methodologies, either implicitly or explicitly [149, Chapter 19; 156]. But these activities occurred out-of-sight and out-of-mind of the economics profession generally. It is only in the past few years, with increasingly widespread use of econometric software and the growing appreciation of the inherent difficulties of insuring numeric reliability, that it is slowly becoming evident that there is appropriately a symbiosis between econometric theory and the software that makes this theory operational [149,223, 229,231,286, p. 315]. As early as 1967, it was known among statistical software developers that textbook formulae were not necessarily reliable computationally [209]. Yet only now is it becoming apparent to even specialists, much less the profession generally, that for reliability econometrically sophisticated techniques must be implemented in numerically sophisticated ways. It also may well be necessary for the average user of econometric software to be taught how to use the available software, although in some respects this may be less true of those under the age of 25. In any case, it has been demonstrated repeatedly in recent years that existing packages do not necessarily provide a reliable basis for applied economic research, particularly to the degree the techniques employed are nonlinear in form and users are not careful when applying the software [38,221–224,226,226,227,229,232,324].

The increasing separation between users and developers of econometric software, as these two roles become more distinct, carries with it a number of implications. In addition to insuring that packages are numerically reliable, there is in particular both a need for this software to be readily useable [52,286] and the requirement to consider the implications of the way in which econometric techniques are implemented [230]. Some years ago, Kenneth Berk pointed out that although statistical "software should [have] the features to do readily what needs to be done," that in fact there is a "tendency for the user to do what is readily available in the software," that ". . . packages have enormous influence over. . . analysis, especially over [that of] the less sophisticated users" [25]. This possibility needs to be much more carefully considered than it has been before. Moreover, there is an increasing need to consider also the relative pedagogic roles now played by textbooks and other printed materials in relation to the existing econometric software and associated manuals. Originally, textbooks consolidated, organized and presented results previously spread throughout the econometrics literature, especially journals. In so doing, they have in the past unquestionably defined current practice, or would have been generally thought to. However, today, it is software that embodies the techniques actually used by economists. All else is purely potential in its effect and to the extent not embodied in software, is likely as the years go by to be increasingly ignored by each new generation that is raised on the microcomputer, not to mention the Playstation, the X-box, and their competitors and successors.

This volume of the *Journal of Economic and Social Measurement* constitutes a first step towards the evaluation of the state of the art of econometrics in terms of the properties of existing software. As indicated, an important aspect of this evaluation is the matter of numeric accuracy, and several of the articles found here address this subject pointedly. However, collectively these articles also raise questions relating to the use of software: implicitly or explicitly, they raise the question whether the software developer's responsibility is limited or unlimited. It is easy enough, in the abstract, to assert that the algorithms that constitute a given program should be numerically sound. However, particularly when nonlinear methods are employed, there are inherent properties of the use process that must be considered. For example, nonlinear problems inherently involve multiple roots, local maxima and minima, and other circumstances that may relate as much to software usability as to strict numeric reliability. There is also the fact that at least two types of packages now exist, at least as polar types: those that offer the user a specific set of techniques, and those that provide him or her essentially a high level econometric programming language, to varying degrees allowing the individual to define the characteristics and properties of the operations performed. A potential pitfall is that, insofar as a package permits the user to determine algorithmically the operations performed, that user takes on the role of a programmer and numeric analyst, shouldering also at least some responsibility to understand the implications of how particular algorithms should be implemented. Unfortunately, relatively few users appear to realize that they have taken on this burden.

The widespread lack of appreciation of potential problems, so much so that a recent special issue on computing in the *Journal of Economic Perspectives* made absolutely no mention of any aspect of such matters, makes such concerns pertinent in a number of contexts. For example, the *Journal of Economic and Social Measurement* is today rare among those indexed by the *Journal of Economic Literature* to require authors to identify the software used, including at least version and platform, as the basis for published applied work; among economics journals specifically, it is the *only* journal. Moreover, as a matter of apparent editorial policy, other economic journals tend to minimize any discussion of computational issues, as well as economic measurement issues [30]. Does this silence not carry with it the implication that applied results presented in those economic journals are somehow invariant to the software used? To be sure, a number of economics journals have adopted some form of replication policy, mandating the archiving of data [67]. A few require authors to provide information or even code pertaining to self-developed software, but generally restricted to software written in a standard programming language [123]. Particularly in a world in which it remains easy to demonstrate that numeric accuracy and other aspects of the use of software potentially pose serious problems, such policies only barely touch the surface of the solution.

2. The historical development of econometric software

2.1. The beginnings

The early development of econometric software can be traced to the first use of the computer by Leontief[5] and Houthakker and colleagues [29,36,165,174,176, 202–204], the conceptual work by Orcutt [27] and Phillips [200,201], and the computational work using electromechanical calculators by Tinbergen, Klein, Goldberger, and others [28,29,124]. In at least one instance in the early days, there was a close association of the development of the computer and economic research. Richard Stone was among those who then saw that computers could become a powerful research tool, and as a result he appears to have plotted a course accordingly [255,261, 325].[6] On the one hand, he pursued close links with the Cowles Commission, then at Chicago, and encouraged the Cambridge visits and work of Houthakker, Prais, Orcutt, and others. On the other, because the Cambridge computer, EDSAC, was both the first stored program computer to begin operation (in May 1949) [7] and during

[5] Leontief's appears to be the first use of a computer by an economist, and therefore deserves pride of place, whether or not his use was otherwise strictly "econometric" in nature. To be precise, Leontief seems to have used the Mark III-IV series of relay/magnetic drum computers at Harvard, which were in part electromechanical, and not actually stored program computers. The development of these was supported by IBM in conjunction with its development of its line of punch card calculating machines. In the interest of full disclosure, from 1980 until his death, Leontief was an Associate Editor and strong supporter of the *Journal of Economic and Social Measurement*.

[6] See, for instance, Stone, Aitchison, and Brown [325], which also outlines a method of programming an expenditure demand model "using a high speed digital machine." The introduction states "It has been adopted as a principle of the research programme of the Department of Applied Economics that the collection and refinement of economic data should go hand in hand with the development of techniques of analysis. . . we subscribe in general to the belief that a refinement in analytical method requires testing against adequate data before we can decide to proceed further along the same lines or to change the direction of our advance" (p. 1). See also Pesaran and Harcourt [255].

[7] "Beginning operation," as a characteristic of EDSAC, needs to be carefully qualified. In a May 2003 email [313], Lucy Slater writes "In October [1949], when I got to the lab, it consisted of an oscilloscope

the 1950s operated as a general-purpose academic resource, as Director of the Department of Applied Economics (DAE) Stone integrated it into economic research as soon as possible. An account of the use of EDSAC 1 to estimate Engel Curves is in Prais and Houthakker [269,270], with other details in Aitchison and Brown [6]. The subsequently influential paper by Michael Farrell on productive efficiency measurement also included computations based on the use of the EDSAC 1 [102,106,107, p.265]. A JASA paper by Brown, Houthakker, and Prais on "electronic computation in economic statistics" [36] is a particularly informative account of the process of using an early computer (EDSAC), including a description of the context of that work and a comparison of the role of the computer, sorting machines, and the desk calculator to make various types of calculations; this account also provides references to work with the computer by others, as well as references to discussions of the "engineering aspects" of the EDSAC.

The most immediate developmental link, beginning in the mid 1950s, was Lucy Slater, who was both in the DAE, because of Stone, and had helped to establish the programming of EDSAC 1. Working with Farrell, she wrote early regression and matrix algebra packages for the EDSAC 1 and EDSAC 2 [102,316, p. 265], apparently the first instance of econometric software, also later developing for the DAE a program called REX,[8] a single equation regression program, and GEM, a programming language for matrix calculations [17,308–311]. Both REX and GEM relied entirely on numeric input, and required the use of specific operator codes – these codes are briefly described in the Milestones paper by Slater in this volume [316]; aspects of numeric codes and other types of interfaces are discussed in the Stokes

and a toggle, so that you could enter in binary patterns and see if they produced the correct resulting pattern. By October 1950, it could send a pattern to an old electric typewriter to be checked and read in a pattern by a five hole paper tape reader. Much of the hardware was obtained from American Air Force sales of redundant equipment after the war, so it was a case of 'what have we bought today, and what use can we make of it?' Hence the paper tapes. The Lorentz factory in Germany was the source of much of this equipment, which had been used in stock exchanges. [But] by 1951, the first book about EDSAC had been published, 'the Preparation of Programs for an Electronic Digital Computer' by Wilkes, Wheeler, and Gill." See Wilkes et al. [350], which describes the capabilities of EDSAC and its characteristics, and the short article by Slater in this volume [316]. In his historical survey of electronic computers, Rosen [291] indicates that the first general purpose stored program computer "the EDVAC, was started at the Moore School [of Engineering of the University of Pennsylvania] in 1946. The first to be completed was the EDSAC (Electronic Delay Storage Automatic Calculator) at Cambridge University in England [349]. The EDSAC was started early in 1947 by Professor Maurice Wilkes, who had spent the preceding summer with the computer design group at the University of Pennsylvania, attending the 'Moore School Lectures' (http://www.computer50.org/mark1/moore.school/list.html). The EDSAC performed its first computations, the first performed by a stored program computer anywhere, in May 1949. The completion of the EDVAC was delayed by (among other things) the fact that Professors Eckert and Mauchly left the University of Pennsylvania to form their own computer manufacturing company." A 1970 paper by Donald Knuth [182] provides other details on the EDVAC in particular, including certain engineering details, and also describes the earliest existant program for a stored program digital computer, written in 1945 by John Von Neumann; Knuth's paper also provides a number of other interesting references.

[8]The earliest currently available documentation for this program, but of a later version ported to the Titan (a successor to the EDSAC), is the program manual published in 1967 [317].

paper on software design [323]. The EDSAC 1 was of course an exceedingly primitive machine by today's standards.[9] It used mercury delay lines for memory, which was limited initially to 1 kilobyte,[10] but the EDSAC 2 in 1957 was a powerhouse: William Peterson [261], who joined the DAE subsequently, reckons that it had at least 32K of memory! And it was powerful enough for Stone to consider using it for a 31 sector Input-Output model; the restriction to 31 sectors because a 31 × 31 matrix can just barely fit into 1KB storage. Work on this model was the subject of 12 reports entitled *A Programme for Growth*, the first of which was published in 1962, and some of these reports discuss computational issues. Other materials still exist at the Marshall Library in Cambridge, including a paper by Stone and others about computing.

However, from a worldwide perspective, it is nonetheless true that the development of software for general use by economists began in the mid to late 1960s. At least as a first approximation, it is possible to identify specific centers for this early development, including the Brookings Institution, the aforementioned Cambridge University, the Economic Council of Canada, the London School of Economics, the Massachusetts Institute of Technology, and the Universities of Auckland, Michigan, Pennsylvania, and Wisconsin. With certain exceptions, such as the work done at Auckland by Rex Bergstrom's students [266],[11] at the LSE by James Durbin, David Hendry, Dennis Sargan, Mike Wickens and others [147,156], at MIT by Robert Hall and others and at Wisconsin by Arnold Zellner, Art Stroud, and colleagues, at the beginning the stimulus for the development of this software was usually to support the estimation and construction of large macroeconometric models. Even in the case of McCracken, it was a move to the Economic Council of Canada in 1965 that provided the incentive to increase the scope of his work. Moreover, particularly in the late 1960s and early 1970s, there was close collaboration between those working on the Brookings Model at many institutions; the Wharton model at the University of Pennsylvania; the MIT-Penn-Federal Reserve model at MIT,

[9] In fact, the context of its use required a certain hardiness. Slater indicates that the machine itself was not in the DAE, but instead "on the top floor of the Anatomy block and was part of the faculty of mathematics." This was near "the physics buildings as Prof. Hartree [who directed day to day operations] was a professor of mathematics and physics, but part of the DAE was in a hut near these buildings so it was easy to get those in the hut interested, long before the rest of the DAE in similar huts at West Road." The "connection with the DAE was a man on a motor bike, Charlie Fienstien who went across from Corn Exchange street, to West Road every morning to fetch us our work and every evening to take back our results. The lady who was my assistant, Ruth Loshak, married him!" [314,315].

[10] In an earlier version of this paper, I described the EDSAC 1 as initially having 2 kilobytes of memory. However, having read that version, Slater indicates that, in fact, initially it had just 1 kilobyte, and only later was this enhanced by an extra magnetic tape or other external memory, thus adding a second kilobyte of memory. Engineering details concerning the EDSAC can be found in the book by Wilkes et al. [350].

[11] Which work is described by Phillips and Hall in some detail later in this journal issue [266]. Apparently the work described also involved, to at least some degree, the development of the Bergstrom model, thus was in part model related. However, it was only after the present paper was substantially written that this information, provided by Phillips and Hall, came to my attention, too late to be fully incorporated here.

the University of Pennsylvania, and the Board of Governors of the Federal Reserve System; and the Bureau of Economic Analysis Model at BEA (formerly the Office of Business Economics) [10,59,60,128,159] [98, Chapter 1]. A similar web of contacts existed in the UK and between Canadian and US econometrician-developers. These linkages obviously make it difficult to identify the work occurring at any one place as logically preceding that at any other: early individual contributions were made, such as those by Mark Eisner [87,89], Robert Hall [27], David Hendry [147], Michael McCracken [216], Morris Norman, Ross Preston, George Schink [93,302], Lucy Slater [309–311,317,318], and Arnold Zellner [355,356], but the lack of a developed historical literature makes it difficult to establish strict precedence in the context of an organized and evolving body of knowledge.

Of course, the development of this software during the 1950s and 1960s took place in an even wider environment than simply econometric applications. Supported by IBM and other such firms and organizations, by the early 1960s documented code libraries were being developed and distributed in a systematic way, providing matrix inversion routines, random number generation, and other code; not always bug free and not always incorporating the best algorithms. In a few cases, even as early as the end of the 1950s, IBM supported the creation of estimation programs by Harry Eisenpress and others [86]. More generally, among econometricians during the middle to late 1960s, code fragments were being casually circulated; for example, subroutine listings from TSP were passed around at Brookings and Wharton in the 1969–1970 period, as were also code listings and card decks from BMD and other regression programs that originated in other disciplines. The Census X-11 seasonal adjustment program, both quarterly and monthly versions, became available in 1966–1967, programmed by Bakka, Shiskin, and Sommer [305]. In truth, this was a cooperative learning period, during which such ideas as code modularity, exemplified by TSP, and the need for integrated economic data base management, regression, and model solution capabilities were the common currency of thought. A possible metaphor might be largely independent beehives of programming activities, with an occasional interchange of directional messages. It is also important to recognize that the programs of those days were rather rudimentary externally and usually incomplete beyond the specific algorithms to perform a designated operation. Often there were no user guides, other than the source code.[12] And as Longley's seminal paper demonstrated [209], showing the pitfalls of single precision and the straightfoward

[12]For example, I still have a 15 page description of the input card deck used to operate a solution program of the mid to late 1960s which is entitled: *THE SIM MODEL SOLUTION PROGRAM by Morris Norman. Description Interpreted from the Fortran by Harold Shapiro With Modifications and Corrections by R.H. Rasche* (there is no date on this document, but it is an earlier variant of [249]). Shapiro's name is footnoted "Please send Professor Norman five cents for every successful run. You may bill him an equivalent amount for every failure." Similarly, the brief write ups of the AUTO and ECON regression programs that are among the treasures of my economics library, dated 1968–1969, describe the control cards to operate the programs, but also the Fortran subroutines used to read the data from cards, as well as the outline of the subroutine to be used to transform the variables for the regression using these data.

implementation of standard textbook formulae, programs then beginning to be used widely were not error free.

The work at the Brookings Institution in the 1960s incorporated several related themes, ranging from the creation of databases by James Craig [80] – based upon programming by Mark Eisner and later partially utilizing the NBER database created by Charlotte Boschan and others [31,279], to the creation of software to condense Input-Output tables by McCarthy and Renfro [215], to the early development of econometric modeling packages such as MODLER [277,284,286] and PLANETS [32,33]. The first task to which MODLER was applied, and which initially caused its creation, was the estimation of the approximately 200 equation "condensed" Brookings model [116, 117].[13] PLANETS, which became generally available at Brookings in 1971, was used subsequently at Wharton Econometric Forecasting Associates, under the name DAMSEL; it was used until 1987, just before the merger of that organization with Chase Econometric Forecasting Associates. However, in 1966–1970, model solution was the paramount cutting edge problem: in addition to somewhat isolated efforts to consider particular aspects of model solutions, such as those reported contemporaneously by Holt [162] and Nagar [242], there was a general effort during that time to determine how best to code, de-bug and solve a large scale model [92,93,215]. Early attempts involved even drastic model linearization and heavy reliance on block recursive model structure [163]. Of the first attempts, using the earlier Klein-Goldberger model as a pattern, Charles Holt recalls, "Solving that small model reliably [using the computer] proved to be extremely difficult, so the [initial] solution system [for the Brookings Model] was designed to incorporate five powerful optimization methods including a new algorithm for decomposing the model into its recursive blocks. If we were having trouble solving 20 simultaneous nonlinear equations, [what] about the difficulties that we could face with 300 equations?" [164]. But slowly during this period the method of Gauss-Seidel became generally adopted, based upon recognition by George Schink [302] and Ed Kuh [29, p. 516], possibly mutually independently, of the applicability of the method, first for the Wharton Model [93,118,302], leading

[13] Prior to 1969, the several versions of the Brookings model not only were the "large" version, but as systems of equations also conceptually represented an after-the-fact attempt to merge into a coherent model the independently developed sectors described in the first two Brookings volumes [80,81] and elsewhere [244]. In contrast, the "condensed" model represented at its creation an attempt to evaluate how the degree of aggregation affected the properties of a model, but estimated by Fromm and Renfro at Brookings, in consultation with Klein, Kuh, and others, as a coherent model by initial design, albeit taking into account the sector specifications of the "large" model [114,116]. This model was to a degree subsequently re-estimated in the very early 1970s by Schink during the process of his coding it into a Fortran language simulation package; two variants were created in this process. The need to estimate the condensed version (in those days, at 200 equations, a big model) with a comparatively minimal human input both sparked the initial development of the MODLER software and helped to define the necessary characteristics of an interactive econometric modeling language to support the development and use of large-scale models; extensive conversations with Douglas Bracy and George Schink were also formative.

to the creation of relatively robust model solution programs by the early 1970s. [14] The concept of an online data base as a central element was transmitted to Lexington, Massachusetts in 1968–1969, taking root with the creation of the aptly named Data Resources, Inc.

As described earlier, the Department of Applied Economics (DAE) at Cambridge University was the site of work done by Orcutt [27] in the 1940s, and Farrell, Houthakker [165], Slater, Stone and others in the 1950s. Terry Barker and William Peterson report that in the 1960s there was considerable use of the computer for one-time projects, particularly after the EDSAC 2 was replaced by the Titan in 1965 [17]. Independently, the Titan was also used to implement an early time-sharing system, certainly one of the first [291, p. 31-32]. As a major activity, in 1960, Alan Brown and Richard Stone established the Cambridge Growth Project in the DAE. Stone's Cambridge Growth Model, which initially began in 1962 [326], progressively developed over the next ten to fifteen years into a notably large model that involved a considerable programming effort to both manage its data base and solve it [262]. A characteristic of this model, as it evolved, was its size and complexity. By 1979, for example, the model both numbered approximately 2500 equations and was multi-sectoral, among other things combining aspects of both macroeconometric models and Input-Output models [16]. The dynamically expanding computational problem, seen in terms of the need to solve the joint problems of data base maintenance, numeric computational issues, and presenting results in an organized and intelligible way, was for that time immense. This and other modeling and policy analysis efforts that required computational support at the DAE created a lively environment for software development [11,51,260]. Among the results, Slater and Pesaran developed algorithms and programs for parameter estimation [258], out of which ultimately came the present day MicroFit package [256,257].

The first stage of innovation is proof-of-concept. Subsequently, focus tends to shift from simply doing, however crudely, to doing easily or well. Often, an element of this transition is the relief of tedium: there will always be tediousness associated with some portion of research, but the degree to which this can be minimized can obviously affect the output obtained. The Economic Council of Canada is notable for being the

---

[14] Since writing this paragraph, I have obtained a manual for "Program Simulate II" [163], apparently written at the University of Wisconsin and published in April 1967. It seems to be the earliest still existing documentation of an econometric model simulation program. It refers both to Newton-Raphson and Gauss-Siedel and generally takes account of the technologies that were then being considered towards solving the problem of solving macroeconometric models. The program the manual describes appears to have had a designed limit of 200 equations and it is not clear to what degree it was ever used in the solution of any actual model. Furthermore, it refers to the assistance of Mark Eisner, identified as then a member of the Brookings Model project, who apparently "helped to establish the IBM compatibility." (p. 8); in particular, a difference between CDC Fortran and IBM Fortran then was the point at which the first checking is done to evaluate whether or not looping limits have been reached. It is not entirely evident exactly how the development of SIMULATE II fits into the overall history of the development of model solution software.

site of the first sustained attempt to define the various aspects of the econometric model building, maintenance, and use process as a computationally integrated activity [216, 217,219]. Essentially, this was the result of McCracken moving his DATABANK system there and expanding on his earlier work. This system, as its name implies, was designed to manage an economic data base, moreover a substantial one containing as many as 5000 time series or more.[15] The principles of its design therefore attempted to address the multiple storage, retrieval and maintenance problems that such large scale data management implies – even now, and much more so in the mid 1960s, during the fetal stage of large-scale data base management. Programs with evocative names such as MASSAGER [216] and SIMSYS were first created then. As will be described later, subsequently this software, ultimately under the name MOSAIC, was further developed as a coordinated set of procedures intended to provide the support necessary to enable the estimation, construction, and use of large-scale macroeconometric models, including the organization and maintenance of its data base. At the end of the 1960s, this project was only in its early days, but a generation of Canadian economists, including James MacKinnon, are quick to recall their first use of MASSAGER and its siblings.

During the 1960s, the work at the London School of Economics incorporates several distinct contributions. In the earlier 1960s, Durbin, Sargan, Wickens and others used the computer for various purposes including programming estimator algorithms, an example being the effort by Wickens referenced above. This early use, on the one hand, reflected an attempt to make the new technology more easily accessible: to this end, the Statistics Department established general computing support for faculty and graduate students in the form of Ray O'Brien and Wickens, who were given the job of providing the human interface with the University of London's Atlas [346]. On the other hand, achieving technical progress requires a willingness to learn and to innovate. as recounted in a just published article in *Econometric Theory* [153], Hendry describes how "Dennis Sargan hand wired/programmed the computer in the very early 1960s for his 1964 paper. Then he wrote Atlas autocode in the mid 1960s

[15]This project was more ambitious in its aims and scope than it might today appear to have been. For perspective, it should be noted that this work is contemporary with what are now regarded as early attempts by computer scientists to define the principles of data base management [285,304,340]. It is indicative of the pioneering nature of McCracken's contribution that volume 1 of the ACM Transactions on Database Systems was only published in 1976, even if other ACM publications do contain papers on this topic dating to the 1960s.

for more 'friendly programs'... [151].[16,17] In a similar spirit of innovation, during the mid-1960s, working with Terence Gorman, Bill Phillips, and Sargan, Clifford Wymer created several programs that were subsequently widely used.[18] Hendry himself of course also fell victim to the seductive charms of the machine and his Ph.D. work, begun in the late 1960s, led first to the creation of a software library [147] and subsequently to the creation of a series of programs, culminating in the PcGive and PcFIML packages.[19] In addition to these efforts, the work of Phillips, in the form of the Phillips Economics Computer, is enshrined in the UK Science Museum in South Kensington, London, as a computing milestone [201]. As described by Hendry [153], LSE in the period from 1950 to the 1970s incorporated both distinct points-of-view concerning the precise role of economics, quantitative economics, and econometrics and a practical, hands-on tradition.[20]

[16]The EDSAC and the Atlas both were programmed, or could be programmed, using autocode. However, these machines were not directly related. As described earlier, the EDSAC was created at Cambridge University. The Atlas was a second generation machine developed by Ferranti Ltd and the Universities in Manchester [291]. However, there were connections: in a recent email (May 2003), Lucy Slater says, "the language used was Autocode on Edsac1 in the early 1950s and was taken over to Edsac2 which was a bigger version of a similar design, which used ferrite cores instead of valves and so was very much faster. Edsac2 started running in 1958. It was much bigger than Edsac1 as we called the old machine. Whereas Edsac 1 had 512 short 16 bit words at its complete store, Edsac 2 had 2048 32 bit words and was about 10 times faster in its input and output. By this time, most electronic companies had a computer under construction or in the design stage. Ferranti served the Manchester Laboratory, and The Hollorith punched card company, which later became ICL, served our laboratory. J.C.Lyons produced a version of Edsac 2 for commercial sale, as did Elliots and English Electric. The Ferranti company which had made its name during the war, with radar and similar devices, now produced a commercial machine called Mercury, which was followed by Pegasus. And then the Atlas series, by 1962. The Atlas ... in London was one of these. Its autocode was very similar to the old code which had been used in Cambridge and Manchester, with of course the needed additions to deal with magnetic tape readers, and enlarged backup storage devices. The third machine in Cambridge was Titan, which started work in 1965 and was an upgraded version of an Atlas."

[17]Other such recollections exist. Sargan customarily lectured without notes. Referring to this, Tim Harrison remembered recently an occasion that, as a student, he was in Sargan's office when the phone rang – someone from the Atlas computer center reporting a problem – whereupon Sargan quickly dictated new code over the phone. There is no guarantee that the program then immediately worked, but it may have.

[18]These include Resimul, developed in 1967/68 as a Full Information Maximum Likelihood estimator of coefficients consisting of nonlinear functions of parameters, initially using a modified version of Durbin's Newton-Raphsen procedure; Continest, developed in 1968 to calculate eigenvalues and their asymptotic standard errors; and Predic, developed at the same time to calculate asymptotic standard errors of dynamic or static forecasts. The programs were subsequently used in Australasia, Europe, UK, and the US. For further details, see the entry for WYSEA in the software compendium at the end of this volume and the references found there.

[19]The development of these more recently has of course been transferred to Nuffield College, Oxford [75,154]. The package called here PcGive was called PC-Give up to version 6.x and PcGive from version 7 onwards. PcGive has been adopted here as the name. A similar nominal transformation occurred in the case of PcFIML.

[20]As a case in point, M.Sc. students choosing the mathematical economics option in the middle to late 1960s not only battled their way through such things as the Kuhn-Tucker saddlepoint and Radner

This practicality may in fact be more of a marker than might appear at first sight. Worldwide, the period from the late 1940s to the late 1960s was a formative and fertile period for the development of econometric theory [240,272]. However, two phenomena in particular can be identified with the last ten years of this period and also the 1970s. The first is the initial development of software to actually implement the conceptual constructs of the Cowles studies [173,183]. The second is the growing disquiet that the specification search process had encountered something of a dead end, roadblocked by both the problem of non-nested hypotheses and other aspects and assumptions associated with the implementation of the "traditional" approach [68]. However, in contrast to the angst expressed by Leamer [199] and the nihilism by Sims [307],[21] at the LSE the development of the methodology of specification search became a challenge, rooted in the Sargan paper of 1964 [66,153,296], but also the countervailing influences of Friedrich von Hayek, Karl Popper, A.W.H. Phillips, Lionel Robbins, and the Staff Seminar on Methodology, Measurement and Testing (M2T), among others. Throughout the 1960s and subsequently, there was at the LSE the closely related development of software.

Somewhat earlier, the first use of the computer with econometric models apparently occurred at the University of Michigan in conjunction with the estimation of the Klein-Goldberger Model [174].[22] Initially, this model was estimated and solved using desk top calculators, applying the methods described by Goldberger later in this volume [124]. But by 1954, as recounted by Klein, computation "was partially shifted to electronic computers for the estimation of moments in preparation for parameter estimation" [29,176, p, 516]. A similar methodology was subsequently used at the Oxford Institute of Statistics for the Klein-Ball-Hazelwood-Vandome model [177]. Solution of the Klein-Goldberger model posed a problem that was resolved in part by simplification. The model was linearized, as described by Suits [328, chapter 2], preparatory to solving it using a Monroe electromechanical desk calculator, employing "an iterative procedure that [Klein] had devised" [329]. Experience with the solution of this model provided a starting point for considering the solution of the Wharton and Brookings models, as mentioned earlier. However, later 1950s and early 1960s Michigan models were also linearized and then solved by matrix inversion. Subsequently, in the early to mid 1960s, an attempt was apparently made to create a general solution program for the Michigan models of that time on an

turnpike theorems, as well as those associated with separating hyperplanes, but were also called upon (in an examination setting) to compute numerically a reasonably detailed Simplex solution, presumably in order to demonstrate a mastery of the associated computational process.

[21] T.C. Liu of course earlier made a somewhat similar argument to that put forward by Sims, concerning the identifiability of macroeconometric models [207]; however, see also Liu's qualification in the 1975 Brookings volume [208].

[22] However, see in addition Phillips and Hall [266], who indicate that Bergstrom, at the University of Cambridge, was also an early user of the computer to support parameter estimation during roughly the same time period.

early IBM mainframe, a program called Obake, Japanese for "ghost," but the details are now phantasmic [29,329, p. 515].

At MIT, prior to the installation of the IBM 1620 and the 407 card reader, Marchant desk calculators were to be found in the basement of Sloan. David Belsley recalls that "even a small project could tie up a couple of people for several days just producing the input for the normal equations," not to mention the mistakes that could be made, Franklin Fisher stopping by from time to time for a tally [22]. Robert Hall began the development of TSP in 1966 on the 1620 [141] and continued this development at Berkeley on a CDC 6400 and a remote Univac 1108. Associated with Hall in this program development were Ray Fair, Robert Gordon, Charles Bischoff and Richard Sutch.[23] Under the general direction of Edwin Kuh, a series of programs were subsequently developed at MIT, including GREMLIN [18] and TROLL [87, 89,195]. Hall recalls learning from Mark Eisner "how to do symbolic differentiation," as well as developing matrix routines for TROLL, and subsequently developing "nonlinear estimation procedures using analytical differentiation, in the time and frequency domains," as a bi-coastal research assistant for Kuh and Dale Jorgenson both in Cambridge and at Berkeley [142]. For some years, MIT was preeminently the site of a considerable amount of work on computer algorithms [62–64,160,190,191], as well as work on regression diagnostics that was closely related to this algorithm development [19,20,24]. Kuh was not then the only person who understood the promise of the electronic computer, as we have seen, but one of his significant contributions was his willingness to act on his belief that econometric computation was and is in principle an intellectual activity on a par with the development of theoretical econometrics. Belsley recalls that the ethos of the Center "directly reflected the strong interdisciplinary nature of Ed Kuh. Ed had an amazing ability to see when two researchers doing seemingly unrelated things were actually doing the same sort of thing" [22].

At the Economic Research Unit (ERU) at the University of Pennsylvania, even in the 1970s desktop calculators could still be found – apparently by then disused, although there was a rumor that in the dead of night Lawrence Klein might still be observed cranking one from time to time, just to verify that the IBM 360 was producing the right numbers. But at nearly all hours in the early to mid 1960s, the ERU and its "spin-off" Wharton Econometric Forecasting Associates, under the direction of Klein and Gerry Adams, was the site of innovative work by Morris Norman, Ross Preston and George Schink that led to the development not only of parameter estimation packages, such as Norman's AUTO and ECON, based upon initial programming by Preston [2,248], but also early work on the development of model solution algorithms [34,129,249,302]. Both the Brookings and Wharton

[23]Later, at Princeton, Ray Fair and J. Phillip Cooper contributed to the development of TSP [139]. Fair remembers that "at MIT, I programmed TSCORC and TSHILU into TSP, which was two stage least squares with first order autoregressive errors" [97,99].

models were solved there in the mid-to-late 1960s initially using the Newton method [93, Chapter IV; 215, especially footnote 9], which was later replaced by the Gauss-Seidel method, being less cumbersome; the programs to do this were created by George Schink [302] working with Vijaya Duggal, Michael McCarthy and Ross Preston.[24] A substantial number of other, more supplementary, programming projects were also undertaken in connection with the various large and small model building efforts then under way at Penn [10,113], not to mention a variety of more generalized empirical investigations [185–187]. One such was the updating of the Wharton Indices of Capacity Utilization, programmed by Renfro in 1972 under the direction of Robert Summers [3,178]. This project was an extension of the earlier work by Klein and Summers, programmed by Ross Preston and others in 1966 [179,180]. A difference was that in 1972 this work was intended to provide software that could be used generally; surprisingly, the resulting program continued to be used at Wharton EFA for at least the next 15 years. Although not then demanding computationally, and thus not in a league with the creation of solution programs, the significance of this type of support programming is that it nonetheless made possible the non-tedious generation of useful statistics. Fifteen to twenty years prior to that, the handling of calculations to determine relative peaks and other characteristics of the raw data would have been truly burdensome [29, p. 510–514].

However, in order to appreciate these developments fully, then and subsequently, it is necessary to understand certain aspects of the context of the 1960s and later mainframe computing environment. Throughout its first 40 to 50 years, the mainframe computer was hot, literally. It generated a substantial amount of heat that needed to be dissipated, reflecting initially the use of vacuum tubes, but more generally the heat energy from the close proximity of many electrical components, large and individually heat-producing – large particularly in comparison with today. Always, the computational speed of the electronic computer has depended upon minimizing the distance between components, and hence even today heat generation remains a critical issue. But in the early days, which certainly included the 1960s, computers were housed in a (normally) glass enclosed, air conditioned environment.[25] Within

[24]In his 1992 *Econometric Theory* article, McCarthy provides a slightly confusing report about this effort, indicating that the Newton method was not used, because it was too formidable computationally: "No one in the 1960s (or the early 1970s) had any intention of using Newton methods, though they were cited in [the Cowles Commission] Monograph 10; the computational burden simply seemed too formidable." However, he immediately thereafter states that the method used was that reported in Evans-Klein [93], which was first programmed by Schink, as just described, and was in fact a Newton method [215]. The contradiction is more apparent than real, for McCarthy later indicated in private conversation that when he wrote this article he was thinking of a simultaneous solution of the full model, which was never attempted at this time. For details of the methodology, see the article by Schink [302] in the Milestones section of this volume.

[25]Normally, but not invariably. Lucy Slater recalls that originally, "in the room where the first Edsac lived, there was no air conditioning, not even a fan, but we had a door to the roof outside and several large windows which opened wide. In summer the temperature was frequently up to 100. In the room

that environment, the machine's operator(s) tended the machine, monitoring its operation, rebooting it whenever necessary, mounting and dismounting tapes (and later removable hard disks), and sometimes performing such other tasks as distributing any printed output – which in those days was the intelligible result of the operations performed. Sometimes, other, subordinate operators would be responsible for distributing the printed output of the machine, which as the years wore on increasingly took place at remote sites, that is in other (usually nearby) buildings, although by the early 1980s such printers might be located even 500 (or more) miles away. But, particularly in the early years, only the operator had a live video monitor and the output of that was rather esoteric. The revolutionary aspect of the first networked machines was that individual users did have their own screens (or paper-based terminals with keyboards), displaying their own typed input and results, but even in this case the operator of the central machine needed to be contacted to mount tapes and perform other critical operations. Of course, at this time, such networked machines were rare.

More characteristically, in those days, particularly when IBM machines were used, programs were input in the form of a sequence of punched cards (collectively called card decks) via a machine known, logically enough, as a card reader. The cards, each three and one quarter inches by seven and a three-eights in dimension, were conceptually subdivided into 80 columns and 12 rows, ten of which were numbered, with rectangular holes punched in particular columns, achieved using a somewhat typewriter-like keyboarded machine called a keypunch. The absence of any holes in a particular column would be interpreted by the computer as a blank character, or a zero, as appropriate. In many cases, more than a single hole would be punched in a column. These card decks would consist of "job control" cards that indicated to the machine the name (and usually account number) of the user and characteristics of the machine resources required by that "job", followed by cards that consisted of the user's program, followed by the data used by that program. [26] As the years passed,

which held Edsac II there were several large fans which could be turned on and off as well as several large windows to open. The room which held the Titan was however, completely enclosed and air conditioned. There the main problem was the fast paper tape reader, which was very sensitive to ladies' face powder, or a flying insect . . . " [312].

[26]The RGR program, written by Arthur Stroud at the University of Wisconsin at the beginning of the 1960s offers an interesting example of data input [125,327]. The data were organized on the punch cards "by observation": one after another, for each given observation in time, data on each variable was punched onto a card, organized in fixed column fields, with that time period's observation on each variable thus being punched onto each card progressively, so that the first field referred to the first variable, the second to the second, and so on. The effect was, as the cards were read, that the observations were then located in a matrix, held in memory, itself organized so that the columns were variables and the rows observations. It was apparently possible to then select a subset of the observations (by choosing the beginning and ending rows) and a subset of the variables, if wished, in order to control the subsequent computation of the sums of squares and cross products (raw moments) matrix from which then the particular variables used in the regression were in turn selected so as to form the matrices and vectors directly used to compute parameter estimates. This process of forming the relevant matrices is not so very different to that used even today, although inasmuch as the cards consisted of only 80 columns, there was immediately a problem concerning

the program might be stored on a tape, or even a removable hard disk unit, and the job control cards would then provide instructions to the machine operator, indicating the tape(s) or hard disk unit to mount. In this case, the card deck would contain just job control cards and the data for the program, although this configuration was much more common in the 1970s than in the 1960s. Referring to the early 1970s, Mike Young recently recalled the days "when the entire database and code for the FRB-Penn-MIT model existed in a complete form in two boxes of cards which lived in the trunk of my 1958 Plymouth Fury. It never occurred to me that an accident might well have destroyed about 10 man years worth of research" [351]. By the end of the 1970s, the card deck, if used, would be likely to contain only cards directing how the computer should perform the "job": the data too would be stored on tape or hard disk. This innovation, had it occurred earlier, would have saved Michael McCarthy the dismay of watching his card boxes actually being run over by a delivery truck in the early 1970s [215, p. 388].

Self contained jobs would be run as just described. However, it was also possible even in the 1960s to store the data on tapes. In 1966–1968, econometric software used with large scale econometric models at Brookings and elsewhere took the form of separate but related programs: for instance, one for data base maintenance, one to make transformations, and one to perform regressions. The data base was normally stored on a tape and, in order to manage it, the maintenance program addressed the tape and added or revised individual series observations, in the process writing a new tape. The transformations program extracted series from the revised data base on this second tape, performed transformations and wrote these to a third tape. This third tape was then read by the regression package and the regressions were performed, the results printed out somewhat cryptically using a "line printer," the object referred to earlier as producing the printed output, so-called because it printed (at Brookings)

---

how to read in data sets that might contain more than 8–16 variables (assuming that each number required a field of 10 to 5 spaces). However, this was a relatively minor problem that could be solved by permitting 2 or more cards per observation as the data deck was read in. Much more troublesome was explaining to the program user exactly how to control these (unseen) operations in order to select both dependent and regressor variables. As a consequence, the user's guide not only explains to the user the process of forming the matrices, but provides forms to fill out that corresponded to the control cards that actually directed these operations. The user is told [125]:

"From your point of view this means that you must give the data deck to the programmer and inform him as to the following:

a) Where the variables are on the data deck.
b) For each correlation problem: which variables are to be selected, which observations are to be selected, and which output is to be printed.
c) For each regression problem: under which correlation problem it is to be subsumed, which variables are to be used and in what order, which (if any) intermediate regressions you want, and which output is to be printed. You will also include various identifying information.

The programmer will translate your information into a form intelligible to the program and computer. A standard format for presenting your information to the programmer has been developed."

At times during this process, a ram may have been sacrificed, or various incantations recited.

a 132 character line essentially simultaneously – inasmuch as there was ordinarily one line printer per machine at that time, output speed was important.[27] The printed output was cryptic not so much because of any characteristic of the line-printer, which was capable of printing a perfectly human-intelligible document (although not with the range of typefaces the laser printer is capable of), but rather because in those days the programmer and consumer were usually one and the same. Programmers, aka young economists performing the role of research assistants, would be separately responsible for writing out the results by hand, in standard written notation, so that others could see what results had been obtained. Only once others began to use the software did it become important to begin to format the output so that it would be intelligible generally.

The card decks themselves could be printed out, using the computer and the line printer, so as to provide a listing of the operations performed. However, this listing tended to be difficult to decipher. For example, individual time series were usually identified in this context by number, that number normally being the record number of the variable on the tape. When transformations were performed, the type of transformation would also be identified by a number, so that a representative transformation instruction might take the form:

```
42   22   3   16
```

having the interpretation that the observations on the variable in record 22 should be multiplied (operation 3) by the observations on the variable in record 16 and the result stored in record number 42. It is immediately evident that a deck of 400 cards, each having such an instruction punched into it, was both difficult to interpret after the fact (even by the person who originally created it) and likely to contain at least one error, often a number of errors. Modern econometric software packages permit the user to write an instruction like:

$$GDP = C + I + G + X - M$$

but such an instruction must be interpreted by the program, usually converting it into a set of machine instructions telling the computer to retrieve observations from a

[27]In fact, one of the important aspects of the historical development of the electronic computer that is often overlooked has been the lagging development of peripheral devices. As noted in passing by Rosen [291], early computers did not print output directly, but instead often either punched cards or in some cases produced tapes, which then were used to produce printed output. For instance, the UNIVAC I had a particularly advanced buffered magnetic tape system, but initially incorporated a device "the Uniprinter, which operated at electric typewriter speed directly from magnetic tape" (p. 11). "The early scientific computers were designed in accordance with a philosophy that assumed that scientific computing was characterized by little or no input or output. The [IBM] 701 and early installations of the 704 used an on-line card reader (150 cards per minute) for input and printed output could be obtained only from an on-line printer that could print 150 short lines or 75 full lines per minute" (p. 15). It was only in the 1960s that input and output began to be efficient, and that only by the standards of those days.

sequence of record locations, perform specific operations, and then to store the result in a particular record. Anyone familiar with a spreadsheet program will immediately realize that even today some vestiges of the 1960s environment remain, inasmuch as such instructions still refer to rows and columns, even if the operators are specified as $+$, $-$, $*$, $/$. On the other hand, only an economist is likely to understand the GDP identity and be able instantly to identify its components.

In the late 1960s, the computational challenge for those who would subsequently develop today's econometric software can be characterized as follows. First, there was the most basic computational challenge: algorithms, which is to say the sequence of operations necessary to perform some recognizable set of mathematical/statistical calculations. These had to be created so as to enable anyone to use the computer to generate results corresponding to those described in some journal article or textbook or defined by the user. This development of algorithms was begun in the 1960s, but only begun. It has not been completed yet, both because econometrics is a still developing discipline and because this is difficult work, not all the implications of which are yet understood. Second, there was the problem of marshalling the resources of the computer, so as to permit a sequence of operations to be performed in a coordinated way. In the case of substantial projects particularly, data bases obviously need to be organized and maintained. Even to perform a minimal amount of work, the data need to be managed and transformed. For example, the estimation of parameters usually involves some transformation of the original data. Finally, the user of the computer, particularly if he or she did not wish to spend a substantial amount of time learning to program, needed a way to communicate with the machine easily in order to tell it what operations should be performed, where to find the data to use, and how to display the results, to name only certain of the things that have to be done.

Characteristically then, and also even today, programs to support macroeconometric models were usually developed with the stress placed upon the harnessing of computer resources and with a focus on making these programs generally usable – in those days ordinarily reflecting the need to support a team of economists. Programs developed as a response to an economist's personal needs tend to be much less developed in terms of data management support and the human interface, with the stress placed upon such things as algorithms associated with particular types of parameter estimators. The initial orientation is often important as a potential, if implicit, design restriction: subsequently, it is usually relatively easy to add a new estimation method to an existing program, but it can be difficult to modify a program originally developed for a specialized purpose to support use in a larger-scale context or use that involves a high degree of process integration – in much the same sense that once a building has been constructed it is normally feasible to modernize particular rooms, but much more difficult to increase the number and purpose of rooms without affecting the usability of other existing rooms.

Of course, hardware was an issue, and the experience at the DAE in Cambridge, although not necessarily precisely typical, is illustrative. As mentioned, the Titan replaced EDSAC 2 in 1965, and was finally to gain a Fortran compiler in 1970, but the machine was designed to be programmed in Autocode, a proprietary high-level language. Autocode provided the capability to do serious econometrics, but restricted the ability of the software to circulate outside Cambridge. Interestingly, although the speed and core memory (RAM, that is) appears limited in retrospect, at the time the principal noticeable constraint was not either of these attributes, but instead the storage space – hard disk in later years. Peterson reports that "when I started on the Growth Project, the allocation for an 8-person project was only 300K bytes" [261]. Similarly, across the Atlantic, until 1970 at Brookings the machine was an IBM 7040, which provided tape storage, but no hard disks, and core memory hardly greater than the maximum the original IBM PC permitted to be installed on its motherboard, namely 64 KB. Word size variations between machines, and perhaps faulty human memory, makes specific magnitude comparisons difficult. But the idea is not too misleading: certainly there was no one, anywhere, with any machine containing a 512MB RAM chip and a 60 GB hard drive, much less a notebook. In fact, across the Pacific, working on the IBM 1130 in the late 1960s, Peter Phillips had to contend with the limitation that "the machine had only 7K core storage and so the program had to be written in segments that were linked together using Call Link statements in Fortran, the data from one stage being written to disk and then read back from disk when the next stage of the program was loaded. On one occasion, the line printer jammed and in order not to lose my operator's license I had to spend the rest of the night reading the technical manual in order to learn how to dismantle the line printer, unravel, clean and rewind the 80 feet of printer ribbon so that the machine was operational when the day shift arrived at 8:00am" [265]. Evidently, at the end of the 1960s, in order to use a computer, it was generally necessary to be a "programmer," if not always an actual licensed computer operator; this changed, to a degree, in the 1970s.

2.2. The promise of the 1970s

The 1970s and into the early 1980s are now remembered for Stagflation and related problems, but computationally, it was a formative period. In Canada and the United States, the establishment of firms such as Data Resources, Chase Econometrics, and Wharton Econometric Forecasting Associates and the development of macroeconometric models in governmental organizations, such as the Economic Council of Canada and the US Department of Commerce, led to the creation of sizeable data bases and dial-up mainframe time-sharing use of software to access those data bases; this was also the period during which government agencies in Canada and the United States began in earnest to develop data distribution initiatives that today have migrated to the Internet [267,279,285,332]. In Europe, but most specifically in the UK, the Cambridge Growth Project, the London Business School and the National Institute of Economic and Social Research played similar roles to economic forecasting firms in the United States. The Treasury Model and that of the Bank of

England represented the public sector. In addition, a number of individual projects were undertaken that have since led to important computational developments on both sides of the Atlantic, including work done by Fair at Princeton and Yale; Hendry and colleagues at the London School of Economics; and Barker, Pesaran, Peterson, Slater, and colleagues at Cambridge University.

One of the difficulties in assessing the development of econometric software even during this period is that of determining the extent of original, independent research. Not only has important work often been undocumented in the standard economics literature, but as indicated earlier a considerable amount of technology transfer also occurred. The result is that it is hard to determine who first did what when, for it is generally true that econometric models require local programming support, or at least did in the "old days," whether or not independently inspired software development took place. A comprehensive history of the period would take into account, in Canada and the US, the support work done at places such as Indiana University, UCLA, and other university and organization-based macroeconometric model projects [90]. Software development was also required in order to support the development of microsimulation models [251,293], as well as INFORUM at the University of Maryland [8]. In Europe, there have obviously been computational projects associated with econometric models in a number of countries [29]. In various other parts of the world, there have also been a number of software development projects, some of which are described for the first time in this volume [264,266]. The degree to which the present account is comprehensive as regards past innovative work will only be evident in the years to come, assuming of course better reporting.

As mentioned earlier, particularly during the 1970s, the Center for Computational Reseach in Economics and Management Science at MIT, under the direction of Edwin Kuh and Roy Welsch, was an important center for econometric software development that both directly and indirectly sponsored a number of subsequent initiatives. The flagship system was TROLL [43,195,352], begun by Eisner in 1968 and which became operational in 1972 [87,89]. [28] During the 1970s there were a number of new facilities incorporated into it, such as GREMLIN, containing David Belsley's nonlinear estimation algorithms, and the "Regression Diagnostics"

[28] The earliest software development work on a prototype system, TROLL/0, apparently began in 1966. However, as Eisner announced in 1972 [87], "In the fall of 1968 work was begun on a completely redesigned and much expanded system. This system TROLL/1, is now programmed and operates on the IBM 360/67." Eisner has indicated, in telephone conversations during August-September 2003, that TROLL/0 was in concept much more restrictedly oriented towards the development of model solution capabilities, based upon Gauss-Seidel and Newton algorithms. In contrast, TROLL/1 was designed to be then state-of-the-art in its file management, including file sharing, capabilities, as well as being explicitly designed to serve as a research environment for the development of sophisticated parameter estimation techniques in the context of a multi-person research team. The file management characteristics of TROLL is reckoned by Eisner to have had an influence on the early development of UNIX, in this regard. In summary, in 1972, the data management and file management infrastructure of TROLL/1 had been developed and was then utilized during the succeeding years of the 1970s to permit the embedding of nonlinear estimation and other algorithms into TROLL, including the experimental CLOUDS facilities [43,195,352].

of Belsley, Kuh, and Welsch [18,23,24]. However, the Center's work was far more generally based: in the early 1970s, a cooperative association with the National Bureau for Economic Research [189], then led by John Meyer, resulted, among other things, in the publication of the journal *Annals of Economic and Social Measurement*, which during its six or seven year lifetime published a series of important articles on software and data base development and some of the seminal work on economic control theory applications that would later lead to the founding of a second journal, the *Journal of Economic Dynamics and Control*, as well as to the creation in the 1990s of the Society for Computational Economics, largely at the instigation of Hans Amman and David Kendrick [172], and the journal *Computational Economics*.

The three major econometric forecasting firms operating initially in the United States, Data Resources, Chase Econometrics, and Wharton Econometric Forecasting Associates, provide interesting contrasts in the way they each developed software for their own and clients' use. Data Resources Inc. (DRI) was founded in 1968 by Otto Eckstein, Gary Fromm, and others. It distinctively promoted the concept of providing large scale data bases to a wide market, but essentially business economists, the restriction reflecting the cost of the services provided. The contemporaneous development of mainframe-based dial-up and dedicated-line telecommunications capabilities meant that, beginning in approximately 1970, it became possible for DRI to offer online time sharing computing services, mixing software and a substantial time series data base that grew to literally millions of time series [279]. To offer these services required the development of a supporting software system. DRI's first such system, started in 1968, combined an adaptation of TSP by Robert Hall, called EPL [142] with a separate model solution program. The second, under the name EPS, was developed during the 1970s, principally by Robert Lacey, but with important design contributions by Hall and Edward Green [55,56]. These systems, developing sequentially over time, provided DRI clients with the capability to perform regressions, display tables and graphs, and, by 1980, even solve some models, although in fact the model solution facilities were never a fully integrated feature, particularly to the degree of being able to handle DRI's larger models as a matter of course [29,168,274].

Chase Econometric Associates, founded in 1970 by Michael Evans with the backing of the Chase Manhattan Bank, was also strongly oriented towards the business economics community and slowly developed similar online data and software support for its clients. As a consequence of the development of EPS by DRI, Chase contracted with Mark Eisner, Robert Pindyck, and others in the late 1970s to obtain the use of XSIM, a commercial adaptation of TROLL, as a competitive response. [29] XSIM incorporated a number of the matrix routines originally developed by Robert

[29] The institutional details concerning the development of XSIM and its final disposition are beyond the scope of the present paper, but are also quite involved. Eisner, Pindyck, J. Phillip Cooper, and others formed the firm Dynamic Associates beginning in or about 1972 in order to enable the development of XSIM. Subsequently, Chase contracted with Dynamic Associates to obtain the use of XSIM. Dynamic

Hall for TROLL as well as the symbolic differentiation routines developed by Eisner and Hall [89,142]. XSIM, which reached full flower during the period 1980–1983, was a much more integrated econometric modeling package than EPS, and considerably more user friendly than TROLL [84,103].[30] Although Chase Econometrics was essentially an economic consulting and forecasting firm, an associated entity, Interactive Data Corporation, provided a broad range of computer technology-related services and products, a number of which were created using the macro language and facilities of XSIM, although other econometric packages were also offered, such as AUTOBJ, now known as Autobox [288].

Wharton Econometric Forecasting Associates (Wharton EFA), traces its roots to the first Wharton model forecasts in 1963–64. Until about 1980 a non-profit corporation wholly owned by the University of Pennsylvania, it was somewhat less successful than its competitors in the development of state-of-the-art online systems during the late 1970s and early 1980s. However, beginning in the very early 1970s, Wharton EFA was the innovator in the development of software and models embedded in software that were made available on 9-track computer tapes to its clients [34,129]. The clients included not only business economists but also research centers at a number of universities [181]. The programs developed by Wharton EFA were generally less sophisticated in the range of parameter estimation facilities, but in the early 1970s more developed in their model solution capabilities, which influenced work at other US locales, including MIT [214,249]. The DAMSEL system, which as noted earlier was essentially a re-badged PLANETS, was developed in the mid to late 1970s by Douglas Bracy and others at Wharton EFA to provide parameter estimation facilities in an online database context, but never attained the degree of integrated processing of either EPS or XSIM later in that decade.

In the UK, at the DAE in Cambridge, the 1970s were years of fruitful activity. The Titan was replaced by an IBM 370 in 1972, which among other things permitted programs to be written in Fortran; so did the Titan, but only from 1970. Most importantly, packages driven by a series of numeric codes were replaced by those with more modern interfaces. Peterson developed IDIOM (Internal Dynamic Input-Output Model) and MREG (Matrix and REGression package), both with command line interfaces [262]. These were batch programs, reflecting the IBM's limited

Associates was, in or about 1981, absorbed into Interactive Data Corporation (IDC), owned by the Chase Manhattan Bank, and at about that time Chase Econometric Associates became a subsidiary of IDC. Later, in 1987, when Wharton Econometric Forecasting Associates was merged with Chase Econometrics to form the WEFA Group, the ownership of XSIM may have in fact stayed with IDC.

[30] In recent telephone conversations, September 2003, Eisner today characterizes XSIM in the early 1980s as internally less sophisticated than mainframe TROLL in the 1970s, lacking TROLL's hierarchical file system and other academic research support facilities, but with a much cleaner front end, more OnLine Analytic Processing (OLAP) tools, more "quick and easy" commercial user-oriented regression facilities, and most importantly a much more developed macro language. XSIM was effectively designed as a "language," almost an econometric programming language – in the sense that this term is used and described later in the present article.

interactive capabilities then and there. Peterson feels that "a dedicated FORTRAN program was [then] the only way to write a program which was sufficiently fast and compact" to support the development of the Cambridge Growth Model, which already was beginning to bulk up in size, dwarfing most other econometric models [261]. The quantity of data associated with this model, as well as its size, posed a succession of software design challenges, ranging from the need to efficiently maintain and update a substantial number of data series, to the need to provide immediate access to the data for estimation and simulation [17,260,263].

More generally in the UK in the 1970s, there were a number of computational initiatives: a model solution system called NIMODEL was developed at the National Institute of Economic and Social Research (NIESR), principally by Richard Pierse. This package was somewhat integrated with a data base system but without parameter estimation capabilities, and in modernized form is still available today [143,330]. At Imperial College, University of London, Berc Rustem, John Prescot and Sean Holly developed control algorithms for large econometric models [161]. At the Treasury, David Ramsden and others also developed model solution software. The Klein-Ball-Hazelwood-Vandome model, created at the Oxford Institute of Statistics, was transformed into the London Business School model by Ball and others. Models were created also at Liverpool and Southampton and elsewhere in the UK [13,333]. Essentially, during this period, the existence of any working large-scale econometric model implied also the existence of programming support, but as mentioned earlier the developmental linkages are not well documented in most cases, although the work at Southampton in particular was finally to cross the Atlantic in the early 1980s and blossom in Philadelphia in 1985 as AREMOS.

Meanwhile, at the LSE, the development of software that began as a software library called AUTOREG [147] increasingly became the handmaiden of what has emerged since as the LSE methodology. As Hendry recounts, "initially the programs focused on 'optimal estimation' based on the implicit assumption that dynamic models under study were more or less correctly specified. The tests offered were mainly tests of model specification, where the null was just a special case of an already estimated more general model. Then an increasing number of diagnostic tests was included for misspecification... gradually leading to the implementation of 'model building' procedures." [149, p. 314] Hendry's development of AUTOREG thus shines forth as software with a purpose, possibly in contrast to other software development, which can be seen as often undertaken simply to perform a specific task of the moment. On the other hand, it is also possible to observe, in considering other software systems, that when (metaphorically speaking) bullets are flying, large tasks are performed without introspection that may nonetheless later appear to have led to a coherent and well-defined result. When comparing AUTOREG to other systems, there is an interesting question whether these others should be regarded as embodying a contrasting philosophy or a neutral concept.

Towards the end of the 1970s, AUTOREG evolved into David Hendry's Give. In the process, this program began to affect other programming efforts in UK, reflecting the growing influence there of the LSE General to Specific methodology. At the National Institute, REG-X was created by Stephen Hall and others as direct clone of Give [143]. At that time, Give was a mainframe program. REG-X as initially developed was a Fortran-based program that ran on a Tandy microcomputer and produced essentially the same output structure as Give. When the National Institute purchased a mini-computer, Hall ported REG-X to that, where it ran from card image files and was extensively used locally. Whether this reflects a quintessential English desire to hold on to the past or not, REG-X is possibly the only example of an econometric software package ported as a replacement from a microcomputer to an older class of machine.

In Canada, at the Economic Council of Canada and later at Informetrica, there was further development of MASSAGER, SIMSYS, and other software to support the creation and solution of macroeconometric models, particularly the CANDIDE and TIM models, the first during the period from 1971 to the mid 1980s and the second beginning in 1979. From the 1960s, MASSAGER was also used by other Canadian government agencies, including the Bank of Canada and the National Energy Board. Finally, MASSAGER "73" was released into the public domain. During this time, SIMSYS emerged as a package for model solution and "equation maintenance." A distinguishing feature was general support for model maintenance and solution, with the equations initially specified in an algebraic format that was translated by the system into Fortran code, which then became an integral component of the solution software [289]. At Informetrica, founded by Michael McCracken, the MOSAIC system incorporating such features was developed subsequently, becoming operational in or about 1979 [167]. MOSAIC was designed as a group of distinct but related subsystems or procedures controlled by a common mathematical-textual language [218]. The subsystems consisted of program control, data management, basic arithmetic, regression analysis, and Forecasting and Seasonal Adjustment. Organized in a somewhat similar manner as SAS, MOSAIC's program control module served as a command interpreting interface between the user and the several applications subsystems.

During this period, there were also individual software development efforts that are best viewed independently of any particular organizational context. Ray Fair's work is an example: this work spans the development of software for both parameter estimation and particular types of model solution and its philosophy is today embodied in the FP (Fair-Parke) program [97,100,101]. Characteristically, during the 1970s, Fair's models were re-estimated frequently, using specific estimation techniques, and were solved without the use of constant adjustments [94,95,97]; this particular orientation is reflected in the properties and progressive development of the associated software. In contrast, TSP continued to develop as a broadly-based package, inherently general in its implied philosophy [78,140], as did also MODLER [79,284]. However, in the case of TSP, the focus was specifically estimation and within this context relatively comprehensive in scope. TSP's nonlinear and system estimation algorithms, in particular, were affected by results presented at the MIT

Center for Computational Research: Bronwyn Hall recalls as fundamental to the development of TSP an important conference on nonlinear estimation methods held at the MIT center, a number of the papers from which were published in the October 1974 issue of the Annals of Economic and Social Measurement and elsewhere [139, 273]. MODLER's development during the 1970s represented a third way, stressing instead the broader aspects of the process of model construction and use as an integrated activity. Neither as specifically methodological as Fair's approach, nor quite so general in its estimation facilities as TSP, MODLER began from the concept that ideally the computer could provide the ability to interpret mathematical-textual instructions as if written on a piece of paper, with the fundamental difference that in a computer context these would instead be operational. This orientation reflected the interactive context of MODLER's early development: the PDP-10 at the end of the 1960s, which provided the individual user with a remote terminal that included a keyboard and CRT screen, making this concept immediately appealing as a goal. To realize this goal required the development of a natural language interpreter and the solution of a number of process integration problems in order to permit an isomorphic representation of the model code on the screen and in machine language [284,289].

However, not everyone focused quite so directly on equation systems. Packages that began to be developed during the 1970s include Autobox, B34S, BRAP, LIMDEP, RATS, and SHAZAM. In common with many other programs, each of these appears to have been created initially either in reaction to the absence of other, appropriate software, or to solve a particular problem. LIMDEP began in 1974 at the University of Wisconsin as an implementation of Nerlove and Press's multinormal model. Later it also implemented Ray Fair's EM algorithm for the tobit model [96].[31] It has finally become "an integrated program for the estimation and analysis of linear and nonlinear single equation models, using any of three types of data: cross section, time series and panel data" [135]. The forerunner of RATS was SPECTRE, written by Christopher Sims and others. This package was developed "to overcome some limitations of existing software that affected Sims' research in the 1970's, by providing spectral analysis and also the ability to run long unrestricted distributed lags." [71]. Tom Doan added ARIMA and VAR capabilities and subsequently looping and other programming features and changed its name to RATS. As a mainframe package, RATS was written in Fortran, but was re-written in C in 1991, after it had already been converted for use on the PC. The earliest development of SHAZAM traces to Kenneth White's undergraduate days at Northwestern, but the program's main development began at Wisconsin in the early1970s on a UNIVAC 1108. It survived

[31]This characterization is Bill Greene's. In a recent email, Marc Nerlove [246] has pointed out that, particularly in the statistics literature, it is generally accepted that the origin of the EM algorithm is Dempster, Laird and Rubin [61] and Rubin [292]. However, in response, Bill Greene noted that, in his 1977 Econometrica paper, Fair produced, apparently independently, an algorithm that is equivalent in its characteristics to the EM method, but quite specific to the tobit context, and that this is the method used in LIMDEP [134].

transplantation to the IBM 370 at Rice, Michigan and the University of British Columbia [344,345]. Autobox was also begun at Wisconsin, being an extension of the original "Pack Program" created by David Pack under the direction of George Box in the late 1960s; among other things, David Reilly added a "a rule-based heuristics system that is today the Autobox approach to ARIMA modeling." Design aspects of the development of B34S, among other packages, are considered by Stokes elsewhere in this volume [323], but this program was begun at the University of Chicago essentially to meet local needs and has since developed into a relatively comprehensive estimation package.

Considering these individual initiatives collectively, it is possible to highlight several salient areas of their development. On the one hand, econometricians began to incorporate into their packages both additional parameter estimation techniques and more sophisticated methods that involved nonlinear algorithms [18,273]. Linear-in-parameter estimation algorithms generally center on the inversion of a matrix, in the simplest case the symmetric matrix of sums of squares and cross products, and the best algorithms achieve both the inverse and, simultaneously, the parameter estimates. Nonlinear estimation involves a number of further considerations, including the need to compute derivative values accurately, usually in the context of a Hessian matrix. Nonlinear estimators, including Full Information Maximum Likelihood, provided a challenge that was then hard for econometric developers to resist, although nonlinear estimators were not commonly used in applied work until perhaps recently, particularly with the development of GARCH and other special application techniques [230, 273]. Meanwhile, in the case of software being developed within macroeconometic model projects, the focus tended to be on the integration of large data bases with estimation and display capabilities, and in a few cases, also the integration of model solution components, reflecting both that not everything can be done at once and that OLS and other linear methods were those most commonly used for large scale econometric models. Thus in the 1970s, the still continuing pattern was firmly set of some developers choosing to incorporate mathematically sophisticated techniques, and others developing packages involving different but similarly computationally challenging features such as program control via natural language commands – involving the need to parse and evaluate inputs and translate conventional mathematical expressions, as written, to polish notation and other more computationally tractable representations – as well as implement large-scale data base management, tighter process integration, and other such features.

However, as the established programs in the 1970s became progressively more feature-rich in their particular ways, other packages began to be created that reflected econometricians' desire to perform specific operations not included in the readily available packages. In certain cases, as with SHAZAM, the original stimulus for development was that packages readily to hand such as BMD, developed out of the Biometric tradition, were not especially suitable to econometric applications specifically. In other cases, as with LIMDEP (which is obviously a play on LIMited DEPendent variable), packages were developed as extensions within the econometric environment. Context is important: starting in the 1970s, panel data began to become more prevalent, with the development of longitudinal data bases associated with the National Longitudinal Surveys, the Panel Survey of Income Dynamics, and more recently the Survey of Income and Program Participation in the United States, or the Household Panel Survey, the National Child Development Survey, or the Social Change and Economic Life Initiative in the United Kingdom [213,245, 285,331]. These are of course simply examples, and, ultimately, a number of public use microdata samples have become available, drawn from tax records and other administrative data collection programs as well as surveys intentionally undertaken to support research [39,235,276].

Simultaneously, there were important extensions in coverage. For example, in 1972, Arnold Zellner and a number of colleagues began to develop BRAP and other programs, in order to provide a solid computational foundation for Bayesian estimation and analysis [1,353]. This case is an obvious example of an instance in which existing packages may well not cater to the interests and needs of a specific group of econometricians. One issue that this type of software development raises is whether there is a need, in such cases, to allow users to add facilities to existing programs? In the absence of this capability, anyone with a minority interest must respond by creating not only algorithms to perform a particular task, but in fact a complete program. Yet there is no difference necessarily between the Bayesian and other approaches as regards such things as data base maintenance facilities and many of the other ancillary program features. In the 1970s, it was sometimes possible of course to obtain source code from an existing program, and simply to embed a particular technique in it, but this process still required programming skills. However, need is not always a bad thing: especially in the early days, when program features were not well developed, the creation of additional programs was in itself socially beneficial, inasmuch as it created a cadre of people interested, however initially grudgingly, in software development.

These general comments introduce the embedding concept and identify possible applications, but the development of BRAP is also worth examining in slightly more detail in order to reveal more specifically what might be involved in the process of embedding a particular set of techniques as a component of an existing program. The earliest version of BRAP was in fact embedded in B34S,[32] then an existing program with the necessary facilities to load and mange data, having a structure very much like TSP at that time, combined with a user interface that could display results [322]. In this context, the data loading element of B34S essentially functioned as a preprocessor

[32] In the interest of expositional simplicity, this description involves a degree of poetic license in the use here of the word "earliest." To be absolutely precise, in 1967, in its original incarnation, BRAP was created as an integral part of B34T, the predecessor of B34S. In 1972, Zeller and others developed a standalone BRAP, in the process separating its code from (then) B34S. It was this earliest standalone version of BRAP that was operationally embedded as here described, permitting the programs to be operated jointly, but without any further actual intermingling of code.

to prepare the data for use by the BRAP add-in. It then executed BRAP. Finally B34S used its facilities to produce for the user the output from BRAP. As explained in the Stokes paper on software design elsewere in this volume [323], this type of embedding is relatively easily accomplished in the context of a procedure-driven program, such as B34S. Nevertheless, although this arrangement formed only a temporary way station in BRAP's development, it is still interesting as a example of both developmental relationships between programs and a relatively early attempt to minimize program development time in order to produce a result. In a Windows context, an essentially similar development has occurred recently with the development of GiveWin as a front end interface to not only PcGive, but also the current version of TSP.

The econometric software developments of the 1970s taken as a whole, even if they did not necessarily become fully realized then, do reflect that those years – particularly the early years – were a time of creative expansion. And although not always in a consciously coordinated way – in fact more often than not just the opposite – the effect of the various individual efforts in multiple countries and many contexts has ultimately resulted in a remarkable, jointly-developed software edifice. There was both a broadening and a deepening in the range of econometric techniques. Successive editions of econometric textbooks over the past 40 years, such as those of Johnston in 1963, 1972, 1984 and Johnston-DiNardo in 1997, as well as the generational development of textbooks by students of earlier textbook authors, obviously demonstrate changes in emphasis in the estimators described, but they also map both a broadening and deepening of the subject coverage. And to a degree, simply the existence of the computer undoubtedly facilitated this expansion. Thus, for example, in 1970, Edward Prescott, at Brookings temporarily from the University of Pennsylvania, was then in the early stages of the formulation of his method of stochastic parameter estimation and was interested to discover how to embody this concept in software [48,271]. Although only a relatively small subset of all estimators described in the econometrics literature have been included in econometric software packages generally, it has been common since the 1960s for econometricians to use the computer when developing estimators and methodologies, as for example in the cases of Durbin, Sargan, Wickens, and Zellner mentioned earlier. Moreover, particularly in the case of econometric software packages developed out of and for academic use, much of the software development has reflected the perceived individual needs of the econometricians doing the development.

However, lest any inference be drawn that the decade of the 1970s was manifestly a golden age, it needs also to be said that econometric software development then was distinctly a minority sport. For one thing, it is important to realize just how much smaller the number of prospective users was then as compared to now, and to recognize that the computer was not ubiquitous, nor even particularly intensively used by economists. Not every economist spent the weekend in the keypunch room; indeed, for most economists, the pencil was the most important applied research tool. Moreover, there were certain market conditions that limited prospects. Econometric software is the focus of this account and so far the focal point has been the supply side. But it is also pertinent to consider this software in its role as statistical software, a broader classification that includes also SAS and SPSS. In the 1970s and before, the market for such software was very much affected by the fact that computers then tended to be organizationally owned and managed, making it generally desirable that any software acquired should be broadly applicable. Regression, as a statistical technique, fits this requirement. But it is also true that in these years, particularly the early years, even among economists the demand was often for regression as a technique, rather than for an econometric software package per se. In the mainframe and even minicomputer applications software market, statistical software that included regression capabilities proved a natural contender, provided that it also included a wide range of other statistical techniques and options. Packages such as SAS and SPSS became widely used in both universities and elsewhere, even in comparison to other categorical types of software.

Reflecting the commercial imperative, SAS and SPSS, among others, were developed to satisfy the apparent needs of a broad range of users. However, inasmuch as these users were not homogenous in their interests and requirements, in time such packages progressively began to be developed to meet the perceived demands of identifiable categories; for example, the SAS/ETS (SAS/Economic Time Series) module was created at the end of the 1970s and included both frankly econometric techniques and an econometric model solution facility [7,294,299–301]. It was possible to buy the SAS/ETS user guide in many, if not most university bookstores, particularly in those instances that SAS/ETS was mounted on one or more machines there. In a few cases, econometric software packages became reasonably widely used, and TSP is an example of this. However, Hendry speaks both for himself and others when he said that "most econometric software has embodied an implicit methodology and modeling approach, but widely distributed programs have usually lagged some years behind the state-of-the-art technical econometric frontier" [149, p. 315]; particularly in certain cases, this lag spurred local software development. General statistical packages may have been the more marketable, but the need to serve a broad market also meant that actively developing market segments were not necessarily well served.

During this time, there was also development for additional computing "platforms," including the minicomputer. IBM mainframes were pervasive, at least in the United States, but during the 1970s the Digital Equipment Corporation began to develop its VAX minicomputers, following the PDP series of time sharing machines that began in the 1960s. The minicomputer provided a somewhat more intimate environment for software development, being conceived as a machine for a smaller group of users, a "department" rather than the "enterprise." In an academic context, the university might be served by one or more mainframes, but the economics department might be better served by one or more minicomputers. It is not clear that the minicomputer per se noticeably influenced the character of econometric software development to the degree that this machine type deserves to be considered separately; however there is little doubt that it made computing more widely available and, at the very least, permitted development to begin that might not have otherwise, either at that time or perhaps even ultimately. The econometrician who begins to program at the age of 50 or later is unusual, to say the least; it is far more common to begin younger. Therefore access to a machine (or not) is generally a critical element in the career of econometricians who also program. Another aspect of the computing environment at this time, which also bears on the issue of access to a computer, was the fact that programs did not always cross national boundaries.

Even within countries multiple frustrations existed. In the UK, for example, IBM computers were not so common at university computing centers as in the US; ICL and CDC machines were, particularly ICL. As a consequence, TSP and other packages from across the pond were not readily available, leading to the local development of programs such as HASH and, later, DEMOS, both developed by Tim Harrison, then at the University of Southampton. However, remote job entry (RJE) terminals that linked provincial universities to the University of London computer center, or to the University of Cambridge, did exist and provided some degree of cooperative development nationally. If the focus of this paper were impediments to the development of econometric software during the 1970s, quite a lot could be said about the balkanization effects created worldwide by incompatibilities among operating systems and among machines from different manufacturers. For example, it could be difficult using an IBM machine to read a tape created by a CDC machine, or a tape from an IBM using an ICL. In addition, everywhere, the resource constraints were binding: some computing centers made it difficult to obtain turnaround in less than 4 hours for jobs that required even 128 K of RAM; in almost any institutional setting crossing the 512K boundary, or sometimes an earlier trip-point, could mean a 12 or even 24 hours wait. Even into 1980s, such problems persisted.

2.3. The last days of empire: Mainframe developments in the 1980s

It is difficult to summarize the state of play at the beginning of the 1980s. The year 1980, or any near year, is not a natural dividing line. The first generally available, albeit build-it-yourself microcomputer, the Altair 8800, was introduced in January 1975, but as a type the microcomputer did not of course supplant other machines until well into the 1980s. As with any new development, even one that captures widespread attention, the adoption process takes time, particularly in those instances in which the implement, which is to say the hardware, is not in itself ready to use, and not only evolves rapidly for the next 20 years and more, but requires the development of a complementary product, the software, in order to be used effectively and widely. In or about 1980, the Apple microcomputer was already well known and as a somewhat experimental object was being adopted: Apples could be found adjacent to mainframe computers, usually in a separate room. In headquarter office settings, they sometimes could be found: in Texas, for example, the King Ranch was making productive use of an Apple in 1982–1983. But even in the case of the IBM PC, it took 3–4 years from introduction before it began to be adopted widely in an everyday context. Just as in 1915 the horse was still commonly used in transportation, during at least the first half of the 1980s, the mainframe computer continued to be used at least as widely as before, if not more so. Actually, although the term "supplant" has been used, for ease of exposition, in fact the microcomputer did not supplant the mainframe so much as become a tool widely used by people most of whom had never before used a computer. There was a change in the compositional mix of mainframe applications, reflecting the migration of particular types of applications to the PC. And certainly, for econometric applications, the microcomputer moved analytic processing out of the glass house and onto the desktop, but even in this case the vast majority of people who began to use it had never operated a keypunch nor loaded a card reader.

Francis Diebold has recently asserted that "Structural Keynesian macroeconomic forecasting, based on postulated systems of decision rules, enjoyed a golden age in the 1950s and 1960s following the advances in Keynesian theory in the 1930s and 1940s" [70]. It is not entirely obvious how to interpret this statement, either in context or out of it, but if it is a statement about the use of structural macroeconometric models, the dates are obviously wrong. Notwithstanding the problems encountered incorporating stagflation into these models beginning in the mid 1970s, the golden age of this type of model (if it has yet occurred) is much more appropriately identified with the years from 1975 to 1985 or later – measured in terms of either money spent to purchase access to forecasts made using them or the number of models active. Until 1985, almost all this activity took place in the context of mainframe econometric software, even if in 1985 there was a rush to implement microcomputer software in order to construct and solve such models.

One of the implications of the popularity of forecasts during this period may be that, had there been no revolutionary development, caused by the microcomputer in the 1980s and the Internet in the 1990s, it is likely that for mainframe econometric software the early 1980s might stand out as the beginning of a period of consolidation and refinement, much as the Edwardian era appears in the aftermath of World War I had there been no war. Or perhaps, given this revolution, such an interpretation is actually quite appropriate. There is good information on the state of the art of econometric software at the beginning of the 1980s. As well as in individual articles and books [23,247,258,284], it is contained in such publications as the 1980 supplementary volume *Computation in Econometric Models* of the *Journal of Econometrics* and the special issue on modeling languages in the 1983 *Journal of Economic Dynamics and Control* that documented the June 1981 annual meeting of the Society for Economic Dynamics and Control in Copenhagen [65,171,320].

In North America, at the beginning of the 1980s, integrated mainframe econometric modeling systems such as EPS, MODLER, and XSIM were organized as online data and software systems in the context of wide area telecommunications-linked networks [279]. In addition, in Canada, Statistics Canada's CANSIM provided a substantial online data base of Canadian data. For the US, although not yet online, the Bureau of Labor Statistics' LABSTAT system had been developed and contained disaggregated time series data on employment, prices, and other related statistics [236,

237,281]. As yet, there were organizational details to be worked out concerning the mechanisms for the distribution of US government produced data versus the "data vendors" such as DRI, Chase Econometrics, Haver Analytics, Wharton EFA and others [42,46,82]. However, even at the regional level there were systems, such as those in Indiana and Kentucky, that provided dialup and networked access to data resources and computing facilities by academic, government, and other users [4,5, 280,283,285].

In Europe, the proliferation of macroeconometric models [29] had resulted in the establishment of at least one organization in almost all countries that supported the development of models and software, as well as, in some cases, some form of online data base system, such as that produced in Calabria by Pitagora SpA, a subsidiary of the San Paulo bank. Not all these organizations were in the process of developing extensive telecommunications-linked networks. But DRI, Chase, and Wharton EFA each had offices in a number of countries, and in many countries, particularly in Europe, there was at least one indigenous firm. And of course at universities and governmental organizations, models were operating. A number of these models were participants in the LINK project, which resulted in the distribution and development of software on a fairly broad scale [12], although not always in the independent development of software. In particular countries, somewhat similar cooperative efforts were established in order to foster technology transfers as a subordinate goal: in 1983, at Warwick University, the ESRC Macroeconomic Modelling Bureau was founded to "to improve the accessibility of macroeconomic models of the UK economy, to promote general understanding of the properties of these models, and to undertake its own comparative and methodological research" [336–339], including a distribution mechanism for model solution software and facilities. Quite naturally, the focus at Warwick at the outset was mainframe computing facilities.

In the UK, as has been discussed, there were in particular a number of economic model-based forecasting and policy analysis organizations that developed during the post-1960 period, especially during the 1970s and 1980s. Those that were notably prominent in the development of software for model estimation and solution were the Cambridge Growth Project and the National Institute of Economic and Social Research, as indicated earlier. Both in Cambridge and at the NIESR software development continued into the 1980s. In each case, this development reflected the size and the characteristics of the embedded models, as well as the particular way in which these models were expected to be used. During the first half of the 1980s, Stephen Hall created a new model solution package CEF, that was an extension of Richard Pierse's NIMODEL. CEF was created in addition to REG-X, mentioned earlier. The CEF software has continued to be developed at the NIESR and in microcomputer form is today used with the Institute's UK and World models, the latter called NIGEM. This software is tailored to these models particularly, and approximately 30 central banks around the world subscribe to NIGEM embedded in it. However, if software persists, scholars are peripatetic. Progressively developed by Hall, CEF and REG-X moved with him to the Bank of England in the late 1980s and to the London Business School Centre for Economic Forecasting in the early 1990s, where the DataView component of MODLER was used to provide the data base management support – which combination may illustrate several aspects of the technology transfer process. Sean Holly, similarly, appears to have traveled from London to Sheffield to Cambridge with code. "Have code, will travel" might well be the motto of many econometricians of the second half of the 20th century, and by no means only in the UK.

Today, the thought of anyone setting up a buggy whip factory in 1910 seems whimsical. So too, setting up mainframe-based facilities in the early 1980s already appears in a somewhat similar light. However, this interpretation is entirely a matter of hindsight. From the perspective of 1981 or even 1983, the microcomputer appeared still toy-like to many observers; in late 1983, many organizations kept PCs in separate rooms as shared facilities and an organization that employed 1000 or more people might have but a single machine. A famous article in *Datamation* magazine in 1983 was one entitled "Real programmers don't use Pascal," a panegyric on the joys of mainframe Fortran and its manly properties [268]. At the 1981 American Economic Association annual meeting, Otto Eckstein, commenting as the discussant for a paper that in part described early work on the use of the IBM PC [282], characterized the microcomputer as needing at least 5 years of development before it could be considered seriously. Even with hindsight, the Eckstein comments are perfectly justifiable as a prediction of the time when the microcomputer was likely to become generally used for analytic work in preference to the mainframe – although these comments also possibly help to explain the change in DRI from a computing leader in the 1970s to a distinct follower in the next 20 years. It is important to be ahead of the curve during revolutions.

The image of British exports to the United States in the 1960s and 1970s centers on the Beatles, the Rolling Stones, and other, even more Hardrock groups. However, in the 1980s there were software exports as well. As mentioned earlier, in the late 1970s, Tim Harrison began the development of DEMOS (Dynamic Econometric MOdelling System) at the University of Southampton to support the modeling effort there. Subsequently, his work came to be supported by the French Atomic Energy agency, CiSi. In 1980, CiSi purchased Wharton Econometric Forecasting Associates, one of the aims being to marry an extension of the DEMOS package with the Wharton models. Later renamed AREMOS, this software was developed first as a mainframe package, with a considerable emphasis on data base management. The mainframe version has since continued to be developed, but during 1984–1985, a microcomputer version was also developed, very much in conjunction with the mainframe version, but also to a degree influenced by the properties of MODLER, the microcomputer version of which was then being used by Wharton EFA and a number of its clients. AREMOS, in its early development, was an interesting system particularly because of the close integration of the mainframe and microcomputer versions, enabling the user of the PC version to extract data series from the mainframe in a relatively effortless way. When Chase Econometrics was merged with Wharton EFA in 1987, AREMOS became the software of choice of the new entity, the WEFA Group, and XSIM fell by the wayside, although for internal company use it was not quite such a walkover as this may sound. During the past year, with the merger of the WEFA Group and what was originally DRI, to form Global Insight, AREMOS is in the process of apparently superceding the now rather antiquated EPS.

The development of MODLER as a mainframe system until 1981 and a microcomputer system since is described in considerable detail elsewhere [284,286]. However, briefly, the mainframe version of this software was made available during the second half of the 1970s and the early 1980s on two wide area networks. One of these was maintained by the Kentucky state government, and was used by its employees and, to some degree, the Council of State Governments and other national organizations. The other formed the Kentucky Educational Computing Network (KECNET) and was used mainly by state-supported universities and related organizations throughout Kentucky. MODLER was implemented in the context of a slightly more general software system, known as the Online Retrieval and Computational Language for Economists (ORACLE) that was an extension of the 1973 version of MODLER. The data base contained a substantial amount of national, state, and local area time series data [279,280], including approximately 14,000 monthly, quarterly, and annual time series for the state and its subdivisions [278]. The overall system was known as the Kentucky Economic Information System (KEIS) and from the beginning of 1976 its purpose was to provide data and software facilities, including cartographic displays, to both academic and governmental users, but also the public at large at various specific sites and via telephone links [4,5,278,290]. In that context, MODLER was used to estimate, build, and solve a variety of econometric models, mainly models of the state of Kentucky and certain of its component geographic areas. MODLER ceased to operate in this context towards the end of 1981, but the KEIS continued to operate as a mainframe data distribution system until the middle of the 1990s.

These online data base and analytic processing systems tended as a group to be less well known among academic economists. Historically, there are three reasons for this. The first is that they either cost too much for widespread academic use, with the fees for software often included in subscriptions for model forecasts and charges for access to data and consulting, or else to be local to their particular environment. The second is that they characteristically did not attempt to provide either leading-edge estimation capabilities or solution facilities for models that incorporated rational expectations and other academically interesting solution features. The context in which these systems operated tended to restrict development to those features likely to be used immediately and intensively by a broad group of people. Third, as software, with the exception of MODLER, from early 1983, and AREMOS, from 1985–1986, these systems were available during the 1980s only as mainframe-based time sharing systems, using either dial-up telecommunications or much more expensive T-1 lines, or else as custom installations on corporate and other institutional mainframes; in the case of XSIM and EPS, these custom installations could cost hundreds of thousands of dollars. Paradoxically, the average user of these systems, particularly when operated as mainframe systems, often used them to perform simple OLS regressions, if that, or to display graphs, charts, or tables, not for particularly sophisticated work. The use to which the systems have been put, being focused on light analytics, has meant that since the late 1980s both AREMOS and EPS in the PC environment have been placed at a competitive price disadvantage to Excel and other spreadsheet packages and, since the early 1990s, also to EViews.

From an academic perspective, it is easy to dismiss the type of system exemplified by AREMOS, EPS, or XSIM. Being "commercial," and responding to their user base first and foremost, these packages have always tended to offer less sophisticated estimation facilities than the "most advanced" academically rooted systems, systems such as MicroFit, PcGive or TSP, among the general systems, or other more particular and more specialist systems, such as those developed by Fair and colleagues. However, that said, it is also true that when typical users are taken into account, the offerings of AREMOS, EPS, and XSIM in the 1970s and 1980s, like the more ubiquitous Excel or even Word in the 1990s, are possibly more representative of the econometric facilities actually used by economists. Day-to-day average use does not involve as sharp a difference between the worlds of the business and the academic economist as might be thought from a theoretical literature review. Of course, the migration of the LSE methodology across the Atlantic has resulted in some changes, but best practice and actual use are not the same thing – in truth, it is not hard to overestimate the comfort of the average user, academic or otherwise, with cutting edge technologies. It also needs to be taken into account that during the 1970s and 1980s, in fact until the second half of the 1990s, most econometric software packages, of whatever classification, offered a relatively unsophisticated range of supplementary statistics [286]; the distinctions between such systems, in terms of parameter estimation facilities, centered almost wholly on the range of estimation methods offered. Moreover, it is still true that in the contest for greatest use, FIML still finds OLS hard to beat.

An additional interesting case is the development of software used in conjunction with the staff research work for the Board of Governors of the Federal Reserve System.[33] In the early 1970s and throughout much of that decade, the software used to support the development of the Federal Reserve-MIT-Penn model was obtained from the Economic Research Unit at the University of Pennsylvania or its affiliated company, Wharton EFA, or was created by extending the features of that software, as well as those of other well-known software packages. However, at the end

[33] In keeping with the overall focus of this paper on econometric software as defined earlier, the emphasis here is on the modeling software at the Board of Governors. However, other, quite closely related software has been developed at the Fed, including for example W.P. Cleveland's weekly seasonal adjustment program, in part based upon earlier programming work done by David Pack and Mike Grupe at the University of Wisconsin. Ideally, such work should also be considered in the present context, but time and space considerations place limits. However, this omission should not be inferred to imply a qualitative judgment; only a definitional restriction.

of the 1970s, a software system called Modeleasy began to be developed as an extension of an existing non-econometric system, Speakeasy [45], originally created by Stanley Cohen, then a theoretical physicist at the Argonne National Laboratory. Modeleasy incorporates the Speakeasy system and in the early 1980s was "defined as the Speakeasy processor enhanced with an FRB econometric vocabulary called FEDEASY" [47]. The development of this system subsequently has been the work of James Condie, then at the Board of Governors, Andrea Cividini and Giuseppe Bruno at the Bank of Italy, and William Teeters at the Econometric Modeling & Computing Corporation, although it also incorporates some work of Alfred Norman and others [47, p. 75].

Of course, as indicated, it is likely that the mainframe software system most used by economists during the 1980s was SAS. The mainframe version of SAS offered not only its standard regression facilities, but also the ETS supplement, as mentioned earlier, which permitted the creation and use of small macroeconometric models. For the estimation of parameters, and general statistical work, SAS was undoubtedly the most used single system. For the creation and use of large macroeconometric models, there is very little evidence of the use of this system, reflecting that during all the past 50 years relatively few large scale econometric models have been created independently. The 1983 article by Drud [79], describing the individual model solution capabilities of then existing software systems, also provides essentially a census of the mainframe econometric model support software systems at the start of the 1980s, but not all the systems described there have ever been used with any any known model.

2.4. The advent of the microcomputer

The microcomputer has its origins in the early to mid 1970s, but insofar as econometric software is concerned, the critical development was the introduction in August 1981 of the IBM Personal Computer. At its introduction, the original IBM PC offered only 16KB of RAM, with the option to add a further 48KB (at a price of at least $100), for a total of 64KB. This machine also offered removable storage in the form of 160KB single sided diskettes. The early programming languages available included Assembler, Interpreted Basic, Fortran, and Pascal. By design, floating point operations were supported in hardware by a separate supplementary FPU chip, the 8087, which adopted the IEEE standard and offered the possibility of performing numerically accurate computations not only faster than using software arithmetic emulation, but with a native level of precision beyond that of contemporaneous mainframes.[34] The primary CPU, the Intel 8088, was a hybrid, internally a 16 bit chip, but externally 8 bit, running at a blinding 4.77 MHz. Today, these specifications

[34]The 8087 FPU chip performed operations with a single instruction that to perform with the 8088 alone might require many. The taking of logs and exponentiation, in particular, were therefore speeded up substantially. Some idea of the difference can be gained from knowing that the multiplication of two

are exceeded by that of most PDAs and possibly even some digital cameras, but at the time the introduction of the PC was exhilarating.

In addition to having been introduced by IBM, which provided an aura of seriousness, the most significant feature of the IBM PC was its open architecture. Constructed of essentially off-the-shelf parts, the machine could be enhanced by its users. Consequently, within 6 months, third party manufacturers were offering memory boards that expanded the available RAM to as much as 320K, then 540 Kb (limited by a Bios quirk), and shortly thereafter to 640Kb. In 1982 IBM began to offer dual-sided diskette drives that provided 320Kb of removable storage; with the introduction of DOS 2.0 in 1983, the capacity of these immediately increased to 360 Kb. But not until March of 1983, with the introduction of the IBM PC XT with its 10 megabyte hard drive [40,253], did the PC become sufficiently advanced to support truly "large-scale" computing. Even then it was the introduction of the PC AT in September 1984, with DOS 3.0, a 6 MHz CPU, a 1.2 Kb diskette drive, and a 20 MB hard drive, that set the stage for subsequent hardware developments [41]. However, in 1984, a PC with dual 360 Kb diskette drives, an 8087 FPU, and 640 Kb of RAM did provide the capability to permit the solution of the PC-Mark7/MODLER 250+ equation Wharton Quarterly Econometric Model for 12 quarters in less than 4 minutes [284]. And by October 1984, the 1200 baud (1.2 Kbs) modem was a reality, even if not present on many desks at that time [306]. Of course, this brief account ignores the creation of a variety of clones and nearly PC-compatible machines during the 1981 to 1984 time period that, together with the PC, actually launched the revolution, but descriptions of these are readily available elsewhere.

Actually, the first attempt to perform a regression on the microcomputer predates the IBM PC. In fact there were apparently at least three early attempts: at the end of the 1970s, prior to his better known work on Lotus 1-2-3, Mitch Kapor created a microcomputer regression program for the Apple II, loosely based on TROLL, which he called Tiny Troll [88].[35] At about that time, in the UK, Stephen Hall

two-byte numbers would take 32 microseconds using the 8088 alone, whereas the 8087 could perform this operation in 27 microseconds. However, this is a best case for the 8088, which was a 16 bit chip (16 bits equals two bytes and 16 bits can hold only numbers that fall within the range –32768 to 32767). The 8087 in contrast contained 80 bit registers, obviously giving it a leg up as the necessary bit length of numbers increased. Moreover, the standard arithmetic operations (add, subtract, multiply, and divide), as well as the calculation of square roots, tangents, arctangents, logs, and base 2 exponents on numbers up to 18 digits in length were built into the hardware. In addition, various constants including zero, one, π, and standard log representations are included in the 8087's instruction sets. Consequently when such things as exponentiation or the taking of logs are considered, the 8087 was as much as 100 times faster than the 8088. Today's Pentium III and Pentium IV CPUs incorporate floating point operations and thus it is no longer necessary to purchase and install (or have installed) a separate FPU chip. Further details on the 8087 are provided in Startz [321] and in a useful article by Sarnak and Jaffe in the PCTech journal [298]. Another view of the 8087 is provided by Stephen Fried [111]. The adoption of the IEEE standard was important because it established a trans-platform standard for floating point computations, among other things allowing the PC to be adopted as a scientific tool.

[35] Kapor at this point became the product manager for VisiCalc and aparently took the plotting facilities

implemented REG-X on a Tandy microcomputer [143], as described earlier. In 1981, in California, David Lilien implemented MicroTSP on the Apple II using interpreted Basic. For Lilien, in particular, the attraction of this specific machine was its bitmapped screen and high resolution color graphics. He recalls, "because I wanted MicroTSP to support graphics and to have a full screen interactive interface I chose the Apple II as my development platform" [205]. However, despite these efforts, once the IBM PC was introduced, in short order it became the platform of choice for econometric software. Not only did it quickly define its market, but among other things the Apple did not offer numeric processing capabilities sufficient to make this alternative more than mildly attractive to developers of computationally intensive software. Notwithstanding that more than a decade was to pass before the Windows machine in the 1990s became even marginally visually competitive with earlier Apple computers, for a variety of well-known reasons the IBM and compatibles became generally market dominant even in the early 1980s. Consequently, before long, as had Kapor, MicroTSP migrated to the PC, becoming a compiled Basic program in 1984, at which point support for its Apple II version ceased [205]. In general, although there are modern examples of econometric software packages being developed for the Apple, including – since 1990 – a version of TSP, for the past 22 years the PC has been where the main action is.

In the beginning, the transition of econometric software packages from mainframe to microcomputer was nevertheless relatively slow to occur. Ivor Francis' 1981 compendium of mainframe statistical software packages [109] included several econometric programs, among them B34S, MODLER (in the context of KEIS/ORACLE), SHAZAM, TROLL, and TSP (2 separate versions). Of these packages, only MODLER is present in the Elsevier microcomputer software catalog of Fall 1983,[36] produced from the International Software Database [69], although both listings also include the more general statistical programs SAS and SPSS. These compilations are not necessarily comprehensive, so that exclusion of any particular program is not

from Tiny Troll to provide the basis for VisiPlot. Tiny Troll itself then evolved into VisiTrend. Having sold the rights to these products to VisiCorp, Kapor left and then began the development of Lotus 1-2-3. See http://www.crn.com/sections/special/supplement/763/763p63_hof.asp for additional details.

[36]The fact that a significant portion of MODLER's initial software design occurred in the context of the IBM 7040 and the DEC PDP-10, both 1960s era machines with comparatively minimal RAM and other computational resources, was of considerable benefit 11 years later when MODLER was ported to the original IBM PC. Its consequently parsimonious use of resources, not to mention its implementation on a variety of IBM 360/370 and later machines under several different operating systems, may help to explain why this complex and comprehensive program was one of the first previously mainframe-resident programs to be successfully ported to the microcomputer with all its facilities essentially intact. MODLER was (and still is) capable of performing all its operations, including solving simultaneous models of as many as 1000 equations in less than 460K RAM, without overlays, although the Windows version, making use of a Visual Basic front end as a user interface, now takes up much more RAM including that interface. Both overlays and the need to maximize RAM efficiency were a feature of life in the case of the IBM 7040 and the PDP-10. Of possible incidental interest, Bill Gates and Paul Allen wrote the first version (dialect) of BASIC for a personal computer using an 8080 emulator running on a PDP-10.

indicative per se, but rather simply illustrative of the speed of development of microcomputer programs and their conversion from the mainframe environment. Early microcomputer compilers for Fortran, Pascal and other compiled programming languages were notoriously difficult to work with, in contrast to their mainframe equivalents. Furthermore, recall that it was not until early 1985 that most organizations began to buy PCs in any quantity.

However, by the end of 1985, econometric software programs began to proliferate. By then, AREMOS, AutoBox (then called AutoBJ), PcGive, RATS, Shazam, and Soritec were operating on both the mainframe and the PC. Gauss was generally available on the PC and, as mentioned, MicroTSP had been converted from the Apple. By the later 1980s, with the introduction of microcomputer compilers that permitted a direct port of mainframe programs, a number of additional econometric packages were converted to the PC, or else directly developed there, including such still-existing packages as LimDep, MicroFit, REG-X, Stata, and TSP, as well as packages such as EAL, ESP and Workbench, which apparently no longer exist. All these were of course initially implemented in a DOS environment. Meanwhile, several previously widely-used mainframe packages either ceased to be maintained or only much later were converted, particularly EPS, TROLL and XSIM, the last two of which have not been, although a new program, "portable" TROLL, was created in the early 1990s based upon the original.[37] At the margin of what might be classed formally as econometric packages, in the sense of being used by econometricians, various other packages were also developed for the personal computer or converted from mainframe versions. These include such general statistical packages as SAS and SPSS, as mentioned earlier, but also MatLab, some aspects of the use of which is considered by Herbert in this volume [158]. Other near relatives include GAMS, which, among its characteristics, provides support for modeling linear, nonlinear and mixed integer optimization problems. But it is difficult to describe the history of the development of such programs in the present context without carrying the story far afield.

Focusing on econometric software, there is some degree of minor controversy as to whether the porting of a number of the previously mainframe programs to the PC were "straight ports" that took little or no advantage of the characteristics and potential of the PC. This debate's full ramifications are best left to after-hours gatherings of the cognoscenti. The significant feature of the microcomputer for econometric software development is the combination of a machine on every desk and a machine on every

[37] It is stated clearly in the description of "TROLL" in the software compendium [288], that description itself written by the current developer Peter Hollinger, that "portable" TROLL is "totally new." Notwithstanding that, as indicated there, "portable" TROLL may provide some or all the capabilities of the original program, it is obviously true that when a computer program is newly written in a different programming language for a different platform (or multiple platforms) by one or more people who are not the authors of an earlier program of the same name that in fact the programs are different programs, even if the later program is based on the earlier.

desk, in much the same sense that house price is said to be determined by location, location, location. The simple ability to acquire a machine that even in its early days offered the capability to perform nearly any task the econometrician might conceive, if not then, certainly in the near future, obviously provided stimulus to econometric software development. However, there was also a "push" factor in many cases. The turnaround time associated with mainframe batch processing has been mentioned. But even in the case of time-sharing systems, mainframes posed problems for their users. At Chase Econometrics in 1983, for example, it was not unusual to watch an economist type in a sequence of commands at a terminal, one by one, then in each case wait for even as much as a half-hour or more for the machine to respond, at least during busy times of the day. The original PC was not the equivalent of the mainframe in processing power, but neither was it shared. As a consequence, given the improvement in the PC's facilities during its first three years, it was certainly well within that time that this microcomputer became the effective equivalent of a share of a mainframe. An aspect of this distinction is provided by Stephen Fried, who in 1983 related: "a PC user recently discovered that his CRAY [super]computer executed one of his applications a factor of 180 faster than his PC. But because the CRAY was serving 100 users, the [actual] turnaround time was only a factor of 2 better than the PC" [111, p. 197].

The fact of the rapid adoption of the PC, particularly in the widespread way it occurred, starting in about 1985, clearly provided a potential market for econometric software. This market was and is small in comparison with the market for Excel, inasmuch as the number of economists worldwide is certainly less than 100,000, however loosely "economist" might be defined. But this number is obviously greater than the number of mainframe installations serving any collection of economists in 1980. Moreover, whereas economists in many cases usually had only a minority vote in the selection of mainframe software packages, as a user of a PC he or she has dominant influence, particularly to the degree that the software is purchased personally. What may be surprising, actually, is that the number of software packages listed today on the American Economic Association's Resources for Economists website (www.rfe.org) is not greater than it is, especially in comparison with the number of mainframe econometric software packages in Francis' 1981 compendium, mentioned earlier [109].

Broadly considered, the development of econometric software packages for the microcomputer, and in particular for the PC, can be seen as an extension of mainframe-based development in the 1980s. There was a transitional hiatus in the 1980s, but once developers adapted to the environmental characteristics of the PC compared to the mainframe or the minicomputer, the direction of movement, in terms of more and "better", was unambiguously forward. In the 1990s, once packages began to be converted from DOS to Windows, a hurdle that forced developers to focus temporarily but rather intensively on non-econometric aspects, there was an acceleration in their incorporation of additional econometric techniques. Various new estimators have been incorporated, including those for GARCH and other processes and methodologies introduced into the econometrics literature since 1980. For many packages, particularly noticeable has been the incorporation of facilities supplementary to the computation of parameter estimates. Test statistics have proliferated: in 1986 the test statistics provided by most packages generally did not differ much from what was offered in 1976, or even 1970. In North America specifically, this accelerated accumulation essentially represents another British invasion, with some flanking support from certain Canadians: Hendry's PcGive and the Pesarans' MicroFit have been in the van of the charge, even if the leading edge may have been a series of British and Canadian econometric methodology papers and monographs [44,53,54, 119,149,157,212,240,259]. These publications both espoused the ideas behind PcGive and MicroFit and provided critical details, which also influenced the latest crop of econometrics textbooks. The exogenous counterthrust by Granger and his allies encountered little resistance, and as a consequence a great deal of cointegration has ensued [14,91,126,127,343]. Of course, there are still econometricians who remain to be convinced, as a matter of methodology, but the point here is simply one of software features becoming available.

However, in addition to such time series-related development, there was generally a broadening of offerings. For instance, the development of B34S and LIMDEP illustrates this, each expanding the offerings of probit, ordered probit, and logit. In the 1980s, LIMDEP in particular incorporated the computations described in Heckman's seminal 1979 paper, specifically Heckman's estimator [130,131,146], as well as the tobit EM algorithm mentioned earlier. In addition, estimators for McFadden's conditional logit model were added, as well as a limited information maximum likelihood estimator for the nested logit model. Beginning in 1990, discrete choice models became such a well-defined subcomponent of LIMDEP that a now-separately distributed package, named NLOGIT, was spawned. One of Greene's stated aims was to automate "a very large number of related limited and discrete dependent variable models as well as a constellation of nonlinear econometric techniques" [135]. In the late 1990s, major areas of program development have been the incorporation of panel data estimation facilities and the estimation of stochastic frontier models: "The main feature of the package is a suite of more than 100 built-in estimators for all forms of the linear regression model, and stochastic frontier, discrete choice and limited dependent variable models, including models for binary, censored, truncated, survival, count, discrete and continuous variables and a variety of sample selection models. Beginning in 1990, a large and growing segment of the package was built for analysis of data on discrete choice (multinomial logit and probit models)" [135].

Other packages showed similar developmental traits. As indicated earlier, the development of EViews has been entirely on the microcomputer and occurred in two phases. The first incarnation, under the name MicroTSP, was developed originally for the Apple II and later ported to the PC. EViews itself, the development of which began in 1990, was released as an original Windows program at the beginning of 1994; Lilien is the original author, but more recently development of the program has become a collaborative effort [205]. During the past almost 10 years, EViews has progressed far from its origins as essentially a regression program. It offers a number of single equation time series techniques and options, supports VAR models, and now offers support for the development and use of structural models generally comparable to that of packages such as BETAHAT or Modeleasy+. The data base management capabilities of EViews have likewise become much more comprehensive, although not yet competitive with programs that have been specifically developed for large scale data base management [285]. EViews is now quite broad in coverage, much more so than more focused packages such as BETAHAT, FP, LimDep, Modeleasy+ or Stata. It appears to aim to support nearly all current econometric "schools," ranging from Box-Jenkins, to GARCH, to a fairly wide range of linear and nonlinear "traditional" single equation and structural equation estimators, to VAR.

This increase in features and usability is not limited to only the newest programs. As one of the "originals" and with a history of being represented on a wide variety of platforms, including mainframes, minicomputers, and workstations, TSP retains some obvious vestiges of its past. More importantly, the program has consistently been found to provide numerically accurate results and to provide its users with the necessary facilities to perform complex operations in a flexible, user controlled way, features that are particularly important when performing nonlinear estimation [230]. One of the program's salient features is that, whenever relevant, its estimation algorithms use analytic derivatives – supplied by the program, not the user – which partially explains why TSP has been found to provide more accurate estimation results than many other programs [223]. In native mode, TSP is operated using free-format commands and offers all the standard econometric estimation methods, including ordinary least squares, two and three stage least squares, GMM, LIML, FIML, ARIMA, Kalman filter, ARCH and other time series techniques. It also provides a "roll-your-own" maximum likelihood estimator, where the likelihood function can be evaluated either by a single equation or using a user-programmed procedure. Supporting the estimation facilities, TSP provides a variety of diagnostic and testing facilities, including a procedure to test nonlinear hypotheses. In addition the program also incorporates programming capabilities, including support for matrix algebra and user-written procedures that permit users to apply TSP to the development of new econometric techniques. However, the program now also has an alternative operating mode: it has "joined the Ox-metrics family of packages," using GiveWin as an interactive Windows shell. Essentially, what is implied by this phrase is that GiveWin can now function as a user interface for TSP: in response to user directives GiveWin generates the equivalent TSP commands, which then are processed by TSP itself. Operating in this context, TSP can be run either as a batch program or interactively. In addition, TSP for MAC OS version X is expected to be released in the late summer or early autumn of 2003.

As the foregoing indicates, most econometric software packages tend to provide an intentionally broad range of facilities, and some strive to be econometrically all encompassing. One that breaks this mold is BACC, the principal authors of which are

John Geweke and William McCausland. BACC was created in the early 1990s with the goal of making tools for Bayesian econometrics "as accessible to practitioners as are those for classical econometrics." In the beginning it was made available for use in a DOS environment as a standalone program. However, one of the notable features of the software is that in 1999 it was re-issued in the form of a Dynamic Link Library (DLL), which has the effect of enabling it to be "called" from other programs as a set of Bayesian techniques, either instead of classical techniques or as a complement to those techniques. Therefore, it can function as an "add on" to a program that otherwise handles the all the basic data management tasks and provides other such user support that is non-specific to the particular Bayesian estimation and directly related operations. This approach results in a different type of "embedding" than that described earlier in the case of BRAP and B34S, but operationally it obviously has some of the same properties.

Stata in contrast is an example of a program from the statistical software world. Originally designed by William Gould, it was initially developed as a DOS program in the mid-1980s and first released in 1985. It is today being developed by "a team of statisticians, econometricians, and computer scientists" [348]. Available for both the Apple and the PC, versions of Stata exist for multiple operating systems, including Apple, Linux, Unix, and Windows. Since the beginning 1990s, Linux and/or Unix have been supported on a variety of machine types, including the HP/9000, DEC RISC, IBM RS/6000, and Sun (Solaris); in 1995, the program was ported to Convex supercomputers under ConvexOS. Stata is designed to provide data base management, graphical analysis support, and a range of statistical techniques for time series, cross section, and panel data. It is cast as a more general "statistical platform with strong support for econometrics – including panel-data, survival, survey data, and time-series – and complete programming facilities for data management, new estimators, graphics, and GUI development" [348]; this is the selective description of capabilities. The developers of Stata encourage user participation in its development through "journals, email list servers, software archives, and special program features" [348].

Another type of recent development is that exemplified by WinSolve, a program developed by Richard Pierse specifically to solve models of various types, among them both structural and Real Business Cycle (RBC) models, using a variety of different algorithms, including both Newton and Gauss-Siedel. This package can be viewed as competitive with CEF, MatLab and other packages that offer both model solution options and facilities to support optimal control techniques. Its lack of capability to actually perform a regression may raise a question in some minds of its present relevance, but if there was any doubt WinSolve places itself firmly in the context of econometric software by offering the capability to read proprietary data files from EViews, MicroFit, MODLER, PcGive, RATS, and TROLL, among others. The package also provides the capability to solve models so as to incorporate model consistent expectations and other rational expectations schemes. In addition, it incorporates a Stacked Newton algorithm that permits the solution of models such as the Ramsey [275] and Koopmans [184] optimal growth models. It also offers such standard structural model forecasting features as support for "ragged edge" solutions, and both constant and multiplicative adjustments, including the Type 1 and Type 2 "fixes" beloved of Treasury modelers in the UK.

Finally, although there is no free lunch, there are freeware econometric software packages, among them EasyReg, FP, and TSMOD.[38] Interestingly, these packages exhibit diversity in several respects, ranging from their econometric characteristics, to the source languages used to write them, to the operating systems under which they run. The primary author of EasyReg is Herman Bierens and it is a Visual Basic program, thus a Windows package. It is seemingly comparable in its econometric facilities to the standard estimation packages, but ranks among the less developed packages in terms of its data management and other creature comforts. The authors of FP are Ray Fair and William Parke. FP is a Fortran program that runs under DOS and is closely keyed in its facilities to Fair's books and his models. The author of TSMOD is James Davidson and it can be run under either Windows or Linux, and apparently involves some degree of use of Java. The program is described by its author as "a new project, still very much under development," however at present, econometrically, the program appears to be specialized to single equation time series modeling. These packages are described in more detail in the supplementary compendium, found at the end of this volume.

It should be evident from this description of a selection of existing programs that, although the initial conversion of mainframe packages to the PC may have represented at first a step backwards in some respects, particularly during the period from 1981 to 1987 – reflecting less advanced operating systems and language compilers, and other such aspects of the 1980s PC environment – by the later years of the decade the forward progress had resumed. Particularly from 1984, the PC offered screen graphical facilities that were vastly superior to those generally available on either mainframes or minicomputers. The RAM available to PC users matched or exceeded that generally available to individual users of either mainframes or minicomputers in 1983, and without the execution delays experienced by individual mainframe users. In fact, by the mid 1980s, the problems posed by the PC for developers were much more the result of an attempt to do more computationally than had ever been done before than a consequence of the PC offering a less enabling environment. Rising aspirations of developers, combined with the increased expectations of users, many of whom had a "Madison Avenue" inculcated view of what the computer was supposed to be, colors many developers' retrospective view of the problems of conversion from the mainframe or minicomputer to the PC.

[38] The use of the term "Finally" reflects not only the order in which these packages are described in this section of the present paper, but also the fact that their authors provided necessary information about them only after the paper was essentially written. Thus their composite (and brief) description reflects much less their common characteristic as freeware than it does the production deadline for this volume. Soritec is yet another program current information about which was received too late to include here, but which is described in the compendium.

Of course, there were certain weaknesses. For example, under DOS a number of packages were weak in terms of their display of graphs and other such "visuals." However, in retrospect it is now very easy to see that DOS was a difficult environment in several respects. Reflecting this environment, it might even be appropriate to apply this criticism of weakness in visual displays, in varying degrees, to all econometric software of that time. But having identified this problem, what is particularly important to understand is its source: the source of the problem is essentially that a DOS program, and its developers, must take responsibility for each of the peripherals used by it and attached to the computer, either directly or via a network connection, including monitors, printers, and plotting devices. Successfully supporting users who might variously own an Epson, a Hewlett-Packard, or a Techtronics printer consequently required the developer to write specific code for each of these, especially to the degree that it became desirable to make each of these devices sing and dance, which of course it was to their particular owners. This requirement to support specific peripherals individually was of course a distraction to the econometrician-developer trying to provide a suitable set of parameter estimation and other econometric facilities.

In contrast, whatever else one might say pro or con about the Windows operating system, a fundamental characteristic is that it takes responsibility for all the hardware devices used by any computer running under it. The programmer of an applications package, an econometric software package in particular, need only make a tight link between it and Windows for the user to be able to use quite successfully any attached peripheral that is supported by Windows. In this process hardware vendors must have earnest talks with Microsoft, but if these folk form a happy family, the user of the econometric software package can change from one monitor to another, from one screen resolution to another, and still find that the program works. To be sure, certain screen resolutions may provide a more satisfactory result than others, but at least something intelligible normally shows up on the screen. The same cannot necessarily be said for DOS and an arbitrarily chosen pixel graphics monitor. There is a lesson in this, when considering multi-platform software implementations: different platforms provide different levels of developer support affecting differentially the use of the software – to the degree that the developer does not do extra work to counteract this.

The entire saga of the conversion of econometric software packages from DOS to Windows is too lengthy a tale, but certain aspects are pertinent. Recall from the earlier discussion that EViews, the successor to MicroTSP, was one of the first econometric software packages to be converted to Windows. All development of MicroTSP ceased in 1990, and a new program was begun using C++ as the programming language for the Windows environment. The Windows version was released at the beginning of 1994 as EViews. A revealing comparison can be made between EViews, on the one hand, and AREMOS and MODLER on the other that illustrates a possibly general characteristic of software development and user reactions. The conversion of these other programs also occurred during the middle 1990s, but took longer and, interestingly enough, both these programs still have users who are steadfast in their determination to stay with the DOS version as long as possible, notwithstanding that various special modifications have to be made to allow these versions to run satisfactorily under Windows 98 and Windows ME, or Windows 2000 and XP, and notwithstanding the DOS and peripherals problem. One of the reasons for the slower pace of the conversion, and certainly the acceptance of the converted versions by users, is apparently that both AREMOS and MODLER are long established and quite reliable as DOS programs, provided of course that the user owns the "right" machine with a standard peripherals configuration. However, users of the DOS versions fully understand their quirks, know the command languages of these programs, and apparently find that the adoption of the Windows version involves a learning curve they would prefer to avoid. In contrast, EViews is a much more capable, comprehensive, and robust program than MicroTSP. From a long-term user's perspective, other than interface, there is possibly less difference in capabilities between the DOS and Windows versions of AREMOS and MODLER than between MicroTSP and EViews. In short, User inertia is an important aspect of the software experience.

The conversion from a command line to graphical interface is specifically an issue that needs to be considered. Actually, the DOS to Windows conversion need not involve this interface conversion: it would be perfectly possible to write a Windows program that within the program's "window," the visual area of that program on the screen, looked essentially the same as its previous DOS command line incarnation, assuming that under DOS this was the program's interface. The reason that this type of conversion is an unusual approach is of course that users (and developers) expect a Windows program to look like a Windows program. And demonstrably this convention applies even more widely than just the Windows environment. From Apples to Linux to Windows, there is a "right" style and that style is now broadly the same across all these operating systems, at least in comparison to a DOS command prompt. Today, most people demand a WIMP interface – Windows, Icons, Menus, and Pointing devices – because there is now a near-reflex reaction against command line interfaces.

One of the commonly perceived defects of a command line is that it requires abstract knowledge: for a particular command, there is no button on the screen to "click on," thus the learning curve may be sufficiently steep as to repel absolutely any new users. Part of the reason for this repulsion today is simply that this interface lacks visual excitement; ostensible modernity is a powerful molder of taste and opinion. However, as an antidote to embracing unreservedly the WIMP interface, consider, for instance, the implications of trying to use a word processing package by successively clicking on scrollable lists of words in order to form sentences and paragraphs, rather than typing them letter-by-letter. Obviously, typing is better; but this conclusion of course reflects the presumption that people already know both the letters and most of the words they might want to use. And this knowledge is of course also the reason why, in the case of word processing programs, the menus and icons appear at the window margins: they supplement the principal data entry process, the typing of the letters and words into the main, usually white, space of the program.

In the case of econometric software, there is unquestionably a role to be played by menus and pointing devices: certain types of operations, such as selecting various default settings or working with graphical displays, are particularly amenable to "point-and-click." However, specifying equations may be an activity more like word processing. In addition, the case can be made that even for menu or click-appropriate operations, a command line alternative should be offered as well: econometric research often involves repetitive operations performed at regular intervals, such as making certain data transformations, estimating or re-estimating equations, and the like. Such operations may be able to be performed interactively, but after a few repetitions it becomes evident to anyone that simply executing a macro once a week or once a month is preferable. During the initial DOS to Windows conversions, the WIMP interface was sometimes seen as a be all and end all, but as time has gone on, there has been a steady and perceptible move back towards at least partial command line operation. In the context of econometric software, a fundamental reason is that the command line is the basis for allowing a user to specify the precise operation that he or she wishes to perform.

Much more could be said about these particular issues, but these comments have been made principally to illustrate that interface design plays a part in econometric software development that should not be ignored, especially to the extent that the program is created for other people to use. Another inference to draw from this description is that conversion to a new operating system environment is a significant step in the life of a program. Furthermore, the Windows environment has two very important additional characteristics. First, it is not static: Windows 3.x, Windows 9.x, Windows ME, and Windows XP are related operating systems, but not the same operating system. Each change in operating system insures that some program feature that worked before will not work now, at least as advertised. Even in those cases that successive operating systems represent improvements, the change nonetheless imposes the need to change the applications programs, if only to take full advantage of the particular new features of the new operating environment. The second important Windows characteristic is that most machines that run Windows also run MS Office, as a matter of course. In part because Microsoft makes Microsoft Office, as well as Windows, and because users change their versions of Office when they change operating systems – and use Office in preference to its competitors in many cases – in practice there is a requirement for a software developer both to make econometric software packages work with Windows and Office and to change the versions of their packages whenever Windows and Office change. It is also not insignificant that government statistical agencies and other providers of the data that econometric software packages use commonly make that data available in Excel spreadsheets. Such contextual issues are important in explaining why it is that it took most of the 90s for econometric software developers to adapt fully to the change from DOS to Windows, assuming that they have fully adapted.

The degree to which the PC has progressively become more competitive with the mainframe is an additional important story. Lest there be any question, there is good evidence from the LINPACK benchmark results [74] that the RS/6000, the IBM workstation machine of the early 1990s, was faster than the Cray SV-1 supercomputer, offering peak performance of 1800 Megaflops per second, compared to 1200 for the Cray. However, the current 2 gigahertz Pentium 4, which is available on a number of notebook computers, offers peak performance of 4 Gigaflops per second [73]. Furthermore, notebooks with 60 GB hard disks are not uncommon and some notebooks sport screens that offer as much as 1600 × 1200 pixel resolution on the notebook screen, not to mention 2048 × 1536 maximum on a suitable monitor that might be attached. Some of these machines in addition support 100 megabit or better network connections and may incorporate both Bluetooth and WiFi (802.11× wireless networking). Obviously, not every user has a machine with these capabilities, but they will have, and in the next year or two, in the case of most users. During the past 20 years, the PC has changed from a machine, in terms of peak performance, that was 180 times slower than the Cray SV-1 to one that is now more than 3 times faster and fits in a briefcase.

3. Econometric practice: The econometric software package today

Classically, econometric software packages have taken the form of programs that offer a specific set of selectable options. This was particularly true of regression packages of the 1970s and 1980s, and it is still true of Autobox, CEF, MicroFit, REG-X, and other Windows packages that fundamentally offer a "point and click" user environment. It is less true of packages such as AREMOS, B34S, LIMDEP, MODLER, RATS, and Stata, among others, which each incorporate a programmable command language that permits the creation of macros to several levels of nesting and, to varying degrees, offer features found in computer languages like Basic, Fortran, Java, or Pascal. Such a facility allows the user to perform operations that either constitute composites of the program's standard offerings or extend those offerings. Sometimes, such as in the case of the DOS version of MODLER, these embedded languages have even permitted the generation an interposable interface that changes fundamentally the program's external appearance, allowing it to do such things as display on the screen a tailored menu rather than a command prompt, offer expert features to less knowledgeable users, and otherwise control the overall operation and look of the package. Both the Economist Workstation, a mid-1980s joint product with DRI, and the later PowerStation offered with text in several human languages by consulting firms in Europe and the US – are examples of such MODLER implementations [15].

However, in order to be able to evaluate properly the implications of such developments, as just described, it might be useful to stop briefly and ask: how exactly did we get here and what does it mean? This approach risks the danger of a pseudo-historical, somewhat Hobbsian or Rousseau-like explanation, complete with early econometric software developers cast as rather primitive creatures, noble or otherwise. Nevertheless, the original stimulus for the development of such macro programming capabilities can be seen as arising from the need to perform various tasks repetitively in an interactive setting. The obvious disadvantage of purely interactive processing, compared, say, to using physical decks of cards, is that commands once processed no longer exist – unless of course these are saved in a file on some storage device and then later executed, or re-executed, by reading that file as a batched set of commands. In the simplest case, a macro is no more, and no less, than a file containing commands of some sort, used in this way. However, there is commonly a need to perform the same transformation on a number of different variables, or flexibly to create moving averages or other such transformations involving lagged values of variables or the like, so that a natural next step is to define a programming syntax that will permit such a macro file to begin to take on the characteristics of an interpreted program, which is then executed by the command processor of the parent econometric software package. Developed in this way, the parent program's macro language progressively becomes a means of symbolically processing variables as data and is enriched to the point that it takes on the characteristics of an actual programming language. The motivation for such developments, by implication, is obviously to improve and enhance the usability of the parent package, so that this type of development has tended to occur in contexts in which the stress has been placed on the broad usability of that program. A good example of an econometric software package enhanced in this way is XSIM: XSIM, having a particularly well-defined macro language, became capable of supporting quickly developed, quite sophisticated macro-based programs to perform specific tasks, utilizing the facilities of the parent program, that simultaneously also simplified the use of the parent program, by providing task-based solutions to particular users' needs – in very much the same sense as today a macro can be used to operate Excel, giving it a temporary persona, or new menu entries can be added to Word for Windows, for example permitting it to generate PDF files or execute another program to fax the document just created, or perform any of a variety of other such user-determined operations.

However, this characterization of the logic of the development of a program's command language is appropriate only in certain cases. In contrast, with the development of Gauss since the mid 1980s and much more recently Ox, another type of package has emerged, essentially an econometric software package that explicitly promotes itself first and foremost as a high level programming and matrix language, and which thereby potentially permits the user to define new econometric constructs. LIMDEP, RATS, Stata, and TSP, among others, also present themselves as sharing this last characteristic, although perhaps not so much as a leading concept. On his Internet "work page," Jurgen Doornik, the principal author of Ox, describes it as "an object-oriented matrix language with a comprehensive mathematical and statistical function library. Matrices can be used directly in expressions, for example to multiply two matrices, or to invert a matrix. Use of the object oriented features is optional, but facilitates code re-use. The syntax of Ox is similar to the C, C++ and Java languages. This similarity is most clear in syntax items such as loops, functions, arrays and classes." Considered on its own out of context, Ox might not qualify as an econometric software package, being only potentially applicable to econometric problems, but its econometric nature becomes apparent when such Ox "applications" as G@RCH and PcGets are taken into account [155,196]. TSMOD is another Ox application, as are also ARFIMA, DPD, MSVAR and STAMP, each described in the econometric software compendium at the end of the current volume. Similarly, CML and GaussX, also described there, are examples of Gauss applications. In addition to Gauss and Ox, there are of course other programming language packages, including Mathematica, MatLab, R, and S-Plus, that can be used by econometricians for this type of development [9,21,357]; MatLab in particular has been used by economists interested in control theory [158]. MathStatica, also described in the compendium, is an "add-on" to Mathematica.

An obvious implication of the econometric programming language approach is that an econometrician using one of these packages no longer necessarily needs to wait for some developer to add a new econometric technique. Within limits, he or she is able to accomplish this directly. Of course, it has always been possible to learn to program [50], but an important aspect is the "high level" nature of this environment. In effect, a program like Gauss or Ox provides an entry point that does not require the econometrician to learn how to program at the more fundamental level of C, C++, Pascal or Fortran, each of which *computer* programming languages involves the need to program with reference to the operating system. It might even be appropriate to see this high level econometric programming language environment as providing a richer approach to the concept mentioned much earlier, that of permitting the economist to approach the computer screen as he or she might a sheet of paper, but with the operational consequence that what is symbolically represented actually occurs. If you will, AREMOS, MODLER, and XSIM are examples of econometric *modeling* languages (EML) [289], but Gauss, Ox and possibly other similar packages are effectively econometric *programming* languages (EPL). The critical distinction is the object being worked with: an econometric modeling language has as its objects specific, well-defined types of estimators, time series variables, model equations, and models, but also variable transformations, which in a data base maintenance context are simply formulae that generate other variables and in a model context may be identities. In contrast, an econometric programming language offers as objects matrices, vectors, operators, implicit functions, a looping syntax, and a particular grammar, among other characteristics.

Evidently, econometric software can now be classified into standard estimation packages, often menu oriented, that provide an economist with the ability to perform a given set of operations that are specifically defined by the software developer: the user of such a package selects from a set of options. There is next a mid-range, which most obviously includes the econometric modeling languages, with the characteristic that the economist is required not only to make certain selections but also to control how particular operations are performed: he or she must put equations together, by combining variables and operators, and by so doing *build* a model. These models can be *solved or simulated.* The results can be *plotted* or displayed as tables. Advanced estimation packages (AEP) that both offer a selection of choices and incorporate a macro language capability should also be included in this classification. Finally, the econometric programming language in turn offers less in the way of prefabricated statistical and mathematical objects, but more scope to *create* new econometric, statistical and mathematical forms. It also might be possible to infer that an econometric programming language is most suited to use by econometricians, as creators of emerging techniques, as opposed to applied economists, who are more likely to use established methodologies, hence another type of package. Obviously, these sharp distinctions are most meaningful when considering polar examples of these package types.

In practice econometric programs may not be so neatly classifiable. In order to probe the state of the art, using the existing programs as observations, it is possible to consider a taxonomy that establishes as aspects three central characteristics: Interface, Language Orientation, and Purview. The types of Interfaces can be categorized as:

- Menus and Icons (the now classic graphical WIMP interface)
- Menus and Icons Can Generate Interactive Commands
- Interactive Command mode
- Menus and Icons can invoke Batch (Macro) Commands
- Batch Operation of a Macro

The successive differences are as follows: in the Menus-Icon case, the program is operated directly by the user selecting a menu item or icon, which in particular instances may cause a dialog box to appear, but always involves a direct link between this interface and the operating structure of the program. For example, this method is essentially how Word and Excel operate in interactive mode: click on the open file icon, a list of available files appear, double click on the name of one of these. The file is opened for access, and its contents (usually) are displayed on the screen, at least in part. In the second case, the critical difference is not necessarily what appears to the user, but how control is effected: the menus and/or icons, when selected, generate one or more (usually at the time hidden) commands that actually operate the program. That is, the commands directly cause the operation of the program, but are generated individually, in response to a particular menu or icon selection, and the program responds in "real time" as each command is issued. In contrast, when the program is operated in the third mode, by Interactive Commands specifically, the commands are issued by the user explicitly, without touching either a menu or an icon, and the program responds to the commands individually, as these are issued. The fourth case is distinguished by the generation of a file, a macro file, containing a set of commands, which are generated using menus and/or icons, but this file is then "executed" as a "batch" operation, with the commands then causing the program to perform a sequence of actions, generally without further user intervention. Finally, in the case of the Batch Operation of a Macro, the user writes this macro file, employing Notepad, Wordpad or some other text editor, which in the case of some programs may be built into its interface. Once the macro file has been created, the user submits it for execution. The macro itself directly causes the program to operate, as the program successively reads each of the included commands, generally without further user intervention. As shown in Table 1, which displays the responses of the developers of the programs listed, it is common for individual econometric software packages to offer two or more of these interface modes. Another, much less common, mode involves the generation of a command file by one program that is then used remotely by another related program, as in the case of MODLER and Stata, [39] or that controls the operation of the other program, as in the case of GiveWin and TSP, or B34S and BRAP, as described earlier.

The Language Orientation of the existing econometric software packages can also be displayed in tabular form, but the issue of Language Orientation involves somewhat greater subtleties. The first language classification characterizes a econometric software package as having the property of allowing its users essentially to select among a given set of specific econometric and related options. Fundamentally, the critical element of language in this context is the objects of the commands: the objects may be an OLS, 2SLS, or other distinct regression command. Alternatively, the object could be a command that opens a model file or causes the solution of a model. Note that here, as discussed earlier, the objects of the language category are types of regressions, equations, models, and the like: essentially econometric entities that are specified by the user in order to cause the program to perform a series of quite well-defined operations. Of course, the specific computations may in fact be unknown by the user, inasmuch as algorithmic details are normally not published by individual developers, although they are generally understood to correspond to known econometric techniques or processes. [40]

However, the "language" as such does not need to be enunciated: in the particular case of econometric software operated interactively by Menus and Icons, the program's user language per se is actually an abstraction. In this case it exists

[39] In the case of MODLER, plot files and other such macros can be used to generate the same plots as in MODLER in the context of both other MODLER "family" programs, such as DataView and MODLER BLUE, and a specific unnamed plotting program that was used in past years to permit plots to be generated by other microcomputers, including Apple machines, used to support dedicated commercial publishing software for the production of very high quality reports [319,341]. In the case of Stata, the process works in reverse using what is called an automatic "do-file" or "ado file." It is this facility that lets users add commands to Stata that appear as built-in commands without having to load a "package" at run time [347].

[40] It is of course common for developers to describe, in standard textbook notation, the operations ostensibly performed. MicroFit, for example, is accompanied by a thick, and very useful, manual that describes in detail the econometrics of the package. Similarly, particularly in recent years, Hendry and Doornik have put considerable effort into the documentation accompanying PcGive, Hendry indicating that "we see our 'PcGive' books as textbooks with a strong computational bent (and use them that way), rather than 'manuals'." [152] But what is referred to here is the algorithmic implementation of the various econometric techniques – that is, the precise way these are actually coded as instructions to the computer.

Table 1
Interface Characteristics of Econometric Software Packages

	WIMP interface	Icons/menus can generate interactive commands	Interactive command mode	Menu/icon can generate batch (macro) commands	Command operation of a macro
Independent Econometric Software Packages					
AREMOS	X	X	X	X	X
AutoBox	X	X		X	
B34S		X	X		
BETAHAT	X		X		X
CEF	X		X	X	
EasyReg	X				
EViews	X	X	X	X	X
FP		X			
gretl	X	X	X	X	X
IDIOM		X		X	
LimDep		X	X	X	X
MicroFit	X				
Modeleasy+	X	X	X		X
MODLER	X	X	X	X	X
MODLER BLUE	X	X	X	X	X
MOSAIC		X		X	
NLOGIT		X	X	X	X
PcGets	X	X		X	X
PcGive	X	X		X	X
PcNaive	X				
RATS		X	X	X	
REG-X	X				
SHAZAM		X	X	X	X
SORITEC	X	X	X	X	X
STAMP	X	X		X	X
STATA	X	X	X	X	X
TROLL		X	X		X
TSP		X	X	X	
WinSolve	X		X	X	
WYSEA	X		X	X	
Econometric Programming Libraries					
BACC			X		X
MLE+			X		
Econometric and Mathematical Modeling Languages					
Gauss			X	X	
LINDO/LINGO		X	X		
Ox		X	X	X	X
Econometric Programming Language Applications					
ARFIMA		X			X
CML					
DPD		X			X
G@RCH		X			X
GaussX	X				X
mathStatica	X	X	X		
MSVAR		X		X	X
TSMod32	X	X			X

ephemerally, as a shadow of the progressive use of the menus and/or icons by the user. To be obvious, a language normally must involve explicit commands, and a grammar and syntax, and must cause specific actions. But in fact, as just indicated, these commands do not necessarily need to be typed by the user; they could just as easily be generated by the selection of menu items or icons. The essential issue is the type of objects manipulated. However, for purposes of classification, it is nevertheless pertinent to distinguish, as sub-categories, between an implicit language facility, taking the form of menus and icons, and an explicit command language, for although in each case the same operations could be performed and the same objects manipulated, these modes differ in the way a user of a program is likely to regard the program's manner of operation, not to mention its flexibility to be used in either interactive or batch or quasi-batch modes. It would be possible to go further in this vein, to make even finer distinctions, for as discussed earlier there are programs, including both Excel and particular econometric software packages, that permit the user to generate macro commands as a by-product of using menus or icons.

The second language category also incorporates sub-categories that refer to either an implicit – menus and icons based – or explicit command language, but in this case the objects are vectors, matrices, and other mathematical and/or statistical entities. In this context, the language can be expected to be higher level than Fortran or Pascal or C/C+, but nevertheless a form of programming language. The ostensible effect of language at this level is to give the user greater control over the operations performed. The presumption is that the user will now control to a finer degree the specific operations performed by the computer, although in fact this need not actually be the case: it is possible for the package developer to cause the user's commands to be interpreted intelligently and then converted and executed in a manner determined by the developer.[41] As before, the specific computational operations are unlikely to be known by the user, inasmuch as these algorithmic details have generally not been published by individual developers. At issue is not just the user's ability to specify the characteristics of an arithmetic or algebraic operation, which may be supported, but also the way in which various conditions are evaluated, such as, for instance, the degree of convergence in the context of an iterative nonlinear process, or the user's freedom to precisely set initial values [229,230].

However, for classification purposes, it can be presumed that the user of this command language at this second category level does not affect the interface that he or she or some other user may see in order to operate the program. Only in the case of the final language category should the available facilities be interpreted to consist

[41] This sort of intermediation occurs, for example, in the case of optimizing compilers, which are of course designed to recognize the user's coding inefficiencies and then to produce "corrected" machine language code that produces faster execution, but presumably no other functional differences – in terms of the operations performed and the numeric values generated – but this is only a presumption. McCullough, Vinod, and others have recently argued, in effect, that economists and econometricians may be too generous in their presumptions [231,232].

of a command syntax, grammar, and structure that has high level objects, but also permits the generation of onscreen objects that may be organized so as to create an interface for the ultimate user of the program – irrespective of whether or not that user is the person doing the language writing or someone else. This capability may involve a higher level language than that of Visual Basic, or Visual C/C+ and other such development environments, but the effect is nevertheless similar in the sense of providing an environment that results or can result in the creation of an application that is operated by menu, icons, explicit commands or any combination of these jointly or severally. Table 2 displays the language orientation of existing econometric software packages, constructed on the basis of responses by the developers of the programs listed.

The issue of Purview, or the range of types of operations performed and facilities incorporated, is just as subtle as language. For many economists, the essence of an econometric software package is that it will permit regressions to be performed, usually in such a way that this facility can be seen as supporting the estimation of the parameters of some equation specification that has economic content. Judging the degree to which an operation is "econometric" is obviously as particular as the various econometric "schools." However, within this classification there are clearly single equation versus system estimators: Ordinary Least Squares (OLS), at one extreme, versus Full Information Maximum Likelihood (FIML) at the other. There is also the time series approach that at one extreme consists of the Box-Jenkins methods and at the other, the dynamic time series approach associated with modern econometrics. However, it is also possible to distinguish between these essentially time-oriented methods and cross-section and panel data methods – and also to make distinctions within each of these classifications. Within the time-oriented approach, it is for example possible to consider methods that are associated with a more detailed specification of the associated error process, such as GARCH. Within cross-section and panel data methods, logit, Poisson, probit, tobit, and other techniques can be distinguished, involving fixed and random effects. There are several ways of examining the classifications of estimators and, historically, at least in the case of linear estimators, the most natural for econometricians is to consider progressively the implications of the failure of each of the particular assumptions that together result in the attainment of Best Linear Unbiased Estimates – although today the diversity has become too great for this particular pedagogic approach to be applied as generally as it was in textbooks, say, in 1980.

Beyond the estimation of parameters, existing econometric software packages include several possible levels of support for data base management. At the most basic level, all programs permit data to be loaded into the program. In the 1960s, data management generally took the form of simply reading the data from cards into a matrix with observations on one axis and variables on the other. Today, almost without exception, all packages not only permit the loading of data, usually in a much more sophisticated way than in years past, but also the creation of new variables, at least constant terms and dummy variables. Most also permit new variables to be created by

Table 2
Language Features of Econometric Software Packages

	Operates by explicitly manipulating econometric objects		Operates by explicitly manipulating mathematical and/or statistical objects		Has programming language features that modify and control the user interface
	Using menus and icons	Using command language	Using menus and icons	Using command language	
Independent Econometric Software Packages					
AREMOS	X	X		X	
AutoBox	X				
B34S		X		X	
BETAHAT	X	X			
CEF	X				
EasyReg	X	X		X	
EViews	X	X		X	
FP		X		X	
gretl	X	X			
IDIOM				X	
LimDep	X	X		X	
MicroFit	X	X			
Modeleasy+		X		X	X
MODLER	X	X	X	X	X
MODLER BLUE	X	X	X	X	X
MOSAIC		X		X	
NLOGIT	X	X		X	
PcGets	X	X			
PcGive	X	X			
PcNaive	X	X			
RATS	X	X	X	X	X
REG-X	X				
SHAZAM		X		X	
SORITEC				X	
STATA	X	X	X	X	X
STAMP	X	X			
TROLL		X		X	
TSP		X		X	
WinSolve	X	X			
WYSEA		X		X	
Econometric Programming Libraries					
BACC				X	
MLE++				X	
Econometric and Mathematical Programming Languages					
Gauss			X	X	
LINDO/LINGO	X			X	
Ox				X	X
Econometric Programming Language Applications					
ARFIMA		X		X	
CML	X	X			
DPD		X		X	
G@RCH	X			X	
GaussX	X			X	
mathStatica	X			X	
MSVAR	X			X	
TSMod32	X				

transformation of the variables loaded. Some permit not only transformations to be performed on those data prior to their use in parameter estimation and other contexts, but also provide rather comprehensive data management, to the point in a few cases of allowing tens of thousands or even millions of variables to be managed as the elements of a data base. Programs, such as EPS, MODLER and XSIM, that were developed in a context of widespread use by people not all of which were necessarily economists, were among the first to offer substantial and sophisticated data management capabilities, including in certain cases the ability to embed transformations in regression, plot, table generation and other commands. Increasingly, especially during the past ten years, such capabilities have become much more widespread among econometric software packages generally. However, to the extent that data base management is well developed in the context of econometric software packages, this well-developedness is generally restricted to the management of time series data, as has been considered in some detail elsewhere [279,285]. An area of remaining weakness is the management of cross-section and longitudinal data bases, which for optimum use should be supported by software that permits the selection of samples from a larger data set, among other operations; only a few attempts have been made to begin to satisfy this need [57,58,285].

The general development of "modeling" capabilities is an aspect of purview. Packages that are specialized to single equation techniques almost as a matter of course have nearly always included support for forecasting and even "regression" packages have offered in a similar way the capability to generate out-of-sample projections; this feature was present in some packages as early as the late 1960s, such as versions of the AUTO/ECON package originally created by Ross Preston and Morris Norman. However, as regards the solution and simulation of multi-equation models, with the exception of the still surviving econometric modeling language packages from the mid-1980s or earlier – such as AREMOS, FP, MODLER, and MOSAIC – integrated solution and simulation components, including the necessary supporting data base maintenance facilities, have only been developed for other econometric software packages, to anything near the same degree, just in the past ten years or so.[42] In certain instances, as in the case of CEF or WinSolve, particular packages have been developed that are specialized to the solution of models.

A fundamental issue here is model size: as the size of the model solved or simulated increases, in particular, a number of design problems arise.[43] First, there is the problem of the organization and management of the equations that form the

[42]Notably, the solution of econometric models is a topic that for the most part is only occasionally considered in the econometrics literature proper. It is generally treated as either computational or as a topic within the area of mathematical economics [72,77,79,101,105,120–122,166,243,252]. Klein's 1974 textbook is one of the few econometrics textbooks to describe the techniques used to solve such models [175], although Hendry's recent text does mention Gauss-Seidel in passing [150].

[43]Of course, equation complexity – as this increases – may involve similar issues. At present, the aim is not to exhaustively consider the design of an econometric modeling language, but simply to describe particular issues that should be more generally considered.

model, which some packages have dealt with by permitting the user to name the equations and then, using these names, specify a model by generating a file that is effectively a list of such names, and essentially functions as an indexed list that points to the location of the equations themselves. Other packages define models as explicit sets of equations contained in files, individually usually called a "model file." These files may contain the model's equations either as a group of distinct equations, sometimes in ASCII format, or in a compiled, solution-ready form. The strength or weakness of each approach is in part a question of whether the user wishes to focus attention upon model building, considering a number of alternative model specifications, or upon the repetitive use of a given model as an entity.[44] Associated with the creation and management of a multi-equation model is the question of how to deal with the problem of debugging the model: developing a 300 equation model, or indeed even a much smaller model, has some of the characteristics of software development. Although individual equations may on their own appear to be well-founded, interactive effects between equations can cause a model to crash and burn. Even a model that has been used successfully for a long period of time can suddenly cease to solve, particularly under stressful conditions. As a consequence, the capability to monitor the solution process closely is important, but adequate monitoring facilities have not always been included in solution packages. Similarly, once the model has been solved, if it contains a large number variables, say 300 or more, there is the problem of presentation of the results. The creation of such facilities is far removed from the practice of econometrics, perceived as a matter of estimator choice or specification search, but is critical to the capability to use econometric models effectively.

In the present context, these types of issues are relevant not only in themselves, but also to bring to the fore, using a fairly concrete example, the role of software design as an active determinant of the degree of usability of econometric software. Given the problem of designing software to support the construction and use of large scale econometric models, it is relatively easy to determine broadly the set of activities that might be involved, which then provides something of a generalized road map to guide the subsequent development. For this particular case, salient historical aspects of that development have been sketched out elsewhere in this volume [289] and can be seen as having occurred in a consciously top-down fashion that has then had a general impact. In contrast, other econometric software has more often tended to be created bottom-up, with specific econometric algorithms implemented first, and other facilities then added subsequently, each addition purposeful no doubt, but also often selected in somewhat ad hoc fashion. It is thus more difficult in this more general case

[44] It should also be pointed out that some econometric modeling language software operates in a different way than either of these approaches [289]. MOSAIC, for example, generates models as – essentially – modules of the software package itself, converting algebraic representations into Fortran source code, which is then compiled, using a Fortran compiler, to produce the solvable model. Of course, the purpose of the present paper is not to describe all the possible varieties and variation of econometric software.

to draw immediate inferences from past developments so as to demonstrate easily the way in which particular feature choices uniquely affect software usability. Detailed classifications of types of estimators and tests can of course be made as a statement of econometric content, but given the compendium, further description of this sort may not at the moment be necessary.

What exists today is obviously the result of the past 50 years' development and the range and detail of the offerings clearly express the various aspects of current econometric practice. Future developments can of course only be dimly perceived, but it is possible nevertheless to reflect on the fact that changes in econometric practice do occur and with some degree of frequency. Recall Ed Prescott's interest in testing a new estimator computationally in 1970. It happens that the latest editions of both the Greene and Johnston-DiNardo econometrics textbooks have coincidentally reduced their coverage of variable parameter estimation, compared to earlier editions. The 2003 edition of Greene also excludes such topics as certain latent variable models, which were included in one or more previous editions. Inevitably, the pressure to keep the size of a textbook manageable causes some degree of churn in the topics presented. In contrast, for the software developer, leaving out previously supported techniques in subsequent versions of the package is not as easy, inasmuch as code changes can be problematic, but at the very least, user guides and manuals can be revised so as to downplay what are considered out-of-date facilities. Both econometric software developers and textbook authors naturally wish to reflect current practice. An interesting question for dinner time debate is what establishes "current practice"?

Greene himself argues that it is not econometric software that drives current practice, although such packages as EViews and LIMDEP may affect what practitioners view as "feasible" – as opposed to just theory. Greene asserts that, when considering each new textbook edition, he examines the journals, and interacts with practitioners directly and through conferences "to see what people are doing." As with the famous Supreme Court definition of obscenity, current practice may be hard to define, but can be recognized when seen. In response to the suggestion that econometric software may determine current practice, Greene responds: "saying that software is central to determining econometric practice may be a bit of a stretch. Surely there is give and take. Keep in mind that to say that software leads practice is to claim that developers of software are the leaders in the proposal of new techniques. I am not sure of that" [136]. It is good to think that among econometric software developers there is at least a modicum of modesty, but is he right? Certainly it is the exception rather than the rule that a software developer per se is the proposer of a given technique, but such a person may have some effect on whether anyone but the proposer ever uses the technique. Is it possible that Keynes presciently had in mind econometric software developers when he referred to "madmen in authority?" He was of course known to have a somewhat jaundiced view of econometrics, as well as of politicians.

An alternative point of view is expressed by Stephen Hall, who responded to an earlier version of the present paper by noting "I think you raise a very interesting point about what defines current economic practise and my view is that software plays a much greater role than either we realise or than it really should. There are clearly a number of quite distinctive econometric methodologies around, a very clear statement of this is a paper by Adrian Pagan which was given at one of the world econometric society meetings... He pointed out that three main intellectual methodologies were the LSE dynamic modelling approach, the Sims VAR approach and the Leamer extreme bounds approach. In fact there are very few examples of the Leamer approach being put into practise because there is no readily available software to do it, while the dynamic modelling software and the VAR (RATS) software meant that everyone could [apply the associated methods] easily. When cointegration came on the scene a key feature of taking it up so widely was that you could do the Engle Granger 2 step procedure easily in any package. If we had been given the Johansen reduced rank regression first, I believe that cointegration would have taken years longer to catch on, if at all. Another good example is the contrast between the Quandt disequilibrium models that were around in the 70s and 80s and the Hamilton Markov switching. These two models are actually very closely related but the Quandt models never caught on because essentially Dick Quandt never gave out the software to implement them. Hamilton on the other hand gave out GAUSS code for everyone to do it and so created a whole industry. The basic point is that econometric practise is defined by what most econometricians [are easily able to] do. Another example would be the Hoderick-Prescot filter, which has been heavily critiscised by almost every good econometric theorist who has looked at it, but people still use it because its easy" [143].

In fact, the major determinants of current econometric practice is not a debate that needs immediate conclusive resolution. At the moment, it does not really matter exactly the degree to which econometric software conditions current practice. That it affects it at all is the most important point, and there is little doubt that this is true. It is also significant that the economics profession appears to be depending upon a relatively small number of econometricians to provide this software, many of whom are "part time programmers," to use Hendry's phrase [149, p. 315]. Of course, from some perspectives, the thought of "programmer power" is a little frightening. There is occasionally dark talk of "automated, pre-programmed, context-free, instant analyses requiring only a single keystroke." But such a characterization of the situation also tends to suggest that the consideration of software design is the exclusive preserve of some small group of "programmers" when in fact the proper inference to be drawn is that it matters to the development of econometrics as a discipline that consideration be given by economists collectively as to how best to develop this resource for the future. It should be evident that, at the least, this is not a topic that should be relegated to the back rooms of the discipline.

4. A brave new world

Much like Monsieur Jourdan, Moliere's character in *Le Bourgeoise Gentilhomme* who was surprised to discover that for forty years he had been unconsciously speaking prose, we are possibly at risk of discovering the need to consciously consider the effects of computing on our practices and behavior. Today, if a poll were to be taken, it is likely that the general presumption of economists would be found to be that the computer has made certain lines of inquiry feasible, but otherwise that it has had no significant effects on the discipline beyond permitting faster calculations. Such an inference is easily drawn from Alan Krueger's introduction to the Fall 2001 *Journal of Economic Perspectives* special issue on computing. Referencing the play *Copenhagen*, in which Niels Bohr and Werner Heisenberg are portrayed as having consciously discussed quantum physics in a way that Bohr's non-physist wife could understand, Krueger introduces what is billed as a "symposium on econometric tools," with the idea that "If Broadway actors can attempt to explain the Heisenberg Uncertainty Principle to a lay audience, then surely econometricians and applied economists can explain recent developments in econometric tools to the diverse audience that makes up the readership of [*JEP*]." (p. 3). It is not clear from this introduction which is to be regarded as more simple, the tools or the expected audience, but the pervading sense that toddlers can safely play is unambiguously present: there are no demons in Krueger's toolbox, nor any sharp edges.

A closer consideration of the development of these "tools" reveals both important changes during the past fifty years and various ways in which applied economics has been influenced, both positively and negatively. In his comparatively recent description of the use of the computer by economists, Klein portrays that use in the 1950s as being an extension of the use of electromechanical desk calculators [29, 176]. Both reflecting the characteristics of the computer itself, at that developmental stage, as well as that people naturally initially tend to incorporate the new into their lives in an "old" way, in the case of the Klein-Goldberger model the computer appears to have been employed for what was then perceived to be the most difficult and tedious part of regression calculations, the calculation of sample moments [29, p. 511]. Once these were calculated, the remainder of the work was done using more familiar devices, including not only desk calculators but also punched-card tabulating machines. In contrast, modern computers, particularly those with today's relatively high-resolution, graphically oriented screens, are not used simply as number crunching devices. They are now treated as having an important role to play in terms of the presentation of multi-colored charts, graphs and images, as well as data management and – finally – performing calculations, which now of course transparently embed any necessary calculation of sample moments and other such intermediate results. At its most advanced, the computer has progressed from being a calculating machine to the means whereby a user can direct the process of analysis, almost in the role of a conductor, with the calculations usually an unseen (and unsung) element in the action.

The early days of computing were also characterized by a shared computer environment, which has not entirely vanished, inasmuch as the Internet today provides nearly instant worldwide contact between colleagues and even family members. But the new shared environment is different: in addition to being asynchronous – not dependent upon a central device – the modern environment is a matter of communication between intelligent devices, as much as anything else. The machine on the desktop, or laptop, is first and foremost an intelligent device. So much so that, as described, the latest generation of notebook computers is now much more than simply competitive with the number-crunching supercomputer of only 20 years ago. Among other features, such a notebook may contain a 60 GB hard drive or more, thus offering the storage capacity of even several mainframes of yesteryear – supercomputers of course characteristically use a mainframe for data storage and pre-computational organization. With this growth of power and resources on the laptop or desktop, almost all analytic processing by economists has migrated to the microcomputer. The mainframe is, in most interactive uses, simply a distributive Internet node, and it might be difficult in practice for most econometric software users to conceive of an econometric problem that would require the use of a modern supercomputer, although computationally intensive econometric applications, beyond the comfortable capabilities of individual microcomputers, still very much exist [75].

However, it is also important to take into account the implications of the change in the fundamental screen display then and now. The modern graphical interface shields the user from contact with the rudiments of computing, intentionally so. And inasmuch as a graphics interface, in some form, is likely to be with us for at least the foreseeable future, if not forever, an obvious question is how to view the early days of the PC, which are now fading fast from collective memory. One option might simply be to view the earlier implementation of econometric software packages in a DOS environment as having been transitional, and therefore essentially of only historical interest. That is, during the DOS era, the apparatus of computing on the microcomputer developed from its initial, rudimentary state to the point of being essentially equivalent to that of the mainframe. In 1993, to choose a date arbitrarily, microcomputer Fortran, Pascal, and other compilers were fully the equal of their mainframe equivalents in 1983. From the point of view of an end user, the computer became smaller and personal, rather than larger and shared. In short, on this view, the mainframe moved to the desktop. Since then, the dogs have barked and the caravan has moved on.

Yet the DOS era remains important notwithstanding. One reason is that it was a period during which interactive and distributed computing unambiguously became the dominant paradigm. Time-sharing, interactive processing was widespread in the mainframe world, but not overwhelmingly dominant, which did affect the mainframe programmer's environment and perspective. Similarly, networked mainframe computers were also widespread: as briefly described, networked, interactive computing existed as early as the late 1960s (and, on an experimental basis, before that) – and in a number of its characteristics was not so different from operating in a networked environment today. However, the intelligence that the DOS microcomputer placed at the point of user contact meant that, almost inevitably, screens became all points addressable, rather than single line oriented; pixels, not characters, became the atomistic screen units. Line oriented file editors became WYSIWYG word processors.

In a DOS world, the graphics environment, such as it was, existed within programs, rather than programs existing within a graphic environment, as in the case of the current Apple or Windows operating systems. But, so long as the user learned the command language, DOS provided the capability to operate programs in a flexible and powerful way. Progressively, irrespective of operating system, whether DOS, Windows, Mac, or Linux, removable storage and other critical facilities were placed at the user's point of contact with the network.

But this is the stuff of romance. For the practical, end-user economist or econometrician who simply views the computer as a tool, the DOS era remains important for the simple reason that the DOS command interface still conditions the operation of most, if not all econometric packages. This is in part because of the desirability of a macro capability, as indicated earlier. For one thing, macros, essentially text files containing commands for a program and executable by that program, have the property of being re-usable. They therefore permit periodic re-execution of particular commands or groups of commands. Or the econometrician may wish to perform a set of operations that inherently involve more than a single command, yet can be viewed as being a single thing, a composite. Alternatively, a set of commands can be used to establish context: the process of initially establishing the computational context – the data source or sources, a date range, and other such settings preliminary to a particular "econometric" operation – can be executed as a composite operation using a macro file invoked by a single command, or even a click on an icon. Just as important, certain types of estimators, particularly system estimators, can involve a sequence of commands. In addition, econometric models, in machine readable form, are sets of equations that may be collected into a text file, if not when in use then at least when being transferred from one environment to another. The written or printed page, expressing thoughts in a mathematical and textual format, is a natural environment to the econometrician, and the closest ex post analogue to that may be the command macro, particularly when the need for repetition is taken into account. Of course, such macros must be created manually, but it is easy to imagine, if not today, then sometime in the future, a tablet-oriented notebook computer, which of course exist today if only recently, but on which in the future an eonometrician might write a series of mathematical expressions, which are then, effortlessly, operated on by the computer.

This ideal is enticing, but although very much the stuff of science fiction and Star Wars, not to mention TV advertisements by the Microsoft Corporation, it inevitably abstracts from reality: to be operational, a symbol representing a variable must refer to a vector of numbers, located somewhere, and located there because of some prior operation. Indeed, there is a danger in such enthusiasm about recent computational developments – in speaking out loud in such broad generalities: which is that those who happen to overhear may come to think that the commands that populate the macros, that are represented in the menus and are evoked by the icons, occur simply by wishing. Econometricians who develop software quickly discover at the outset that in fact these housekeeping operations take up the bulk of programming time, both when writing the code and when designing how all this fits into the packages, generally and in detail. The algorithms that define the econometric operations form only a small portion of the total package code. To the econometric theoretician, the majority of code is as plumbing might be to a king, perhaps important to well being, but not very interesting. However, what needs to be more generally recognized is that – by marshalling the data, parsing the input, presenting the output and at some point making some calculations, among other operations – it is mastery of the housekeeping that offers the possibility that in the end what is now drudgery can become a pleasure. *The single greatest limiting factor today on the amount of applied economic research that economists can do collectively is the time they spend preparing to do the interesting part of the research.* To alleviate drain on the economist's energy and enthusiasm, and to minimize the costs involved, is a matter of focusing the attention of both economists and econometric software designers – the demand and supply – not only upon particular estimators, particular constructs (such as the Hodrick-Prescott filter, the Dickey-Fuller tests and the like), and the other issues that dominate the econometrics journals, but also upon the mechanisms of data transmission from the government agencies and other original data sources, as well as upon the design of the software interface.

However, at the moment, the environment does not generally exist in which economists can consider collectively such issues, or more broadly how econometric software packages should be designed so as to better facilitate applied economic research. At least part of the reason is the still prevailing professional sentiment that to talk about such ancillary issues is not what economists do. Therefore, these topics are not addressed in the most widely-read journals, seemingly as a as a matter of course. What is addressed instead is the ongoing development of econometric and economic constructs, but in an atmosphere in which these are divorced from the underlying computational environment; as an immediate case in point, carefully examine, for instance, the aforementioned *Journal of Economic Perspectives'* recent special issue on computing. There is nothing wrong per se in indulging in happy talk about "harnessing increased computing power for improved statistical tests" (*JEP*, Fall 2001, pp. 129–141), but the level of the discussion there and throughout the literature needs to be more penetrating. In the absence of a full and frank discussion of software design, what is happening is not only the piecemeal and unevaluated use of econometric software but also its piecemeal development, usually in response to vague perceptions of demand: thus in various small rooms in the dead of night, a few more tools are progressively being added to already ladened econometric software packages, perhaps at the suggestion of some user, but finally at the whim of the software designer, or an assistant, rather than because of a well considered collective sense of what specifically is needed.

Yet, the matter is not quite that simple. The issue is not only choices between particular econometric features or where the data are obtained. One of the most significant issues involved in the design of current and future econometric packages is the fundamental representational characteristics of computer numbers, both in terms of the conversion of packages from, say, the mainframe environment to the microcomputer, or simply when considering the microcomputer on its own. As is well-known to computer scientists and should be known by applied economists and econometricians, numbers in a computer are inherently approximates to the set of real numbers: they both need conversion from base 10 to base 2 and require representation by a finite number of digits, which in many cases (one might actually say, an infinite number of cases) inherently involves approximation. Aspects of the implications of this conversion requirement have been discussed in the *Journal of Economic Literature* by McCullough and Vinod [231], but notwithstanding that journal's reach among economists, the importance of the need to represent numbers in a restricted way may not yet have been absorbed by economists generally. The point is that, to the degree that the computer is the mechanism by which econometric theory becomes operational, this fact of number representation essentially calls into question the way that theoretical econometrics presents itself. If numbers could be represented infinitely precisely in the computer, then the standard statement of the OLS estimator:

$$\beta = (X'X)^{-1}X'Y$$

would have operational significance. However, in reality, this is not how the estimator is calculated today in econometric software packages, or at least not in those that define the state-of-the-art. Of course, it can be argued that what these packages do is to replace the steps implied by this formula (and the other relevant formulae) with operations designed to produce a result that approximates as closely as possible the spirit of the written formula – but that is still not the same thing. At some point, at least in the econometric textbooks, it will become necessary to begin to present the computational process as it is performed by the programs that the students are likely to use. When nonlinear estimators come to be considered, presenting the computational facts of life becomes that much more important. To preserve purity of thought, the Victorian bride may have gone to her wedding night unprepared for the unspeakable horrors of the event, but this is no reason to leave the modern student unprepared for what he or she may face in the night.

Coming to grips with the essential nature of the computer and its representational characteristics is an important, and overdue, first step. However, it is also generally important to adopt the right perspective concerning both the history of econometric computation and what is now possible. It is relevant to note that the advent of the microcomputer occurred at a time of controversy among econometricians. Leamer in 1983 [199] crystallized and focused some of the discontent evident in conference proceedings ten years earlier [37], and in Orcutt's earlier presciently voiced concerns [85,250, p. 197ff]. He expressed as well the dismay implicit in the general absence of answers to critical methodological questions [68,198]. Sims' 1980 attack on structural models as being unidentified and unwarrantedly dependent on identifying restrictions for their estimation, led ultimately to the development of an alternative form of model, the VAR model [297,307]. [45] The Lucas critique, arguably independently foreseen by Orcutt [85,250] and Phillips [49], of course was published even earlier, in 1976 [210], although elaborations of it came subsequently and only during the 1980s sponsored considerable debate. Finally, but similarly, the contributions that coalesced as the General-to-Specific Methodology, by Davidson, Hendry, Mizon, Sargan, Srba, Yeo, and others, were published mainly prior to 1980, but it was in the 1980s that the methodology began to achieve widespread acceptance in the UK and abroad. More recently, the methods advocated by Kydland and Prescott [192–194], variously described as computational experimentation or as the Real Business Cycle approach, are put forward by them as econometric in nature in the broadest sense [194, p. 70], although Cripps and others may have an equal claim to aspects of the idea [51].

A possibly more charitable view of the state of econometrics in 1980 than that expressed by the proponents of these various critiques and methodologies – and particularly certain of their adherents (see, for example, Charemza and Deadman [44] or Diebold [70]) – proceeds directly from an appreciation of the inability that existed in the 1950s throughout even most of the 1980s to realize computationally the insights of the Cowles Commission work, and thus to refine, confront, and elaborate it appropriately. The computational advances from the late 1960s and through the 1970s created a situation in which it had become possible, but not necessarily always easy, to make these computations – taking into account all aspects of the process, from acquiring and managing the data, to estimating parameters, to forming and solving models, and then presenting the results. It is only today that the doing has become sufficiently manageable that it is now possible to focus attention much more centrally on the whys and wherefores of the process. This argument should not be interpreted as being in any sense a justification of econometric practices of anyone during the past half century, but instead simply as explanation. The accounts of the various sins of "traditional econometrics," as the strawman is commonly called, often betray an astonishing level of ignorance of the actual historical events, such as the degree of use of the Brookings Model to make "forecasts," or even the actual forecasting accuracy of any models historically: there are dozens of complications associated with any scientific evaluation of forecast accuracy, but it can also be argued that, without very careful qualification, it is bogus to attempt to establish the validity of any model or method on the basis of *ex ante* forecasts that are produced by it and/or its handlers. Effectively, what has been done during the past 25 years is to throw the baby out with the bath water.

[45] If the idea is not too impudent, the question can be raised whether economists who use it really believe that the VAR representation is the best achievable, in an abstract intellectual sense, or whether the attraction of the VAR approach more reflects the small amount of data required, relatively speaking, and a manageable computational problem, which the structural model certainly did not – for most economists – twenty years ago? To what degree do the subsequent innovations in this approach reflect computational improvements during the past twenty years or so?

It also needs to be recognized, as pointed out by McCarthy [215, p. 386], that the Cowles Commission theorists "really did not have a lot to say about model selection." This phrase, "model selection," is quite revealing about the "traditional approach" that emerged in the 1950s and held sway until approximately 1980, inasmuch as "selection" essentially implies that there is something to select from, which of course may relate to the idea that it was economic theory that in the early days of econometrics was seen as providing the specifications to be tested. The more modern term "specification search" does not have the same connotation. There are many things that can be said in retrospect about the model building process of the 1970s, in particular, none of which are quite so telling as the relative poverty of the data base then as compared to that available today. In another context [286] it has previously been remarked that, considering just macroeconomic processes, the past 40 years has been a period of considerable economic diversity (for the US economy, among others) and it is not obvious that this data base has yet been exploited to the degree that it can be. The data base available to any economist in 1968, for example, was neither as extensive as that available today nor as potentially rich in content, notwithstanding any data quality issues [138]. Today's data base is comparatively richer, both in terms of types of data and in the varieties of economic behavior potentially capable of being revealed. For example, the 1970s and 1980s, in particular, displayed price and interest rate behavior quite different from that seen in the 1950s and early 1960s. It is perfectly valid to decry the quality of the data, certainly as compared to alternative measurement states of the world. However, economists cannot truthfully say that they have exhausted the potential information content. And if longitudinal and other microeconomic data are additionally considered, the scope is even greater. This comparative data treasure trove may not be enough, on its own, to will into existence improved software (or careful economic research), but it should serve to provide some stimulus once the potential of the combination is sufficiently widely recognized.

5. The evaluation of software and its process

It has been said somewhat waggishly that naïve users of software characteristically expect the software to be error free, but that experienced users are surprised by any correct result. As noted earlier, several of the articles in this volume evaluate the performance of econometric software packages, and to date, in the economics literature, such evaluation has only rarely been done, especially in contrast with the statistics literature [26,108–110,206,254,334,335,342]. In a *Journal of Economic Literature* article published in 1999 [231], McCullough and Vinod report that their survey of the set of economics and econometrics journals most likely to publish software reviews identified a total of 120 reviews during the period 1990–1997. Of these, they find that only 3 paid any attention to numeric accuracy and only "two applied more than a single test of numeric accuracy."[46] During the period since, following from earlier articles by McCullough and Renfro, published independently in 1997 [220,286], a more organized evaluation process has been started that has led to the publication of this particular volume, as well as evaluative articles in other journals. It is useful to consider some of the findings so far.

The 1999 McCullough-Vinod article considers generally some of the sources of numeric error. The location of this article in a widely-read, essentially non-specialist journal has appropriately gained it a degree of attention it would not have received in an econometrics journal, but has not yet led to any apparent change in the way economists report the use of software. At almost the same time, McCullough and Renfro published a specific examination of a currently popular topic, GARCH estimation [229], followed by a related article in the next year [230]. The important aspect of the first McCullough-Renfro article is not just the specific findings, but also the discovery that, with two exceptions, developers who were presented with the findings had difficulty making the programmatic changes to insure numeric accuracy. Moreover, the case examined was essentially the simplest possible case; more complex GARCH representations are not likely to lead to happier findings. Part of the reason for the discovered problems is that the world does not match the ideal: just as there is no reason to expect that a model's specification is necessarily correct *a priori*, there is no necessity for estimation spaces to be nicely regular and beautifully quadratic. The McCullough-Renfro article points directly to the need to improve real world nonlinear estimation methodology, and it is not obvious that there is a simple solution. Meanwhile, the rage is to implement ever more complex nonlinear estimation schemes, as the basis for reported applied economic research results.

In the current volume, McCullough [228] once again steps into the ring and applies to a number of econometric software packages a set of tests originally developed by Leland Wilkinson in the context of more general statistical packages. These tests are designed to evaluate such things as a program's algorithms that implement the computation of correlation matrices, which actually have two aspects. First, it can be demonstrated that the specific way in which a correlation coefficient is computed does matter. But, second, the way in which the Wilkinson's test is implemented essentially requires that the tested program stores data in high precision, generally double precision. The McCullough paper presents important results that need to be carefully considered by econometric software developers, but it also raises some general issues concerning both program design and the limits of evaluative testing.

[46] Because of such findings, the stress here is upon numeric accuracy specifically. However, if accuracy is a fundamental consideration, it is also not the only consideration. In particular, it should not be inferred from the present emphasis that software evaluations that do not primarily probe issues of numerical accuracy are per se any less valuable. At the end of the day, there is as much need to consider evaluatively the features and use of econometric software generally. For illustration, see for instance the book by Harris [144], which in an appendix evaluates the degree to which alternative packages make it convenient to implement a particular technique, or the article by Mackie-Mason [211], which compares the use characteristics of alternative packages for a particular purpose.

Given the inherent imprecision of economic data, most famously examined by Morgenstern [241], there is a question whether memory space should be devoted to high precision storage (as opposed to calculation in high precision) simply to insure that a package passes a particular set of tests. The bar can always be set too high, when framing evaluative tests, so as to result in too many packages failing. Obviously, it can also be set too low. Therefore, there is a need for some active discussion among econometric software developers and evaluators, and the editors who guard the publication portals, about the appropriateness of any particular set of tests. It is also open for debate whether tests should be created specifically for econometric software packages, or if it is useful to import them from other, albeit closely related, disciplines.

The Bruno-De Bonis study [38] is avowedly a response to the 1999 McCullough-Vinod paper, but focuses on the specific examination of existing packages that permit the estimation of panel data. The authors note the absence of any readily available benchmark for panel data estimates, which essentially prevents the tester from declaring more than that the same results have or have not been obtained for all packages tested, thus limiting the benefits of the evaluation. At the same time, it is certainly true that when all packages subjected to a particular battery of tests generate the same results, this finding inspires some confidence in the underlying calculations. Equally, when packages differ in the results they generate, this finding points to the need to examine why. The Bruno-De Bonis study is also interesting as an example of a common phenomenon: the interaction between developers and evaluators leading to some disquiet, at least on the part of developers [137]. It is common that when software packages are evaluated, the results are made known to the developers of the packages tested. Characteristically, as mentioned earlier, the developers immediately attempt to correct any computational errors revealed. If, at this stage, the evaluators do not report the results, the effect can be that all programs involved now work properly, in at least the tested context, but evaluators gain nothing but the satisfaction of having advanced the discipline. On the other hand, if the results are publicly reported, at least some users may reach the conclusion that, *ex post*, the programs differ in their accuracy.

Of course, this paradox is only apparent. Given that the packages tested are in use by economists generally, it is important to know which versions of those packages exhibit particular flaws. So long as the testing done is essentially fair and even handed, more published information is better than less. But at the same time, the fact that one version of a program significantly differs from another also argues for the importance of any published results obtained using the package being prominently reported. Moreover, this consideration leads also to the argument that information about program descriptions and documentation deserve to be considered an integral part of the normal reporting process of economists' research findings. Hooke's construction of the microscope is normally termed a "discovery" and is usually given the prominence in the history of Biology that Mendel's or Darwin's discoveries are. Galileo and Newton's work with telescopes and glass prisms are basic to the foundation of the discipline of physics. On several levels, it is shameful that any discipline that prides itself on being "scientific" in its fundamental ethos should not also publish prominently information that allows applied research results reported in the past to be properly evaluated subsequently (not to mention replicated). In this context, talk of space pressures and the need to save paper are entirely misplaced. Equally, those who develop econometric software have an obligation to do their best to document and describe their work to the best of their ability; it is a two way street.

A particularly interesting aspect of Stokes' paper [324] considering the evaluation of two or more programs together is that it demonstrates, among other things, the fact that it pays to look carefully at results, as well as to approach any particular estimation problem from more than one direction, as the title of his paper implies. The most significant finding of this paper is that the properties of estimators critically depend upon the context in which they are applied, and that routine applications may be as likely to involve inherent computational problems as those of greater ostensible complexity. The paper furthermore demonstrates the importance, after the fact, of a full reporting of computational details, at least to the degree of identifying the software used, including also the platform and version used. Stokes' investigation begins with his discovery of a conflict between results reported by Maddala 15 years previously and his calculations made using SAS. For many years his own software had replicated the Maddala finding with the exception of one coefficient which he though to be a typo in the printed paper. However, when the SAS result was found to differ, a detailed investigation of the problem led to the finding that for this particular class of problems, the convergence tolerance used made a major difference. The ultimate resolution of the problem can in one sense be regarded as a matter of software evaluation: an implication of Stokes' paper is that developers need to pay particular attention to detecting and reporting anomalies. On the other hand, it also demonstrates one of the ways in which econometric software development can assist in the further development of econometric theory and confirms the symbiosis. Moreover, inasmuch as Stokes is himself an econometric software developer, the paper additionally demonstrates that the careful documentation of one's own package can be educational.

The final specifically evaluative paper in the current issue is that by Herbert [158], which considers the use of MATLAB in a somewhat broader setting than econometrics as normally defined. MATLAB is an example of a specialized programming language that, as Herbert points out, fits "between the conventional programming languages (such as C++ and Java) and the higher level applications packages." As discussed earlier, in the past 15 years or so, several programs have appeared, such as Gauss and more recently Ox, that in principle permit the econometrician to exercise greater control over the results obtained, at the cost of taking on more of a programmer's role. MATLAB is a member of a class of packages, such as GAMS and others, that generally do not support parameter estimation, particularly the variety of econometric methods, yet permit the construction and use of models. Inasmuch as parameters can be estimated in one package and the estimated equations then transferred to a package such as MATLAB, there is clearly an overlap between this program and econometric modeling packages. The Herbert paper does not evaluate the numeric characteristics of MATLAB – particularly issues of numeric accuracy – so much as consider aspects of the applicability of packages like this to economic modeling, to include the application of control theoretic techniques.

Collectively these papers are both interesting and important. Moreover, it is incumbent upon us to recognize that the evaluation of software is as fundamental to the developmental process as is the original coding. Furthermore, it needs to be generally accepted that this is a task that should be mutually shared between developers and users – and not regarded as being just the province of those who independently, actively set out to test. It has been said before, both here and by others [231], that the precise way in which algorithms are implemented can be as critical to the result as the properties of the algorithms themselves, considered abstractly. Just as important, as an inherent characteristic of the use process, how users apply a package can also determine its numeric accuracy, particularly to the degree that complex, especially nonlinear, operations are performed.

It is important to view both the evaluation and use of software in the proper perspective. The original testing of a package naturally occurs as a part of its development, but this "alpha" testing is limited by the developer's imagination, which is already battered by the design and coding process, making it unlikely that such testing will be performed under a particularly diverse set of conditions. Especially in the case of a newly written program, the context of its use can affect the results obtained: the order in which particular operations are performed determines the specific numeric values located in memory at each point in time, in effect potentially providing the initial conditions for the next step. If the "right" values are there, the program might generate the correct results, but if not, errors may occur. In addition, users quickly discover their own idiosyncratic style of use: rare is the developer who has not discovered that users soon find ways to do things that he or she never imagined, with an effect impossible to conceived in advance. This trait is especially characteristic of packages that can be operated using commands and macros. The corollary of both these circumstances is that independent users may encounter "bugs" that the developer would not.

During the software's creation, the testing cycle begins early and inevitably involves step-by-step testing, inasmuch as the developer obviously needs to know that each component of a package, tested separately, does what it is supposed to do. As the package takes shape, emerging finally as a recognizable and usable program, the developer will then normally attempt to replicate known results. Unfortunately, these known results are relatively scarce. Zellner and others who have proposed estimators have often also provided estimates, but not all econometricians have been so practical. Furthermore, as the evaluative papers in this issue demonstrate, it is beneficial to have multiple tests of estimators and these can be hard to come by. Berndt's 1991 text [27] is almost unique in what it does, although in recent years Greene [132,133], Johnston-diNardo [170], and other econometrics textbooks have increasingly provided both worked examples and diskettes or CDRoms containing the data. But it is very rare to find parameter estimates in the literature that include both the parameter estimates themselves and a full complement of associated statistics. As recently discussed by Renfro [286], there remains a substantial burden on developers not only to create packages, often without much feedback, but also to determine what facilities and tests to include, and then finally subject all these to evaluative software tests.

However, as indicated, the developer's testing, no matter how intensively done, is of limited utility. An additional reason is that any developer, being either an individual or a group of people, creates a package that suits that developer's own work habits. Someone else needs to confront the software independently, before it is possible for anyone to say that the software is to any degree likely to be reliable; the parallel with the out-of-sample testing of an econometric model is obvious. This "beta" testing phase is common to all software, and nowadays has been institutionalized. However, when Microsoft releases a beta version of Windows or Office, literally thousands of developers mount the software on their machines. When a new version of EViews, MicroFit, PcGive or TSP is released, the testing frenzy is considerably less. Yet there is actually no evidence that the numeric reliability of, say, Excel is any greater than that of virtually any econometric software package; quite to the contrary [233,234]. The difference is probably that with econometric software, beta testing may be less widespread, offset by more care on the part of the developers and perhaps more rigor on the part of the subset of users who provide the evaluative feedback.

Finally, once the software is "released" it is, by implication, validated for general use – unfortunately, this is the common misperception. In fact, in the case of all software, not only is a just-released package not yet validated, but over time, with each new release, there is always constant change in the facilities offered, which can result in options that worked previously no longer working, or working badly. Furthermore, what matters most in the case of the use of software is context, context, context. It is possible to say now, with some confidence, that after 20 years of general use WordStar 3.3, which dates to 1982 or thereabouts, and has not been changed in the meantime, is very nearly bug free – or at least the bugs have become known "features" and can be either adored, for their charm, or avoided. But this is a simple program, in modern terms, and rather limited in its facilities; today, ironically, it is also not much used. Microsoft Word 2000, in contrast, remains something of an adventure.

6. Demand and supply: The market for econometric software

As with any product, the initial cost of developing an econometric software package for widespread use essentially consists of the direct development costs plus the marketing and sales costs; in common with most other software the in-production variable production cost is a relatively smaller consideration. It is obviously possible to continue in this vein and to talk in terms of a market for this product; and among economists what could be more natural than to talk of markets – indeed, there is an almost immediate tendency for academic economists, in particular, to describe econometric software as "commercial" and as being produced by "commercial vendors," and there are certainly some of those. However, the specific characteristics of this market should be noted at the outset. A fundamental one is that, with only a few exceptions, the programs are each created and maintained by at most a handful of people, and in some cases one or two, not as "large-scale" commercial propositions – particularly in contrast to Adobe, Corel, Lotus or Microsoft, the econometric software "industry" is a cottage industry. Furthermore, the extent to which this software should be viewed as being created, maintained, and sold (or leased) in a free market environment is not obvious; for instance, a number of packages benefit from a variety of both explicit and implicit subsidies. Considering the demand side, an obvious characteristic is that the market is small. As suggested earlier, the number of economists worldwide is unlikely to be in excess of 100,000, howsoever "economist" is defined. Of course, the limit of this market might be viewed as being somewhat larger if undergraduate students, taking an economics course, are included. On the other hand, it is certainly smaller if it is regarded as being limited to "applied economists," or just econometricians. But whatever number is attached as an approximation, the market is obviously not a mass market. Finally, if a value judgment might be permitted, it can be argued that for the good of economics as a discipline, this market should ideally be vibrant and innovative, whatever its size – and, in addition, it might be further argued that those on the demand side have an incentive to prevent market failure.

In the Windows environment especially, there are significant constraints on cottage software development for widespread use. Hendry [149, p. 315] has described the difficulties as including the development of code in a menu-driven, graphics-oriented interactive world in which users have both grown "accustomed to excellent and powerful general packages for word processing, databases, and spreadsheets, and [demand] similar quality products in econometrics. A part-time programmer [cannot] easily attain the required standards," particularly as users demand "superior and detailed documentation, including explanations of the econometrics as well as the software." Against this backdrop, it is not out-of-place to suggest, as a related consequence, that the discipline of the market threatens econometricians with the possibility that at some time in the future the sole remaining regression-capable program could be Excel, which has yet to achieve either a range of parameter estimation methods, a satisfactory set of supplementary statistical tests or even an adequate level of numeric reliability [233,234]. Excel does in fact permit regressions to be performed, so that arguably it is a market participant, and there are countless examples during the past 10 years of the operation of the dictum that the "good is the enemy of the best." Possibly, and fortunately, the limitedness and specialty of the econometric software market may actually be a preserving characteristic against the onslaught of this giant, as it was with SAS.

Considering the econometric software packages themselves, it might be possible to view them as each having specific traits: the compendium of existing packages included in this volume provides a means of directly comparing and contrasting them. It is evident from this compendium that only to a degree are they close substitutes for each other. In particular, the market is not a "toothpaste" market: Colgate versus Crest, both offering essentially the same thing that competing marketing departments attempt to represent as something quite different. For one thing, the philosophy that specific packages embody creates actual differences: for example, PcGive can be viewed as reflecting a different approach to the representation of economic phenomena than does Stata, in fact a different philosophy. MicroFit is more specialist in orientation than EViews. And insofar as econometric software packages are used in an academic context, the fact that packages are philosophically competitive may be a reason to license both, rather than one in preference to another.

Apart from philosophy, there are several reasons why packages differ. One of these is the disincentive on the part of any one developer to offer every facility that a user might demand. In some cases, this disincentive might originate in the developer's perception that there is an infinitesimal benefit-cost to offer, for example, every regression option ever described in the literature; this restriction to particular techniques may therefore cause specialization. Or it may be that certain facilities simply are not logically compatible with others, to the point that inclusion of both adversely affects the program's overall design. The initial historical choice of particular techniques thus may maintain specialization subsequently: for instance, packages that support the construction and use of large-scale macroeconometric models, and are viewed by their developers as specialized to this, may be potentially less likely to contain many options very closely associated with single equation models or, perhaps even more, with cross-section micro data. For these reasons, the presence of distinguishable and persistent market segments might be viewed as an inherent characteristic of the econometric software market.

However, there is also a countervailing tendency: from the user's perspective, diverse facilities within a given package may make a great deal of sense, at least prima facie. Just as with newspapers, where the cost of the paper is not really the purchase price, but rather that of the time taken to read it, the cost of maintaining a library of econometric software packages today is not so much the license fees to obtain them, but the time it takes to learn to use them. Among mass market products, the aforementioned Excel might be a good example of a package the users of which try to apply it universally, rather than employ other programs for specific purposes. One of the consequences appears to have been the demise of a number of specialist programs: for instance, who now remembers Harvard Graphics? Similar behavior can be observed with respect to econometric software packages: a screw can be driven by a hammer as well as a screwdriver, although not always with as good effect.

Recognizing this market imperative, a developer might therefore be inclined to try to preserve his barriers to entry by offering a somewhat larger set of facilities than otherwise, so long as the additional ones are viewed by developers and users as representing current econometric practice. The market segments may be fuzzy sets, or it might be that certain techniques are technically similar, notwithstanding an ostensibly different application, thus permitting broader coverage than would be the case otherwise [18,148].

An important determining factor is of course developers' perceptions of market demand. In advance of the marketwide penetration of a particular new technique, to a software developer there is usually not much feedback favoring its adoption. The first indication of the technique's existence can be an overture from its proud proposer that it would fit very nicely into the developer's package. Sometimes this suggestion will be accompanied by off-prints, algorithmic suggestions and occasionally machine-readable test data. However, once a particular technique is established in the canon, users may demand its inclusion and developers may include it even in the absence of evident user demand, simply to avoid being caught short. Alternatively, the diffusion of techniques can occur endogenously when a particular developer acts as a promoter of those techniques, as has occurred most famously with PcGive. Exogenously, as the earlier quote from Greene implies, techniques can be added by a developer who, sniffing the air, determines the next new thing. In fact, the birth and death of implemented techniques might make an interesting study, but at present would be difficult to pursue if for no other reason than that econometric software packages are not well documented in the literature.

Of course, comparative software reviews have been published from time to time during the past twenty and more years, but reliance on these is likely to be misleading: the techniques actually implemented in each program, as opposed to what the developer might have indicated, have only seldom been independently verified by compilers of such reviews; vaporware is not unknown in the econometric software market. However, once published, comparative reviews sometimes become a guide to the developer interested in keeping pace, notwithstanding the disinformation they may provide, and thus *ex post* may be to some degree self-validating.

A careful consideration of the characteristics of the existing packages reveals certain distinct categories and these classifications may provide some insight into the design principles of at least some packages. Autobox will never be confused with MODLER, nor LimDep with MicroFit, nor PcGive with RATS. However, relatively few developers have gone on record to declare their particular design intentions and it is therefore not clear to what degree the design-undeclared econometric software packages are simply ad hoc accumulations of techniques. The relative restrictedness in the number of possible users has definitely had an effect on the facilities offered, particularly in the case of the more commercially minded developers. All other things equal, small markets of course do not support a high degree of specialization. Developers who wish to hire assistants may need to boost revenues and consequently need to provide a greater number of techniques in order to attract more users. Obviously, to the degree that there is doubt among users and developers as to what constitutes econometric practice, some confusion ensues and consequently there is a greater tendency for developers to add marginal techniques just in case. There is presently evidence that this has occurred, to at least some degree. Of course, it also must be borne in mind that the market for econometric software is not isolated: for example, particular econometric techniques have been developed for and by those interested in financial theory applications, and with the relatively recent comparative growth of this specialty, some econometric software packages have stretched to cover on the one hand structural models, on the other VAR models, and on the third GARCH and other specific financial econometric techniques [238,239].

To be sure, as indicated earlier, users are sometimes inclined to view more as being better. And this attitude extends to other aspects of the software, including for instance the "platforms" on which a given package is available. It is not uncommon to find a particular program presented as being available on Apples, PCs, minicomputers, and mainframes, at least in years past. And in one sense this availability undoubtedly exists: for the right price, developers generally stand ready to port their programs. Hubris can also play a part. But there are also important disincentives: the truth of the matter is that while multiple platforms in principle provide the user with a high degree of perceived flexibility, for the developer the incremental cost can be substantial. In the context of any knowledge or skill-based activity, there is both a cost and a reduced proficiency associated with generality. For the developer to offer a package on two or more platforms may mean, for instance, either limiting the package's capabilities to only those that can be supported on every platform, or producing a different package for different platforms. Today, a computer that supports Windows can be counted on to offer Internet Explorer as a possible browser. Other machines may not. Similarly, Linux offers some attractive characteristics, but to the developer also represents a step back into a DOS-type world inasmuch as in this context peripherals may once again need to be considered explicitly. Few potential users who advocate movement to Linux then say in the next breath, "I'll pay twice the price you charge for the Windows version, and I'll have 500 copies."

Similarly, the attraction to the developer of being able to offer a more comprehensive set of techniques on any given platform comes at the cost of having to pay for the development of the additional techniques. This cost is proportionately greater to the degree that those techniques lie outside the core competency of the developer. And, in this case, the happy solution is not always to hire another assistant: it is well known that multiplying the number of programmers by n does not decease the time of development by the same factor: restructuring a program to include additional techniques is difficult enough for the person who created the program. Including several additional people in the project involves the need both to take time to train these people and to pay the organizational costs of the increased degree of joint development. In addition, to find another assistant involves search costs, not to mention the problem of trying to fit a square peg into a round hole when the ideal person cannot be found easily: that is, there may be a difference in result between hiring an economist able to program and hiring a computer scientist or other person in the hope of training him or her to try to think like an economist. Particularly in the case of applications that involve concepts that are familiar to economists but perhaps not others, this is an important consideration. First class mathematicians, for example, can find even the notion of a time series emotionally difficult. Computer scientists knowledgeable about relational data bases find it easy to consider multiple-key searches, but sometimes difficult to come to grips with the idea that economic data base systems do not necessarily require the same degree of record-locking as do airline reservations systems. Such expansion problems as these, combined with users' notorious lack of concern about numeric accuracy, at least until recently (possibly), provide some temptation for econometric software developers to paper over the cracks and hope that no one steps there: you may think it possible to maintain an extremely comprehensive package, that is highly numerically accurate, and bug-free, on four different platforms for pennies a year, but if you do, you are probably not an econometric software developer.

The realities of the situation are that most econometric software developers need to watch their costs rather carefully. One of the inferences to be drawn by developers from this consideration might be that a greater attempt should be made collectively to harmonize packages in particular non-competitive areas, especially in those instances that the basic usability of the package is at issue, and proficiency is expected as a matter of course. A particular problem that exists for both developers and users is the availability of data. Considered generally, particularly in comparison with yesteryear, data are abundant and easy to acquire. However, it is ordinarily still quite difficult for anyone to download data from the Internet in a way that the observations become immediately usable. There are of course technical difficulties confronting harmonization, when considering different types of data, say time series versus cross-section, but certainly within categories of data, there is no reason why software developers should not work together to improve the situation.

In the case of data downloads specifically, it remains true today that the process of extracting data from the Internet is still much more longwinded than it need be, especially to the degree that the data are obtained from different sources. As an example, go to the Federal Reserve Board website and try to download the Industrial production index data on the US economy for the period from 1945 to the present day. The data are available as Excel spreadsheets, but it can take all but the most data proficient as much as a week to create a data base containing all, or even a sizeable selection of the available series in a form that would be immediately usable in an econometric software package. The situation becomes worse if an attempt is made to create a composite data base containing data from the Federal Reserve Board, the Bureau of Economic Analysis and the Bureau of Labor Statistics. Currently, there is a tremendous multiplicity of effort among users of such data, which cries out for the adoption of a common approach. It should be possible for a user of one econometric software package to trade data with the user of another package, or for the same user to use both packages, with a minimum of conversion effort. What makes the present situation particularly frustrating is that, given the Internet, it is now not only technologically possible for data sources to make observations available in such a way so as to absolutely minimize the time between the download and first analytic use, but once such an (at least quasi Pareto) optimum were attained, the cost to the original data sources would be essentially the same as maintaining the present system [285,287]. Furthermore, with the possible exception of Canada, the situation expressed by the example of US data may represent the best case.

7. The next new thing

Classically, during most of the past 30 years, econometric software developers have stood ready to provide all comers with a sensible selection of econometric techniques, and for the average applied economist, this continues to be a defensible stance. However, there is an alternative view, alluded to earlier and not necessarily directly contradictory, that every serious econometrician should have at hand a package, such as Gauss, MatLab or Ox (some would include in this list, instead or as well, Mathematica, S-Plus or R), that provides the facilities to program whatever facilities are needed at the moment. It is worth examining this alternative view, and an argument might be made in the following terms: there is, to be sure, the need for facilities that permit the development of new estimators and new statistical tests, just as there is a need for facilities that permit the study of the solution characteristics of various types of multi-equation models in various contexts. But considering the broad range of applications, there is a role for every type of package: different people may wish to drive different automobiles, but to teach a son or daughter to drive, it is not necessary to build a car piece by piece. To win the Grand Prix, it is. As argued earlier, the skill set to program an econometric technique in a numerically accurate and efficient way, and to generate the various associated test statistics, may in the end rule out widespread use of econometric programming languages. More generally, there is a wide range of applications of econometric software, and given the relatively small number of active developers, it makes sense for both developers and users to recognize that there is a variety of contexts in which the software is applied, and a variety of needs for particular types of facilities.

The counter argument is that packages such as Ox, as econometric programming languages, can provide an environment for the development of a series of applications, programmed in the Ox language, that collectively can provide economists with the research tools they need. This thesis has been advanced more or less as a self-evident truth, and several "Ox packages" have been developed by econometricians. One such Ox package is PcGets, which presents itself as "implementing automatic general-to-specific (Gets) modeling for linear regression models based on the theory of reduction, as in Hendry [150, chapter 9]" [155]. Another is the Arfima package 1.0 for Ox [76]. A third is G@RCH 2.2 [196]. In effect, Ox is seemingly being used in these cases in an analogous fashion to Visual Basic, Visual C+, and other Windows developmental environments, to provide a basis for the creation a series of end user packages that provide specific applications.[47] Conceptually this is not so different from the PowerStation created on the basis of the DOS version of MODLER, so that it may be difficult for someone who has indulged to be too critical of the idea. But one is reminded of Samuelson's invocation of La Rochefoucauld in the context of another introduction [295, p. 7]: "The old give us good advice when they can no longer set us a bad example."

Pursuing this course, a package like Ox (or Gauss, or S-Plus or other such) sets itself up as a third layer of code: Windows first, the developmental language used to write Ox second, and then Ox. Windows, in this context, might itself be regarded as two layers, inasmuch as the Dynamic Link Libraries (DLLs) that form the Windows API, generally written in C and Assembler, sit on top of the Bios kernel. Each layer may provide an easier environment in which to program, but each simultaneously and successively places restrictions on the freedom of the programmer(s) at each level to control exactly how the coding at that level is done. Furthermore, each layer can introduce bugs. Consequently, the approach is not without its pitfalls. Commendably, in the case of G@RCH 2.2 in particular, the authors have provided some evidence of numeric accuracy, comparing results with the benchmark established by Fiorentini, Calzolari, and Pannattoni [104] and the particular model presented in the evaluative studies by McCullough and Renfro [229] and Brooks, Burke, and Persand [35]. The authors even evaluate 8-step ahead forecasts and note that "Contrary to EViews, Matlab, and SAS, G@RCH 2.2 hits the benchmarks for all steps to the third decimal (note that GAUSS, MicroFit, and RATS also do)" [196].[48] Inasmuch as these authors apparently are not associated with the development of Ox, these results tentatively validate the concept of third party use, although the discussion in McCullough and Renfro is quite relevant to this judgment and should not be ignored [229].

Similarly, it is possible to identify stages of processing and to argue in favor of an approach that provides users with flexibility and variety. For example, in the case of macroeconometric models, there are a number of different computational

---

[47] PcGive, PcGets and the next version of STAMP are all written in Ox, but function as standalone programs, requiring GiveWin as an interface, but not requiring immediate access to Ox itself to run; they are in effect "compiled" Ox programs. In contrast, packages such as Afima, G@RCH, and MSVAR require access to Ox to be used, although G@RCH is shortly to be released as a standalone program.

[48] In the case of EViews, the implied fault has since been determined to be correctable in the latest version of the package. The source of the problem is apparently what can be construed as an unconventional set of default initial conditions in EViews 3.1 and EViews 4, which can be controlled by the user in EViews 4, provided that he or she is aware of this capability and the particular default [197]. Once this circumstance is taken into account and the initial conditions are set appropriately, EViews 4 apparently produces acceptable results. Historically, there has actually been more than one instance in which EViews has been reviewed and subsequently it has been discovered that the results produced by the program have been affected by nonstandard user protocols. To provide another particular example: contrary to standard mathematical convention, versions of EViews at least as late as 3.1 apparently evaluate $-x^2$, where $x = 1$, as 1, rather than –1. It can be argued that "gotchas", such as this one, should be regarded as being grounds for identifying a program as producing incorrect results, inasmuch as users should be able to expect standard mathematical conventions to be adhered to by the developers of a widely used program.

tasks that must be performed: parameters must be estimated, models need to be organized, validated, and then solved and validated again. These tasks can be performed by one program, and at least for standard cases, a good argument can be made for the use of a single program for many users. However, as mentioned earlier, from the user's perspective there is a logic that might argue for the ability to use a multiplicity of specialized programs to estimate the parameters of different equations of a particular model, on the one hand, and to solve the model in a multiplicity of different ways on the other. Unfortunately, any attempt made to put this into practice today would run up against the absence of common representational standards. This lack of standards not only restricts users, but it also impedes the development of economics and econometrics as disciplines, inasmuch as the result is to create significant disincentives to potentially interesting research initiatives.

Comments such as these could be interpreted as criticism directed at econometric software developers. However, they should not be. Although recent evaluative studies have identified some numeric problems that are as yet unresolved, those who have taken the trouble to evaluate econometric packages have discovered that developers generally react almost immediately to reported problems. As McCullough and Vinod indicate [231, footnote p. 635] "some developers are remarkably quick to respond to reports of errors and many of the errors we recount were fixed even before our article went to press." It is true that sometimes there are systemic problems, and for this reason it would be better for there to be more widespread testing of the software than there is: software development is inherently difficult. Econometric software programs can contain a million or more lines of source code, and even the simplest can contain thousands. Any single line can contain one or more errors. Errors are therefore to be expected, particularly to the degree that users wish to push the envelope and developers attempt to keep up with the development of econometric theory by enhancing and changing their programs. But the evidence so far is that the most difficult problems lie mainly at the margin. Of course, it is at the margin that much innovation occurs.

Finally, once more it needs to be said that both the likelihood and the incidence of errors implies the need for users of software to identify precisely the software used when publishing books and journal articles. The general lack of computational knowledge on the part of most economists, the relatively restricted opportunities for economists to publish articles dealing with computational issues in tenure track journals, and the seeming unwillingness on the part of editors of economics and econometrics journals generally to require authors to disclose information about computational details has sometimes led economists to present their work as computationally well founded, based upon powerful techniques and facilities, whereas the reality is more akin to smoke and mirrors. There is growing evidence that a careful replication of applied results published in many journals might reveal a disconcerting number of problems [232]. Moreover, this evidence points to the likelihood that the greatest problems can be expected to be associated with the use of leading edge computational techniques, which if true is likely to mean a high correlation with the research reports and articles most likely to be considered as a basis for tenure and promotion.

8. Conclusion and prospective

The period of development of econometric software spans the professional careers of almost all working economists. At each step along the road, what constituted "the present" at that time seemed to offer both promise and the sense of being at the forefront. With such thoughts in mind, it is interesting to read Daniel Suit's 1963 monograph [328, p. 7] describing the construction and use of econometric models. Writing in 1962, he asserts that "in the days before large digital computers, individual relationships generally had to be kept simple, and the number of equations that could be used in a system was rather small. Today, with the aid of high speed electronic computers, we can use models of indefinite size, limited only by the available data." This is of course a reference to a marvel of that day, the IBM 1620, which now seems decidedly less impressive a machine. Yet the quote also masks in its enthusiasm a deeper reality, for shortly thereafter, Michael Evans was using a Marchant mechanical calculator to solve interactively the mid-1960s versions of the Wharton US Quarterly Model. Modern nonlinear model solution techniques, which is to say in this case the Gauss-Seidel method, were not used to solve the Wharton Model until 1968–1969. The Brookings Model was not solved in this way until the early 1970s [115–117,302, 303]. In the light of these computational circumstances, it is interesting to read many years later [44], an assertion that the predictive performance of the Brookings Model was poor, notwithstanding that no version of that model was ever used to make an actual ex ante prediction.

However, although it is easy to demonstrate by these examples both the limitedness of the technology of yesteryear and, even then, the degree of its non-application, as well as that the absence of published descriptions of the actual computational facts serves only to create false inferences years later, it is nonetheless true that in the 1960s heady optimism was the order of the day. For their part, today's software developers need to keep firmly in mind those halcyon, salad days of economic forecasting, when good feelings concerning the apparent success of the Kennedy tax cuts led to a seemingly general optimism that the economy was both finely controllable and its future performance eminently predictable. Of course, these were not the sentiments of those proposing the policies nor of those making the forecasts. A careful reading of the publications of the model builders and forecasters of that period make it clear that at the time they felt that their work was tentative and experimental, that each finished model was no more than an hypothesis to test. Nevertheless this work has been in more modern times excoriated as being Icarian in the extreme.

Today, we believe that we are beyond that, that we are on a firmer footing, and likewise in our hubris we might be inclined to echo Suits that "with the aid of high speed electronic computers, we can use models of indefinite size, limited only by the available data" in order to tout our modern software. It is of course on the basis of the econometric software packages individually described in the compendium found later in this volume, which have been developed during the past ten years – either newly or as an extension of previous work, together with the software being developed today, that the economics profession will in the near term undertake applied research. And in parallel with the economic forecasting experience of the late sixties and early 1970s, there is a danger that flaws, real or imagined, due to negligence or as a result of pure accident, or even caused by other parties, could lead to a sense of betrayal and outrage on the part of users. This is the Democlean sword that hangs above the software developer's head.

The threat is actually broader than simply whether or not the software is accurate and suitable to the task, in the hands of a knowledgeable and experienced user. There is an implied responsibility to produce software that can be used by any economist. As a consequence, software developers, particularly those who set out to develop software for widespread use, need to consider their role. As Johnston has recently noted [169],

> the number of suggested estimation, testing, and diagnostic procedures has proliferated, perhaps to the point where even econometric theorists are not fully cognizant of the nature, advantages and disadvantages of the various procedures, and certainly beyond the point where the average applied econometrician can hope to make sensible judgments about what research procedure to implement. It is thus all too possible for someone to activate an econometric software package, of which he has only a dim understanding, to apply it to data of whose nature and provenance he is ignorant, and then to draw conclusions about an economic situation, whose historical and institutional realities he has, perhaps, not studied in any depth.

And this view seemingly assumes no software flaws. The issues that Johnston raises are too profound to be considered in any detail at this stage, but the implications are obvious. Software developers face the problem not just of developing numerically sound packages containing a well defined, given set of features, but of designing and developing packages that are numerically sound and conceptually well founded in a context in which there is little or no external guidance beyond the lure of the next new thing. Johnston's words are not simply an assessment, they are also a challenge.

References

[1] *Annual Report of the H.G.B. Alexander Research Foundation*, Graduate School of Business, University of Chicago, Chicago, 1995.

[2] F.G. Adams, *Email re software used in the Economics Research Unit, Department of Economics, University of Pennsylvania*, C.G. Renfro, recipient, 7 August 2003.

[3] F.G. Adams and R. Summers, The Wharton Indexes of Capacity Utilization: A Ten Year Perspective, in: *Proceedings of the American Statistical Association: Business and Economics Statistics Section*, 1973.

[4] M.O. Adams, The Kentucky Economic Information System: a resource for government, academic, and private sector researchers and libraries, in: *National Online Meeting Proceedings – 1981*, M.E. Williams and T.H. Hogan, eds, Learned Information, Medford, NJ, 1981.

[5] M.O. Adams, The Kentucky Economic Information System, in: *Exemplary Systems in Government Awards '85-'86: the State of the Art*, Urban and Regional Information Systems Association, 1986, pp. 144–158.

[6] J. Aitchison and J.A.C. Brown, *The LogNormal Distribution*, Cambridge University Press, Cambridge, 1957.

[7] A.T. Allen, ed., *SAS/ETS User's Guide: Econometrics and Time Series Library*, 1982 Edition. SAS Institute, Inc., Cary, NC, 1982.

[8] C. Almon, *The Craft of Economic Modeling*, Fourth Ed., Department of Economics, University of Maryland, College Park, MD, 1999.

[9] H.M. Amman and D. Kendrick, Programming Languages in Economics, *Computational Economics* **14**(1-2) (1999), 151–181.

[10] A. Ando and R. Rasche, *Equations in the MIT-Penn-SSRC Econometric Model of the United States*, Department of Economics, University of Pennsylvania, Philadelphia, PA, 1971.

[11] A.G. Armstrong and L.J. Slater, A computerised data bank, in: *The Econometric Study of the United Kingdom*, K. Hilton and D.F. Heathfield, eds, London, Macmillan, 1970.

[12] R.J. Ball, ed., *The International Linkage of National Economic Models*, North Holland/American Elsevier: New York, 1973.

[13] R.J. Ball and S. Holly, Macroeconometric model-building in the United Kingdom, in: *A History of Macroeconometric Model-Building*, R.G. Bodkin, L.R. Klein and K. Marwah, eds, Edward Elgar, Aldershot, 1991, pp. 195–230.

[14] A. Banerjee et al., *Co-integration, Error Correction, and the Econometric Analysis of Nonstationary Data*, Oxford University Press, New York, 1993.

[15] F. Barber, Statistical Software for the PC: PowerStation, *PC Magazine* **8**(5) (1989), 214–216.

[16] T.S. Barker, Economic policy formulation in a large-scale model, in: *Optimal Control for Econometric Models*, S. Holly, B. Rustem and M.B. Zarrop, eds, St Martin's Press, New York, 1979, pp. 286–299.

[17] T.S. Barker, W. Dada and W. Peterson, Software developments in the Cambridge Growth Project 1960–1976: The origins of software for space-time economics, *Journal of Economic and Social Measurement* **29** (2004), 183–187, this volume.

[18] D.A. Belsley, Estimation of systems of simultaneous equations, and computational specification of GREMLIN, *Annals of Economic and Social Measurement* **3** (1974), 551–614.

[19] D.A. Belsley, Centering, the Constant, First-Differencing, and Assessing Conditioning, in: *Model Reliability*, MIT Press, Cambridge, MA, 1986, pp. 117–152.

[20] D.A. Belsley, *Conditioning Diagnostics*, Wiley, New York, 1991.

[21] D.A. Belsley, Mathematica as an environment for doing economics and econometrics, *Computational Economics* **14**(1–2) (1991), 69–87.

[22] D.A. Belsley, *Email re the relation of GREMLIN to TROLL and other issues*, C.G. Renfro, recipient, 22 March 2003.

[23] D.A. Belsley and E. Kuh, eds, *Model Reliability*, MIT Press, Cambridge, MA, 1986.

[24] D.A. Belsley, E. Kuh and R.E. Welsch, *Regression Diagnostics*, Wiley-Interscience, New York, 1980.

[25] K.N. Berk, Effective microcomputer statistical software, *American Statistician* **41**(3) (1987), 222–228.

[26] K.N. Berk and I. Francis, A review of the manuals for BMDP and SPSS, *Journal of the American Statistical Association* **73** (1978), 65–71.

[27] E.R. Berndt, *The Practice of Econometrics: Classic and Contemporary*, Addison-Wesley Publishing Company, Reading, MA, 1991.

[28] R.G. Bodkin, Computation in macroeconometric model-building: Some historical aspects, in: *Advances in Econometrics, Income Distribution, and Scientific Methodology: Essays in Honor of Camilo Dagum*, D.J. Slottje, ed., Physica-Verlag, New York, 1999, pp. 41–60.

[29] R.G. Bodkin, L.R. Klein and K. Marwah, *A History of Macroeconometric Model-Building*, Edward Elgar, Brookfield, VT, 1991, p. 573.
[30] J.L. Bona and M.S. Santos, On the role of computation in economic theory, *Journal of Economic Theory* **71** (1997), 241–281.
[31] C. Boschan, The NBER Time Series Data Bank, *Annals of Economic and Social Measurement* **1** (1972), 193–209.
[32] D. Bracy, *PLANETS: Programming Language for the Analysis of Economic Time Series*, Social Science Computing Center, Brookings Institution, Washington, DC, 1970.
[33] D. Bracy, *PLANETS: Programming Language for the Analysis of Economic Time Series*, Social Science Computing Center, Brookings Institution, Washington, DC, 1972.
[34] D. Bracy et al., eds, *Computer Programs Available for Distribution*, Wharton Econometric Forecasting Associates, Philadelphia, PA, 1975.
[35] C. Brooks, S. Burke and G. Persand, Benchmarks and the accuracy of GARCH model estimation, *International Journal of Forecasting* **17** (2000), 45–56.
[36] J.A.C. Brown, H.S. Houthakker and S.J. Prais, Electronic computation in economic statistics, *Journal of the American Statistical Association* **48**(263) (1953), 414–428.
[37] K. Brunner, *Problems and issues in current econometric practice*, College of Administrative Science Ohio State University, Columbus, 1972.
[38] G. Bruno and R. De Bonis, A comparative study of alternative econometric packages with an application to Italian deposit interest rates, *Journal of Economic and Social Measurement* **29** (2004), 271–295, this volume.
[39] M. Brynin and R. Smith, Mapping the Household, *Journal of Economic and Social Measurement* **20** (1994), 1–17.
[40] Byte, Guide to the IBM Personal Computers, *Byte: The small systems journal* **9**(9) (1984).
[41] Byte, Inside the IBM PCs, *Byte, the small systems journal* **11**(11) (1986),
[42] D.W. Cartwright, The regional economic information system: Data management problems and solutions, in: *Annual Conference of the Association for University Business and Economic Reseach*, San Antonio, TX, 1979.
[43] Center for Computational Research in Economics and Management Science, *TROLL Primer*, 3rd Ed., MIT Center for Computational Research in Economics and Management Science, Cambridge, MA, 1979.
[44] W. Charemza and D.F. Deadman, *New Directions in Econometric Practice*, Edward Elgar, Aldershot, 1993.
[45] S. Cohen and S. Pieper, *The Speakeasy III Reference Manual*, Speakeasy Computing Corporation, Chicago, 1979.
[46] E.J. Coleman and D.W. Cartwright, Toward a REIS System for the 1980s, in: *Association for University Business and Economic Research Annual Meeting*, Big Sky, Montana, 1980.
[47] J.M. Condie et al., A brief description of the FRB MODELEASY/FEDEASY econometric language, *Journal of Economic Dynamics and Control* 5(1) (1983), 75–79.
[48] T.F. Cooley and E.C. Prescott, Varying parameter regression: a theory and some applications, *Annals of Economic and Social Measurement* **4**(2) (1973), 463–474.
[49] R. Court, The Lucas Critique: did Phillips make a comparable contribution, in: *A.W.H. Phillips: Collected Works in Contemporary Perspective*, R. Leeson, ed., Cambridge University Press, Cambridge, 2000, pp. 460–467.
[50] F. Cribari-Neto, C for Econometricians, *Computational Economics* **14**(1–2) (1999), 135–149.
[51] T.F. Cripps and M. Fetherston, Cambridge economic policy group methodology, in: *Economic Modelling*, P. Ormerod, ed., Heinemann, London, 1979, pp. 40–52.
[52] R.N. Cuff, On Casual Users, *International Journal of Man-Machine Studies* **12** (1980), 163–187.
[53] K. Cuthbertson, S.G. Hall and M.P. Taylor, *Applied Econometric Techniques*, University of Michigan Press, Ann Arbor, 1992.
[54] A.C. Darnell and L. Evans, *The Limits of Econometrics*, E. Elgar, Aldershot, 1990.
[55] Data Resources, *EPS Reference Manual*, Data Resources, Inc., Cambridge, MA, 1978.
[56] Data Resources, *EPS On-Line: An Example Session*, Data Resources, Inc., Cambridge, MA, 1979.

[57] M.H. David, Managing Panel data for scientific analysis: the role of relational database management systems, in: *Panel Surveys*, D. Kasprzyk et al., eds, New York, John Wiley, 1989, pp. 226–241.

[58] M.H. David and A. Robbin, *Building New Infrastructures for the Social Science Enterprise: Final Report to the National Science Foundation on the SIPP Access Project, November 1984–December 1991*, Institute for Research on Poverty, Madison, WI, 1992.

[59] F. de Leeuw and E. Gramlich, *The Federal Reserve-MIT Econometric Model*, Federal Reserve Bulletin, 1968, pp. 11–29.

[60] F. de Leeuw and E. Gramlich, *The Channels of Monetary Policy*, Federal Reserve Bulletin, 1969, pp. 472–491.

[61] A.P. Dempster, N.M. Laird and D.B. Rubin, Maximum likelihood from incomplete data via the EM algorithm, *Journal of the Royal Statistical Society, Series B* **39**(1) 1977, 1–38.

[62] J.E. Dennis and R.E. Welsch, Techniques for Nonlinear Least Squares and Robust Regression, *Communications in Statistics* **7** (1978), 345–359.

[63] J.E.J. Dennis, D.M. Gay and R.E. Welsch, An Adaptive Nonlinear Least-Squares Algorithm, *ACM Transactions on Mathematical Software* **7** (1981), 348–368.

[64] J.E.J. Dennis, D.M. Gay and R.E. Welsch, Algorithm 573 NL2SOL–An Adaptive Nonlinear Least-Squares Algorithm, *ACM Transactions on Mathematical Software* **7** (1981), 369–383.

[65] W.T. Dent, ed., Computation in econometric models, *Journal of Econometrics: Annals of Applied Econometrics* **12** (1980).

[66] M. Desai, D.F. Hendry and G.E. Mizon, John Dennis Sargan: An obituary, *Economic Journal* **107** (1997), 1121–1125.

[67] W.G. DeWald, J.G. Thursby and R.G. Anderson, Replication in empirical economics: the Journal of Money, Credit and Banking Project, *American Economic Review* **76**(4) (1986), 587–603.

[68] P.J. Dhrymes et al., Criteria for the evaluation of econometric models, *Annals of Economic and Social Measurement* **3**(1) (1972), 291–324.

[69] C.J. Dickerson, ed., *The Software Catalog: Microcomputers, Fall 1983*, Elsevier, New York, 1983.

[70] F.X. Diebold, The Past, Present, and Future of Macroeconomic Forecasting, *Journal of Economic Perspectives* **12**(2) (1998), 175–192.

[71] T. Doan, *Email Message*, C.G. Renfro, recipient. 10 March 2003.

[72] H. Don and G.M. Gallo, Solving large sparse systems of equations in econometric models, *Journal of Forecasting* **6** (1987), 167–180.

[73] J. Dongarra, *Email re The LINPACK Benchmark*, C.G. Renfro, recipient, 22 March 2003.

[74] J. Dongarra, P. Luszczek and A. Petitet, The LINPACK Benchmark: Past, Present, and Future, *Concurrency: Practice and Experience* **15** (2003), 803–820.

[75] J.A. Doornik, D.F. Hendry and N. Shephard, *Computationally-Intensive Econometrics Using a Distributed Matrix-Programming Language*, 2002.

[76] J.A. Doornik and M. Ooms, *A Package for Estimating, Forecasting, and Simulating AFRIMA Models: Arfima 1.0 for Ox*, Discussion Paper, Nuffield College, Oxford, 1999.

[77] A. Drud, *An Optimization Code for Nonlinear Econometric Models Based on Sparse Matrix Techniques and Reduced Gradients*, Matematisk Institut Danmarks Tekniske Højskole, Lyngby, 1977.

[78] A. Drud, Interfacing Modelling Systems and Solution Algorithms, *Journal of Economic Dynamics and Control* **5** (1983), 131–149.

[79] A. Drud, A survey of model representations and simulation algorithms in some existing modeling systems, *Journal of Economic Dynamics and Control* **5** (1983), 5–35.

[80] J.S. Duesenberry, G. Fromm, L.R. Klein and E. Kuh, *The Brookings quarterly econometric model of the United States*, Rand McNally, Chicago, 1965.

[81] J.S. Duesenberry, G. Fromm, L.R. Klein and E. Kuh, *The Brookings Model: Some Further Results*, Rand McNally & Company, Chicago, 1969.

[82] J.W. Duncan, *Seeking a Strategy, in Report on the Conference on Cataloging and Information Services for Machine-readable Data Files, Arlie House, Warrenton, Virginia, March 29–31, 1978*, Data Use and Access Laboratories, Arlington, VA, 1978, pp. 118–119.

[83] J. Durbin, Maximum Likelihood Estimation of the Parameters of a System of Simultaneous Regression Equations, *Econometric Theory* **4** (1988), 159–170.

[84] Dynamics Associates, *Economic Forecasting in XSIM User's Guide*, Interactive Data Corporation, Waltham, MA, 1979.

[85] J.B. Edwards and G. Orcutt, Should aggregation prior to estimation be the rule, *Review of Economics and Statistics* **51**(4) (1969), 409–420.

[86] H. Eisenpress, *Forecasting by Generalized Regression Methods*, Limited-Information Estimation Procedure IBM 704 Program IB LI, International Business Machines Corporation. Data Systems Division, New York, 1959.

[87] M. Eisner, TROLL/1 - an interactive computer system for econometric research, *Annals of Economic and Social Measurement* **1** (1972), 95–96.

[88] M. Eisner, *Email re econometric software*, C.G. Renfro, recipient, 27 August 2003.

[89] M. Eisner and R.S. Pindyck, A generalized approach to estimation as implemented in the TROLL/1 system, *Annals of Economic and Social Measurement* **2** (1973), 29–51.

[90] M.E. Ellis, Social Science Computing at the University of Wisconsin, *Annals of Economic and Social Measurement* **1**(2) (1972), 237–248.

[91] R.F. Engle and C.W.J. Granger, *Long-Run Economic Relationships: Readings in Cointegration*, Advanced texts in econometrics, New York, Oxford University Press, Oxford, 1991.

[92] L.C. Erdman, *Recursive Simulation of the Brookings Quarterly Econometric Model of the United States*, Master Thesis. Massachusetts Institute of Technology, Cambridge, MA, 1966.

[93] M.K. Evans and L.R. Klein, *The Wharton Econometric Forecasting Model*, Economics Research Unit, University of Pennsylvania, Philadelphia, 1967.

[94] R.C. Fair, *A Short-Run Forecasting Model of the United States Economy*, Lexington Books, D.C.Heath and Company, Lexington, MA, 1971.

[95] R.C. Fair, On the robust estimation of econometric models, *Annals of Economic and Social Measurement* **3**(4) (1974), 667–678.

[96] R.C. Fair, A note on the computation of the Tobit estimator, *Econometrica* **45**(7) (1977), 1723–1727.

[97] R.C. Fair, *Specification, Estimation, and Analysis of Macroeconometric Models*, Harvard University Press, Cambridge, MA, 1984.

[98] R.C. Fair, *Specification, Estimation, and Analysis of Macroeconometric Models*, Second Ed., Harvard University Press, Cambridge, MA, 1994.

[99] R.C. Fair, *Email re History of econometric software*, C.G. Renfro, recipient, 17 June 2003.

[100] R.C. Fair and W.F. Parke, *The Fair-Parke Program for the Estimation and Analysis of Nonlinear Econometric Models*, New Haven, CT, 1993.

[101] R.C. Fair and J.B. Taylor, Solution and maximum likelihood estimation of dynamic nonlinear rational expectations models, *Econometrica* **51** (1983), 1169–1185.

[102] M.J. Farrell, The measurement of productive efficiency, *Journal of the Royal Statistical Society, Series A (General)* **120**(Part III) (1957), 253–290.

[103] D. Fay, *&Forecast: General Model Simulator User's Manual and Reference Manual*, Regional Economics, Chase Econometric Forecasting Associates, Bala Cynwyd, PA, 1981.

[104] G. Fiorentini, G. Calzolari and L. Panattoni, Analytic derivatives and the computation of GARCH estimates, *Journal of Applied Econometrics* **11** (1996), 399–414.

[105] P.G. Fisher and A.J. Hughes Hallett, Iterative techniques for solving simultaneous equations systems: a view from the economics literature, *Journal of Computational and Applied Mathematics* **24** (1988), 241–255.

[106] F.R. Førsund and N. Sarafoglou, On the origins of data envelopment analysis, *Journal of Productivity Analysis* **17** (2002), 23–40.

[107] F.R. Førsund and N. Sarafoglou, *The Tale of two Research Communities: The Diffusion of Research on Productive Efficiency*, Memorandum No. 08/2003, Department of Economics, University of Oslo, Oslo, 2003.

[108] I. Francis, A comparison of several analysis of variance programs, *Journal of the American Statistical Association* **68** (1973), 860–865.

[109] I. Francis, ed., *Statistical Software: A Comparative Review*, North-Holland, New York, 1981.
[110] I. Francis, R. Heiberger and P.F. Velleman, Criteria and Considerations in the evaluation of statistical program packages, *American Statistician* **29** (1975), 52–56.
[111] S.S. Fried, Evaluating 8087 performance on the IBM PC, *Byte* **9**(9) (1984), 197–208.
[112] M. Friedman and A.J. Schwartz, Alternative approaches to analyzing economic data, *American Economic Review* **81** (1991), 39–49.
[113] I. Friend and P. Taubman, A short-term forecasting model, *Review of Economics and Statistics* **46**(3) (1964), 229–236.
[114] G. Fromm, Survey of United States Models, in: *The Brookings Model: Perspective and Recent Developments*, G. Fromm and L.R. Klein, eds, American Elsevier Publishing Company, New York, 1975, pp. 376–414.
[115] G. Fromm and G.R. Schink, Short and long-term simulations with the Brookings Model, in: *Econometric Models of Cyclical Behavior*, B.G. Hickman, ed., National Bureau of Economic Research, New York, 1972.
[116] G. Fromm and G.R. Schink, Aggregation and Econometric Models, *International Economic Review* **16** (1973), 1–32.
[117] G. Fromm and G.R. Schink, An evaluation of the predictive abilities of a large model: post-sample simulations with the Brookings Model, in: *The Brookings Model: Perspectives and Recent Developments*, G. Fromm and L.R. Klein, eds, North-Holland, New York, 1975.
[118] G. Fromm, P. Taubman and Brookings Institution, *Policy simulations with an econometric model*, Brookings Institution, Washington, 1968.
[119] C.L. Gilbert, Professor Hendry's econometric methodology, *Oxford Bulletin of Economics and Statistics* **48** (1986), 283–307.
[120] M. Gilli, Causal Ordering and Beyond, *International Economic Review* **33**(4) (1992), 957–971.
[121] M. Gilli, *Computational economic systems: models, methods & econometrics*, Advances in computational economics, Vol. 5. Kluwer Academic Publishers, Boston, MA, 1996.
[122] M. Gilli and G. Pauletto, Krylov methods for solving models with forward-looking variables, *Journal of Economic Dynamics and Control* **22** (1998), 1275–1289.
[123] W.L. Goffe and R.P. Parks, The future information infrastructure in economics, *Journal of Economic Perspectives* **11**(3) (1997), 75–94.
[124] A.S. Goldberger, Econometric computation by hand, *Journal of Economic and Social Measurement* **29** (2004), 115–117, this volume.
[125] A.S. Goldberger and V. Hofer, *A Users Guide to the Multiple Regression Program RGR*, Systems Formulation and Methodology Workshop Paper 6207, Social Systems Reserach Institute, University of Wisconsin, Madison, WI, 1962.
[126] C.W.J. Granger, *Modelling Economic Series: Readings in Econometric Methodology*, Clarendon Press, Oxford, 1990.
[127] C.W.J. Granger, *Empirical Modeling in Economics: Specification and Evaluation*, Cambridge University Press, Chapter xii, Cambridge, New York, 1999, p. 99.
[128] G.R. Green, *SIMEMOD: A General Purpose Computer Program to Simulate and Forecast with Econometric Models*, BEA Staff Paper in Economics and Statistics, Bureau of Economic Analysis, US Department of Commerce, Washington, DC, 1970.
[129] G.R. Green and I. Green, eds, *The Wharton Short Term Forecasting System Computer Programs*, Wharton Econometric Forecasting Associates, Philadelphia, 1973.
[130] W.H. Greene, Maximum likelihood estimation of econometric frontier functions, *Journal of Econometrics* **13** (1980), 27–56.
[131] W.H. Greene, On the asymptotic bias of the ordinary least squares estimator of the tobit model, *Econometrica* **48** (1980), 505–514.
[132] W.H. Greene, *Econometric Analysis*, Upper Saddle River, Prentice Hall, NJ, 2000.
[133] W.H. Greene, *Econometric Analysis*, 5th Ed., Upper Saddle River, Prentice Hall, NJ, 2003.
[134] W.H. Greene, *Email re EM Algorithm*, C.G. Renfro, recipient, 26 June 2003.
[135] W.H. Greene, *Email re LIMDEP Characteristics*, C.G. Renfro, recipient, 18 March 2003.
[136] W.H. Greene, *Email re Randomly Varying Parameters*, C.G. Renfro, recipient, 17 March 2003.

[137] W.H. Greene, Reply to “A comparative study of alternative econometric packages with an application to Italian deposit rates”, by G. Bruno and R. De Bonis, *Journal of Economic and Social Measurement* **29** (2204), 297–305, this volume.

[138] Z. Griliches, Productivity, R&D and the data constraint, *American Economic Review* **84** (1994), 1–23.

[139] B.H. Hall, *Email re the History of Econometric Software Development*, C.G. Renfro, recipient, 28 February 2003.

[140] B.H. Hall and R.E. Hall, *Time Series Processor*, Version 3.5, User’s Manual, 1980.

[141] R.E. Hall, *TSP: Time Series Processor*, Source listings of various Fortran routines, 1968.

[142] R.E. Hall, *Email re History of Econometric Software Development*, C.G. Renfro and B.H. Hall, recipients, 27 February 2003.

[143] S.G. Hall, *Email message*, C.G. Renfro, recipient, London, 2003.

[144] R.I.D. Harris, *Using Cointegration Analysis in Econometric Modeling*, Prentice Hall/Harvester Wheatsheaf, London, 1995.

[145] J. Hausman, An instrumental variable approach to full information estimators for linear and certain nonlinear econometric models, *Economica* **43**(4) (1975), 727–738.

[146] J.J. Heckman, Sample selection bias as a specification error, *Econometrica* **47**(1) (1979), 153–162.

[147] D.F. Hendry, *The Estimation of Economic Models With Autoregressive Errors*, Deparment of Economics, London School of Economics, University of London, London, 1970.

[148] D.F. Hendry, The structure of simultaneous equation estimators, *Journal of Econometrics* **4** (1976), 51–88.

[149] D.F. Hendry, *Econometrics: alchemy or science?: essays in econometric methodology*, Cambridge, B. Blackwell, Oxford, UK, 1993.

[150] D.F. Hendry, *Dynamic Econometrics*, Oxford University Press, Oxford, 1995.

[151] D.F. Hendry, *Email re Econometric Software on the Microcomputer*, C.G. Renfro, recipient, 16 March 2003.

[152] D.F. Hendry, *Email re Final Version of Software Survey Paper*, C.G. Renfro, recipient, 4 September 2003.

[153] D.F. Hendry, J. Denis Sargan and the origins of the LSE econometric methodology, *Econometric Theory* **19** (2003), 457–480.

[154] D.F. Hendry and J.A. Doornik, The impact of computational tools on time-series econometrics, in: *Information Technology and Scholarship*, T. Coppock, ed., British Academy, London, 1999, pp. 257–269.

[155] D.F. Hendry and H.-M. Krolzig, *The Properties of Automatic Gets Modelling*, 2003, p. 20.

[156] D.F. Hendry and F. Srba, AUTOREG: a computer program library for dynamic econometric models with autoregressive errors, *Journal of Econometrics* **12** (1980), 85–102.

[157] D.F. Hendry and K.F. Wallis, *Econometrics and quantitative economics*, Oxford, B. Blackwell, New York, NY, 1984.

[158] R.D. Herbert, Modelling programming languages – appropriate tools? *Journal of Economic and Social Measurement* **29** (2004), 321–337, this volume.

[159] A.A. Hirsch, M. Liebenberg and G.R. Green, *The BEA Quarterly Econometric Model*, BEA Staff Paper, Bureau of Economic Analysis, US Department of Commerce, Washington, DC, 1973.

[160] P.W. Holland and R.E. Welsch, Robust Regression Using Iteratively Reweighted Least-Squares, *Communications in Statistics* **6** (1977), 813–827.

[161] S. Holly, B. Rustem and M.B. Zarrop, eds, *Optimal Control for Econometric Models, An Approach to Economic Policy Formulation*, St. Martin’s Press, New York, 1979.

[162] C.C. Holt, Validation and application of macroeconometric models using computer simulation, in: *The Brookings Quarterly Econometric Model of the United States*, J.S. Duesenberry et al., eds, Rand McNally & Company, Chicago, 1965, pp. 637–650.

[163] C.C. Holt, *PROGRAM SIMULATE II, A User’s and Programmer’s Manual*, Social Systems Research Institute, Madison, WI, 1967.

[164] C.C. Holt, *Email re Econometric Software*, C.G. Renfro, recipient, 18 March 2003.

[165] H.S. Houthakker, Some calculations on electricity consumption in Great Britain, *Journal of the Royal Statistical Society* **Series A**(No. 114, Part III) (1951), 351–371.
[166] A.J. Hughes Hallett and L. Piscitelli, Simple reordering techniques for expanding the convergence radius of first-order iterative techniques, *Journal of Economic Dynamics and Control* **22** (1998), 1319–1333.
[167] Infometrica, MOSAIC: A New Tool for Economic Analysis and Forecasting, Infometrica Ltd, Ottawa, 1979, p. 6.
[168] M.D. Intriligator, R.G. Bodkin and C. Hsiao, *Econometric Models, Techniques, and Applications*, 2nd Ed., Upper Saddle River, Prentice Hall, NJ, 1996.
[169] J. Johnston, Econometrics Retrospect and Prospect, *Economic Journal* **101** (1991), 51–56.
[170] J. Johnston, *Econometric methods*, 4th Ed., McGraw-Hill, New York, 1997.
[171] D. Kendrick and A. Meeraus, Special Issue on Modeling Languages, *Journal of Economic Dynamics and Control* **5**(1) (1983).
[172] D.A. Kendrick, *Research Opportunities in Computational Economics: Report of the NSF Workshop on Research Opportunities in Computational Economics, Washington, DC, March 6, 1991*,Center for Economic Research, Department of Economics, Austin, TX, 1994.
[173] L.R. Klein, Economic Fluctuations in the United States 1921–1941, *Cowles Commission Monograph*, Vol. 11, John Wiley & Sons, Inc., New York, 1994.
[174] L.R. Klein, Single equation vs. equation systems methods of estimation in economics, *Econometrica* **28** (1960), 866–871.
[175] L.R. Klein, *A Textbook of Econometrics*, Second Ed., Prentice-Hall, Englewood Cliffs, NJ, 1974.
[176] L.R. Klein, *The History of Computation in Econometrics*, manuscript, 1989.
[177] L.R. Klein et al., *An Econometric Model of the United Kingdom*, Basil Blackwell, Oxford, 1961.
[178] L.R. Klein and V. Long, Capacity Utilization-Concept, Measurement, and Recent Estimates, *Brookings Papers on Economic Activity* **3** (1973), 743–756.
[179] L.R. Klein and R. Preston, Some New Results in the Measurement of Capacity Utilization, *American Economic Review* **57**(1) (1967), 34–58.
[180] L.R. Klein and R. Summers, *The Wharton Index of Capacity Utilization*, Economics Research Unit, Department of Economics, Wharton School of Finance and Commerce, University of Pennsylvania, Philadelphia, PA, 1966.
[181] J.L. Knapp, T.W. Fields and R.T. Jerome, *A Survey of State and Regional Econometric Models*, Tayloe Murphy Institute, University of Virginia, Charlottesville, VA, 1978.
[182] D.E. Knuth, Von Neumann's first computer program, *ACM Computing Surveys* **2**(4) (1970), 247–260.
[183] T.C. Koopmans, Statistical Inference in Dynamic Economic Models, Cowles Commission, *Monograph*, Vol. 11, First Ed., John Wiley & Sons, Chapter xvi, New York, 1950, p. 438.
[184] T.C. Koopmans, *On the concept of optimal economic growth, in The Econometric Approach to Development Planning*, North-Holland, Amsterdam, 1965.
[185] I.B. Kravis, Comparative studies of national incomes and prices, *Journal of Economic Literature* **22**(1) (1984), 1–39.
[186] I.B. Kravis, A.W. Heston and R. Summers, Real GDP Per Capita for more than one hundred countries, *Economic Journal* **88** (1978), 215–242.
[187] I.B. Kravis and R.E. Lipsey, Export prices and the transmission of inflation, *American Economic Review* **67**(1) (1977), 155–163.
[188] E. Kuh, A progress report, in: *The Brookings Model: Some Further Results*, J.S. Duesenberry et al., eds., Rand McNalley & Company, Chicago, 1969, pp. 3–16.
[189] E. Kuh, Some Notes on the Research Program at the NBER Computer Research Center for Economics and Management Science, *Annals of Economic and Social Measurement* **1**(2) (1972), 233–236.
[190] E. Kuh, J. Neese and P. Hollinger, *Structural Sensitivity in Econometric Models*, John Wiley & Sons, New York, 1985.
[191] E. Kuh and R.E. Welsch, Econometric Models and Their Assessment for Policy: Some New Diagnostics Applied to the Translog Energy Demand in Manufacturing, in: *Proceedings of the*

Workshop on Validation and Assessment Issues of Energy Models, S. Gass, ed., National Bureau of Standards, Washington, DC, 1980, pp. 445–475.

[192] F.E. Kydland and E.C. Prescott, The econometrics of the general equilibrium approach to business cycles, *Scandinavian Journal of Economics* **93**(2) (1991), 161–178.

[193] F.E. Kydland and E.C. Prescott, Hours and employment variation in business cycle theory, *Economic Theory* **1**(1) (1991), 63–81.

[194] F.E. Kydland and E.C. Prescott, The computational experiment: an econometric tool, *Journal of Economic Perspectives* **10**(1) (1996), 69–85.

[195] T. Lane, ed., *TROLL Reference Manual (Standard System). Second ed*, MIT Center for Computational Research in Economics and Management Science, MIT Information Processing Services: Cambridge, MA, 1979.

[196] S. Laurent and J.-P. Peters, *GARCH 2.0: An Ox Package for Estimating and Forecasting Various ARCH Models*, 2001, 33.

[197] S. Laurent and J.-P. Peters, Correction, *Journal of Economic Surveys* **17** (2003), 113–114.

[198] E.E. Leamer, *Specification Searches: Ad Hoc Inference with Non-experimental Data*, Wiley, New York, 1978.

[199] E.E. Leamer, Let's take the con out of econometrics, *American Economic Review* **73** (1983), 31–43.

[200] R. Leeson, A.W.H. Phillips M.B.E. (Military Division), *Economic Journal* **104**(May 1994), 605–618.

[201] R. Leeson, ed., *A.W.H. Phillips: Collected Works in Contemporary Perspective*, Cambridge University Press, Cambridge, 2000.

[202] W. Leontief, Structural matrices of national economies, *Econometrica* **17**(Issue Supplement: Report of the Washington Meeting) (1949), 273–282.

[203] W.W. Leontief, Computational problems arising in connection with economic analysis of industrial relationships, in: *Proceedings of a Symposium on Large-Scale Digital Calculating Machinery*, Harvard University Press, Cambridge, MA, 1948.

[204] W.W. Leontief, *The Structure of the American Economy*, Oxford University Press, New York, 1949.

[205] D.M. Lilien, *MicroTSP and Eviews*, C.G. Renfro, recipient, 17 March 2003.

[206] R.F. Ling, General considerations in the design of an interactive system for data analysis, *Communications of the Association for Computing Machinery* **23** (1980), 147–154.

[207] T.C. Liu, Underidentification, structural estimation and forecasting, *Econometrica* **28** (1960), 855–865.

[208] T.C. Liu, Survey of United States models: discussion, in: *The Brookings Model: Perspective and Recent Developments*, G. Fromm and L.R. Klein, ed, American Elsevier Publishing Company, New York, 1975, pp. 415–418.

[209] J.W. Longley, An appraisal of least squares programs for the electronic computer from the point of view of the user, *Journal of the American Statistical Association* **62** (1967), 819–841

[210] R.E. Lucas, Jr, Econometric policy evaluation: a critique, in: *The Phillips Curve and Labor Markets*, K. Brunner and A.H. Meltzer, eds, North-Holland, Amsterdam, 1976.

[211] J.K. Mackie-Mason, Econometric software: a user's view, *Journal of Economic Perspectives* **6** (1992), 165–188.

[212] J.G. MacKinnon, Model specification tests and artificial regressions, *Journal of Economic Literature* **30** (1992), 102–146.

[213] W.F. Maunder and M.C. Fleming, Reviews of United Kingdom statistical sources, *Journal of Economic and Social Measurement* **14** (1986), 271–276.

[214] M.D. McCarthy, *The Wharton Quarterly Econometric Forecasting Model Mark III*, Economic Research Unit, Department of Economics, Wharton School of Finance and Commerce, Philadelphia, PA, 1973.

[215] M.D. McCarthy, The Cowles Commission, the Brookings Project, and the econometric services industry: successes and possible new directions: a personal view, *Econometric Theory* **8** (1992), 383–401.

[216] M.C. McCracken, A computer system for econometric research, *Social Science Information* **5** (1967), 151–158.
[217] M.C. McCracken, Data administration in an information system, in: *Conference on Government Information Systems*, Economic Council of Canada, Ottawa, 1967.
[218] M.C. McCracken and K. May, Issues in the development of early solution facilities for very large macroeconometric models, *Journal of Economic and Social Measurement* **29** (2004), 167–171, this volume.
[219] M.C. McCracken and C.A. Sonnen, A system for large econometric models: management, estimation, and simulation, in: *Proceedings of the Association for Computing Machinery Annual Conference, August 1972*, Association for Computing Machinery, 1972.
[220] B.D. McCullough, A review of RATS v4.2: Benchmarking numeric accuracy, *Journal of Applied Econometrics* **12** (1997), 181–190.
[221] B.D. McCullough, Assessing the reliability of statitistical software: Part I, *American Statistician* **52**(4) (1998), 358–366.
[222] B.D. McCullough, Assessing the reliability of statistical software: Part II, *American Statistician* **53**(2) (1999), 149–159.
[223] B.D. McCullough, Econometric software reliability: Eviews, LimDep, Shazam, and TSP, *Journal of Applied Econometrics* **14**(2) (1999), 191–202.
[224] B.D. McCullough, The accuracy of Mathematica 4.0 as a Statistical Package, *Computational Statistics* **15** (2000), 279–299.
[225] B.D. McCullough, Experience with the StRD: Application and Interpretation, in: *Proceedings of the 31st Symposium on the Interface: Models, Prediction, and Computing*, Interface Foundation of North America, Fairfax, VA, 2000.
[226] B.D. McCullough, Is it safe to assume that software is accurate? *International Journal of Forecasting* **16** (2000), 349–357.
[227] B.D. McCullough, Some details of nonlinear estimation, in: *Numerical Methods in Statistical Computing for the Social Sciences*, M. Altman, J. Gill and M. McDonald, eds, Wiley, New York, 2003.
[228] B.D. McCullough, Wilkinson's tests and econometric software, *Journal of Economic and Social Measurement* **29** (2004), 261–270, this volume.
[229] B.D. McCullough and C.G. Renfro, Benchmarks and software standards: a case study of GARCH procedures, *Journal of Economic and Social Measurement* **25** (1998), 59–71.
[230] B.D. McCullough and C.G. Renfro, Some numerical aspects of nonlinear estimation, *Journal of Economic and Social Measurement* **26** (2000), 63–77.
[231] B.D. McCullough and H.D. Vinod, The numerical reliability of econometric software, *Journal of Economic Literature* **37**(2) (1999), 633–665.
[232] B.D. McCullough and H.D. Vinod, Verifying the solution from a nonlinear solver: a case study, *American Economic Review* **93**(3) (2003), 873–892.
[233] B.D. McCullough and B. Wilson, On the accuracy of statistical procedures in Microsoft Excel 97, *Computational Statistics & Data Analysis* **31** (1999), 27–37.
[234] B.D. McCullough and B. Wilson, On the accuracy of statistical procedures in Microsoft Excel 2000 and Excel XP, *Computational Statistics & Data Analysis* **40** (2002), 713–721.
[235] R.H. McGuckin and S.V. Nguyen, Public use microdata: disclosure and usefulness, *Journal of Economic and Social Measurement* **16** (1990), 19–40.
[236] R.C. Mendelssohn, The BLS computer language for quantitative economic research, in: *Conference on Government Information Systems, October 5–6, 1967*, Economic Council of Canada, Ottawa, 1967.
[237] R.C. Mendelssohn, The New on-line BLS database and information system, in: *Readings in Business and Economic Research Management: Execution and Enterprise*, J.D. Fischer, ed., Office of Research Administration, School of Business, University of Wisconsin, Madison, WI. 1980, pp. 86–89.
[238] T.C. Mills, *The Econometric Modeling of Financial Time Series*, Cambridge University Press, Cambridge, 1993.

[239] T.C. Mills, *The Econometric Modeling of Financial Time Series*, Second Ed., Cambridge University Press, Cambridge, 1999.

[240] M.S. Morgan, *The History of Econometric Ideas. Historical Perspectives on Modern Economics*, Cambridge, UK; New York: Cambridge University Press, Chapter xv, 1990, p. 296.

[241] O. Morgenstern, *On the Accuracy of Economic Observations*, Princeton University Press, Princeton, NJ, 1960.

[242] A.L. Nagar, Stochastic Simulation of the Brookings Econometric Model, in: *The Brookings Model: Some Further Results*, J.S. Duesenberry et al., eds, Rand McNally & Company, Chicago, 1969, pp. 425–456.

[243] P. Nepomiastchy and A. Ravelli, Adapted methods for solving and optimizing quasi-triangular econometric models, *Annals of Economic and Social Measurement* **6**(5) (1978), 555–562.

[244] M. Nerlove, A tabular survey of macroeconometric models, *International Economic Review* **7** (1966), 127–175.

[245] M. Nerlove, History of panel data econometrics 1861–1997, in: *Essays in Panel Data Econometrics*, Cambridge University Press, Cambridge, 2002.

[246] M. Nerlove, *Email re EM algorithm*, C.G. Renfro, recipient, 26 June 2003.

[247] A.L. Norman, L.S. Lasdon and J.K. Hsin, A comparison of methods for solving and optimizing a large non-linear econometric model, *Journal of Economic Dynamics and Control* **6**(1/2) (1983), 3–24.

[248] M. Norman, Multiple Regression Program (AUTO: functional description and instructions for use), in: *The Wharton Short Term Forecasting System Computer Programs*, G.R. Green and I. Green, eds, Wharton Econometric Forecasting Associates, Philadelphia, PA, 1973, pp. 1–26.

[249] M. Norman, H. Shapiro and R. Rasche, *The SIM Model Solution Program*, MIT Center for Computational Research in Economics and Management Science, MIT Information Processing Services, Cambridge, MA, 1967.

[250] G. Orcutt, Toward partial redirection of econometrics, *Review of Economics and Statistics* **34** (1952), 195–213.

[251] G. Orcutt, S. Caldwell and R. Wertheimer, *Policy Exploration Through Microanalytic Simulation*, Urban Institute, Washington, DC, 1976.

[252] G. Pauletto, Computational solution of large-scale macroeconometric models, *Advances in Computational Economics*, Vol. 7, Kluwer Academic Publishers, Chapter xiv, Boston, 1997, p. 161.

[253] PC Age, IBM takes a spin on the hard disk: Big Blue announces a hard disk PC and new DOS expansion, in: *Personal Computer Age*, 1983, pp. 94–95.

[254] J. Pease and R. Lepage, *An Evaluation of Selected Microcomputer Statistical Programs, Working Paper 15*, Department of Agricultural Economics, Michigan State University, 1984.

[255] M.H. Pesaran and G.C. Harcourt, Life and Work of John Richard Nicholas Stone 1913–1991, *The Economic Journal* **110** (2000), F146–F165.

[256] M.H. Pesaran and B. Pesaran, *Microfit. A Interactive Econometric Software Package*, User Manual, Oxford University Press, Oxford, 1987.

[257] M.H. Pesaran and B. Pesaran, *Microfit 3.0. An Interactive Econometric Software Package. User Manual*, Oxford University Press, Oxford, 1991.

[258] M.H. Pesaran and L.J. Slater, *Dynamic Regression: Theory and Algorithms*, Ellis Horwood, Chichester, 1980.

[259] M.H. Pesaran and M. Wickens, *Handbook of Applied Econometrics. Blackwell Handbooks in Economics*, Blackwell, Oxford, UK, Cambridge, MA, 1995.

[260] W. Peterson, Computer software for a large econometric model, in: *The Cambridge Multisectoral Dynamic Model of the British Economy*, T.S. Barker and W. Peterson, eds, Cambridge University Press, Cambridge, 1987, pp. 105–121.

[261] W. Peterson, *Econometric Computing in Cambridge*, C.G. Renfro, recipient, 20 March 2003.

[262] W. Peterson, T. Barker and R. van der Ploeg, Software support for multisectoral dynamic models of national economies, *Journal of Economic Dynamics and Control* **5**(1) (1983), 81–108.

[263] W. Peterson, T.S. Barker and L.A. Winters, IDIOM, an International Dynamic Input-Output Model, in: *Proceedings of the 7th International Input-Output Conference, 1979*, UNIDO, New York, 1984.
[264] P.C.B. Phillips, The Structural Estimation of a Stochastic Differential Equation System, *Econometrica* **40**(6) (1972), 1021–1041.
[265] P.C.B. Phillips, *Email re the History of Econometric Software*, C.G. Renfro, recipient, 28 March 2003.
[266] P.C.B. Phillips and V.B. Hall, Early development of econometric software at the University of Auckland, *Journal of Economic and Social Measurement* **29** (2004), 127–133, this Volume.
[267] G. Pilozzi, A new approach to the dissemination of CANSIM data, *Canadian Statistical Review* **51** (1971), 5–8.
[268] E. Post, Real programmers don't use Pascal, *Datamation* **29**(7) (1983).
[269] S.J. Prais, The estimation of equivalent-adult scales from family budgets, *Economic Journal* **63**(252) (1953), 791–810.
[270] S.J. Prais and H.S. Houthakker, *The Analysis of Family Budgets*, Cambridge University Press, Cambridge, 1955.
[271] E.C. Prescott and T.F. Cooley, Estimation in the Presence of Stochastic Parameter Variation, *Econometrica* **44**(1) (1976), 167–184.
[272] D. Qin, *The Formation of Econometrics: A Historical Perspective*, Clarendon Press, Chapter xii, Oxford, UK, 1993, p. 212.
[273] R.E. Quandt, Computational Problems and Methods, in: *Handbook of Econometrics*, Z. Griliches and M.D. Intriligator, eds, North-Holland, Amsterdam, 1983, pp. 699–764.
[274] W. Raduchel and O. Eckstein, Economic Modeling Languages: the DRI Experience, *Journal of Economic Dynamics and Control* **5**(1) (1983), 59–74.
[275] F.P. Ramsey, A mathematical theory of savings, *Economic Journal* **38** (1928), 543–559.
[276] A. Reisman et al., On the voids in U.S. national educational statistics, *Journal of Economic and Social Measurement* **14** (1986), 357–366.
[277] C.G. Renfro, *An Interactive Regression Program for the PDP-10. Description and User Manual*, Brookings Quarterly Model Project, Brookings Institution, Washington, DC, 1970.
[278] C.G. Renfro, On the development of a comprehensive public data base for aggregate state and local economic data, *Review of Public Data Use* **7**(5/6) (1979), 1–10.
[279] C.G. Renfro, Economic Data Base Systems: Some reflections on the state of the art, *Review of Public Data Use* **8**(3) (1980), 121–140.
[280] C.G. Renfro, An on-line information system for aggregate state and local area economic data, *Journal of the American Society for Information Science* **31**(5) (1980).
[281] C.G. Renfro, Reflections on a theme by Mendelssohn: the LABSTAT data base system, in: *Readings in Business and Economic Research Management: Execution and Enterprise*, J.D. Fischer, ed., Office of Research Administration, School of Business, University of Wisconsin, Madison, WI, 1980, 86–90.
[282] C.G. Renfro, *The Computer as a Factor of Production in Economic Data Provision and Research*, paper presented at the American Economic Association Annual Meeting, 30 December 1981, Washington, DC.
[283] C.G. Renfro, The design of an information system for state and local government planning and analysis, in: *Proceedings of the Eighth European Urban Data Management Symposium*, Norwegian Ministry of the Environment, Oslo, 1981.
[284] C.G. Renfro, On the Development of Econometric Modeling Languages: MODLER and its first twenty-five years, *Journal of Economic and Social Measurement* **22**(4) (1996), 241–311.
[285] C.G. Renfro, Economic Data Base Systems: Further reflections on the state of the art, *Journal of Economic and Social Measurement* **23**(1) (1997), 43–85.
[286] C.G. Renfro, Normative Considerations in the development of a software package for econometric estimation, *Journal of Economic and Social Measurement* **23**(4) (1997), 277–330.
[287] C.G. Renfro, Macroeconometric models and changes in measurement concepts: an overview, *Journal of Economic and Social Measurement* **24**(2) (1998), 63–82.

[288] C.G. Renfro, ed., A compendium of existing econometric software packages, *Journal of Economic and Social Measurement* **29** (2004), 359–409, this volume.
[289] C.G. Renfro, The early development of econometric modeling languages, *Journal of Economic and Social Measurement* **29** (2004), 145–166, this volume.
[290] C.G. Renfro and P.A. Coomes, *The Kentucky Economic Information System User Manual*, Office for Research, College of Business and Economics, University of Kentucky, Lexington, KY, 1976.
[291] S. Rosen, Electronic Computers: A historical survey, *ACM Computing Surveys* **1**(1) (1969), 7–36.
[292] D.B. Rubin, Inference and missing data, *Biometrika* **63**(3) (1976), 581–592.
[293] G. Sadowsky, *MASH: A Computer System for Microanalytic Simulation for Policy Exploration*, Urban Institute, Washington, DC, 1977.
[294] J.P. Sall, SAS Econometric and Time-series Library. Preliminary Test Version for SAS 79.2, in: *SAS Institute Technical Report*, SAS Institute, Inc., Raleigh, NC, 1979.
[295] P.A. Samuelson, The art and science of macromodels over 50 years, in: *The Brookings Model: Perspective and Recent Developments*, G. Fromm and L.R. Klein, eds, North-Holland, Amsterdam, 1975, pp. 3–10.
[296] J.D. Sargan, Wages and prices in the United Kingdom: a study in econometric methodology, in: *Econometric Analysis for National Economic Planning*, P.E. Hart, G. Mills and J.K. Whitaker, eds, Butterworths, London, 1964, pp. 25–63.
[297] T.J. Sargent and C.A. Sims, Business cycle modeling without pretending to have too much a priori economic theory, in: *New Methods of Business Cycle Reserach*, Federal Reserve Bank of Minneapolis, Minneapolis, MN, 1977, pp. 45–109.
[298] N. Sarnak and E. Jaffe, 8087 performance considerations, *PCTech Journal* **1**(2) (1983), 30–47.
[299] SAS, SAS/ETS user's guide, version 5 edition, SAS Institute, Cary, NC, 1984.
[300] SAS, SAS/ETS user's guide, version 6, 2nd Ed., SAS Institute, Cary, NC, 1993.
[301] SAS, SAS/ETS user's guide, version 8, SAS Pub, Cary, NC, 1999.
[302] G.R. Schink, Simulation with large econometric models: The quest for a solution, *Journal of Economic and Social Measurement* **29** (2004) 135–143, this volume (incorporates Paper originally presented to the Association for Computing Machinery meetings, Denver, Colorado, 12 June 1970).
[303] G.R. Schink, The Brookings Quarterly Model: An aid to longer term economic policy analysis, in: *Econometric Model Performance: Comparative Simulation Studies of the U.S. Economy*, L.R. Klein and E. Burmeister, eds, University of Pennsylvania Press, Philadelphia, PA, 1976, pp. 307–321.
[304] M.E. Senko, Information systems: records, relations, sets, entities, and things, *Information Systems* **1** (1975), 3–13.
[305] J. Shiskin, A.H. Young and J.C. Musgrave, *The X-11 Variant of Census Method II Seasonal Adjustment, Technical Paper No. 15*, Bureau of the Census, U.S. Department of Commerce, Washington, DC, 1967.
[306] J. Siegel, Moving data between PCs and mainframes, in: *Byte Guide to the IBM PC*, 1984, pp. 248–255.
[307] C.A. Sims, Macroeconomics and reality, *Econometrica* **48** (1980), 1–48.
[308] L.J. Slater, Regression analysis, *Computer Journal* (1962), 1–5.
[309] L.J. Slater, *Fortran Programs for Economists, Department of Applied Economics Occasional Paper 13*, Cambridge University Press, Cambridge, 1967.
[310] L.J. Slater, *More Fortran Programs for Economists. DAE Occasional Paper 34*, Cambridge University Press, Cambridge, 1972.
[311] L.J. Slater, *GEM: A General Econometric Matrix Program. DAE Occasional Paper 46*, Cambridge University Press, Cambridge, 1976.
[312] L.J. Slater, *Email re Air Conditioning*, C.G. Renfro, recipient, 1 July 2003.
[313] L.J. Slater, *Email re EDSAC and the DAE*, C.G. Renfro, recipient, 2 May 2003.
[314] L.J. Slater, *Email re Your paper and follow on*, C.G. Renfro, recipient, 10 June 2003, 3:22 PM.
[315] L.J. Slater, *Email Re: Re: Your paper and follow on*, C.G. Renfro, recipient. 10 June 2003, 3:28 PM.

[316] L.J. Slater, EDSAC: Recollections on early days in the Cambridge Computing Laboratory, *Journal of Economic and Social Measurement* **29** (2004), 119–122, this volume.
[317] L.J. Slater and T.S. Barker, *Regression Program for Titan*, Department of Applied Economics, University of Cambridge, Cambridge, 1967.
[318] L.J. Slater and T.S. Barker, *REX Regression Program for Titan*, Department of Applied Economics, University of Cambridge, Cambridge, 1971.
[319] B. Smith, *Showtime in the City*, DTP Desktop Publishing: Professional Presentation Solutions, 1988, 22–23.
[320] Society for Economic Dynamics and Control, News Item: Third Conference of the Society for Economic Dynamics and Control (Program), *Journal of Economic Dynamics and Control* **3** (1981), 393–395.
[321] R. Startz, *8087: Applications and Programming for the IBM PC and Other PCs*, Robert J. Brady Company, Bowie, MD, 1983.
[322] H.H. Stokes, *Email re Bayesian Program*, etc., C.G. Renfro, recipient, 31 August 2003.
[323] H.H. Stokes, The evolution of econometric software design: A developer's view, *Journal of Economic and Social Measurement* **29** (2004), 205–259, this volume.
[324] H.H. Stokes, On the advantage of using two or more econometric software systems to solve the same problem, *Journal of Economic and Social Measurement* **29** (2004), 307–320, this volume.
[325] R. Stone, J. Aitchison and A.J.C. Brown, Some Estimation Problems in Demand Analysis, *The Incorporated Statistician* **5**(4) (1955), 1–13.
[326] R. Stone and A. Brown, A Computable Model of Economic Growth, in: *A Program for Growth*, Vol. 1, R. Stone, ed., Department of Applied Economics, Cambridge, 1962.
[327] A. Stroud, *The Multiple Regression Program RGR*, Social Systems Research Institute, University of Wisconsin, Madison, WI, 1961.
[328] D.B. Suits, *The theory and application of econometric models*, Center of Economic Research, Chapter xiii, Athens, 1963, p. 147.
[329] D.B. Suits, *Email re Solution of the Klein-Goldberger model and early software used at the University of Michigan*, C.G. Renfro, recipient, 28 March, 2003.
[330] M.J.C. Surrey, *The Analysis and Forecasting of the British Economy*, Cambridge: Cambridge University Press, 1971.
[331] R.C. Taeuber and R.C. Rockwell, National social data series: a compendium of brief descriptions, *Review of Public Data Use* **10**(1-2) (1982), 23–111.
[332] P.N. Triandafillou, CANSIM/SIS–A new phase of development, *Canadian Statistical Review* **50** (1975), 4–6.
[333] G. Uebe, G. Huber and J. Fischer, *Macro-Econometric Models – An International Bibliography*, Gower, Aldershot, 1988.
[334] P.F. Velleman and R.E. Welsch, On evaluating interactive statistical program packages, *Communications in Statistics, Part B–Simulation and Computation* **5** (1976), 197–208.
[335] P.F. Velleman and M.A. Ypellar, Constructing regressions with controlled features: a method for probing regression performance, *Journal of the American Statistical Association* **75** (1980), 839–844.
[336] K.F. Wallis et al., *Models of the UK Economy*, Oxford University Press, Oxford, 1984.
[337] K.F. Wallis et al., *Models of the UK Economy: A Second Review by the ESRC Macroeconomic Modelling Bureau*, Oxford University Press, Oxford, 1985.
[338] K.F. Wallis et al., *Models of the UK Economy: A Third Review by the ESRC Macroeconomic Modelling Bureau*, Oxford University Press, Oxford, 1986.
[339] K.F. Wallis et al., *Models of the UK Economy: A Fourth Review by the ESRC Macroeconomic Modelling Bureau*, Oxford University Press, Oxford, 1987.
[340] A.I. Wasserman, Information system design methodology, *Journal of the American Society for Information Science* **31** (1980), 5–24.
[341] R.F. Wescott and M.V. Yates, The PC Corner: desktop publishing is for economists, *Business Economics* **24** (1989), 51–53.

[342] G.B. Wetherill et al., The design and evaluation of statistical software for microcomputers, *The Statistician* **34** (1985), 391–427.
[343] H. White, R.F. Engle and C.W.J. Granger, *Cointegration, Causality, and Forecasting: A Festschrift in Honour of Clive W.J. Granger*, Oxford University Press, Oxford, New York, 1999.
[344] K.J. White, A General Computer for Econometric Models–Shazam, *Econometrica* **46**(1) (1978), 239–240.
[345] K.J. White, *Email*, C.G. Renfro, recipient, 11 March 2003.
[346] M. Wickens, *Email re early computing at the LSE*, C.G. Renfro, recipient, 24 April 2003.
[347] V. Wiggins, *Email re Interface versus organization*, C.G. Renfro, recipient, 9 April 2003.
[348] V. Wiggins, *Email re Stata entry for Compendium for econometric software*, C.G. Renfro, recipient, 1 April 2003.
[349] M.V. Wilkes and W. Renwick, The EDSAC, an electronic calculating machine, *Journal of Scientific Instruments* **26** (1949), 385–391.
[350] M.V. Wilkes, D.J. Wheeler and S. Gill, *The Preparation of Programs for an Electronic Digital Computer: With special reference to the EDSAC and the use of a library of subroutines*, Addison Wesley, Cambridge, MA, 1951.
[351] R.M. Young, *Email re the history of econometric software*, C.G. Renfro, recipient, 25 March 2003.
[352] W.Zafft, G. Solomon and R. Perron, *TROLL Reference Manual, in installments*, National Bureau of Economic Research, New York, 1973–1976.
[353] A. Zellner, PCBRAP: A PC Bayesian Regression Program, *American Statistician* **43**(1) (1989), 124.
[354] A. Zellner, *Email re History of Econometric Software Development*, C.G. Renfro, recipient, 27 February 2003.
[355] A. Zellner, A. Stroud and L.C. Chau, *Program for Computing Seemingly Unrelated Regressions Estimates*, Social Systems Research Institute, Department of Economics, Madison, WI, 1963.
[356] A. Zellner, A. Stroud and L.C. Chau, *Program for Computing Two and Three Stage Least Squares and Associated Statistics*, Social Systems Research Institute, Department of Economics, Madison, WI, 1963.
[357] E. Zivot and J. Wang, *Modelling Financial Time Series with S-PLUS*, May 22, 2002 ed., Insightful Corporation, Seatle, WA, 2002.

Some Milestones in Econometric Computing

Journal of Economic and Social Measurement 29 (2004) 111–114
IOS Press

Introduction

Charles G. Renfro
601 West 113th Street, #12G, New York, NY 10025, USA
E-mail: cgrenfro@modler.com

The short articles in this section are, for the most part, memoir descriptions of econometric computing in its various phases during the early days from about 1953 to the period of sustained expansion during the 1970s. The year 2003 essentially marks the 50th anniversary of the first development of econometric software, including the publication, that year, by Brown, Houthakker, and Prais of a still informative article on electronic computation in economic statistics in the *Journal of the American Statistical Association*, as well as early computational work towards the development of the first regression package by Lucy Slater, working with M.J. Farrell, all at the Department of Applied Economics at the University of Cambridge, and the use of the computer by Klein, Goldberger, and colleagues at the University of Michigan to calculate moments in preparation for parameter estimation. However, whereas this collective milestone marks the first step, in actuality it took another 10 years before the use of the computer began to become at all general. Throughout the 1950s, and even into the 1960s, the standard computing device remained for economists the electromechanical desk calculator. The 1960s were the period of transition, the point in time that the computer became a common applied research tool, and economists moved beyond applying it to calculations that were in principle possible using hand methods to those that fundamentally either required a computer or else a literal lifetime to perform a single (albeit complex) task.

The first milestone article is by Arthur Goldberger, who describes aspects of the pre-computer era and recalls some of the trials and tribulations associated with the desk calculator. These devices could occasionally be seen on desks in economic departments as late as the 1970s, but not much later. Consequently, anyone much younger than 50 is unlikely to have seen such a device in operation, with the possible exception of someone who has visited a museum. However, a point of interest of the Goldberger memoir is not just the glimpse of a bygone era it affords, but also a sense of the continuity of applied economic research. The calculations still performed today, in their operative characteristics, are the same as those performed then. The differences are the speed with which they are performed (not to mention the associated human ease of the modern laptop computer) and certain algorithmic differences that reflect the need to deal with roundoff and other numeric errors in a somewhat different way in each context. Of course, because of the speed with which calculations can now be performed, much can be done today that simply could not even be attempted then.

Lucy Slater's memoir begins the description of the use of the computer, but as you turn to her contribution do not expect to be brought face to face with a machine anything like what you may be used to, for this is $t = 0$. The machines then, the EDSAC at the University of Cambridge, the ENIAC and the EDVAC at the University of Pennsylvania, or the Whirlwind at the Massachusetts Institute of Technology, all predate both the Cathode Ray Tube (CRT) terminal, and the line printer, each of which of course themselves much predate the flatscreen monitor or the modern inkjet or laser printer. The particular machine that is here described is one that until about 1951–52 was both input- and output-challenged, and cobbled together from scavenged parts. This machine also marks the dawn of programming, which itself then needed to be defined in its characteristics as an activity: this was the pre-Formula Translation (FORTRAN) and pre-transistor era, not to mention the real Johnny-come-latelies, such as C or C+. Tape drives, disk drives, printers, and other computer peripherals (with the notable exception of punch card devices) were then at best only twinkles in the eyes of their creators. Moreover, even at the end of that decade, IBMfls then latest and greatest machine, its first transistor-based computer, was oil-cooled.

The year 1960 roughly defines the point at which computers, as collections of transistor circuits and what today would be easily recognized assemblages of peripheral devices, began to be manufactured and installed for widespread use. These second generation machines were the first to offer their users software tools, such as ALGOL, COBOL, FORTRAN and other compilers, as well as object libraries, that enabled young economists at various universities around the world to begin to develop econometric software. The memoir by Charles Holt describes one of the results of having available one of the later first generation computers, the IBM 650, which permitted the first computer implementation of the then rather computer-challenging Holt-Winters forecasting technique by Winters in 1959–60. Fortunately, the technique was not particularly demanding in terms of memory requirements, inasmuch as the IBM 650 offered only 2K of 10 digit word storage. Interestingly, Although the Holt-Winters technique has had widespread practical application during the past more than 40 years, the theoretical basis of this technique has not yet actually been published in the literature. Today, Holt's original article can be obtained as a research memorandum from the University of Texas Engineering Library, but stimulated by Holt's memoir, it will now be published in 2004.

Rex Bergstrom, as a graduate student, was present in Cambridge during the period described by Slater's memoir and used EDSAC. In antipodal New Zealand, in the early 1960s, his graduate students began to use the IBM 1620 to program linear and non-linear, single and simultaneous equation parameter estimation algorithms. The memoir by Peter Phillips and Viv Hall describes computing at the University of Auckland during the 1960s, not only the development of models of the New Zealand economy, but also the characteristics of two of the IBM computers of that time and some interesting and even amusing aspects of their hands-on operation. These authors also provide additional retrospective on the use of EDSAC at Cambridge by Bergstrom.

At more or less the same time, but in the United States, development of progressively larger scale models at, principally, the University of Pennsylvania and the contemporaneous development of the Brookings Quarterly Econometric Model of the United States by scholars at a number of institutions, not all in the United States, lead to the need to develop efficient computer algorithms to solve these large scale models. Even as late as 1968, and in possibly one or two cases even later, models estimated using the computer were still being solved on desk calculators. The article by George Schink published here addresses this quest for efficient solution and in fact incorporates verbatim a never-before-published paper, he originally presented at an Association for Computing Machinery meeting in June of 1970. The present day introduction by Schink describes the context of this paper, but the paper itself conveys a good sense of the process of the discovery of an appropriate model solution algorithm during those years.

In contrast to the early stages of the use of the computer, which generally involved the development of specific algorithms, as described in the foregoing memoirs, in the middle 1960s, with the development of increasingly large scale econometric models, it became important to create software systems that not only performed the necessary computations, but also managed the process of econometric model construction and use. The next memoir, by Charles Renfro, traces the development of econometric modeling languages, during the period beginning in the mid-1960s through the middle 1980s. A characteristic of the advent of this type of software system was the progressive development of a quasi-algebraic, more or less natural command syntax and at the same time an increasing degree of process integration. This description is buttressed by the next memoir, by Michael McCracken and Keith May, which focuses more specifically on a particular example of an econometric modeling language, one that today is known as MOSAIC. This software system began its development in the early to mid 1960s as a data base management system, known as DATABANK, and has progressively developed into an integrated econometric modeling language designed to support the construction and use of large to very large econometric models.

Following the take off phase in the 1960s, the 1970s were in general a time of noticeable expansion in the use of the computer, in terms of both wider use and for progressively more intensive applications. The memoir by Terry Barker, Wagner Dada and William Peterson focuses on the Cambridge Growth Model, and the software system MREG/IDIOM that was developed over a 20 year period to support it. A notable aspect of this model was its sheer size, ultimately numbering in excess of 2500 equations. Such size requires the maintenance of a substantial database, as well as overcoming a number of computational hurdles. Significantly, the Growth Model began to be developed during the time that even a 300 equation model taxed the capabilities of existing mainframes. The effectively available RAM in those days was normally less than 512 K, and contiguous disk storage was limited to – at best – 10–30 megabytes and often much less. The disk storage capacity of the present day Apple IPOD easily competes with, if not dominates, that of the 1970s era computers, and even a digital camera may offer 512 megabytes of storage. The challenge of mounting the entire Cambridge Growth Model on a Pocket PC PDA is possibly less now than the challenge then of mounting and maintaining it on an IBM mainframe.

The final Milestone memoir, by Houston Stokes, addresses in contrast the issue of the interplay between the computer and the first development of econometric techniques. Often, perhaps usually, econometric theory has been perceived as being developed with pencil in hand, and not with the computer. However, even in the past, this perception has not always been accurate. The development of the Theil BLUS technique is a specific example of a two-way relationship between econometric theory and software design. In particular, the fact that the sum of squares of the N-K BLUS residuals is equal to the sum of squares of the N OLS residuals was first observed experimentally and subsequently proved in theory. Increasingly, such a symbiosis may become common, perhaps in ways that cannot yet even be imagined.

Journal of Economic and Social Measurement 29 (2004) 115–117
IOS Press

Econometric computing by hand

Arthur S. Goldberger
Department of Economics, University of Wisconsin Madison, 1180 Observatory Drive, Madison, WI 53706-1393, USA
E-mail: asgoldbe@facstaff.wisc.edu

The electronic computer was first created in the 1940s, but was expensive to purchase and slow to spread. Throughout the 1950s and even into the earlier 1960s, electromechanical desk calculators were generally the only means whereby economists could compute regression parameters or solve econometric models. Some of the trials and tribulations of econometric computing by hand are described in this brief memoir of the context in which the Klein-Goldberger model was developed and used.

In September 1951, I arrived at Michigan to begin graduate studies in economics. The electromechanical desk calculators – Marchant, Friden, and Monroe – were the size of the typewriters of those days, and had a moving carriage as well. A 10 $\times$ 10 keyboard was used for input, and an odometer-style display gave the output. My recollection is that the Monroematic was the most compact and preferred. To calculate a square, one entered the number, hit the multiply key, and then the equal key. To get a sum of squares, a cumulative-multiply key was at hand. Moving to linear regression, I soon learned a trick for dealing with paired observations, provided each variable was recorded to only 1 or 2 digits. For example, with $x = 13$, $y = 23$, I could enter the artificial 10-digit variable 1300000023, square it to get 1690000059800000529, in which $169 = x$-square, $529 = y$-square, and $598 = 2$ times x times y. These could be cumulated – provided the sample was not too large – to produce the key statistics of linear regression, sum of x-squared, sum of y-squared, and (twice) the sum of x times y.

Even when sample sizes were small, data entry was occasionally interrupted by visitors, telephone calls, and other distractions. One would lose one's place while going down the columns of observations. A powerful innovation was introduced by Professor Paul Dwyer of the Mathematics Department, the computational guru. He hooked up a simple counter that would increment by one each time an observation was entered.

I'm speaking of electromechanical calculators. But Professor Daniel Suits (later my thesis supervisor) had an affection – or affectation – for a manual-mechanical version, reminiscent of a coffee grinder, which had a handcrank to be turned repeatedly clockwise (if memory serves) for multiplication and counterclockwise for division, those operations being repeated addition and subtraction respectively. There are

0747-9662/04/$17.00

museums and websites devoted to calculators of those and earlier days. One such is http://www.syssrc.com/html/museum/

Of course, calculating moments was merely the prolegomenon to the real task, running least-squares linear regressions. The method of choice for matrix inversion and solution of the normal equations was the Doolittle method. On large sheets of green accountant-ruled paper, the table of moments would be entered, and then a sequence of mysterious operations engaged in (when I later took a matrix algebra course, I learned that these were implementing elementary row operations to first reduce the matrix to triangular form ("forward solution"), and then recursively solving ("back solution")). As each successive element of the tableau (as it was called) was produced on the odometer, I pencilled it in neatly in the appropriate row and column of the large ruled sheet.

The potential for error in punching the wrong key or copying the wrong number was rife. Protection was offered by the use of an artificial check-sum column. A new column was added to the table of moments; it consisted of the sum of the elements of the preceding columns. The same mysterious operations were performed on that column as one went along. The check was that the sum of results in a row should equal the result of the sum, at each stage. Understand that it might take several days of part-time work to complete a regression with 4 or 5 variables.

It turned out that a foolproof method is not proof against a fool. On one noteworthy occasion, everything was going well until I got down to the 8th row when the check-sum failed to check. Several days were spent in redoing that row over and over to no avail. At long last – after Larry & Sonia Klein had both intervened, I discovered that the error had occurred on the previous row, but gone unnoticed because the two 10-digit numbers had looked identical, but in fact one had the middle digits 18 and the other had them transposed as 81. (Curiously enough, I was recently informed by the IRS that in my 2001 income tax return I had transposed two digits in reported amount withheld).

Some indication of computational progress over the years can be garnered by looking at texts. The first edition of Klein's Textbook of Econometrics [2] devotes pages 144 to 159 to least-squares computation, including the Doolittle method in gory detail, along with an ingenious "progressive digiting" trick for computing moments, when the data are on punch cards, a trick that used only a card sorter and a tabulator. My 1964 Econometric Theory [1, pp. 182–191] covered the Doolittle method in similar gory detail, but scratched the punch card trick. By 1991, in A Course in Econometrics, I finally felt comfortable disposing of least-squares computational matters with a line or two of GAUSS code, like $Q = X'X; QI = \text{invpd}(Q)$; $b = QI * X'y$.

It has been argued that the incredible revolution in computing was more bane than boon. Researchers no longer needed to actually look at their data before processing it, nor to think long and hard before trying a (costly, in time and money) alternative specification. Occasionally, I see some merit in that argument.

References

[1] A.S. Goldberger, *Econometric Theory*, John Wiley & Sons, New York, 1964.
[2] L.R. Klein, *A Textbook of Econometrics*, Prentice Hall, Englewood Cliffs, 1953.

Journal of Economic and Social Measurement 29 (2004) 119–122
IOS Press

EDSAC: Recollections on early days in the Cambridge Computing Laboratory

Lucy Joan Slater
Department of Applied Economics, University of Cambridge, Sidgwich Avenne, Combridge CB3 9DE, UK
E-mail: LJSWardle@aol.com

Economists were among the earliest users of the programmable electronic computer, when it was made available for general use in the early 1950s. The first operating programmable electronic computer was the EDSAC, developed at Cambridge University. This memoir describes the context of the development of the first econometric software package, a regression program developed by the author, working together with M.J. Farrell, as well as a number of other aspects of the early computing environment at the Department of Applied Economics at Cambridge.

The first computing machine, which I can remember seeing in action, was a device at Imperial College, London University, which could play noughts and crosses. This must have been about 1948. It always won! But it made me want to go to Cambridge, where they were building a true computing machine which would be able to do addition, subtraction, multiplication and division, in an order predetermined by the user.

In spring 1949, I made my first visit to Cambridge and saw this machine. It was called an Electronic Delayed Storage Automatic Calculator, or EDSAC for short. So I determined to go to Cambridge and in October I got my way, a grant enough to live on, acceptance in the University, Girton College, and the Computing Laboratory, and somewhere to live in Cambridge.

A description and a photograph of EDSAC is given in the 1951 book by Wilkes, Wheeler, and Gill, which is also the first book that described the process of programming a computer [8]. The authors were the chief brains behind the development of EDSAC. Stan Gill died young, but David Wheeler and Maurice Wilkes, now Sir Maurice, live within a quarter of a mile from my home and we are still friends. Sir Maurice will be 90 at the end of June this year, 2003.

When I first saw EDSAC, an oscilloscope was the only way to communicate. Patterns were input by the user operating toggles, and the result came back as a pattern on the screen. Later, when I was allowed to try to use it, there was an old electric typewriter to input orders and numbers, and a ticker tape machine to output answers on five hole paper tape. Sid Barton was our engineer, the man with the soldering iron, and he went round American air bases, which at that time were auctioning off surplus war equipment, including very many valves. So it was not a case of designing something and then getting special bits made up from the design. Instead it was a case of using what we had, to extend the machine and see what it could be made to do. Hence the electric typewriter, the ticker tape machines, and why it used so very many valves. The room where EDSAC stood, was on the top floor of an old building which had been used as an anatomy laboratory in the past. The ropping hooks were still in the walls of one room. The EDSAC room was very hot indeed, with a usual temperature of about 100 degrees. We frequently cooked eggs in a frying pan on the top of the case containing the delay storage lines, to the horror of Sid Barton. It was a good thing that I liked being warm.

The program code used was a gnomic one from the earliest days. Thus A stood for add, S for subtract, M for multiply, and D for divide. Soon the machine had the ability to read in a program which would repeat a cycle of orders a given number of times, while varying the address of one of the items of data. Thus it could add numbers stored in locations 1 to 10, and put the result into location 11. The details of processes like these are described in detail in Wilkes, Wheeler and Gill.

About 1953, I was asked by Alan Brown, of the Department of Applied Economics at Cambridge, if I could provide a short program to carry out a repetitive calculation for him over many values of the input data. He needed these calculations for the book he was working on with Prais and Houthaker. Aspects of this work are described best in a 1953 article in the *Journal of the American Statistical Association* [2]. By this time, the computer could calculate and print decimals with the point in the correct place. The main difficulty was that double length floating point numbers were only just being developed and the calculation required the difference of two nearly equal sums of squares, that is the difference of the sum of squares of the observed data and the sum of squares of the theoretical data. There was a lot of programming and testing work for me to do before I got a routine which could do that calculation fairly accurately. Then Alan's data went through quite rapidly, in minutes instead of woman days, which is what it took when it was done in the Faculty of Economics, on Marchant electric calculators.

In March 1953, the first symposium about Automatic Digital Computation in England was held at the National Physical Laboratory, Teddington, and the proceedings were published by H. M. Stationary Office in 1954 [1]. These proceedings contained forty papers by all the leading brains working in the field at that time; in particular, The opening address by Professor Hartree, The EDSAC by M.V. Wilkes, Conversion routines by E.N. Mutch and S. Gill, Getting programs right by S. Gill, Applications of electronic machines in Pure Mathematics by J.C.P. Miller, Marginal checking by M.V. Wilkes and S.A. Barton. Anyone seriously interested in the early days of computers, should read these proceedings. In 1954, a booklet was prepared by Professor Hartree and Stan Gill as a teaching aid for people attending summer schools. In September 1955, this booklet was greatly extended and reprinted to help to teach people how to use EDSAC. It was called *Introduction to Programming for* the EDSAC and it was so popular that it had to be reprinted in September 1956 with an addition by Eric Mutch about the new B-box facilities.

About this time I was working on a Cambridge Ph.D. thesis about the solutions of the Schrodinger equations under the direction of J.C.P. Miller. The special cases of these solutions had never been worked out accurately and Houselander in America was taking an interest in these equations, as they were used in calculations for atomic bombs. It turned me cold when I realised just how my numbers might be used, and I declined the offer of a job at the National Bureau of Standards in Washington DC. At that time the Bureau was being run by Milton Abramovitz, so I asked him if I could stay in Cambridge and do his work here, where I already knew how to use the computer. Also plans were being made for a second machine called EDSAC II, to be built in our laboratory, which gave me an added incentive to stay in Cambridge. EDSAC II was to use ferrite cores, instead of values, and also it was going to be very much bigger and at least ten times faster.

I finished my Ph. D. thesis on the calculations of the Whittaker functions and Cambridge University Press published my book *Confluent Hypergeometric Functions* [3], which contained tables of some of these functions over a restricted range of values. These tables were calculated on EDSAC I and then checked by being recalculated on EDSAC II. I wanted the printing of these tables to be done directly from the punched paper tapes which contained the numbers, but that was too much for the Press to swallow, so they actually reset the tables in type, from the type written text and then had to check the tables all over again by hand.

I got some money for this work but a secure income was becoming vital, so I became a Junior Research Officer at the newly formed Department of Applied Economics in Cambridge. I felt that while a mistake in calculations in Economics may lead to a small disaster, a mistake in Atomic calculations could be a very big disaster indeed.

The first work I did in this post, was an analysis of the British coal mines for Mike Farrell. There were 818 coal mines in Britain at that time. The data for these had been punched on 80 column Holorith cards and we had to do an analysis which again involved sums of squares and cross products and the formation of the theoretical sums of squares and the actual sums of squares. The details of what the program had to do were written up by Mike Farrell, and as far as I know, this was the first attempt in England to produce a program which could do an elementary regression analysis. This program quickly became very popular among other research units in the University, such as the Department of Agricultural Economics, and the Medical Statistics Unit under Bob Carpenter. It seemed that every one had a set of data which they wanted to put through EDSAC's regression program which was called Reg I. This quickly became Reg II, Reg III, and so on, as other ideas were incorporated and EDSAC developed other facilities such as an early magnetic tape unit [4–6]. Also I made a program called Matrix manipulation program or MM I. This was limited to the addition , subtraction and inversion of a three by three matrix, but it was later developed further [7]. These early efforts were severely limited by the lack of storage space in EDSAC so, by 1958, the whole laboratory was looking forward to the advent of EDSAC II . But that is another story.

References

[1] Automatic Digital Computation Symposium, *Proceedings of the Symposium held October 1953 at the National Physical Laboratory, Teddington*, H.M.S.O., London, 1954.

[2] J.A.C. Brown, H.S. Houthakker and S.J. Prais, Electronic computation in economic statistics, *Journal of the American Statistical Association* **48** (1953), 414–428.

[3] L.J. Slater, *Confluent Hypergeometric Functions*, Cambridge University Press, Cambridge.

[4] L.J. Slater, 1962 Regression Analysis, *Computer Journal* (January 1962), 1–5.

[5] L.J. Slater, *Fortran Programs for Economists*, DAE Occasional Paper 13, Cambridge University Press, Cambridge, 1967.

[6] L.J. Slater, *More Fortran Programs for Economists*, DAE Occasional Paper 34, Cambridge University Press, Cambridge, 1972.

[7] L.J. Slater, *GEM A General Econometric Matrix Program*, DAE Occasional Paper 46, Cambridge University Press, Cambridge, 1976.

[8] M.V. Wilkes, D.J. Wheeler and S. Gill, *The Preparation of Programs for an Electronic Digital Computer: With special reference to the EDSAC and the Use of a Library of Subroutines*, Addison Wesley, Cambridge, MA, 1951.

Journal of Economic and Social Measurement 29 (2004) 123–125
IOS Press

Some Milestones in Econometric Computing

Forecasting seasonals and trends by exponentially weighted moving averages

Charles C. Holt
Graduate School of Business, University of Texas at Austin, 1452 Wild Basin Ledge, Austin, TX 78746, USA
E-mail: ccholt@mail.utexas.edu

This brief memoir describes the context of the original development of the well-known Holt-Winters exponentially weighted average forecast methodology, both in terms of its concepts and its first computer implementation in 1960. The original motivation for the development of the methodology by Holt was the widespread need for a feasible technique that could be applied to the forecasting of sales on a product by product basis. Once introduced, the method has come to be widely applied as a practical technique. The Holt-Winters methodology also played an important part in stimulating the work of J.F. Muth on what came to be called rational expectations. Notwithstanding this implact, the methodologyfls theoretical basis has not before now been described in the literature, however as a result of the development of this memoir for this special issue of the Journal of Economic and Social Measurement on the history and evaluation of econometric software, by arrangement the original theory paper will now be published in a forthcoming issue of the International Journal of Forecasting.

Four researchers with widely varied backgrounds, Holt, Modigliani, Muth and Simon, were supported in the 1950's by the Office of Naval Research on the project, Planning and Control of Industrial Operations. Decisions on production and inventories would require forecasts that were both cheap and accurate, and melded into an integrated system.

Forecast accuracy is important because a high forecast leads to excessive inventories, and a low forecast leads to stockouts. Thus forecast errors can produce excessive inventories and stock outs.

Not only are forecast errors costly, but the process of making forecasts is costly as well. Often business firms produce a tremendous number of different products each of which may require forecasts. An extreme example illustrates this point. The research team encountered a small sandpaper manufacturer that employed 75 workers. The factory produced many different types of sandpaper – different shapes, grits and weights. Each month the company needed sales forecasts of over 200.000 different products. Accurate forecasts of sales for so many products virtually requires efficient computerized forecasting. Holt , who had taken on this problem, followed the forecasting literature, and visited R.G. Brown at Arthur D. Little [2].

Exponentially weighted moving averages, EWMA, were, at the time, widely used as a simply-computed formula for smoothing data. It was recognized that a random variable smoothed by an EWMA constituted a limited kind of forecast. It was a

0747-9662/04/$17.00

way to suppress random variation of a forecast variable – a useful mathematical formula–but little more.

One weekend in April of 1957 it dawned on Holt that the EWMA concept might be used not only as a way to smooth the level of a variable, but also might be used to smooth trends, seasonals, and other components each of which could be forecasted. By Monday he had written a ten page paper [5] that demonstrated that the EWMA formula could be extended, easily and flexibly, to forecasting multiple components in a variety of combinations. The new system could handle: multiplicative seasonals, additive seasonals, multiplicative trends, additive trends and standard errors. The new system had the following desirable characteristics: it was easy to program, fast to compute, required minimal data storage, put declining weight on old data, used simple initial conditions, had robust parameters, was automatically adaptive, model formulations were easy, and the math was tractable.

The question then was: how accurate would the new forecasts be? P.R. Winters, a graduate student, was recruited to answer that forecast performance question. With time series data drawn from a variety of fields Winters easily programmed the forecast formulas in FORTRAN for an IBM 650 [10] and found that the formula forecasts were surprisingly accurate. Winters published his results under the same title as Holt's theory paper three years earlier, and the Holt forecasting formulas came to be called the Holt-Winters forecasting formulas.

The problem of obtaining adequate forecasts appeared to be adequately "solved" by the Holt formulas – at least they were under control – so the research team went back to work on the unsolved decision problems of optimizing inventories, production and work force. New mathematical tools were needed there as well. Under pressure to complete the HMMS book, the basic theory paper was never published.

J.F. Muth [9] then picked up the simple EWMA model and explored the question – under what conditions does the EWMA formula yield optimal forecasts. Muth found that if each period an independent random variable occurred with a fixed distribution about its expected value, and if a constant fraction of that random deviation persisted as a shift in the expected value of that distribution, then the EWMA is the (smoothed) expected value for the next period. His analysis contributed significantly to understanding the design of the Holt forecasting models.

Tests of forecast accuracy found that George Box's statistically rigorous forecast system [1] did marginally better that the Holt formulas, but at considerably higher costs of professional administration. A great many researchers have followed up in extending and validating Holt's forecasting research. Accuracy comparisons were reported in [4], and also in Makridakis et al. [8]. A 1985 overview of exponential forecasting was given in Gardner [3]. Variations on the Holt forecasting models and their very creditable performances were given considerable attention in this featured review. Gardner's paper on exponential forecasting is the first comprehensive overview of the field. It cites more than a hundred research references on exponential forecasting. Gardner systematically examines all of the issues familiar to econometricians: specifying model structures, estimating seasonal adjustments, programming and computing models, measuring and tracking model performances, optimizing parameters, making parameters adaptive, and system uses.

Even though Holt's original paper [5] went unpublished, word of its forecast performance and ease of use quickly spread and Holt was deluged with requests from the U.S. and overseas for copies of the theory draft. The Holt and Holt-Winters formulas were quickly incorporated in commercial software systems for forecasting. EWMA formulas were reported to be more widely used for computerized forecasting in the US than any other forecasting system. Source and verification of that report? Although unpublished, the theory paper still is cited after almost 50 years. While Holt's research stressed practical statistics and flexibility rather than theoretical elegance, it, like much of operations research, has contributed significantly to business and engineering productivity.

The team of Holt, Modiglini, Muth and Simon went on to complete their research and report the results comprehensively in a book [7] that was widely used in MBA programs and was reviewed retrospectively in Holt [6]. Modigliani and Simon did research that earned them Nobel prizes in economics, and Muth wrote the paper that formulated the concept of rational expectations – and made him famous.

The graduate School of Industrial Administration at the Carnegie Institute of Technology in the early 1950's developed a conscience strategy of teaching and research that attempted to influence American business education in the direction of quantitative theory and analysis. The Carnegie Tech research on forecasting seems to have had considerable success in implementing that strategy.

References

[1] G.E.P. Box and G.M. Jenkins, *Time Series Analysis, Forecasting, and Control*, Holden Day, San Francisco, CA, 1970.

[2] R.G. Brown, *Statistical Forecasting for Inventory Control*, McGraw Hill, New York, 1959.

[3] E.S. Gardner, Jr., Exponential Smoothing: The State of the Art, *Journal of Forecasting* **4** (1985), 1–28.

[4] C.W.J. Granger and P. Newbold, *Forecasting Economic Time Series*, Academic Press, New York, 1977. 2nd Ed., 1986.

[5] C.C. Holt, Forecasting Seasonals and Trends by Exponentially Weighted Moving Averages, ONR Research Memorandum No. 52, Available from the Engineering Library, University of Texas at Austin, 2003.

[6] C.C. Holt, Learning How to Plan Production, Inventories, and Work Force, *Operations Research* **50**(1) (January-February 2002), 96-97.

[7] C.C. Holt, F. Modigliani, J.F. Muth and H.A. Simon, *Planning Production, Inventories, and Work Force*, Prentice-Hall, Eglewood Cliffs, NJ, 1960.

[8] S. Makridakis et al., *Forecasting Methods and Applications*, 2nd Ed., Wiley, New York, 1983.

[9] J.F. Muth, Optimal Properties of Exponentially Weighted Forecasts, *Journal of the American Statistical Association* **55** (June, 1960), 299–306.

[10] P.R. Winters, General Exponential forecasting: A Computer Program for the IBM 360 ONR Research Memorandum No 71, August 1960.

[11] P.R. Winters, Forecasting Sales by Exponentially Weighted Moving Averages, *Management Science* **6** (1960), 324–342.

[12] *Models of Man. Essays in Memory of Herbert A. Simon.*, MIT Press, 2003.

Journal of Economic and Social Measurement 29 (2004) 127–133
IOS Press

Early development of econometric software at the University of Auckland

Peter C.B. Phillips[a,b,c] and Viv B. Hall[d]
[a]*Cowles Foundation, Yale University, P.O. Box 208281, New Haven, CT 06520-8281, USA*
Tel.: +1 203 432 3695; Fax: +1 203 432 6167; E-mail: peter.phillips@yale.edu
[b]*Department of Economics, University of Auckland, Auckland, New Zealand*
[c]*Department of Economics and Related Studies, University of York, York, YO10 5DD, UK*
[d]*School of Economics and Finance, Victoria University of Wellington, P.O. Box 600, Wellington 6001, New Zealand*
E-mail: viv.hall@vuw.ac.nz

Over the period 1964–1970, graduate students of Rex Bergstrom at the University of Auckland in New Zealand developed econometric computer programs to conduct estimation and inference for dynamic linear models, dynamic simultaneous equation models and systems of linear stochastic differential equations. Linear and nonlinear multiple equation regression programs were written in Fortran; and simulation experiments and empirical applications were performed on two small IBM mainframe computers.

The first electronic computer at the University of Auckland was an IBM 1620, which was acquired by the department of physics in 1963.[1] This was followed a few years later in 1967 by the installation of an IBM 1130, which remained the university's central computer until a Burroughs B6700 was acquired during 1973 in a joint arrangement with other New Zealand universities. The 1620 and 1130 were small mainframe computers designed principally for scientific use. Like earlier generations of computer, and unlike the IBM 360 series (launched in 1964), these computers had non-modular designs, so that their main components were wired or soldered rather than plugged together. The modularity design of the 360 contributed greatly to its commercial success[2] and the concept proved even more successful, of course, with the now famous introduction of the IBM PC 5150 in 1981.

For a time, the 1620 was housed in a room in Choral Hall (in the University of Auckland city campus) across the road from the department of economics in no. 4 Alfred Street, from where, with considerable excitement, we saw it being lifted in

[1]The first digital computer in New Zealand was an IBM 650, which was acquired by the New Zealand Treasury department in 1960. This and other interesting historical details (including a discussion of the number system used in Maori culture) can be found in Garry Tee's [15] fascinating account of the pioneers of early computing and connections to New Zealand.

[2]The IBM 360 series changed the nature of mainframe computing and had a huge commercial impact on IBM's market share and profitability. Baldwin and Clark [2] discuss the impact of the IBM 360 series on computing design and the power of modularity in the commercial development of the computing industry.

by crane. The 1130 and its peripherals occupied a room in the newly constructed chemistry building, a convenient block's walk up Symonds Street from the department of economics; and in 1968 the 1620 was moved to a room adjacent to the 1130 in the same building. The console on the 1130 had a futuristic look, complete with flashing lights in hexadecimal code that gave it the appearance of something out of an early science-fiction movie. The main demand for these two machines in the 1960s came from physics, engineering, chemistry, mathematics and economics. [3] Summary statistics on the use of the 1130 were printed each month and these reported individual usage by different departments in the university. During the late 1960s the department of economics was often the heaviest user. At that time, several members of the economics department were running simulation experiments with econometric models and doing applied econometric research for masters and doctoral theses.

The developmental period for this work in econometrics was 1964–1970. Over this period, a succession of graduate students in the department of economics embarked on empirical studies of the New Zealand economy that involved the estimation of dynamic linear models, dynamic simultaneous equation models and systems of linear stochastic differential equations. All of this work was computationally intensive, involving data manipulation and filtering (e.g. for seasonal adjustment), econometric estimation, diagnostic evaluation and statistical testing. With the arrival of the 1620 and 1130, the computational burden in this empirical work shifted from desk calculators to the new computing machines. A series of computer programs were written in Fortran to carry out the necessary computations. By 1970 the department of economics had developed a suite of econometric regression programs to calculate OLS, 2SLS, and 3SLS estimators, some associated test statistics and diagnostics, as well as a multiple equation nonlinear regression program that was based on a Gauss-Newton iterative procedure.

Not all the computational work was done on the 1620 or 1130. The department of economics had some Facit (electric and mechanical) calculating machines and from 1967–1968 an electronic calculator for which there was high demand and for which we queued for access. All of these machines we routinely used for subsidiary calculations and sometimes even major computations (such as large matrix inversions or inversions of complex matrices) when the computers were down or otherwise unavailable. In anticipation of such needs, it was usual practice to obtain fairly complete printouts of subsidiary calculations done on the computer at each run, so that these could be used to cross check results, debug programs and to get work done during the turnaround cycle.

Both computers, but particularly the 1130 (which offered tape and disk storage as well as line printer output), were in heavy demand. Large batch jobs were normally run overnight and there was a special lunchtime service offering quicker

[3] The University of Auckland had no separate department of statistics in the 1960s. Faculty with research interests in statistics ranged over several departments, including mathematics and economics.

turnaround for short jobs lasting less than 5 minutes, which was convenient for program development and debugging. Otherwise, it was necessary to obtain an operator's license to use the 1130, something that was essential for simulation work where large numbers of repeated runs were required.

To become a computer operator you had to undergo a training program and sit a practical test. The "driving test" took about 15 minutes. In this time, you had to cold-start the machine, put in disk and tape drives, activate the line printer (the size of a large household refrigerator) and run a special batch job through the card reader that was designed to throw up every conceivable problem that might be encountered while running the machine on your own. For example, some cards in the test batch were too thick and they deliberately jammed the card reader. You had to identify this problem and others by reading and interpreting the hexadecimal error codes that showed up in flashing lights on the main console. Once the problem was identified you had to resolve it – in the card reader case by opening the reader and extracting the faulty card. Some cards called you to load tapes or disks. Some caused problems in the processing unit and freeze-ups that required a warm restart. Others set the printer into an endless print cycle that had to be aborted at the main console. Running the operator's license batch job was an ordeal of tribal initiation that the machine technicians had dreamed up to test your understanding of the system components and to deal with non-critical system shutdowns.

This driving test gave us all our first exposure to computer frustration. But every second of tension was worth it when the thrill of the first night's operating shift came along. The excitement of a hands-on computing experience alone in the computer room for 10 hours overnight was an extraordinary intellectual adventure: turning up with flask and sandwiches in the evening, booting up the 1130, loading a simulation in the hopper and waiting for the thunder of the line printer to stamp out thesis results. Nothing short of nirvana to a young scientist!

The individuals involved in the early econometric software development work at Auckland were Derek Ford, Hessel Baas, Viv Hall, Keith Carpenter and Peter Phillips, all students of Rex Bergstrom who was professor of econometrics and the intellectual force behind the research program in econometrics. Derek was the first person to use the 1620 and he wrote an OLS and 2SLS regression program in Fortran around 1964. Derek tutored Hessel and Viv on using the 1620. Over 1965–1967 Hessel developed Derek's programs further and subsequently helped Viv write a LIML program. Viv adapted a seasonal adjustment program originally written by Rex Bergstrom[4] for quarterly data so that it was suited to semi-annual data. Peter worked on the 1620 and 1130 over 1968–1969 and wrote a 3SLS program that allowed for across-equation parameter restrictions and a multiple equation nonlinear regression program with facilities that enabled its use in estimating the exact discrete model corresponding to a system of linear stochastic differential equations.

[4]We recall that Rex wrote this program, punched the cards and was so meticulous in doing so that the batch job ran correctly first time.

The results of this research are reported in the dissertations and research papers listed in the references. Hessel, Viv and Peter each had an operator's licence for running the 1130 after hours. Peter was the largest user, having a large nonlinear estimation simulation experiment to conduct as part of his master's dissertation [11, 12]. Each simulation took about 30 minutes of computing time on average, amounting to around 250 hours of computing time in total for this simulation experiment with 500 replications. Booking the 1130 for two evenings of 10 hours a week meant that some 3 months of computing time was required for this simulation, leaving aside the additional time involved in program development.

Some of the practicalities of programming in the 1960s are worth recalling. Only tiny memory capacities were available. The 1130, for instance, had just 8 kilobytes of memory.[5] It was therefore necessary to tailor programs carefully so that they would fit into memory. In Viv's work with the LIML estimation of a six-equation simultaneous equations macroeconomic system, it was necessary to feed in and estimate the model equation by equation; so not all jointly determined variables were in the system at once, in true limited information style. Peter's work involved multiple equation nonlinear regression with across-equation parameter restrictions and matrix exponential nonlinear functions, which could not be treated equation by equation. In that case, it was necessary to use Call Link statements in Fortran to link segments of the code together and write and recall essential numbers to and from disk so that they were available as subsequent segments of the program became active.

There were tape and hard disk facilities on the 1130 and a fast line printer and card reader. A room outside the 1130 housed three IBM card-punch machines,[6] which were always heavily booked. There was therefore considerable advantage when running simulations to use the computer itself to punch cards (e.g., for subsequent simulations) that could be run as batch jobs during the day, thereby reducing labor input and maximizing computer capital usage. Dimension statements for arrays had to be carefully tailored so that programs would fit in memory. Using variables to dimension arrays helped in this regard, but often it was necessary to put in specific dimensions and change them with each application in order to avoid program crashes and needless waiting time for reruns. Standard protocol in the 1960s was to check draft program and data input carefully in order to avoid needless 24-hour turnaround delays arising from avoidable errors. By contrast, modern desktop hardware, multi-processing and software aids like debuggers and powerful text editors all contribute enormously to expedite program development. In consequence, present day software development is a vastly accelerated and very different experience.

[5]Some 7K memory was available for practical use after the operating system loaded. According to folklore at the computing center in the 1960s, Brian Hicks and a small group of systems operators downloaded the operating system of the 1130 in machine code, rewrote it more efficiently and succeeded in substantially enhancing the 1130's performance characteristics to an extent that astounded IBM system engineers when they revisited the machine.

[6]Over time these variously included IBM 026, IBM 560 and IBM 870 machines, but frequently only one, and occasionally none, of these was operational.

The econometric research program at Auckland in the 1960s was conducted under the mentorship of Rex Bergstrom, who was supremely well qualified for the task. Rex's own thesis work was done in Cambridge over the period 1952–1954. It involved the empirical implementation of a 27 equation model of New Zealand exports that had 55 parameters which were estimated by both OLS and LIML. With the help of Alan Brown in the department of applied economics, Rex used the EDSAC computer at Cambridge to invert the moment matrices needed for the calculation of the LIML and OLS estimates. As Rex points out in his interview with *Econometric Theory* [13, p. 307], the EDSAC frequently broke down and it was necessary to invert some 10 by 10 matrices on a desk calculator to complete his work. This study was the most ambitious empirical implementation up to that time of the new Cowles Commission econometric methodology and it showcased the advantages of the new techniques, particularly in the context of small samples of data and in making predictions.

Another important member of the Auckland student econometric group in the 1960s was Clifford Wymer. Cliff was ahead of Derek Ford and completed his master's thesis in 1964 using Facit desk calculators for his empirical work. Cliff also did the number crunching on a Facit to estimate the Bergstrom and Brownlie [3] model of the New Zealand economy (a small dynamic aggregate simultaneous equations model) which involved some 7 by 7 matrix inversions. Cliff did not use the 1620 at Auckland. He left for the LSE to do doctoral work and, starting in 1965, began to develop there a suite of Fortran-based econometric software for the estimation, analysis and use in prediction of linear simultaneous equations models with general analytic restrictions on the coefficients. These programs were developed in modules and were used extensively by later students at the LSE, at other universities in the UK and at the IMF and other international economic agencies. One remarkable feature of this suite of econometric software was their built-in facility for symbolic differentiation of any specified function, so that the score and Hessian were set up automatically. All that the user had to do was to type in the functional form of the equations on cards. This development appears to have been the first of its kind in econometric software. A summary of these programs and some of their properties is given in the Appendix of Bergstrom and Wymer [4].

On the face of it, much has changed since the early days of econometric software development in the 1960s. Nowadays, several user-friendly packages of econometric software are available that make it easy to perform quite complicated tasks of data manipulation, parameter estimation, testing, model evaluation, prediction and even simulation. These packages are routinely used in undergraduate and beginning graduate courses in econometrics to train students in empirical econometric research. Many applied researchers also place heavy reliance on them. Nonetheless, the need for high-end software facilities has not disappeared and has, in fact, grown stronger over the years as econometric technique has become more widespread. New models and data sets often present peculiarities that demand special treatment in the way of modified procedures or new econometric methods, which in turn need programming because they do not fit within the confines of existing packages. In consequence, matrix programming languages like Gauss, Matlab, S+, R, and Ox have become popular among advanced students and researchers in econometrics because of the flexibility they offer with respect to the incorporation of new econometric methodology, not to mention the simplicity with which existing procedures can be programmed. Gauss provides some elegant instances in this regard with supremely simple codes like that for a multivariate least squares regression, viz., b = y/x. The growth of applied econometrics has been so extensive in recent years that this process seems destined to continue.

Just as early researchers in the 1960s coded programs for new estimation procedures like 2SLS and 3SLS in Fortran to complete their empirical projects, present-day researchers code the new programs they need for more recent econometric methods using efficient object oriented and matrix programming languages. The programming tools and hardware at the disposal of the econometrician continue to grow more powerful and are conveniently portable. But the manner of the research process itself has changed less and has many broad similarities with the past: questions are asked, hypotheses are formulated, data is collected, methods are developed and implementation is accomplished using appropriate computational software. When the latter is not available, it needs to be written, just as it did in the 1960s.

Web communications and online support groups now make it much easier to problem solve and to share and download code. A new possibility is also emerging that permits the interactive use of advanced econometric methods by way of a web browser. Rather than use a local software package, users may access a suite of econometric methods and data sets online. Simple web browser selections then initiate econometric software algorithms and results are returned online and by file and graphics downloads. Some possibilities along these lines are outlined in Phillips [14], and a prototype of web-based econometrics for forecasting the NZ economy was developed at the University of Auckland in 1999.

Acknowledgement

Thanks go to Hessel Baas, Rex Bergstrom, Roger Bowden, Alan Creak, Bob Doran, Garry Tee, and Cliff Wymer for helpful conversations and recollections about the computing environment at the University of Auckland in the 1960s. Donggyu Sul and John Hilas helpfully supplied information about Auckland economics theses. Phillips thanks the NSF for research support under grant SES 0092509.

References

[1] H.J. Baas, *The demand for New Zealand's imports, 1950–1967*, M.Com thesis, University of Auckland, Auckland, 1969.

[2] C.Y. Baldwin and K.B. Clark, *Design Rules: The power of modularity*, MIT Press, Cambridge, 2000.

[3] A.R. Bergstrom and A.D. Brownlie, An econometric model of the New Zealand economy, *Economic Record* (1965), 125–126.

[4] A.R. Bergstrom and C.R. Wymer, A model of disequilibrium neoclassical growth and its application to the United Kingdom, in: *Statistical Inference in Continuous Time Economic Models*, A.R. Bergstrom, ed., North-Holland, Amsterdam, 1976, Chapter 10, pp. 267–327.

[5] K. Carpenter, *Wage and Labour Mobility in New Zealand*, M.Com Thesis, University of Auckland, Auckland, 1968.

[6] D.J. Ford, *Consumption in New Zealand*, M.Com thesis, University of Auckland, Auckland, 1966.

[7] V.B. Hall, *Money wage determinants in New Zealand: 1947–1965*, M.Com thesis, University of Auckland, Auckland, 1968.

[8] V.B. Hall, Determinants of the Minimum Money Wage Rate in New Zealand, 1947–1965, *New Zealand Economic Papers* **3** (1969), 14–26.

[9] V.B. Hall, *A Model of New Zealand's Post-War Inflation*, Ph.D. thesis, University of Auckland, Auckland, 1971.

[10] V.B. Hall, Simultaneous Equation Wage Determination in New Zealand, *New Zealand Economic Papers* **6** (1972), 29–51.

[11] P.C.B. Phillips, *The Structural Estimation of a Stochastic Differential Equation System*, M.A. thesis, University of Auckland, Auckland, 1971.

[12] P.C.B. Phillips, The Structural Estimation of a Stochastic Differential Equation System, *Econometrica* **40** (1972), 1021–1041.

[13] P.C.B. Phillips, The ET Interview: Professor A.R. Bergstrom, *Econometric Theory* **4** (1988), 301–328.

[14] P.C.B. Phillips, Laws and Limits of Econometrics, *Economic Journal* **113** (2003), C26–C52.

[15] G.J. Tee, New Zealand and the Pioneers of Early Computing, *New Zealand Journal of Computing* **1** (1989), 5–10.

[16] C.R. Wymer, *A liquidity preference function for New Zealand*, M.Com thesis, University of Auckland, Auckland, 1964.

Journal of Economic and Social Measurement 29 (2004) 135–143
IOS Press

Some Milestones in Econometric Computing

Simulation with large econometric models: The quest for a solution

George R. Schink
LECG, LLC, 1725 Eye Street, N.W., Suite 800, Washington, DC 20006, USA
Tel.: +1 202 973 9885; Fax: +1 202 466 4487; E-mail: George_Schink@lecg.com

This paper describes the development of algorithms to solve large-scale macroeconometric models. The bulk of this paper was written in 1970 when the problem of finding solutions for these large-scale models was still an issue. During the 1960s, large powerful (for that time period) computers became available for use by economists who proceeded to use this powerful new tool to develop and apply econometric software to the problem of estimating large-scale macroeconometric models such as the Wharton Quarterly Model and the Brookings Model. Having succeeded in estimating these models, the next problem was to find a way to solve them either in the context of simulation experiments or forecasting exercises. During the late 1960s, the author investigated the problem of solving these large-scale models and found several acceptable methods which are presented in this paper.

1. Introduction

I first was exposed to the problem of estimating a large-scale econometric model of the US economy by Lawrence R. Klein when I was a graduate student. In 1966, I spent an entire summer of long days attempting to estimate Klein's specification for a new Wharton Quarterly Model. I often sought Klein's guidance when the data refused to behave in accordance with economic theory. By the end of the summer, the new version of the model was estimated and ready to use to perform simulation experiments and to generate forecasts. I assumed, because the previous version of the Wharton Quarterly Model was being used to generate forecasts, that there was an existing computer software package that was being used to solve the model. I was mistaken.

The previous version of the Wharton Quarterly Model was solved to produce a forecast by Michael Evans using a Marchant mechanical calculator. Evans would spend many hours, often into the early hours of the morning, to judgmentally iterate to a solution using a process that only he understood. The solution obtained was approximate and it was not feasible to solve the model using numerous alternative sets of assumptions. The model was used to assess the implications of potential major policy changes, but the lack of a computer algorithm to solve the model severely limited the number and scope of the "what if" forecast period scenarios that could be evaluated.

I was tasked with implementing a computer program that would solve the new Wharton Quarterly Model. Klein, I think with the assistance of Michael McCarthy, had devised an approach to solving these models which were nonlinear in the endogenous variables. The solution involved "linearzing" the model through the use of a Taylor expansion. To produce a Taylor expansion of the model, the matrix of first derivatives of the model's equations with respect to all the endogenous variables had to be defined and calculated based on the estimated model equations, on initial estimates of the endogenous variables, and on the values of the exogenous/predetermined variables. The initial estimates of the endogenous variables in a forecasting context would be the value for the previous period and, in a simulation context, would be the actual data value. The Taylor approximation to the model could be solved using standard linear model solution techniques. These techniques involve large-scale matrix inversion for which computer algorithms were readily available. However, the solution to the Taylor expansion of the model provides only an approximate solution to the actual model. Newton's iterative solution method was used to find the solution to the actual model. The mathematics of this process are discussed in the body of this paper.

My assignment was to develop a computer program to implement the Newton method for the newly-estimated Wharton Model. The matrix of first derivatives from the Wharton Model was very large which made its inversion a large task for the computers of that time. A simplification of the Newton method, which is called the interacting linear blocks method, was developed. This method took advantage of the simple nature of the nonlinearities in the macroeconometric models; namely, the "price times quantity" type nonlinearities which allowed the partitioning of the matrix of first derivatives into a "quantity" block and a "price" block with a limited number of nonzero entries in the price-quantity interaction section of the matrix of first derivatives. This simplification essentially assumed that there was no interaction between the "price" and "quantity" blocks which cut the size of the matrix to be inverted approximately in half. This made the matrix inversion problem tractable for the computers of that time. The mathematics of the interacting linear blocks method are described below.

The method of interacting linear blocks was successfully applied by the author to the Wharton Model [2] and by Ross Preston to the Brookings Model [4]. It was also implemented for a larger revised version of the Brookings Model at the University of Pennsylvania under Klein's direction by the author and Vijaya Duggal. While the method of interacting linear blocks posed a tractable computer problem, it posed a horrendous implementation problem because the first partial derivatives for all the model equations with respect to all the endogenous variables had to be calculated by hand and then programmed by hand. There was no way to use the computer to check whether the program code was correct except by trial and error which took a long time.

In an effort to find a less cumbersome approach to solving large macro-econometric models, in late 1967, I researched the literature from the physical sciences to see if there were less cumbersome to implement methods available. The simplest methods discussed in this literature were the Jacobi and Gauss-Seidel methods [3]. The physical sciences literature indicated that these methods did not work well for the extremely nonlinear problems that had to be solved in these disciplines. However, macroeconometric models do not have the extreme nonlinearities that were present in the physical science models. Therefore, I implemented both the Jacobi and Gauss-Seidel methods for the Wharton Model. Implementation was much simpler because there was no need to take partial derivatives or to invert large matrices. All that was required was to translate the estimated equations into computer code. For the Gauss-Seidel method, one has to find an equation ordering that produces a structure that is as close as possible to recursive. If one were to take partial first derivatives of the ordered equation system, one would want the matrix for the ordered equations to be as close as possible to lower triangular. I found, as did others who used the Gauss-Seidel method, that one could find a sufficiently good order for the equations without undue effort. One of the best features of the Jacobi and Gauss-Seidel methods, from an implementation perspective, is that one could check the model coding by calculating the residuals from the coded equations and comparing them to the residuals produced by the regression program. This made checking the implementation of the model code much easier. Therefore, the time required to generate and check the computer code necessary to solve a model under the Jacobi or Gauss-Seidel methods was much less than for the interacting linear blocks method. [1] Further, the computer time required to solve the models was much less than for the interacting linear blocks method. Therefore, the Jacobi and Gauss-Seidel methods quickly displaced the interacting linear blocks method.

The remainder of this paper, with the exception of a brief postscript, was written and presented at an ACM conference in Denver in June of 1970. Other than making some minor corrections and adding a few citations, it is unchanged.

2. Origins of large models

Econometricians have been building models of the United States economy for a long time, starting with the pioneering work of Tinbergen [5]. Prior to the development of generally accessible high speed computers, these models were of necessity small by present day standards. The functional forms were restricted to be linear in both the parameters and the variables. Estimation and solution (simulation) of these models were only accomplished after a good deal of tedious manual labor.

Following the development of large high-speed computers, approximately coincident with the derivation of tractable estimation techniques for large systems of

---

[1] In addition, the same computer code for a model could be used for either the Jacobi or Gauss-Seidel methods.

equations (specifically two-stage least squares), econometricians proceeded to build much larger and more complex models. These models were restricted to be linear in the unknown parameters. This linearity restriction, in some cases, represented an accommodation of economic theory to the existing estimation techniques. However, the estimation techniques placed no restrictions on the dependent variables in the system and various non-linearities were introduced. Most of the non-linearities were simple such as price times quantity or ratios of prices. Production functions are the prime area where the more complex non-linearities were introduced involving log transformations of the dependent variables.

Two large quarterly econometric models of the United States economy were estimated during the early to mid-1960s: the Wharton Model [2] and the Brookings Model [1]. Both models were built with the intention of performing sample period simulations and predictive experiments. Unfortunately, all the methods in common usage in econometrics for solving models were designed for linear systems. The nonlinearities which caused no problems in estimation now impeded use of these models as forecasting tools.

Before considering the series of techniques which have been used in solving large non-linear models, consider the following general specification of a model:

$$f(y_t, x_t, e_t) = 0 \quad t = 1, \ldots, T \tag{1}$$

or

$$y_t = g(y_t, x_t, e_t) \tag{2}$$

where y_t is a vector of jointly dependent variables, x_t is a vector of predetermined variables (given constants for our purposes), and e_t is a vector of random disturbance terms. Expression (2) is a transformation (normalization) of expression (1). The functions f and g involve unknown parameters. Estimates of f and g will be denoted as $\hat{f}$ and $\hat{g}$ respectively. Individual elements of the vectors y_t, x_t, and e_t will be written as y_{it}, x_{it}, and e_{it} respectively. The individual functions corresponding to y_{it} will be written as f_i or g_i. The value of y_t on the k th iteration will be denoted as y_t^k with the initial estimate (guess) denoted as y_t^o and the solution value denoted as y_t^s. When solving for the y_t, the usual procedure is to replace e_t by its expected value of zero. The matrices of first partial derivatives of f and g with respect to y will be denoted as F and G respectively.

3. Evolution of iterative solution techniques

Econometricians turned to the literature in the physical sciences and numerical analysis to find potential methods of solution for systems such as Eq. (2). In the physical sciences applications, it had been found that fairly demanding solution techniques such as the Newton method combined with a good initial estimate were required for solving their systems of the form given in Eq. (2). The nonlinearieties in their functional forms were much more complex than in the typical functions contained in the econometric models. The majority of the nonlinearities in econometric functions were in the form of simple products and ratios. Only in the production functions were there more complex nonlinearities: namely, log-log functions.

Lawrence Klein, who, with Michael Evans, constructed the Wharton Model, developed, with this author's assistance, a solution technique to take advantage of the simple form of the nonlinearities in econometric models, which is called the interacting linear blocks method [2]. This technique is best viewed as an approximation to the Newton Method. To see how this works, it is helpful to rewrite expression (1) as:

$$h(y_t, x_t, e_t) = b(x_t) \quad \text{for } t = 1, \ldots, T \tag{3}$$

An estimate of h will be denoted by $\hat{h}$ while the matrix of first partial derivatives of h with respect to y_t will be denoted as H. Application of the method of interacting linear blocks requires that a partition of y_t be found, say $y_t = (p_t, q_t)$, such that: $\hat{H}(y_t, x_t, 0) = \hat{H}(y_t, x_t)$ can be expressed as:

$$\hat{H}(y_t, x_t) = \hat{H}(p_t, q_t, x_t) = \begin{bmatrix} A(q_t, x_t) & B(p_t, q_t, x_t \\ C(p_t, q_t, x_t) & D(p_t, x_t) \end{bmatrix} \tag{4}$$

The ability to define an expression such as Eq. (4) hinges on finding a partition (p_t, q_t) such that no single function h_i contains terms both of the form p_{it}, p_{jt} and q_{kt}, q_{it}. Terms of the form p_{it}, q_{it} are acceptable in any h_i. Log-log functions defy such a partition and must be approximated by a Taylor's expansion. [2] Finding a partition (p_t, q_t) satisfying Eq. (4) is, in practice, not very difficult but nonetheless tedious.

Given the existence of a partition $(p_t,\ q_t)$ such that Eq. (4) can be defined, the function h may be written as:

$$h(p_t, q_t, x_t) = \begin{bmatrix} A(q_t, x_t)p_t + r(q_t, x_t) \\ D(p_t, x_t)q_t + s(p_t, x_t) \end{bmatrix} \tag{5}$$

If the Newton method were used to solve for (p_t, q_t), the iteration scheme would be:

$$\begin{aligned} (p_t^{k+1}, q_t^{k+1}) - v(p_t^k, q_t^k, x_t) \\ = (p_t^k, q_t^k) - H(p_t^k, q_t^k, x_t)^{-1} \left[h(p_t^k, q_t^k, x_t) - b(x_t)\right] \end{aligned} \tag{6}$$

[2]The Taylor's expansion can be constructed about either an initial estimate, or about the previous iterations value, on the k th iteration. In practice, the latter expansion has proved more accurate without leading to problems of instability.

The method of interacting linear blocks approximates H^{-1} with:

$$E(p_t, q_t, x_t) = \begin{bmatrix} A^{-1}(q_t, x_t) & 0 \\ 0 & D^{-1}(p_t, x_t) \end{bmatrix} \tag{7}$$

The necessary and sufficient conditions for convergence of Eq. (6) when H^{-1} is replaced by E require that all the characteristic roots of $V(p_t^s, q_t^s, x_t)$ have modulus less than one where V is the matrix of partial derivatives of v with respect to p_t and q_t. In addition, the initial guess, (p_t^0, q_t^0), must be sufficiently close to the solution. If H^{-1} were not replaced by E, the necessary and sufficient conditions could be re-expressed in terms of the second partials of h with respect to p_t and q_t. However, when the approximation E is used, the characteristic roots of V depend not only on the second partials of h but also on the accuracy of the approximate inverse E. The accuracy of E, in turn, depends, in some sense, on how "close" the off diagonal blocks of H are to zero. In practice, it is possible to find a partition (p_t, q_t) such that E is a sufficiently good approximation to H^{-1}.

The actual iteration scheme can be shown to reduce to:

$$\begin{aligned} p_t^{k+1} &= -\left[Aq_t^k, x_t\right]^{-1}\left[r(q_t^k, x_t) - b_p(x_t)\right] \\ q_t^{k+1} &= -\left[D(p_t^{k+1}, x_t)\right]^{-1}\left[s(p_t^{k+1}, x_t) - b_q(x_t)\right] \end{aligned} \tag{8}$$

where b_p and b_q are corresponding partitions of b. The iteration scheme given by Eq. (8) was successfully applied to both the Brookings and Wharton models. Convergence typically occurs in less than ten iterations with the average being approximately six. The time required to complete these iterations obviously depends on the machine. However, on the IBM 7040, solution of the Wharton Model required, on the average, 30 seconds of machine time per period. While 30 seconds is not very much time, it must be noted that these models are solved many times. A typical forecasting experiment requires eight or ten solutions.

After using the method of interacting linear blocks for more than one year, several more or less simultaneous attempts were made at finding a more efficient solution technique. Two techniques emerged which, surprisingly, given the bad experiences in the physical sciences, worked very well. The Jacobi method (or simultaneous iteration) and the Gauss-Seidel method (or successive iteration) were found to be very stable. Since these two methods are quire similar, they will be presented together. Expression (2) will be used here with $g(y_t, x_t, e_t)$ replaced by $g(y_t, x_t, 0) = g(y_t, x_t)$. The method of Jacobi is given by:

$$\begin{aligned} y_{1t}^{k+1} &= g_1(y_{1t}^k, \ldots, y_{nt}^k, x_t) \\ &\vdots \\ y_{nt}^{k+1} &= g_n(y_{1t}^k, \ldots, y_{nt}^k, x_t) \end{aligned} \tag{9}$$

while the Gauss-Seidel method is given by:

$$\begin{aligned} y_{1t}^{k+1} &= g_1(y_{1t}^k, y_{2t}^k, \ldots, y_{n-1t}^k, y_{nt}^k, x_t) \\ &\vdots \\ y_{2t}^{k+1} &= g_2(y_{1t}^{k+1}, y_{2t}^k, \ldots, y_{n-1t}^k, y_{nt}^k, x_t) \\ &\vdots \\ y_{nt}^{k+1} &= g_n(y_{1t}^{k+1}, y_{2t}^{k+1}, \ldots, y_{n-1t}^{k+1}, y_{nt}^k, x_t) \end{aligned} \tag{10}$$

The necessary and sufficient conditions for convergence of the Jacobi method require that all the characteristic roots of $G(y_t^s, x_t)$ which is the matrix of first derivatives of g with respect to y, have modulus less than one. Defining G_A and G_B as:

$$G_A = \begin{bmatrix} 0 & 0 & & 0 & 0 \\ \frac{\partial g_2}{\partial y_1} & 0 & . & . \ 0 & 0 \\ \vdots & \vdots & & \vdots & \vdots \\ \frac{\partial g_n}{\partial y_1} & \frac{\partial g_n}{\partial y_2} & & \frac{\partial g_n}{\partial y_{n-1}} & 0 \end{bmatrix} \quad \text{and } G_B = G - G_A \tag{11}$$

The necessary and sufficient conditions for convergence of the Gauss-Seidel methods require that all the characteristic roots of:

$$[I - G_A(y_t^s, x_t)]^{-1} G_B(y_t^s, x_t) \tag{12}$$

have modulus less than one. In addition, convergence of both the Jacobi and Gauss-Seidel methods requires the initial guess y_t^o be in a sufficiently small neighborhood of y_t^s.

Even though the Jacobi and Gauss-Seidel methods are similar, for any given function g, their convergence criteria are obviously quite different. As can be observed from expressions (11) and (12), the Gauss-Seidel method is sensitive to the ordering of the equations while the Jacobi method is not. Both methods are affected by the normalization chosen (i.e., the definition of g which need not be unique).

The Jacobi technique, as expressed in (9), failed to converge for both the Brookings and Wharton models. However, a slight modification produced convergence. This modified Jacobi method is given by:

$$y_t^{k+1} = v(y_t^k, x_t) \tag{13}$$

or, more specifically,

$$y_{it}^{k+1} = y_{it}^k(1-d) + dg_i(y_t^k, x_t) \text{ for } i = 1, \ldots, n. \tag{14}$$

where d is a real scalar.

Defining V as the matrix of first partial derivatives of v with respect to y, the necessary and sufficient conditions for the scheme (13) or (14) to converge requires that all the characteristic roots of V have modulus less than one. If r is a characteristic root of G and s is a characteristic root of V, the two satisfy the following relation:

$$r = d(s - 1) + 1 \tag{15}$$

The modification of the Jacobi method given by (13) or (14) does not guarantee convergence. However, there are a large number of situations where the largest of the roots s has modulus greater than one while a proper choice of d will insure that the largest of the roots r has modulus less than one.

In applications of the modified Jacobi method to both the Brookings Model and the Wharton Model, the best value of d was approximately 0.7. For values less than this, the systems converged more slowly while for marginally larger values, the systems occasionally failed to converge. In general, for values of d greater than 0.8, the systems almost always failed to converge.

Application of the Gauss-Seidel method to the Brookings Model and Wharton Model required several experiments with various equation orderings. As can be seen from expressions (11) and (12), an optimal ordering of the equations entails making the matrix of first partials, G, as "close" to lower diagonal as possible. While the matrix G was never computed, simple examination of the equations was sufficient to produce a good ordering. Econometric models fortunately are essentially constructed in a block recursive manner which makes finding the proper ordering relatively easy.

Of the two methods, the Gauss-Seidel method is the fastest. Solution of the Wharton Model or the Brookings Model require 10–15 iterations and approximately 1–2 seconds of computing time on the IBM 7040 per period. The Jacobi method is slightly slower. For the Wharton Model 15–20 iterations and 2–3 seconds computing time on the IBM 7040 per period are required to solve the Wharton Model (the Jacobi method was not applied to the Brookings Model). The short time required to solve these large models has opened the way to more sophisticated simulation experiments.

4. Recent uses of simulation

In addition to extensive use of the large-scale econometric models for sample period simulations and post-sample prediction experiments, numerous more demanding experiments have been performed. As was stated above, the random disturbance term is usually set equal to zero when solving a model. However, using a technique developed by Michael D. McCarthy, pseudo-random disturbance terms can be generated with the same asymptotic properties as the observed disturbances. Both sample period and post-sample period stochastic simulation experiments have been performed to more properly assess the dynamic characteristics of the system. Stochastic simulation has been used by the author to compute small sample estimates of expected forecast error for the Wharton Model. The list of applications, both current and potential, is too long to enumerate here. However, the above brief sample should give some indication of the potential.

5. Postscript

The previous section was written in 1970. The modified Jacobi and Gauss-Seidel methods are still being used to solve large-scale macroeconometric models. The current computer software will automatically generate computer instructions to solve these models including finding the "best" ordering for the equations under the Gauss-Seidel method. I remained involved in the process of developing the computer programs to solve these large-scale macroeconometric models until the late 1980s. My last effort was to develop the computer algorithms used to find the "best" order for the model equations under he Gauss-Seidel method for a software package that was developed at WEFA.

References

[1] J.S. Duesenberry, G. Fromm, L.R. Klein and E. Kuh, *The Brookings Quarterly Econometric Model of the United States*, Rand McNally and North-Holland, New York, 1965.

[2] M.K. Evans and L.R. Klein, programmed by G.R. Schink, *The Wharton Econometric Forecasting Model*, Economics Research Unit of the University of Pennsylvania, Philadelphia, 1967.

[3] V.N. Faddeeva, *Computational Methods of Linear Algebra*, translated by C.D. Benster, Dover Publications, New York, 1959.

[4] G. Fromm and P. Taubinan, *Policy Simulations with An Econometric Model*, The Brookings Institution, Washington, DC, 1968.

[5] J. Tinbergen, *Statistical Testing of Business-Cycle Theories*, 2 vols, League of Nations, Geneva, 1939.

Journal of Economic and Social Measurement 29 (2004) 145–166
IOS Press

The early development of econometric modeling languages

Charles G. Renfro
601 West 113th Street, #12G, New York, NY 10025, USA
E-mail: cgrenfro@modler.com

This article considers certain salient aspects of the development of software specifically created in order to support the construction, maintenance and use of macroeconometric models. As a type, the individual packages are commonly classified as econometric modeling languages. This nomenclature reflects that the command structures used to operate this software are language-like in many of their characteristics, particularly in the case of those commands employed to express a model's relationships, state variable transformations, and perform other essentially mathematical or statistical operations. The focus of this article is both the evolution of language structure, as an expression of the process of creating and using econometric models, and the concomitant increased degree of functional integration that has accompanied it.

1. Introduction

One of the consequences of the development of econometric modeling language software during the past 35 years has been a significant increase in the applied research productivity of economists, both actual and potential. A measure of this increase can be seen in the difference in the manpower and time required to construct and solve a large scale macroeconometric model then and now. In 1972, for example, McCracken and Sonnen [45] estimated that to build a sizeable model – in those days certainly anything in the neighborhood of 200 equations or more – required 10–15 economists and a construction horizon of a year or more. Left unstated was the likelihood that at the end of this time the model would exist, but might require a further period of re-estimation and re-working – a significant consideration, inasmuch as the transition from model estimation to a solvable model was particularly time consuming in those days, reflecting in large part the need to correct errors inevitably made when manually coding equations into the solution package. In contrast, in 1987, Frank Cooper [16, 55] reported that, using this type of software and a Compaq 386 Deskpro personal computer, on his own he was able to construct and solve the approximately 300 equation Merrill Lynch quarterly model of the US in less than a week, albeit starting with an already created data base. He then immediately demonstrated the use of the model by providing three alternative and rather distinct model solutions in a period of approximately 30 minutes. Further model modification, involving the estimation and replacement of even numerous equations might then have taken at most a further week of time and effort. Obviously, not every economist brings to this work the same experience and proficiency as did Cooper, but the point made is still generally valid. Of course, today, microcomputers are faster, easier to use, and offer greater storage and connectivity than in 1987; in addition, there has also been further improvement in software technologies.

However, the effects of the development of this software are not limited to the more efficient construction and use of models. One of the salient characteristics of this development has been the premium it necessarily placed upon both process integration and a general improvement in the software interface, later affecting the design of all econometric software. Many of the time-saving features of econometric modeling language software, first introduced in the years between 1965 and 1985, are now commonplace. These include not only the embedding of expressions and implicit functions into program operating commands, but also the capability to convert from one observation frequency to another more or less automatically and to produce high quality graphics displays, not to mention the noticeably higher degree of underlying process integration that now exists. Particularly during the past twenty years, there has been a general improvement in econometric software interface standards, involving such things as more natural language commands, the capability to use programming language constructs, support for the creation and use of command macros, and the like – all of which are characteristic of state-of-the-art econometric modeling languages since the early 1970s. Of course, simultaneously there have also been important exogenous enabling changes, specifically as a consequence of the introduction and subsequent evolution of the microcomputer. The result has been a transformation in the computing environment, leading to new methods of program control – in the form of menus, icons, pointing devices, high-resolution color screens and other features of the graphical user interface – as well as a pervasive hardware revolution that has affected all econometric software development.

This depiction of econometric modeling language software development as path breaking should not be interpreted to mean that one group of econometricians has played the role of pioneer software developers and others that of followers. Obviously, to a certain degree this has occurred, inasmuch as someone writing a first program in 1980 or 1990 will have been influenced, pro and con, by the available software produced by those who began earlier. However, the point that is being made is much more that during the past 35 years there has been a general development of a set of program features that have increasingly become common to all econometric software, and that these are particularly characteristic of the earlier development of econometric modeling languages as highly integrated software systems. As is well demonstrated by the contributions to the present volume, econometric software development has in fact proceeded on a broad front during the past fifty years with many different people focusing on a variety of different objectives. Consequently, it would be easy to recast the present narrative so as to describe the ways the development of other types of econometric and other software have affected and are now affecting the development of econometric modeling languages.

The first econometric modeling languages began to be developed during the period from 1965 to 1970 and the earliest examples are MASSAGER/SIMSYS, MODLER, MREG/IDIOM, PLANETS, and TROLL. In certain respects, these are similar in design: most notably, they share the characteristic of having been consciously designed as computer software systems to support the construction, maintenance, and use of multi-equation, generally macroeconometric models. In other respects, they differ, reflecting both individual design characteristics and developmental histories. MASSAGER and SIMSYS began as distinct programs, but have progressively been merged into the present day MOSAIC. MODLER has also evolved, but as an integrated system, retaining its original overall design. MODLER and MOSAIC nonetheless share the common trait of development continuity, of still being, fundamentally, Fortran programs, containing portions of original source code, and still being developed by and under the direction of their respective original principal authors. In comparison, MREG/IDIOM is more bespoke in its design and other characteristics, having been created specifically to support the construction and use of a given model, the Cambridge Growth Model [51,52,63]. This software developed very much in pace with the progressive development of this model, and its design reflects both the model's ultimate size and multi-sectoral nature. More metamorphic than evolving, MREG/IDIOM has roots in the 1960s, but as a specific body of code dates from the later 1970s [2]. Conversely, PLANETS no longer exists and was never completed, but the data management and parameter estimation components were operated as DAMSEL by Wharton Econometric Forecasting Associates from the early to mid 1970s through the mid 1980s. In contrast, although TROLL still exists as a brand, and in its present "portable" form is intended to provide in "a more flexible package" the capabilities of its mainframe progenitor, as a body of code it is "totally new," re-written in a different computer language during the 1990s by a later principal developer [57, p. 388].

Additional systems, also with a variety of characteristics, have been developed in the interim. In the 1970s these included: EPS, as a system to support the economists and clients of Data Resources, Inc. (DRI); FP, essentially to support the estimation and use of Ray Fair's models; and XSIM, as an extension and elaboration of mainframe TROLL circa 1973. XSIM was later used by Chase Econometric Associates' economists and clients. In the early 1980s, another, generally oriented system began to be developed at Wharton EFA in order to replace DAMSEL: AREMOS, which began operation in the mid 1980s and is based upon HASH and DEMOS, originally created at the University of Southampton during the late 1970s. Of this generation, only AREMOS and FP continue to be actively supported. However, as the software compendium found elsewhere in this volume attests [57], several other packages have been created since 1985 that, apparently by design, have at least some of the characteristics of econometric modeling languages.

The purpose of this account is not really to consider these econometric modeling languages individually, but rather the prototypical characteristics of this type of software and the historical context that led to its development. The date of the first operative system was in the early to mid 1970s, but which system can claim this honor is possibly debatable. Although there are two, perhaps more, candidates, inasmuch as the appropriate criterion is not functionality per se, but the degree of integration and extensiveness of functionality, both subjective traits, an unbiased judge might find it difficult to make the choice, and then only after a careful and extensive investigation. What is beyond question is that the first articles to be published that describe the specific needs, and hence define the broad characteristics of such systems, are those by McCracken [41,42], followed by McCracken and Sonnen [45, 46]. Furthermore, with the exception of MODLER and PLANETS, TROLL and XSIM, the development of these systems occurred mutually independently. Only in 1978 or thereabouts, did there begin to be any significant degree of publication of descriptions of their properties as modeling languages [19,21,22,28,36,39,52,54,66], although there was always some knowledge among the developers of the existence of other systems beginning in the early 1970s.

2. The definition of needs

From the beginning, what was known in common by the authors of these packages were the tasks that needed to be performed, inasmuch as each of these people was associated with the construction of one or more macroeconometric models, either before or during the development of the software. In order to support the construction and use of large econometric models, ranging in size of up to 1000 equations or more, there are basically five multifaceted activities that must be supported:

- The simple creation and maintenance of a data base, in the restricted sense of storing, editing and retrieving observation values obtained from original, external data sources, often but not always government statistical agencies, international organizations, and trade associations.
- The more general development and management of that data base, in the sense of establishing accounting relationships, making transformations and otherwise creating variables directly used in the models. Such transformations can involve the manipulation of primary economic variables, or they can take the form of frequency conversions, or even the original generation of values, as in the case of dummy variables, pseudo random variates, and other such constructs.
- The creation of one or more models, including the specification of its equations and the estimation of unknown parameters.
- The formation of solvable versions of these one or more models and the generation of solutions.
- The display of the data and results in the form of graphs, tables, and other such visual presentations.

Considered as a body of techniques, this catalogue of activities incorporates not only the whole of applied econometrics pertaining to macroeconomic models, but also a considerable variety of more general statistical and mathematical methods.

In the process of constructing or using an econometric model, these activities are in fact computationally quite highly interrelated, and only to a certain degree uniquely distinguishable as stage-of-process tasks. For example, the equations of an econometric model incorporate arithmetic operators and often various types of mathematical functions, such as logarithms. These same operators and functions can also appear in the statement of transformations, or in graphics and other display commands. Similarly, in the context of a model, a particular equation might be viewed as an identity whereas in a data base management context, it can be viewed as a constructive transformation – but in each case it is the same equation.

As a matter of software design, the immediate implication is that a properly formed econometric modeling language must consist of both a command interpreter of some sort, to translate the actions to be performed – as instructed by the user – into a series of specific internal software commands, and a set of callable procedures to perform the tasks, in such a way that the context of each task is recognized by the program. Furthermore, the results of each relevant operation must be stored in such a way as to be capable of being used as an input to the next task. As a matter of program usability, the command interpreter must also be capable of dealing with "illegal" or misstated commands, and in these circumstances ideally return to the user intelligible error messages, to allow mistakes to be corrected and processing to continue, at least to the degree that the software is operated interactively [17].

Reflecting the need to learn by doing, as well as their scale and complexity as software, econometric modeling languages were not the first model support programs to be developed. The first programs created to support the construction of econometric models, created during the mid-1960s, were both batch oriented and single purpose, so much so that particular activities, such as estimating an equation's parameters, might require the use of two or more separate programs, with the data passed between using some sort of storage device as the transfer medium [45,58]. In the 1960s and in some cases even as late as the 1970s, these programs, on cards or paper tape, were operated by selecting among options, using numbers as selection indicators, ordinarily in fixed fields. This process of setting up for a run was time consuming, and to get it right might take multiple attempts; given slow job turnaround, possibly taking 24 hours or more. Furthermore, it was not at all intuitive – usually requiring the direct use of some sort of reference manual (sometimes in the form of handwritten sheets of paper) and possibly an explicit coding form. Subsequently, the transmission of results of one stage of a model's construction to the next was equally vexatious as a task, if not more so, generally requiring manual transcription.

Until the middle to late 1960s, when the first solution programs began to appear [44, 58,60], the only econometric software programs were task-specific data management programs or relatively rustic regression programs, judged by their software features. Worldwide, task specificity persisted in many cases even well into the 1970s [9,20,

31,62]. Essentially, the reason for this characteristic is simply that separate, focused, programs are relatively easy to write. This isolation also permitted the use of human intelligence to organize the output of one activity so as to provide the input to the next, so that although tedious to the user, it made sense – in the beginning – to construct separated building blocks, which then at least permitted computationally intensive tasks to be performed in days or weeks that using the desk calculator methods described earlier by Goldberger [30], might otherwise have taken months or years.

Functional integration occurred somewhat slowly, inasmuch as achieving this goal required innovation, including the development of efficient command parsing techniques. In 1968, three separate programs might be required to run a regression [58]. Starting then, an obvious initial enhancement was to incorporate data transformation facilities into the regression program itself. Almost immediately, some progress was made: in order to perform these transformations, certain new packages of that time, such as AUTO and ECON, permitted, indeed ordinarily required their users to write Fortran or other such computer language data transformation subroutines that were then compiled as a part of the program. However, the downside was that logical coding errors were not necessarily thereby noticeably reduced: in the context of a computer algorithm, observations on time series variables are normally organized as elements of arrays – that is, matrices – with particular variables and their observations referenced by row and column location, much as present day spreadsheet transformations use cell references. Prototypically, transformations involved, on the right-hand-side, row references in order to specify contemporaneous and lagged observations and column references particular variables. On the left-side-side, the column reference identified the variable created by that transformation, yielding visually a source code statement like:

$$X(I,32) = X(I,7)/X(I-1,16)$$

But if this coding style is still generally familiar to someone who uses Excel, a difference that needs to be noted is that neither was this coding done interactively, with the successive transformations interpreted and recorded more or less instantly, nor was there any logic error checking being done, so as to resolve – or at least alert the coder to – circular references.

Of course, there is also the question of how the data got there in the first place. Prior to the transformation stage, observations must be loaded into the program. Decks of cards or paper tapes, with the data series observations punched on them, were common until even the mid-1970s, perhaps even later in some cases. But at the leading edge, by or about 1970 – on computers that supported the technology – packages were being created that used random access data files in the context of some form of leased, owned, or otherwise privately-controlled direct access device, the most familiar analogues of these today being the microcomputer hard drive or a Zip disk. Here, random access refers to the capability to define a file as composed of (normally) equal length records, each of which records were then independently accessible by record number, relative to the start of the file. As collections of economic time series organized by some common grouping characteristic, these files came to be called "data banks," and were organized so that a given record contained both the documentation and observations on a particular series. However, this format was not universal: in a number of cases, a data bank might consist of two files, one containing observations and the other documentation. This configuration most likely reflects that series documentation was originally an afterthought, so that in such cases it was most natural to add later a second, parallel "documentation" file.

The next problem was that of retrieval. Other than in the head of the user or in the form of a numerically-ordered printout of series, there was at this point no link between a particular variable name, such as GDP, and the record location of its corresponding observations. Only as alphabetic and other indexes were added to each data bank – usually consisting of ordered lists of mnemonic names and corresponding record pointers – did it become possible for the program user to begin to retrieve series, other than by knowing a priori the number of the record containing their observations. For general perspective, it is relevant that, at this time, there was little difference in the state-of-the-art between econometric software and other packages: it is indicative that it was only in 1970 that E.F. Codd began to publish the set of seminal papers that would provide the concepts for the subsequent creation of modern data base management packages such as ACCESS, DB2, FoxPro, ORACLE, and Sybase [10–14], and only in 1973 that IBM introduced the 3340 disk drive, offering 30 megabytes of removable mainframe disk storage.

During the time period beginning in the mid 1960s and leading up to these data storage innovations, for most individual economist-developers the computer's principal attraction was its direct computational capabilities in the context of self-contained batch "jobs," for example as described elsewhere in this volume by Phillips [53]. Permanent or semi-permanent readily-accessible data storage was limited, especially in comparison with today, and "on-line" access was not yet even a concept. Although in the 1960s a computer might contain a hard disk, as Phillips mentions in passing – IBM having introduced the Model 1301 Advanced Disk File in 1962 – its purpose almost always was to provide temporary storage during program execution. Usually, only magnetic reel tapes, mounted for the duration of each job by the central computer operator, or card decks or rolls of paper tape, provided a means of long-term data storage. None daunted, McCracken began in the mid 1960s with a program called DATABANK [40,41] recognizing correctly that if the aim is to support the construction of a large-scale econometric model, a machine-resident library of time series data is fundamental. Others, as they began to come to grips with the practicalities, soon recognized this truth. Therefore, it is not surprising that as the model project started to be organized at the Brookings Institution in the mid-1960s, the management of data was similarly a focal point. On Brookings' IBM 7040, James Craig, Mark Eisner, and others organized a tape resident data bank, with a computer program to manage it; later the NBER data bank, created in 1967 by Charlotte Boschan and others [8,

54], was incorporated. However, in the prevailing 9-Track magnetic tape-oriented batch-processing computer environment of the 1960s, the management of this data base involved reading one tape, revising a series, and then writing the result to another tape. Such an environmental characteristic obviously limited the development of more integrated systems at this time, inasmuch as the lack of interactive computing necessarily fostered a set piece approach.

Nevertheless, some things could be done: in particular, the first step leading to the development of MODLER took the form, in 1968, of the creation of a regression program on the IBM 7040 that – as well as offering such techniques as OLS, 2SLS, and LIML – featured the capability to read the Brookings data bank series directly from magnetic tape as well as to both transform retrieved time series and create additional variables, including dummy variables. One of the data management problems that needed solution was how to select variables from the tape, from among hundreds or possibly even more time series, then manage the selected subset in the context of a computer with a small fraction of the RAM memory capacity of a modern Palm PDA. The crucial element was essentially that of symbolically simultaneously referencing locations on the tape and in the program's matrix of observations, in the absence of variable mnemonic names – and in a before-the-fact batch-operated context, for the user of course had to set up the job *before* the run. The simple fact of batch processing thereby limited the benefit of solving this problem.

TSP, beginning in 1966 one of the very few programs of that era to feature a symbolic language interface, permitted its users to specify transformation commands using its keyword GENR command [18,32], variable names and operators. Robert Hall was able to implement such an innovation then because TSP was free standing, but the version of MODLER implemented two years later was not, inasmuch as the tape-based data file from which the observations were retrieved lacked the proper series documentation, particularly mnemonic names. In 2003, programs that retrieve data on the fly from Excel spreadsheets and other such sources that lack such individual variable identification are still likely to be limited by this lack, although the option now exists, much more so than then, to supply a separate variable names file, in the form of an Alias file, that will permit the assignment of mnemonic names to each relevant set of observations. But even in this case, it is obvious that the selection of a subset of the variables in the file imposes the requirement to establish a protocol to achieve this selection.

Fortuitously, the technology changed. It was Brookings' acquisition of a Digital Equipment Corporation PDP-10 time-sharing, networked computer, activated on or about 1 January 1970, that enabled the development of the first interactive version of MODLER, which incorporated the ability for each individual user to manage directly a random access data bank, using a parsed free-format symbolic language format and mnemonic series names, permitting both "real time" operation and the long-term storage of both primary series and a variety of transformations; this program was in use throughout Brookings by March of 1970, as a consequence of the location of terminals near or in many individual offices. Then and now, MODLER transformations are recognized not by a leading keyword, such as GENR, but by their evaluated properties as commands. Inasmuch as this 1970 version is apparently the first instance of interactive statistical or econometric software, and an early example of such software in general, this event illustrates the importance of the environment to software innovation. The PDP-10 in 1969–1970 was actually not all that different as a programming and user environment from a "diskless" PC-based local area network in the mid 1980s – then using machines with Intel 286 CPUs but with only the server containing a permanent storage device – although the RAM memory available on the PDP-10 was much less and personal random access was supported through the use of DECtapes, rather than a much faster and more capacious hard disk.

The development of TROLL/1 during the period 1968 to 1972 [23,24] was similarly inspired by the need to achieve this type of functional integration, but with the distinction that in the 1970s its design goals became far more ambitious. Particularly once its development became generously funded by the National Science Foundation, the underlying concept conditioning the design of TROLL was that it should be developed to provide a multi-user computer-based research platform to undergird the research activities of the MIT Center for Computational Research in Economics and Management Science. Significantly, the name TROLL derives from Timeshared Reactive OnLine Laboratory. The essential intention was to create a time-shared software system that could be used simultaneously by an indeterminately large group of econometricians involved in the development of algorithms and econometrically-inspired computer techniques. Because of the involvement, in addition, of the National Bureau of Economic Research, whose associates might at some later time conceivably connect to the system remotely, its use was not expected to be limited to only those at MIT [37]. This focus led to an emphasis on design issues associated with mutual file sharing in such a context and the development of a sophisticated hierarchical file management system to support this – verging on operating system type functionality; in fact, this work to some degree appears to have been associated with and to have influenced the subsequent design of UNIX. However, although in later years the use of TROLL elsewhere has often been identified with large scale models, the particular way in which its development progressed at MIT during the early to mid 1970s reflects that, at that time, the research output of those associated with the Center more characteristically involved what came to be called "regression diagnostics," interactive data analysis, and the development of sophisticated nonlinear parameter estimation algorithms [3–7,24,33,38]. Nevertheless, the capacity to support the construction and use of simultaneous equation econometric models was very much a TROLL design consideration from the start. Moreover, the fact that user manuals for solution programs created elsewhere, such as Morris Norman's SIM, were published by the Center [50] and the source code circulated there, obviously implies active interest in the techniques of model solution.

However, this description risks getting ahead of the story. The first successful solution of a large-scale econometric model using a computer occurred in 1967 [25,

26,60]. TROLL/0, developed during the period 1966 to 1968 as a precursor to TROLL, was apparently another early attempt to develop this type of program [23, 58], as was also the seemingly related development of SIMULATE II [35]. Beginning in late 1967, the first generation of model solution packages began to appear and by the early 1970s such programs were becoming widespread [9,31,44,50,62,65]. Characteristically, these were written in Fortran and were single task by design. In the nature of nonlinear solutions, the econometric model solution process, whatever its particular algorithmic form, involves iterating from a set of initial values to a set of converged values – to the degree of course that convergence can be achieved. The particular wrinkle here is that, due to solution speed considerations, it was common for users in the late 1960s and early 1970s, when manually coding a model's equations as Fortran code, to pick apart many, if not most, model equations, separating them into two parts. One part included predetermined variables, which obviously did not vary from iteration to iteration. The other part included those that did. The equation portions that were constant over iterations were then segregated into certain subroutines and those that varied went in others. In addition, because of computer memory limitations, it was also necessary to minimize RAM usage in various ways, including using program overlays. The net effect of such coding practices, whatever benefit they provided in actually making it possible to solve a large model then in a reasonable amount of time and possibly less than 128Kb of memory, was simultaneously to increase the coding errors dramatically. Simply reading an estimated equation from a regression printout of those days, and writing it down anywhere, offered considerable potential for transcription error; thus in every way, the context of the use of a first generation solution package involved error possibilities. Moreover, when the time came to consider how to merge solution capabilities into a unified package, these previously established coding conventions provided something of a mental roadblock to surmount.

Assembling these separate functions into a unified package had a particular pattern. The first stage in the development of econometric modeling languages generally involved the integration of the first three model construction activities identified earlier. This was a natural first step, inasmuch as the particular activities of data base management, the display of data in the form of tables and graphs, and parameter estimation (including transformations, regression and related statistical operations) essentially fit within the usual conception of what econometrics is about. However, in addition, the model solution process not only involved the problems just described, but is algorithmically distinct from the calculations associated with transformations and parameter estimation, especially linear parameter estimation. Moreover, model solution can also present a somewhat different type of data management problem: for one thing, the solution process generally involves dealing with particular dated cross-sections of time series observations, and may involve constant and multiplicative adjustments – and other such variables – not commonly encountered functionally in other contexts. There is in addition the fact that no longer is the data management problem restricted to observations on time series variables, but now can be construed to include also the management of such entities as estimated equations and identities, among the things to be treated as "data".

3. The transition to modeling languages: Interface development

Although the foregoing description is rather brief, it should be evident that the transition from a distinct set of single task programs to an integrated modeling language involves both process integration and the creation of an appropriate human interface. This interface in fact plays two roles. The first is the simple communication of instructions to the software to perform various tasks. The second is to provide a means both to simplify the process of creating, maintaining and solving econometric models and to minimize the possibility of error. Error in this context takes two particular forms. The first type is the variety associated with the communication of instructions, and includes also coding errors in both transformations and model formation. The second type is more generally mathematical, and is associated with the fact that a given set of simultaneous equations may or may not solve; that is, iterate to convergence. Furthermore, this inability to solve may be either general or specific: a newly created model may not solve under "normal" conditions, as a general finding. However, if it solves initially, a model used for some period of time may later suddenly not solve, especially when confronted with some type of "stressful" circumstance, such as a particularly different set of initial conditions or "unusual" values of the exogenous variables.

Considering first the communication of instructions, the nature of an econometric model as a set of equations led early to the recognition that an attractive command interface would be one that replicated as closely as possible what an economist might write on a sheet of paper. However, in saying this, it is important to distinguish between general and specific representations. It is true that in certain contexts, such as an Input-Output table, generic matrix representations provide a concise notation that can serve to simplify conceptually, but this simplification is most useful in circumstances in which the elemental details are conceptually secondary, thus capable of being subsumed by the notation and thereby ignored in favor of focusing on the mathematical operations performed. When it is the details that are the focus, a naming convention that identifies one variable, indexed over I, as the vector XX(I,23) and another as XX(I,42), makes it difficult to keep in mind, or to recognize at a glance, which is which. Thus, in general, the statement of an identity that incorporates mnemonic names of variables, such as:

$$\mathbf{GDP} = \mathbf{C} + \mathbf{I} + \mathbf{G} + (\mathbf{X} - \mathbf{M})$$

or a regression command, such as:

$$\ln(\mathbf{C}) = f(\ln(\mathbf{YPD}), \ln(\mathbf{C}(\ \ 1)))$$

or their near equivalents, are immediately conceptually attractive as model building program control commands; here, $\ln()$ should be interpreted as a natural log implicit function, and the syntax $y = f(x_1, x_2)$ as a directive to regress y on x_1 and x_2. To the degree that a user of an econometric software package recognizes the mnemonic names and can immediately identify the variables involved, the above GDP identity lifted off the page of a book and typed into a computer is a rather comfortable way to tell the program what to do. However, it should also be noted that certain changes in interpretation may be required: here the variable names are to be interpreted as referencing *vectors* of observations, not as symbols referring to scalar values at some time t. Because of the vector representation, the time reference is implicit, which also explains why $\mathbf{C}(-1)$ should be interpreted as referencing a vector of values lagged one period.

It is easy to see that once a data source has been specified, a date range given, and the observation frequency chosen, to be able – using a single command – to direct the computer to calculate GDP, by first retrieving observations on each of the right-hand-side variables, carrying out the operations specified, and then storing the result in a particular nominally assigned data record, is a giant step from the situation described earlier. There are still issues associated with the naming of variables and their retrieval from the large-scale data bases that big models need [54], but notwithstanding such considerations, from the perspective of an economist as a program user it is obviously conceptually attractive to be able to "soft code" equations, using recognizable variable names, operators, implicit functions, and the like, and in the process to leave it to the computer to sort out the associated housekeeping details.

Of course, as a general proposition, it is only to a certain degree possible to allow the computer to manage the housekeeping by default, inasmuch as a program's usefulness normally depends on its degree of flexibility: for instance, alternative and supplementary commands are needed to select among regression methods, different sets of associated statistical tests, and various displays of results. From this need for variety stems complexity, given that each permitted variation generally requires a specific command or variant command. In fact, there is no alternative: initially it might appear that, today, such explicit commands could be dispensed with, in favor of menu choices, icons, and dialog boxes, except that do this completely would imply the general inability to create macros, as sets of program commands to perform particular replicable operations. Model maintenance, if not the original creation of a model, essentially implies the need for a reasonably extensive command language whatever the operating system used. Moreover, it is notable that modern spreadsheet programs display a similar developmental characteristic in their transition over the past nearly 25 years from essentially interactive software in the early 1980s to packages that now incorporate extensive macro languages. At least in part, this transition has occurred in order to permit their users to perform maintenance or complex repetitive operations – or to fit the use of the program into a particular context.

4. The transition to modeling languages: Integrated processing

This description is in fact not precisely chronological. Historically, the interface development of econometric software initially involved the transition from commands coded as numbers in fixed fields on IBM cards or paper tape to free-formatted keywords. Such keywords are still commonly employed to establish observation frequency, date ranges and other environmental conditions of a program's operation, as well as generally to identify the operations to be performed. These were the starting point, and only at a later stage did the parsing of commands that involve algebraic expressions become common. Furthermore, supplemental keyword commands are still necessary: no matter how well thought out and elegant the command structure and syntax of an econometric modeling language, it is impossible to create an operative language that exactly corresponds to the printed page, and the reason of course is that any operative computer language must function as a detailed set of directives. The question is in fact not so much, "why keywords?" as, "why embedded algebraic expressions?"

It is at the point of process integration that a simple keyword language structure fails, for here the ability to capture as input to a later activity the output of an earlier one obviously becomes critical. The capability to embed expressions in commands, and to symbolically evaluate equations, involves much greater design complexity and much more programming that is not directly related to econometric techniques per se. This extra work can be avoided if the aim is just to display the results of a single processing stage, but the use at a later stage of expressions generated earlier requires the ability to interpret them. An econometrician writing a regression package might be able to finesse such complexity, inasmuch as the human user in this context has the capability to pre-parse and otherwise organize the input to suit the machine, but the developer of an econometric modeling language, forced to consider a more comprehensive set of operations, does not have the same freedom.

On the other hand, once this more sophisticated facility exists, a side benefit is of course that it is then possible to create almost immediately a richer, more flexible user interface, inasmuch as soft-coded expressions provided by the program user can then also be evaluated. A well-developed interface of this type is itself generally beneficial, inasmuch as it additionally implies minimization of the need to redo what has already been done before. As a case in point, quite clearly, it is time saving to be able to perform a regression and then, by default or with a single command, direct that the estimated equation be either inserted into a model or otherwise saved for later use. However, not only is this type of process integration a matter of saving time in the doing, but as discussed before it can also help to minimize errors, saving time on that score too. What is more, once a result has been verified as correct and then stored – including not only an estimated equation, but also a procedure such as a macro – it can be regularly re-used with some assurance it will thereafter continue to be correct. Of course, making this inference presumes the procedure's results are not context dependent and therefore in the event may required additional verification.

The integration of the model formation and solution procedures into an econometric modeling language that otherwise incorporated facilities for data base management, as well as regression and other such computational operations, began to occur in the early 1970s, as indicated earlier. One approach to this integration appears to be characteristic of the later development of MOSAIC and takes the form of Fortran (or other computer language) statements that are generated from soft-coded identities and estimated equations [44]. In effect, the computer is used to write computer source code by a process that involves first interpreting text that expresses the individual equations of a model. The resulting Fortran (or other computer language) code is then compiled and linked to standard modules that manage the model solution process, thus creating a solution package that in a general sense is equivalent to one that might have otherwise been created by hand coding, as described earlier.

An alternative approach is for a program to interpret the estimated equations, and any identities or other soft-coded equations supplied directly by the model builder, in much the same fashion as just described, but for it to generate instead a series of more primitive computer instructions that by their sequential order of execution cause the solution of a model. This approach is characteristic of AREMOS, MODLER, and TROLL, broadly considered, although the three involve implementation differences, not only between each other, but also because of the distinction between the pre-1990 "mainframe" TROLL and the post-1990 "portable" system, based upon the pre-1990 version, but actually a new program. Such intra-package complications will not be considered further here. It is generally true of TROLL that from the beginning Newton-Raphson has tended to be the default simulation algorithm. The standard procedure has apparently been to compile residual and partial-derivative expressions directly into machine language, with equations and other expressions then maintained as binary trees. Consequently, whereas, in the case of MOSAIC, the "compiled" model is a compiled Fortran program, in the case of TROLL, the solution-ready model is a binary file. Among other things, the result is to integrate the model solution process, rather than to support (or require) the use of an external solution module or package.

MODLER also compiles solution-ready models into binary files. In this case, the binary file is called a "Compiled Model File" (with the extent CMF) and the result of this model "compilation" process is two vectors and a matrix, the latter expressed in a form called a "tattered lag." To solve a model, these arrays are then processed by an integrated module that carries out a series of binary operations, using a stack, progressively pushing values onto this stack, and then popping them and performing individual floating point operations, as appropriate. This approach is essentially equivalent to coding the entire model directly into machine language. One of the effects – indeed the motivating purpose – is the parsimonious use of RAM: even today, MODLER requires significantly less than 512 KB of RAM, and no overlays, to solve a model of as many as 1000 equations. During this process, a solution file, containing observations on the model's variables, is occasionally read and written, effectively minimizing the use of the one (slow) mechanical element, the hard drive

– or, originally, floppy disk. Nowadays this file is always located on the user's hard drive or possibly a "Ram drive," but all these files are relatively compact and each will still fit easily on a 1.2 Kb diskette, and in most cases even on a 360 Kb diskette. In fact, models created in MODLER in 1983–1984 still work with the very latest, 2003 Windows version of the program, although a model created in a mainframe version of MODLER prior to that time will not. In broad terms, the compilation and solution process is essentially the same today as in 1972 – then optimized to take account of the use of mainframe 9-Track tapes, before the introduction of the IBM 3340 Winchester removable hard disk, but specific changes needed to be made in 1983–1984 to permit large models to be solved in MODLER on the original IBM PC.

As these examples illustrate, the approach taken in each case obviously reflects the different contexts and perspectives of each developer, and these differences would become much more evident if each approach were to be examined in more detail. Focusing on aesthetics or issues of solution speed or perhaps flexibility in the treatment of different model characteristics or even particular ways in which a model can be used, different developers will argue in favor of a particular method as "best." However, neither the AREMOS/MODLER/TROLL nor the MOSAIC approach is necessarily logically superior, nor in any sense necessarily "better," out-of-context. In fact, in the 1980s, an optional utility was added to mainframe TROLL that alternatively allowed the creation of a Fortran program from a TROLL model.

Most importantly, computationally, the numeric results obtained by the different methods can be the same. MODLER has never been tested against MOSAIC, nor TROLL, but it was extensively tested in 1984–1985, model for model, against models coded into the Wharton Econometric Forecasting Associates' workhorse mainframe solution package SIMPLE [65]. SIMPLE was written in Fortran, and is otherwise very similar in its general algorithmic structure to the MOSAIC solution facility, as well as to earlier Wharton solution packages. This testing was done to insure that MODLER would produce the same results for the Wharton Mark7 and Mark8 models as would SIMPLE, and in repeated testing this comparability was found to be the case, notwithstanding numeric representational differences between the personal computer, the CPU of which complies with the IEEE standard, and IBM mainframes of the 1983–1985 time period and earlier, the CPUs of which did not [29,59,64]. Subsequently, in 1985, as it came on line, AREMOS was then tested at Wharton EFA against MODLER, as the standard for numeric solution results on the PC at that time.

Of course, as might be expected, the size of the model that the language is designed to manage and solve can affect the detailed implementation. MOSAIC and MREG/IDIOM are both optimized to be used with models that number in the thousands of equations. Both are designed to be used with multi-sectoral models, essentially incorporating Input-Output structures. As a consequence, these systems characteristically tend to represent models using a matrix notation. As Terry Barker has pointed out, a "key differentiating feature of IDIOM and MREG (c/f MODLER) is that variables can be treated as time series of vectors and matrices, not just time series of scalars. In effect a huge system of single equations can be estimated and solved as a small system of matrix equations. This poses different problems of aggregation and time/size of model solution, so the software development has followed a different path – mainly because it is much more specialized" [1]. Or, to rephrase slightly, the specialization of MODLER is the construction of medium to large macroeconometric models, with the largest model ever solved in it topping out at about 3000 equations, but using a particular version of the program, whereas MREG/IDIOM is specialized to the construction of very large models, with no effective conceptual size limit. As indicated, MREG/IDIOM integrates the Input-Output structures. In contrast, MODLER usually incorporates Input-Output constructs, whenever necessary, via a separate module, called effectively as a dynamic link library during model solution [47–49,61,67], although in a few cases the related equations have been integrated into the main model [15]. Furthermore, MREG/IDIOM is designed to be used with specific models whereas MODLER is designed to be used with a more general class of models, and has been used to construct and solve a wide variety of these, including those created by economists at Chase Econometric Associates, Data Resources, and Wharton Econometric Forecasting Associates, as well as individual economists in various countries and contexts – many of these models have numbered in excess of 100 equations, but few more than 800 equations. Unfortunately, there is very little such comparative information about the models historically used with them available for the other packages that would allow these models' characteristics also to be described here.

However, a key element in the definition of an econometric modeling language is, curiously enough, not so much the ability simply to manage and solve a model in various ways as it is the provisions made for model debugging. McCracken recently recalled, "a conversation with Charlie Holt many years ago – perhaps around 1969. It was in reference to the program [SIMULATE II], which had been written at the University of Wisconsin to solve econometric models. The Klein-Goldberger model was their test-bed and increasingly sophisticated methods were introduced, but to no avail. Finally, it was determined that one of the coefficients was off by a scale of 1000 (probably due to different data scaling). When this fix was put in place the model solved quickly with Gauss-Seidel. Econometric models, like real economies, are not complex structures with multiple optima nearby. The lesson I took was to introduce substantial error detection into the simulation software we developed..." [43].

It is characteristic of the solution of nonlinear systems of equations that, except in the very early stages of model construction, the particular error associated with the instant that the model crashes is almost always purely symptomatic. The reason for the crash is usually found in an earlier iteration, or even an earlier solution time period. Thus the ability to display computations at various points, to trace which variables converge first or last, and other such debugging aids is the sine qua non of a true, professional quality, econometric modeling language. Even for a relatively simply-specified 300 equation model, each iteration may involve in excess of 5000 separate computational operations, and for such a model there are likely to be at least 8–10 iterations at each point in time of the solution. At the instant the model begins to go wrong, the deflection involved, compared to a successful solution, can be very small and thus difficult to spot. The ability to construct a model quickly and efficiently can be touted as a measure of the elegance of one package compared to another, but there is nothing quite so frustrating as having estimated a model, compiled it, and then told it to solve, only to find that it will not, but without knowing why.

5. The display of results

At each stage of the process of model construction and use, the display of results is an important aspect, and to some degree also relates to the point just made about error detection facilities. There are generally two types of display, default and designed. Default displays are encountered by the user at each stage of the model construction, maintenance and use process, but it is particularly at the model solution stage that such displays become especially important. At that stage, inasmuch as the solvability of the model may be in doubt, particularly in the case of a new model, to be able to look at variable values, sets of model equations, and other such items, before and after a solution is attempted, is obviously important. It can be argued that default displays, together with the particular set of results shown, should be carefully considered in the design of any software package [56], inasmuch as these displays provide the user with the information that forms the basis for decisions, including decisions to request further information and perform additional computations and tests.

The issue is not regression results: the results associated with parameter estimation are in principle no different for an econometric modeling language than for any other econometric software package. Where the divergence tends to begin is at the point of displaying transformation and other data management results. Packages specialized to parameter estimation tend to be used with relatively small data sets. In contrast, particularly as the size of a model increases, a larger proportion of a modeling language user's time will be spent on data entry, data transformations, and other operations that make it desirable to be able to view substantial tabular displays. Similarly, the capability to display a complete set of model equations, or some particular subset of these, comes to the fore as interest moves from the consideration of alternative regression specifications to the model as a set of various types of equations. Ideally, a package designed to support the construction and ongoing management of a large scale econometric model should provide considerable capabilities to document each step of the process, although packages are seldom described in terms of their provision for this type of documentation support, possibly because of a general lack of recognition on the part of economists of its importance.

Of course, as the model grows progressively larger, the display problem increasingly becomes that of displaying specific information, especially to the degree that screen displays are involved. In the 1970s and before, 132 column by 60 row, or greater dimensioned, line printer sheets tended to be utilized to simply "dump" results. In that context, it generally did not matter whether the output consisted of 50 pages or 500. In contrast, scrolling though 500 screen pages of output can be daunting, even on the most modern personal computer. Given that most screens display, at any one time, no more than about 30 lines of output, taking account of blank lines between entries, a glossary for a data bank containing 3000 time series might itself require something in the neighborhood of 500 screen pages if each entry requires 5 lines. Similarly, a 300 equation model might require 50 or more screen pages to display the complete model. For such a model, the set of tables required to display solution results in an organized fashion might consist of 30–40 tables.

Of course, display elegance may also be an issue today. The transition from a line printer dump of results in the early 1970s to a beautifully formatted set of tables, complete with multiple fonts and other embellishments, is a further aspect of the development of econometric modeling languages, particularly in the context of the need to present results that meet the standards established by modern word processing and spreadsheet software. Such details are beyond the scope of the present article, but it is obvious that all aspects of presentational facilities require careful thought.

6. Conclusion

This description of the historical development of econometric modeling languages obviously does no more than hint at the various detailed computational and design issues that have been involved in the development of these systems during the past 35 years. If the onion of their development were to be peeled further, the degree of variety would become progressively even more obvious There is, for example, a distinction to be made between systems, such as AREMOS, that define models as a list of equations, creating the solvable version by a process of compiling the given set of equations specified by the list into a final solvable form, but without an earlier organization of that set of equations as a "model," versus other systems that collect equations into a file containing the set of equations and then operate on that file to generate the solvable model. TROLL's facilities, as a another example, can be compared to AREMOS or MODLER on the one hand, or to MOSAIC on the other, for, as indicated earlier, certain versions can be made to generate solvable model files that either exist as "compiled" model files, roughly comparable in style to AREMOS or MODLER models, or as Fortran source subroutines, in the spirit of MOSAIC. This investigation, if pursued, would lead naturally into a more thorough comparison of the various properties of these systems, including some not yet mentioned: for instance, because of the present focus, only the Gauss Seidel and Newton-Raphson model solution methods have so far been identified, but some packages currently offer in addition the capability to generate model consistent forecasts [27,34], involving not just the solution of a model as a set of nonlinear equations, but also a particular conception of the way that economic agents form their expectations. Considering systems developed more recently, there are also points of developmental continuity: some later developed packages, such as Modeleasy/Speakeasy [57], follow the MOSAIC approach and write models as Fortran source code. In the process of describing such characteristics and assessing their individual significance, it would not be difficult to fill an entire journal issue, or perhaps even a complete volume, that took as its subject this ongoing development, with the aim of bringing the story up-to-date, as well as filling in the details that have been ignored here.

Acknowledgement

I am grateful for comments and suggestions made by a number of people. In particular, I am grateful to Terry Barker, Mark Eisner, Ray Fair, Stephen Hall, Tim Harrison, Peter Hollinger, Charles C. Holt, Michael McCracken, Marc Nerlove, William Peterson, George Schink and Houston Stokes for their assistance. I am wholly responsible for all errors and omissions and for all opinions stated.

References

[1] T.S. Barker, *Email re the design of MREG/IDIOM*, C.G. Renfro, recipient, 9 August 2003.

[2] T. Barker, W. Dada and W. Peterson, Software developments in the Cambridge Growth Project 1960–1976: The origins of software for space-time economics, *Journal of Economic and Social Measurement* **29** (2004), 173–182, this volume.

[3] D.A. Belsley, Estimation of systems of simultaneous equations, and computational specification of GREMLIN, *Annals of Economic and Social Measurement* **3** (1974), 551–614.

[4] D.A. Belsley, Centering, the Constant, First-Differencing, and Assessing Conditioning, in: *Model Reliability*, D.A. Belsley and E. Kuh, eds, MIT Press, Cambridge, MA, 1986, pp. 117–152.

[5] D.A. Belsley and E. Kuh, eds, *Model Reliability*, MIT Press, Cambridge, MA, 1986.

[6] D.A. Belsley, E. Kuh and R.E. Welsch, *Regression Diagnostics*, Wiley-Interscience, New York, 1980.

[7] E.R. Berndt, B.H. Hall, R.E. Hall and J. Hausman, Estimation and inference in nonlinear structural models, *Annals of Economic and Social Measurement* **3** (1974), 653–665.

[8] C. Boschan, The NBER Time Series Data Bank, *Annals of Economic and Social Measurement* **1** (1972), 193–209.

[9] B.W. Brown, WEFA batch solution program, WEFA program usage guide #2, in: *Computer Programs Available for Distribution*, D. Bracy, B.W. Brown, J.M. Golderer, M.O. Proctor, D.M. Rowe, G.R. Schink and W. Serad, eds, Wharton Econometric Forecasting Associates, Philadelphia, PA, 1975.

[10] E.F. Codd, A relational model of data for large shared data banks, *Communications of the Association for Computing Machinery* **13** (1970), 377–387.

[11] E.F. Codd, A data base sublanguage founded on the relational calculus, in: *Proceedings of the Association for Computing Machinery SIGFIDET Workshop on Data Description, Access, and Control*, 1971.

[12] E.F. Codd, Normalised data base structure: A brief tutorial, in: *Proceedings of the Association for Computing Machinery SIGFIDET Workshop on Data Description, Access, and Control*, 1971.

[13] E.F. Codd, Further normalization of the data base relational model, in: *Data Base Systems, Courant Computer Science 6th Symposium*, R. Rustin, ed., Prentice-Hall, Englewood Cliffs, NJ, 1972.

[14] E.F. Codd, Relational completeness of data base sublanguages, in: *Data Base Systems, Courant Computer Science 6th Symposium*, R. Rustin, ed., Prentice-Hall, Englewood Cliffs, NJ, 1972.
[15] P.A. Coomes, D.O. Olsen and D. Glennon, The interindustry employment demand variable: an extension of the I-SAMIS technique for linking input-output and econometric models, *Environment and Planning* **23** (1991), 1063–1066.
[16] F. Cooper, Modeling the U.S. trade sector, Paper presented to the *1987 MODLER Users Conference*, Philadelphia, PA, 21 October 1987.
[17] R.N. Cuff, On Casual Users, *International Journal of Man-Machine Studies* **12** (1980), 163–187.
[18] C. Cummins, *Email re TSP and Symbolic processing*, C.G. Renfro, recipient, 30 September 2003.
[19] Data Resources, *EPS Reference Manual*, Data Resources, Inc., Cambridge, MA, 1978.
[20] A. Drud, Interfacing Modelling Systems and Solution Algorithms, *Journal of Economic Dynamics and Control* **5** (1983), 131–149.
[21] A. Drud, A survey of model representations and simulation algorithms in some existing modeling systems, *Journal of Economic Dynamics and Control* **5** (1983), 5–35.
[22] Dynamics Associates, *Economic Forecasting in XSIM User's Guide*, Interactive Data Corporation, Waltham, MA, 1979.
[23] M. Eisner, TROLL/1 – an interactive computer system for econometric research, *Annals of Economic and Social Measurement* **1** (1972), 95–96.
[24] M. Eisner and R.S. Pindyck, A generalized approach to estimation as implemented in the TROLL/1 system, *Annals of Economic and Social Measurement* **2** (1973), 29–51.
[25] M.K. Evans and L.R. Klein, *The Wharton Econometric Forecasting Model. Programmed by George R. Schink*, Economics Research Unit, University of Pennsylvania, Philadelphia, 1967.
[26] M.K. Evans and L.R. Klein, *The Wharton Econometric Forecasting Model. Programmed by George R. Schink*, 2nd Enlarged Ed., Economics Research Unit, University of Pennsylvania, Philadelphia, 1968.
[27] R.C. Fair and J.B. Taylor, Solution and maximum likelihood estimation of dynamic nonlinear rational expectations models, *Econometrica* **51** (1983), 1169–1185.
[28] I. Francis, ed., *Statistical Software: A Comparative Review*, North-Holland, New York, 1981.
[29] S.S. Fried, Evaluating 8087 performance on the IBM PC, *Byte* **9**(9) (1984), 197–208.
[30] A.S. Goldberger, Econometric computating by hand, *Journal of Economic and Social Measurement* **29** (2004), 115–117, this volume.
[31] G.R. Green, SIMEMOD: A General Purpose Computer Program to Simulate and Forecast with Econometric Models, in: *BEA Staff Paper in Economics and Statistics*, Bureau of Economic Analysis, US Department of Commerce, Washington, DC, 1970.
[32] B.F. Hall, *Email re TSP and Symbolic processing*, C.G. Renfro, recipient, 30 September 2003.
[33] P.W. Holland, The Data-analysis project, April 1974, *Annals of Economic and Social Measurement* **3**(2) (1974), 440–442.
[34] P. Hollinger, The Stacked-Time Simulator in TROLL: A Robust Algorithm for Solving Forward-Looking Models, Paper presented at the *Second International Conference on Computing in Economics and Finance, Geneva, Switzerland, 26–28 June 1996.*
[35] C.C. Holt, et al., *Program Simulate II: A User's and Programmer's Manual*, Social Systems Research Institute, University of Wisconsin, Madison, WI, 1967.
[36] J. Kirsch, *Troll Primer*, Third ed., MIT Center for Computational Research in Economics and Management Science, Cambridge, MA, 1979.
[37] E. Kuh, Some Notes on the Research Program at the NBER Computer Research Center for Economics and Management Science, *Annals of Economic and Social Measurement* **1**(2) (1972), 233–236.
[38] E. Kuh, Introduction, *Annals of Economic and Social Measurement* **3**(4) (1974), i–iii.
[39] T. Lane, ed., *TROLL Reference Manual* (*Standard System*), Second Ed., MIT Center for Computational Research in Economics and Management Science, MIT Information Processing Services, Cambridge, MA, 1979.
[40] M.C. McCracken, *DATABANK System: Users' Manual*, Economic Council of Canada, Ottawa, 1966.

[41] M.C. McCracken, A computer system for econometric research, *Social Science Information* **5** (1967), 151–158.
[42] M.C. McCracken, Data administration in an information system, in: *Conference on Government Information Systems*, Economic Council of Canada, Ottawa, 1967.
[43] M.C. McCracken, *Email re MOSAIC development*, C.G. Renfro, recipient, 22 July 2003.
[44] M.C. McCracken and K. May, Issues in the development of early solution facilities for very large macroeconometric models, *Journal of Economic and Social Measurement* **29** (2004), 167–171, this volume.
[45] M.C. McCracken and C.A. Sonnen, A system for large econometric models: management, estimation, and simulation, in: *Proceedings of the Association for Computing Machinery Annual Conference, August 1972*, Association for Computing Machinery, 1972.
[46] M.C. McCracken and C.A. Sonnen, *MASSAGER User's Manual*, Statistics Canada, Ottawa, 1973.
[47] B. Meyer, A neo-classical input-output model based on make and use tables, *Empirical Economics* **14** (1989), 1–19.
[48] B. Meyer and G. Ewerhart, Die saubere Dienstleistungsgesellschaft. Eine konsistente projektion, in: *Okointegrative Gesamstrechnung – Potentiale, Problem und Prognosen*, H. Schnabt, ed., Berlin, 1994.
[49] B. Meyer, G. Ewerhart and T. Siebe, *Dollarkurs und Beschaftigung, Eine Empirische Analyse für die Bundesrepublik Deutschland*, Berlin, 1990.
[50] M. Norman, H. Shapiro and R. Rasche, *The SIM Model Solution Program*, MIT Center for Computational Research in Economics and Management Science, MIT Information Processing Services, Cambridge, MA, 1967.
[51] W. Peterson, Computer software for a large econometric model, in: *The Cambridge Multisectoral Dynamic Model of the British Economy*, T.S. Barker and W. Peterson, eds, Cambridge University Press, Cambridge, 1987, pp. 105–121.
[52] W. Peterson, T. barker and R. van der Ploeg, Software support for multisectoral dynamic models of national economies, *Journal of Economic Dynamics and Control* **5**(1) (1983), 81–108.
[53] P.C.B. Phillips and V.B. Hall, Early development of econometric software at the University of Auckland, *Journal of Economic and Social Measurement* **29** (2004), 127–133, this volume.
[54] C.G. Renfro, Economic Data Base Systems: Some reflections on the state of the art, *Review of Public Data Use* **8**(3) (1980), 121–140.
[55] C.G. Renfro, On the Development of Econometric Modeling Languages: MODLER and its first twenty-five years, *Journal of Economic and Social Measurement* **22**(4) (1996), 241–311.
[56] C.G. Renfro, Normative Considerations in the development of a software package for econometric estimation, *Journal of Economic and Social Measurement* **23**(4) (1997), 277–330.
[57] C.G. Renfro, ed., A compendium of existing econometric software packages, *Journal of Economic and Social Measurement* **29** (2004), 359–409, this volume.
[58] C.G. Renfro, Econometric Software: The first fifty years in perspective, *Journal of Economic and Social Measurement* **29** (2004), 9–107, this volume.
[59] N. Sarnak and E. Jaffe, 8087 performance considerations, *PCTech Journal* **1**(2) (1983), 30–47.
[60] G.R. Schink, Simulation with large econometric models: The quest for a solution, *Journal of Economic and Social Measurement* **29** (2004), 135–143, this volume. Originally a paper presented to the Association for Computing Machinery meetings, Denver, Colorado, 12 June 1970.
[61] A.E. Scowcroft, The mechanics of joint cross sectional time series modelling, Paper presented to the *1988 MODLER Users Conference*, Philadelphia, PA, 15–16 November 1988.
[62] D. Sheinson, SOLVEM model solution program, in: *The Wharton Short Term Forecasting System Computer Programs*, G.R. Green and J. Green, eds, Wharton Econometric Forecasting Associates, Philadelphia, 1973.
[63] L.J. Slater, Computing the state of the economy, *Computer Journal* (1966), 11–15.
[64] R. Startz, *8087: Applications and Programming for the IBM PC and Other PCs*, Robert J. Brady Company, Bowie, MD, 1983.
[65] Wharton Econometric Forecasting Associates, *Wharton User Manual for SIMPLE*, Wharton Econometric Forecasting Associates, Philadelphia, PA, 1983.

[66] Wharton Econometric Forecasting Associates, *WEFA User Guide: DAMSEL Program Section*, Wharton Econometric Forecasting Associates, Philadelphia, PA, Circa 1980.

[67] S. Wright, C.G. Renfro and A.E. Scowcroft, Toward A Generic Macroeconomic Modelling Environment. A paper presented at the *Society for Computational Economics Third International Conference on Computing in Economics and Finance, Stanford University, 30 June–2 July 1997.*

Journal of Economic and Social Measurement 29 (2004) 167–171
IOS Press

Issues in the development of early solution facilities for very large macroeconometric models

Michael C. McCracken and Keith May
Informetrica Limited, P.O. Box 828, Station B, Ottawa, Ontario, Canada K1P 5P9
E-mail: staff@informetrica.com

The SIMSYS simulation system was first developed at the Economic Council of Canada in 1970/71 to support its development of the large-scale CANDIDE econometric model. The size of the model raised many concerns, particularly about the "correctness" of the model implementation, equation ordering and run-time performance. This article describes the modeling language and coding scheme used in SIMSYS to address these issues.

1. Introduction

The SIMSYS system was first developed at the Economic Council of Canada in 1970–1971 to support the development of the CANDIDE model [1]. This model was an ambitious project for the time: the specification called for a model of about 1500 equations, including embedded I-O models for both industry GDP and final demand prices.

The MASSAGER/DATABANK [3–5] system had been in use at the Council and other government departments for some time to provide time series database management and estimation support, so that software was already at hand for these modeling tasks. The main software problem was that of model solution. Several concerns drove the design of the software:

- Coding equations in a "raw" programming language was inherently error prone. The development team was acutely aware of the painful experience at the Bank of Canada of a lengthy delay in their model development project due to coding errors. Heavy emphasis was placed on having some method of guaranteeing correctness of the model code.
- There were worries about equation ordering with the Gauss-Seidel [2] algorithm. Since re-ordering the equations of such a large model would cause significant delays the inclusion of the Ritz, or Jacobi [2] solution method in the solution software was considered an important "fall back". At the very least, it would

identify whether convergence difficulties arose from ordering or starting value problems.[1]

- Parts of the model were highly dynamic. It was important to be able to test the model with both actual and calculated lags to determine if the dynamic structure of the model was stable.
- Due to the size of the model, there was a clear need for segmenting it into "blocks" of equations that could be independently coded and tested. This would allow individuals to work independently on separate parts of the model and a "layered" approach to debugging it (for example the real and price sides of the model were tested and debugged separately before being simulated together). This segmentation also afforded some control over equation-ordering problems.
- The computing budget was a particular worry, since it was unknown how expensive the solution of such a large model would be. Heavy emphasis was placed on run-time efficiency of the software. In particular, memory use was heavily "taxed", so a small memory footprint was essential.
- Finally, the model was to be used by many parties. Documentation was important to have and to keep current. It was decided to make the model "self-documenting" by using files readable by people as inputs to the computer program. Thus, the model code was not unlike a description in an econometrics article. The mnemonic table included a description of each mnemonic as well as the block and equation numbers. Cross-reference files could be generated for use both by analysts and by programs designed to analyze the block recursive structure of the model.

The overall architecture decided on was a general-purpose solution component that would call one or more "blocks" of equations (subroutines) and take care of solution method (Ritz or Gauss Seidel), updating of lags (actual or calculated), convergence checking, starting value initialization, etc.

The most important design decision was to have equations coded in an algebraic-like language using "mnemonics" for variables, which would then be translated into a coding scheme in the underlying language (FORTRAN). Thus users could code equations as:

$$\mathrm{CONSUM} \;= \mathrm{EXP}(\mathrm{B} + \mathrm{B} * \mathrm{INCOME} + \mathrm{B} * \mathrm{INCOME} < -1 >)$$

instead of something like:

$$\mathrm{V}(508, \mathrm{T}) = \mathrm{EXP}(\mathrm{B}(38) + \mathrm{B}(39) * \mathrm{V}(96, \mathrm{T}) + \mathrm{B}(40) * \mathrm{V}(96, \mathrm{T} - 1)).$$

[1] The Gauss-Seidel method used the most current iteration value for right-hand side variables while Ritz used the previous iteration values only, updating them at the end of the iteration. Ritz solved more slowly but was independent of the equation order.

While such a feature provided obvious benefits to equation coders, the separation of the equation language from the underlying code gave the software developers complete freedom in specifying the coding scheme. The scheme suggested from the above line of code, while simple, doesn't lend itself easily to solving the equation using current/last iteration values, or with actual/calculated lags. Also, the minimum required size of the array "V" depends on the length of the longest lag used in the model. The coding scheme actually used separated contemporaneous references from lagged ones, and right-hand references from left-hand sides. So, the actual code generated looked like:

$$\mathrm{S(403) = EXP(B(38) + B(39) * E(96) + B(40) * EL(909))}$$

With this scheme, solving the model with Ritz vs. Gauss-Seidel simply requires the solution software to call the subroutine with the last iteration values for "E", vs. current iteration values. Actual vs. calculated lags are a simple decision on what way the solution software updates the "EL" array. Also the separation of lagged references from contemporaneous ones allows for minimal memory use from lag references and avoids the overhead in index calculation for two-dimensional arrays (one index addition per variable reference – yes, we did think this was significant overhead given the model size).

So the coding scheme provided for good run-time performance and a complete separation of the model equation code from the general-purpose solution software.

In addition to equation translation, it was considered important for coders to have complete access to the programming language – that is, to be able to "mix in" raw code with the equations. Thus the coding language was in fact designed as a superset of FORTRAN which allowed "pure" FORTRAN" to be mixed with equations, and even mnemonic references within otherwise "pure" FORTRAN statements. This allowed for specialized calculations, such as for the I-O subsystems, along with more mundane conditional statements such as:

$$\mathrm{IF\ (TIME\ .GT.\ 1991)\ldots}$$

mixed in with equations. The "TIME" variable reference in the above FORTRAN would be translated to the appropriate array reference.

While the use of a symbolic language for equation coding greatly reduced coding errors it didn't eliminate them. As mentioned above, the solution software supported the Ritz solution method. A special kind of simulation was defined (called a "Residual Check") which was a single iteration Ritz simulation with historical data as initial values. The result of such a simulation is, in the case of behavioral equations the calculated values from the regressions, and in the case of identities, the data on the historical database. The "Check" involved running a utility to compare the simulation results with the estimation results and database. Discrepancies here would reveal "obvious" kinds of errors such as missing terms in identities, or the use of a different variable in the model code vs. the regression. However, it would also reveal more subtle errors, such as equations that had been estimated using the wrong vintage of database. The Residual Check provided a guarantee that the coded equations were consistent with estimated results and the database.

The SIMSYS system was later adopted by Informetrica, which continued the development of the software and is still in use today as part of the company's MOSAIC system.[2] While the software has undergone substantial change since its original development, the most durable feature has been the generation of code using the original coding scheme and equation coding language. The main reason for this is that the performance afforded by a model running "natively" on its host machine is in some sense unbeatable. This, along with access to the underlying programming language has given modelers great freedom in pushing the envelope on model size and complexity.[3]

The move to the VAX and PCs has also stimulated other developments. A SCAN program has been developed that allows for the comparison of simulation runs in a very sophisticated fashion. It has proved invaluable in analyzing results, tracing back to equation specifications, and following through the effects of model impacts. The system is designed for interactive use with a few keystrokes and is the most heavily used module during simulation studies.

An additional, and unanticipated, benefit of producing an "executable" model has been in exploiting "component" technologies (such as Microsoft's COM (Component Object Model) technology). At its simplest level, this has allowed configuring the model as a DLL (Dynamic Link Library) callable by third-party software through one/more interfaces. For example, the Informetrica model has been integrated "as-is" with other models using a simple interface allowing for two-way communications between models. A less complicated application might include driving the model through the VBA (Visual Basic for Applications) macro language of Excel to provide a simplified or special-purpose user interface for the model.

References

[1] R.G. Bodkin, L.R. Klein and K. Marwah, *A History of Macroeconometric Model-Building*, Edward Elgar, Brookfield, VT, 1991, p. 573.

[2] G. Dahlquist and A. Bjorck, *Numerical Methods*, Prentice-Hall, Englewood Cliffs, NJ, 1974.

[3] M.C. McCracken, *DATABANK System: Users' Manual*, Economic Council of Canada, Ottawa, 1966.

[2]The rest of the MOSAIC system was developed in the late 1970s to replace DATABANK-MASSAGER. The emphasis was on database management, estimation, manipulation of data, report generation, etc. The program was designed for use on interactive platforms, including VAX systems. It is now available for PCs.

[3]The current Informetrica annual macro model, with over 8,000 equations and a large embedded I-O subsystem, solves for 30 years in about 10 seconds on a 1 GHz PC. Doubling the run time of the model will still be tolerable for the modelers.

[4] M.C. McCracken and C.A. Sonnen, *A system for large econometric models: management, estimation, and simulation, in Proceedings of the Association for Computing Machinery Annual Conference, August 1972*, Association for Computing Machinery, 1972.

[5] M.C. McCracken and C.A. Sonnen, *MASSAGER User's Manual*, Statistics Canada, Ottawa, 1973.

Journal of Economic and Social Measurement 29 (2004) 173–182
IOS Press

Software developments in the Cambridge Growth Project 1960–1976: The origins of software for space-time economics

Terry Barker, Wagner Dada and William Peterson
Department of Applied Economics, University of Cambridge, CB3 9DE, UK
E-mail: Terry.Barker@econ.cam.ac.uk

The Cambridge Growth Project (CGP) 1960–1987 developed its own software packages for (1) single-equation then matrix-equation regression analysis and (2) matrix manipulation, then full dynamic non-linear model solution. The hardware used by the project was the successor to EDSAC, the Titan computer, succeeded by an IBM mainframe, and one of the first personal computers, built by Acorn a local Cambridge company, which was replaced by the standard personal computer running under DOS. The development of the matrix approach to modelling stemmed from the emphasis on social accounting associated with the work of Richard Stone. The software was developed around the concept of the zero-, one-, two- or three-dimensional tensor (scalar, vector, matrix, or 3D tensor) a powerful way of organizing data that are both cross-section and time-series. The programs, written in FORTRAN, that were developed over the period 1973–1978 MREG and IDIOM are still in use today, although they have gone through many versions, they are able to manage much larger data sets, and they have become much faster in operation.

1. Introduction

One of the most widely accepted contributions of the Department of Applied Economics (DAE) at Cambridge to the field of Economics is in the area of econometric methods and their applications. Begg and Henry [6, p. 2] noted that the "DAE can reasonably claim to have spawned 'Durbin-Watson' and 'Cochrane-Orcutt' techniques for handling problems of serially correlated errors, amongst other widely used tools of the trade". The DAE was also pivotal in the development of large model econometric software in the 1960s and 1970s as rightly noted by Renfro [14]. Smith [26] also argued that the DAE played a major role, especially in matrix algebra, regression packages and computational methods for the large-scale modelling required by the Growth Project.

In what follows, we provide an historical account of these developments in the DAE, tracing how the requirement in the 1970s for a commercial service based on the CGP model led to the development of more general software that was able to manage large-scale space-time economic data-sets (panel data) as well as to solve space-time economic models (regionalized, dynamic, endogenous solutions).

2. Background

The development of econometric software to support the construction and use of large-scale models at the DAE can be traced back to the Cambridge Growth Project (CGP), which began in 1960 under the leadership of Richard Stone and Alan Brown. Prior to the commencement of the CGP, however, the DAE had already been experimenting with the use of electronic device in econometrics. The first documented use of an electronic device in econometric regression calculations was by Houthakker [8, p. 366]. The Cambridge electronic calculator, the Electronic Delay Storage Automatic Calculator (EDSAC) was used to carry out estimation of Ordinary Least Squares (OLS) equation in investigating the determinants of electricity consumption in Britain. EDSAC was developed and constructed by the Cambridge University Mathematical Laboratory. The Mathematical Laboratory under the leadership of Dr. Maurice Wilkes, Stan Gill and David Wheeler developed the system, which was completed in May 1949.

3. Early computing in the DAE

Richard Stone, the then Director of the Department of Applied Economics in Cambridge, saw the opportunity to adopt the use of the EDSAC machine in economic research. Commenting on the efficiency of the EDSAC, Brown et al. [7] said that about 70 hours of labour by a human computor with an electric desk machine was replaced by 7 minutes of machine time. The first program for the inversion of large matrices (using the Choleski method) was developed by Houthakker and Prais. Wilkes et al. [29], Prais and Houthakker [13] and Aitchison and Brown [1] contain a full description of the use of EDSAC.

Stone later appointed Lucy Slater to the DAE in 1956 to assist in the development of regression programs to be used on the EDSAC I computer. Slater had been engaged in research work in the Mathematical Laboratory at Cambridge, studying the calculation of the confluent hypergeometric functions, and the applications of the Electronic Computers EDSAC I and EDSAC II since 1951.

4. The Cambridge Growth Project (CGP)

In 1960, Richard Stone together with Alan Brown started the Cambridge Growth Project. The main purpose of the CGP was to study quantitatively, in as great detail as practicable, the structure of the British economy and its future prospects and the possibility of influencing these prospects by policy measures. To these ends, the team designed and built a succession of large-scale disaggregated models of the economy. The intention [28] was to build two models: one was static concerned with steady-state growth; the other was dynamic concerned with fluctuations in the economy.

However, the main thrust of the research went into the static model, with projections made of the British economy to 1980 (see Barker [2]). The dynamic model did not get beyond a theoretical specification [28] and no projections of fluctuations in the economy were published.

The static and dynamic models were merged into one dynamic model in the mid 1970s, and the concept of the steady state and the equilibrium year for the base and for the 10-year projection were abandoned [2]. The dynamic model involved estimating a year-by-year model at the level of disaggregation required of the target projection and simulating the economy year-by-year. This development introduced the time element into the model; also it was later extended to incorporate various regions of the UK, so introducing the spatial element. A corresponding model for regions of the EU (E3ME) was developed in the 1990s.

Stone's social accounting matrix which was developed during his work on national accounting systems, and for which he was awarded the Nobel prize in 1984, provides the framework for the these models.

5. The evolution of software developed by Lucy Slater and used by the CGP

Lucy Slater took responsibility for developing computer software and programmes to be used on the Cambridge machines, first on the EDSAC machines, and later on the TITAN (Atlas MK II) and IBM 360, 370, 3081 and 3084 computing systems, in basic machine code and a wide range of higher level machine languages.

The first computer used by the CGP was EDSAC I. Slater [22] notes: "the program code for EDSAC was a gnomic one from the earliest days. Thus A stood for add, S for subtract, M for multiply, and D for divide. The machine also had the ability to read in a program which would repeat a cycle of orders a given number of times, while varying the address of one of the items of data. Thus it could add numbers stored in locations 1 to 10, and put the result into location 11". The construction of the successor EDSAC II computer was completed in 1958. It was built using ferrite cores, instead of valves, was much bigger and at least ten times faster. It also had some data storage space, thus partly overcoming some of the difficulties of EDSAC I.

Reg I was the first regression program developed in the DAE for use on the EDSAC machine. It was developed by Lucy Slater in collaboration with Michael Farrell, then also in the DAE. Reg 1 was an elementary regression package, with successive versions called Reg II, Reg III, ..., up to Reg X. The Reg programs are well described in Slater [15,17,19], Slater and Barker [17] and Slater and Rendle [25]. The Reg regression package was initially developed to work on the EDSAC machine. The final version of REG was the tenth version, REG X, which was eventually re-titled REX.

The REX program was designed to provide a simple and quick way to carry out multiple regression analysis on large or small sets of data. The program is stored within the computer, the users supply a short steering program punched on a pack of cards or on a paper tape, and they then have only to draw up a list of the steps in their proposed calculations, very much as they would do when preparing their computing work to be done on a desk calculating machine. The user looks up to the numbers in the REX control list for the steps in his calculations. These are then punched together with their data onto cards or tape, and added onto the end of the steering program, which is then run through the computer.

The University TITAN mainframe machine later succeeded EDSAC II machine. Although EDSAC II was ten times faster than EDSAC I, the CGP models required a faster machine than the EDSAC II, which was comparatively slow, running at about one million multiplications a minute, and had limited memory, thus posing a limit to the number of product groups that could be analysed simultaneously. On the comparative speed of EDSAC II and the TITAN computers, Slater [16] noted that EDSAC II originally required about one hour to perform a complete machine run of the CGP model calculations, when it was reprogrammed in Extended Mercury Autocode (EMA), the same calculation took 25 minutes; with the arrival of the Cambridge Titan machine, and the new Titan Autocode compiler, one complete machine run took only 110 seconds!

When Terry Barker joined the CGP in 1965, he worked with Lucy Slater in developing her REG X program, which was written in Autocode (a high level machine language) that ran on the TITAN mainframe. Terry Barker extended the REG X program to handling two-stage least squares and a stepwise regression procedure [17]. In 1969, REG X became REX and included forecasting tests, adjustment for serial correlation and an instrumental variable procedure [24]. REX was developed by Slater, Barker, Rendle, Coe and several other assistants.

REX was set up to compute sum of squares, which were used to carry out multiple regression residuals. To do this, it used the Jourdan process (described in Barron and Swinnerston-Dyer [5]), the standard routine used by the Cambridge University Mathematical Laboratory to construct matrix inversion routines, which took up minimal storage space. If the data sets are large, an auxiliary storage such as a magnetic tape is used. The operation of the program consumed little time, however much of the operation time was spent on reading in the data and putting out the results. REX was re-written in FORTRAN for an IBM370 mainframe in 1972, thus giving users as much control over the regression analysis as possible. The strength of REX was that any number of regressions, transformations or other calculations could be carried out in one run, an important consideration when the turn-around period (from sending the problem to the central computer to receiving the printed output) was normally one day.

By 1972, various other computer programs written in FORTRAN had been developed at the DAE. These programs could perform inversion of large triangular matrices (TRINV), optimal surface calculations (OPTSUR), standard consumer demand calculations (program S10F), probit analysis (program PA4F), and more advanced regression technique known as the Effroymson process (program REFER), as well as techniques used in demographic accounting (program DAP4F); see Slater [18].

Hashem Pesaran who had joined the DAE as a Junior Research Officer in 1971 developed 4 package programmes for dynamic time series modelling in 1975 (see [9]). The packages, AR, ARMA, DL1 and DL2 were all written in FORTRAN, and could be used to estimate and predict single equation dynamic economic models. The programmes were complementary to his PhD thesis, which he had written at Cambridge and submitted in 1972. The packages could compute Ordinary Least Squares (OLS), Cochrane-Orchutt procedures, forecasting tests, AR1, AR2, among others.

In 1972, Lucy Slater reprogrammed the REGINA software, which had been written by David Champernowne into FORTRAN. REGINA was designed to fit regression equations containing more than one endogenous variable. It was used to solve simultaneous equation models. However, it could only fit parameters in a model consisting of a set of simultaneous equations each of which is "exactly identifiable".[1] It did not provide estimates of regression coefficients in an equation, which is under-identified, nor in one that is over-identified (see [20]).

In 1976, Slater developed the General Econometric Matrix Program (GEM) databank, which was the result of her work over the period 1961–1976 in the DAE. GEM was a databank matrix designed to store, manipulate and present data in the form of matrices, vectors and scalars. It consisted of a set of computer subroutines in FORTRAN that enables a user with little experience of computers to carry out extended sets of calculations on matrices and vectors and to maintain his or her own computerized databank on a magnetic tape, or a disc file. GEM could manage about one hundred matrix and vector operations, each of which was identified by a control number (an integer). The user had to only write out the steps of his or her calculations as a list of these control numbers. The main limitation of the GEM databank was that it was unsuited to the IBM hardware. Another limitation was that matrices in the databank have their dimensions stored within them and so the dimensions of the databank matrices were not provided to GEM by the user. This limitation was overcome in later versions of GEM with refinements and contributions from Brian Shearey, Geoffrey Rendle, Roger Smith, William Peterson, Terry Barker and Eduardo Martinez. For instance, GEM3 was a dynamic version of the original GEM in that the size of the matrix and vector stores, the size of the workspace and the printing level can be determined by the user in the first four numbers read into the program.

6. The development of Multisectoral-Model-Solution and Matrix-Regression Software (IDIOM and MREG)

In 1975 and 1976 a new dynamic model was developed by the CGP to replace the two-model (static and transient) system. This was and is named the Multisectoral

[1] An equation is exactly identified when the number of endogenous variables included in it is exactly one greater than the number of exogenous variables excluded from it. This includes of course, the important case where there is just one endogenous variable included and no exogenous variable is excluded.

Dynamic Model (MDM) of the UK economy and is written in FORTRAN. This new model led to the production of new solution and estimation packages, which were more suited to a large-scale dynamic econometric model than packages that estimate equations one-at-a-time. The MDM FORTRAN routines were embedded in a new solution package, IDIOM, developed by Terry Barker, William Peterson and Alan Winters, 1978–1980 under a contract from UNIDO. Database management and estimation tasks were handled by a new package, MREG (Matrix REGression package), which superseded REX and GEM (MREG was mainly developed by William Peterson).

Models such as MDM can simulate period-by-period development of national economies, and are usually very large with numerous equations and variables. For example, the first version of MDM, which solved a 40-industry annual dynamic model of the UK economy, had 7,272 variables, of which 2,551 were endogenous and 4,721 were predetermined [27]. As noted by Peterson et al. [11], most general-purpose estimation, solution or optimal control packages cannot adequately handle such multisectoral models with their substantial data structures and huge estimation requirements. Thus the CGP had to construct customized packages, such as IDIOM and MREG, for the estimation and simulation of these models. A third package implementing optimal control techniques was also developed to allow the synthesis of economic policy from large-scale non-linear econometric models. In particular, it performs policy optimisation exercises in the course of a single computer run. These packages were developed for the IBM computer systems operated by the University of Cambridge Computing Service.

The MREG package was responsible for data handling and estimation. MREG offered the user an estimation package capable of matrix operations and sophisticated facilities for iteration and the conditional execution of commands, thus allowing for considerable flexibility. IDIOM on the other hand was a model simulation and solution program. Separating the functions of the two packages allowed for organisational simplicity, and was efficient given the limited memory available on the Cambridge IBM system at the time. However both packages contributed to the estimation and solution of the MDM models. Commenting on the potential problem of such separation, Peterson, Barker and Van der Ploeg [11, p. 6] stated: "provided that communication between the two packages, via the database or temporary disc files follows a common set of protocols, and provided the command input to the two programs is synthetically similar, no problems are likely to arise from this separation".

To overcome this problem, data was stored in matrices to make it more compact, and was stored in binary form in databanks (direct access data sets) accessed using IBM FORTRAN direct access routines, which were common to both packages. The databanks contained both time series and cross sectional data used for model construction and estimation: there were also facilities for holding character data (used for tabulating results). Because both IDIOM and MREG were based on variables arranged as matrices, so that (for example) time series data on employment by industry is treated as an array with one dimension the number of industries and the other the number of observations, the number of databank entries was comparatively small and indexing relatively simple. IDIOM and MREG shared a common command syntax, and many of the utility routines for decoding commands and evaluating expressions were based on the same code. The programs had only a limited distribution outside Cambridge. Following the move to Windows, MREG is no longer supported and its functions are largely replaced by Ox applications.

However IDIOM, the model simulation package, is available and continues as a software platform for large-scale macro-econometric models by the commercial company Cambridge Econometrics. IDIOM is in effect an expert system that implements the lessons which the Cambridge Growth Project learnt from constructing a large dynamic input-output model of the British economy. The original aim was to design software, which would be applicable to the general task of model-building for local and national (and now global) economies with very different industrial and institutional structures. IDIOM was developed as a separate package, in preference to extending the MREG package to performing forecasting and model simulation, because a simulation package for large non-linear models is inevitably an expensive program to run, since it may have to solve several thousand highly non-linear equations for each period, and under various assumptions about structural changes in the economy. In order to perform this solution process efficiently, IDIOM was designed as a hybrid system. The equations which actually define the model are written by the user as FORTRAN subroutines, and must therefore be rewritten and recompiled whenever an entirely new model is developed. However IDIOM provides a separate interpreted command language interface, which not only handles tasks such as reading input and tabulating results, but also allows the user to chose between alternative pre-programmed versions of selected model equations without recompilation. Allowing this flexibility through run-time commands makes it possible to 'freeze' the compiled program for long periods, and thus reduces the amount of time spent in model development and debugging. For a full description of IDIOM, see Barker et al. [4] and successive User's Manuals published by Cambridge Econometrics.

Although the CGP was closed in 1987, development of later versions of the IDIOM program has continued to be carried out by Cambridge Econometrics, which began as the commercial arm of the Growth Project. The latest version of IDIOM (the 8th version released in 2002) is a FORTRAN90 program designed for the specification and solution of large-scale econometric non-linear simulation models incorporating a wide range of relationships, including input-output equations. IDIOM has been revised and extended by Cambridge Econometrics as the software platform for a number of econometric models covering economic, energy and environmental models for countries and regions, namely, the UK models MDM-E3 and LEFM, the Europe regional E3 model E3ME, and the global model E3MG. In 1989, IDIOM was re-written for compilation and solution using the Salford FORTRAN compiler FTN77 and the operating system DBOS, so that it could run models unconstrained by the 640k limitations of the IBM-PC-compatible 386 and 486 PCs. In 1997 the software was further developed so that it could be used as part of a user-friendly system for solving models under Windows 95. The latest version uses the Salford compiler FTN95.

Various features of IDIOM are common across all the models built and solved using the package (the housekeeping routines) and are described in the model manual. Other features have to be provided by the model builder as specific to his or her particular model. Builders of models should prepare a separate manual for model users; and users of the models should consult the appropriate model manual for details of a particular model.

IDIOM differs from other economic modelling solving packages, such as MODLER, AREMOS, EViews, or TROLL in two respects. Firstly the organising concept and principle of IDIOM is that of matrix algebra, rather than the individual series. In this it is more like the GAUSS or Ox packages than MODLER and others. The specification of equations can be in terms of industries or regions or both, so that one line of commands can replace many lines required by a package organised around scalar variables and equations for each such variable. This is particularly useful for cross-section, time-series econometric modelling involving large datasets. Secondly, IDIOM does not provide facilities for estimating equations or managing associated databanks. These tasks must be done using the MREG software package or the Ox programmes developed by Cambridge Econometrics.

The main benefits from such specialisation are time-saving in computer calculations and ease of managing large models by organising solutions about matrix variables. IDIOM can solve and store large-scale E3 models (e.g. involving about 10,000 estimated equations and over a million variables) taking a few seconds for each year of solution on a year on a PC with Pentium 3, 1Ghz processor and 192MB RAM. IDIOM operates by interpreting directives from the model-builder defining the specification of the model required and the computations to be performed. Since these directives are interpreted rather than compiled, substantial changes in the model structure can be made without knowledge of the internal program structure. In addition, the provision of facilities for the conditional or repeated execution of directives provides the model-builder with much of the control over the models normally obtained by writing in a conventional high-level computer language.

7. Conclusion

While hardware limitations impeded the development of econometric software during the CGP, improvements in the quality of available hardware appears to have been associated with further software development, which in turn impacted on the design of CGP packages. To illustrate, hardware improvements from EDSAC1 to EDSAC2, to the TITAN machines, and later to IBM computers are associated with similar improvements in the software, noticeable by the movement from gnomic machine codes to TITAN Autocode to FORTRAN, a portable high-level language. Because FORTRAN had facilities for character manipulation which Autocode lacked, MREG and IDIOM could adopt a syntax for commands in terms of simple keywords (such as OLS or REPLACE), rather than integer control numbers, and could implement techniques such as the parsing of algebraic expressions which made the specification of operations much more transparent to the user.

The experience of the CGP shows that there is a strong element of learning-by – doing in research. Research requirements were clearly a driving force in the development of software at the CGP. As the Growth Project evolved from being static to being dynamic, there was the need for improvement in the available software needed to carry out the new analyses. Programming techniques to deal with large bodies of data quickly and efficiently also emerged. Software developed during the CGP can be classified into 2 categories, the first being general software which could be easily adapted for use in other econometric analysis, such as REX and MREG; and the other category being software of a more specialised nature which can only be adapted for use by similar large disaggregated macro models, such as the GEM and IDIOM. Several other ideas emerged from the CGP as noted by Renfro [14], and the research requirements of the CGP led to the development of algorithms and programs for parameter estimation by Pesaran and Slater [10], out of which ultimately came the present day MicroFit package now supplied by Oxford University Press.

IDIOM and the models (including whole-system models) built using the package are the main software legacies of the CGP. The approach using this software is now, in Europe at least, the main alternative to the Computable General Equilibrium approach conventionally used in economic-system analysis.

References

[1] J. Aitchison and J.A.C. Brown, *The LogNormal Distribution,* Cambridge University Press, Cambridge, 1957.

[2] T.S. Barker, The Cambridge Economic Growth Project Model, in: *The Medium Term Models of the British Economy,* G.D.N. Worswick and F.T. Blackaby, eds, N.I.E.S.R., London, 1974.

[3] T.S. Barker, Making the Cambridge Growth Project Model Dynamic, in: *Medium-Term Dynamic Forecasting, Proceedings of 1975 London Conference*, W.F. Gossling, ed., Input-Output Publishing Company, London, 1977, pp. 96–109.

[4] T.S. Barker, A.W.A. Peterson and A. Winters, An international dynamic input-output model, in: *Proceedings of the Seventh International Conference on Input-Output Techniques*, UNIDO, ed.,United Nations, New York, 1984, pp. 183–192.

[5] D. Barron and H.P.F. Swinnerston-Dyer, Solution of Simultaneous Linear Equations using a Magnetic-Tape Store, *The Computer Journal* **3** (1960), 28.

[6] I. Begg and S.G.B. Henry, *Applied Economics and Public Policy,* Cambridge University Press, Cambridge, 1998, pp. 1–11.

[7] J.A.C. Brown, H.S. Houthakker and S.J. Prais, Electronic computation in economic statistics, *Journal of the American Statistical Association* **48**(263) (1953), 414–428.

[8] H.S. Houthakker, Some calculations on electricity consumption in Great Britain, *Journal of the Royal Statistical Society* **A114**(Part III) (1951), 351–371.

[9] M.H. Pesaran, *AR, ARMA, DL1, DL2: Programmes for Small Sample Estimation of Dynamic Economic Models,* mimeo, Department of Applied Economics, Cambridge, March 1975.

[10] M.H. Pesaran and L.J. Slater, *Dynamic Regression: Theory and Algorithms,* Ellis Horwood, Chichester, 1980.

[11] A.W.A. Peterson, T.S. Barker and R. Van der Ploeg, Software support for Multisectoral dynamic models of national economies, *Journal of Economics Dynamics and Control* **5** (1983), 109–130.

[12] A.W.A. Peterson, Computer software for a large econometric model, in: *The Cambridge Multisectoral Dynamic Model of the British Economy,* T.S. Barker and A.W.A. Peterson, eds, Cambridge University Press, 1987.

[13] S.J. Prais and H.S. Houthakker, *The Analysis of Family Budgets,* Cambridge University Press, Cambridge, 1995.

[14] C.G. Renfro, Econometric software: The first fifty years in perspective, *Journal of Economic and Social Measurement* **29** (2004), 9–107, this volume.

[15] L.J. Slater, Regression Analysis, *The Computer Journal* (January 1962), 1–5.

[16] L.J. Slater, Computing the State of the Economy, *The Computer Journal* (May 1966), 11–15.

[17] L.J. Slater, *Fortran Programs for Economists,* DAE Occasional Paper 13, Cambridge University Press, Cambridge, 1967.

[18] L.J. Slater, *More Fortran Programs for Economists,* DAE Occasional Paper 34, Cambridge University Press, Cambridge, 1972.

[19] L.J. Slater, *Program REXF: Notes on the Re-programming of REX in Fortran IV (ASA),* mimeo, Department of Applied Economics, Cambridge, July 1972.

[20] L.J. Slater, *REGINA: A Beginner's Program for fitting Regression Equations to Time-series: Translated into Fortran,* 2nd Ed., mimeo, Department of Applied Economics, Cambridge, 1972.

[21] L.J. Slater, *GEM A General Econometric Matrix Program,* DAE Occasional Paper 46, Cambridge University Press, Cambridge, 1976.

[22] L.J. Slater, EDSAC: Recollections on early days in the Cambridge Computing Laboratory, *Journal of Economic and Social Measurement* **29** (2004), 119–122, this volume.

[23] L.J. Slater and T.S. Barker, *Regression Program for TITAN,* mimeo, Department of Applied Economics, Cambridge, May 1967.

[24] L.J. Slater and T.S. Barker, *Regression Program for TITAN,* 6th Ed., mimeo, Department of Applied Economics, Cambridge, September 1971.

[25] L.J. Slater and G. Rendle, *A Guide to the Regression Program REX for Users of the IBM 370/165 Computer,* 2nd Ed., mimeo, Department of Applied Economics, Cambridge, September 1973.

[26] P.R. Smith, The development of econometric methods at the DAE, in: *Applied Economics and Public Policy,* I. Begg and S.G.B. Henry, eds, Cambridge University Press, Cambridge, 1998, pp. 88–103.

[27] R. Stone, The evolution of the Cambridge Growth Project, Lecture given at the Institut fir Siedlungs- und Wohnungswesen der Westfälischen Wilhelms-Universität Münster, in: *Beiträge zur Strukturpolitik, Materialien zum Siedlungs- und Wohnungswesen und zur Raumplanung*, No. 18, Münster; Hungarian translation, *Statistikai Szemle* **56** (1978), 236–249.

[28] R. Stone and A. Brown, A Computable Model of Economic Growth, in: *A Programme for Growth,* R. Stone, ed., Chapman and Hall, London, 1962.

[29] M.V. Wilkes, D.J. Wheeler and S. Gill, The *Preparation of Programs for an Electronic Digital Computer: With special reference to the EDSAC and the Use of a Library of Subroutines,* Addison Wesley, Cambridge, MA, 1951.

Journal of Economic and Social Measurement 29 (2004) 183–187
IOS Press

Some Milestones in Econometric Computing

Econometric software as a theoretical research tool

Houston H. Stokes
Department of Economics, University of Illinois at Chicago, 601 South Morgan Street (M/C 144), Chicago, IL 60607, USA
E-mail: hhstokes@uic.edu

It is common that the discovery or development of a statistical finding precedes its implementation, but in certain cases this is not true. The development of the Theil BLUS technique is a specific example of a two-way relationship between econometric theory and software design. In particular, the fact that the sum of squares of the N-K BLUS residuals is equal to the sum of squares of the N OLS residuals was first observed experimentally and subsequently proved in theory.

1. Introduction

In the Forward to his classic econometrics textbook, Theil [13, p. 5] suggests, "Nobody believes that he can become a chemist by attending lectures and reading textbooks and journal articles. He should devote time and energy to the real work in the laboratory. In the same way, nobody should believe that he will be able to handle statistical data in econometrics without touching actual data." In the spirit of this thought, the present note outlines how the analysis of data in one case gave rise to new theory, a phenomenon that is common in hard sciences such as physics and chemistry but less so in econometrics.

Prior to writing his textbook, in an important paper Theil [11] had already laid out the theory for the BLUS (best, linear, unbiased, scalar covariance matrix) residuals. The essential objective behind the development of the BLUS concept was to transform the sample OLS residuals in such as way as to provide these new residuals with a scalar covariance matrix–so that exact tests could be performed for a variety of problems such as heteroskedasticity, serial correlation nonlinearity and normality. Theil first proved that there could be at most N-K BLUS residuals, where N is the sample size and K is the number of right hand side variables. The problem then became how best to determine which K residuals to place in the base from which to calculate the N-K BLUS residuals. For each problem, there would be a number of possible bases that should be considered. As a result of detailed empirical analysis, Theil solved this selection problem by developing a structured way to determine the most appropriate base for various statistical tests.

2. A brief review of BLUS residual theory

To begin, it might be helpful to recall certain results. Assume y is a N-element left hand side variable, X is a N by K matrix of exogenous variables, β is a K by 1 matrix of coefficients and u is the N element population residual. Then consider the linear model:

$$y = X\beta + u \tag{1}$$

The OLS estimate of the coefficient vector is of course

$$\hat{\beta} = (X'X)^{-1}X'y \tag{2}$$

from which we can define the vector of estimated or sample residuals $\hat{u}$ as

$$\begin{aligned}\hat{u} &= y - X\hat{\beta} \\ &= X\beta + u - X(X'X)^{-1}X'y \\ &= X\beta + u - X(X'X)^{-1}X'(X\beta + u) \\ &= u - X(X'X)^{-1}X'u \\ &= (I - X(X'X)^{-1}X')u\end{aligned} \tag{3}$$

The presently important implication of the result shown as Eq. (3) is that even if the population residual u has a scalar covariance matrix, the sample residual will not. As a consequence, the sample residuals will not have this (assumed) ideal property of the original errors.

However, Theil [11] realized that fortuitously there exists a vector $\hat{\varepsilon}_1$ defined for the subset of T-K observations associated with the data sub-matrix X_1, that is also an estimator of the population residuals, but which has a scalar covariance matrix. After some work, Theil [12] simplified the estimation of these BLUS residuals to

$$\hat{\varepsilon}_1 = u_1 - X_1 X_0^{-1} \left[\sum_{h=1}^{K} \frac{d_h}{(1 + d_h)} q_h q_h' \right] u_0 \tag{4}$$

as is described in greater detail in Theil [13], where X_0 is the K by K matrix of observations in the base and d_i and q_i are the eigenvalues and eigenvectors of the matrix $X_0(X'X)^{-1}X_0'$. The $N - K$ by K matrix X_1 is the observations that are not in the base.

3. Properties of the BLUS residuals

In his original presentation, Theil [11] does not mention the fact that the sum of squares of the N OLS residuals is the same as the sum of squares of the N-K BLUS residuals. However, two years later, Koerts [3], who worked with Theil in Rotterdam on the calculations, published this result simply as a calculation checksum. By this time Theil had moved to the University of Chicago. Shortly thereafter Thornber [15, 16] had incorporated BLUS calculations into B34T, the then standard econometric estimation program at Chicago, developed by him there. In 1972, Stokes took over development of B34T, which became B34S and in which these calculations were then incorporated.[1]

Subsequently, in 1977, Stokes was asked by Theil to work on a BLUS example of nonlinear detection, while he was in the process of revising his textbook. This work was intended to be included in a revision of Chapter 5 (Theil [14]). During this collaboration Theil told Stokes orally that the result

$$\sum_{i=1}^{T-K} \hat{\varepsilon}_{1i}^2 = \sum_{i=1}^{T} u_i^2 \tag{5}$$

had first been discovered experimentally, and only later proved. This revised version of Chapter 5 was completed, but the complete book was never published. The reason was apparently Theil's unwillingness to cannibalize his earlier work: Kenneth Clements, who worked with Theil in the 70', informed Stokes that in the 1980's Theil told him he had abandoned the revised edition since he would be "competing with himself."

The BLUS example Theil and Stokes developed has however been published, in Stokes [6,7]. Its development involved use of the logic of problem 5.2 in Theil [13] which had been moved into the text of the revised chapter 5 in Theil [14] as a part of this example. The importance of Eq. (5) as a result is a consequence both of its value as a computational check and the fact that it is related to the Theil [13] and Koerts [3][2] result that the minimum expected sum of squares of the N-K BLUS errors is

$$E[(\hat{\varepsilon}_1 - u_1)'(\hat{\varepsilon}_1 - u_1)] = 2\sigma^2 \sum_{i=1}^{K}(1 - d_i). \tag{6}$$

Inasmuch as Theil [12] proved that the maximum eigenvalue was at most 1.0, it follows immediately that Eq. (6) directly implies that the expected error of the T-K BLUS estimates of unobserved population vector u_1, for the non-base observations, will be minimized the larger is

$$\sum_{i=1}^{K} d_i \tag{7}$$

[1] Stokes [8,9] documents the B34S whose history and development is discussed in Stokes [10] in the context of Renfro [7].

[2] See Theil [13] Theorem 5.4. A slightly different formulation is given in Koerts [3].

thus forming the theory basis for using the sum of the square roots of the eigenvalues as the BLUS selection criteria whenever there is a possibility of alternative appropriate bases (X_0).

4. Summary

The BLUS technique continued to be listed in econometric books such as Chow [1] and Maddala [5] into the 1980's. Theil [14], although never published, contained a response to Koerts and Abrahamse [4] that had questioned the power of the BLUS test. At issue was the use of a non-optimum BLUS base. In Theil's view and the experience of Stokes [8,9], it is a serious error not to utilize Eq. (7) to select the appropriate BLUS base. It remains to be seen if errors in BLUS base selection is the cause of some of the lack of power in the BLUS procedure found by Huang and Bolch [2] and Ramsay [6] and cited in Maddala [5].

Acknowledgement

The author is indebt to Charles Renfro for a number of excellent suggestions that have substantially improved this paper. Any remaining errors are the responsibility of the author.

References

[1] G. Chow, *Econometrics*, McGraw-Hill, New York, 1983.
[2] C.J. Huang and B.W. Bolch, On the Testing of Regression Disturbances for Normality, *Journal of the American Statistical Association* **69** (1974), 169–183.
[3] J. Koerts, Some Further Notes on Disturbance Estimates in Regression Analysis, *Journal of the American Statistical Association* **62** (1967), 169–183.
[4] J. Koerts and A.P.J. Abrahamse, On the Power of the BLUS Procedure, *Journal of the American Statistical Association* **63** (1968), 1227–1236.
[5] G.S. Maddala, *Econometrics*, New York, McGraw Hill 1977.
[6] J.B. Ramsey, Classical Model Selection through Specification Error Tests, in: *Frontiers in Econometrics*, P. Zarembka, ed., New York, Academic Press, Inc., 1974.
[7] C.G. Renfro, Econometric software: The first fifty years in perspective, *Journal of Economic and Social Measurement* **29** (2004), 9–107, this volume.
[8] H.H. Stokes, *Specifying and Diagnostically Testing Econometric Models*, 1st Ed., Quorum Press, Westport, 1991.
[9] H.H. Stokes, *Specifying and Diagnostically Testing Econometric Models*, 2nd Ed., Quorum Press, Westport, 1997.
[10] H.H. Stokes, The evolution of econometric software design: A developer's view, *Journal of Economic and Social Measurement* **29** (2004), 205–259, this volume.
[11] H. Theil, The Analysis of Disturbances in Regression Analysis, *Journal of the American Statistical Association* **60** (1965), 1067–1079.
[12] H. Theil, A Simplification of the BLUS Procedure for Analyzing Regression Disturbances, *Journal of the American Statistical Association* **63** (1968), 242–251.

[13] H. Theil, *Principles of Econometrics*, Wiley, New York, 1971.
[14] H. Theil, Chapter 5: The Analysis of Residuals, prepared in 1977 for publication in the revised edition of *Principles of Econometrics* which never came out.
[15] H. Thornber, Manual for B34T (8 MAR 66)-A Stepwise Regression Program, University of Chicago Business School technical report 6603, 1966.
[16] H. Thornber, BLUS Addendum to Technical Report 6603: Manual for B34T-A Stepwise Regression Program, *University of Chicago Business School* **1** (August 1968).

Journal of Economic and Social Measurement 29 (2004) 189–203
IOS Press

Programming languages: A short history for economists*

Marc Nerlove
Department of Agricultural and Resource Economics, University of Maryland, College Park, MD 20742, USA
Tel.: +1 301 405 1388; Fax: +1 301 314 9032; E-mail: mnerlove@arec.umd.edu;
URL: http://www.arec.umd.edu/mnerlove/mnerlove.htm

> The White Rabbit put on his spectacles. "Where shall I begin, please your Majesty?" he asked. "Begin at the beginning," the King said gravely, "and go on till you come to the end; then stop."
>
> Lewis Carroll, Alice's Adventures in Wonderland, XII

The development of programming languages as a means of communicating with digital computers is surveyed with emphasis on those languages and characteristics of particular relevance to economists and statisticians. There are several different types of software: (1) True programming languages which are used for many purposes in communicating with the machine, such as FORTRAN. (2) Software with greater specificity in purpose and function such as MATHEMATICA, GAUSS, MATLAB and MAPLE. (3) "Libraries" or collections of special purpose algorithms designed to be used within programs written in one of the major languages, e.g., the LINPACK, MINPACK, EISPAC, and IMSL libraries. (4) Collections of programs, sometimes called packages, linked together and designed for special purposes. These generally must be used within some of the languages one step removed from the basics. Examples include MATLAB Toolboxes. (5) Finally, there are programs which although made generally available cannot be used stand-alone in any sense.

*Research supported by the Maryland Agricultural Experiment Station. I am indebted to my colleagues Hanan Samet and Marvin Zelkowitz, Department of Computer Science, University of Maryland. Charles Renfro has made numerous detailed comments based on first-hand knowledge of the last 50 years of programming and computation in econometrics. Browyn Hall set me straight on the origins of TSP. The usual disclaimer applies. This account is based mainly on my personal recollections and is far from definitive. Errors undoubtedly remain and details may be inaccurate. I would appreciate any corrections of substance or interpretation. My story is written from my standpoint as an economist and applied econometrician and for economists. The definitive treatment of the history of programming languages is contained in the two volumes of conference proceedings: Wexelblat [46] and Bergin and Gibson [4]. A very good brief treatment from a general perspective may be found in a standard textbook on programming languages widely used in computer science departments, Pratt and Zelkowitz [32]. The history of computing and of software is an area of active research; for example Ceruzzi [7] and Campbell-Kelly [5]. The very popular exposé, Cringely [9], on which a PBS miniseries, "Triumph of the Nerds" was based, is a delight to read. An amusing fictional account is the novel, Gibson and Sterling [17]. Two important papers by Charles Renfro [33,34] published in this issue deal more specifically with econometric software, supplement my discussion.

0747-9662/04/$17.00

The Encyclopedia Britannica [16] defines a computer programming language as "... any of various languages for expressing a set of detailed instructions for a digital computer. Such a language consists of characters and rules for combining them into symbols and words.

The history of the development of computer languages shows an evolution towards an ever closer approximation to natural or mathematical language. This history in the last half of the twentieth century is summarized in the table at the end of this paper.

Computers only recognize yes-no or 0–1 or off-on internally. Von Neumann's great contribution to computation was the idea that a machine could be programmed to follow a sequence of instructions stored in its memory as off-on's. In 1946, at the University of Pennsylvania's ENIAC, the switches were really set by hand. [1] In the early days, circa 1956, I vividly recall Hy Weingarten of our group at the USDA actually writing simple programs in machine language, i.e., binary bits, which was equivalent to setting these internal switches "by hand." This clumsy and time-consuming method was quickly supplanted by the first assembler programs which established a one-to-one correspondence between machine code and easily remembered "words."

At first, programmers, Hy among them, would first write out what he wanted the machine to do in semi-symbolic form, assembly language, and then laboriously translate these instructions into appropriate patterns of bits (binary numbers) to be stored in the machine's memory, used by the machine actually to execute Hy's program. Of course, it was pretty silly to have a human being do the laborious translation. What was needed was a standard symbolic representation of the algorithms to be implemented so that the machine itself could do the grunt work of translation. These programs are called *assemblers*. What an assembler does is to translate each of the symbols in the assembly language program into machine language symbol of binary bits. By collecting all of these machine language symbols, the assembler produces a machine language program that sets the switches as the programmer intended. Hy could now write statements like "Add A B" instead of "1011010100111010010111010" in order two numbers.

Assembly languages are direct word for word translations of machine language. For each machine language instruction, there is a symbol that indicates what it is used for; and for each storage location in memory, there is a symbol that tells what it is meant to contain. After some experimentation with assemblers, it became apparent that computer programs could do much more than just translate word for word; it is also possible for the translation program to rearrange the words so that the syntax of the language is different from the syntax of the machine language. The ability to change the syntax of the language lets the programmer write statements like $a = 1+1$, rather than a sequence of instructions to the hardware, that will store one in a memory location, add that location to itself, then store the resulting value in a new location.

[1] EDSAC at the University of Cambridge, constructed under the direction of Maurice Wilkes, came along about the same time, as did the Mark 1 at Manchester, Davis [11, p. 194].

Thus were invented the first *programming languages*: FORTRAN in 1957 by IBM,[2] and ALGOL in 1958 by a European consortium,[3] COBOL (Common Business OrientedLanguage) in 1960,[4] and LISP, in 1958, for basic list processing, by John McCarthy, then at MIT.[5] LISP, however, is a rather different sort of creature and I will discuss it more thoroughly below. These languages are known in the trade as high-level languages (HLL), that is, a programming language which provides some level of abstraction above assembly language. They normally use statements consisting of English-like keywords such as "FOR", "PRINT", or "GOTO", where each statement can correspond to several machine language instructions. It is much easier to program in a high-level language than in assembly language though the efficiency of execution depends on how good the compiler or interpreter is at optimizing the program. There is an important distinction between compiling a program and interpreting it.[6] But, in the end the program has to be expressed in a manner the machine can understand. Whereas assembly languages let programmers express things directly in machine

---

[2] *FORmula TRANSlation*, John Backus, IBM, 1954–1957.

[3] ALGOL (ALGOrithmic Language) is one of several high level languages designed specifically for programming scientific computations. It started out in the late 1950's, first formalized in a report titled ALGOL 58, and then progressed through reports ALGOL 60, and ALGOL 68. It was designed by an international committee to be a universal language. Their original conference, which took place in Zurich, was one of the first formal attempts to address the issue of software portability. ALGOL's machine independence permitted the designers to be more creative, but it made implementation much more difficult. Although ALGOL never reached the level of commercial popularity of FORTRAN and COBOL, it is considered the most important language of its era in terms of its influence on later language development. ALGOL's lexical and syntactic structures became so popular that virtually all languages designed since have been referred to as "ALGOL – like"; that is, they have a hierarchical in structure with nesting of both environments and control structures. See Backus [1,2], Baumann, Feliciano, Samelson [3], Naur, Backus, Bauer, Green, Katz, McCarthy, Perlis, Rutishauer, Samelson, Vauquois, Wegstein, van Wijngaarden, and Woodger [28a] and many subsequent papers. The papers by Naur and Perlis in Wexelblatt [46, pp. 75–139] give a very comprehensive discussion of ALGOL's history on both sides of the Atlantic. Although ALGOL was implemented on a new powerful Boroughs machine in about 1960 (IBM wouldn't have anything to do with it), it was originally intended as a language for the expression and communication of *algorithms* in general; at one time, *Communications of the Association for Computing Machinery* published algorithms in ALGOL.

[4] "Grace Hopper led a group at Univac to develop FLOWMATIC in 1955. The goal was to develop business applications using a form of English like text. In 1959, the US Department of Defense sponsored a meeting to develop Common Business Language (CBL), which would be a business-oriented language that used English as much as possible for its notation. Because of divergent activities from many companies, a Short Range Committee was formed to quickly develop this language. Although they thought they were designing an interim language, the specifications, published in 1960, were the designs for COBOL (Common Business Oriented Language). COBOL was revised in 1961 and 1962, standardized in 1968, and revised again in 1974 and 1984." Pratt and Zelkowitz [32, p 6].

[5] The original version was LISP 1, invented (some historians prefer the use of the word "discovered") by John McCarthy at MIT in the late 1950s. McCarthy [28,29]. LISP is actually older than any other high level language still in use except FORTRAN, and has undergone considerable change over the years. Modern variants are quite different in detail. See below.

[6] Compilers transform an entire program from one language to another (e.g., the assembly language) for subsequent execution; interpreters execute a program sequentially, translating at each step. Compiled programs almost always run faster than interpreted programs but are a lot harder to debug

terms in a different way than in terms of binary bits, they still tell the machine what is to be put in memory locations and what is to be done with the contents of these memory locations. The actions that can be expressed are closely tied to the actions the machine can do, such as, putting the contents of one memory location into a register and adding that number to another in another location. HLLs bring us much closer to natural language.

At about this time, many of the early econometric programs were written. These were not general purpose programs designed to do a variety of statistical and econometric tasks but were rather limited, and were, moreover, machine-specific. In following the history of programming languages, one has to distinguish among several different types of software although the boundaries between them are often blurred. On the one hand, there are true programming languages which are used for many purposes in communicating with the machine, beginning with the first versions of FORTRAN, ALGOL, etc., and ranging all the way in recent times to FORTRAN90, C, C++, and Java. The most recent versions of Mathematica, while emphasizing doing computer assisted mathematics and graphics, nonetheless aim for this level of general use. At the next level, one finds somewhat greater specificity in purpose and function. Examples of particular interest to economists include S, S+, R, GAUSS, MATLAB and MAPLE. Modern versions of TSP, SAS, SPSS, LIMDEP and STATA, among others, come close to falling in this category. Then, there are what I would call "libraries" or collections of special purpose algorithms designed to be used within programs written in one of the major languages, e.g., the LINPACK, MINPACK and EISPAC, IMSL Libraries of Visual Numerics and the NAG Fortran Library Subroutines of the Numerical Analysis Group, first developed in the 1960s. There are, in addition, collections of programs, sometimes called packages, linked together and designed for special purposes. These generally must be used within some of the languages one step removed from the basics. Examples include MATLAB Toolboxes many of which are written by third parties. Finally, there are programs which although made generally available cannot be used stand-alone in any sense. Soon after the development of FORTRAN and ALGOL, econometricians and statisticians began writing and making available to colleagues programs for doing basic statistical analyses such as regression. Special mention should be made of the regression program written by Stroud [43] at the University of Wisconsin, the programs by Zellner, Stroud and Chau [47,48] for computing seemingly unrelated regressions estimates and two and three stage least squares, and a program by Eisenpress [14] for limited-information maximum likelihood. Regression programs became common. Five OLS regression programs dating from that era were evaluated in Longley [27]. In this period, the once widely used package TROLL (Timeshared Reactive OnLine Laboratory) was developed at MIT under the guidance of Ed Kuh by Mark Eisner [13], although the first readily available version wasn't released until 1972 (see Renfro [33]). Mitch Kapor, later of Lotus 1-2-3 fame, developed a version for the early Apple PC called Tiny TROLL.

IBM developed PL/I, a precursor of C, in the 1960's.[7] PL/I (Programming Language One) was an attempt to combine the best features of FORTRAN, COBOL and ALGOL60 was developed by George Radin of IBM in 1964. PL/1 provided the foundation for development of the SAS system on IBM operating systems. Later SAS was rewritten in C so as to be portable to other systems.

The influence of LISP (John McCarthy [28,29]) on all further developments in the evolution of programming languages has been fundamental and pervasive. LISP and its variants have been very important in the development of data base management and word processing programs – and in the development of still higher level HLLs. WORD, WordPerfect, and LaTex, in many respects have their origin here. In his essay on the history of LISP, Herbert Stoyan [41], writes:

"LISP is understood as the model of a functional programming language today. There are people who believe that there once was a clean 'pure' language design in the functional direction which was comprised by AI(Artificial Intelligence)-programmers in search of efficiency. This view does not take into account, that around the end of the fifties, nobody, including McCarthy himself, seriously based his programming on the concept of mathematical function. It is quite certain that McCarthy for a long time associated programming with the design of stepwise executed 'algorithms'.

"On the other side, it was McCarthy who, as the first, seemed to have developed the idea of using functional terms (in the form of "function calls" or "subroutine calls") for every partial step of a program. This idea emerged more as a stylistic decision, proved to be sound and became the basis for a proper way of programming – functional programming (or, as I prefer to call it, function-oriented programming). We should mention here that McCarthy at the same time conceived the idea of logic-oriented programming, that is, the idea of using logical formulae to express goals that a program should try to establish and of using the prover as programming language interpreter."[8]

For my purposes in this paper, however, a more important related development was the development of FORMAC (FORmula MAnipulation Compiler) at IBM in the early 1960's (Sammet and Bond [36]). This was the first step in extending the

---

[7]With the introduction of its new 360 line of computers in 1963, IBM developed NPL (New Programming Language) at its Hursley Laboratory in England. After some complaints by the English National Physical Laboratory, the name was changed to MPPL (Multi-Purpose Programming Language), which was then shortened to just PL/I. PL/I merged the numerical attributes of FORTRAN with the business programming features of COBOL and the syntax of ALGOL. PL/I achieved modest success in the 1970s, but its use today is dwindling as it is replaced by C, C++ and Ada. The Cornell University educational subset PL/C achieved modest success in the 1970s as a student PL/I compiler.

[8]For a an explanation "... in the simplest possible terms [of] what McCarthy discovered...," see Graham [19]. But this paper is not so simple for one who does not already know a lot about computer programming! There is some controversy, however, about where exactly the concept of subroutine originated. See Giloi [18], who cites the early work of Konrad Zuse [49] in 1943–1945, published only in 1972, and see Graham [19], also Sebasta [37, p. 55]. I suspect that all this is an example of Stigler's Law of Eponymy [39, p. 277-290] Whoever originated the idea, it is McCarthy's influence that has been pervasive.

use of computers to do formal mathematics, as distinct from numerical mathematics. MAPLE and MATHEMATICA, which are discussed here, are the "children" of FORMAC. But all modern HLLs, whether designed primarily for numerical or for symbolic manipulation, incorporate list processing elements and the ideas of John McCarthy.

At this point in the history of programming languages, the ideas behind the development of ALGOL came to dominate: algorithmic and information structures. Algol68 was released in 1968, after having been under active development by a group associated with A. van Wijngaarden in the period 1965–1968. Intel was founded by Robert Noyce, Andrew Grove and Gordon Moore in 1967. Donald Knuth's multivolume landmark [24] began publication in 1968. [9] The now widely-used "econometric software packages," e.g., SAS, SPSS and TSP, were created about this time, and have since grown into major commercial enterprises. [10] BASIC (Beginner's All-purpose Symbolic Instruction Code) was designed by John G. Kemeny and Thomas E. Kurtz at Dartmouth College in 1963. It first ran on an IBM 704 in 1964 and was designed for quick and easy programming by students and beginners. BASIC exists in many dialects, and is popular now on microcomputers with sound and graphics support. [11]

At about this time (the mid-1960's), a number of groups began to develop libraries of computer routines, which could be incorporated in other programs and which were efficiently written from a numerical point of view. By the early 1970's, EISPAC, LINPACK and MINPACK by Argonne National Laboratories, in the public domain, and the IMSL Libraries of Visual Numerics and the NAG Fortran Library Subroutines of the Numerical Analysis Group, which are proprietary, were available. [12] These

[9] And is projected to run to seven volumes, of which only three have so far appeared: 1. *Fundamental Algorithms*, 1968; 2. *Seminumerical Algorihtms*, 1969; 3. *Sorting and Searching*, 1973. Volumes 1 and 2 have gone into third editions (1997). Volume 3 is now in its second edition (1998). According to Knuth's homepage, Volume 4 is in "beta test" version.

[10] SAS software was originally written as a by-product of a university project to analyze agricultural data at North Carolina State University in the early 1970's. The first references to SAS appear in 1972. SAS Institute Inc. was formed in 1975. SPSS Inc. was founded in 1968. The development of TSP is described in some detail by Browyn Hall in a recent e-mail: "The original TSP was developed in 1965/66 by Robert Hall with the help of several other graduate students at MIT (Robert Gordon, Charles Bischoff, Richard Sutch, etc). Bob took a version to Data Resources Inc in 1969/70 and it became the basis for their first interactive econometric program. I did not really do any development for them, although I worked on a different program (capital budgeting) as a consultant briefly. The current TSP is based on a version I found in the basement of Littauer in 1970 (on cards) which was sent by Dale Jorgenson from Berkeley to Harvard when he moved. It was developed and distributed by me at Harvard until 1977 and became a commercial product in 1977 when we moved to Stanford (basically because of customer demand for better support and service and the need to finance it). Thus although the official name of the company was adopted in 1982, the actual start date was 1977."

[11] Visual Basic is a derivative peculiar to Microsoft Windows applications. The role of BASIC in the origin of Microsoft (and Bill Gates' rise to fame and fortune) is described by Campbell-Kelly [5, pp. 204–205].

[12] These originated in the work of the NATS Project (National Activity for Testing Software), sponsored by the National Science Foundation in the 1960's, and are precursors of BLAS (Basic Linear Algebra

collections of standard numerical analysis results, written in FORTRAN or in C, but have to be put together within still higher level programming languages in order to be useful to statisticians and econometricians. These subroutines are the building blocks of GAUSS and MATLAB, and many other still higher level packages for doing statistical and econometric calculations, such as, inter alia, SAS, TSP, and LIMDEP.[13]

PASCAL, after the French mathematician Blaise Pascal (1623–1662) was a programming language designed by Niklaus Wirth around 1970. PASCAL was designed for simplicity and for teaching programming in reaction to the complexity of ALGOL 68. It emphasizes structured programming constructs, data structures and strong typing. PASCAL has been extremely influential in programming language design and has a great number of variants and descendants.

The next major development in the evolution of computer languages was C, a programming language designed by Dennis Ritchie at AT&T Bell Labs ca. 1972 for systems programming on the PDP-11 and immediately implemented in the Unix operating system.[14] C++ is an updated version designed by Bjarne Stroustrup [42].[15]

Subprograms), a collection of high quality "building block" routines for performing basic vector and matrix operations. Level 1 BLAS do vector-vector operations, Level 2 BLAS do matrix-vector operations, and Level 3 BLAS do matrix-matrix operations. Because the BLAS are efficient, portable, and widely available, they're commonly used in the development of other high quality linear algebra software. Lawson, Kincaid, Krogh [26]. A modern version is LAPACK, which is written in Fortran77 and provides routines for solving systems of simultaneous linear equations, least-squares solutions of linear systems of equations, eigenvalue problems, and singular value problems. The associated matrix factorizations (LU, Cholesky, QR, SVD, Schur, generalized Schur) are also provided, as are related computations such as reordering of the Schur factorizations and estimating condition numbers. Dense and banded matrices are handled, but not general sparse matrices. In all areas, similar functionality is provided for real and complex matrices, in both single and double precision. http://www.netlib.org/lapack/index.html, accessed 06/17/03.

[13] According to Charles Renfro [34], LIMDEP began in 1974 at the University of Wisconsin as an implementation of a RAND Corporation report by M. Nerlove and S. J. Press on multivariate loglinear and logistic models for the analysis of categorical data. RATS was also launched about this time as well.

[14] Subsequently described in Kernighan and Ritchie [23].

[15] Opinions, however, are not uniformly laudatory. One critic describes C++ as "a huge, bloated, hack-ridden monster." C++ is a fairly complicated object-oriented language derived from C. The syntax of C++ is a lot like C, with various extensions and extra keywords needed to support classes, inheritance and other object-oriented features. C++ was originally developed as an extension to C, but quickly evolved into a separate language.
Object-oriented languages define not only the data type of a data structure, but also the types of operations (functions) that can be applied to the data structure. In this way, the data structure becomes an *object* that includes both data and functions. In addition, programmers can create relationships between one object and another. For example, objects can *inherit* characteristics from other objects. One of the principal advantages of object-oriented programming techniques over procedural programming techniques is that they enable programmers to create modules that do not need to be changed when a new type of object is added. A programmer can simply create a new object that inherits many of its features from existing objects. This makes object-oriented programs easier to modify.
The original object-oriented language, Smalltalk, was developed by Alan Kay in 1973. Modern variants include Java as well as C++, Dictionary of Programming Languages [12].

C is terse, low-level and permissive. Unix is written in C. Partly due to its distribution with Unix, C became immensely popular outside Bell Labs after about 1980 and is now the dominant language in systems and personal computer applications programming. It has grown popular because of its simplicity, efficiency, and flexibility. C programs are easily adapted to new environments. C has been acerbically described as "a language that combines all the elegance and power of assembly language with all the readability and maintainability of assembly language." A modern variant is C++, which has become since its introduction, the language of choice for many programming applications such as MATLAB and GAUSS.[16] Cribari-Neto [1999] recommends that all serious econometricians do at least some C or C++. My own view, is that it's not a bad idea to do at least some C++ programming because all of the third-level programming languages may be slow for repetitive calculations such as are common in bootstrapping or estimation by simulation.[17] On the other hand, in the last few years many of these third-level languages have been greatly improved with respect to speed and numerical accuracy, so that for many econometric purposes resort to C, C++, or FORTAN may no longer be necessary. Moreover, MATLAB, GAUSS, and MATHEMATICA now support the use of C and C++ for user extensions, that is C or C++ programs may be called directly from programs written in these three higher level languages.

Throughout the 1970's there was intensive development of "packages" of all sorts, especially for statistical and econometric analysis. In a recent paper, Charles Renfro [34] gives a thorough summary of these developments.[18] Many of these packages have since fallen by the wayside, but a large number still have their loyal adherents. As mentioned above, SAS and TSP among others were largely developed in this period. Graphics got off to a slow start during this period but gained momentum in the next decade with the development of Postscript by Adobe Systems in 1982, the release of the first version of WINDOWS (1984), and by the release of the Adobe Illustrator (1985) and Video Graphics Array in 1987. Improvements to FORTRAN (FORTRAN77), to PASCAL, and to BASIC (first introduced in 1964) were made during the 1970s. But the most momentous development, with the most far-reaching consequences, was the introduction of the first personal computers by Apple in 1977, followed closely first spreadsheet program, developed by Dan Bricklin, Dan Fylstra and Bob Frankston in 1978 and launched as VisiCalc in 1979, and by DOS (Disk Operating System), developed sometime before 1978. Spreadsheets and an easy to implement system for handling files turned the personal computer into a real tool

[16]These languages themselves are largely written in FORTRAN, C and C++.

[17]Speed comparisons do not bear out MATLAB's lack of speed in comparison to GAUSS; while MATLAB is slightly slower for many calculations, it is faster for some. The newest versions (6+) represent a significant improvement in this respect over the versions evaluated by Cribari-Neto [8], and by Küsters and Steffen [24a].

[18]In a paper also in this issue, Houston Stokes [40] describes his development of B34S which evolved from an LS regression package beginning in about 1968.

from what had been basically a toy.[19] Mention should also be made here of S, a high-level procedural language designed and used for statistics, numerical modeling, data analysis, and simulation, designed to provide powerful interactive statistics and data analysis. S was developed during the period 1974–1978 by a group which included R. A. Becker and John Chambers at what was then AT&T Bell Labs.[20]

The 1980s were a period of extremely rapid development and innovation. C++, mentioned already, was developed in this period by Bjarne Stroustrup [42]. In order to compete with Apple, IBM introduced its first PCs in 1981, and this development was followed the next year by numerous clones.[21] In the same year Osborne introduced the first truly portable PC,[22] i.e., Notebook, Microsoft released the first FORTRAN for DOS, and WordPerfect was first introduced. The following year, 1983, Microsoft WORD and Lotus 1-2-3 were released, followed in 1984 by EXCEL and WINDOWS 1.0 and the first networking software. In 1985, Adobe released Illustrator, and the Video Graphics Array (VGA) was introduced in 1987. Fast laser printers became common in the 1980s; color inkjet printers and MicroSoft PowerPoint were introduced in 1988. For the purposes of this essay, however, the most significant development of the 1980s was the almost simultaneous founding of the companies that market GAUSS, MAPLAB and MATHEMATICA: Aptech was

[19] Ceruzzi [7], Chapter 7, "The Personal Computer, 1972–1977, "pp. 207–242, especially pp. 236–237; Campbell-Kelly [5] "Early Development of the Personal Computer Software Industry, 1975–1983," pp. 201–230. The early history of DOS is somewhat convoluted: IBM had something called DOS for its mainframe computers before 1971, Ceruzzi [7]. The Altair 8800, manufactured by Micro Instrumentation Telemetry Systems (MITS), was not the first microprocessor-based computer, but it was enormously influential. It was sold in kit form to computer hobbyists. Its appearance, according to Ceruzzi, on the January 1975 cover of *Popular Science* is "perhaps the best-known event in the folk history of the personal computer. There were imitators of course, but more importantly there were bright "kids" like Bill Gates, Paul Allen and Gary Kildall who developed software for these machines. But the defining event was the launch of Apple II in April 1977. It was this machine for which Visicalc was created by Dan Bricklin, Dan Fylstra, and Bob Frankston and released in the fall of 1979. The "'electronic spreadsheet" it created transformed the perception of the PC as a hobbyist's dream to a serious business machine.

[20] The successor to AT&T Bell Labs, Lucent Technology has not maintained the language, but it is available commercially as S-PLUS and as a freeware version (http://www.r-project.org/). Both are very widely used today in statistics applications. There are several useful books: Venables and Ripley [44,45]; Dalgaard [10].

[21] Cringely [9] says that these clones were made possible by the technique of "reverse engineering" which IBM had used to produce a non-patent-infringing version of the Apple using components available off the shelf, but such a characterization appears nowhere else that I have been able to find. However, Kildall and IBM did develop a key element crucial to the wide-spread use of the PC, which was spread by "reverse engineering," the code they called BIOS (for Basic Input/Output System). This code, or modifications of it, permitted essentially the operating system to run on many different clones. (Ceruzzi [7, pp. 238–239].)

[22] There were antecedents, of course: IBM created a machine in 1975, the Model 5100, with a proprietary IBM cpu, which is sometimes described as the first portable, but it weighed about 50–60 pounds, so is questionably described as "portable. The Model 5100 incorporated in one piece all the parts, including the screen, the keyboard and the system unit. It is this one piece construction that suggests its portability. The Osborne 1, released in 1981, although it weighed in at 24 pounds, could be described as the first "Notebook."

founded by Sam Jones in 1983 and the first version of GAUSS was released in mid-1984. The MathWorks was founded by Jack Little and Cleve Moler in 1984 and the first version of MATLAB released that year. Although MAPLE was the product of a decade-long research project at the Department of Computer Science, University of Waterloo, Ontario and, later with the collaboration of a group at the Eidgen össische Technische Hochschule, Zürich, it was first released commercially in 1985. Stephen Wolfram founded Wolfram Research in 1987; the first version of MATHEMATICA was released in 1988. These programming languages are one step up from FORTRAN and C and make extensive use of the LINPACK, MINPACK and EISPAC, IMSL Libraries of Visual Numerics and the NAG Fortran Library Subroutines of the Numerical Analysis Group, first developed in the 1960s and discussed above. But, more importantly they are infinitely more flexible and powerful, than the statistical and econometric packages commonly in use. These languages have become the way to disseminate statistical and econometric research. Many mathematical, statistical, and econometric texts are now written making extensive use of one of these languages. The range and extent of these languages and packages, their differences and capabilities, are spelled out in some detail by the two papers by Renfro appearing in this issue.

It is interesting to speculate on the reasons for the efflorescence of languages and packages occurred in the 1980s why, in particular, "third-level" programming languages appeared almost simultaneously in the mid-1980s, followed then and through the 1990s by the development of a large number of econometric software packages. It seems to me that these developments are a classic case of Adam Smith's famous theorem that the division of labor is limited by the extent of the market, Stigler [38]. By the end of the 1970s, use of mainframe computers had become very expensive; for academic users at any rate; high priority and consequently rapid turn-around was virtually restricted to those supported by the AEC and Defense Department. The rest of us ran at low priority and usually at night. Because any original programs required, and still require, extensive debugging, many runs were usually required. While two or three runs might under the best of circumstances be possible at most university computer centers in the course of a night, only those with a low value of time were able to camp out at the computer center the requisite hours. It might take several weeks to debug even a relatively simple program. Such high time costs greatly reduced the incentive of many of us to learn programming skills and to do econometrics and statistics requiring more than extant statistical packages. The very success of packages like SAS and TSP, available at that time in mainframe versions, which do more or less everything but which produce huge volumes of output which have to be pored over, was more or less a response to the high value of time and high time costs of "doing one's own thing." But the development of the PC and the rapid evolution of both hard- and software technology for personal computers changed all this.[23] The dramatic fall in costs, both pecuniary and more importantly

[23]Of course, on-line use of mainframe computers through remote terminals had been possible since

time costs, greatly expanded the market for computation of all sorts and opened a niche for satisfying the demands of those who wanted to do "hands on" mathematics, econometrics and statistics, wanted more than the "hands off" computational power provided by packages such as SAS and TSP, but did not want to engage in "serious" programming by writing their own in C++ or FORTRAN. Successful packages did, of course, adapt to the PC in order to survive, but retain to this day more than vestiges of their origins. Perhaps this accounts for the roughly simultaneous appearance of the four programming languages considered above in the mid-1980s.

Finally to bring the story down to the present day, the decade of the 90s, just finished, has witnessed continued technological improvements in hardware: greatly increased storage capacity and accessibility and considerable increases in speed, but software development seems to have slowed as compare with the previous decade. Recently, however, the third-level languages, in particular, MATLAB, GAUSS, MAPLE and MATHEMATICA have begun to converge in capabilities. MATLAB and GAUSS have added symbolic manipulation capabilities, while MAPLE and MATHEMATICA have added enhanced numerical capacity and, more importantly, speed.[24] These languages in turn have spurred the development of many specialized packages by third-party programmers. The reader need only to consult the websites of the companies that provide these languages to discover the extent and variety of third-party applications. The major change through the nineties has been the explosive growth of the internet, the communit of users all sharing programs and tips, and the associated development of object-oriented programming languages such as JAVA (http://java.sun.com), which take full advantage of the network infrastructure provided by the internet.[25] The implications of the profound changes in the economic information structure which are taking place and are expected in the near future for the economics profession are explored in a recent paper by Bill Goffe and Bob Parks [20]. Of major significance in the present context is the availability, on line, of extensive machine-readable economic data bases and of programs and add-ons supporting all four of the third-level programming languages discussed.[26] Several journals, notably the *Journal of Applied Econometrics* and the *Journal of Economic*

---

virtually the beginning. TSP, for example, was further developed as part of an on-line system for data retrieval and analysis via telephone to what was then an advanced Borroughs computer at DRI headquarters in Lexington, Massachusetts. But these systems were far too slow for interactive "programming," which became attractive only with the advent of the stand alone and relatively cheap personal computer. Many of the econometric software packages in use today, began as mainframe packages later "ported" to PCs or Macs, but widespread use is much more recent.

[24]Many computations can be best done by first expressing the result one wants analytically and then evaluating the analytical result numerically for some specific values of the arguments. This convergence is surely an example of the Hotelling principle in which hot dog vendors competing on a finite beach with a uniformly distributed demand converge toward the center of the beach. Hotelling [22].

[25]Eliens [15]. C++ and FORTRAN90 both have some element of object-oriented programming, which basically assures portability independently of programming environment, Cary, et al. [6].

[26]A good source for accessing such resources is Bill Goffe's Resources for Economists on the Internet: http://wuecon.wustl.edu/cgi-bin/ufs/03/EconFAQ.html.

and Business Statistics have established data archives for all of the articles they now publish, making replication of results possible at long last.

Implicit in my account of the history of programming languages with particular relevance to econometric research is the idea that there is a continuum of languages, ranging at one extreme from machine and assembly language, through FORTRAN and C and the ISML and NAG libraries, through third-level languages such as GAUSS, MATLAB, MAPLE and MATHEMATICA, to software such as SAS, TSP or LIMDEP at the other extreme. There is another dimension as well, that is languages such as MAPLE and MATHEMATICA emphasize symbolic manipulation, GAUSS and MATLAB emphasize numerical calculation, although as indicated above they are converging. All four of these languages will do econometrics and statistics, but some will be more efficient for our purposes than others for reasons related to their location on this dimension of the spectrum. Specifically econometric software is generally designed for a limited range of tasks, although there has always been a tendency for the developers to expand this range and to incorporate more and more methods.

It is apparent that there has been a constant interplay between the development of programming languages and econometric software. In turn, the availability of ever more powerful software and more especially the increasing power and ease of accessibility of programming languages have enhanced the capacity of econometricians to write programs for the solution of specific problems. As the availability of a variety of data sets has increased, so has the range of econometric problems considered and methods developed. It would not be fair, however, to say that the development of programming languages has been influenced by econometric developments, but the opposite is surely true.

Appendix: Major dates in the history of programming languages

1946	ENIAC, first stored programmed machine
1950's	Assembly language programs
1957	FORTRAN
1958	ALGOL
1960	COBOL, LISP
1963–1964	BASIC
~1964	FORMAC
1964	PL/1, IBM introduces the 360
mid-1960's	EISPAC, LINPACK, MINPACK, FFTPACK, and later BLAS
1965–1968	Algol68
1968	SPSS, TSP, first volume of Donald Knuth, *The Art of Computer Programming*
1970	SAS
1971	PASCAL
1972	C
1973	Smalltalk, the first object-oriented programming language, developed by Alan Kay
1977	First micro computer introduced by Apple, FORTRAN77, Prolog, S
1978	First spreadsheet program, VisiCalc, TeX

~1978	DOS
1981–1982	IBM introduces the PC, Osborne introduces the first Notebook, FORTRAN for DOS
1982	Postscript
1983	WORD, Lotus 1-2-3
1984	EXCEL, WINDOWS 1.0, first networking software, GAUSS, MATLAB
1985	C++, Adobe Illustrator, MAPLE
1987	VGA (Video Graphics Array)
1988	MATHEMATICA
1990	FORTRAN90
1990's	The Internet, JAVA, etc., etc.

Sources:

- Encyclopedia of Computer Science, 4th Ed., Macmillan, London, 2000, Timeline of Computing, http://www.macmillanreference.co.uk/Science/ ComputerScienceTimeline1.htm, accessed 06/14/03.
- Dictionary of Programming Languages, 2000, http://cgibin.erols.com/ziring/cgi-bin/cep/cep.pl, accessed 06/14/03.

References

[1] J.W. Backus, *The Syntax and Semantics of the Proposed International Algebraic Language of the Zurich ACM-GRAMM Conference on Information Processing*, UNESCO Paris, June 1959, pp. 125–132.

[2] J.W. Backus, F.L. Bauer, J. Green, C. Katz, J. McCarthy, A.J. Perlis, H. Rutishauser, K. Samelson, B. Vauquois, J. H. Wegstein, A. van Wijngaarden, M. Woodger and P. Nauer, Revised report on the algorithm language ALGOL 60, *Communications of the ACM* **6** (January, 1963), 1–17.

[3] R. Baumann, M. Feliciano, F.L. Bauer and K. Samelson, *Introduction to ALGOL*, Prentice-Hall, Englewood Cliffs, 1964.

[4] T.J. Bergin and R.G. Gibson, eds, *History of Programming Languages – II*, Academic Press, New York, 1996.

[5] M. Campbell-Kelly, *From Airline Reservations to Sonic the Hedgehog: A History of the Software Industry*, MIT Press, Cambridge, 2003

[6] J.R. Cary, S.G. Shasharina, J.C. Cummings, J.V.W. Reynders and P.J. Hinker, Comparison of C++ and Fortran 90 for Object-Oriented Scientific Programming, Los Alamos National Laboratory, Report No. LA-UR-96-4064, 1996, *Computer Physics Communications* **105** (September, 1997), 20–36.

[7] P.E. Ceruzzi, *A History of Modern Computing*, 2nd Ed., MIT Press, Cambridge, 2003.

[8] F. Cribari-Neto, C for Econometricians, *Computational Economics* **14** (1999), 135–149.

[9] R.X. Cringely, *Accidental Empires,* Harper Information, New York, 1996.

[10] P. Dalgaard, *Introductory Statistics with R*, Springer, New York, 2002.

[11] M. Davis, *The Universal Computer: The Road from Leibnitz to Turing*, Norton, New York, 2000.

[12] Dictionary of Programming Languages, 2000, http://cgibin.erols.com/ziring/cgi-bin/cep/cep.pl, accessed 06/14/03.

[13] M. Eisner, TROLL/1 – an interactive computer system for econometric research, *Annals of Economic and Social Measurement* **1** (1972), 95–96.

[14] H. Eisenpress, *Forecasting by Generalized Regression Methods, Limited-Information Estimation Procedure IBM 704 Program IB LI*, International Business Machines Corporation, Data Systems Division, New York, 1959.

[15] A. Eliens, *Principles of Object Oriented-Software Development*, Addison-Wesley, Reading, MA, 1994.

[16] Encyclopædia Britannica, Computer Programming Language? Retrieved June 12, 2003, *from Encyclopædia Britannica Online*, http://www.search.eb.com/eb/article?eu=25460.

[17] W. Gibson and B. Sterling, *The Difference Engine*, Bantam Books, New York, 1992.
[18] W.K. Giloi, Konrad Zuse's Plankalkül: The First High-Level non von Neumann Programming Language, *IEEE Annals of the History of Computing* **19** (1997), 17–24.
[19] P. Graham, *The Roots of LISP,* http://www.paulgraham.com/rootsoflisp.html.
[20] W.L. Goffe and R.P. Parks, *The Future Information Infrastructure in Economics,* 1997, http://econwpa.wustl.edu/eprints/mic/papers/9704/9704001.
[21] T. Hopkins and B. Horan, *Smalltalk: An Introduction to Application Development Using VisualWorks*, Prentice Hall, 1995.
[22] H. Hotelling, Stability in Competition, *The Economic Journal* **39** (1929), 41–57.
[23] B.W. Kernighan and D.M. Ritchie, *The C Programming Language*, Prentice-Hall, Englewood Cliffs, NJ, 1978, 2nd Ed., 1988.
[24] D. Knuth, *Art of Computer Programming*, Addison-Wesley, Reading, MA, *Vol. 1, Fundamental Algorithm, 1968; Vol. 2, Seminumerical Algorithms, 1969; Vol. 3, Sorting and Searching, 1973*; projected to run to seven volumes.
[25] U. Küsters, Matrix Programming Languages for Statistical Computing: A Comparison of GAUSS, MATLAB, and Ox, with Jens Peter Steffen, in: *SoftStat'97*, F. Faulbaum and W. Bandilla, eds, Lucius & Lucius, Stuttgart, 1997.
[26] C.R. Lawson, D.K. Hanson and F. Krogh, Basic Linear Algebra Subprograms for Fortran Usage, *ACM Transactions on Mathematical Software* **5** (1979), 308–325.
[27] J.W. Longley, An Appraisal of Least Squares Programs for the Electronic Computer from the Point of View of the User, *Journal of the American Statistical Association* **62** (1967), 819–841.
[28] J. McCarthy, *An Algebraic Language for the Manipulation of Symbolic Expressions*, MIT AI Lab, AI Memo No. 1, Cambridge, September, 1958.
[29] J. McCarthy, Recursive Functions of Symbolic Expressions and Their Computation by Machine, *Communications of the ACM* **3** (1960), 184–195.
[30] P. Naur, J.W. Backus, F.L. Bauer, J. Green, C. Katz, J. McCarthy, A.J. Perlis, H. Rutishauer, K. Samelson, B. Vauquois, J.H. Wegstein, A. van Wijngaarden and M. Woodger, Revised Report on the Algorithmic Language ALGOL 60, *Communications of the ACM* **6**(1) (1963), 1–17.
[31] M. Nerlove and S.J. Press, *Univariate and Multivariate Log-Linear and Logistic Models*), RAND Corporation R-1306-EDA/NIH, RAND Corporation, Santa Monica, 1973.
[32] T.W. Pratt and M.V. Zelkowitz, *Programming Languages: Design and Implementation*, 4th Ed., Prentice-Hall, Upper Saddle River, NJ, 2001.
[33] C.G. Renfro, Econometric software: The first fifty years in perspective, *Journal of Economic and Social Measurement* **29** (2004), 9–107, this volume.
[34] C.G. Renfro, A compendium of existing econometric software packages, *Journal of Economic and Social Measurement* **29** (2004), 359–409, this volume.
[35] D. Ritchie, *The C++ Programming Language*, Addison-Wesley, Reading, MA, 1986.
[36] J.E. Sammet and R.E. Bond, Introduction to FORMAC, *IEEE Transactions on Electronic Computers* **EC-13**(4) (August, 1964), 386–394.
[37] R. Sebesta, *Concepts of Programming Languages*, Addison Wesley Publishing Company, 1996.
[38] G.J. Stigler, The Division of Labor Is Limited by the Extent of the Market, *Journal of Political Economy* **59** (1951), 185–193.
[39] S.M. Stigler, *Statistics on the Table: The History of Statistical Concepts and Methods*, Harvard University Press, Cambridge, 1999.
[40] H.H. Stokes, The evolution of econometric software design: A developer's view, *Journal of Economic and Social Measurement* **29** (2004), 205–259, this volume.
[41] H. Stoyan, *Early LISP History (1956–1959)*, http://www8.informatik.uni-erlangen.de/html/lisp/histlit1.html, accessed 1 September 2003.
[42] B. Stroustrup, *The C++ Programming Language*, Addison-Wesley, Reading, MA, 1986.
[43] A. Stroud, *The Multiple Regression Program RGR*, Social Systems Research Institute, University of Wisconsin, Madison, WI, 1961.
[44] W.N. Venables and B.D. Ripley, *S Programming*, Springer, New York, 2000.

[45] W.N. Venables and B.D. Ripley, *Modern Applied Statistics with S-Plus*, 3rd Ed., Springer, New York, 1999.
[46] R.L. Wexelblat, ed., *History of Programming Languages*, Academic Press, New York, 1981.
[47] A. Zellner, A. Stroud and L.C. Chau, *Program for Computing Seemingly Unrelated Regressions Estimate*, Department of Economics, Social Systems Research Institute, Madison, WI, 1963.
[48] A. Zellner, A. Stroud and L.C. Chau, *Program for Computing Two and Three Stage Least Squares and Associated Statistics*, Department of Economics, Social Systems Research Institute, Madison, WI, 1963.
[49] K. Zuse, Der Plankalkül, *Gesellschaft für Mathematik und Datenverarbeitung* **63** (1972), BMBW-GMD 63.

Journal of Economic and Social Measurement 29 (2004) 205–259
IOS Press

The evolution of econometric software design: A developer's view

Houston H. Stokes
Department of Economics, College of Business Administration, University of Illinois at Chicago, 601 South Morgan Street, Room 2103, Chicago, IL 60607-7121, USA
E-mail: hhstokes@uic.edu

In the last 30 years, changes in operating systems, computer hardware, compiler technology and the needs of research in applied econometrics have all influenced econometric software development and the environment of statistical computing. The evolution of various representative software systems, including B34S® developed by the author, are used to illustrate differences in software design and the interrelation of a number of factors that influenced these choices. A list of desired econometric software features, software design goals and econometric programming language characteristics are suggested. It is stressed that there is no one "ideal" software system that will work effectively in all situations. System integration of statistical software provides a means by which capability can be leveraged.

1. Introduction

1.1. Overview

The development of modern econometric software has been influenced by the changing needs of applied econometric research, the expanding capability of computer hardware (CPU speed, disk storage and memory), changes in the design and capability of compilers, and the availability of high-quality subroutine libraries. Software design in turn has itself impacted applied econometric research, which has seen its horizons expand rapidly in the last 30 years as new techniques of analysis became computationally possible. How some of these interrelationships have evolved over time is illustrated by a discussion of the evolution of the design and capability of the B34S® Software system [55] which is contrasted to a selection of other software systems.

The goal of the present paper is to discuss, from the perspective of a developer, statistical software development as a design issue with emphasis on some of the historical reasons why there have been changes over time. Depending on the end user's application, quite different software systems designs are appropriate. Common to all well founded econometric software systems are the attributes of accuracy, speed, flexibility and extendibility. The main points of this paper are illustrated by using examples from a small subset of econometric software consisting of B34S ®, GAUSS, LIMDEP, MATLAB, RATS, SAS®, SCA, SPEAKEASY, SPSS®, and TSP whose

0747-9662/04/$17.00

design will be contrasted.[1] To set the stage for a more detailed discussion of the issues, a brief discussion of the historic and modern software environment is presented. The main body of the paper consists of a discussion of the effects of changes in hardware and proprietary operating systems on software, the impact of differences in software design, the evolution of software and a discussion of the advantages of procedure driven and programming language based systems. Software implementation issues are discussed and as well as the issue of developer recognition. Finally a number of recommendations for the future are considered.

Other pertinent contributions in this topic area are those by Bodkin [6] and Renfro [51], who provide an overview of the development of econometric software generally, and Bodklin, Klein and Marwah [5], who provide a history of macroeconometric modeling. The development of other individual software systems is the focus of recent papers by Hendry and Doornik [23] and Renfro [48].[2]

1.2. A brief look at historic software characteristics

As a general phenomenon, software controls the operation of a computer. The overall control is exercised by a particular example of software known as the *operating system*, a fundamental characteristic of which is that it directly controls access to

[1]Cohen-Pieper [11] documents the SPEAKEASY system which was developed for physics applications, but has been extended to have a number of econometric strengths. SPEAKEASY is a programming language that was developed in the late 1960s that contains numerous user extended commands. MATLAB is documented in numerous manuals, such as [22] and [34], which discusses the capabilities of the basic system as of version 6.0. MATLAB has strengths in optimization and programming. Most MATLAB commands are actually scripts that can be inspected and modified by the user. GAUSS, another programming language, is documented in Edlefson-Jones [14] and has been quite widely used as an econometric development language, especially in time series. B34S, documented in Stokes [55], has a long history going back to the 1960s, and has strengths both as a traditional procedure-driven (to be defined later) programming system and a programming language. RATS, which is documented in Doan [12], is a widely used time series package with programming capability. RATS has strengths in maximum likelihood estimation and other nonlinear applications, especially in time series. RATS has some programming capability but is not a true programming language, such as MATLAB and GAUSS. SAS [3], SPSS [45] and TSP [21] are procedure-driven programming systems that date back to the 1970s or earlier. Programming capability has been added in later years. SCA [32] and LIMDEP [19] represent more specialized software systems with strengths in time series and limited dependent variable problems, respectively. These systems have more limited programming capability but are rich in preprogrammed procedures.

[2]The Hendry-Doornik [23] paper contains a discussion of the evolution of the PcGive system as it progressed from a card-input driven program to a modern software system with a GUI (Graphical User Interface). While PcGive is primarily an estimation program, MODLER, which is discussed in the more detailed paper by Renfro [48], is a large-scale model estimation and simulation system. Both these systems have had a long history, with the history of MODLER going back to the 1960s. In contrast with these excellent papers, the present paper looks more at hardware and compiler developments and how they affect software design. Bodkin, Klein and Marwah [5] traces the history of Macroeconometric Model building. More detail is provided in Bodkin [6], which looks at the history of large-scale modeling starting with a discussion of calculation techniques such as the "Doolittle method" in the pre-computer period. Renfro [49] discusses estimation issues common to all software systems while Renfro [51] provides an overview of the current state of econometric software with emphasis on much of the history.

the machine's resources, including the hardware. The modern computer consists of specific hardware components. These include the Central Processing Unit (the CPU), various types of storage media, for either temporary or permanent storage of data, and a variety of peripherals, at minimum video monitors and printers. It can be argued that the operating system is the consciousness of the machine and that modern machines are more aware than earlier ones. Early computers had rudimentary operating systems at best. In contrast a modern PC operating system (such as Windows /XP, Unix/Linux or Mac OS/X) provides a wide range of services to software running on the system and is relatively immune from being "crashed" or brought down by an applications program. Applications programs, such as econometric software packages, word processing packages, and even Internet browsers, perform their work by interacting with the operating system, which permits or denies that program the capability to invoke the execution of some particular action.

Over the years there have been significant changes in both operating systems and applications programs. While modern software can be classified in various ways, such as whether the program runs from a Graphic User Interface (GUI) interface or whether it runs from a *script* or sequence of commands written in accordance with a specific grammar, this has not always been the case. In the 1960's the typical econometric program used 80 column input cards that were prepared on keypunch machines and fed into a card reader that read 600 cards per minute, at least in the absence of a card jam. Statistical software, which was usually written in Fortran II, was first *compiled* (translated) into an *object* deck, which was punched on cards. Inasmuch as it was then not possible to save a program as an *executable file* on disk, every time a job ran the user had to input both the *object decks* (which had to be *linked* into the program) and the *control file*, which instructed the program to make the desired calculation. Without a video terminal to allow the user to see what was being submitted, and just a keypunch to prepare the cards, great care was needed to set up a run, since the commands that controlled the execution of the program were often merely numbers in specific card columns. In that era CPU use was expensive, turn around time was measured in hours, or even days, and users spent a great deal of time in preparing and waiting for their runs. The *operating system* available was rudimentary or non-existent and provided little in the way of support to the developer.

In contrast, in the modern computer hardware (CPU, memory etc) is managed by a complex operating system (MVS, CMS, VM, Unix, Linux, Windows 2000 etc). On top of this control layer, the *applications program* (SAS, SPSS, MATLAB etc) runs under control of the user. Depending on the sophistication of the applications software developer, the resulting program can make a variety of system calls to obtain resources from the operating system.[3] A relatively stable operating system such as

[3]On Windows, for example, an API (Applications programming Interface) call allows the developer to open windows and perform other operating system specific tasks. On Unix other types of calls are needed. Such customization of software to an operating system inhibits portability, a theme that will be discussed later but allows added capability to be standardized for that platform.

Windows XP, is less likely to be brought down (crashed) by an applications program, although this is still possible. An example shows how far we have come: In the 1960's at the University of Chicago, users were warned not to place the Fortran statement `stop` in their programs since it would physically stop the entire mainframe machine. Users were told to use instead the command `call exit`, which would call in turn a customized termination program and thus would protect the operating system. In contrast, no matter how the applications program is written and whatever it may try to do, the operating system controls the limits of its own operation.

A similar evolution has occurred in the case of applications programs, and in particular econometric software packages. One particular example is B34S, which was originally created by Thornber [57–59] and has been developed since 1972 by Stokes [55]. B34S, in common with almost all other packages in 1960–1970 and even as late as 1980, was initially developed simply to implement basic econometric techniques such as OLS, generalized least squares and rudimentary residual analysis, as described by Renfro [49]. At that time, both hardware limitations and the column dependent input control language impeded the implementation of more advanced features. Furthermore, many researchers in that era, conditioned by their experience with mechanical calculators, tended to see software as just a faster way to do what had been done in a prior period by hand. The fact that computers were scarce and costly and of low power, even at major universities, precluded much of the experimentation with more advanced techniques.[4] But as years passed research needs changed, hardware improved and costs fell. The statistical capability of the B34S software system expanded and its design was enhanced.[5] The many influences that stimulated these changes will be considered as this paper proceeds.

1.3. Characteristics of computing in the modern environment

In contrast to the past, when the applications program interface simply took the form of punched cards with commands represented by rectangular holes in fixed columns, the most immediately obvious aspect of modern software is that it has true interface characteristics; that is, the user and the software mutually interact in any (or all) of a variety of ways. These forms of interaction can range from the modern Graphical User Interface (GUI) whereby using a visual system of often overlapping windows, the user conducts a dialogue with the software, to an interactive command line interface, as was particularly typical of the PC operating in the DOS environment

---

[4] Renfro [51] documents the vast increase in computing power that has occurred and provides a number of interesting historical examples of what it was like to perform econometric analysis in these early days

[5] Table 1 shows the changing features of Econometric Software over time. The needs of purely statistical software are not treated, although there is some overlay with econometric software. It can be argued that although SAS contains econometric capability, the original focus of the software was statistical. Table 4, which is discussed in Section 2, shows the econometric capability of B34S in different periods and the source of the code base.

Table 1
Changing features of representative econometric software

Pre-operating System Period (1960s to early 1970s)

- Software driven by scripts that required column dependent codes.
- Premium placed on saving memory results in data saved in files, not in memory.
- Variance covariance matrix saved between regression steps to save CPU time.
- Problems in precision across platforms limits portability.
- Quality utility subroutine libraries not generally available.
- Most applied econometric researchers forced to write their own Fortran code.
- SPEAKEASY a 4th generation object oriented programming language was developed to supplement Fortran.

Rise of Programming Languages for Procedure Software (1970s – early 1980s)

- C programming language developed and used to port Unix to various platforms. Programs becoming more portable. Specific hardware less a factor in software availability. CPU costs falling.
- TSP, SAS and SPSS and other software developed using "higher" level languages.
- EISPACK, LINPACK, FFTPACK, IMSL and NAG high-quality utility libraries developed.
- Applied researchers increasingly rely on packages, not custom Fortran applications.
- SAS, SPEAKEASY and other systems designed with dynamic links to commands that were separate programs. Users encouraged to extend these systems, since dangers of strange "bugs" in other commands being introduced were reduced.
- MATLAB developed to facilitate use of LINPACK.
- GAUSS developed to exploit the 8088/8087 chip on IBM PC/XT.

Major Software Systems Develop Extensive Programming Capability (1980s -)

- Cutting edge research begins to be distributed in the form of GAUSS, MATLAB and other programming languages where the end user can follow the calculation.
- Windows? spurs the development of point-and-click GUIs. Old programs retrofit to new "standard" with varying success.
- Workstations running Unix and PCs free users from stranglehold of mainframe computer centers.
- Most software runs from either point and click (Excel) or scripts (SAS). Some software uses GUI to write scripts hidden from the user. A number of systems allow running from a GUI or from a script.
- Menu-building commands allowed in some systems such as SAS, RATS, MATLAB and B34S, allow user customization of the GUI. System integrators increasingly utilize these features.
- Optimization subroutines that allow users to customize model specification spur applied econometric research that was formerly trapped in packages. Users can see and modify the calculation. Calculation less a "black box."

during the 1980s and early 1990s, to batch operation, whereby a program is controlled using a command, or script, file containing a series of commands that are executed sequentially by the program without further human interaction during that phase. Batch operation is of course most akin to the original method of program control of yesteryear, except that the punched cards have been replaced by a command script file, a subtle yet crucial distinction.

In fact, each of these types of interface remains a valid, and even modern, form of program control. On the face of it, the dominant interface today is the Graphical user interface. However, what you see is not always what you get. Often a GUI program is not actually controlled by this interface: in many cases, underneath the "point-and-click" visual interface, the program can be quietly building a script of some sort and it is the execution of this script that actually causes the program's operations to be performed. Alternatively, even in cases that the software is run from a *script* (being commands in a file that follow a distinct grammar), this script can be, and often is, submitted from an interactive window.[6] What makes this mixture of interface modes particularly modern is that while the program may turn a friendly GUI face to the user, behind the scenes the ability to operate it using scripts provides additional power. For example, script commands can either call other commands from a list of procedures or can even form a programming language that might allow the user to customize the calculation or extend the capability of the basic system.

Other aspects of modern software that are similarly behind-the-scenes include the way in which programs manage data, as well as their particular "number crunching" algorithms. Of these two, this last aspect is the most evident, in large part because most software systems are described by the functions they perform. Thus even the most casual user will be aware that whereas many econometric systems such as RATS and LIMDEP are relatively specialized in terms of econometric scope, general systems such as SAS and SPSS provide a wide variety of capability. Nonetheless, hidden from the average user are many major design differences. Program descriptions characteristically list their functional options in a way that emphases the implied correspondence between these operations and their textbook descriptions. But the user generally has no way of knowing precisely the degree to which the operations performed are actually those advertised. It is uncommon for developers to publsh details of the actual algorithms used, so that the user normally must accept on faith that the developer is a competent programmer.

Other aspects of the design of the numerical processing component of modern software will be discussed in more detail later. But it is worth noting here that an important, related change during the past 30 to 40 years has been development of subroutine libraries that make available to developers a variety of number crunching facilities, such as nonlinear constrained and unconstrained optimization and nonlinear least squares routines. The availability of high quality subroutine libraries such as LAPACK [1], LINPACK [13], EISPACK [53] and IMSL [46] provide the modern developer with ready-made software development tools, with the result that it is no longer necessary to create software packages entirely from scratch.

Similarly, the way in which programs manage data is for the most part hidden from the user, yet changes in the management of data have been an important area of program development during the past 30 years. Due to memory limitations, systems developed in the early period such as SAS, B34S and SPSS saved data in files and brought in variables as needed for a calculation. Programs developed later, such as RATS and MATLAB, were designed to load all data in memory, in common with such well known mass market packages as Excel and Lotus 1-2-3. Various data base management aspects of program design have been recently considered by Renfro [50],

[6]Examples of what a *script* means and how this differs from a *macro* will be discussed later. Examples of both these terms are given in the glossary. Rats, SAS and B34S represent windows interface examples where scripts are submitted from a window environment. Excel is a counter example.

who discusses in detail the optimum characteristics of a database system and how developments in this important area have affected a number of software systems. But the issue is not just how programs manage data internally, but also the provisions that are made for data input and output, the transfer of data between programs, as well as the entry of new observations or the revision of existing ones. SAS is an example of a software package that has characteristically supported a substantial number of input formats, many geared to the corporate world. Similarly, although it does not support nearly the same range of data input formats, RATS is an example of a package that currently contains options to read important third party data formats, such as the NBER format. It also provides it's own portable database format, which has in turn been incorporated into other packages, such as B34S.

In some cases, programs have been designed not just to read particular data transfer formats, such as the NBER or Lotus Printfile format, but also to organize their data in keeping with standards established by third party data vendors, such as Data Resources or Wharton Econometric Forecasting Associates. For example, in the 1970's B34S was modified to read a Wharton style data base, which took the form of a random access file, a format that allows individual data series to be extracted. This type of data organization is particularly suitable for data bases that contain a large number of data series, numbering in the tens or hundreds of thousands, or even millions. It is to be noted that the RATS portable format is not random access and is not suitable for large numbers of series.

Mass market packages have also directly affected the design of statistical software packages, both because of their prevalence and because these packages sometimes store data in a useful way. In particular, due to the needs of the market, in the late 1990's most software systems were modified to read Excel files, which were both widely understood and allowed users to visually modify the data. However, Excel has its limitations, including the restriction to a maximum of 256 data columns and 65536 rows. Consequently, software systems such as the SAS FSP product and the B34S data viewer were developed to look at and/or modify data points in files that contained more that 65536 observations, the upper limit of Excel. It may well be that the increasing use of Excel as an input format during the past ten years is a step backwards, for not only does it have size limitations, but it also offers few of the desired database characteristics considered by Renfro [50]. In the context of data base documentation is haphazard at best and data base management in this environment does not provide an audit trail of the way the data has been constructed. In contrast, if there was an agreed upon database structure along the lines suggested by Renfro [50] software systems could be modified to save and retrieve data and its documentation in an agreed upon format. In time, such data base issues may be resolved with the new XML format that is under development.

1.4. Procedure driven systems vs. programming languages

The several types of modern interfaces have been briefly described and the point has been made that the interface the user sees is not always indicative of the way in which the program actually operates. In fact, at present, the Graphical User Interface itself is not of particular interest, and the reason is that the specific way in which the user communicates with the program can be divorced from actual program control, as mentioned earlier. The focus here will be specifically upon aspects of program control, rather than the design of an optimal human interface. Program control can be considered by focusing upon command scripts, without any loss of generality, inasmuch as such scripts can be produced either using a text processor, or as a result of the program operator selecting from the objects that populate a graphical user interface, be they menu items or icons, or by typing responses as text into dialog boxes.

The scripts that run a modern software system fall into two basic types: procedure driven systems and programming language based systems. Procedure-driven systems use sequences of commands based on a syntax or grammar to perform a specific task. For example, the SAS commands

```
PROC REG;
MODEL Y = X1 X2 X3;
RUN;
```

run a regression of Y on X1, X2 and X3, using the procedure (PROC) called REG, which obviously performs regressions. In contrast to such a procedure driven system, a software system containing a *programming language*, such as MATLAB, allows the user to customize and control operations at a more detailed level. In the days when most software systems were procedure-driven, if particular techniques were not available, research was limited unless a custom Fortran or C program was written by the researcher. A software system that offers a programming language by its very design does not limit experimentation with alternative statistical techniques. Furthermore, in many language-based software systems the programming language is close to the form of the underlying mathematics, reducing the learning curve. Using a programming language the user of course has complete control over how the calculation is done. For example, the OLS coefficient vector estimated more or less automatically in the SAS REG procedure can be calculated specifically in MATLAB as

```
beta = inv (x'x)*x'*y;
```

provided of course that x contains X1, X2, X3 and the constant and y contains Y, the left hand side variable. The above example, although it may not represent current "best practice," also illustrates the difference in level of knowledge needed to use a procedure-driven system compared to that required to run a programming language based system.[7] By using a procedure-based system the user relies on the developer

[7]It should be noted that McCullough and Vinod [36, 648] and others suggest that the QR or SVD approach is a much superior way to estimate an OLS model. Judd [28,58,59] contrasts the advantages of the QR approach, the LU factorization and the Cholesky factorization, which is more stable than the LU factorization.

to select the very best approach to a given calculation. In contrast, when a language based system is used, it is up to the research to know what specific algorithm to use, implying as well that that given users may select the wrong technique for their problem.

1.5. Data handling and script processing

Typically programming languages load data into named storage or workspace, although file reading during the calculation is possible. As indicated earlier, while legacy procedure-driven systems read data from files, many modern systems such as RATS load data directly into memory. Because it has been designed to handle massive datasets, SAS continues to maintain datasets in files although it allows the procedures to copy selected variables into the workspace. B34S has been designed in a similar way. The actual differences implied may also depend upon the specific operation: while many procedures run from files and do not require workspace to save the data file in workspace, other commands such as the matrix command typically load all data into workspace or named storage.

Similarly, it was noted that many software systems that appear to have a GUI are actually writing a script that is later run. While most scripts are parsed (translated) or interpreted at run time, many advanced software systems actually provide the ability to compile (translate into machine code) the script into an executable file. The IBM MVS implementation of the SAS data step in the 1970's was an example of this later capability. MATLAB currently provides a way to convert its programming language commands to C++ code that can be compiled into a stand alone program. Software designed to compile a user written script into an executable or program increases the speed of execution at the expense of complexity.

These comments are intended to emphasize that what a software system does may very much depend upon context, and therefore that it is not always possible to characterize one system as doing one thing and another as doing something else. But the point of course is to identify the various modes of operation.

1.6. An overview of software design features

A number of influences have impacted the development of procedure-based econometric software systems and programming language base systems. Consider again the software systems GAUSS, MATLAB, SPEAKEASY, B34S, LIMDEP, RATS, SAS, SCA, SPSS, and TSP. While the first three systems are primarily programming languages, the last seven are procedure-based although they are also general-purpose software systems that contain various degrees of programming capability. B34S and SAS, for example, have procedures **matrix** and **iml** that provide an extensive programming language along the lines of GAUSS, MATLAB and SPEAKEASY. The rest of B34S and SAS is procedure-driven. Other systems, such as RATS and LIMDEP, integrate a more limited programming capability inside essentially a procedure-driven software system.[8] The difference between systems is to some degree a matter of degree: while calculations can be programmed, the means by which this is done is not always by using a full-fledged programming-based language along the lines of MATLAB. The power and extendibility of these systems is enhanced to a large degree by the programming capability available that allows manipulation of the output of the built-in procedures.

Of course, the fact that language based systems require the user to not just choose between operations, but also to specify the precise operations performed raises the obvious question, how do these system differ from standard programming languages like Fortran or C? The answer is that while SPEAKEASY, MATLAB and GAUSS are programming languages, they also provide a somewhat more user-friendly context, limiting the programming required to specific types of operations: their object orientation and availability of specialized commands, among other things, makes them substantially easier to use than Fortran and C. In a sense, these (as they are called) 4th generation languages, actually themselves embody data and program control procedures for the purpose of simplifying other computer operations, while leaving open for the user the choice of programming statistical and other research oriented operations. In contrast, Fortran and C impose the requirement that the person doing the programming needs to program each and every operation, at all levels of program operation.

The distinction between true programming languages, 4th generation programming languages and procedure based systems is thus essentially the degree of programming required of the user. At the same time, to the degree the user is willing to program, the more control he or she has over the specific results obtained. In past years, there was also the consideration that careful programming, from the ground up, could make a fundamental difference in speed of execution. However, today, with faster CPU's, the advantage of a program written in a language such as Fortran or C that compiles into a executable file and executes quickly, is offset by the reduction in time and training needed to write an essentially self documenting application in a 4th generation language. The design issues raised by these alternative approaches are discussed further below and throughout the paper.

Table 1 outlines how the features in econometric software have changed over time. These changes are discussed from the point of reference of the author's experience as the developer of the B34S Software System whose evolution in capability is shown in Table 4.[9] It is argued that these changes have been driven by:

---

[8] Sections 5.1 and 5.2 discuss the distinction between programming capability and a programming language in more detail and provide examples.

[9] In the spirit of Renfro [48,49], the present paper looks at design issues in the development of statistical software and explores how these have changed over time. The present paper extends Renfro [49] by providing more detail on the effect of compiler (Fortran and C) and operating system changes on econometric software. Since many of their users are econometricians, for the purposes of this paper GAUSS, SPEAKEASY and MATLAB are considered to be econometric/statistical software systems.

- Changes in hardware (CPU speed, memory).
- Changes in operating systems (rise of portable operating systems, such as Unix).
- Changes in platforms (mainframe to work station to PC, text-based to graphics screen).
- Changing needs of applied econometric research.

We first turn to a brief discussion of the effects of changes in hardware and operating systems.

2. The effects of changes in hardware and proprietary operating systems on B34S

2.1. Historical notes on the development of B34S in the pre-operating system period

The history of the development of B34S, whose evolution of capability is shown in Table 4, can be used to illustrate the effect of changes in hardware on software design. The modern B34S program began to take shape at the University of Chicago (U of C) in the 1960s. In 1966 B34T, which had been developed from the BIMED34 program by Hodson Thornber [57–59], was released. Thornber had added Bayesian capability, BLUS residuals and generally improved the operation of the BIMED34 program. B34T later became B34S in 1972, when Stokes undertook development. The computing environment was primitive and very limited by modern standards. [10] Since econometric software from the 1960s relied on numbers in specific columns to control what features were used, it was very hard to use and debug. In this era software was severely limited by hardware and compiler capability. Not being able to store the compiled program on disk was a major problem.

2.2. IBM mainframe operating system development and its impact

The evolution of the IBM mainframe operating system impacted the development time line of number of software systems including B34S. As noted, in 1972 Stokes began B34S development work, using the 3000 lines of Fortran II code in B34T as a basis. Table 4 shows when features were added. Portability problems involved in moving the source to the Fortran IV standard on an IBM 360/50 included: removing

[10] In the 1960's the U of C used the 7040/7094 "Operating System," which consisted of linking together two computers: an IBM 7040 to input and print jobs and an IBM 7094 to run jobs. There was no disk storage available. For every run, the user had to input an object deck (which had been compiled from Fortran) on cards, *link* the program with the Fortran II run time library to form a *load module* or *executable program* and try to run a job that had been punched on 80-column cards. There were usually numerous problems reading the cards, especially in damp weather when things expanded. The U of Chicago computer center staff modified the existing IBM Fortran II compiler and made important contributions to the IBM Fortran Run Time library.

nonstandard Fortran II code,[11] replacing a BAL (basic assembler language) routine used for eigenvalue calculations with EISPACK routines (**tred2**, **imtql2**) and converting the program to double precision.[12] Prior to that time the program had been written in single precision except for source lines with a "D" in column 1 that were calculated in double precision under the Fortran II standard.

The IBM 360 series machines were a major step forward in a number of important ways. They were *scalable* (could be made bigger without changes in software having to be made), and *optimizing compilers* such as Fortran H were made available that both increased speed of execution and, more important, encouraged developers to code for speed. Poorly written code either ran slowly or incorrectly due to compiler-generated code movement [43]. The next generation and upwardly compatible IBM 370 series machines had *virtual memory*, where *paging* (the operating system moving blocks of memory to disk during run time) allowed the operating system to simulate more memory than was available. Prior to the development of virtual memory operating system software, developers had to program code movement in from the disk in stages as the program ran. With the advent of virtual memory, such *overlays* were now replaced by operating system-initiated overlays, or paging. In those days IBM had two major operating systems. The IBM MVS operating system was optimized for batch processing while the CMS operating system was optimized for time-sharing use. While the development of virtual memory obviated the use of overlays, a developer with code that jumped around in the address space would still suffer a speed loss as the operating system paged in and out sections of code. Programming skills that optimized design around overlays or potential page breaks was still an important, although neglected, skill. Subroutine libraries, such as LINPACK [13] and EISPACK [53], were developed to minimize paging and provide high accuracy and were a major step forward.

In 1982, before the PC market had stabilized into its Apple and Intel-compatible camps, IBM ported its time-sharing operating system CMS to a card in the original PC. The author saw the full CMS SAS running on an IBM PC/XT at the SAS Users Group International (SUGI). Before long IBM marketing killed this "innovation" that they regarded as a threat to mainframe profit margins. The history of computing might have been quite different had IBM allowed the 360 instruction set to be run on a PC board, or possibly on a PC. In hindsight it is probably a good thing that this

[11] The University of Chicago had modified the Fortran compiler to accept RIT and WIT for READ INPUT TAPE and WRITE INPUT TAPE, respectively. Such nonstandard modifications hurt portability of code.

[12] EISPACK, a library of Eigenvalue routines developed at Argonne National Laboratory, was one of the first high-quality public domain Fortran libraries [53]. EISPACK was followed later by LINPACK for linear algebra [13], BLAS for basic linear algebra calculations and FFTPACK for FFT calculations. In the 1990s LAPACK [1] combined the functions of EISPACK and LINPACK for super computers and made use of block algorithms to increased speed on large problems. These routines found their way into the commercial IMSL [46] and NAG libraries in various forms and made possible the development of quality software.

did not happen since the current Intel chips meet the IEEE [26] accuracy standard, while the 360 series chips, which are less accurate, did not. In 1982 the IBM VS Fortran Compiler was far superior to anything available on the PC. Only later did the PC compilers catch up and exceed the performance of the mainframe compilers of those days. The current IBM RS/6000 workstation chips are far superior to the 360/370/390 chips for numerical calculations, both in speed and accuracy. By 2000 most econometric work was done on IEEE standard-conforming chips rather than the older 360 series chips. IEEE standard- conforming chips are found in Intel PCs, and Unix machines such as Sun, IBM RS/6000, HP and others.

2.3. Dynamic linking and its influence on the development of software sytems

In the early 1970s two dominant software systems, SAS and SPSS, chose different hardware-driven development paths that had major long-run effects. While SAS chose the dynamic linking model, SPSS stuck with a more traditional design. SPSS was written in Fortran and *statically linked* so that it could more easily be ported to run on many hardware systems. There was one executable that contained all the procedures in SPSS, The SPSS manual of that era outlined how the software could be extended by *relinking* SPSS with the new commands. There was a detailed discussion of how key program variables were passed between the Fortran subroutines using *named commons* that had to be placed in user routines. Nie, Hull, Jenkins, Steinbrenner and Brent [45, pp. 631–660] discuss the structure of the SPSS program in some detail. Using this documentation Philip Burns at the University of Illinois at Chicago (UIC) added variable lagging, though such changes were very dangerous. With new code being linked into SPSS, it was easy to create subtle bugs that could unexpectedly compromise accuracy in apparently unrelated commands.

In contrast to SPSS, SAS was written in PL/1 and had been developed to run on IBM hardware using the MVS operating system. The SAS design, shared and influenced by the SPEAKEASY design that had been developed in the 1960s at Argonne National Laboratory, involved a base system that made dynamic links to commands that were each separately compiled programs. For example, unless you called the SAS procedure **spectra**, there was no way that a possible bug in **spectra** could have any effect on another command in SAS since the **spectra** command was not a part of the base SAS executable in any way. This was not true for a statically linked program such as SPSS. In fact, with a statically linked program even changes made by the software developers in one procedure ran the risk of causing other unexpected changes. Every time a change was made, all commands in the system had to be exhaustively tested. The SAS design only required a massive testing when the base executable was changed. The more complex a software system, the greater the advantage of the SAS design.[13]

---

[13]The danger of introducing a bug into statically liked software can be reduced by design changes. If

Both SAS and SPEAKEASY encouraged users to develop *procedures* (or in SPEAKEASY terms: *linkules*) that are separate programs. SPEAKEASY was extended at the Federal Reserve, which added FEDEASY to provide econometric capability. All the SPEAKEASY linkules had a common calling sequence that allowed the user to access and create variables in the SPEAKASY named storage or workspace. Users, who met once a year in Chicago at the annual conference, added many other commands. A printed proceedings was distributed each year. Stokes implemented over 40 commands in SPEAKEASY to allow use of the Fortran libraries LINPACK and FFTPACK. These contributions were accepted by the SPEAKEASY developers and later became part of the base product.

SAS did not have a named storage like SPEAKEASY, except within the **iml** procedure, but did support multiple datasets at the same time. A user-written SAS procedure could access datasets and create datasets. Given the SAS design, it was easy to add capability. These user-contributed procedures were documented in a special SAS manual distributed by the parent corporation. Many later found their way into the base SAS product. In the late 1970s and early 1980s there was rapid expansion of the SAS system from the user community. The new user additions were discussed in the annual (SUGU) Conference where the papers describing these advances were circulated.

During this period B34S had a dynamic link capability that allowed specification of a nonlinear model in a user Fortran program. At run time the user's Fortran program was called by the base system. Here the dynamic link was used to pass back a computed vector of residuals, given a vector of parameters and data passed in. Unlike the SPEAKEASY and SAS dynamic links, the B34S dynamic link required no specific library to be used. Stokes [55, Chapter 11] further documents this feature. The **model** subroutine listed next illustrates how a 2 and 3 factor CES production function might be coded in Fortran in that period.

```
      subroutine model(nprob,th,f,nob,np,x,nvar,nobs1)
      implicit real*8(a-h,o-z)
      dimension th(np),f(nob),x(nob,nvar)
c
c     set up for ces production function
c     nprob = 1  **** a 2 factor model without time
```

the various sections of a software system are all driven by subroutines and there is limited or no use of named common, the risk of inducing bugs can be lowered, however there is always unexpected problems, even in a system with no named common. In the early 1970's at UIC when removing the banner page in TSP to save print costs, we discovered that the order of listing routines in the overlay structure was the difference between TSP running certain procedures or not. This subtle bug appears to have been due to one routine accidentally being over written by another during execution. This example in no way is meant to denigrate TSP, an excellent system. It is used only to illustrate the perils of field modifications of a statically linked system. It should be noted that the risks go up exponentially the more developers working on a system.

```
c       nprob=2 -- a 3 factor model
c
        if(nprob.eq.2)go to 100
c
        do i=1,nob
        th222=1.0d+00 - th(1)
        f(i)=((th(1)*(x(i,1)**th(4)))+(th222*(x(i,2)**th(4))))**
        (th(3)/
       *th(4))*th(2)
        enddo
c
        go to 99
c
    100 do i=1,nob
        th333=1.0d+00 -th(1)-th(2)
        f(i)=((th(1)*(x(i,1)**th(4)))+(th(2)*(x(i,2)**th(4))) +
       * (th333*(x(i,3)**th(4)))  )**(th(5)/th(4) )*th(3)
        enddo
     99 return
        end
```

In the current B34S **matrix** command, the user Fortran routine has been replaced with a user program written in the B34S programming language. The complete setup for a CES estimation now is

```
b34sexec matrix;
call loaddata;
* Sinai-Stokes RES Data ---  Nonlinear Models ;

program res72;
yhat=a*(g1*k**r+g2*l**r+(1.0 g1-g2)*(m1/p)**r)**(v/r);
/$ Optional statements to monitor solution
call outstring(3,3,'Coefficients');
call outstring(3,4,'g1 g2 v r');
call outdouble(34,4,g1);
call outdouble(50,4,g2);
call outdouble(34,5,v);
call outdouble(50,5,r);
return;
end;

call echooff;
call nllsq(q,yhat :name res72 :parms g1 g2 a r v
```

```
              :maxit 50 :flam 1. :flu 10. :eps2 .004
              :ivalue array(:.27698 .7754 1.,-.05 1.8)
                   :print result residuals);
b34srun;
```

Here the B34S **matrix** program **res72** specifies the model. The optional calls to **outstring** and **outdouble** allow the user to monitor the convergence process by writing to the screen at a column and row under control of the user. The call to *nllsq* passed in the names for which in this problem are called q and yhat and the name of the matrix program that contains the model (**res72**). In the B34S implementation the nllsq command is a compiled Fortran program that at run time calls the B34S **matrix** program **res72**. The only speed loss is the parse of the model program. If the optional calls were not used, the user program would be:

```
program res72;
yhat=a*(g1*k**r+g2*l**r+(1.0-g1-g2)*(m1/p)**r)**(v/r);
return;
end;
```

which is substantially less complex that the Fortran it replaced. Since **res72** is a program, not a subroutine, the variables are taken from the workspace and do not have to be supplied in the call. The optional call to **echooff** turns off listing of the commands as they execute. This could be removed if debug information was needed.[14]

The dynamic link in SPEAKEASY, SAS and B34S serves the same function as a DLL (dynamic link library) on a modern Windows NT/95/98/2000/XP platform, except that the calling sequences were fixed. By having the calling sequence fixed, the user did not have to know anything about the design of the calling program, which could change without having to change the users program. Utility routines were supplied by SAS and SPEAKEASY that could be called within the users external program to enhance its use. Recently MATLAB has carried this design a step further. The MATLAB program is extended by either *.m files, which are scripts of written MATLAB commands, or *.mex files which are compiled programs rather like a SPEAKEASY Linkule. What is unique about the current MATLAB design is the release of a toolkit that allows a series of MATLAB commands in a script to be automatically translated into C/C++ and then automatically compiled into a

[14]The above two examples contrast implementation of a nonlinear model using a dynamic link to a compiled Fortran problem with a “link” to a B34S **matrix** command subroutine. Note that in both cases the code to actually estimate the model is a compiled Fortran program. MATLAB, GAUSS and other systems use an alternative strategy that codes the nonlinear estimation routines in their language. The advantage of having 100the calculation “exposed” in routines is that is documents the calculation, the disadvantage is the parse overhead of interpreting rather that compiling the nonlinear estimation routine each time it is run.

*.mex file. Such a design allows the user to develop high performance additions to MATLAB without having to master C/C++. This new capability represents a major advance.

The importance of dynamic links to software design cannot be over emphasized. With this capability, software can be enhanced without fear of unexpected bugs in other procedures. Second, a dynamic link capability allows many users to all work independently. Third, in the case of nonlinear estimation, a dynamic link substantially speeded up modeling, since the model was compiled into a load module and executed instead of having to be interpreted during estimation. Given the hardware limitations at the time, speed of the calculation was most important. Now with more powerful hardware, it is not so important to compile the specification of the model to be estimated. In the Windows world, while the closest equivalent to the dynamic link is the DLL, the OLE (object linking and embedding) capability is an alternative way to link programs. Hendry and Doornik [23] discuss these alternative approaches in some detail. In their view, the advantages of OLE are that the modules run in their own address space, the modules can use remote procedure calls, and the modules can be used as stand-alone programs. Against these advantages, the disadvantages they stress are: loss of speed, the need to transfer all data and the major limitation that OLE links are one way only. DLL links run in their own address space, which is mapped to the main process, provide two-way communication and run substantially faster than an OLE link but cannot run stand- alone. To give the non-technical reader an idea of what is happening, Microsoft Word® communicates with Microsoft Excel® via OLE links. Both programs can run stand-alone. The Windows operating system itself uses many DLLs to dynamically share with other programs many of its functions. Hendry and Doornik do not mention that the design of the DLL and OLE link capability is specific to the Microsoft Windows platform and is not in the C and Fortran language standards. It would be good to have a platform-independent way to implement a dynamic link that would be integrated into the major programming languages in a standard way. If such a standard were developed, it would make software integration much easier. Further issues regarding dynamic linking are discussed later.

The decision to develop a software system, with or without a dynamic link, appears to be market driven. SPSS targeted a variety of platforms and adopted a design that would allow a 100% Fortran implementation to facilitate portability at minimal expense. Having user additions was not a priority. In the 1970s and early 1980s SAS was confined to IBM mainframe machines due to the PL/1 implementation of the system. SAS developers added the dynamic link using a custom software interface. With the rise of Unix, SAS had to migrate its system to other platforms. With version 6.xx of SAS, the complete system was rewritten in C, which made it possible to port to a variety of machines, including most Unix platforms. SAS had a large staff and had to develop their own C compiler to make the move. Even after these changes, ports were expensive. At the SAS users group meeting in the 80's, a SAS VP stated that their costs for a port to a new system, such as the DEC Alpha Unix machine, were in the area of $1,000,000. Once SAS became widely available, SPSS stagnated as a development platform for cutting edge econometric research but continued to be a production workhorse. Due to cost differences and markets, there appears to be room for both types of systems. In the next section some hardware-driven design issues are discussed.

2.4. Hardware changes impact programming style

The IBM 370 series architecture created a *virtual machine* and represented an advance in design over the 360 series machines that allocated physical memory to running programs. This hardware change required the software developer to change focus in a number of ways. With the 370 series machines, the operating system made the paging decision. The software engineer now had to anticipate what the operating system might do and, wherever possible, design code to avoid paging. Poorly designed programs **trashed** or excessively paged and ran very slowly. The key to avoiding **trashing was**, wherever possible, to confine calculations to addresses near each other. Since Fortran saves a matrix by rows, going across a row was more costly than going down a column since with a large matrix you were more likely to go over a page boundary and get your job swapped out of the system.

On large IBM systems, multiple operating systems could run on the same machine. The VM operating system ran on top and controlled the other operating systems. MVS (designed for batch jobs) and CMS (designed for time-share jobs), and at times IBM Unix (AIX) could be run under VM. Flexibility had arrived at the cost of some operating system overhead.[15]

The advent of these virtual machines required changes in programming. By the middle and late 1970s programmers began to use the Basic Linear Algebra Subroutine Library (BLAS) and many other tools that would help a program stay in the CPU by avoiding going over a page boundary. A program that stays in the CPU forces other executing programs to wait their turn and thus completes more quickly.[16] Many researchers did not understand these issues but by calling utility subroutines for linear algebra from high quality libraries they were protected in some sense.

[15]This technology is now on the PC. In 2001 the developer of B34S used PC VM software to run both Windows 2000 and Linux at the same time on a PC. After booting Windows 2K as the operating system the program VM is started that in turn loads Linux. The same PC has two IP addresses and is in effect two machines. External users can be logging into the Linux side of the machine while on the Windows side the local user is doing normal PC tasks.

[16]The BLAS was a major advance. BLAS routines are used in LINPACK and LAPACK to speed up low-level calculations. While Fortran versions of the BLAS are available, many vendors provide custom libraries for the BLAS that exploit special features of the hardware. These special libraries can be linked into user programs. The BLAS is such an important development that the IMSL library includes these routines and maintains their calling sequences [13]. The LAPACK guide [1] preface traces the importance of level 2 and 3 BLAS on LAPACK routine performance.

2.5. Dynamic memory allocation and its effect on software design

Dynamic memory allocation allows a properly written software system to expand to handle ever-larger problems without having to be re-linked. In the 1970s on IBM equipment, B34S used a modification of the Harwell routine **iao1as** to dynamically allocate memory at an address pointing to *subpool zero*. Subpool zero was maintained by the operating system for scratch space at a location in memory outside the program. There were a number of advantages of this design. First, the working storage of the program could be expanded to meet a particular problem. Second, by having only one work array whose pointers were managed inside the program rather than having many fixed dimension arrays, it was possible for the software designer to keep the address of arrays used at the same time near each other and thus avoid a page break. Finally, with this design, there was no way that the execution code could be overwritten by a work data array, since the address of the work array was outside the address space of the load module. With larger memory allowed and dynamic memory allocation, software could now be written to allow large datasets to be kept in memory without increasing the load module size for all users. Many software systems that had kept the data in scratch files were redesigned. Since the Fortran 77 standard did not allow dynamic memory management, dynamic memory allocation required custom assembler routines that were not portable and had a habit of having to be modified as hardware changed.

Wherever possible, internally B34S used fully packed adjustable arrays. Assume a program needs an array of size 1000 as an upper limit but usually the space used is much less, say 30. If the array is fixed at 1000, there is a great deal of unused space. By tightly packing all data arrays into one large array with address pointers passed to the calculation routines, space use is optimized as well as paging being reduced since the arrays being used are closer together. Dynamic memory management required existing routines to be rewritten to take advantage of this design. An alternative to using fully packed arrays is to have the software developer allocate arrays equal to the maximum size allowed for the software. Most user applications were usually run with problems that used way under this upper limit. Since the arrays were never fully packed, often as the problem got bigger the code would unexpectedly fail if there was a hidden error in the way an array was used. If the array had been packed tightly, the logic of the program would have been tested for any size. The above discussion suggests that taking advantage of dynamic memory management allows software to handle bigger problems, run faster and be more bug-free than the older fixed design that had many fixed dimension arrays. By Fortran 1990, memory allocation was in the standard, as it had been with C. Prior to Fortran 1990, many PC compiler vendors, such as Lahey, had implemented extensions to allow for memory management that anticipated the Fortran 90 convention.

In a programming language the management of *named storage* is most important for both efficiency and accuracy reasons. Named storage saves all the active variables, all the temporary variables and all the programs being executed. Named storage in

B34S is a one dimensional array where, as the **matrix** command executes, various utility routines allocate space for objects, release space no longer being used and, where necessary, compress the work space to remove unused space. In such an environment there is the danger that an undetected bug or error in the program logic will modify an object in named storage and this change will go unnoticed. To try to reduce this possibility, B34S, like many other systems, binds a *header* and *footer* to the storage of each object. The footer duplicates information in the header. If a bug were to overwrite an array, it would be likely that the header or footer would be damaged and the next time a command tried to access that object, it would be easily detected as the header and footer were tested and found not to match. The longer a command runs, the more likely a problem will be detected using this design.

2.6. The development of C and its impact on unix and software development

In 1978 Kernighan and Ritchie [30] developed C and published *The C Programming Language*. From their forward, "C was designed for and implemented on the Unix Operating System on the DEC PDP-11 by Dennis Ritchie." The goal was to have a portable operating system that would be able to run on any hardware. This was a revolutionary idea. C was an improvement to B, which had been written by Thompson at Bell Laboratories to port the early Unix to the PDP-11. Since Unix was as close to being truly portable as was possible, it was a major break with the past and was not welcomed by IBM and other vendors who wanted to protect their user base by maintaining barriers to a user moving to another vender. In the end Unix, a portable operating system, made substantial inroads into markets formerly the preserve of proprietary operating systems. Prior to this date, operating systems were written in assembler language and could not be moved. The development of Unix by its very design promoted competetition, with the result that hardware prices were driven down at a faster rate. Software written in C or in Fortran calling C libraries was portable, yet could do operating system tasks, such as open windows, that were not possible in the Fortran language.

2.7. Linux, OpenBSD and the rise of the open source movement from its unix roots

Among the many strengths of Unix was its design and implementation in C which facilitated portability and extendibility. Unix was released to the software community and was extended in university settings, especially at the University of California, Berkeley and at MIT which developed X-Windows and other important additions. In the beginning AT&T had given away the code for Unix. As Unix became more commercial, there was pressure for a new and better "university Unix." In 1991 Linus Torvalds, at the University of Helsinki, developed Linux, a "free" Unix. The days of the 1970s began again. Linux runs on Intel, Sun and DEC ALPHA, all types of IBM and many other machines. More ports are planned. IBM has announced it will support both its own operating systems and Linux on all platforms. Sun has made similar claims.[17] As of 2001, hardware vendors were trying to maintain their installed base against the falling of CPU prices and expanding of CPU power on PCs. By that time Linux had become very stable, was fast and had become a formidable competitor to Microsoft Windows 95/98/NT/2000/XP. Linux seems to have replaced the early Microsoft Unix flavor XENIX and won many converts. BSD Unix became OpenBSD and attracted a loyal following, becoming the basis for Apple OS X, which from all reports is substantially more stable than the prior Apple operating system. For many Mac users the Apple supplied GUI was all that they needed or wanted to know, yet they welcomed the added stability provided by the Unix base of the operating system.

Linux is at the heart of the *Copy Left Software Movement.* The only restriction on any user is that the source of any advancement must be freely distributed. This is like the National Science Foundation (NSF) requirement that all source code developed under a grant be freely distributed. What is driving the Linux movement is the Worldwide web, which allows software to be fixed and distributed at close to zero cost. The "high priests" of the Linux movement have the right to add any good changes to the Linux distribution. The whole thing is very like economic research in which good ideas become part of the accepted theory and bad ideas are dropped. By 2003 due to its reduced cost and availability on powerful Intel CPU's, Linux had seriously eroded Unix as the platform of choice for econometric computing.

2.8. Fortran compilers and the evolution of the fortran language and libraries

An essential tool for software development is the availability of a reliable and stable compiler. The early Fortran compilers only compiled the source. Optimization was for the future. The IBM 360 Fortran level G had a limited debug facility, but retained a terrible run-time diagnostic procedure. If a program failed with a *traceback*, or operating system generated diagnostic printout, the user had to subtract two hex numbers to determine where in the code the program stopped. A modern Fortran compiler such as Lahey LF95, in contrast, will give a line number in the source where execution failed. Powerful debug tools are also available. In the early 1970s the IBM Fortran H compiler compiled Fortran source slower than the level G compiler, but produced faster execution code. Users soon found that accuracy could change depending on the degree of optimization. The reason was that the optimizing compilers kept values in registers where there was more accuracy, while the compilers that did not optimize the calculation copied each value to memory as it was calculated. Software developers began to write to the compiler but had to take care that their software continued to run correctly as a result of optimization. The software developer could now program to take advantage of the new compiler

[17] Free BSD (Berkeley Standard Distribution), which was developed from the old Berkeley Unix code base, still is running but has been overshadowed for the most part by Linux, which is technically more advanced and appears to have more momentum in the market as of early 2001.

technology. The developers of EISPACK [53] found that under some situations, one routine ran faster than another on one machine but the reverse was found on another machine.[18] These differences were traced to hardware differences between models in the IBM 360 family. During this period, the B34S code was developed to run at the highest level of optimization possible. A Fortran *optimizing compiler* will move blocks of invariant code backwards to speed the calculation and use other techniques. Metcalf [43] provides an excellent discussion of this issue from the compiler and from the user perspective. If such *code movement* was found to cause a problem, the B34S code was redesigned to avoid this problem. The goal of the developer of B34S was accuracy and speed, in that order. B34S was designed to make use of the BLAS for utility tasks, such as array copies and inner products etc.

The IBM Fortran H-extended compiler was a still further improvement over the older Fortran H and was a mainstay for professional programmers in the IBM world for many years. Stan Cohen and the SPEAKEASY development team optimized the SPEAKEASY linkule facility to minimize on space. The linkules were all precompiled programs on their own and were dynamically loaded when they were called from an executing SPEAKEASY program. In Cohen's view it was wasteful to link in the Fortran run-time functions, such as **dsin** and **dcos**, into each linkule. SPEAKEASY developed their own stub replacements for most of the IBM run-time library. The stub call to the replacement library allowed the linkule to reach back into the SPEAKEASY processor to execute the processor version of **dsin**, not the linkule version (which was only a stub that facilitated the link with the processor copy). This design was a clever way to save on precious disk space.

Trouble arose when IBM developed the vector versions of the VS series of compilers, where they made many run-time calls entry points. While the IBM VS Fortran compiler was developed to exploit the IBM vector facility, the changed design prevented SPEAKEASY from reaching back into the processor to access run-time routines because of multiple subroutines with the same name being found at the link step. This bit of computer history illustrates an example of unintended consequences of compiler design changes. As discussed earlier, the B34S dynamic link facility for nonlinear model building was very fast but did not rely on reaching back into the processor. The user had to write a small Fortran subroutine with fixed arguments that calculated the residual vector based on the values of the parameters at that time. The advantage of the dynamic call in B34S was that the user could express a nonlinear model in Fortran and not pay the parse overhead that would have slowed the solution on the machines of those days. The fact that the model subroutine was compiled into

[18] Smith, Boyle, Dongarra, Garbow, Ikebe, Klema and Moler [53] Table 30 on page 156, reports that the speed of reducing a 40 by 40 matrix from full to real symmetric tridiagonal form with **tred2** and **tred3** was 1.9 to 1.5, respectively, on the CDC 6400 at Northwestern University. The same problem on the Univac 1110 at the University of Wisconsin listed in Table 42 on page 168 gives the relative speeds as 1.9 to 2.0. Hence, it can be said that on this machine, in contrast with the CDC, **tred3** is slower! Many more such cases have been documented.

a stand-alone program meant that the user avoided having to relink the B34S every time a model had to be changed.[19] The assembler routine that provided this "magic" worked well for over 15 years. Using this design, the B34S processor and the dynamically called program were able to share the same output file. Suddenly, with the VS compiler, IBM disabled this capability. The B34S dynamically linked routine could no longer produce output on the calling program output file using standard Fortran I/O routines. Since the dynamically linked program was designed to express a model and not produce output, this sudden loss of capability was not fatal. These few examples show how a hardware vender can make a change that will adversely impact a software developer who has been pushing the envelope with regards to software development. This problem can now be avoided to some extent since Fortran, C and C++ and been extended to have more built-in capability and some of the operating system related tasks can be handled by the large number of portable libraries such as IMSL [46] and Interacter [62] which are now available. In the Windows world many programs use Visual Basic as a menu builder. While Microsoft as of 2001 promises that Visual Basic will be portable across other platforms using the .NET technology, as of now this capability has not been released except in beta form.

2.9. *Issues regarding the vectorization of programs*

In order to increase speed of execution without a faster CPU, in the 70's and 80's many vendors such as IBM made available *vector facilities* that were part of a CPU on a mainframe and allowed parallel execution of instructions. The problem was that most if not all the of the code base then run on such machines had not be designed with this in mind. However with IBM VS Fortran, it was possible to have the compiler produce code that was *vectorized* and would run faster on a *vector facility*. A *vector facility* is actually a large number of added numerical CPUs linked to one CPU and controlled under a mask. A mask controls whether or not one of the added CPUs is to do a calculation. Assume a user has two vectors of data and wishes to add these vectors to form a third vector. In a *serial* machine, each calculation is done at a time and the result saved in the output vector. In a vector facility with 256 processors, up to 256 elements of the two input vectors are loaded and calculated at the same time. If all elements are to be added, a mask is set to turn on each of the vector CPUs. At UIC we had an IBM 3090 with 4 CPUs, each linked with its own 256 vector facility. In theory, if one were to add two columns of a matrix with the number of elements a multiple of 256, there could be a speed up of 256 times. The speed up would be drastically less if two rows of the same Fortran matrix were added because the

[19] MODELEASY++, an extension of SPEAKEASY first developed at the Federal Reserve, carried this a step further. The large-scale model code, specified in a high-level language, was automatically translated to Fortran, compiled, linked and made available to the system without the user quite realizing what had happened. This design resulted in a substantial increase in speed of model solution without requiring the user to know Fortran. The tradeoff was underlying software complexity and portability.

elements added were not stored in memory contiguously and the vector facility mask had to turn off many adds. In theory, with a 256 by 256 matrix, an add between two rows to be placed in another row would not speed up at all if done on such a vector machine.

In the 1980s B34S made use of IBM custom libraries of BLAS routines (ESSL) that were designed for the CMS vector machine. In B34S these libraries replaced the compiled versions of BLAS routines. To study what could be achieved in a vector facility, using code that had been optimized for a *scalar* or one CPU machine, IBM requested that it be allowed to inspect the B34S code and see if it could be optimized further. The test case involved estimation of a large VARMA model. J. P. Fasano at IBM was able to speed up the solution five times. This impressive gain was offset by the fact that Fasano had optimized the source specifically for exactly that size test case and that the five-fold speed up was not scalable up or down without source changes. A big part of the gain was the IBM ESSL library of tuned BLAS routines that exploited the IBM vector facility. The ESSL library was able to detect whether it was running on a 128 vector, a 256 vector or a 512 vector and make the appropriate changes. At UIC the CMS B34S linked in the ESSL BLAS routines for speed gains throughout the package, but these were not of the order of a five times speed-up. The downside was that this B34S load module would not run on those CMS systems that did not have a vector facility.

The B34S vector facility test problem became an IBM benchmark for changes to the hardware, the compilers, the linker and the ESSL library. J. P. Fasano and the IBM team attended the SPEAKEASY conference for a number of years and discussed their Fortran optimization experience. On a number of occasions, Fasano and others had found that the B34S test problem had slowed unexpectedly, although no code changes had been made, with the exception of a recompile and a relink. On these occasions, the speed loss was traced to design problems in proposed "improvements" to the ESSL library, the Fortran compiler or the Fortran run time library, that were soon corrected by IBM before they were released. The project leader of the ESSL team also attended the annual SPEAKEASY conferences and expressed his willingness to make ESSL run on more than just IBM equipment. ESSL was designed so this was in fact possible. Making ESSL portable apparently was turned down by marketing at IBM. Except for the BLAS ESSL implementation that used open source argument lists, the rest of ESSL used calling sequences and names that were unique to ESSL. This apparently marketing-driven decision was designed to "trap" users into staying on IBM 370 or RS/6000 platforms by making their source not portable without changes. The ESSL routines were complex to use and replacing them would not have been easy. The developer of B34S avoided this problem by staying with LINPACK, EISPACK and FFTPACK, which were in the public domain and of very high quality, and only used the vectorized BLAS from ESSL which had the open source calling sequence.

Software design at the smallest level in the university and at the biggest computer vender in the world consists of one person making small changes and making run after run to test timing and accuracy. At IBM the procedure to test for speed is to make at least five to ten runs with every test problem on a machine with no other jobs running and keep detailed timing records. It is essential to have many test problems to continue to benchmark the system. The developer of B34S has followed the same pattern. B34S is supplied with over 600,000 lines of test datasets and test problems. All procedures and **matrix** commands have running examples. Since B34S can call other systems, it is easy to test other systems on the same problems and many of the test problems do just this.

Testing of software is important for a number of reasons. First, it is imperative that the results be accurate. Second, speed is also of major interest. In the past, since most users were running canned procedures, there were limited things that could be done to improve performance. On MVS and CMS, it was possible to optimize the block sizes of the scratch files, depending on the hardware characteristics of the hard drives used. For years, to test accuracy knowledgeable software developers have used various test datasets, such as Longley [33]. Recently, the Statistical and Engineering Division of the National Institute of Technology (NIST) has collected a library of datasets for which they have "known" answers. The file stattest.mac, which is distributed with B34S, has test setups for all the linear and nonlinear problems. In many cases these jobs call RATS to provide a comparison. While there is increased interest in software testing, starting with Longley [33], much of the literature on the subject, for various reasons, does not identify which software had the problem. A modern example is the paper by McCullough and Vinod [36], which tests a number of software systems but in footnote 2 remarks, "We have elected not to identify software packages by name for two reasons. First, we regard published software reviews as a more suitable vehicle for providing full and fair assessments of individual packages. Second, some developers are remarkably quick to respond to reports of errors." It might be useful if we could tell which software and which version had the problem, although I see their point. With regard to FIML, the above paper reports quite different answers obtained by three researchers. While the software they used is not identified, interested readers can test their systems against what was found.

In the late 1990s, with the increasing use of programmable systems, such as MATLAB and GAUSS, the testing of user-written procedures has become more important. A poorly coded MATLAB M file runs very slowly. Users were forced to confront programming design issues that would impact speed. Due to the fact that the eigenvalue and inversion routines in most programming languages such as MATLAB were well designed, accuracy issues were less of a problem unless the user failed to properly scale the problem. There can be a downside from doing research using programming languages rather that procedure-driven systems. A novice user can make subtle and often not so subtle errors that invalidate the research. A common error is for the novice to attempt to code inversion and eigenvalue routines based on theory and ignore the advances that are available in LAPACK [1] and LINPACK [13]. Using a procedure-driven system of high quality, the researcher is protected by the skill of the developer of the software. Despite some restriction on capability, the user is more assured that the calculation is correct. The above suggests that both types of systems will continue to be needed.

2.10. The impact of Lahey Fortran compilers on porting fortran programs to the PC

Early research on the PC was hampered by both the technical limitations of the machine and the poor Fortran compilers that were available. This all changed with the Lahey F77EM32 compiler that used Phar-Lap technology to place 386-class PC machines in "protected mode" so that direct addressing of a large memory space was possible. Tom Lahey, who led the team that developed the compiler, was a long-time member of the Fortran technical committee that set the Fortran standards. His compilers had advanced features, such as pointers, dynamic memory allocation and other design enhancements, that were beyond the Fortran 77 standard. Lahey compilers were fast, had good diagnostics and could compile large subroutines. The Lahey LF90 compiler, which replaced the F77EM32 compiler, generated intermediate code that was fed into the Intel "crawler." The crawler would take the intermediate code and optimize the object deck for the target chip. Substantial speed gains were realized over the now dated F77EM32 compiler.

In 1998 Lahey teamed up with Fujitsu to produce the LF95 compiler. Speed gains of up to five times have been achieved on some types of problems over what was obtained with the LF90 compiler. In the summer of 1999, Lahey distributed the LF95 Linux compiler. Programs built on Linux appear to run up to 18% faster than the same program built with the LF95 compiler running under Windows 98. With PCs now containing larger CPUs and thus running faster than many workstations, econometric research has new tools with which to build software. The large reductions in cost of such systems, especially when spread over large numbers of users, should stimulate interest in heavily numerically intensive research projects.

3. Econometric software design differences and their impact

3.1. A brief look at the historical evolution of econometric software

Greene's [20] discussion of software provides an outline of some of the major software systems. What follows is a discussion of the basis of some of the design changes that have occurred and how they directly or indirectly impact the user. Some of these changes are summarized in Table 1. The discussion, while making no attempt to be complete, is intended to contrast software designs with specific reference to various systems for illustration purposes.

Early econometric programs required the user to code in specific columns. While fast to parse, this design made for many hard-to-trace user errors. TSP [21] was one of the first general-purpose software systems to have a more natural programming language. SPSS [45] was another early system that had a more limited programming front end, but became immediately popular with the user base because of ease of use.

As discussed earlier, SPSS [45] was built in Fortran and all commands were statically linked into the executable for reasons of portability. This design did not allow for easy extension of the system since any new command could potentially introduce a bug that would cause unexpected problems with another command. For the SPSS user base, this disadvantage was out weighed by the ease of use of SPSS and its availability on many platforms in addition to IBM.

SAS [3] was built at North Carolina State in the 1970s. As discussed earlier, SAS was designed to run with a dynamic link to each procedure or PROC, which was a distinct program. The SAS design allowed many users to add to the system. No user had to know what the other was doing. Unless a PROC was called, it could never negatively impact the system. John Stall, one of the SAS developers, had worked with and knew about SPEAKEASY, which had a similar design. The SAS **data** step on IBM actually wrote object code on the fly to increase execution speed. The SAS **data** step instructions were not interpreted during execution. The initial SAS system design was truly a work of art but it was not portable. A SAS PROC is similar in capability with what the Windows 95/98/NT/2000 world now calls a DLL except for the fact that the PROC had a common interface with the base SAS program. To provide the user with the ability to program calculations that were not available in the distributed commands, SAS developed PROC **matrix**, which became PROC **iml** in later releases of SAS. PROC **iml** was a programming language within a procedure-driven software system. Econometric systems, such as LIMDEP, B34S, RATS, like SAS, added programming capability to what were originally procedure-driven systems. MATLAB, GAUSS and SPEAKEASY, in contrast, started out as programming languages and over time added specialized commands that could be programmed. While providing the advantage of allowing user contributions, the disadvantage of the SAS/SPEAKEASY/MATLAB design is the greater complexity of the system and the size of the install in terms of files.

In the 1980s, SAS developed the *macro facility*, a programming language on top of the basic SAS language. This was a great advance forward since SAS programs could automatically write their own SAS code at execution time. The macro facility allowed users to customize their applications without writing source code. B34S has such a facility modeled after the SAS implementation but modified for use in calling and writing the command structure of other systems as well as B34S. A simple example of the B34S macro facility is the code fragment that defines a B34S macro **print** that when run will generate executable code:

```
%b34smacro print;
  %b34sdo i=&start,&end;
    b34sexec list ibegin=%b34seval(&i) ; b34seend;
  %b34senddo;
%b34smend;
```

The macro call command

```
%b34smcall print(start=1 end=4);
```

results in the following B34S code being generated at execution time.

```
b34sexec list ibegin=1 ; b34seend;
b34sexec list ibegin=2 ; b34seend;
b34sexec list ibegin=3 ; b34seend;
b34sexec list ibegin=4 ; b34seend;
```

as the B34S LET variable &i takes the values 1, 2, 3 and 4. This small example gives the flavor of a macro language or a language on top of a lower command language. In order to have a macro language facility, the software parser has to be able to suspend execution of the sequential statements and expand all macro statements (that begin with `%b34s`) before resuming execution of the program. This mode of operation is contrasted with a more traditional program that executes one line at a time. With the advent of the SAS **macro** facility, the **cb34s** SAS **proc** that passed data from SAS to B34S was replaced by a platform-independent SAS MACRO **cb34sm** that performed the same role.

Macro languages in systems such as SAS and B34S are of interest to expert programmers who want to develop production systems. Most users are content to produce lines of commands, saved in a script, that are sequentially executed. Such users typically call macros from the library and obtain the advantage of these advances without having to code them directly. Many users are not aware of the availability of the macro facility.

3.2. Interfacing with specialized econometric software

High-quality, more specialized programs, such as SCA (Liu), RATS (Doan) and LIMDEP (Greene), were developed in the areas of time series and limited dependent variables to fulfill a growing research need. The B34S was modified to branch to these excellent and more specialized systems, which became in effect B34S subroutines since they were called from under a running B34S program. The B34S **pgmcall** command allowed the user to pass the data and the exact commands needed for these systems to a file. The B34S **dodos** and **dounix** system commands are designed to call the other program that does not realize that it is being run under the B34S. The other program's output file is captured and placed in the B34S output file. As far as the user is concerned, this output looks as if it had come from executing an internal B34S procedure. The learning curve for using the link is kept low and the B34S user does not have to worry about moving the data and command files between the programs. An example of **pgmcall** is a branch from B34S to RATS, which is listed next:

```
b34sexec options ginclude('gas.b34'); b34srun;

b34sexec robust;
         model gasout gasout{1 to 6} gasin{1 to 6};
         b34srun;

b34sexec options open('rats.dat') unit(28) disp=unknown;
 b34srun;
b34sexec options open('rats.in')  unit(29) disp=unknown;
 b34srun;
b34sexec options clean(28);       b34srun;
b34sexec options clean(29);       b34srun;

b34sexec pgmcall;
  rats  passasts
pcomments('*  ',
          '* data passed from b34s(r) system to rats',
          '*  ') ;
pgmcards;
* rats commands here
* rats linreg is used to run a regression

 linreg gasout / resids
# constant  gasin{1 to 6} gasout{1 to 6}
*
* save residual in rats to a portable file
*
open copy myrun.por
smpl
copy(format=portable) /  resids
* rats commands end

b34sreturn;
b34srun;

b34sexec options close(28); b34srun;
b34sexec options close(29); b34srun;
b34sexec options dodos(start /w /r rats32s rats.in /run')
                 dounix('rats     rats.in rats.out');
                  b34srun;
b34sexec options npageout
    writeout('Output from rats',' ',' ')
    copyfout('rats.out')
```

```
    dodos('erase  rats.in','erase rats.out','erase
    rats.dat')
    dounix('rm    rats.in','rm    rats.out','rm
     rats.dat')
    ;
    b34srun;

/; reads rats extract files into b34s
b34sexec options open('myrun.por') unit(45) disp=unknown;
 b34srun;
b34sexec scainput; getrats ratsunit(45);
         b34srun;
b34sexec matrix;
call loaddata;
call graph(resids);
b34srun;
b34sexec options close(45); b34srun;
```

Data are first loaded into B34S and a **robust** regression is run. Next, the files 'rats.in' and 'rats.dat' are opened and processed by the B34S **pgmcall** command. The **rats** sentence after the line **b34sexec pgmcall**; triggers B34S to pass the data in a format that RATS expects. All data is passed as time series. All statements after the B34S command **pgmcards**; and before the B34S command **b34sreturn**; are executed by RATS, which makes a RATS portable file 'myrun.por' containing the residuals. In the third part of the job the B34S **matrix** command is used to do a graph of the residual calculated by RATS. While the tasks here are simple, the example gives the flavor of how closely B34S and RATS systems work together. Key to implementing this mode of operation is the fact that B34S can read and write RATS datafiles so that RATS can run efficiently. This use of RATS requires no special modifications to the RATS program. The interface is leveraged from capability already built into RATS. The job as set up will run under Windows or Unix since the command **dodos**( ) only passes the command string to the system under Windows, while the command **dounix**( ) only passes the command string to the operating system under a Unix platform. The goal is to have the job be completely platform-independent.

Since SAS can call B34S, at UIC B34S became the gate from SAS to these other programs. As a further refinement, the B34S **matrix** command allows other programs to be repeatedly loaded and run from under a B34S **do** loop. As seen from the B34S user, such systems are a part of the B34S program. System integration is most important since no one program can do everything that is needed. The B34S design allows such integration without any changes to the called program. This topic is visited further below in section 5.3 in the context of software implementation.

3.3. Evolution of some representative software systems

Many important econometric software systems in use today were built from improved and updated versions of other excellent "research programs." For example, SCA incorporated the Wisconsin multiple times program version 2 (WMTS-2) and various Box-Jenkins routines into a time series package. B34S incorporated WMTS-1 (Tiao-Box-Grupe-Hudak-Bell-Chang [61]) with added nonlinear testing options suggested by Hinich [25] and others. Stokes [55] documents in more detail the origin of many of the other B34S commands. Table 4 of this paper provides references. RATS was originally developed from the Minnesota SPECTRE program that was written by Sims and extended by Geweke. RATS has become the standard for nonlinear time series model building. LIMDEP, written by Greene [19], has become the premier limited dependent variable software. In the 1990s all these systems were ported to the PC. SCA, B34S and LIMDEP have used various Lahey Fortran compilers for their implementation, while in recent years RATS has migrated to C. In the late 1990s B34S and LIMDEP released student versions.

SAS was originally written in PL/1 with some Fortran. In the late 1980's SAS saw the rise of non-IBM systems and with version 6, converted to C. The program is now available on PCs and widely available on most Unix systems. In recent years SAS has increased the number of manuals and reduced its focus on the development of statistical applications, especially time series procedures. The usefulness of the system for more than data building and basic statistical techniques is reduced although PROC **iml** has continued to be enhanced. Due to the proliferation of manuals and its command driven interface, SAS use in teaching statistics has been replaced to some extent by Excel®. In view of the accuracy problems of the statistical routines in Excel documented by McCullough and Wilson [38], this development may be a step backwards in many ways. The cost of the SAS system and the requirement that it be licensed every year have also reduced use.

SPEAKEASY was built by Stan Cohen [11] with help from others in the 1960s at Argonne National Laboratory. It has always been in Fortran. FEDEASY, an extensive linkule library, was built at the Washington Federal Reserve and provided an extension to SPEAKEASY in the area of econometrics. The old FEDEASY and MODELEASY+ additions to the system were extended by the Bank of Italy and Bill Teeters at SPEAKEASY. The advantage of the MODELEASY+ system over TROLL is that the full programming capability of SPEAKEASY is available to allow the system to be extended and complex calculations to be made. This brief history is in no way complete. It outlines how a number of software systems have evolved over time and some of the reasons for these changes. The B34S history is given next in more detail.

4. Development of B34S as a case study of software evolution

4.1. Brief review of early history

The B34S design has had a number of phases. Table 4 shows when features were added and references for the code that was converted and extended. Up until 1987, B34S linked together a number of procedures, such as logit, tobit and Box-Jenkins, many of which had been developed by others. The system was designed so that most procedures could be run stand-alone as long as the data were placed on a scratch file on Fortran unit 8 in real*8 unformatted form. Using this expert mode, users could either link their Fortran main program with the B34S library to attach a routine and start executing a command, or run the command using the B34S program itself. To run a command under a user Fortran program only required that variable names, a work array, the numbers of lags and the numbers of observations be passed to the B34S procedure subroutine. As mentioned, the user would have had to place the data on Fortran scratch unit 8. If the B34S command read switches, these could be provided on a file that could be rewound and reread if the command had to be run many times. Commands to run B34S procedures are passed in on Fortran unit 5, which was built by the B34S **setup** subroutine. Unlike most Fortran routines, B34S has always read off a control file on unit 3, which was then copied to unit 5. By this design Fortran unit 5 could be rewound during the job and modified to be used again. Since all input from Fortran unit 5 for the procedure switches was column-dependent, no parsing was required.

The usual way B34S was run in that period was with a command file that would instruct B34S to build the data using the appropriate transformations. The B34S main routine read each line, it was scanned and the appropriate procedure was called depending on key letters in specific columns. B34S had a dynamic link capability for nonlinear modeling that allowed expert users to write the model to be estimated in Fortran. Since the Fortran subroutine is linked into a distinct program, unless this executable was called, it could not impact the B34S system negatively. B34S also allowed new commands to be added in dynamic programs. In 1970s the **pgmcall** procedure in B34S supported links to other systems, such as SAS, RATS, LIMDEP, SCA and SPEAKEASY, which themselves were seen as B34S commands. B34S provided a gateway into these systems without the user having to reformat the data. The called program was loaded in memory under B34S and would run from a command file that had been built. When the called program completed, the output was added to the B34S output. Section 3.2 shows a link with RATS using the more modern B34S control language. The implications of this design are further discussed in section 5.3.

In the 1970s in response to user demands to "go the other way," the SAS PROC **cb34s** was built, allowing B34S to be seen as a SAS procedure. B34S output would be seen in the SAS output file as if it came from a production SAS procedure. Using this PROC, B34S was used by many at UIC to call LIMDEP and other programs from SAS. PROC **cb34s** ran until SAS 6 changed the PROC interface. Now the SAS to B34S call is made with the SAS macro **cb34sm**, which is distributed with B34S and runs on all SAS systems using the SAS **macro** facility. The speed loss of the interface is more than made up by portability that is now required in a many-vendor Unix world.

4.2. B34S parser: A program generator

By 1987 the B34S *parser* [54] had been developed to convert a "historic" column-dependent interface to a modern key-word-driven interface. The problem was how to best make the change without giving up features and advantages of the old design. Upward portability and limiting bugs were major objectives. Unlike most other programs, the B34S parser was designed as a *script generator*, rather that being directly integrated into the procedure. The B34S parser can either write the column-dependent commands that actually run the B34S procedures or other programs, or it can make direct calls to run procedures. This design has a number of advantages. First, existing procedures do not have to be changed. Second, the column- dependent commands can be saved and reused, saving a parse step. Third, new procedures, based on the code of others, can be quickly added since the command syntax needed to run the added procedure does not need to be changed since it can be written by the B34S parser. From the perspective of the user, the command structure of B34S is consistent. Finally, since the B34S parser just is writing a script of commands, it can easily be used to write the commands of other external programs that are not part of B34S.

Soon after the B34S parser was developed, the B34S **macro** facility was added. Like a similar capability in SAS, the B34S macro facility allows B34S and other program commands to be written and then executed. The need for a macro facility was discussed and an example was given earlier in section 3.1. The basic B34S command syntax consists of groups of commands called execs that start with **b34sexec cdname** where cdname is a command name. There is no line continuation character, since each sentence ends in a **$** or **;**. The exec ends with the statement **b34srun**; or **b34seend;** (B34S Exec End). Data loadings is similar to SAS. For example a simple job to load data, calculate correlations, list the data and run an OLS, L1 and Minimax regression is:

```
b34sexec data corr $
label x = 'age of cars' $
label y = 'price of cars' $
input x y $
datacards $
1  1995  3   875  6   695
10  345  5   595  2  1795
b34sreturn $
```

```
b34seend $
b34sexec list $ b34seend $
b34sexec robust $
model y=x $
b34seend $
```

The parser was designed to make life easy for the user. Parameters can be passed as noob(10) or noob=10 and in most places the comma is optional. Error messages point to the line in question and detailed diagnostics are given in the log. Every effort is made to assist in identifying and correcting the problem.

4.3. The impact of the PC

As research moved off mainframes, B34S followed and in 1991 was ported to the Lahey F77EM32 compiler and moved to the PC. Before this time the lack of a suitable compiler and hardware limitations inherent in the PC prevented this move. Initially, the program ran only in batch mode. Phar-Lap technology was used to run the system in "protected mode," which gave B34S the large memory space it needed. Memory was dynamically allocated with Fortran 90 additions then present in the Lahey Fortran, replacing the **ia01as** memory allocation routine whose use was discussed in section 2.5. Graphic and menu facilities were soon added with the use of the Graphoria and Spindrift Libraries which were Lahey add-on libraries. Initially the GUI menus ran only in text mode under DOS. The B34S GUI and graphics routines were soon replaced with the Interacter Subroutine Library (ISL) [62], which provided menu and graphics support for PC (Windows 95/98/NT/2000/XP) and Unix (Linux, RS/6000 and Sun) systems *without a code change*. A key design decision was made to not build the B34S GUI for Windows alone. The B34S GUI had to work in both text and graphics mode, depending on the need. A B34S user on a dial-up line into a Unix machine was not forced to a command line interface, as was the case for most systems not designed with this flexibility. Depending on the environment, the B34S Display Manager or GUI will come up in graphics or text mode. The Interacter Library provided more than just a platform independent way to implement a GUI with just Fortran based calls. With the proper software design is became possible to build custom menus in real time.

Unlike programs that "hard wire" menus into the executable program, menus that run procedures in B34S are generated "on the fly" with the **makemenu** command. A generated menu can be thought of as a "data entry screen" or "form." These forms are generated and controlled from a running B34S **makemenu** command, which itself writes another B34S command script. The menu allows an end user to run a B34S command from a "point-and-click" screen. MATLAB has a similar, although less flexible, capability in this area, as does SAS with the AF command. RATS also has a limited capability in putting up a user menu. By allowing users control of the menus, an expert can build a custom GUI front-end to a system. In B34S, all menus that run procedures are thus outside the executable and can be easily fixed or extended in the field since they are just running B34S programs. Permitting user interfaces to be developed independent of the software developer allows the GUI face of B34S to be as varied as the user desires. Having this capability in a software system is most important.

In 1998, an early version of the B34S **matrix** command was released. The **matrix** command provides a full programming language, including full support for complex variables, user subroutines, programs and functions. While all user subroutines and functions have local variables, programs use global variables. The subroutine **desc**, which uses the built-in functions **mean** and **variance**, provides an illustration of how to add a new command to the **matrix** language:

```
subroutine desc(name,mean1,var);
mean1=mean(name);
var=variance(name);
return;
end;
```

The following code fragment uses **desc**:

```
x=array(5:1 2 3 4 5);
call desc(x,m,v);
call print('Variable  mean Variance', x,m,v);
```

As in Fortran, the variable x is passed into the subroutine and the variables m and v are calculated. Unlike Fortran which passes only an address, here a copy of the variable (object) and its full description are passed. The variables m and v are created as the subroutine runs. A user program to produce the same result would be **desc2**:

```
program desc2;
m=mean(x);
v=variance(x);
return;
end;
```

Here the variable x is known by the program. The advantage of a program over a subroutine is that there is no overhead in passing the data. The disadvantage is that a variable name in the program could by accident modify a variable with the same name currently in named storage. In the implementation of the optimization routines and the nonlinear least squares routines, due to the need for speed at all costs, programs rather than subroutines were used. If a subroutine was needed, the program could call a user subroutine. The following code fragment uses the **desc2** program.

```
x=array(5:1 2 3 4 5);
call desc2;
call print('Variable Mean Variance', x,m,v);
```

Note that in this case the actual names are needed to be used inside DESC2 since the name domain is at the global level. The same result can be obtained with use of a user function. The function **desf** will return the mean, although in this case this is not needed due to the built-in function **mean**. A function can return both a result and change an argument in a manner similar to Fortran.

```
function desf(x);
m=mean(x);
return(m);
end;
```

The following code fragment uses **desf**

```
x=array(5:1 2 3 4 5);
amean=desf(x);
```

These examples show the basic structure of the language and how it can be extended beyond the built-in subroutines and functions. Like MATLAB and GAUSS users, B34S users have libraries of their own extensions to the language to augment the distributed libraries of commands.

The **matrix** command has facilities to call other programs inside the language. The user can specify nonlinear models in a high-order language similar to SPEAKEASY and, by writing to the screen, monitor the solution progress. Section 2.3 has an example of this use. The nonlinear solver can be a B34S subroutine or a Fortran-based B34S **matrix** command subroutine. Both approaches are distributed, although the latter is substantially faster. All B34S **matrix** commands have running examples and help documents that can be viewed from the Display Manager, or edited with a user-selected editor or the B34S editor. This design has been copied from SPEAKEASY, where all commands have help files and most commands have example files. The feature of the B34S design gives users complete control of the help and example files, which can be edited in the field.

5. The implementation of procedure and programming capability in software

5.1. Overview

Modern econometric software must be accurate, flexible and able to do both production tasks and research tasks. It should be able to be called from another systems, it must be user extendable, which means that it should have a programming

Table 2
Desired characteristics of modern econometric software

- Accuracy and documentation of all calculations.
- Program contains both built-in procedures and access to a full programming language.
- GUI and script operation possible.
- Program runs the same on multiple platforms from both a script or a GUI. Program not trapped on Microsoft platforms.
- Program provides high resolution 2D and 3D graphics that are output in formats suitable for inclusion in word processors, such as Word® and Word Perfect®
- Program enables users to modify help files and example files in the field.
- All procedures have help files and running example files accessible from either a GUI interface or from a script.
- Program allows users to modify menus that can build and execute scripts, which can be captured for future use.
- Program contains a MACRO language, which allows real-time generation of scripts.
- Where possible, GUI works from graphics screen or in text-mode from a dial up Unix session.
- Program contains an editor and/or allows access to a user editor such as pico, vi or emacs to lower the learning curve.
- Program is able to display and modify the current dataset in a spread sheet form.

capability. It is desirable that the software be able to run in batch mode from a script or from a GUI in point-and-click mode. The GUI point-and-click mode is widely used by novice users who graduate to building scripts once they gain confidence. This suggests that underneath the GUI there should be a script that is actually running the system. Only by having a script can the calculation be audited and/or documented. Table 2 summarizes a number of valuable characteristics of a modern econometric software system. Table 3 lists a number of desirable features in a higher-level programming language.

MATLAB and GAUSS are programming languages, each of which has its own advantages. These software systems are not procedure driven programs along the lines of SPSS, SAS and other legacy systems. The nature of the revolution in programming style that MATLAB and GAUSS represent will be illustrated next by contrasting different systems. SAS and B34S are examples of software systems that provide both procedure driven commands and a user programming language. These two important aspects of a modern econometric software system are illustrated by a number of code fragments. As an example of a procedure driven system, the B34S command

```
b34sexec reg;
model gasout=gasin{0 to 20} gasout{1 to 20}; b34srun;
```

runs a regression of gasout on gasin and 20 lags of gasin and 20 lags of gasout. To use such a command requires minimal programming skill. The same command in RATS is

```
linreg gasout
# constant gasin{0 to 20} gasout{1 to 20}
```

Table 3
Desirable characteristics of a programming language

Basic Functionality
- Accuracy and speed in all calculations, such as inverse, FFT, eigenvalues, etc.
- Support for real*8, complex*16, real*4 and integer*4 data types.
- Ability to manipulate character*1 and character*8 data.
- Allow subroutines and functions access to local and global data.
- Provide high-resolution graphics with 2D and 3D plot capability.
- Provide ability to run under a GUI or from a script.
- Provide ability to define and manipulate user-defined data types.
- Programming language should allow structured indexes to promote vectorization.
- Provide a wide variety of optimization routines, such as nonlinear programming with nonlinear constraints, maximization/minimization and nonlinear least squares where the user has total control over the form of the model. It is desirable that the underlying routines be compiled code from libraries, such as IMSL and NAG, but be able to branch to user-written model specification code written in the programming language. Note that MATLAB meets this requirement since the m files can be optionally compiled into C++ code.
- Give the users the ability to add subroutines and functions to enhance the system.
- Give users ability to add or modify help or example files that are accessible from a GUI interface.
- Provide complete running examples for all commands.

Advanced Features
- Ability to compile the programming language into C or Fortran for speed.
- Ability to have user commands written in C or Fortran and dynamically linked at run time

A B34S **matrix** command code fragment illustrates the programming approach to estimation of an OLS coefficient vector.[20] The command

```
beta=inv(transpose(x)*x)*transpose(x)*y;
```

solves for the OLS coefficients in the variable beta provided that x is an n by k matrix of independent variables and y is a vector containing n observations on the independent variables. The user must know what is being calculated or that $\hat{\beta} = (X'X)^{-1}X'Y$. Unless there is a bug in the software, there is full knowledge of how the result was obtained. An alternate is

```
beta=(1./(transpose(x)*x))*transpose(x)*y;
```

In SAS **iml** the same command would be

```
beta=inv(t(x)*x)*t(x)*y;
```

or

```
beta=inv(x'*x)*x'*y;
```

[20] As mentioned earlier, the QR approach should be used to insure high accuracy. In B34S the **inv** command uses the LU factorization to invert a general matrix. It is possible to specify switches if it is known that the matrix to be inverted is symmetric or symmetric positive definite. It is also possible to indicate whether a LAPACK or LINPACK routine is to be called.

Table 4
Econometric capability and original source of B34S by different periods

1967

- OLS, Generalized Least Squares using two pass technique Thornber [57]
- BLUS residuals. Limited Bayesian capability. Thornber [58,59]
- Data Building and Display using residual plots

1977

- Probit and Multinomial Probit Models McKelvy-Zavoina [39,40]
- Logit, and Multinomial Logit Models (Nerlove-Press [44], Kawasaki [29]
- Tobit
- Error Component Analysis Henry-McDonald-Stokes [24]
- Two and three Stage Least Squares Modeling Jennings [27]
- LINPACK [13] and EISPACK [53] used extensively.

1987

- Program runs with command language, not values in card columns.
- Macro Language developed.
- Recursive Residual Analysis.
- QR Approach to regression models supported.
- Nonlinear Estimation using a Dynamic link. Meeter [41,42]
- Markov Probability Models Lee-Judge-Zellner [31]
- ARIMA and Transfer function models Pack [47]
- VAR and VARMA models Tiao-Grupe-Hudak-Bell-Chang [61]. Tiao-Box [60]
- Frequency decomposition of VAR Model Geweke [17,18]
- Optimal Control Models Chow [7–10]
- State Space Modeling Aoki [2]
- Two way links with SAS, SPEAKEASY and other systems

1995

- Graphical Interface on PC in addition to batch support
- Users can customize menus using B34S Language
- Mars and PISPLINE Models Friedman [16] Brieman [4]
- High Resolution Graphics including 3D plots
- Spectral Analysis
- Numerous nonlinearity tests

2001

- Full 4th generation programming language. Support for Real*8 and Complex*16 data types and well as character array processing with over 175 commands and 177 functions.
- Programming language contains extensive nonlinear estimation and optimization capability up to and including solution of nonlinear programming problems with nonlinear constraints
- Extensive simulation capability.
- Robust (L1, MINIMAX, Quantile) Estimation
- Linear Programming
- GUI runs on Windows NT/2K/XP, Linux, RS/6000 and Sun in graphics and text mode.

In MATLAB

```
beta=inv(x'*x)*x'*y;
```

while in SPEAKEASY

```
beta=inv(transpose(x)*x)*transpose(x)*y
```

or

```
beta=(1/(transpose(x)*x))*transpose(x)*y
```

which is seen to be the same as B34S but without the ; at the end of the line. For common tasks like OLS, running a procedure is often easier than running a program written in a programming language such as Fortran or C. A compromise is a higher level command inside a programming language. For example, inside the B34S **matrix** command is a built-in higher level command

```
call olsq(gasout gasin{0 to 20} gasout{1 to 20}:print);
```

which is easier to use. The **olsq** command automatically makes vectors of the coefficients (`%coef`), the standard errors (`%se`) and the t scores (`%t`) and other summary measures of the model that can be used in the next **matrix** command. An optional switch `:QR` can be set to make the calculation using the QR method.

5.2. Object-oriented programming implementations

All of the above programming examples rely on the software knowing the characteristics of objects. This was not possible in the early computer languages, such as Fortran, except to a very limited extent. In both B34S and SPEAKEASY, the command `y = x*x` will be solved to produce a different answer, depending on whether x is a scalar, a vector, a 1D array, a 2D array, or a matrix. In computer math the operators +, −, * and/perform addition, subtraction, multiplication and division respectively. In MATLAB, the use of *overload operators* or placing the character. in front of the operator *, allows `y = x*x` to refer to matrix math, while `y = x.*x` refers to element-by-element math. In MATLAB it is easy to leave off the overload operator and write `y = x*x;` in place of `y = x.*x;` with disastrous and often undetected consequences. The B34S and SPEAKEASY language design, by having more object types, avoids the use of overload operators at the cost of a proliferation of object types. To implement MATLAB command `x.*x`, in SPEAKEASY and B34S requires "array math" in place of "vector math." Array math requires that the object be an array, not a vector or matrix. In B34S and SPEAKEASY, a matrix can be made from a 2D array with the command `x = mfam(x);` while an array can be made from a matrix with the command `x = afam(x);`.[21]

Between the extremes of a programming language software system, such as MATLAB, and a strictly procedure-driven system lies software typified by RATS. RATS contains programmable procedures with a great deal of power. Complex nonlinear models can be specified at the cost of using rigid programming conventions that are not like the underlying math. A sample of the rigid programming style required for complex objects in RATS is the suggested code contained in the RATS Manual for a high-pass filter assuming a series x is loaded

[21] The command **afam**( ) means array family while **mfam**( ) means matrix family.

```
FREQ 2 256
RTOC
#    X
#    1
FFT 1
CSET  1  =  %Z(T,1)*(T>64.and.T<=192)
IFT  1
```

The variable x is first loaded in a complex array 1, using the RATS RTOC (real to complex) command. Next, the FFT is taken on complex vector 1 and a number of elements are zeroed out using the RATS if type statement. Finally, the inverse FFT is calculated. While the above represents "programming," it is not a programming language in the usual sense of the word. For more detail on these points see the Glossary of Key Terms at end of this paper. For B34S, the complete **matrix** command for this task, including data generation, comments and graphics, is

```
b34sexec matrix;
* Uses FFT to High Pass Random Series;
/;
/; Illustrate with random numbers. Spectrum is inspected
/; before and after the filter is applied
/;
n=296;
x=rn(array(n:));
spec=spectrum(x,freq);
call graph(freq,spec :plottype xyplot
          :heading 'Spectrum of Random series');

cfft    =fft(complex(x,0.0));
fftnew  =cfft*complex(0.0,0.0);

i=integers(64,192);
fftnew(i)  = cfft(i);
nseries=afam(real(fft(fftnew :back)))*(1./dfloat(norows(x)));
call tabulate(x,nseries);
call graph(freq,spectrum(nseries,freq) :plottype xyplot
           :heading 'Spectrun of filtered Random
           Series');

b34srun;
```

The B34S code first generates a random series x whose spectrum is plotted. Next, the FFT is taken and saved in a variable `cfft`. The complex array fftnew initially contains all zeros. The integer array i ($i = [64, \ldots, 192]$) is used to copy only a subset of the `cfft` elements into `fftnew` with the command `fftnew(i) = cfft(i);` and illustrates a vectorized instruction. The newly filtered series is calculated with the inverse FFT and scaled. Next, it is tabulated and its spectrum calculated. The B34S example illustrates moving series back and forth from real to complex and working with structured index addressing. Such a system shows the logic of the calculation. The fact that a modern programming language can document a calculation in the language of math is one of a number of major advances.

Although very easy to use, SPEAKEASY has far fewer contributed subroutines than MATLAB. For what it does, SPEAKEASY is very powerful and flexible and can be extended by user linkules (compiled commands) and subroutines as was discussed earlier. The fact that it has to be programmed limits its use by the point-and-click generation that is used to GUI interface systems. In capability SPEAKEASY is closest to MATLAB. The B34S **matrix** language follows as closely as possible the SPEAKEASY language for basic operations. While SPEAKEASY has many hard science functions, the B34S **matrix** language is geared to econometric and time series operations. Both programs use the same portable savefile format.

5.3. Software integration issues

Since no one software system can possibly fulfill all needs of a researcher, software integration is needed. We next turn to how this requirement was implemented in the B34S design. Section 3.2 provided an example showing how RATS could be called from the B34S system and the results obtained back in the calling system. For this example to work a number of capabilities had to be available in the calling program (B34S) and the called program (RATS).

- The called program had to be able to be run from a script.
- The calling program had to be able to issue a system call to execute RATS, the called program.
- The calling program had to be able to pass the data in a form usable to RATS and had to be able to pass a script of RATS commands.
- The calling program had to be able to reuse the RATS results.

In this example the RATS development team was not involved in any way. The B34S developer had to make changes in B34S to both read and write a RATS portable file. If the suggestions of Renfro [50] on a database interface standard are accepted and all software developers support the standard, such integration will only involve passing the called program script and making the system call to execute the program. [22] Allowing one software system to easily execute commands in another software

[22] B34S, SAS, MATLAB, SPEAKEASY, SCA are systems which are known to be able to issue systems calls and which have successfully been shown to be able to call B34S. As of this date RATS lacks this capability.

system will facilitate validation of nonlinear estimation results a point stressed in Stokes [50].

The below listed example shows a link from SAS to B34S that is discussed further in Stokes [55]. Here B34S is being called. The SAS job includes macro files cb34sm.sas that are used to facilitate the passing of commands to B34S from SAS. [23]

```
* This job uses the SAS MACRO CB34SM;
%include 'c:\b34slm\cb34sm.sas';
data junk;
input x y;
cards;
11 22
33 44
55 66
99 77
77 88
;
proc means; run;
* Clean files **********************************   ;
options noxwait; run;
data _null_;
command ='erase  myjob.b34';
call system(command);
* End of clean step ****************************   ;
* Place B34S commands next after %readpgm ;
%readpgm
cards;
b34sexec list $ var x $ b34srun $
b34sexec regression $ model y = x $
                      b34srun $
b34sexec describe $ b34seend $
;
run;
  %cb34sm(data=junk, var=x y, u8='myjob.b34',
                              u3='myjob.b34',
                        options=nohead)
options noxwait; run;
```

[23] In the 1970's the SAS PROC CB34S was developed to simplify the running of B34S under SAS. This program was able to place the B34S log into the SAS log and the B34S output into the SAS output file. The PROC CB34S ran for a number of years on MVS for a number of SAS releases. When SAS version 6 was released, it no longer ran and was replaced with the SAS macro cb34sm. This macro runs unchanged on three unix platforms (RS/6000, Sun, Linux) and Windows 2K/XP.

```
*  This step calls b34s and copies files     ;
data _null_;
command ='b34s myjob';
call system(command);
run;
endsas;
```

SAS first loads a very simple dataset. Next the command '`erase myjob.b34`' is executed from SAS to clean out any prior B34S control files. The SAS Macro `%readpgm` is supplied in cb34sm.sas and loads the B34S command script which here lists the data, runs a regression and describes the data. The SAS macro `%cb34sm` builds the b34s data loading step and is explicitly told to pass the series x and y. In this job both the data (U8) and the commands (U3) are placed in the same file. The importance of this example is that is shows how a powerful software system (SAS in this case) has built in the programming power to allow a third party (not a SAS developer) to develop an interface with another system (B34S) to leverage the power of SAS. The next job, shown below, goes the other way, with B34S now on top and SAS being called. B34S is started and the gas data studied by Tiao-Box [58] is loaded. The built-in B34S command **pgmcall** is used to build the SAS data loading step in the file testsas.sas and copy the SAS commands **reg**, **autoreg** and **arima**. B34S then closes this file, which was assigned to unit 29, and executes SAS. Note that either the B34S commands **dodos** or **dounix** will be executed depending on the platform. After the SAS job runs the B34S commands **copyfout** and **copyflog** copy the SAS output and log to the B34S output and log files respectively. Here again the B34S user has been able to leverage its programming capability by a branch to SAS. In jobs not shown, it is easily possible to make a branch to another software system while inside a B34S **matrix** command do loop.

```
b34sexec options ginclude('gas.b34'); b34srun;
b34sexec options open('testsas.sas') unit(29)
 disp=unknown$ b34srun$
b34sexec options clean(29)$ b34seend$
b34sexec pgmcall idata=29 icntrl=29$
  sas    $
* sas commands next ;
pgmcards$
proc reg; model gasout=gasin; run;
proc autoreg;
     model gasout=gasin / method=ml nlag=1; run;
proc arima;
     identify var=gasout(1); run;
b34sreturn$
b34srun$
```

```
b34sexec options close(29)$ b34srun$
b34sexec options dodos('start /w /r    sas testsas' )
                 dounix('sas testsas' )
                         $ b34srun$
b34sexec options npageout noheader
 writeout('   ','output from sas',' ',' ')
 writelog('   ','output from sas',' ',' ')
 copyfout('testsas.lst')
 copyflog('testsas.log')
   dodos('erase testsas.sas','erase testsas.lst','erase
   testsas.log')
 dounix('rm    testsas.sas','rm    testsas.lst','rm
 testsas.log')
 $ b34srun$
b34sexec options header $ b34srun$
```

No one software system is able to fulfill all econometric needs nor should this be a goal. In addition the complexities of nonlinear estimation suggest that it is most important for research to be validated by two or more econometric systems. Passing data and command files between software systems thus is increasingly important. Such links between programs can be driven by scripts or by menus that in turn write scripts. What is important is the availability of capability to move between software systems. The B34S **pgmcall** capability has been available since the middle 1970's. It would be helpful if other software systems develop such capability or, better still as in the case of SAS, provide sufficient programming capability that allows third party developers to build these links. In summary, system integration will be increasingly important in the future.[24]

5.4. *Software capability enhancements driven by hardware and research needs*

If trends continue, in the future it appears that, econometricians will be running more programmable enabled systems. If this is not the case, then, at the very least, existing systems will be made to work better together so that calculations can seamlessly move between systems to leverage capability. Rather than learning Fortran, as in the past, researchers will master one or more of the programming systems. While producing an application that runs slower than a Fortran or C program, the ease of use of the programmable system more than makes up for the speed loss, especially as CPUs get more powerful. In macroeconomics today,

[24]Examples where MATLAB and SPEAKEASY run B34S and in turn have the ability to execute SAS and RATS etc have not been shown due to space limitations. Stokes [56] illustrates a probit model using a number of systems. The job that runs all these systems under B34S is on the web in www.uic.ed/~hhstokes and should be consulted by interested users.

basic software to be mastered includes knowing either GAUSS, SPEAKEASY or MATLAB, plus a procedure-driven software system such as RATS. B34S combines both types of systems in one software package. The days of forcing the analysis of a research problem into what the software system can perform are basically over. However much econometric work involves "production calculations" that are done with procedure driven systems since the techniques are widely known. In the applied research world, it is quite common for the subroutines of MATLAB, RATS and GAUSS to be distributed over the world wide web. The logic of the calculation is clearly visible which helps logic errors to be found quickly.

While the average researcher may not develop Fortran or C software, there continues to be a major role for software developers to maintain the basic platforms upon which the production analysis is done. A major weakness of applied researchers is to trust their software. Many bugs still remain in major programming systems and are undetected for long periods of time. In compiled systems these bugs can only be detected by use of carefully constructed test problems. McCullough and H. D. Vinod [36] survey the extent of the reliability problem that still remains. Increased use of nonlinear methods of analysis has only made matters worse.

5.5. *Evolution of current software systems*

The proceeding paragraphs have outlined the major changes that have occurred in statistical computing over the past 30 years. Of interest is why over such a period older systems have not been radically rewritten. The experience of SAS and SPSS is most interesting. The SAS of the 1970's was written in PL/1 and ran only in batch mode on the IBM MVS operating system. SAS was later rewritten in C but the grammar of the program did not change, only evolved. The user investment in production programs, or scripts, was maintained and the vast SAS user base continued to grow. B34S has followed this route. Every effort has been made to allow older programs or scripts to continue to run and limit the startup time for users to learn the system. New capability that was added did not impact older uses. SPSS, in contrast to SAS, went through at least three phases. The grammar of the original program was changed to SPSS-X, which became the modern system (before the GUI). At this juncture, many users rather than learning a new system, switched to the more stable SAS. At around this time SPSS tried to interest users in an interactive version of the program called Conversational SPSS, but few users changed since the grammar was still different. The SPEAKEASY and RATS interfaces have evolved rather than been changed although, hidden from the user, the underlying program has changed. In contrast to a script-based system, a GUI-based system has a shorter learning curve which allows new users to try it with less cost. On the other side there is less cost to leaving such a system. The learning costs suggest that script based systems are more likely to evolve by maintaining their older interface, while GUI systems may be more likely to change radically. Even GUI programs face user resistance to changes. The Windows version of the editor KEDIT, that is a PC version of the IBM CMS editor, still maintains an option whereby the user can select the "classic interface" over the newer "Windows style" interface. Windows XP allows a user to maintain the Windows 2000 interface. Old habits die hard!

While a new user may be up and running faster with a GUI interface, the demands to replicate results mandate a script[25] be saved. To adapt to the new group of users who have grown up using Windows products, many older script based systems developed menus that generate scripts.[26] A software system that provides a number of menus for various tasks but is able to generate a script system may well become the norm in the future since it encompasses the best of all worlds.

As mentioned earlier, Renfro [50] outlines the need for a database interface standard. With increasing amounts of data being available and downloadable from the web, a common interface format is needed. Once agreed upon, software system could be modified to read and write into this format. The present trend to use Excel as database manager or web extract format is clearly a least common denominator that involves substantial negative tradeoffs. In the future Excel and other user systems should be able to read and write the data interchange standard that should be portable over all hardware systems. It is hoped that there will be moves in this direction in the years ahead. It remains to be seen if the proposed XML data interchange standard will begin to address some of the above concerns.

5.6. *Future trends*

While it is dangerous to attempt to predict the future, the unfolding history of software development suggests a number of trends. First and foremost the increasing power of CPU's suggests that a whole range of new econometric techniques, formerly not possible, will be developed. It is clear that software systems with a programming capability with a steep learning curve are increasingly required to implement many of these techniques. It is also clear that software systems that provide a GUI interface must produce scripts that can be saved to provide a calculation audit trail. It is increasing desirable that the GUI interface be able to be modified by the user in the field. The rise of the open software movement and particularly the Linux operating system suggests that for software to stay relevant it must be portable and flexible. Microsoft is being challenged on the desktop as Unix is being challenged on the server side. We have seen an older system such as SAS successfully reinvent itself and be reprogrammed into C to facilitate portability. Many other older systems may be forced to reinvent themselves.

---

[25] Both a procedure-driven software system and a programming language software system run from a script. Of interest is how this script is initially written.

[26] The SAS **AF** facility generates menus that write scripts. MATLAB contains a facility that allows the user to build GUI menus that produce MATLAB command language. The B34S **makemenu** command generates menus that produce the B34S procedure scripts or programming language scripts. In contrast to Excel menus that just produce answers, the above three examples allow the user to save the generated script.

While many software systems on the PC have initially used Microsoft Visual Basic to provide the GUI, such a design limits portability. Other software systems such as B34S have relied on third party libraries such as Interacter to maintain a GUI across different CPU's.[27] Perhaps MATLAB points the way to the future using an alternative path. Starting with version 6, MATLAB redesigned the user GUI using Java.[28] A Java virtual machine is installed with every MATLAB on the PC. Java has been integrated into MATLAB to such an extent that Java classes, objects and methods can be accessed from the MATLAB command line and from MATLAB functions. Such a design maximizes portability and user flexibility. While most of the MATLAB commands are run as m files which are scripts of commands, the fact that MATLAB provides the ability to either automatically compile these scripts into an executable mex file or build a mex file in C or Fortran allows the system to be expanded with new features that can execute very fast. The key point is that the additions can be added in the field by researchers all working independently. The latter advantage partially explains why in engineering and other applications MATLAB programming skills have replaced programming skills in Fortran, C and C++ to a large extent for many if not most of the students.

A final desirable feature of future software systems will be to allow the system to be run as an engine that can be called from other systems. MATLAB again shows us the way, although there are other systems that have this feature. There are now a number of third party Excel commands that allow complicated calculations to be performed from a spreadsheet by providing a two-way link with the MATLAB engine. In the future such system integration will be increasingly important since there is little likelihood that it would be possible to develop one ideal all purpose software system.

5.7. Developer recognition

One peculiar aspect of statistical software development in academic life is that in most cases it is not highly rewarded. Most academic economists appear relatively unaware of the various design issues that go into software development. As noted by Bodkin [6], many in academic life view software development as mere translation of mathematical formulas into software.[29] While in many cases the implementation of the mathematics into computer code does not matter, when software is pushed hard,

[27] On Unix based systems the Interacter [62] Library calls X-Windows while on Windows Microsoft DLL's custom c routines are automatically called. The user is unaware of these differences and calls a common interface in Fortran.

[28] Hanselman and Littlefield [22] chapter 35 provides a very clear and comprehensive discussion of how MATLAB can be extended using the built-in Java capability. Of more interest is the hints at what will be coming down the road in later releases.

[29] Bodkin [6, pp. 55–56] notes "... program development (particularly the development of comprehensive programs for the management of a macroeconomic model project) has often not benefited from the prestige that it warrants, if not been subject to outright neglect! This is unfortunate. In the various fields

design weaknesses may show up. Possibly because software design is not a priority, most applied researchers seem relatively unconcerned about the technical aspects of their software and rarely document packages they have used in their calculations.[30] Of still more concern is the difficulty in replicating results and the reliability or accuracy of software in general.[31] One unfortunate result of the dearth of academic rewards for software development is the incentive it gives for experts in this field to leave the academy for the business world.

6. Conclusion

In the last 30 years econometric software design has been influenced by massive reductions in CPU costs and impressive speed gains. Moore's Law states that CPU speed doubles every 18 months. With the advent of new, 4th generation programming languages, new econometric theory has been put into practice much sooner than in the days of research implementations in Fortran or C. The computationally intensive GUI has been developed to speed specification of models and lower the learning curve for new users. User programmed column-dependent batch based software of the 1960's has been replaced by interactive systems, such as MATLAB, GAUSS and SPEAKEASY, which have opened programming to a wider audience than the Fortran and C professionals of the prior era. In many fields of applied econometrics, it has become increasingly more difficult to publish in major applied journals without building custom applications. While the 1960s and early 1970s saw the rise of the modern software packages, in the late 1970s and early 1980s many economists could get along with only the procedures in a software system, such as SAS. With the

of pure mathematics, I understand that often high credit is bestowed on the simplification of the proof of a theorem agreed to be true, or at least the rendering of such a proof more easily understandable or capable of an intuitive interpretation. This should be the case for econometric computation; the field should be recognized as a legitimate subject of intellectual endeavor." A similar point has been made forcefully by Renfro [49].

[30] Longley [33] first sounded the alarm concerning software accuracy. A number of poorly coded OLS packages were shown to break down when tested on a dataset with high multicollinearity. Longley's message was that we need to test for rank problems and, when solving an OLS model, should use a procedure like the QR that is known to be more stable than the usual text book approach. Renfro [49] provides a survey of many of the papers that have been written concerning software development since Longley. His seminal paper [48] was written from his perspective as the lead developer of MODLER.

[31] McCullough and Vinod [36] is an excellent survey of this problem. McCullough and Vinod [37] provides convincing evidence that most articles even in the most prestigious journals cannot be replicated. As a result of these findings the *American Economics Review* has recently implemented a policy that requires all accepted papers to submit their data and control scripts to facilitate and insure replication. Perhaps this new policy will change the focus of the profession and lead to great weight placed on developer contributions. A number of recent papers have been written concerning estimation problems. These include McCullough and Renfro [35] which documents various problems in nonlinear estimation and Stokes [56] which recommends that nonlinear models be estimated by two or more software systems to insure accurate answers that are free from the hidden effects of software default values.

advent of Unix workstations and PCs, together with modern compilers and higher level languages, there has been a resurgence in software development and exchange. Documented MATLAB M-files, or GAUSS programs, which can be distributed easily over the world wide web and modified by the end user, provide a new way to both communicate new methods and perform the required calculations.

While programming languages are suitable for the development and dissemination of cutting edge research, in the applied field there is a growing need for flexible, procedure-driven software that allows production jobs to be run on a regular basis without too much of a learning curve. Properly designed, such systems should protect the end user from computational errors. Recent papers by McCullough-Vinod [36, 37], McCullough-Renfro [35], Stokes [56] and others suggest a need for more testing of computational accuracy of all software.

Appendix. Glossary of Key Terms and More Detail on their Significance

Dynamic link. Programs that have all the object decks bound in one executable are said to be statically linked. An alternative is a dynamically linked program that picks up sections at run time. These sections can be developed independently. In the Windows world, many programs dynamically link to dll files.

Load Module/Executable. Self contained file that runs a program. A load module is made by linking object decks that were created from the compiling of a source file in a language such as C or Fortran.

Macro. The term Macro refers to a facility in a software system whereby script statements are generated. SAS [52] provides a detailed description of how this capability was implemented in SAS. Section 3.1 of this paper shows a B34S example. For an example of a SAS macro see SAS [52, 69].

```
%macro du(num);
%put beginning macro du: num is &num;
%do %until(&num>3);
  %put *** &num***;
  %let num=%eval(%nun+1);
%end;
%put ending macro du: num is &num;
%mend du;
```

the command

```
%du(2)
```

produces

```
beginning macro du: num is 2
***2***
***3***
ending macro du: num is 4
```

The SAS and B34S macro facilities allow automatic generation of a script that will actually run the program. For a discussion of script see below.

Object Deck. A compiler for the C or Fortran language translates a source file into an object deck which is then *linked* into a load module. It is possible to link object decks make from different source languages.

Parser. A parser consists of a set of subroutines that tokenize a string for further processing. Each token or logical string in the sentence is classified for further processing at a later time. For example a **matrix** command such as

```
y=x/(z-10.);
```

is seen by the parser as sentence consisting of 10 tokens. Of these 10, three are variables (y, x, z) and 6 are special characters (=, /, (–,), ;) and one is a floating point number (10.). The parser checks for such things as matching ( ) during the first pass. Each token is assigned an identifying integer number and the parse tree shows the location of the beginning of each token in the string and its length. The sentence is further processed at a later time. For example in the **matrix** command the above 10 tokens are recognized as an analytic sentence. The system has to detect if x and z are active variables. The real*8 floating point variable is first converted to a temp variable and the expression `(z-temp1)` resolved. The next task is to parse `y` = `x/temp2` and make sure `temp2` ≠ `0.0`. Finally the expression `y` = `temp3` moves the answer to named storage. At every stage the parser is an integral part of the process.

Procedure. A self contained command, callable using a program syntax, that performs a specific task such as estimation of an OLS model. For example, a SAS regression procedure REG is called as:

```
proc reg;
model y = x g;
run;
```

Programming Language. A 4th generation language that allows users to more easily customize a operation that if the same calculation was attempted with Fortran of C. MATLAB and GAUSS are programming languages. Such systems typically have a number of commands that have packaged calculations. In contract, to Fortran and C are strictly programming languages. For example MATLAB and GAUSS sell optimization add-ons that allow uses to estimate maximum likelihood models using likelihood functions programmed in GAUSS or MATLAB. The B34S **matrix** command and the SAS **iml** procedure are programming languages that are callable from a software system that contains a number of procedures. For example the OLS coefficients can be recovered from a SVD (singular value decomposition) of the N by K X right hands side matrix. Using math, we first decompose $X = U\Theta V'$ where $U'U = I$ and $V'V = I$ and Θ is a diagonal matrix. The OLS coefficients of the model predicting y given X can be calculated as $\hat{\beta} = V\Theta^{-1}U'y$. Using the MATLAB programming language, the commands

```
[U,S,V]=svd(X,0);
beta=V*inv(S)*U'*y;
```

illustrate clearly how this calculation can be made using a programming language. Note that the objects X and y are processed where their dimensions are known by the system. Next the commands **svd**( ) and **inv**( ), which are supplied with the MATLAB system, are used to calculate the singular value decomposition and inverse respectively. Finally the convention U' is used to perform the transpose. The MATLAB syntax is very close the underlying mathematics and is a far cry from coding the same calculations in C or Fortran. Inspection of the MATLAB commands documents the calculation.

Programming Capability. All programming languages by definition provide programming capability but the reverse in not true. For example the recommended RATS commands to place a series X in a complex array and take the fast fourier transform

```
RTOC
#  X
#  1
FFT 1
```

provide programming capability in that the user can customize the command but are not a programming language such as GAUSS and MATLAB. No one would optimally use such a "language" to illustrate a calculation.

Script. A file containing a sequence of commands that are executed by a running program. Programs run by scripts are inherently self documenting. The term macro as used in this paper is in the sense of SAS [52] and refers to a facility found in SAS and B34S that generates a script to be run later. Section 3.1 of this paper shows a B34S Macro and what happens then it is run. For further detail see Macro is this glossary.

System Integration. System integration refers the process by which a number of distinct programs are made to work together as if they are one system. At the low end, system integration could be a number of programs called in sequence under control of a script. At the high end, system integration could mean one software system increasing its apparent capability by being able to pass data and control instructions to a second system and retrieve the results back for further processing.

Acknowledgements

Diana A. Stokes provided editorial assistance. Lawson Wakefield, George Yanos and Stan Cohen read an earlier draft of this paper and made a number of excellent suggestions. An earlier draft of this paper "The Relationship Between Hardware Developments, Operating System Evolution and Econometric Software Design" was presented to the Illinois Economic Association 23 October 1999. This draft has benefited from extensive suggestions from Charles Renfro who read a number of drafts very closely and made a number of substantial suggestions that improved the present draft in many ways. Bruce McCullough made many helpful suggestions, all of which were incorporated in the present draft. A number of unnamed referees made helpful comments. The author is responsible for any remaining errors.

References

[1] E. Anderson, Z. Bai, C. Bischof, J. Demmel, J. Dongarra, J. Du Croz, A. Greenbaum, S. Hammarling, A. McKenney, S. Ostrouchov and D. Sorenson, *LAPACK User's Guide*, Siam, Philadelphia, 1992.

[2] M. Aoki, *State Space Modeling of Time Series*, Springer-Verlag, New York, 1987.

[3] A.J. Barr, J.H. Goodnight, J.P. Sall and J.T. Helwig, *A User's Guide to SAS 76*, SAS Institute, Raleigh, NC, 1976.

[4] L. Breiman, The Π Method for Estimating Multivariate Functions From Noisy Data, *Technometrics* **33**(2) (May 1991), 125–143.

[5] R.G. Bodkin, L.R. Klein and K. Marwah, *A History of Macroeconometric Model-building*, Edward Elgar, Aldershot, 1991.

[6] R.G. Bodkin, Computation in Macroeconomic Model-Building: Some Historical Aspects, in: *Advances in Econometrics, Income Distribution and Scientific Methodology*, J.D. Slottje, ed., Springer-Verlag, New York, 1999.

[7] G. Chow and E.H. Butters, *Optimal Control of Nonlinear Systems Program User's Guide*, Research Memorandum 209, Mimeo, Econometric Research Program, Princeton University, Princeton, NJ, 1977.

[8] G. Chow, *Analysis and Control of Dynamic Economic Systems*, Wiley, New York, 1975.

[9] G. Chow, *Economic Analysis by Control Methods*, Wiley, New York, 1981.

[10] G. Chow, *Econometrics*, McGraw-Hill, New York, 1983.

[11] S. Cohen and S. Pieper, *The Speakeasy III Reference Manual*, Speakeasy Computing Corporation, Chicago, IL, 1979.

[12] T. Doan, *RATS User's Manual*, Estima, Evanston, 1992.

[13] J. Dongarra, C.B. Moler, J.R. Bunch and G.W. Stewart, *LINPACK User's Guide*, Siam, Philadelphia, 1979.

[14] L. Edlefson and S. Jones, *GAUSS*, Aptech Systems, Kent, WA, 1985.

[15] A. Freiden, A Program for the Estimation of Dynamic Economic Relations From a Time Series of Cross Sections, *Annals of Economic and Social Measurement* **2**(1) (January 1973), 89–91.

[16] J. Friedman, Multivariate Adaptive Regression Splines, *Annals of Statistics* **19**(1) (1991), 1–67.

[17] J. Geweke, *Multiple Time Series Manipulator (MTSM). 8208 ed.: User's Guide*, Mimeo, Carnegie Mellon, Philadelphia, PA, 1982.

[18] J. Geweke, Measurement of Linear Dependence and Feedback Between Multiple Time Series, *Journal of the American Statistical Association* **77** (June 1982), 304–313.

[19] W. Greene, *LIMDEP Version 7.0*, Econometric Software, 1998.

[20] W. Greene, Econometric Software, *International Encyclopedia of the Social and Behavioral Sciences*, O. Ashenfelter, ed., Pergamon Press, 2001.
[21] B.F. Hall and R.E. Hall, *Time Series Processor, Version 3.5, User's Manual*, typescript, 1980.
[22] D. Hanselman and B. Littlefield, *Mastering MATLAB 6: A Comprehensive Tutorial and Reference*, Prentice Hall, Upper Saddle River, NJ, 2001.
[23] D. Hendry and J. Doornik, The impact of computational tools on time-series econometrics, *Information, Technology and Scholarship*, T. Coppock, ed., The British Academy, 1999, pp. 257–269.
[24] N. Henry, J. McDonald and H.H. Stokes, The Estimation of Dynamic Economic Relations From a Time Series of Cross Sections: A Programming Modification, *Annals of Economic and Social Measurement* **5**(1) (January 1976), 153–155.
[25] M. Hinich, Testing for GAUSSianity and Linearity of a Stationary Time Series, *Journal of Time Series Analysis* **3**(5) (1982), 169–176.
[26] IEEE, *Standard for Binary Floating-Point Arithmetic, ANSI/IEEE Standard 754-1985*, NY Institute Electrical and Electronics Engineers, 1985; reprinted in *SIGPLAN Notices* **22** (1987), 9–25.
[27] L. Jennings, Simultaneous Equations Estimation, *Journal of Econometrics* **12**(1) (January 1980), 23–39.
[28] K. Judd, *Numerical Methods in Economics*, MIT Press, Cambridge, MA, 1998.
[29] S. Kawasaki, *Manual to Accompany LOGLIN 31*, Mimeo, Northwestern University, Evanston, IL, 1978.
[30] B. Kernighan and D. Ritchie, *The C Programming Language*, Prentice Hall, New Jersey, 1978.
[31] T.C. Lee, G.G. Judge and A. Zellner, *Estimating the Parameters of the Markov Probability Model From Aggregate Time Series Data*, North Holland, New York, 1970.
[32] L.M. Liu and G. Hudak, *The SCA Statistical System: Reference Manual for Fundamental Capabilities*, Scientific Computing Associates, Chicago, 1991.
[33] J. Longley, An Appraisal of Least Squares Programs for the Electronic Computer From the Point of View of the User, *Journal of the American Statistical Association* **62**(319) (1967), 819–841.
[34] *MATLAB: The Language of Technical Computing*, Mathworks, Natick, MA, 2000.
[35] B.D. McCullough and C.G. Renfro, Some Numerical Aspects of Nonlinear Estimation, *Journal of Economic and Social Measurement* **26** (2000), 63–77.
[36] B.D. McCullough and H.D. Vinod, The Numerical Reliability of Econometric Software, *Journal of Economic Literature* **37** (June 1999), 633–665.
[37] B.D. McCullough and H.D. Vinod, Verifying the Solution from a Nonlinear Solver A Case Study, *American Economic Review*, forthcoming.
[38] B.D. McCullough and B. Wilson, On the Accuracy of Statistical Procedures in Microsoft Excel 97, *Computational Statistics and Data Analysis* **31**(1) (1999), 27–37.
[39] R. McKelvey and W. Zavoina, An IBM Fortran IV Program to Perform N-Chotomous Multivariate Probit Analysis, *Behavioral Science* **16** (March 1971), 186–187.
[40] R. McKelvey and W. Zavoina, A Statistical Model for the Analysis of Ordinal Level Dependent Variables, *Journal of Mathematical Sociology* **4** (1975), 103–120.
[41] D. Meeter, *Problems in the Analysis of Nonlinear Models by Least Squares*, Ph.D. diss., University of Wisconsin, 1964.
[42] D. Meeter, *Non-Linear Least Squares* (*GAUSHAUS*), Mimeo, University of Wisconsin Computing Center, Madison, WI, 1964.
[43] M. Metcalf, *Fortran Optimization*, Academic Press, New York, 1985.
[44] M. Nerlove and S.J. Press, *Univariate and Multivariate Log-Linear and Logistic Models*, RAND Corp. Report R-1306-EDA/NIA, Santa Monica, CA, December 1973.
[45] N. Nie, C.H. Hull, J. Jenkins, K. Steinbrenner and D. Bent, *SPSS Statistical Package for the Social Sciences*, 2nd Ed., McGraw, New York, 1975.
[46] V. Numerics, *IMSL Stat/Library and Math/ Library*, IMSL, Houston, TX, 1987.
[47] D. Pack, *A Computer Program for the Analysis of Time Series Models Using the Box-Jenkins Philosophy*, Mimeo, Department of Statistics, Cleveland, Ohio State University, 1977.
[48] C. Renfro, On the development of econometric modeling languages: MODLER and its first twenty-five years, *Journal of Economic and Social Measurement* **22** (1996), 241–311.

[49] C. Renfro, Normative considerations in the development of a software package for econometric estimation, *Journal of Economic and Social Measurement* **23** (1997), 277–330.

[50] C. Renfro, Economic database systems: further reflections on the state of the art, *Journal of Economic and Social Measurement* **23** (1997), 43–85.

[51] C. Renfro, Econometric software: The first fifty years in perspective, *Journal of Economic and Social Measurement* **29** (2004), 9–107, this volume.

[52] SAS, *SAS Guide to Macro Processing, Version 6.0*, 2nd Ed., SAS Institute, Cary, NC, 1990, p. 319.

[53] B.T. Smith, J.M. Boyle, J.J. Dongarra, B.S. Garbow, Y. Ikebe, V.C. Klema and C.B. Moler, *Matrix Eigensystem Routines – EISPACK Guide*, 2nd Ed., Springer-Verlag, Berlin, 1976.

[54] H.H. Stokes, Two-Level Parsing in B34S: A Large-Scale Econometric Package, *IEEE Workshop on Languages for Automation*, IEEE Computer Society Press, Washington, DC, 1987, pp. 235–236.

[55] H.H. Stokes, *Specifying and Diagnostically Testing Econometric Models*, 2nd Ed., Quorum Press, Westport, 1997.

[56] H.H. Stokes, On the advantage of using two or more econometric software systems to solve the same problem, *Journal of Economic and Social Measurement* **29** (2004), 307–320, this volume.

[57] H. Thornber, *Manual for B34T (8 MAR 66)-A Stepwise Regression Program*, University of Chicago Business School technical report 6603, 1966.

[58] H. Thornber, *BAYES Addendum to Technical Report 6603: Manual for B34T-A Stepwise Regression Program*, University of Chicago Business School, 15 September 1967.

[59] H. Thornber, *BLUS Addendum to Technical Report 6603: Manual for B34T-A Stepwise Regression Program*, University of Chicago Business School, 1 August 1968.

[60] G. Tiao and G.E.P. Box, Modeling Multiple Time Series With Applications, *Journal of the American Statistical Association* **76** (1981), 802–816.

[61] G. Tiao, G. Box, M. Grupe, G. Hudak, W. Bell and I. Chang, *The Wisconsin Multiple Time Series (WMTS-1) Program, A Preliminary Guide*, Mimeo, Department of Statistics, University of Wisconsin, Madison, WI, 1979.

[62] L. Wakefield, *Interacter 5.0 Subroutine Reference*, vol. I and II, Interactive Software Ltd., Huntington Staffs, UK, 2000.

Journal of Economic and Social Measurement 29 (2004) 261–270
IOS Press

Wilkinson's tests and econometric software

B.D. McCullough
Department of Decision Sciences, Drexel University, Philadelphia, PA 19104, USA
E-mail: bdmccullough@drexel.edu

The Wilkinson Tests, entry-level tests for assessing the numerical accuracy of statistical computations, have been applied to statistical software packages. Some software developers, having failed these tests, have corrected deficiencies in subsequent versions. Thus these tests have had a meliorative impact on the state of statistical software. These same tests are applied to several econometrics packages. Many deficiencies are noted.

Keywords: Numerical accuracy, software reliability

1. Introduction

The primary purpose of econometric software is to crunch numbers. Regrettably, the primary consideration in evaluating econometric software is not how well the software fulfills its primary purpose. What does matter is how easy it is to get an answer out of the package; whether the answer is accurate is of almost no importance. Reviews of econometric software typically make no mention whatsoever of accuracy, though Vinod [14,15], Veall [13], McCullough [7,8], and MacKenzie [5] are exceptions.

In part, this lack of benchmarking during reviews may be attributed to the fact that, until quite recently, no one ever collected the various benchmarks in a single place (see the NIST StRD at www.nist.gov/itl/div898/strd). A reviewer may well have been aware of a few scattered benchmarks, but including only a few benchmarks is hardly worth the effort. This view is supported by the fact that while the statistics profession has a long history of concern with the reliability of its software, software reviews in statistical journals rarely mention numerical accuracy. However, there is one collection of tests which has been widely applied in the statistics literature: Wilkinson's [16] *Statistics Quiz: Problems which reveal deficiencies in statistical programs*, which is discussed in detail in Sawitzki [10]. These tests have been profitably employed by Sawitzki [11], who uncovered errors in SAS, SPSS, and S-PLUS, among other packages, and also by Bankhofer and Hilbert [1,2]. To date these tests have not been applied to econometric software.

The Wilkinson tests are not meant to be realistic: they were purposefully designed to expose specific errors in statistical packages. Their elegance is three-fold.

- First, they are simple. Therefore, they can reasonably be applied to most any statistical or software package.

- Second, the flaws they are designed to expose have well-known solutions. That is, these are tests which any package *could* pass. If a software package fails a particular test, there exists a known method of obtaining the correct answer.
- Third, they examine the maintained assumptions of the software we use, and which we rarely pause to question. When we have our program read a file, we assume that it is read correctly. When we graph a variable, we assume that the graph accurately represents the data. When we calculate a number, we assume the calculation is accurate and that missing values are "correctly" accounted for.

Statistics Quiz presents six suites of tests: reading an ASCII file; real numbers; missing data; regression; analysis of variance; and operating on a database. The first and last suites are for packages that claim to be general-purpose, and not suited to specialized econometric packages; also, analysis of variance is not much used in economics. The other three suites are relevant to econometric software, and so we apply them to more recent versions of several of the packages that MacKie-Mason [6] evaluated for user-friendliness: E-Views v3.0, LIMDEP v7.0 for Windows 95, RATS v4.3, SHAZAM v8.0, and TSP v4.4.

In applying these tests, we distinguish between "miserable failure" and "catastrophic failure" [9]. A program fails miserably when it refuses to complete the task and the user is informated that the task has not been completed. By contrast, a program fails catastrophically when it incorrectly completes a task without advising the user that something is amiss.

2. The data

Table 1 displays the data set "Nasty", whose values are all well within the range of representable numbers for 32-bit double precision. The values for BIG are less than the US population, while the values of HUGE are the same order of magnitude as the national debt.

Table 1
Data Set NASTY.DAT

LABLE$	X	ZERO	MISS	BIG	LITTLE	HUGE	TINY	ROUND
ONE	1	0	.	99999991	0.99999991	1.0E12	1.0E-12	0.5
TWO	2	0	.	99999992	0.99999992	2.0E12	2.0E-12	1.5
THREE	3	0	.	99999993	0.99999993	3.0E12	3.0E-12	2.5
FOUR	4	0	.	99999994	0.99999994	4.0E12	4.0E-12	3.5
FIVE	5	0	.	99999995	0.99999995	5.0E12	5.0E-12	4.5
SIX	6	0	.	99999996	0.99999996	6.0E12	6.0E-12	5.5
SEVEN	7	0	.	99999997	0.99999997	7.0E12	7.0E-12	6.5
EIGHT	8	0	.	99999998	0.99999998	8.0E12	8.0E-12	7.5
NINE	9	0	.	99999999	0.99999999	9.0E12	9.0E-12	8.5

Table 2
Results of Test IIA

	E-Views	LIMDEP	RATS	SHAZAM	TSP
print ROUND	p	p	p	p	p

3. The tests

3.1. Wilkinson's Test II. Real numbers

Test IIA. Print ROUND with only one digit. This does not mean truncate or round to one digit and then print; it means print displaying only one digit, so that the rounding is done by the program rather than the user. The use of FORMAT statements may be necessary. The answer should be the numbers from 1 to 9. All packages pass. See Table 2.

This is a test of the package's ability to round numbers. Some compilers round numbers inconsistently or use uncommon rounding methods such as round-to-even. Letting R be the rounding function, round-to-even has the interesting property that $R(1.5) = R(2.5)$, for example. An econometric package created with such a compiler may do so, too. Wilkinson presents another test in this section, which is relegated to the appendix for discussion.

Test IIB. Plot HUGE against TINY in a scatterplot. Plot BIG against LITTLE. In each case the answer should be a 45-degree line. The results can somtimes be surprising, as indicated by Fig. 1, which shows the correct graph produced by RATS and the graph produced by E-Views, which failed catastrophically. A common cause of such a result is that computation is in double precision while the graphics routine is in single precision. For such packages, data points may be incorrectly placed or omitted completely, making graphical analysis of data problematic, e.g., visual detection of outliers.

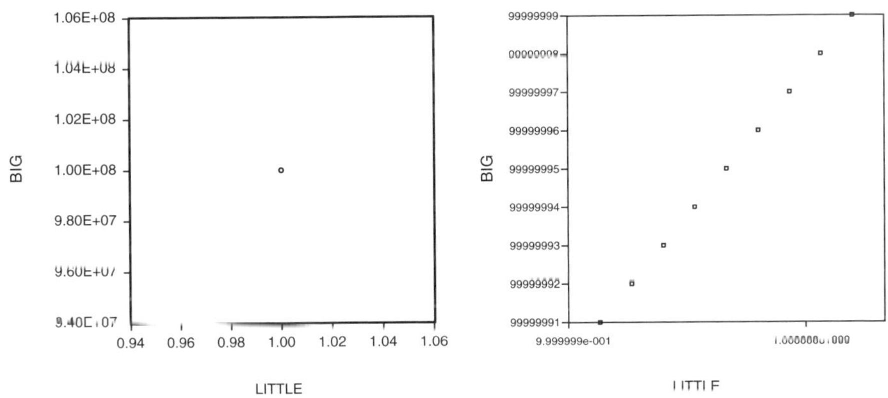

Fig. 1. Test IIB Results for E-Views (left) and RATS (right)

Table 3
Results of Test IIB. †Refused to produce a graph

	E-Views	LIMDEP	RATS	SHAZAM	TSP
HUGE v. TINY	p	p	p	p	p
BIG v. LITTLE	F	p	p	F	p
X v. ZERO	p	†	p	p	p

Table 4
Results of Test IIC – calculate the variance correct answers (indicated by 'p'): NA for ZERO and MISS, 2.738 for all others. †refused to calculate

	E-Views	LIMDEP	RATS	SHAZAM	TSP
X	p	p	p	p	p
ZERO	†	p	p	p	0
MISS	†	†	†	0	†
BIG	p	p	p	2.424	p
LITTLE	p	p	p	2.870	p
HUGE	p	p	p	p	p
TINY	p	p	p	p	p
ROUND	p	p	p	p	p

Plot X against ZERO. The answer should be a vertical line. Some packages, such as LIMDEP, refuse to produce a graph because they are unable to scale the horizontal axis for these data. Since the user is advised that the graph is not produced, this is a miserable failure, rather than a catastrophic failure. SHAZAM's basic plotting routine did not correctly plot big vs. little. (SHAZAM can produce publication-quality graphics by an interface to the "GNUPLOT" program, and these plots pass all the tests.) See Table 3.

Test IIC. Compute basic statistics on each variable. The means should be the fifth value of each variable. Standard deviations should be "undefined" or missing for MISS, zero for ZERO, and 2.738612788 (times 10 to a power) for all other variables (in the table the powers of ten are omitted). Generally, calculation of the means is correct with the following exceptions: SHAZAM returns zero for MISS, when the correct result is 'undefined', while E-Views refuses to calculate for MISS and ZERO. The standard deviation calculations produce some interesting results, as seen in Table 4.

For MISS, SHAZAM returned zero, and the others refused to perform the calculation. The SHAZAM results for BIG and LITTLE can be explained by its algorithm for computing the variance. Ling [4] and Chan et al. [3] analyzed various algorithms for computing the sample variance. The least reliable of these methods was shown to be the 'calculator formula' (so-called because it is used as a shortcut formula in many elementary texts)

$$\hat{\sigma}^2 = \frac{\sum_{i=1}^{n} x_i^2 - \left(\sum_{i=1}^{n} x_i\right)^2 / n}{n-1} \tag{1}$$

whereas the usual formula is

$$\hat{\sigma}^2 = \frac{\sum_{i=1}^{n} (x_i - \overline{x})^2}{n-1} \tag{2}$$

Equation (1) squares the observations themselves, rather than their deviations from the mean, thus unnecessarily using up the computer's finite precision. Indeed, texts on statistical computing (e.g. [12], use Eq. (1) as an example of 'how not to compute the sample variance'.

Test IID. Compute a correlation matrix for all the variables. The correlations for all variables should be unity, except for ZERO and MISS, which should be "undefined" or missing. If MISS must removed from the dataset by the user before the correlations can be computed, this indicates that the package does not "handle" missing observations, but simply deletes them. This turned out to be the case for all the packages but SHAZAM. Results are displayed in Table 5.

The common failure for this test was the calculation of a zero correlation between ZERO and all the other variables. This is clearly an incorrect answer. The correlation coefficient is defined

$$\rho_{wz} = \frac{cov(w, z)}{\sigma_w \sigma_z} \tag{3}$$

where $cov(w, z)$ is the covariance between w and z and and σ_w is the standard deviation of w. Since the standard deviation of ZERO is zero, Eq. (3) has zero in the denominator and so its correlation with any other variable is undefined. Additionally, E-Views and SHAZAM both return correlations greater than unity, which constitutes evidence of an unstable algorithm. SHAZAM computes a correlation of both MISS with itself and ZERO with itself as unity, when the correct answer for both is 'undefined'.

Test IIE. Tabulate X against X, using BIG as a case weight. None of the packages offers this procedure.

Test IIF. Regress BIG on X and a constant. The constant should be 99999990 and the coefficient should be unity. Summary results presented in Table 6 indicate that all programs pass.

Table 5
Results of Test IID. Lower diagonal of correlation matrix: Only incorrect results are displayed

E-Views

	X	ZERO	BIG	LITTLE	HUGE	TINY	ROUND
X							
ZERO	0	0					
BIG	1.13	0					
LITTLE	1.01	0	1.14				
HUGE		0	1.13	1.01			
TINY		0	1.13	1.01			
ROUND		0	1.13	1.01			

LIMDEP, RATS, TSP

	X	ZERO	BIG	LITTLE	HUGE	TINY	ROUND
X							
ZERO	0	0					
BIG		0					
LITTLE		0					
HUGE		0					
TINY		0					
ROUND		0					

SHAZAM

	X	ZERO	BIG	LITTLE	HUGE	TINY	ROUND	MISS
X								
ZERO	0	1						
BIG	1.129	0	1.277					0
LITTLE	1.001	0	1.137	1.013				0
HUGE		0	1.30	1.001				0
TINY		0	1.30	1.001				0
ROUND		0	1.30	1.001				0
MISS	0	0						1

Table 6
Results of Test IIF

	E-Views	LIMDEP	RATS	SHAZAM	TSP
Regress BIG on X	p	p	p	p	p

3.2. *Wilkinson's Test III. Missing data*

Missing values are common in some areas of economics, so it is important to know how they are handled, both in calculations and in logical tests. We draw a distinction between 'handling' missing values and simply excluding all observations.

Test IIIA. Use the data set NASTY on the following transformation:

```
IF MISS = 3
THEN TEST = 1
ELSE TEST = 2
```

TEST should have the value 2 for all cases because MISS does not anywhere equal 3. Another accepted solution is for TEST to be equal to the missing value. Any other

Table 7
Results of Test IIIA

	E-Views	LIMDEP	RATS	SHAZAM	TSP
vectorized	p	p	p	p	NA
do loop	p	p	F	p	p

Table 8
Results of Test IIIB

	E-Views	LIMDEP	RATS	SHAZAM	TSP
vectorized	p	p	p	F	NA
do loop	p	F	p	F	p

answer implies that the software cannot be used for testing logical comparisons when missing values are present.

If the package does not have an ELSE statement, two consecutive IF statements can be used. We distinguish between the vectorized and do-loop versions of the test, where applicable conducting both. They should give the same answer. Sometimes they do not. Results are presented in Table 7. TSP does not offer a vectorized version and returns TEST = 2 for the loop. RATS returns TEST = 1 for the loop and TEST = 2 for the vectorized.

Test IIIB. Use the data set NASTY on the following calculation:

$$\texttt{IFMISS} = <\texttt{missing}> \ \texttt{THENMISS} = \texttt{MISS} + \texttt{1}$$

The correct answer is <missing>, since 1 added to a missing value is still missing. As in the previous test, we distinguish between vectorized and do loop methods. They should give the same answer, but sometimes they do not. Results are presented in Table 8. For the loop, LIMDEP returns MISS = −998. SHAZAM returns MISS = −99998 for both.

3.3. Wilkinson's Test IV: Regression

Test IVA. Using the variable X, compute X1 = X, X2 = X^2, X3 = $X^3, \ldots,$ X9 =X^9. Regress X1 on a constant and X2 through X9. The coefficients, to three significant digits, are: 0.353, 1.14, −0.705, 0.262, −0.0616, 0.00920, −0.000847, 0.0000438, −0.000000974. Since this test is bound to stress the machinery, what is important is not the coefficients but the overall regression. Since this gives a perfect fit, R^2 should be unity. As an added check, the sum of squared residuals should be close to zero as should the integrated squared error evaluated for the estimated coefficients. Results are presented in Table 9. E-Views can perform the the regression only up to X7, refusing to compute for the eighth and ninth degree polynomials. Since it refuses to compute rather than return an incorrect answer, this is a miserable failure rather than a catastrophic failure.

Table 9
Results of Test IVA, †only calculated up to X7

	E-Views	LIMDEP	RATS	SHAZAM	TSP
polynomial regression	†	p	p	p	p

Table 10
Results of Test IVB

	E-Views	LIMDEP	RATS	SHAZAM	TSP
regress X on X	p	p	p	p	p

Table 11
Results of Test IVC

	E-Views	LIMDEP	RATS	SHAZAM	TSP
regress X on BIG, LITTLE	p	p	F	p	p

Table 12
Results of Test IVD

	E-Views	LIMDEP	RATS	SHAZAM	TSP
regress ZERO on X	p	p	p	p	p

Test IVB. Regress X on a constant and X. The constant should be exactly zero and the regression coefficient should be unity. Results are summarized in Table 10: all packages pass.

Test IVC. Regress X on a constant, BIG, and LITTLE. The program should inform the user that this is a singular regression. Results are presented in Table 11. RATS returns coefficients and does not warn about the singularity, which is a catastrophic failure.

Test IVD. Regress ZERO on a constant and X. The program should inform the user that ZERO has no variance or should report both the correlation and sum of squares to be zero. Results are presented in Table 12. All packages pass.

4. Conclusions

Wilkinson's Tests have been applied to five econometric packages, uncovering flaws in all five. These flaws include dropping points from a graph, incorrect calculation of the sample variance, correlation coefficients in excess of unity, and incorrect and inconsistent handling of missing values. These econometrics packages fared about as well as did the statistics packages examined by Sawitzki [11]. Some of these statistics packages improved their performance in subsequent versions, and the same can be hoped for these econometric packages. All the packages assessed in this article have since released new versions. It will be interesting to see whether the developers have fixed known errors.

Table 13
Results of Test IIA

	E-Views	LIMDEP	RATS	SHAZAM	TSP
Y1,Y2,Y3	18,0,0	18,0,0	18,0,0	18,0,0	18,0,0

Appendix

Wilkinson's Test IIA continues in the following fashion. As another test of consistent rounding, note that $\sqrt{2}\sqrt{2} = 2$, and $\exp[\ln(2)] = 2$. Compute the following scalars where INT is the greatest integer function (converts reals to integers by throwing away the decimals), and LOG is the natural logarithm. Wilkinson writes that if a statistical package fails this test, "you cannot trust it to compute any function accurately".

Y1 = INT(2.6*7 – 0.2)	⇒	INT(18.0)	⇒	18
Y2 = 2-INT(EXP(LOG(SQRT(2)*SQRT(2))))	⇒	2-INT(2.0)	⇒	0
Y3 = INT(3-EXP(LOG(SQRT(2)*SQRT(2))))	⇒	INT(3.0-2.0)	⇒	1

Results of this test are presented in Table 13.

According to Wilkinson, none of these packages can be trusted to perform any calculation because all return 0 instead of 1 for Y3. To the contrary, 0 is the correct answer for Y3, and Wilkinson can be excused for this mistake.

Wilkinson's *Statistics Quiz* was published in 1985, the same year that the IEEE-754 standard for computer arithmetic was released, so Wilkinson cannot be faulted for contradicting IEEE-754. In fact, the results displayed in Table 13 are perfectly consistent with IEEE-754.

To see this, recall that in 32-bit double precision the computer has about 16 digits with which to represent any number. In the case of taking square roots that are not exactly representable in 16 digits, the last digit must be rounded. The square root of 2, being an irrational number, cannot be exactly represented in sixteen digits. So the square root of 2 is 1.414213562373095 to sixteen digits, the next four digits are 0488. Let a = the sixteen digit square root of 2. Then a^2 equals not 2 but $2 + 4.44089$E-16.

Similarly, EXP(LOG(SQRT(2)*SQRT(2))) becomes EXP(LOG(2+4.44089E-16)) which equals someting slightly greater than 2, for simplicity call it $2 + \epsilon$.

For Y2, the integer part of $(2 + \epsilon)$ is 2 which, subtracted from 2, yields zero. For Y3, $3 - (2 + \epsilon)$ becomes $1 - \epsilon$ which, when the integer part is taken, becomes zero. Thus, the five packages considered all produce answers that are in accordance with IEEE-754. Hence, rather than indicate a problem with the software, this test suggests that the user be aware of the limitations of finite precision computation.

Acknowledgements

Thanks for comments to J. Doornik, P. Hollinger, and conference participants of the 1999 Boston meeting of the Society for Computational Economics, as well as seminar participants at various bureaus of the Federal Communications Commission and the software developers. Finally, thanks to M. Cornea for an illuminating disucssion of IEEE-754 square root calculations.

References

[1] U. Bankhofer and A. Hilbert, An Application of Two-Mode Classification to Analze the Statistical Software Market, in: *Classification and Knowledge Organisation*, R. Klar and O. Opitz, eds, Springer, Heidelberg, 1997, pp. 567–572.

[2] U. Bankhofer and A. Hilbert, Statistical Software Packages for Windows: A Market Survey, *Statistical Papers* **38** (1997), 393–407.

[3] T.F. Chan, G.H. Golub and R.J. Leveque, Algorithms for Computing the Sample Variance: Analysis and Recommendations, *American Statistician* **37** (1983), 242–247.

[4] R.F. Ling, Comparison of Several Algorithms for Computing Sample Means and Variances, *Journal of the American Statistical Association* **69** (1974), 859–866.

[5] C.R. MacKenzie, MicroFit 4.0, *Journal of Applied Econometrics* **13** (1998), 77–89.

[6] J. MacKie-Mason, Econometric Software: A User's View, *Journal of Economic Perspectives* **6** (1992), 165–188.

[7] B.D. McCullough, Benchmarking Numerical Accuracy: A Review of RATS v4.2, *Journal of Applied Econometrics* **12** (1997), 181–190.

[8] B.D. McCullough, Econometric Software Reliability:EViews, LIMDEP, SHAZAM, and TSP, *Journal of Applied Econometrics* **12** (1997), 191–202.

[9] W. Murray, Failure, the Causes and Cures, in: *Numerical Methods for Unconstrained Optimization*, W. Murray, ed., Academic Press, NY, 1972, pp. 107–122.

[10] G. Sawitzki, Testing Numerical Reliability of Data Analysis Systems, *Computational Statistics and Data Analysis* **18** (1994), 269–286.

[11] G. Sawitzki, Report on the Numerical Reliability of Data Analysis Systems, *Computational Statistics and Data Analysis* **18** (1994), 289–301.

[12] R.A. Thisted, *Elements of Statistical Computing*, Chapman and Hall, New York, 1988.

[13] M.R. Veall, SHAZAM 6.2: A Review, *Journal of Applied Econometrics* **6** (1991), 317–320.

[14] H.D. Vinod, A Review of SORITEC 6.2, *American Statistician* **43** (1989), 266–269.

[15] H.D. Vinod, Review of GAUSS for Windows Including Its Numerical Accuracy, *Journal of Applied Econometrics* **15** (2000), 211–220.

[16] L. Wilkinson, *Statistics Quiz*, SYSTAT, Evanston, IL, 1985.

Journal of Economic and Social Measurement 29 (2004) 271–295
IOS Press

A comparative study of alternative econometric packages with an application to Italian deposit interest rates*

Giuseppe Bruno** and Riccardo De Bonis
Research Department, Banca d'Italia, Via Nazionale 91, I-00184 Rome, Italy
Tel.: +39 06 47924164, +39 06 47922335; Fax: +39 06 4747820, +39 06 47923611;
E-mail: {bruno.giuseppe,debonis.riccardo}@insedia.interbusiness.it

This paper compares alternative econometric packages for the estimation of panel data. Concern has recently been expressed in the literature about the lack of attention paid to numerical accuracy in econometric software. We compare the numerical values of the estimates of three of the most popular econometric packages featuring built-in panel data estimation algorithms: LIMDEP, STATA and TSP. The empirical application consists in looking at the determinants of bank interest rates on deposits in Italy using a data set with more than 10,000 observations. Different specifications have been estimated using fixed- and random-effects models. Fixed- effects estimates are equal in the three packages. By contrast, small differences appear for the random-effects estimators. We discuss the reasons for which the estimators differ and compare the relative efficiency of the random-effects algorithms provided by the three packages using a set of suitably designed Monte Carlo simulations.

1. Introduction

Over the last two decades many software packages have been developed featuring complex estimation procedures that do not require users to have in-depth knowledge of the numerical algorithms or computer science. Most of the econometric and statistical software packages available to the academic and business communities feature both interactive and programmable interfaces. The users of these packages may be unaware of the risk of numerical inaccuracy.

The purpose of this paper is to respond to the *caveats* about numerical accuracy in econometric software raised in McCullough and Vinod [25], who are concerned about the lack of attention paid to numerical precision in the selection of econometric packages. The fear is that the market might place Central Processing Unit (CPU) performance above accuracy. We accordingly decided to compare the numerical precision of some popular econometric software packages by estimating panel data and looking at the estimators' characteristics with fixed-effects and random-effects models.

---

*The views expressed in the paper are those of the authors and do not involve the responsibility of Banca d'Italia.

**Corresponding author.

In contrast to tests of the numerical accuracy of packages using standard data sets [20–22,35], we follow the approach of Newbold et al. [30] and McCullough and Renfro [23] making tests using a specific data set on the determinants of bank deposit interest rates in Italy.

The paper is divided into four sections. Section 2 discusses the issues and introduces the three popular econometric packages featuring the built-in panel-data estimation algorithms we wish to compare: LIMDEP, STATA and TSP (LIMDEP Mainframe version 7.0, STATA 6.0 and TSP 4.4.). Our empirical application is based on a large data set with more than 10,000 observations of the rates paid on deposits by banks in the Italian provinces between 1990 and 1999; we concentrate on static regressions, i.e. without including lagged endogenous variables among the regressors. Section 3 compares the numerical values of the estimates we obtained using LIMDEP, STATA and TSP. Section 4 presents a simulation designed to evaluate the relative efficiency of the three estimators. The main conclusions are set out in Section 5. The Appendix documents some of the program listings we built.

2. Comparing LIMDEP, STATA and TSP in the estimation of panel data: fixed- and random-effects models

2.1. *Some aspects of the research strategy*

The last two decades have seen the rapid development of econometric and statistical software featuring complex estimation procedures that do not require users to have in-depth knowledge of the numerical algorithms used or computer science (for earlier implementation of balanced panel data estimation see for example [14] and [17]). The main selection criteria for these products are usability, availability of the commands most frequently required and cost (we do not address this aspect here).

To the best of the authors' knowledge, there has been only one panel-data software review in recent years [11]. We feel a new study is needed because of the impressive pace at which these packages have been developed in the last few years and the lack of numerical applications in Blanchard's paper. Unlike Blanchard, we do not include the RATS package because it does not address the panel data estimation problem in a straightforward way (although it is possible to build simple programs using the usual algorithms).

For various reasons, the numerical accuracy of the answers supplied by software packages is often overlooked or even neglected. McCullough and Vinod [25] give examples in which the numerical answers produced by several (unnamed) econometric and statistical packages are different. The problem is even more crucial for non-linear applications (see [23,24]) where many different reasons might negatively affect the numerical accuracy. Given the importance of this issue, however, it should be normal practice for users to validate their results. The natural question is how to evaluate the numerical accuracy of a complex algorithm. Here, we simply compare the results obtained using three different econometric packages that are widely available in the research departments of many institutions. The packages compared are:

1) LIMDEP from Econometrics Software, Inc. of Plainview New York;
2) STATA from STATA Corp. (Texas);
3) Time Series Processor (TSP) from TSP Intl. (California).

It should be noted that these packages have been developed to meet special academic research needs and less weight has been given to their user interface, typically simple text. Learning to use these packages represents an important sunk cost for researchers; once a researcher has learnt a package, it is hard to switch to another one, even if the last software is more usable than the former.

The three packages all have a number of panel-estimation commands. The algorithms used for the panel estimation (fixed- and random-effects estimators) can be interpreted as Generalized Least Squares (GLS) estimates. When dealing with panel data a very desired feature is the ability to build sample dataset drawing on the overall database. All the examined packages provide simple programming tools to carry out these tasks.

There are essentially two ways to validate the numerical accuracy of different software. The first compares the numerical robustness of a procedure using an ad hoc data set for which a benchmark is available. The second compares the numerical results achieved with different packages. We have followed the second route, which we feel is the one most relevant to the usual research department equipped with many different packages. Our approach is similar to that of Newbold et al. [30]. These authors compare software for ARIMA models estimation and find different estimates and forecasts depending on which package is used. Sometimes the differences can be explained, due to differences in default options and adopted algorithms. Other times the differences cannot be explained and therefore the need for a benchmark arises. In our paper we explored avenues for increasing the confidence that each one of the examined packages operates correctly. If different estimates appear, their further investigation can lead to results that are useful for applied econometricians.

2.2. *The available data-set and the empirical application*

The empirical example we present here examines the determinants of the interest rates paid on bank deposits in 95 Italian provinces between 1990 and 1999. We focus on these rates because bank deposits are still one of the main ways in which Italian households invest their financial wealth. The data on interest rates have been taken from the Central Credit Register and refer to deposits of 20 million lire or more with a sample of banks.[1]

[1] The sample collects interest rates provided by 41 banks in 1990, 46 in 1991, 47 in 1992, 47 in 1993, 47 in 1994, 47 in 1995, 46 in 1996, 45 in 1997, 44 in 1998, 43 in 1999. Mergers are mainly responsible for these annual changes. Data are available upon request. For confidentiality reasons we cannot provide information on the identity of the individual banks.

Table 1
Summary Statistics (1990–1999)

	Average	Minimum	Maximum
Deposits interest rate* (%)	5.77	0.12	10.97
Herfindahl index**	0.20	0.05	0.56
Concentration ratio** (R3,%)	64.2	34.1	96.5
Banks per province** (number)	26	1	115
Costs/total assets (%)*	2.71	1.24	5.12
Staff costs per employee* (euro)	53827	34119	82894

Summary Statistics for the Five Italian Macroregions: 1990–1999
(number of observations and average values of the variables)

	NorthWest	NorthEast	Center	South	Islands
Number of observations	2980	2899	2117	1689	876
Deposits' interest rate (%)	5.92	5.88	5.74	5.52	5.45
Herfindahl index	0.17	0.22	0.21	0.18	0.24
Concentration ratio	59.7	68.1	67.1	60.2	67.3
Banks per province	33.4	27.4	25.7	16.5	14.1
Costs/assets (%)	2.75	2.69	2.72	2.67	2.66
Staff costs per employee (euro)	53425	53596	54030	54322	54511

*Variables refer to the banks reporting interest rates.
**Variables refer to a larger sample, covering about 92 per cent of total deposits in Italy.

The data set is arranged using the individual code of each bank and the province in which it is active. The unit of observation is a subset of the Cartesian product of the sets of banks and provinces (for example, bank i in province j gives one unit of observation, i.e. the couple i, j). The total number of individuals is obtained by summing the number of banks over the provinces. This number equals 1,298 in our sample. The data set is unbalanced in the sense that not all the individuals are present in all the years 1990–1999. Summing the individuals over the years we get a total of 10,561 observations after removal of outliers; in some rare occasions banks provided interest rates which were economically meaningless.

The dependent variable in the regressions is the average rate on the total deposits of each bank. There has been an extensive debate in the United States on the determinants of interest rates, with two opposing points of view. According to the first, market concentration is still an important factor influencing bank interest rates. According to the second, the link between traditional measures of competition and banking prices disappeared with the deregulation of the banking system. [2]

In this paper two variables are used to measure concentration: the Herfindahl index for deposits and the concentration ratio for the first three banks in the province (R3, the sum of their market shares). The Herfindahl indices and the concentration ratios R3 consider all the different types of banks but the mutual banks. As other indicators

[2]For the debate in the United States see, inter alia [1,7–10,15,18,28,29,31,32,26,33]. For the Italian case see [2] and [13].

Table 2
Determinants of deposit interest rates; panel estimation, 1990–1999

	(i) Fixed effects		(ii) Fixed Effects		(iii) Fixed effects		(iv) Fixed effects		(v) Fixed effects	
HER	−0.22						−0.31			
	(−0.79)						(−1.09)			
R3			−0.33	***					−0.39	**
			(−1.92)						(−2.20)	
NBANKS					−0.004		−0.004	***	−0.005	***
					(−1.59)		(−1.75)		(−1.91)	
COSPER	−6.48	*	−6.47	*	−6.42	*	−6.42	*	−6.40	*
	(−4.50)		(−4.49)		(−4.45)		(−4.45)		(−4.43)	
COSRAT	4.05	*	4.06	*	4.03	**	4.00	**	4.00	**
	(2.35)		(2.35)		(2.34)		(2.32)		(2.32)	
Number of observations	10,561		10,561		10,561		10,561		10,561	
R^2	0.95		0.95		0.95		0.95		0.95	
Sum squared residuals	2,839.1		2,838.22		2,838.58		2,838.22		2,837.09	
Hausman test	136.87		139.47		139.66		141.76		145.17	

Dependent variable: banks' deposit rate in each province.

Independent variables: Herfindahl index for deposits' market shares (HER); concentration ratio (R3), i.e. sum of the first 3 banks' market shares per province; staff costs per employee (COSPER); costs/total assets (COSRAT); number of banks per province (NBANKS). Variables refer to end-of-year data, for the period 1990–1999. Regressions include time dummy variables, whose coefficients are not reported. t – statistics in brackets.

*Significant at 1 per cent.

**Significant at 5 per cent.

*** Significant at 10 per cent.

of competition and diffusion of financial services, we use the total number of banks in each province, irrespective of those included in our sample.

Different control variables are used in the literature to check for the effect of concentration on interest rates. We use per-capita income in each province, which is an indicator of the degree of economic development, and the growth rate of deposits in each province, which may influence the return offered on deposits. Other control variables include banks' costs, which may influence deposit rates on the assumption that banks consider their total costs when fixing deposit rates. Here we consider two aggregates: the ratio between costs and total assets and average staff costs per employee. Descriptive statistics for all the variables are reported in Table 1.

Table 2 reports some initial estimates. The regressions contain yearly dummy variables to control for the effects on deposit rates of changes in the stance of monetary policy and the business cycle. The dummies are significant, evidence of the importance of the evolution of rates over time. The Herfindahl index does not have a statistically significant influence on deposit rates. The results for Italy thus do not appear to confirm the negative relationship often found in America between concentration and deposit rates. A significant negative effect is produced, however,

Table 3
Determinants of deposit interest rates; panel estimation, 1990–1999

	(i) Fixed effects	(ii) Fixed Effects
HER	−0.23	−0.22
	(−0.83)	(−0.78)
COSPER	−5.04 *	
	(−3.86)	
COSRAT		0.75
		(0.48)
N. observations	10,561	10,561
R^2	0.95	0.95
Sum of squared residuals	2,840.86	2,845.4
Hausman test	100.9	131

Dependent variable: banks' deposit rate in each province.

Independent variables: Herfindahl index for deposits' market shares (HER); staff costs per employee (COSPER); costs/total assets (COSRAT). Variables refer to end-of-year data, for the period 1990-99. Regressions include time dummy variables, whose coefficients are not reported. t – statistics in brackets.

* Significant at 1 per cent.

** Significant at 5 per cent.

*** Significant at 10 per cent.

by the concentration ratio R3. It seems that only the market shares of the most important banks in each province are negatively correlated with the level of interest rates.

Average staff costs per employee (COSPER) have a negative effect on the remuneration of deposits: the higher the value of this variable, the lower the deposit rate. The negative sign of COSPER (Table 2) is also found in a regression containing only this variable and HER (Table 3). A possible explanation of this result is that banks with high internal costs try to save on deposit remuneration. The number of banks per province (NBANKS) has mainly a negative but usually not significant effect on deposit rates (Table 2). Deposit growth rates and provincial per-capita incomes do not influence deposit rates (regressions with these variables are not reported). Cross-sections for the period 1990–1999 (Table 4) confirm that the Herfindahl index does not influence interest rates for most of the years examined.

2.3. Comparison among the three packages

We now compare the 3 software packages – LIMDEP, STATA and TSP – we used to estimate the determinants of bank interest rates.

The packages can be used interactively but to preserve reproducibility we use programs written in languages native to the packages. The code fragments for these programs are given in the Appendix. The results shown there refer to the regression reported in Table 3, column (i), for the fixed-effects case. A simple visual inspection

Table 4
Determinants of deposit interest rates cross-sections (OLS), 1990–1995

	(i) 1990	(ii) 1991	(iii) 1992	(iv) 1993	(v) 1994	(vi) 1995
HER	0.14	0.23	−0.21	0.35	−0.07	−0.11
	(0.54)	(0.98)	(−0.6)	(1.44)	(−0.31)	(−0.43)
COSPER	23.31 *	25.77 *	43.92 *	−4.79 ***	−20.35 *	−6.23
	(2.81)	(3.82)	(5.12)	(−1.72)	(−4.95)	(−1.31)
COSRAT	−28.75 *	−10.75 **	1.68	16.77 *	−16.32 *	13.72 *
	(−5.25)	(−2.11)	(0.27)	(3.03)	(−3.70)	(2.74)
COSTANT	7.62 *	6.98 *	6.60 *	6.33 *	7.45 *	6.98 *
	(29.44)	(26.17)	(15.69)	(35.11)	(34.11)	(28.20)
N. observat.	804	928	1,088	1,115	1,150	1,177
R^2	0,03	0,02	0,02	0,01	0,05	0,01
Sum squared residuals	404	388	1260	646	576	740
	(i) 1990	(ii) 1991	(iii) 1992	(iv) 1993	(v) 1994	(vi) 1995
HERF	0.33	0.15	−0.009	0.04	−0.004	0.36
	(1.09)	(0.59)	(−0.02)	(0.17)	(−0.017)	(1.25)
NBANKS	0.001	−0.0006	0.002	−0.003	0.0007	0.005 *
	(1.3)	(−0.57)	(1.17)	(−2.46)	(0.56)	(3.68)
COSPER	22.58 **	25.91 *	44.12 *	−5.11	−20.23 *	−5.60
	(2.72)	(3.83)	(5.14)	(−1.84)	(−4.91)	(−1.18)
COSRAT	−28.42 *	−10.82 **	1.42	16.51 *	−16.28 *	13.13 *
	(−5.18)	(−2.12)	(0.22)	(2.99)	(−3.69)	(2.63)
COSTANT	7.55 *	7.00 *	6.50 *	6.35 *	7.41 *	6.72 *
	(28.70)	(25.82)	(15.13)	(32.94)	(32.20)	(26.25)
N. observat.	804	928	1,088	1,115	1,150	1,177
R^2	0.03	0.01	0.02	0.01	0.05	0.01
Sum squared residuals	403	388	1258	642	576	732

Dependent variable: banks' deposit rate in each province.

Independent variables: Herfindahl index for deposit market shares (HER); staff costs per employee (COSPER); costs/total assets (COSRAT); number of banks per province (NBANKS). Variables refer to end-of-year data, for the period 1990–95. t – statistics in brackets.

*Significant at 1 per cent.

**Significant at 5 per cent.

***Significant at 10 per cent.

of this code shows the similarity of the packages considered in terms of the number of lines of code and the output produced.

The numerical values of the estimated coefficients for the fixed- and random-effects models are checked using the Speakeasy-Modeleasy Plus environment.[3] This general purpose package supplies an interactive shell which permits compact expressions for

[3]Modeleasy Plus, EMCC (Palm Harbor, Florida).

Table 4 (continued)
Determinants of deposit interest rates; cross-sections (OLS), 1996–1999

	(i) 1996	(ii) 1997	(iii) 1998	(iv) 1999
HER	0.22	0.25	0.39 **	0.46 *
	(1.11)	(1.22)	(2.26)	(3.08)
COSPER	−37.44 *	−12.89 *	−25.80 *	−15.42 *
	(−10.39)	(−3.29)	(−7.43)	(−7.02)
COSRAT	−47.66 *	−33.72 *	−38.24 *	−1.76
	(−8.71)	(−7.86)	(−11.09)	(−0.72)
COSTANT	9.25 *	5.97 *	4.76 *	2.38 *
	(33.92)	(22.62)	(20.36)	(16.69)
N. observat.	1,175	1,022	1,056	1,046
R^2	0.12	0.06	0.12	0.05
Sum of squared residuals	438	335	259	184
	(i) 1996	(ii) 1997	(iii) 1998	(iv) 1999
HERF	0.21	0.37	0.62 *	0.46 *
	(0.94)	(1.62)	(3.22)	(2.83)
NBANKS	−0.0001	0.001	0.002 *	0.000
	(−0.15)	(1.23)	(2.71)	(0.08)
COSPER	−37.47 *	−12.59 *	−25.30 *	−15.40 *
	(−10.38)	(−3.20)	(−7.30)	(−6.95)
COSRAT	−47.65 *	−33.89 *	−38.55 *	−1.77
	(−8.70)	(−7.90)	(−11.21)	(−0.72)
COSTANT	9.26 *	5.89 *	4.62 *	2.38 *
	(33.19)	(21.75)	(19.32)	(15.66)
N. observat.	1,175	1,022	1,056	1,046
R^2	0.12	0.06	0.13	0.05
Sum squared residuals	438	335	257	184

Dependent variable: banks' deposit rate in each province.

Independent variables: Herfindahl index for deposit market shares (HER); staff costs per employee (COSPER); costs/total assets (COSRAT); number of banks per province (NBANKS). Variables refer to end-of-year data, for the period 1996-99. t – statistics in brackets.

*Significant at 1 per cent.

** Significant at 5 per cent.

*** Significant at 10 per cent.

matrix processing. This feature allows the users to write and adjust their own algorithms with a high level of flexibility at the cost of an in-depth knowledge of the algorithm itself. Using the matrix language provided by the packages, we have written a program implementing the fixed- and random-effects data transformation and then the usual OLS formulas have been applied on the transformed data. Paragraph 3 presents the details. Speakeasy-Modeleasy Plus yields the same results of the 3 examined packages, increasing the confidence that the results are correct and making

Table 5
TSP, LIMDEP and STATA: comparison between the outputs (parameter estimates and, in parentheses, standard errors)

(*a*) *Fixed effects regressions*

	Herfin	Cosper
TSP	−0.239628	−5.04241
	(0.287650)	(1.30455)
LIMDEP	−0.23963	−5.0424
	(0.28765)	(1.3046)
STATA	−0.239628	−5.04241
	(0.287650)	(1.30455)

(*b*) *Random effects regressions*

	Herfin	Cosper
TSP	0.060432	−5.70928
	(0.139469)	(1.23183)
LIMDEP	0.053140	−5.6567
	(0.14489)	(1.2381)
STATA	0.059021	−5.69863
	(0.141082)	(1.23794)

not necessary the construction of a formal benchmark.

A first glimpse at the regressions' outputs shows that STATA gives a value for the constant, which is irrelevant for the fixed-effects estimator that assumes a restriction on the fixed effects to avoid the dummy variable trap. The constant can be derived from the following formula:

$$\alpha_{\text{within}} = \frac{1}{\sum_{i=1}^{Nfirm} T_i} \cdot (\overline{\overline{y}} - \beta_{\text{within}} \cdot \overline{\overline{X}}) \qquad (1)$$

where: T_i is the number of observations available for firm i, $Nfirm$ is the number of individual firms, $\sum_{i=1}^{Nfirm} T_i = NOBS$ is the total number of available observations, $\overline{\overline{y}}_i = \frac{1}{NOBS} \sum_{i=1}^{Nfirm} \sum_{t=1}^{T_i} y_{it}$ is the scalar grand average of all the observations on the dependent variable, $\overline{\overline{X}}_i = \frac{1}{NOBS} \sum_{i=1}^{Nfirm} \sum_{t=1}^{T_i} X_{it}t$ is the vector of the grand averages of all the observations on the independent variables.

The main goal of our comparison is to validate the numerical results. The regressions' outputs reported in Table 5a show that the fixed-effects estimator, for its implementation simplicity, gives the same numerical value for all three packages to 5 significant digits. By contrast, there are non-trivial differences between the random-effects estimates (see Table 5b; the whole set of econometric results are displayed in the Appendix). From an economic perspective these differences seem small. From a numerical perspective, they are not so small that they can be attributed to rounding errors. Therefore, these differences deserve further investigation.

3. Why do random-effects estimators differ?

The numerical differences for the random-effects estimation are due to the different criteria adopted to estimate the variance components. Baltagi [4] and Maddala and Mount [19] offer a comprehensive survey on the estimation methods for variance-component models. For the examined packages, the information on the individual algorithms have been taken from the manuals. Further details were provided by the developers.

Our analysis focuses on the one-way error model with no time-only component in the disturbance term.

For the random-effects model the lack of knowledge of the true disturbances implies the need of an estimate of their variance-covariance matrix; different algorithms have been proposed in the literature for estimating the variance of the two error terms. Statistical comparisons among the various feasible estimators show their asymptotic efficiency as either T_i or $Nfirm \to \infty$. It turns out that the guiding element for the choice among the different algorithms is the simplicity and numerical robustness of the implementation.

Given the model $y_{it} = \alpha + X'_{it}\beta + u_{it}, i = 1, \dots, Nfirm; t = 1, \dots, T_i,$, with the disturbance term decomposed as: $u_{it} = \mu_i + v_{it}$ and $\sigma_u^2 = \sigma_\mu^2 + \sigma_\nu^2$, and assuming that the idiosyncratic elements μ_i are random, the estimation consists in the application of ordinary least squares to the transformed model:

$$y_{it} - \theta_i \cdot \overline{y}_{i\cdot} = \alpha \cdot (1 - \theta_i) + (X'_{it} - \theta_i \cdot \overline{X}'_{i\cdot}) \cdot \beta + u_{it} - \theta_i \cdot \overline{u}_{i\cdot} \tag{2}$$

where the bar over the variable represents its temporal average. The parameter θ_i determines the amount of quasi-differencing in the GLS transformation; this parameter is a function of the two variance components $\sigma_\mu^2, \sigma_\nu^2$. Limiting values for θ_i are: 1 for the within regression and 0 for the pooled OLS regression. σ_ν^2 (the variance of the residuals component net of the idiosyncratic term σ_μ^2) is achievable from the fixed-effects estimation (within regression). The following alternative equations for σ_1^2 are used by the three packages:

- TSP. $\breve{\sigma}_1^2 = \sigma_{\text{tot}}^2 - \sigma_\nu^2$, where σ_{tot}^2 is the variance of the pooled regression (OLS) given by TSP. If $\breve{\sigma}_1^2$ is negative, TSP resorts to the large-sample formula given by $\breve{\sigma}_1 = (SSR_{\text{OLS}} - SSR_{\text{Within}})/NOBS$, where SSR stands for residuals sum of squares and $NOBS$ is the total number of observations;
- LIMDEP. $\tilde{\sigma}_1^2$ is the following variance computed with LIMDEP:
  $\tilde{\sigma}_1^2 = \left(\sum_i (\overline{y}_{i\cdot} - b_{ols} \cdot \overline{x}_{i\cdot})^2/(Nfirm - k - 1)\right) - \frac{1}{T_{ave}}\sigma_\nu^2$, where b_{ols} is the pooled OLS coefficient vector;
  $Nfirm$ is the number of different groups;
  k is the number of explanatory variables;
  T_{ave} is the arithmetic mean of the set of T_i;
  b_{ols} is replaced by b_{between} when the value of $\tilde{\sigma}_1^2$ turns out to be negative;

– STATA. $\hat{\sigma}_1^2$ is the variance computed with STATA:
$\hat{\sigma}_1^2 = \max(0, \sigma^2_{\text{between}} - \sigma^2_\nu/\overline{T})$, where $\overline{T}$ is the harmonic mean of the set of T_i.

It is clear that all the numerical differences produced by the random-effects estimates are caused by the differences in the small-sample formulas for the computation of the between-regression variance. The parameter θ_i, which distinguishes the behaviour of the three packages, is computed in the following ways:

$$\text{TSP} \quad \theta_i = 1 - \sqrt{\frac{\sigma_\nu^2}{T_i \cdot \breve{\sigma}_1^2 + \sigma_\nu^2}}$$

$$\text{LIMDEP} \quad \theta_i = 1 - \sqrt{\frac{\sigma_\nu^2}{T_i \cdot \tilde{\sigma}_1^2 + \sigma_\nu^2}}$$

$$\text{STATA} \quad \theta_i = 1 - \sqrt{\frac{\sigma_\nu^2}{T_i \cdot \hat{\sigma}_1^2 + \sigma_\nu^2}}$$

Although the three estimators are asymptotically equivalent, they show different small-sample properties (on this subject see [34]). Now we sketch the reasons for the differences in the random-effects model estimation. Starting from model M1, in order to estimate the two variance components σ_μ^2 and σ_ν^2, we consider the following quadratic forms defining the within and between sums of squares (for the theoretical background see for example [5]):

$$q_1 = u'Qu$$

$$q_2 = u'Pu$$

where: u is the residuals vector achieved by the regression, $P = I_{Nfirm} \otimes [\overline{J}_{T_i}]$, $\overline{J}_{T_i}$ is a $T_i \times T_i$ given by

$$\begin{pmatrix} 1/T_i & 1/T_i & \cdots & 1/T_i \\ 1/T_i & 1/T_i & \cdots & 1/T_i \\ \vdots & \vdots & \vdots & \vdots \\ 1/T_i & 1/T_i & \cdots & 1/T_i \end{pmatrix}$$

is the matrix which averages the observations across time for each individual, $Q = I_{Nfirm\ T_{ave}} - P$ is the matrix which obtains the deviations from individuals means.

With these formal instruments and looking at the numerical results provided by the packages (see the Appendix), we draw the following conclusions for TSP, STATA and LIMDEP:

Table 6
Execution times and program sizes

Package	Execution time (sec.)	Lines of Code
TSP	5	30
LIMDEP	12	28
STATA	38	32

1) TSP adopts an algorithm based on the Wansbeek and Kapteyen [37] method, henceforth WK, where the variance components are estimated by replacing the within regression residuals in the quadratic forms q_1 and q_2. The variances are computed from the expectations of q_1 and q_2: $\hat{\sigma}_\nu^2 = \frac{E(q_1)}{(NOBS - Nfirm - K + 1)}$ taking advantage of the fact the $Q + P = I_{Nfirm\ T_{\mathrm{ave}}}$ we get $\hat{\sigma}^2_{\mathrm{between}} = \hat{\sigma}^2_{\mathrm{tot}} - \hat{\sigma}^2_\nu$
2) STATA adopts an algorithm following a generalization of the Swamy and Arora [34] method, henceforth SA, where both the between and within regression residuals are used to estimate the variance component for an unbalanced one-way model. With this method the within regression variance is computed exactly as in TSP while $\sigma^2_{\mathrm{between}}$ is computed using the between-regression residuals.
3) LIMDEP adopts an algorithm that follows the Wallace and Hussain [36] suggestion, henceforth WH, of using the total OLS residuals to estimate the variance components of an unbalanced one-way model (for further investigation see [27]).

Another difference in the numerical results is related to a small problem with the Hausman test computation in STATA. In the context of panel data, the Hausman test checks the null hypothesis of no correlation between the individual effects and the regressors. This test is asymptotically distributed as a χ^2 (see [16], chapter 16). The algorithm adopted by STATA (see the program xthaus.ado) uses an inversion routine suitable for positive definite matrices. This procedure does not warn the user when the matrix obtained as the difference of the variance-covariance matrices is not positive definite. This causes the lack of meaning of the computed Hausman test. On the other hand both TSP and LIMDEP yield a value for the Hausman test which is consistent with their random-effects coefficient estimates.

As a concluding remark, the three software packages have been used to estimate 5 possible model specifications adopting both fixed and random effects. The execution times (on a RISC6000 990b platform) and program sizes are given in Table 6.

The execution times achieved by TSP and LIMDEP are smaller essentially because they use algorithms written in FORTRAN, meanwhile STATA adopts its own interpreted language.

4. A simulation exercise: bias and Monte Carlo variability of the three estimators

As far as the numerical differences of the random-effects estimates are concerned, in this paragraph we analyze the relative efficiency of the small-sample properties of the three estimators. The estimators' efficiency has been studied by running a parametric bootstrap procedure using the OLS residuals in one selected specification (see [6]). Bootstrap procedures are numerical methods developed to improve the accuracy of estimated confidence bands over theoretical models. For an introduction about different bootstrap techniques readers can refer to Brownstone and Valletta [12] who describe the most common implementations. The parametric bootstrap used is not a bootstrap in the usual sense. It consists in a Monte Carlo exercise made up of seven steps:

1) Obtain the OLS residuals;
2) use these residuals to get a biased but consistent estimate of the two variance components[4]
$\sigma_\nu^2 = \frac{1}{Nfirm(T_{\text{ave}}-1)} \sum\sum(\hat{\varepsilon}_{it} - \hat{\varepsilon}_{i\cdot})^2$, $\sigma_\mu^2 = \frac{1}{Nfirm-1} \sum_i(\hat{\varepsilon}_{i\cdot} - \hat{\varepsilon}_{\cdot\cdot})^2 - \frac{\hat{\sigma}_\nu^2}{T_{\text{ave}}}$,
where:
$\varepsilon_{\cdot\cdot} = \frac{1}{Nfirm\sum_i T_i} \sum_i \sum_t \varepsilon_{it}$ and $\varepsilon_{i\cdot} = \frac{1}{T_i} \sum_t \varepsilon_{it}$;
3) run a control random-effect estimation to compute the "true" estimated model; this task is carried out separately for each package and provides a *true value* (a benchmark) for the dependent variable and for the structural coefficients;
4) generate two normal random samples with zero mean and the standard deviations computed in step 2;
5) add the two simulated residuals to the true value of the dependent variable computed in step 3, thus simulating a new draw for the dependent variable;
6) perform a random-effects estimation using this new dataset;
7) compute the mean and the standard deviation of the replications.

This algorithm is called MCA1 (Monte Carlo A1).

The first result of interest in using MCA1 is the CPU time required for the completion of the Monte Carlo experiment. This is shown in Fig. 1, where we compare execution time versus number of replications for the Monte Carlo exercises. TSP is the fastest software.

In order to have comparable results, the programs for the Monte Carlo experiments have been written using the looping features made available by each package (the code for these programs is available upon request).

[4] See [36] for the balanced panel case.

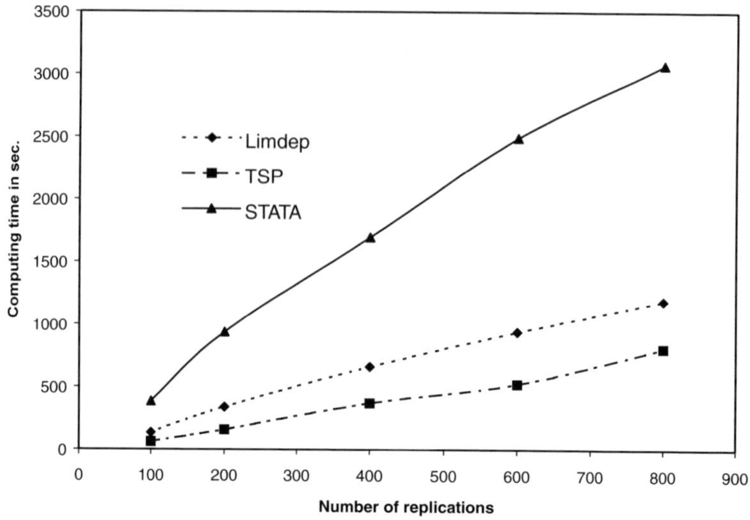

Fig. 1. Execution time versus number of replications.

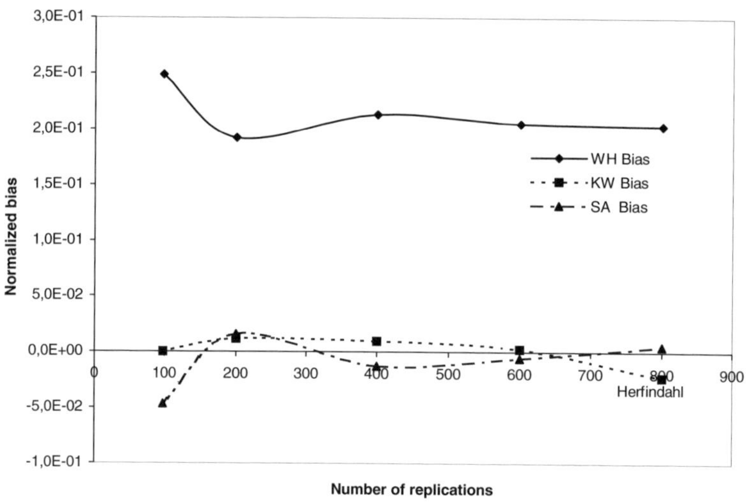

Fig. 2. Normalized bias for the coefficient of the Herfindahl index.

A second and more important insight is the evaluation of the bias and standard deviation for the Monte Carlo replications for each of the packages examined. Figures 2,3,4,5 show the behavior of the bias and the standard deviation around the Monte Carlo mean computed for the coefficients of the Herfindahl concentration index and the normalized cost of personnel.

Before drawing conclusions, we note some details of the Monte Carlo experiment.

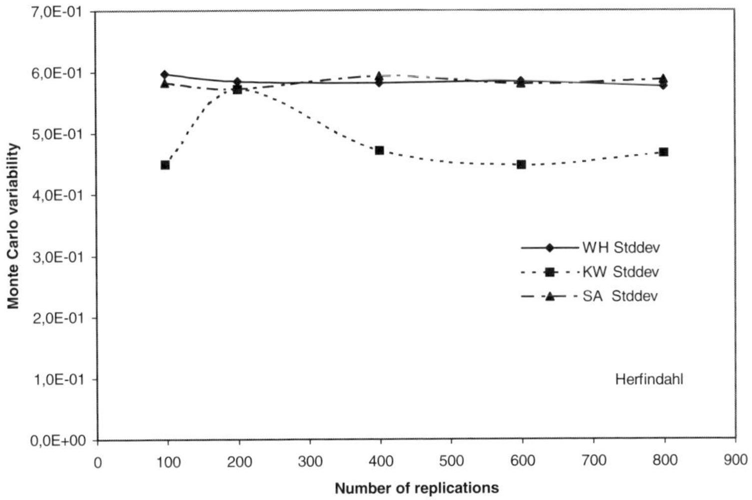

Fig. 3. Standard deviation for the coefficient of the Herfindahl index.

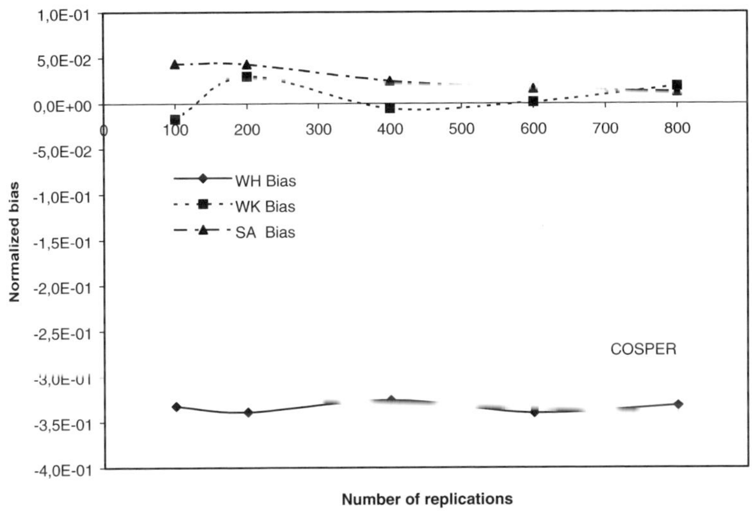

Fig. 4. Normalized bias for the coefficient of the cost of personnel.

1) The data-generation process is given by the fitted value of the random effects estimate for each of the three packages.
2) Each package's own random-number generator was used. Using the same set of residuals would have required a program for the generation and storage of two large files of more than 70 Mbytes each.
3) The total panel length was kept fixed over the different replications.

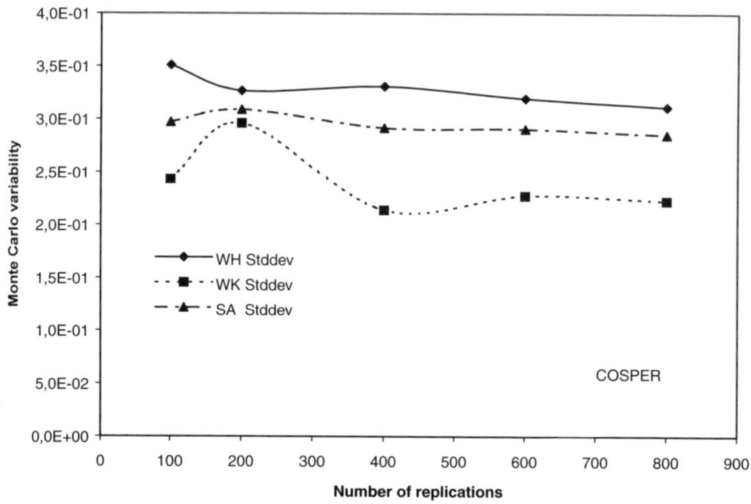

Fig. 5. Standard deviation for the coefficient of the cost of personnel.

Taking into account these experimental conditions, observation of the graphs permits some interesting considerations.

- The WK and SA estimators show about the same behavior for the normalized bias, which appears to approach zero, and the Monte Carlo volatility, which approaches a constant value;
- the WH shows a slightly different behavior: a non-zero bias with a variability comparable to that generated by WK and SA.

It seems reasonable to conclude that WK and SA estimators use a random-effects algorithm having a smaller bias than WH's.

5. Conclusions and directions for further research

This paper compares alternative econometric packages for panel-data estimation. Our purpose was to find an answer to the caveats about numerical accuracy raised in McCullough and Vinod [25] and these authors' concern about the lack of attention paid to the numerical accuracy of the algorithms used by many econometric packages. As far as we know there is no benchmark for panel data. In order to fill this gap we try to increase the confidence in the use of software packages by giving the same problem to three of them: LIMDEP, STATA and TSP. We used the Speakeasy-Modeleasy Plus matrix language to confirm the results of the individual packages. The empirical application considers the determinants of deposit interest rates in the Italian banking system.

As regards the numerical comparison of the estimators in the three packages, the fixed-effects algorithms gave the same numerical results to the available decimal places. The random-effects algorithms yielded slightly different results. We found out that the difference in the estimates can be attributed to the different methods used to compute the between-regression variance. We ran a Monte Carlo exercise to assess the relative efficiency of the random-effects algorithms provided by the three packages. On the basis of this exercise two of the algorithms appeared to be asymptotically equivalent, whereas the third one showed a persistent bias up to about one thousand Monte Carlo replications. Since differences between the packages have been explained, we are reasonably confident about correctness of our results. Therefore, taking into account the set of packages adopted and the confirmation provided by Speakeasy, we feel that the construction of a numerical benchmark is not worthwhile for panel data applications with fixed- and random-effects estimators.

We feel that an interesting topic for further research is the evaluation of the numerical accuracy of panel data algorithms when lagged endogenous variables are included among the regressors. Given a balanced panel of N individuals with T observations for each individual, it is well known that when a lagged endogenous variable appears among the explanatory variables the usual algorithms, such as OLS or fixed-effects, produce inconsistency of the parameter estimates for fixed T, even for N going to infinity. In the last ten years, various alternative estimators have been proposed in the literature to overcome this inconsistency. These estimators belong to two classes: instrumental variables and maximum likelihood. The Dynamic Panel Data (DPD) GAUSS package (see [3]) belongs to the first class; the algorithms implemented in this software are partially available in TSP.[5] STATA version 7 includes the ado file *xtabond* producing different versions of the Arellano-Bond estimator. LIMDEP has recently announced a new version which will provide users with an algorithm for the estimation of dynamic panel data. We leave to future research the comparison between the estimators based on instrumental variables and maximum likelihood.

Acknowledgments

Special thanks are due to Prof. Bruce McCullough and Prof. Charles Renfro for their advices and stimulating suggestions. We also thank Filippo Altissimo, Prof. Carlo Bianchi, Prof. William H. Greene, and an anonymous referee for helpful comments. Clint Cummins (TSP Corp.) and Vince Wiggins (STATA Corp.) provided valuable insights. Edoardo Tagliaferri provided research assistance. Any remaining errors are our own.

[5] Furthermore the Arellano-Bond DPD software itself has now been made available in the Ox package developed by Jurgen Doornik at Nuffield College, Oxford.

Appendix. Program listing

TSP Code

```
OPTIONS CRT NODATE MEMORY=8.4 DOUBLE SIGNIF=11;
NAME DEPORATE 'ESTIMATION OF THE DETERMINANTS OF THE DE-
POSIT INTEREST RATE'
? Unbalanced panel data estimation
SMPL 1 10561;
READ (FILE='newdep99',FORMAT=FREE)
   ABIPRO ANNO RATE HERFIN SHARE3 CCGROW NBRANCH NBANKS
COSRAT COSPER DNWEST DNEAST DCENTRE DSOUTH DISLAND;
FREQ(PANEL, ID=ABIPRO) A;
DUMMY (EXCLUDE) ANNO ANN90-ANN98;
LIST REGRA = HERFIN COSPER ANN90-ANN98;

TITLE(PAGE) 'Number 1) ESTIMATE WITH the COSPER';
PANEL(NOBYID,ID=ABIPRO,WITHIN,NOTOT,NOBET,VARCOM) RATE C R-
EGRA;
```

LIMDEP Code

```
? Limdep program for evaluating the determinants of the deposit rate on the total of
the deposit
?
read; nobs=10561; nvar = 14;
names = abipro, anno, rate, herfin, share3, ccgrow, nbranch, nbanks, cosrat, cosper,
dnwest, dcentre, dsouth, disland);
file=/_saee/brunogi/RICGIUS/dati022000/newdep99; sample=All$

? create the yearly dummy variables.
create ;ann90=anno=1990;ann91=anno=1991;ann92=anno=1992;ann93=anno=
1993;ann94=anno=1994;ann95=anno=1995;ann96=anno=1996;ann97=anno=
1997;ann98=anno=1998 $
create ; tp = anno - 1990 $

namelist;regra=herfin,cosper,ann90,ann91,ann92,ann93,ann94,ann95,ann96,ann97,
ann98$

regress ; lhs=rate; rhs=regra; str=abipro; perido = tp; panel$
```

STATA Code

```
* lettura files
infile abipro anno rate herfin share3 ccgrow nbranch nbanks cosrat cosper dnwest
dneast dcentre dsouth disland using newdep99. , clear

* generazione delle dummies per ogni anno
```

```
for num 90/98: gen annX=(anno==19X)

xtreg rate herfin cosper ann9*, be i(abipro)
xtreg rate herfin cosper ann9*, fe i(abipro)
xtreg rate herfin cosper ann9*, re i(abipro) th
xttest0
xthaus
```

The above program listing show only the first of 7 estimation commands. The following tables also show the result of the first estimation.

TSP Version 4.4

Current sample: 1 to 10561

Number 1) Estimate with the COSPER. Panel Data Estimation

Unbalanced data: NI = 1298, TMIN = 1, TMAX = 10, NOB = 10561.

Within (fixed effects) Estimates:

Dependent variable: RATE

Mean of dep. var. = 5.77473934949
Std. dev. of dep. var. = 2.32240807464
Sum of squared residuals = 2840.86941638
Variance of residuals = 0.307054627797
Std. error of regression = 0.554125101215
R-squared = 0.950121855671
Adjusted R-squared = 0.943070341103
LM het. test = 134.254116419 [0.000]
Durbin-Watson = 1.41901859827 [0.000,.000]

Variable	Estimated Coefficient	Standard Error	t-statistic	P-value
HERFIN	−0.239628158459	0.28765038512	−0.833053494283	[0.405]
COSPER	−5.04241821144	1.30455896612	−3.86522828203	[0.000]
ANN90	6.06869814130	0.03482742309	174.250564693	[0.000]
ANN91	6.22595565809	0.031051519018	200.504060833	[0.000]
ANN92	7.17330853047	0.027027008142	265.412601085	[0.000]
ANN93	5.08795274936	0.025272916498	201.320364028	[0.000]
ANN94	4.28020119680	0.024497423707	174.720462365	[0.000]
ANN95	5.38862732293	0.024116409528	223.442354333	[0.000]
ANN96	4.26015036686	0.024399451758	174.600249592	[0.000]
ANN97	2.84630957934	0.024997887641	113.862003869	[0.000]
ANN98	0.886113711041	0.024424802539	36.2792579233	[0.000]

Variance Components (random effects) Estimates:

VWITH (variance of Uit) = 0.30705
VBET (variance of Ai) = 0.20959
(computed from small sample formula)
THETA (0=WITHIN, 1=TOTAL) = 0.12778
(evaluated at TMAX = 10)

Dependent variable: RATE

Mean of dep. var. = 5.77473934949
Std. dev. of dep. var. = 2.32240807464
Sum of squared residuals = 5453.30855194
Variance of residuals = 0.516950284571
Std. error of regression = 0.718992548341
R-squared = 0.904266722843
Adjusted R-squared = 0.904166896694
LM het. Test = 395.094219831 [0.000]
Durbin-Watson = 0.739612917160 [0.000,.000]

Variable	Estimated Coefficient	Standard Error	t-statistic	P-value
HERFIN	0.06043275854	0.13946962243	0.433304095132	[0.665]
COSPER	−5.7092824493	1.23183946425	−4.63476176488	[0.000]
ANN90	6.05895320644	0.033738206107	179.587295995	[0.000]
ANN91	6.21282810582	0.030203205250	205.700953076	[0.000]
ANN92	7.16433236176	0.026481812328	270.537842089	[0.000]
ANN93	5.08315523214	0.024937322357	203.837250827	[0.000]
ANN94	4.27782267909	0.024231121537	176.542496089	[0.000]
ANN95	5.39269081247	0.023905477139	225.583902014	[0.000]
ANN96	4.27179541420	0.024184477329	176.633770332	[0.000]
ANN97	2.85081595554	0.024855712897	114.694596264	[0.000]
ANN98	0.886993851958	0.024328588909	36.4589107600	[0.000]
C	1.87302261265	0.079070488963	23.6880110041	[0.000]

Hausman test of H0:RE vs. FE: CHISQ(11) = 100.87, P-value = [0.0000]

LIMDEP 7.0 OUTPUT

LIMDEP Estimation Results, Run log line 15, Page 2
Current sample contains 10561 observations.

Least Squares with Group Dummy Variables
Ordinary least squares regression, Weighting variable = ONE
Dependent variable is RATE, Mean = 5.77474, S.D. = 2.3224
Model size: Observations = 10561, Parameters = ***, Deg.Fr.= 9252
Residuals: Sum of squares = 2840.8694, Std.Dev. = 0.55413
Fit: R-squared = .95012, Adjusted R-squared = 0.94307
Model test: F[***, 9252] = 134.74, Prob value = 0.00000

Diagnostic: Log-L = −8051.8082, Restricted(b=0) Log-L = -23883.6573
Amemiya Pr. Crt.= 0.345, Akaike Info. Crt.= 1.773
Estd. Autocorrelation of e(i,t) 0.153372 |

Variable	Coefficient	Standard Error	b/St.Er.	P[|Z|>z]	Mean of X
HERFIN	−0.23963	0.28765	−0.833	0.40481	0.2051
COSPER	−5.0424	1.3046	−3.865	0.00011	0.5383E-01
ANN90	6.0687	0.34827E-01	174.251	0.00000	0.7613E-01
ANN91	6.2260	0.31052E-01	200.504	0.00000	0.8787E-01
ANN92	7.1733	0.27027E-01	265.413	0.00000	0.1030
ANN93	5.0880	0.25273E-01	201.320	0.00000	0.1056
ANN94	4.2802	0.24497E-01	174.720	0.00000	0.1089
ANN95	5.3886	0.24116E-01	223.442	0.00000	0.1114
ANN96	4.2602	0.24399E-01	174.600	0.00000	0.1113
ANN97	2.8463	0.24998E-01	113.862	0.00000	0.9677E-01
ANN98	0.88611	0.24425E-01	36.279	0.00000	0.9999E-01

Test Statistics for the Classical Model

	Model	Log-Likelihood	Sum of Squares	R-squared
(1)	Constant term only	−23883.65713	0.569562D+05	0.0000000
(2)	Group effects only	−23138.24008	0.494577D+05	0.1316532
(3)	X - variables only	−11492.21202	0.545013D+04	0.9043101
(4)	X and group effects	−8051.80801	0.284087D+04	0.9501219

Hypothesis Tests

	Likelihood Ratio test			F Tests			
	Chi-squared	d.f.	Prob.	F	num.	denom.	Prob value
(2) vs (1)	1490.834	1297	0.00012	1.083	1297	9262	0.02700
(3) vs (1)	24782.890	11	0.00000	9062.955	11	10549	0.00000
(4) vs (1)	31663.698	1308	0.00000	134.740	1308	9252	0.00000
(4) vs (2)	30172.864	11	0.00000	13801.767	11	9252	0.00000
(4) vs (3)	6880.808	1297	0.00000	6.552	1297	9252	0.00000

Random Effects Model: v(i,t) = e(i,t) + u(i)
Estimates: Var[e] = 0.307055D+00
Var[u] = 0.236181D+00
Corr[v(i,t),v(i,s)] = 0.434768
Lagrange Multiplier Test vs. Model (3) = 5534.72
(1 df, prob value = 0.000000)
Fixed vs. Random Effects (Hausman) = 92.32
(11 df, prob value = 0.000000)
Estd. Autocorrelation of e(i,t) 0.153150
Reestimated using GLS coefficients:
Estimates: Var[e] = 0.307110D+00
Var[u] = 0.237101D+00
Sum of Squares 0.545356D+04
R-squared 0.904250D+00

Variable	Coefficient	Standard Error	b/St.Er.	P[|Z|>z]	Mean of X
HERFIN	0.5314E-01	0.14489	0.367	0.71382	0.2051
COSPER	−5.6567	1.2381	−4.569	0.00000	0.5383E-01
ANN90	6.0596	0.33825E-01	179.144	0.00000	0.7613E-01
ANN91	6.2138	0.30270E-01	205.282	0.00000	0.8787E-01
ANN92	7.1650	0.26521E-01	270.159	0.00000	0.1030
ANN93	5.0835	0.24961E-01	203.657	0.00000	0.1056
ANN94	4.2779	0.24248E-01	176.421	0.00000	0.1089
ANN95	5.3924	0.23919E-01	225.438	0.00000	0.1114
ANN96	4.2708	0.24199E-01	176.489	0.00000	0.1113
ANN97	2.8505	0.24866E-01	114.634	0.00000	0.9677E-01
ANN98	0.88685	0.24334E-01	36.444	0.00000	0.9999E-01
Constant	1.8715	0.79935E-01	23.413	0.00000	

STATA 6.0 OUTPUT

Fixed-effects (within) regression Number of obs = 10561
Group variable (i) : abipro Number of groups = 1298

R-sq: within = 0.9426 Obs per group: min = 1
between = 0.8056 avg = 8.1
overall = 0.9040 max = 10

F(11,9252) = 13801.77,
corr(u_i, Xb) = −0.0052 Prob > F = 0.0000

rate	Coef.	Std. Err.	t	P>|t|	[95% Conf. Interval]	
herfin	−0.2396283	0.2876504	−0.833	0.405	−0.8034864	0.3242299
cosper	−5.042418	1.304559	−3.865	0.000	−7.599641	−2.485195
ann90	6.068698	0.0348274	174.251	0.000	6.000429	6.136968
ann91	6.225956	0.0310515	200.504	0.000	6.165088	6.286824
ann92	7.173309	0.027027	265.413	0.000	7.12033	7.226288
ann93	5.087953	0.0252729	201.320	0.000	5.038412	5.137493
ann94	4.280201	0.0244974	174.720	0.000	4.232181	4.328222
ann95	5.388627	0.0241164	223.442	0.000	5.341354	5.435901
ann96	4.26015	0.0243995	174.600	0.000	4.212322	4.307979
ann97	2.84631	0.0249979	113.862	0.000	2.797308	2.895311
ann98	0.8861137	0.0244248	36.279	0.000	0.8382357	0.9339917
_cons	1.905405	0.0970433	19.635	0.000	1.715179	2.095632
sigma_u	0.53321461					
sigma_e	0.5541251					
rho	0.48077623 (fraction of variance due to u_i)					

F test that all u_i=0: F(1297,9252) = 6.55 Prob > F = 0.0000

Random-effects GLS regression Number of obs = 10561
Group variable (i) : abipro Number of groups = 1298

R-sq: within = 0.9425 Obs per group: min = 1
between = 0.8066 avg = 8.1
overall = 0.9043 max = 10

Random effects u_i ~ Gaussian Wald chi2(11) = 155123.66
corr(u_i, X) = 0 (assumed) Prob > chi2 = 0.0000

theta				
min	5%	median	95%	max
0.2328	0.3542	0.6297	0.6462	0.6462

rate	Coef.	Std. Err.	z	P>|z|	[95% Conf.	Interval]
herfin	0.0590218	0.1410826	0.418	0.676	−0.2174949	0.3355386
cosper	−5.698637	1.237944	−4.603	0.000	−8.124963	−3.272312
ann90	6.059083	0.0338881	178.797	0.000	5.992663	6.125502
ann91	6.213022	0.030335	204.813	0.000	6.153566	6.272477
ann92	7.164459	0.0265936	269.406	0.000	7.112336	7.216581
ann93	5.083225	0.0250398	203.006	0.000	5.034148	5.132302
ann94	4.277844	0.0243295	175.829	0.000	4.230159	4.325529
ann95	5.392627	0.024002	224.675	0.000	5.345584	5.43967
ann96	4.271596	0.0242821	175.915	0.000	4.224004	4.319188
ann97	2.850745	0.0249551	114.235	0.000	2.801834	2.899656
ann98	0.8869631	0.024425	36.314	0.000	0.839091	0.9348353
_cons	1.872697	0.0795514	23.541	0.000	1.71678	2.028615
sigma_u	0.46327689					
sigma_e	0.5541251					
rho	0.41141204 (fraction of variance due to u_i)					

Breusch and Pagan Lagrangian multiplier test for random effects:
rate[abipro,t] = Xb + u[abipro] + e[abipro,t]

	Estimated results	
	Var	sd = sqrt(Var)
rate	5.393579	2.322408
e	0.3070546	0.5541251
u	0.2146255	0.46327689

Test: Var(u) = 0, chi2(1) = 5534.72, Prob>chi2 = 0.0000.

Hausman specification test			
	Coefficients		
rate	Fixed Effects	Random Effects	Difference
herfin	−0.2396283	0.0590218	−0.2986501
cosper	−5.042418	−5.698637	0.656219
ann90	6.068698	6.059083	0.0096154
ann91	6.225956	6.213022	0.0129338
ann92	7.173309	7.164459	0.0088497
ann93	5.087953	5.083225	0.0047281
ann94	4.280201	4.277844	0.0023576
ann95	5.388627	5.392627	−0.0039995
ann96	4.26015	4.271596	−0.0114457
ann97	2.84631	2.850745	−0.0044354
ann98	0.8861137	0.8869631	−0.0008494

Test: Ho: difference in coefficients not systematic, chi2(11) $= (b-B)'[S^(-1)](b-B)$, S = (S_fe - S_re), chi2(11) = 7.34, Prob>chi2 = 0.7711.

References

[1] L. Allen, A.G. Saunders and F. Udell, The Pricing of Retail Deposits: Concentration and Information, *Journal of Financial Intermediation* **1** (1991), 335–361.

[2] I. Angeloni, L. Buttiglione, G. Ferri and E. Gaiotti, The Credit Channel of Monetary Policy across Heterogeneous Banks: The Case of Italy, Banca d'Italia, *Temi di discussione* **256** (1995).

[3] M. Arellano and S. Bond, Some Tests of Specification for Panel Data: Monte Carlo Evidence and an Application to Employment Equations, *Review of Economic Studies* **58** (1991), 277–297.

[4] B.H. Baltagi, *Econometric Analysis of Panel Data*, Wiley, Chichester, 1995.

[5] B.H. Baltagi and Y-J. Chang, Incomplete panels. A comparative study of alternative estimators for the unbalanced one-way error component regression model, *Journal of Econometrics* **62** (1994), 67–89.

[6] L. Bellman, J. Breitung and J. Wagner, Bias Correction and Bootstrapping of Error Component Models for Panel data: Theory and Applications, *Empirical Economics* (1989), 329–342.

[7] N.A. Berger and T.H. Hannan, The Price-Concentration Relationship in Banking, *Review of Economics and Statistics* **2** (1989), 291–99.

[8] N.A. Berger and T.H. Hannan, Deposit Interest Rates and Local Market Concentration, in: *Concentration and Price*, L.W. Weiss, ed., MIT Press, Cambridge, MA, 1989, pp. 255–265.

[9] N.A. Berger and T.H. Hannan, The Rigidity of Prices: Evidence from the Banking Industry, *American Economic Review* **4** (1991), 938–945.

[10] N.A. Berger and T.H. Hannan, The Price-Concentration Relationship in Banking: A Reply, *Review of Economics and Statistics* **2** (1992), 376–379.

[11] P. Blanchard, Software Review, in: *The econometrics of Panel Data: handbook of theory and applications*, L.Màtyàs and P. Sevestre, eds., Kluwer Academic Publishers, Dordrecht, 1992, pp. 521–546.

[12] D. Brownstone and R. Valletta, The Bootstrap and Multiple Imputations: Harnessing Increased Computing Power for Improved Statistical Tests, *Journal of Economic Perspectives* **4** (2001), 129–141.

[13] R. De Bonis and A. Ferrando, Da che cosa dipendono i tassi di interesse sui prestiti nelle province? Banca d'Italia, *Temi di discussione*, **319** (1997).

[14] A. Freiden, A Program for the Estimation of Dynamic Economic Relations from a Time Series of Cross Sections, *Annals of Economic and Social Measurement* **1** (1973), 89–91.

[15] R.A. Gilbert, Bank, Market Structure and Competition, *Journal of Money, Credit and Banking* **4** (1984), 617–645.

[16] W.H. Greene, *Econometric Analysis*, Second Ed., Macmillan Publishing Company, New York, 1993.

[17] N.W. Henry, J.F. McDonald and H. Stokes, The Estimation of Dynamic Economic Relations from a Time Series of Cross Sections: a Programming Modification, *Annals of Economic and Social Measurement* **1** (1976), 153–155.

[18] W.E. Jackson III, The Price-Concentration Relationship, *Review of Economics and Statistics* **2** (1992), 373–376.

[19] G.S. Maddala and T.D. Mount, A Comparative Study of Alternative Estimators for Variance Components Models Used in Econometric Applications, *Journal of American Statistical Association* **342** (1973), 324–328.

[20] B.D. McCullough, A review of RATS v4.2: Benchmarking Numerical Accuracy, *Journal of Applied Econometrics* **12** (1997), 181–190.

[21] B.D. McCullough, Assessing the Reliability of Statistical Software: Part I, *The American Statistician* **4** (1998), 358–366.

[22] B.D. McCullough, Econometric Software Reliability: Eviews, Limdep, Shazam and TSP, *Journal of Applied Econometrics* (1999), 191–202.
[23] B.D. McCullough and C.G. Renfro, Benchmarks and software standards: A case study of GARCH procedures, *Journal of Economic and Social Measurement* **25** (1998), 59–71.
[24] B.D. McCullough and C.G. Renfro, Some numerical aspects of nonlinear estimation, *Journal of Economic and Social Measurement* **26** (2000), 63–77.
[25] B.D. McCullough and H.D. Vinod, The Numerical Reliability of Econometric Software, *Journal of Economic Literature June* (1999), 633–665.
[26] R. Moore, Concentration, Technology, and Market Power in Banking: Is Distance Dead? Financial Industry Studies, *Federal Reserve Bank of Dallas December* (1998), 1–10.
[27] M. Nerlove, A Note on Error Components Models, *Econometrica* **2** (1971), 383–396.
[28] J.D. Neuberger and G. Zimmerman, Bank pricing of retail deposit accounts and the California rate mystery, *Economic Review Federal Reserve Bank of San Francisco* (1990), 3–16.
[29] D. Neumark and S.A. Sharpe, Market Structure and the Nature of Price Rigidity: Evidence from the Market for Consumer Deposits, *Quarterly Journal of Economics* **2** (1992), 657–680.
[30] P. Newbold, C. Agiakloglou and J. Miller, Adventures with ARIMA software, *International Journal of Forecasting* **10** (1994), 573–581.
[31] D.K. Osborne, Banking Structure and Competition, in: *The New Palgrave: Dictionary of Money and Finance*, Macmillan, London, 1992, pp. 152–155.
[32] R.A. Prager and T.H. Hannan, Do Substantial Horizontal Mergers Generate Significant Price Effects? Evidence from the Banking Industry, *The Journal of Industrial Economics* **4** (December, 1998).
[33] L.J. Radecki, The Expanding Geographic Reach of Retail Banking Markets, Federal Reserve Bank of New York, *Economic Policy Review* (June, 1998), 15–34.
[34] P.A. Swami and S.S. Arora, The exact finite sample properties of the estimators of coefficients in the error components regression models, *Econometrica* **40** (1972), 261–275.
[35] H.D. Vinod, Review of Gauss for Windows, Including its numerical Accuracy, *Journal of Applied Econometrics* **15** (2000), 211–220.
[36] T.D. Wallace and A. Hussain, The use of error components models in combining cross-section and time-series data, *Econometrica* **37** (1969), 55–72.
[37] T. Wansbeek and A. Kapteyn, Estimation of the error component model with incomplete panels, *Journal of Econometrics* (1989), 341–361.

Journal of Economic and Social Measurement 29 (2004) 297–305
IOS Press

Reply to "A comparative study of alternative econometric packages with an application to Italian deposit interest rates", by G. Bruno and R. De Bonis

William Greene
Department of Economics, Stern School of Business, New York University, 44 West 4th Street, New York, NY 10012, USA
E-mail: wgreene@stern.nyu.edu; URL: http://www.stern.nyu.edu/~wgreene
Econometric Software, Inc., 15 Gloria Place, Plainview, NY 11803, USA
URL: http://www.limdep.com

1. Introduction

In this study, Bruno and De Bonis (henceforth BD) analyze the performance of three econometrics packages, LIMDEP, Stata and TSP, in a calculation that, so far as I am aware, has not previously been intensively studied in this fashion. The computations relate to the calculation of fixed and random effects models in a moderately large data set. The three packages produce identical results for the fixed effects estimator, but different results for the random effects estimator. The differences in the latter are traced to the computation of the estimator of the variance of the common (time invariant) random effect. LIMDEP's calculations produced some notable anomalies (see BD's Figs 2–5). The following provides some commentary on the results in the paper and offers some observations about this paper and other software comparisons of the same sort.

2. Summary of the computations

As noted in the introduction, the three packages produce the same results for the fixed effects estimator, so I will not comment on these calculations. The random effects model is estimated by all three packages using a two step feasible GLS procedure (as opposed to maximum likelihood). The random effects model analyzed is a static variant of the linear model,

$$\begin{aligned} y_{it} &= \beta'\mathbf{x}_{it} + v_{it} + u_i \\ &= \beta'\mathbf{x}_{it} + \varepsilon_{it}, \end{aligned}$$

where v_{it} and u_i have zero means, are uncorrelated with each other, with all other draws from their respective populations and with $\mathbf{x}_{it}$, and are homoscedastic with variances σ_v^2 and σ_u^2. Feasible GLS requires estimation of both variance components. As BD discovered, the three packages reviewed used (at the time) three different procedures. It is useful to reiterate the computations.

Feasible GLS is carried out by linearly regressing the partial deviations of y_{it} from its group mean on the same transformation of $\mathbf{x}_{it}$:

$$y_{it}^* = y_{it} - \theta_i \overline{y}_i$$

where

$$\theta_i = 1 - \sqrt{\frac{\sigma_v^2}{T_i\sigma_u^2 + \sigma_v^2}}.$$

Note that the accommodation of unbalanced panels, which is necessary for BD's study, is a trivial extension of the familiar procedures, at least at this juncture. Computation of θ_i requires estimation of both parts of the compound variance

$$\sigma_\varepsilon^2 = \sigma_v^2 + \sigma_u^2.$$

The usual strategy is to estimate σ_ε^2 and subtract from it a consistent estimator of σ_v^2 in order to estimate σ_u^2. Most estimators are based on this simple method of moments, but see Nerlove [4] for discussion of maximum likelihood procedures. [1]

From the construction of the model, it is clear that a variety of estimators are available. Denote by $\mathbf{b}_{\text{OLS}}$ the OLS coefficient (slope) vector obtained by pooled regression of the full sample of $n = \sum_{i=1}^{N} T_i$ observations on y_{it} on $\mathbf{x}_{it}$ and a constant term – denote by a_{OLS} the constant term in this regression. Denote by $\mathbf{b}_B$ the slopes in the group means, or "between groups" regression estimator obtained by least squares regression of the N group means of y_{it} on a constant and the group means of $\mathbf{x}_{it}$ and let a_B denote the constant term in this regression. Note that there are only $N \leqslant n$ observations in this regression. Finally, denote by $\mathbf{b}_W$ the least squares dummy variable estimator (fixed effects), or "within groups" estimator. Note that there is no overall constant in this regression. We use a full set of N dummy variables. The calculations done by the three packages are as follows: First, all three programs base estimates of σ_v^2 on the sum of squared residuals from the dummy variable (within groups) regression; [2]

$$ss_W = \mathbf{e}_W'\mathbf{e}_W = \sum_{i=1}^{N}\sum_{i=1}^{T_i}[(y_{it} - \overline{y}_i) - (\mathbf{x}_{it} - \overline{\mathbf{x}}_i)'\mathbf{b}_W]^2$$

[1] The MLE is not common in commercial software. Given the contemporary aversion to strong distributional assumptions, this is unlikely to change.

[2] The computation suggested by BD as done by TSP has an excessive (by one) correction for degrees of freedom in the denominator of this estimator.

Two consistent estimators based on this are $\hat{\sigma}_v^2 = ss_W/n$ and $s_v^2 = ss_W/(n-N-K)$ where K is the number of regressors, not including a constant term. Likewise, there are two consistent estimators of σ_ε^2, both based on pooled least squares, using

$$ss_{\text{OLS}} = \mathbf{e}'_{\text{OLS}}\mathbf{e}_{\text{OLS}} = \sum_{i=1}^{N}\sum_{i=1}^{T_i}[(y_{it} - \overline{\overline{y}}) - (\mathbf{x}_{it} - \overline{\overline{\mathbf{x}}})'\mathbf{b}_{\text{OLS}}]^2;$$

these are $\hat{\sigma}_\varepsilon^2 = ss_{\text{OLS}}/n$ and $s_{\text{OLS}}^2 = ss_{\text{OLS}}/(n-K-1)$. The next computation produces by subtraction a usable estimator of σ_u^2. All are based on estimating σ_ε^2 and subtracting from that estimator an estimator of σ_v^2. The recurrent problem is that in most instances, nothing in the construction precludes a negative estimate of σ_u^2, and programs differ on what estimators are used. The next step proceeds as follows:

TSP: Two attempts are made. The first estimator is $s_{\text{OLS}}^2 - s_v^2$. This may produce a negative estimate of σ_u^2. If so, the second estimator is $\hat{\sigma}_\varepsilon^2 - \hat{\sigma}_v^2$. This is guaranteed to be nonnegative, because the total sum of squares equals the within groups sum of squares plus the between groups sum of squares. Unless the group means are all identical, which is obviously pathological, this second estimator will be positive.

LIMDEP: Prior to the modification noted below, LIMDEP used an estimator based on the group means (between groups) regression. In the group means regression,

$$\overline{y}_i = \beta'\overline{\mathbf{x}}_i + \overline{v}_i + u_i$$

the (heteroscedastic) disturbance variance is $\sigma_v^2/T_i + \sigma_u^2$. The residual variance in the group means regression estimates the mean of these, which would be simple in a balanced panel, but is ambiguous in an unbalanced panel. The residual variance in the group means regression, corrected for degrees of freedom, is a consistent (in N) estimator of $\sigma_u^2 + \overline{Q}\sigma_v^2$ where $\overline{Q} = \text{plim}(1/N)\sum_{i=1}^{N}(1/T_i)$. (Note that $\overline{Q}$ is not the $(1/T_{\text{ave}})$ suggested in BD's paper. There is a theoretical loose end here concerning the meaning of "large sample behavior" of $\overline{Q}$.) This implies LIMDEP's estimator,

$$\hat{\hat{\sigma}}_u^2 = \frac{\sum_{i=1}^{N}(\overline{y}_i - a_B - \overline{\mathbf{x}}_i'\mathbf{b}_B)^2}{N-K-1} - \overline{Q}\hat{\sigma}_v^2.$$

This calculation can produce a negative estimate of σ_u^2. If so, the computation is retried using the overall pooled regression constant and slope vector, $(a_{\text{OLS}}, \mathbf{b}_{\text{OLS}})$. (DB suggest that LIMDEP used the OLS estimator first, but that is not the case. The group means estimator was tried first, then the OLS vector. LIMDEP's previous estimator was based on Swamy and Arora [?] not Wallace and Hussain [5] as suggested in the study.) After discussion with the authors and review of the results of this paper, LIMDEP was modified so that after March, 2000, LIMDEP's computations are the same as TSP's.

Stata: Stata computes one candidate for σ_u^2,

$$\hat{\hat{\sigma}}_u^2 = \max\left\{0, \frac{\sum_{i=1}^{N}[\overline{y}_i - a_B - \mathbf{x}_i'\mathbf{b}_B]^2}{N-K-1} - \frac{\hat{\sigma}_v^2}{\overline{T}}\right\}$$

$$\text{where } \overline{T} = \exp\left(\frac{1}{N}\sum_{i=1}^{N}\ln t_i\right)$$

(The latter term uses the harmonic mean of the group sizes.) Note that both Stata and LIMDEP, unlike TSP, used group means for the overall variance estimator. It is not noted in BD's paper that the difference between LIMDEP and Stata at this point is not the variance estimator; it is only $\overline{Q}$ in LIMDEP versus in Stata (assuming that Stata made the degrees of freedom correction in the variance estimator in the fixed computation).[3]

At this point, the computations reconverge; all base feasible GLS on these estimators. Before proceeding to some broader questions, some issues seem worth noting.

3. Comments

The computations done in DB's Monte Carlo study do not appear to be based on the estimator actually used by LIMDEP. (The coefficient vector used to compute the group mean residuals and the average reciprocal of the group sizes both differ.) I cannot state whether this casts a cloud over their results or not, or whether their study would change substantively if redone, but for accuracy's sake, it should be noted that, as described above, there are these two substantive differences in their description of the computation of their "biased but consistent estimate of the variance components". First, LIMDEP did not use the OLS residuals, as suggested DB. It used, as did Stata, the group mean regression residuals first. Then, LIMDEP used the group mean residuals based on the OLS coefficients if the computed estimate of σ_u^2 was negative. The second difference concerns the scaling used to eliminate σ_v^2 from the estimator of σ_ε^2. Here, the result may well be substantive. (This point is moot with respect to TSP.) Stata used $1/\overline{T}$ as described above; LIMDEP used $\overline{Q}$; DB in their computations of what they believed LIMDEP was using used $1/T_{\text{ave}}$. It is impossible without their data to ascertain how much difference this makes, but a small experiment is suggestive. DB's data set contained 1298 groups ranging in

[3]DB do not report whether LIMDEP reported a finding of a negative variance estimator at its first attempt, which it would have done in its runlog. Assuming that this problem did not arise, the LIMDEP and Stata estimators differ only in the scaling of the second term.

size from 1 to 10. I generated a random sample of 1298 values from the 10 point discrete uniform distribution and computed $1/\overline{T}$, $\overline{Q}$ and $1/T_{\text{ave}}$. The three values I obtained were 0.2205, 0.2910 and 0.1822, respectively. These differences are large. The fact that $\overline{Q}$ is considerably larger than the other two may yet argue against its use, however, nothing in the literature suggests that either the harmonic mean or the reciprocal of the simple average is a better choice for an unbalanced sample. I am unsure what to conclude from the Monte Carlo study because, as noted, it does not replicate LIMDEP's computations. (These results are explained in lengthy detail on pages 333–337 of the version 7.0 LIMDEP manual. The computation of $\overline{Q}$ is emphasized in particular.)

The study describes the "bias" of the estimators in a certain computation.[4] The so called bias relates to a specific computation in the context of this specific study, so it is unclear what a general readership should infer from what they find here. That the random effects estimator has a small sample bias is true in every setting and indeed, will generally be true of any two step GLS estimator. Oddly enough, if we take the implication that Stata's treatment is not "biased" then it appears that the culprit in the analysis might be the scaling constant $\overline{Q}$, not the underlying variance estimator. But, once again, because DB did not use $\overline{Q}$ and used a different coefficient vector in the computation of the residual variance, this is not established. Nonetheless, LIMDEP has been modified so that it now does the computations the same way that TSP does, so the point is moot. It should be noted, however, that none of the estimators shown above is inappropriate. All are consistent and in principle, all will produce consistent slope estimators of the full model. How they perform in finite samples is a matter for studies such as this one. What the authors have found here certainly constitutes an anomaly worthy of consideration. But, calling it a "bias" as such seems inappropriate. The conclusions state that the algorithm showed a "persistent bias up to about one thousand Monte Carlo replications". This is a strong statement and possibly misleading since it is unclear what it is that is biased. It might be useful for the reader to see in a single place the results of estimation of the model for the three packages analyzed here (see Table 1). The notable difference in the coefficients on Herfin and Cosper certainly caught my attention and do seem worth a hard look, but in the main, the rest of the results seem quite similar across the three estimators, allowing for the now transparent differences in the weighting coefficients, θ_i. "Persistent bias" suggests a somewhat different picture.

My second point is a small one, but I would invite some commentary from readers and other developers. There is a bit of artificial intelligence built into all these

[4] The study also compared some computation times. In the current computing environment, comparisons of computing times are questionable. As an example, consider the computation (using Gauss) of a panel probit model reported by Bertschek and Lechner [1]. Using a less than state of the art machine only a few years later, LIMDEP (see Greene [3]) reproduced the computations in less than one one hundredth of the time. Thus, absolute computing times reported by BD are probably not meaningful. The relative slowness of Stata owing to its different internal representation of the problem, would probably persist in any environment, however.

Table 1

Estimated parameter	TSP	LIMDEP	Stata
σ_u^2	0.20959	0.236181	0.28431
σ_v^2	0.307055	0.307055	0.307055
Constant	1.8730	1.8715	1.8727
Herfin	0.06043	0.05314	0.05902
Cosper	−5.7092	−5.6567	−5.6986
Year90	6.0589	6.0596	6.0591
Year91	6.2128	6.2138	6.2130
Year92	7.1643	7.1650	7.1645
Year93	5.0832	5.0835	5.08323
Year94	4.2778	4.2779	4.27784
Year95	5.3927	5.3924	5.3926
Y ear96	4.2718	4.2708	4.2716
Year97	2.8508	2.8505	2.85075
Year98	0.88699	0.88685	0.88696

computations. First, note that all three produce different second estimators when the first attempt to estimate the variance of u_i turns up negative. TSP generates a second attempt which is guaranteed to succeed, even if the random effects model is itself inappropriate – unless the group means are identical. By overfitting the model, TSP produced a positive estimator of σ_u^2 based on the simple algebra of least squares. Not noted by the authors of this study is that LIMDEP's second estimator could also come up negative. If so, LIMDEP makes no third attempt. The estimator quits, stating that it could not find a positive variance estimator. This is a tip to the user that they might reconsider the random effects specification. Stata (according to this paper) makes a single attempt to find a positive variance estimator and, upon failing to do so, reverts to pooled least squares (which is produced when zero is used as the estimator of σ_u^2). This is an appropriate way to proceed if that is what the user has asked for. The designer of the software must always determine how many such decisions they are willing to make for a user, and programs differ in this regard. A noteworthy example is the decision process of a certain well known program (not named) which will choose for the user to drop one or more variables from a regression upon finding multicollinearity in a data set. (LIMDEP will not do this – multicollinearity stops the estimation and the next step in this case is up to the user.)

There is one last fine point in this that users and developers might consider. All of the preceding tapestry, both DB's and the software as documented, comes unraveled if the sample contains time invariant regressors. In that case, the within groups estimator cannot be computed – the fixed effects estimator is precluded. That leaves the problem of estimating σ_v^2 unsolved. But, this situation presents no obstacle in principle to the computation of a random effects model. The fixed effects estimator is inessential to the computation so long as some other consistent estimator is available, and the group means estimator will suffice in tandem with the OLS estimator. I note at this point that in this specific case, which must be indicated to the user, LIMDEP will use several other resources based on pooled OLS and the group means estimator. I invite the readers of this article and the other software developers to comment on how one should proceed in this case. Note, finally, the problem, while not really uncommon, is moot in most of the literature, as contemporary applications usually build dynamic effects into panel data models. The results of this paper are limited to a static model.

4. Broader questions

I was sent a copy of this paper quite some time before it appeared at this journal. At that time, I had a very fruitful exchange with the authors on the subject which culminated in the revision of LIMDEP to make use of this new (to us) knowledge. That raises a question which occasioned a discussion (initiated by the editor of this journal) among several observers and software developers. Since the package was indeed changed – from early 2000 on forward, LIMDEP uses the same computations as TSP, as documented in this reply – by the time the BD study appears in print, the computations it describes will no longer be produced by the current version of LIMDEP. The question then arises, should this paper, or at least the result that it documents with respect to LIMDEP, be published? The consensus of the aforementioned discussants, myself included, was yes. In an obvious way that is only minor in the larger picture, current users will be interested in the findings. In that regard, it should be noted that the result documented here is not a "failure" as such. The estimator remains consistent. Apparently, it may not be the best use of the data – that does appear to be the case at this point. A second aspect is more important. The development of econometric software is a collaborative process between users, the literature, and the developers. Much of the advance in software simply follows the literature. But, for better or worse, the process of publication in much of the econometrics literature is distressingly slow. The internet and electronic distribution of work in progress has thankfully short circuited that process. But, at least for our purposes at Econometric Software, an equally crucial conduit for information about techniques and the intellectual marketplace is the direct communication between us and our users. The improvement in LIMDEP that this paper led to is simply part of that process. I am pleased to be able to signal to our users, current and future, how active that process is. Users of LIMDEP know well that for its now over 20 years of continuing development, many of its features and most of its nonstandard models (there are many) have been installed as a result of direct suggestions from our users. [5]

The collaboration between users and software developers runs in both directions. LIMDEP users will be the beneficiaries of the efforts of these authors. But, in addition, this sort of exchange helps to highlight the contribution of software and software development to the evolution of econometric practice. In its own way, this

[5] Version of 8.0 was released with version 3.0 of NLOGIT in August of 2002. Users should be able to recognize this ongoing collaboration.

study may discredit the Swamy and Arora (and Wallace and Hussein) estimator(s). There is no other statement in the literature which would produce this opinion. It's a small point, but the contribution of software and its development is not always small. If I may cite just two examples, the development of the LSQ procedure in TSP in the early 1970s produced the platform on which an entire literature on demand systems was able to stand for at least two decades. LIMDEP's estimator for Heckman's sample selection model was cited as the standard computational device for this model for many years. The role of the software in use in econometric applications is routinely given insufficient recognition. Finally, at the risk of moving into pure editorial, I'd note a trend in the literature. To an ever increasing degree, authors are developing new estimating techniques whose theoretical underpinnings are documented in microscopically detailed technical appendices whose length often (and technical depth always, by far) exceeds the paper itself. But the documentation in the same typical paper of how computations are done is essentially what it has always been, thin to nonexistent. This is unfortunate. It conveys the impression that the implementation of models is unimportant; only the development is. Equally disconcerting is the tendency for authors to develop (microscopically) elaborate estimation techniques, then to report, almost as an afterthought an application that contains little more than signs and statistical "significance" of the things that they estimate (or worse yet, nothing more than a forgettable Monte Carlo study in which signs and significance are preordained). All three of these failings could easily be remedied, in ways so obvious as not to require any further commentary from this quarter.

5. Conclusion

The preceding documents a few flaws in DBs analysis of the estimator in LIMDEP. These flaws may be minor, but I am troubled by the combination of the two errors in the same computation. I was more struck by the coefficient estimates of the actual model than the Monte Carlo study which may or may not be informative. The differences that I saw there suggested that on the basis of this study in its totality, it would be appropriate and desirable to modify LIMDEP to do the computations using the OLS estimates rather than the group means estimates. That was done over two years ago. These authors have done us at Econometric Software and the users of LIMDEP a service in pointing out their result. Whether or not the Monte Carlo results hold up or not if done correctly, I believe that results and exchanges such as these always produce improvements in the software.

References

[1] I. Bertschek and M. Lechner, Convenient Estimators for the Panel Probit Model, *Journal of Econometrics* **87**(2) (1998), 329–372.

[2] G. Bruno and R. De Bonis, A comparative study of alternative econometric packages with an application to Italian deposit interest rates, *Journal of Economic and Social Measurement* **29** (2004), 271–295, this volume.
[3] W. Greene, Convenient Estimators for the Panel Probit Model: Further Results, Stern School of Business, Department of Economics, Working Paper 02-06, 2002 (also available at http://www.stern.nyu.edu/~wgreene/panelprobitmodel.pdf).
[4] M. Nerlove, *Essays in Panel Data Econometrics,* Cambridge University Press, Cambridge, 2003, forthcoming.
[5] T. Wallace and A. Hussain, The Use of Error Components Models in Combining Cross-Section and Time-Series Data, *Econometrica* **37** (1969), 55–72.

Journal of Economic and Social Measurement 29 (2004) 307–320
IOS Press

On the advantage of using two or more econometric software systems to solve the same problem

Houston H. Stokes
Department of Economics (MC 144) College of Business Administration, University of Illinois at Chicago, 601 South Morgan Street, Room 2103, Chicago, IL 60607-7121, USA
Tel.: +1 312 996 0971; Fax: +1 312 996 3344; E-mail: hhstokes@uic.edu

This paper illustrates the dangers of relying on just one software system to solve what appears to be a fairly routine probit model. It is shown that quite different results can be obtained using various well known software systems. In this example, at a superficial level of analysis, the differences were traced to the default convergence tolerances that are built into the statistical software. At a deeper level of analysis, the effect of the convergence tolerance on the solution indicates that the maximum likelihood estimate does not exist due to a formerly undetected quasi-complete separation problem. Using a Multivariate Adaptive Regression Splines (MARS) model to relax the assumption of constant coefficients, further implications are drawn from this dataset.

1. Introduction

McCullough and Vinod [18] surveyed the growing literature on the problems of statistical software reliability. In their view, user errors can be caused by poorly designed code, outright errors in the coding or due to misuse of the package. While such problems can and do occur in linear models, as was shown in classic work by Longley [14,15] and others, in nonlinear models the problems can be substantially more acute. With the greater inherent complexity of a nonlinear model comes greater potential for problems. In a recent paper on nonlinear estimation, McCullough and Renfro [17] stress two major areas of concern. First, for many nonlinear models one algorithm might produce an answer while others may fail. Second, even if both algorithms produce answers, one may be more accurate. Their paper traces estimation accuracy difficulties to differences in step length, convergence criterion and the way that derivatives are calculated. The present paper provides an example that documents a case where there was an undetected underlying problem in a nonlinear probit/logit model that had been widely published in various places for many years. The problems of this model were detected by accident during a routine replication exercise. After careful analysis and experimentation, it was found that only by varying the convergence tolerance was it possible to determine that in fact there was no maximum likelihood solution to the model, which turned out to be a undetected quasi-complete separation problem.

The paper starts with a brief discussion of the nature of the problem and how it was found. Next, the symptoms of the problem are investigated. To make sure this

Table 1
Variables in the McManus capital punishment dataset

Variable	Description
T	Median time served convicted murders
Y	Median family income of families in 1949 (thousands of dollars)
LF	Labor force participation rate in 1950 (expressed as a percent)
NW	Proportion of population that is nonwhite in 1950
D2	Dummy Variable, 1 for southern states, 0 for others
PX	Average number of executions 1946–1950/convictions in 1950
D1	Dummy Variable, 1 $PX > 0$, 0 otherwise

Source: Maddala [16]. Original data from McManus [20].

difficulty was not related to one or two particular software packages, a number of well known software systems are tested and their results reported. Since software systems are "black boxes" in that the calculations are hidden in compiled code, the problem was attempted with the IMSL routine DBCONF, which is available in B34S, and FMINUNC, which is available in Matlab. Here the calculation is completely exposed. To facilitate replication on the part of readers, all input control files, data and output and log files are available on-line to facilitate further experimentation and study. For the DBCONF and Matlab results the exact setups are shown in Tables 2 and 3. An important goal is to discuss the symptoms of this problem to alert researchers when their software is not able to detect the exact problem. Finally, a Multivariate Adaptive Regression Splines (MARS) model is used to relax the assumption of constant coefficients.

2. Data and preliminary results

Strange results were obtained when the author used what was thought to be a stable probit test case reported by Maddala [16] to test the SAS PROBIT command. Maddala, then at the University of Florida, had estimated a probit model using data on the deterrent effect of capital punishment that had been reported and analyzed with baysian methods by McManus [20] in 1985 . The dataset consisted of a cross section of 44 states and contained data on capital punishment. Key variables and their descriptions are listed in Table 1.

Maddala [16] in 1988 and later in 1992 reported an OLS model

$$\begin{array}{llllll} \hat{D}1 = 1.993 + & 0.00146T + & 0.658Y - & 0.055LF + & 1.988NW + & 0.343D2 \\ \quad (1.33) & (0.001) & (0.240) & (0.028) & (0.759) & (0.189) \end{array} \quad (1)$$

where standard errors are reported under the coefficients.[1] Maddala next estimated the above model using probit (his results are reported in Table 2 as column 6) and

[1]Maddala actually reported t scores. The SE's were calculated from the t's. Variable names are defined in Table 1.

Table 2
Probit results for extended model

	B34S	SAS	RATS	LIMDEP	Stata	Maddala	B34S	B34S	B34S
Column	1	2	3	4	5	6	7	8	9
CON	6.915406	−6.9155	6.9155	6.9155	6.915513	6.92	6.915403	6.915403	6.915403
	11.32239	11.3225	11.3225	11.32251	11.3225	11.344	11.32242	11.3224	11.3224
T	0.011312	−0.0113	0.0113	0.011312	0.011312	0.0113	0.011312	0.011312	0.011312
	0.005656	0.0057	0.005656	0.005656	0.005656	0.00565	0.005656	0.005656	0.005656
Y	6.461074	−6.4611	6.4611	6.46112	6.4611	6.46	6.46107	6.46107	6.461074
	3.14832	3.1484	3.1484	3.1484	3.1483	3.1512	3.14833	3.14833	3.148326
LF	−0.40928	0.4093	−0.4093	−0.40929	−0.40929	−0.409	−0.40928	−0.40928	−0.40928
	0.257213	0.2572	0.2572	0.2572	0.2572	0.2572	0.257213	0.257213	0.257213
NW	42.49808	−42.4983	42.4983	42.49827	42.4983	42.5	42.49808	42.49808	42.49808
	20.74961	20.7498	20.7498	20.7498	20.7497	20.732	20.7497	20.7497	20.7497
D2	4.39004	−6.8494	8.0863	7.197776	*	4.63	5.256471	6.162708	7.09329
	46.3237	53,170.4	4,647,813	114,550.1	*	115.75	325.662	3,802.26	73,594.5
LogL	−8.64041	−9.01665	−8.64038	−8.64038	−8.64038	na	−8.64039	−8.64039	−8.64039
Tol	1.00E-05	0.001	0.00001	0.0001	1.00E-6	na	1.00E-07	1.00E-09	1.00E-12
Iterations	11.00	na	36.00	29.00	6.00	na	15.00	20.00	24.00
Cond	6.46E+08	na	na	na	na	na	3.86E+10	5.29E+12	1.98E+15

For data sources see Table 1 and text. LogL is the Log Likelihood. Tol = the convergence tolerance used. Tol set to default for all but columns 7–9. Cond is the condition of the variance covariance matrix.

remarked "surprisingly, D2 is not significant but all other coefficients have the same signs as in the linear probability model." Stokes [24] used this model to illustrate probit models using the B34S(R) software in 1991, and later in 1997 did further analysis using the Friedman [9] MARS model. The B34S results for Maddala's Eq. (1) estimated as a probit model are listed in column 1 in Table 2. Here the log likelihood function is reported and the condition of the variance covariance matrix is given as 6.46E + 08. The difference between column 1 and 6 is in the D2 coefficient, which was 4.39 for B34S and 4.63 for Maddala. Initially, the importance of this was thought to be a typesetting error, since in addition to the equation in column 6, Maddala reported a subset probit model that removed D2.

$$\hat{D}1 = 10.27 + 0.0094T + 5.55Y - 0.437LF + 50.25NW$$
$$(10.48)\ (0.0051)\quad (2.817)\ (0.257)\qquad (20.1) \tag{2}$$

which was exactly replicated with B34S for all coefficients and their standard errors.

At a later time in order to benchmark the SAS PROBIT command, Maddala's Eq. (1) was run and is reported in Table 2 as column 2.[2] In comparison with the

[2]Due to software design, SAS calculates the cumulative normal distribution of XB rather than XB,

B34S result listed in column 1, we note the Log Likelihood function is virtually the same and all coefficients except D2 are the same except for a sign change. For D2 SAS had reported −6.8494 with a suspect SE of 53,170.3. Subsequent testing with RATS, reported in column 3, and LIMDEP, reported in column 4, found the same pattern. Again, the Log Likelihood agreed and all coefficients were the same, except D2. For the RATS Linux version 5.01 PRB command, the SE became 4,647,812.5029 while for LIMDEP 7.0 on Linux (compiled with the Lahey LF95 compiler from Fortran), the SE was 114,550.1. Point estimates of the D2 coefficient were 8.0863 and 7.19776, respectively. As a final test of packages, Stata version 7.0 for Linux was tried. Stata reported "note: d2 $\sim=$ 0 predicts success perfectly. d2 dropped and 15 obs not used." The Stata results are shown in Table 2, column 5. The reported coefficients and log likelihood (−8.64038) for this "reduced model" were found to be nearly the same as was found by the other systems for the complete period including D2. What Stata appeared to have done is to just not report the coefficients for D2. The cryptic Stata message might cause some confusion to the average researcher since what Stata reports is *not* Maddala's model (2), which is a probit model estimated for all 44 observations without D2 on the right-hand side. If the Maddala Eq. (2) is run, all programs replicate the results reported by Maddala. In the next section a number of tests are run to attempt to understand the nature of the problem that is causing the different results.

3. A discussion of the symptoms of this problem

The B34S probit command has a tolerance that defaults to 1.0E-5.[3] It was found that if this is reduced to 1.0E-7 (see results reported in column 7 in Table 2), the D2 coefficient increases to 5.256471 and the SE increases to 325.662. Further reductions to 1.00E-9 and 1.00E-12 cause the coefficient of D2 to increase to 6.162708 and

which results in all coefficients having the opposite sign. This is a potential problem for users of this software who do not carefully read just what is being estimated and/or fail to validate the SAS results with other software.

[3]The B34S PROBIT command was originally obtained from Mathematica Policy Research in the middle 1970's. This tolerance is a bit large in comparison with some other software systems. The code has been substantially altered by the developer of B34S, although the basic structure of the program has remained the same. The program is 100% double precision and older inverters have been replaced by the LINPACK [7] Cholesky routines DPOCO/DPOFA/DPODI, which are used to invert and calculate an estimate of 1 over the condition of the variance covariance matrix. This has been converted to the condition. It should be noted that this estimate differs slightly from the estimate provided by LAPACK [3]. SAS is documented in Barr, Goodnight, Sall and Helwig [4], while RATS is documented in Doan [8]. Greene [11] documents LIMDEP, while Stata is documented in [25]. White [26] documents SHAZAM version 8 while EViews is documented in [23]. The versions of the software used were: B34S 8.67E, Rats 5.01, Limdep 7.0 and Stata 7.0. All initial runs were on a PC running Linux Red Hat 7.1. The same runs are made on W2K, slight differences will be observed for the extreme cases, most likely due to run- time library differences. Setups for this problem are distributed with the B34S.

Table 3
Implementation of the probit model in B34S

```
b34sexec matrix;
call loaddata;
mask1 = (d1.eq.1.); mask2 = (d1.eq.0.);

program test2;
xb=(cc+ t_coef*t + y_coef*y + lf_coef*lf
      + nw_coef*nw + d2_coef*d2);
func= mlsum((mask1*probnorm(xb))+(mask2*probnorm((-1.)*xb)));
return;
end;

rvec=array(6:  10., 0.01, 5., -0.4, 40., 3.);
ll=  array(6:-100.,-100.,-100.,-100., -100., -100.);
uu=  array(6:  100.  100.  100.  100.  100., 100.);
call echooff;
call cmaxf2(func :name test2
   :parms cc t_coef y_coef lf_coef nw_coef d2_coef
   :ivalue rvec :maxfun 20000 :maxg 20000
   :maxit 100000 :lower ll :upper uu :print);
b34srun;
```

7.09329 and the SE to rise to 3,802.26 and 73,594.5, respectively, (see columns 8 and 9). If the value of 1.00E-13 is used, the condition check of the hessian matrix fails and the B34S probit command stops because the hessian matrix cannot be inverted. Note that for the B34S equations (columns 1 and 7–9), the condition of the variance covariance matrix is reported. As the tolerance is reduced from the default in column 1 to 1.00E-12 in the equation reported in column 9, the condition increases from 6.46E + 08 to 1.98E + 15. The results of this first experiment suggest that the puzzle is related to the convergence tolerance.

To confirm that these findings were not unique to the B34S, the tolerance in RATS (CVCRIT) was raised from the default of 0.00001 to 0.01 and 0.1, respectively. This change in the opposite direction resulted in the estimated D2 coefficient falling to 7.8911 and 3.3928 and the standard error falling to 1,702,804 and a more reasonable 8.17, respectively. This experiment confirms the sensitivity of the D2 coefficient to the tolerance is not a unique feature of the B34S system. The importance of the experiments with tolerance is that when using default settings many software systems may appear to converge when in fact they have not.[4] If this happens, rank problems

[4]The other possibility is that the default tolerance in a software system is such that a rank message is obtained. The McKelvey-Zavoina [19] program MPROBIT, which is part of B34S, is just such a program. Here, unless the tolerance is increased from the default of 0.1E-5 to > 0.02, the hessian matrix is found to be not full rank. The Press-Nerlove [22] LOGLIN and the Kawasaki [13] MLOGLIN programs, also part of B34S, fail to estimate the problem using logit models when default settings are used. With the default number of iterations, LOGLIN did not converge. When the iterations were increased, a rank error occurred on the hessian matrix. Similar problems were obtained with MLOGLIN. The fact that all three systems fail with default settings protects the user but does not give an insight into the nature of the problem.

Table 4
Implementation of the probit model in MATLAB

```
function y=testcase(x,d1,xx);
% sets up a PROBIT using normcdf function
% x are the coef, d1 is the left hand side
% xx is the data vector

xb=xx*x';
dd=abs(d1-1.);

y=-1.*(sum(d1.*log(normcdf(xb)))+ ...
  sum(dd.*log(normcdf((-1.).*xb))));
guess=[10.  0.01 5.   -0.4 40.   3.   ];
options=optimset('MaxFunEvals', 2000,'MaxIter',2000)
xx=[ones(size(t)) t y lf nw d2];
[x,fval,e,o] =fminsearch('testcase',guess,options, d1,xx);
[x2,fval2,e,o,g,h]=fminunc('testcase',guess,options,d1,xx);

disp('Answers using fminsearch & fminunc for Base Case')
[x' x2']
disp('Log Likelihood Function found')
[fval' fval2']
disp('Gradint');
g
disp('Hessian');
h
ih=inv(h);
se=sqrt(diag(ih));
tstat=x2' ./se;
disp('Coef SE tstat')
[x2' se tstat]
```

Note: The data loading steps have not been shown in Tables 3 and 4.

on the hessian matrix predicted by the theory may not be seen. This problem is investigated first by using the IMSL [21] routine DBCONF, to obtain measurements of the gradient and Matlab [5] to verify the findings. The setups for these runs illustrate the probit calculation in two 4th generation programming systems and are given in Tables 3 and 4, respectively. A probit model takes the form $P(y_i = 1|X_i) = F(X_i\beta)$, where y is a 0–1 left-hand variable and X_i is a set of explanatory variables for the ith observation. $F(\ )$ is the standard Normal c.d.f. The probit model is estimated by maximizing $L = \sum_{Y_i \neq 0} \log(F(X_i\beta)) + \sum_{Y_i=0} \log(1 - F(X_i\beta))$ over β. In the B34S MATRIX command the function PROBNORM is $F()$ while the function MLSUM sums the logs. The mask1 and mask2 variables facilitate vectorization of the problem, since parse costs of the calculation are fixed no matter how large the sample size. The variable rvec sets an initial guess and uu and ll set upper and lower bounds. In the call to CMAXF2, the function name (func) and its program (test2) are passed as well as some switches.

The Matlab implementation requires a function (y) to be specified. Here d1 and dd are the mask variables and NORMCDF the cumulative normal distribution. After

Table 5
Experiments with IMSL routine DBCONF

	Constant	T	Y	LF	NW	D2	LogL	# It	Grad Tol
Setup 1									
Coef	6.9156	0.011312	6.461085	−0.40929	42.4984	4.6838	−8.64038	199	6.06E-06
SE	10.44	0.005358	2.94959	0.23754	17.5124	138.9			
Grad	1.22E-08	−7.86E-07	−2.17E-08	−1.69E-07	7.27E-09	−1.12E-05			
Setup 2									
Coef	6.9155	0.011312	6.461116	−0.40929	42.49827	5.397677	−8.64038	15,585	1.00E-13
SE	0.001132	8.92E-05	2.75E-04	2.09E-04	1.44E-02	3.31E+00			
Grad	2.44E-08	−1.40E-07	−8.69E-09	2.81E-08	6.61E-10	−3.28E-07			

setting some switches with OPTIMSET, the Matlab commands FMINSEARCH and FMINUNC are used to obtain the "solution." From the hessian matrix we calculate the SE and print the results.

As is clear from Tables 3 and 4, to use DBCONF under B34S or FMINUNC under Matlab requires that the user supply the model in a matrix language. Apart from this input, the rest of the calculation is done with DBCONF or FMINUNC. We next discuss the DBCONF results reported in Table 5. Setup 1 listed in Table 5 shows the solution of the model using the default settings for all input parameters. The SE is calculated as the square root of the diagonal of the hessian matrix. Of all the results reported so far, these are closest to Maddala's original findings and may give us a clue about the software settings he used. Inspection of the gradient[5] shows a value −1.12E-5 for the D2 coefficient, which is consistent with the "convergence" that was found with the B34S probit command. Setup 2 substantially lowers the gradient tolerance to 1.00E-13 and results in 15,585 iterations, no change in the Log Likehood and a coefficient and SE of D2 of 5.3976 and 3.305, respectively. The message "Scaled step tolerance satisfied. May be a local solution. Or progress too slow. Adjust STEPTL." suggests problems. The SE's are quite different and should not be taken seriously. The gradient for D2 decreased to −3.28E-07. The fact that changes in the tolerance change the D2 coefficient and its SE is a symptom that is consistent with D2 not being identified.[6] These findings again point up some of the

[5]The suggestion to investigate whether the gradient of the suspect parameter (D2) at the alleged maximum was not zero was made by a reviewer. Using the B34S probit command, the condition for the hessian matrix for equation 1 was 6.46E + 8 and not appreciatively different from the condition found when estimating the subset model in equation (2) that did not contain D2 where it was 1.22E + 8. However, when a smaller tolerance was used, the condition increased. Gould and Sribney [10], who are developers for Stata, discuss on page 119 situations in which as the iterations proceed the negative hessian matrix cannot be inverted and a direction cannot be calculated. They note that in such cases Stata will give a message that the likelihood is "not concave." During the solution of this problem no such message was observed from Stata.

[6]The MATLAB optimization routine FMINUNC [5] was used to verify what was found with DBCONF. Using the default settings the D2 coefficient was 4.1136 with SE 5.7790. If the TolX and TolFun are set to 0.10E-13, the coefficient rises to 15.833, the SE increases to 10,317 and we get a rank warning for inverting the hessian matrix. As the tolerance is lowered, the SE's move for all coefficients due to inversion problems.

pitfalls of running programs with their default values, a point made by McCullough and Renfro [17].[7]

Sorting the dataset with respect to D1, the dependent variable, reveals that when D1 = 0, D2 is always 0 but then D1 = 1, D2 can be 0 or 1. This means that if we find that D2 = 1, we know for certain that D1 = 1. There were 15 such cases. Once the sort was studied, the formerly cryptic message in Stata was understood. All 15 such cases were detected by Stata. What is strange is that if Stata really believed its own message, it would have either reported nothing (the best decision) or reported the subset model in Eq. (2). Just not reporting the D2 coefficient but leaving all other coefficients in the model is a strange and confusing choice. The obvious question was to see if other widely used software systems were able to detect this problem.

If Eq. (1) is estimated using EViews version 3.0, the log likelihood is found to be −8.64038, the model converges after 27 iterations and the D2 coefficient and its SE are 8.591597 and 360,990,038, respectively, suggesting problems to most experienced researchers. However, if SHAZAM version 8.0 is run, we get convergence after 8 iterations with the log likelihood −8.6428 and D2 coefficients and SE as 3.2825 and 7.0084, respectively. SHAZAM reports the tolerance was 0.001. Other coefficients are close to the values found for other systems but still differ. For example, the LF coefficient was −0.40930 with SE 0.25713, while most other software systems found −0.40928 with SE 0.2572. These findings suggest nonconvergence due to the large tolerance that would not be readily apparent to a researcher not using other software systems. TSP [12] Version 4.5 provides a better message to the user. When Eq. (1) is estimated, TSP reports "Quasicomplete Separation: some observations perfectly predicted for choice... D2 > 0.00 perfectly predicts D1 = 1. Delete D2 and all obs. which satisfy this. Estimation would not converge; coefficients of these variables would slowly diverge to +/− infinity – the scale of the coefficients is not identified in this situation." TSP makes reference to Albert and Anderson [1] and Amemiya [2] for a further discussion of Quasicomplete Separation. In the next section this problem is discussed in more detail.

4. Diagnosis of the problem

The key reference to the problem of Complete Peparation and Quasicomplete Separation is Albert and Anderson [1], which is the basis of the reference in Amemiya [2]. No other econometric book seems to address this issue except for Davidson and

[7]The B34S control setup that runs all the tests, the B34S log and the B34S out file for the job are available on the web under the page www.uic.edu/ hhstokes , which points the user to the B34S ftp location. The file names are probit.b34, probit.log , probit.out, probit2.b34 and probit2.out. Complete data and output are given for Tables 2 and 5.

MacKinnon [6], whose book is in press and contains an excellent summary of the problem.[8] Define the probit log likelihood function as

$$l(y,\beta)=\sum_{i=1}^{n}(y_i\log(F(X_i\beta))+(1-y_i)\log(1-F(X_i\beta))) \tag{3}$$

where y_i is the left-hand side variable assumed to be 0-1 and X_i is a vector containing the *i*th observations of right-hand side variables. Complete Separation or a Perfect Classifier Problem occurs if there is a linear combination of variables such that

$$y_t=0 \text{ if } X_t\tilde{\beta}<0 \text{ and } y_t=1 \text{ if } X_t\tilde{\beta}>0 \tag{4}$$

The symptom of this problem is that one or more of the parameters will increase without bound since the log likelihood in Eq. (3) approaches zero if $\beta=\gamma\tilde{\beta}$ and $\gamma\to\infty$. This pattern was not observed. Quasicomplete separation occurs if there is at least one observation with $y_i=0$ and $X_i\tilde{\beta}=0$ and at least one other observation with y_i and $X_i\tilde{\beta}=0$. Recall that the sort showed that for all cases when D1 =0, D2 was 0 and when D1 $=0$, D2 was 0 and when D1 was 1, D2 could take on the value 0 or 1. For the McManus data we can identify all coefficients except D2. There is no unique D2 coefficient, since we can set it to any value and for the case when D2 $=1$ still predict with 100% certainty that D1 was not equal to 0. In this situation the likelihood function is not zero. Although it exists in theory, it can never be reached numerically, since as the D2 coefficient increases in value the density of the cumulative normal distribution approaches zero, which results in rank problems when inverting the hessian matrix. As is noted in Albert and Anderson [1], in such a situation the maximum likelihood estimator does not exist.

5. A strategy of prevention

The main lesson learned in this exercise is to not accept the output of one program without further testing with other software. The default convergence tolerances may give the illusion of convergence when in fact this has not occurred. If one software system is used, it is a good idea to vary the default nonlinear estimation assumptions to see the results as was suggested by McCullough and Renfro [17]. While it is always a good idea to check the gradients, in this case this did not flag the problem. The condition of the hessian matrix should also be checked on a routine basis. If the condition increases as the tolerance is lowered, this is cause for further concern and warrants further checking, since it suggests the hessian matrix may be moving toward singularity, which is a symptom of quasicomplete separation.

[8] Evelyn Lehrer, who worked with Press and Nerlove [22] on LOGLIN, characterized the difficulty as an "empty cell problem." In the context of the sort, this would mean that for the case where D1 $=0$, D2 is never 1. The key chapter in Davidson and MacKinnon [6] is 11.

The dramatic increase in the SE as the tolerance is lowered is another giveaway that the hessian matrix is unbounded. It is clear that the estimated SE's should be inspected closely. The SAS SE of 53,170.39, the EViews SE of 360,990,038 and the RATS SE of 4,647,813 raise red flags to veteran empirical workers. At issue is both the parameterization of the model (if it is probit what variables are on the right?) and the more general question of whether in fact a hyperplane exists for this problem. To obtain some insight into the underlying model, in the next section we relax some of the assumptions of the probit model and investigate interaction terms using MARS.

6. Further results when some assumptions of the model are relaxed

The Multivariate Adaptive Regression Splines (MARS) technique was developed by Friedman [9] to relax the assumption of constant coefficients at all levels of the right-hand side variables. The MARS technique provides a spline-based method to search for interactions and threshold effects in the data that are implicitly assumed away in a more traditional probit model. Only brief discussion of the theory will occur here. More detail is provided in Stokes [24] and Friedman [9]. The first step in identifying a MARS model is to determine the maximum number of basis functions or knots and the maximum number of variables in each basis function. In this analysis the number of variables in each basis function is limited to a maximum of 2. If the maximum was set as 1, a simple spline model with no interactions is estimated.

Define $(x_i - \tau_i)_+ = x_i - \tau_i$ if $x_i > \tau_1$ and 0 otherwise. Assuming a linear model, if a MARS model is fit in a situation in which there is no break in the data, then the model found should be

$$y = \alpha + \sum_{i=1}^{k} \beta_i (x_i - \tau_i)_+ \tag{5}$$

where τ_i is the minimum of the x_i vector for $i = 1, \ldots, k$. The linear OLS model is a special case of the MARS model. If τ_i is not set at the minimum of the x_i vector, we have a knot or in words a change in the coefficient that is related to a particular value in x_i vector. The Friedman MARS software allows estimation of a logit form of this equation, not the probit form.[9] Since logit is similar to probit, a logit MARS model will be used in the next experiment. Define

$$f(X) = f(\alpha + \sum_{i=1}^{k} \beta_i (x_i - \tau_i)_+) \tag{6}$$

[9]While it would be possible to modify the Friedman [9] MARS library Fortran source to add probit, this was not the focus of this paper. In addition, the author did not want to introduce any possible additional sources of error arising from such modifications. The reason to attempt the problem with MARS logit was to investigate dropping the hyperplane assumption and allow modeling interaction points.

The logit MARS model becomes

$$F(Z_i) = (1/(1 + e^{-\hat{f}(X)})) \tag{7}$$

The MARS procedure calculates a modified generalized cross validation statistic (GCV) for the complete model and a GCV_i if the ith variable is removed.[10] If the ith variable was important, then $\mathrm{GCV}_i > \mathrm{GCV}$. If the ith variable did not add to the model, then $\mathrm{GCV}_i < \mathrm{GCV}$ or the penalty of adding that variable was not offset by greater predictive accuracy obtained by including that variable. Such a technique is useful in telling what variables are important in the model. The GCV_i vector can be normalized to form the normalized relative variable importance vector NRVI_i, where each variable is rated on a scale of from 0 to 100.

$$\mathrm{NRVI}_i = (100 * (\max(0, (\mathrm{GCP}_i - \mathrm{GCV})))/A0, \tag{8}$$

where

$$A0 = \max(\mathrm{GCP}_i - \mathrm{GCV}) \tag{9}$$

for $i = 1, \ldots, k$ variables in the model. In the stepwise forward-knot placement phase of model estimation, the GCV is shown as each basis function enters the model. If the basis function adds to the model, the GCV will fall. If the basis function does not add to the model, then GCV can rise. After backward stepwise elimination, the software produces a table that shows the basis functions remaining in the model and the increase in the GCV that would occur if the basis function was removed from the model. In OLS models without interaction terms, there is a one-to-one mapping of basis functions and variables. Once knots are introduced to the analysis, there is the possibility that one variable can enter into the model as part of one or more functions.

For the McManus data the MARS logit model estimated was as follows:

$$\begin{aligned} \mathrm{D1} = {} & 0.9951 - 0.1303(\mathrm{T} - 164.)_{+}(0.061 - \mathrm{NW})_{+} \\ & 0.2788(164. - \mathrm{T}_{+})(0.061 - \mathrm{NW})_{+} \end{aligned} \tag{10}$$

$$\mathrm{GCV} = 0.08529$$

The estimated MARS model was estimated where there was a maximum of 5 knots, and the highest order interaction was 2. Setting the number of knots larger had no effect on the estimated model. Recall that in equation (1) the probability of the state having capital punishment was positively associated with T (medium time served), Y (median family income) and NW (proportion of the population that is nonwhite). While the probit model had three significant variables, the MARS/logit model had only two, T and NW, with Y dropping out. Interestingly, the deterrent

[10] For details on the construction of this statistic and other MARS related questions, see Friedman [9].

effect of time served (T) only affected whether the state had capital punishment if the proportion of the nonwhite population was < 0.061. If this condition was met and if the median time served was > 164 months, an increase in T *lowered* the probability that the state had a death penalty (see coefficient -0.1303). However, if the median time served was < 164 months, then increases in T were positively associated with the state having the death penalty (-0.2788 multiplied by $-$T is positive). Note that the probit model, by construction, was not able to detect these level effects and just found the positive effect. What the MARS logit model suggests is that if the median time served for murders is below 164 months, the population views the death penalty as a complementary punishment with prison time. If the level of sentencing produces longer median sentences above 164 months, the death penalty is a substitute for a prison time.

To access the models estimated, the variance of the residuals was 0.065002 in the probit model and 0.0588775 in the MARS logit model. For the estimated MARS model the relative importance of T and NW was 100%, with the other three variables having 0%. The GCV is lowered to 1704 for the inclusion of both T and NW and 0.08529 for Y, LF and D2. The reason is the MARS logit model depends only on interactions between two variables, T and NW. The other variables were eliminated in the automatic model selection process as the software selects a simplified (less variables on the right) model. The MARS procedure eliminated D2 and Y and LF once the knot was discovered. These results are consistent with D2 being not identified in the usual probit specification.

The MARS analysis, by suggesting that there are knots in the model, gives us some insight into what is probably happening. By forcing the probit model into the constant coefficient assumption and ignoring interactions and adding possibly redundant variables, the researcher may be setting the stage for various nonlinear estimation problems. The fact that these problems are related to the convergence tolerance is of some interest to those working in this field.

7. Conclusions

What started as a replication of probit results reported in Maddala [16] was extended when different results were obtained with the software systems B34S, SAS, RATS, LIMDEP and Stata. The differences were traced to the effect of alternative convergence tolerances on both the rank of the variance covariance matrix and the point estimate of one variable that was caused by Quasicomplete Separation. Only two software systems, Stata and TSP, were able to detect the underlying problem that for this model and these data, the maximum likelihood estimate does not exist, Using a Multivariate Adaptive Regression Splines (MARS) model to relax the assumption of constant coefficients, further implications are drawn from this dataset.

A number of important conclusions emerge from this brief analysis. The most important is that the user should not just accept output uncritically, but probe the solution offered by the computer. It is a good idea to try nonlinear models on a variety of software systems. The experiment will either confirm your original findings or assist in uncovering something that would not have been found otherwise. The sensitivity of the results to the convergence tolerance in software systems suggests great awareness of the implications of these often hidden assumptions of estimation, which are usually ignored. It is important to experiment with the default settings when running nonlinear models. While Complete and Quasicomplete Separation and other problems are known, even experts in the probit/logit field such as Maddala can be fooled if the software system appears to converge and the coefficients and SE's errors appear reasonable. To guard against publishing flawed results it is highly recommended that the condition of the variance covariance matrix or the hessian matrix from which it is derived be available for inspection and possible reporting along with the log likelihood function. The gradient, which is often not available, gives indications concerning whether false convergence has occurred.

It may be the case that the underlying model is not a constant coefficient probit model, no matter what variables are placed on the right. The MARS analysis of the data in this paper suggests that the constant coefficient assumption implicit in the traditional probit model was not met. A simplified but less restrictive model was shown to outperform the more complex (more variables on the right) probit model. The results reported here suggest more analysis is needed of this interesting, real-world example since it appears to contain subtle numerical problems that are not readily apparent to most software systems.

Acknowledgement

Many suggestions received by B.D. McCullough and Charles Renfro are most appreciated and have helped to strengthen the paper in many ways. Evelyn Lehrer read an earlier draft and contributed in a number of ways. Diana A. Stokes provided editorial help. Any remaining errors are my responsibility.

References

[1] A. Albert and J. Anderson, On the existence of maximum likelihood estimates in logistic regression models, *Biometrika* **71** (1984), 1–10.
[2] T. Amemiya, *Advanced Econometrics*, Harvard University Press, Cambridge, MA, 1985.
[3] E. Anderson et al., *LAPACK Users' Guide*, Third Edition, Siam, Philadelphia, 1999.
[4] A.J. Barr, J.H. Goodnight, J.P. Sall and J.T. Helwig, *A User's Guide to SAS 76*, SAS Institute, Raleigh NC, 1976.
[5] T. Coleman and M. Branch and A. Grace, *Optimization Toolbox: For Use with Matlab(r)*, The MathWorks, Natick, MA, 1999
[6] R. Davidson and J. MacKinnon, *Econometric Theory and Methods*, Oxford University Press, New York, 2003.
[7] J. Dongarra, C.B. Moler. J.R. Bunch and G.W. Stewart, *LINPACK Users' Guide*, Siam, Philadelphia, 1979.

[8] T. Doan, *RATS User's Manual*, Estima, Evanston, IL, 1992.
[9] J. Friedman, Multivariate Adaptive Regression Splines, *Annals of Statistics* **19**(1) (1991), 1–67.
[10] W. Gould and William Sribney, *Maximum Likelihood Estimation with Stata*, Stata Corporation, College Station, TX, 1999.
[11] W. Greene, *LIMDEP Version 7.0*, Econometric Software, 1998.
[12] B. Hall and C. Cummins *TSP Reference Manual, version 4.5*, TSP International, Palo Alto, CA, 1999.
[13] S. Kawasaki, Applications of Log-Linear Probability Models in Economics. Ph.D. dissertation, Northwestern University, 1979.
[14] J. Longley, An Appraisal of Least Squares Programs for the Electronic Computer from the Point of View of the User, *Journal of the American Statistical Association* **62**(319) (1967), 819–841.
[15] J. Longley, *Least Squares Computing Using Orthogonalization Methods*, Marcel Decker, New York, 1984.
[16] G.S. Maddala, *Introduction to Econometrics*, MacMillian, New York, 1988, 1992.
[17] B.D. McCullough and C.G. Renfro, Some Numerical Aspects of Nonlinear Estimation, *Journal of Economic and Social Measurement* **26** (2000), 63–77.
[18] B.D. McCullough and H.D. Vinod, The Numerical Reliability of Econometric Software, *Journal of Economic Literature* **37** (June 1999), 633–665.
[19] R. McKelvey and W. Zavoina, An IBM Fortran IV Program to Perform N-Chotomous Multivariate Probit Analysis, *Behavioral Science* **16** (March 1971), 186–187.
[20] W.S. McManus, Estimates of the Deterrent Effect of Capital Punishment: The Importance of the Researcher's Prior Beliefs, *Journal of Political Economy* **93** (April 1985), 417–425.
[21] V. Numerics, *IMSL Stat/Library and Math/Library*, IMSL, Houston, TX, 1987.
[22] J. Press and M. Nerlove, *Univariate and Multivariate Log-Linear and Logistic Models*, RAND Corp., Santa, Monica, CA, Report R-1306-EDA/NIA 1973.
[23] Quantitative Micro Software, *EViews version 3 User's Guide*, Quantitative Micro Software, 1997.
[24] H.H. Stokes, *Specifying and Diagnostically Testing Econometric Models*, Quorum Press, Westport, CT, 1991, 1997.
[25] StataCorp, *Stata Statistical Software Release 7.0*, Stata Corporation, College Station, TX, 2001.
[26] K. White, *SHAZAM version 8.0 User's Reference Manual*, McGraw-Hill, New York, 1997.

Journal of Economic and Social Measurement 29 (2004) 321–337
IOS Press

Modelling programming languages – appropriate tools?

Ric D. Herbert
Faculty of Science and Information Technology, University of Newcastle, Ourimbah, NSW, 2257, Australia
E-mail: ric.herbert@newcastle.edu.au

This paper examines the issue of modelling languages as software tools for the construction and analysis of economic models. Modelling languages are intermediate level software tools that fit between the conventional commercial programming languages (such as C++ and Java) and the higher level applications packages (such as specific econometric packages). They try to blend the advantages of both the higher level and lower level tools. This paper examines these languages for use in the construction of economic models. Specifically, it examines the issue of whether such a language is the appropriate software tool for an economic modeller. It uses the modelling language MATLAB together with a number of illustrative examples to examine the use of these software tools with dynamic economic models.

Keywords: Programming languages, visual simulation, model construction

1. Introduction

This paper examines the use of modelling languages for economic systems. Modelling languages are those high level programming language software tools that are specifically oriented towards the construction and manipulation of mathematical models. They are designed to be used for scientific and technical computing. There is a large range of such software tools. Examples of the more common modelling languages include GAMS [13], GAUSS [4], MATLAB [31], MATHEMATICA [44], MODSIM [7], S-PLUS [26] and VISSIM [43].

Modelling languages are higher level languages than conventional commercial programming languages, like C/C++ and Java, in that they require less detailed programming than those languages. They are, though, programming languages as they have the language structures in common with the conventional languages. [1] Modelling languages are lower level software tools than conventional packaged tools like econometrics packages and spreadsheets. They are lower level in that they operate on smaller software elements and require a more detailed knowledge of programming to achieve similar results. Modelling languages sit between the higher

[1] In many ways modelling languages have more in common with the scripting languages [38], like Perl, than the conventional third generation programming languages, like Fortran, C/C++ and Cobol, as modelling and scripting languages operate with higher level tasks and tend to be interpreted rather than compiled.

level packages and the lower level commercial programming languages, and are aimed at implementing and simulating mathematical models.

Lower level software tools give the user more flexibility and control, but generally take more time and effort to achieve an identical task to that undertaken by a higher level software tool. In recent times the lower level programming languages (such as assembler languages) are less frequently used in developing commercial information systems. There is a tendency for modern programming languages, and software in general, to move to higher levels.[2]

There are trade-offs between using higher and lower levelled software tools. The question arises as to what level of software tool is the most appropriate for economic modellers. Given the aim of constructing and analysing economic and econometric models which software tools should one use? Or, more importantly, which set of tools should one invest time and money in? This is the focus of the paper. The paper specifically examines the question: "are the modelling languages the appropriate software tools for me as an economic modeller?" and "should the focus of my software development reside in only these languages?" If you want a simple direct answer to these questions, then don't read any more. If there were such answers, then there would not be such a range of software tools.

The questions asked here are not new questions. They have been examined in general (e.g., [12]), in software reviews (e.g., [21]) and by econometrics software developers (e.g., [41,42]). The issues are not restricted to economic modellers. Nor are the issues static. With the massive increase in computing power and connectivity,[3] we can predict that software tools of the future will rapidly change. But the question of what tools should be in an economic modeller's tool box will remain.

This paper focuses on the modelling languages that are used in economics and econometrics. In the literature they are often referred to as matrix manipulation languages, and while this may be how they started,[4] they have evolved to a much higher level than simply programming languages with matrix capabilities.[5] Some of the languages, such as MATHEMATICA and S-PLUS, originated in other directions and have evolved towards the languages, such as GAUSS, MATLAB and OX [10], more commonly called matrix manipulation by economists [22].

The spectrum of modelling languages is wide, with some (e.g., MODSIM) being at a much higher level than others (e.g., Ox). There are also different purposes and

[2] An example is the Abstract Windowing Toolkit in Java.

[3] Moore's Law states that the effectiveness of semi-conductor technology (the technology that currently underlies computing power) doubles every 18 months [40]. At present, the capacity of optical-fibre communications systems doubles every 12 months [24].

[4] Matlab, for example, was originated by the numerical analyst Cleve Moler as a software tool to teach matrix algebra.

[5] APL is an early programming language with matrix capabilities, with the addition of a standard numerical library (like LINPACK and NAG) it could be argued that Fortran IV had matrix capabilities. Object oriented languages, like Java, have the capabilities of processing objects like matrices easily. But these languages are not usually considered to be part of the matrix manipulation languages of economists.

philosophies in their design. The commonality is that they all fit in the continuum between the lower level conventional programming languages (like Java) and the higher level econometrics packages and spreadsheets. Modelling languages are designed with modelling and computational science as a predominant consideration.

This paper is not a review or a comparison of the individual software tools (see, e.g., [8,39]); but examines the issue of the appropriateness of modelling languages based on my experience.[6]

2. Are modelling languages the tool for me?

Given that the aim is to construct, analyse and simulate economic models, then is it worthwhile to invest time and energy in a modelling language? Would it be more appropriate to invest in a lower level conventional programming language, or in a higher level software tool like a standard econometrics package? Or is it a combination of all? The selection of a software tool is the same as the selection of any other tool. The skill is to know which is the appropriate tool from the tool box for the particular job.

Here I illustrate the use of modelling languages by illustrating the features of a particular modelling language, MATLAB, which is typical of this type of language. The aim of the illustrations is that you may consider the question of whether modelling languages should be one of the software tools included in your tool box.

Most modelling languages are commercial software and tend to be priced around the level of other commercial packaged software. Many have add-on packages (see below), and if one purchases a number of these then the modelling language can be relatively expensive. In the case of MATLAB the main supplier is *MathWorks* [30], but there are a number of MATLAB-type products available, including the OCTAVE [11,14] (which is available free of charge) and MIDEVA [27]. There is also available reasonably priced student editions [9,16].

Modelling languages tend to be interpreted rather than compiled like conventional programming languages. They then have the advantage that they can produce immediate feedback, including results and syntax errors, to the programmer compared to conventional programming languages. The disadvantage is that interpreters tend to be slower in program execution than interpreters.[7] There is also the issue that interpreters require the actual source code for the programs, so that distributing programs generally requires distributing the source code. Depending upon your point

---

[6]I have a background in computing and economics. I have worked in the commercial computing industry, and currently teach Information systems. I have run courses in many programming languages, including Basic, C, C++, Cobol, Fortran, Java and Pascal. I have taught computational science using MATLAB.

[7]Translators to produce C/C++ source code are avialble for MATLAB [27,28]. In some cases, compiled Matlab can execute up to 100 times faster than the original code [35,36].

of view, restricting access to the actual source code for the program is an advantage or disadvantage.

Modelling languages also tend to be architectural neutral so that they can be easily transferred between different computing platforms (like PCs, Macs and Unix Workstations). This is a considerable advantage in the increasingly networked world, and allows for programmer to easily swap between computing platforms of various power and for the easy distribution of programs amongst programmers. It is also the trend in software in general and in modern conventional programming languages. [8]

Modelling languages tend have multiple layers of programmer sophistication. For example, with MATLAB numeric data can be displayed automatically with no ';' at the end of the statement, with more user control through the use of display statements (disp() method), or at fine level of user control with the fprintf() method. Similarly, graphic output ranges from simple plot statements, to detailed control over finer details such as line thicknesses, through to the construction of complete Graphical User Interfaces. The advantage to the programmer of these multiple layers of sophistication is that more detail and control can be added as the programmer finds the need for it. Quick results can be produced, and more finesse added later.

2.1. Linear least squares example

As the first illustrative example, consider the problem of linear least squares. This example is specifically chosen as this is the type of problem that an econometrics package was designed to solve. Producing parameter estimates and associated test statistics can generally be done with ease using such a package. It will be seen that it is more user effort to solve it a modelling language, but much less effort than is necessary with a conventional programming language. More importantly, the aim of this example is to show how modelling languages are used.

The programming statements used in this example are taken from a script file containing the program. They could equally well have been entered directly at standard language interface of a window containing a prompt. In the later case the statement are interpreted as they are entered. One of the advantages of these languages is that programs can be built up from statements first tested in the command window and then 'cut and pasted' into the program.

Consider the linear least squares problem. Given a design matrix, A, and a set of data observations, y, then the parameter vector, p, can be found by solving the normal equations:

$$A^T Ap = A^T y \tag{1}$$

[8]Java, for example, has the approach of "write once, run anywhere" [33, p. 22]; but whereas most modelling languages rely on the distribution of source code to acheive architectural neutrally, Java distributes a compiled version of the source code called bytecode, which is then interpreted by a run-time environment. MATLAB's p-code has the same objective, and this may be a trend with modelling languages.

where T is the transpose operator. The resulting predictions from the model are:

$$\hat{Y} = \Lambda p \tag{2}$$

It is for such problems that MATLAB was originally designed, for it began as a matrix manipulation language. Consider the programming problem of generating a model in a specific domain; adding some random noise to generate data; calculating the linear least squares parameters; and plotting the data and estimated model. Using this problem I will illustrate some of the power of such a language.

Let the model be given by the quadratic:

$$z = -2 + 3x + 4x^2 \tag{3}$$

and let $x \in [-10, 10]$.

Then the statement

$$x = [-10 : 0.5 : 10]';$$

generates a column vector of grid points from -10 to 10 at 0.5 intervals. The : operator in MATLAB is an implied for loop and can be used to indicate ranges.[9] Here the loop starts at -10 and increments in steps of 0.5 until 10. The variable x is automatically allocated to be a matrix of the correct dimensionality (41×1). The vector is a column vector for the $'$ operator transpose the default row vector. Notice that the variable x was not specifically declared. Most modelling languages use the concept of a default data type, and while this aims at making the programming easier it can be a cause of error (as will be seen below).

The data at each point can be generated by

$$y = -2 + 3 * x + 4 * x.\hat{}2 + 10 * \text{randn}(\text{size}(x));$$

Here the knowledge of matrix algebra can be seen. A vector is multiplied by a scalar $(3 * x)$ and added to a scalar (-2). As vectors cannot be squared, the operator . is used to indicate element by element operations. Thus matrix operation rules, or element by element operations can be chosen by the programmer. The statement also involves two method calls: one to size() which returns the dimensionality of a matrix, and the other to randn() which returns a matrix of normally distributed random numbers of a given dimensionality.

This statement highlights the power of a language that can use matrix objects through its data types and knowledge of the methods of matrix algebra, and where operators can be overridden. In this case, for example, the assignment operator $(=)$ is such that a matrix is assigned to a matrix (as long as they have the same dimensionality). The multiplication operator $(*)$ is overridden so that it is equally

[9] As in many spreadsheets and conventional programming languages like Fortran90.

applicable to scalar multiplication and matrix multiplication. The cost is that for matrix element by matrix element multiplication a new operator is required. The statement reads as an equation, but the assignment operator is for a vector, the addition operator, $+$ is used to add a scalar to a vector, scalar by vector multiplication is used, and matrix element by element operations are undertaken.

Calculating the linear least squares involves generating the design matrix, and solving the normal equations (Eq. (1)) for the parameters can be achieved by the statements

$$A = [\text{ones(length}(x)\text{,1)}, x, x.\hat{\ }2];$$

$$p = \text{inv}(A' * A) * A' * y;$$

Again, these statements read like the mathematics. The matrix A is assigned what is between the square brackets. These are columns (determined by the , (comma) operator) of an appropriately dimensioned unity matrix, the elements of the vector x and its elements squared. The parameter vector, p, is solved by matrix manipulation and a call to the method inv() which returns the inverse of a matrix.

Determining the estimated model for each grid point, and plotting the results uses the following statements:

```
yhat = A * p;
plot(x,y,'o',x,yhat), ...
  title('OLS Parameter Estimation'), ...
  xlabel('x'), ...
  ylabel('y'), ...
  legend('Data','Model')
```

The ... is not necessary but links the statements to be interpreted at once, resulting in a faster final display. The resulting plot is given in Fig. 1.

The example shows how easy it is to quickly generate powerful programs with few statements using a modelling language such as MATLAB. It also is meant to show that there is a lot of work being done by the language itself. The programmer can take the benefits of this work, without having to write it. If the language is optimised to manipulate the raw numbers, then the language can execute quickly. If it has accurate and efficient methods, then the programmer can benefit from them. Most modelling languages emphasise these points.

Modelling languages also focus on computational issues. Data is stored using high precision and the languages incorporate methods designed with emphasis on computational accuracy as well as computational efficiency. For example, it is computationally preferable to use Gaussian elimination rather than matrix inversion in solving the normal equations. This can be achieved by the statement

$$p = (A' * A)\backslash A' * y;$$

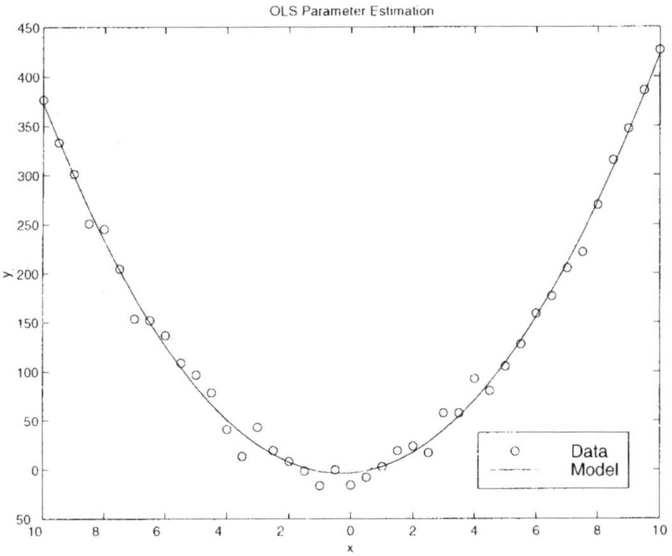

Fig. 1. Linear least squares example.

where a new operator method (left division \) uses Gaussian elimination to solve the system of equations. For the scenario here, the difference between the two resulting parameter sets is marginal ($<10^{-12}$), but this is not always the situation. The effect depends upon the condition of the design matrix.

The design matrix for linear least squares becomes more ill-conditioned as the degree of the polynomial increases. Suppose, for the next illustration, we wish to consider how the condition number of the design matrix changes as the degree of the model polynomial increases. Let each of the coefficients of the polynomial be one, then the condition number as each additional term is added to the model is given by Table 1. It is generated by the following statements:

$x = [-10{:}0.5{:}10]';$

Table 1
Condition number (using the 2-norm) of linear least squares design matrix, A, for the polynomial $y = \sum_{n=0}^{N} x^n$

N	$\kappa_2(A)$	$\kappa_2(A^T A)$
0	1	1
1	6	35
2	70	4965
3	610	4×10^5
4	6891	5×10^7
5	6×10^4	4×10^9
6	7×10^5	5×10^{11}

$A = [];$
$m = 6;$
$C =$ zeros$(m+1, 2);$
for $n = 0{:}m$
  $A = [A, x.\hat{}n];$
  $C(n+1, 1) =$ cond$(A);$
  $C(n+1, 2) =$ cond$(A' * A);$
end

Again, the power of matrix data structures and methods is readily seen. Each iteration of the for loop (from 0 to m in increments of 1) adds a column to the design matrix (starting from the empty matrix). For each design matrix the cond() method is used to return condition number for the matrix, and this is stored in the matrix C. Two matrices are initialised: A to the empty matrix and C to the 7×2 zero matrix. Individual elements in C are addressed in a common matrix format. [10]

Modelling languages also have other features to ease the programming of models. Most allow for complex numbers, and in MATLAB the complex number $3 + 2i$ can be written as $3 + 2i$, $3 + 2 * i$, $3 + 2j$, $3 + 2 * j$ or $3 + 2 * sqrt(-1)$. As with the rules of matrix algebra, the rules of complex number manipulation are built into the language.

The use of complex numbers can be used to illustrate a disadvantage of modelling languages where code is interpreted and no data declaration (typing) is required. Consider the following statements:

$z1 = 3 + 2i;$

$z2 = 3 + 2 * i;$

$i = 6;$

After execution $z1$ and $z2$ will be the same. But executing the statements a second time will result in $z2$ being 15. The complex unit, i has been overridden to be the real number 6 by the execution of $i = 6$ and this value (and implied declaration) remains in the users workspace. While this is a reasonably obvious example, it illustrates the sort of problem that can result from using such languages. Powerful tools can cause powerful problems.

2.2. *Symbolic manipulation – a illustration of packages*

One of the advantages of modelling languages is that there is available a large range of packages or libraries of prewritten software. This add-on software is designed

[10]Compare with C/C++ and Java where square brackets are used for addressing and braces for initialising.

to solve problems in particular areas. For example Mathworks [31] supplies, at additional cost, about 40 packages or “Toolboxes” including Optimization, Statistics, System Identification, Control Systems, Financial, Fuzzy Logic and Neural Nets. Mathtools [27] has available a range of free Toolboxes some of which cover the similar problem domains, but others, such as Genetic Algorithms and Clustering focus on different areas.

In this illustration I use the Symbolic Math Toolbox [37] to linearise a nonlinear model. Modelling languages with symbolic mathematics, use the computer to manipulate symbols, rather than numbers, according to mathematical rules. The advantage of being able to manipulate both mathematical symbols and numeric values, and to move between the two forms, is a powerful feature of modelling languages.

In MATLAB the Symbolic Math Toolbox is an interface between the numeric capabilities of MATLAB and the symbolic capabilities of the MAPLE modelling language [25]. Combining the original features of different modelling languages is the trend in the evolution of these languages, and is an aspect I am deliberately highlighting in this paper.

Consider the Representative Agent Model given by:

$$F(K, L) = aK^{\alpha}L^{(1-\alpha)} \tag{4}$$

$$\Lambda(q) = \frac{q-1}{2bq} \tag{5}$$

$$\frac{\dot{K}}{K}\Lambda(q)[1 - b\Lambda(q)] \tag{6}$$

$$\dot{q} = \{r - b[\Lambda(q)]^2\}q - F_K \tag{7}$$

$$\dot{C} = (r - \Theta)C - p(p + \Theta)[qK - D + B] \tag{8}$$

$$\dot{D} = C - F(K, 1) + G + K\Lambda(q) + rD \tag{9}$$

$$\dot{B} = G - T + rB \tag{10}$$

Details of the model are not relevant here, but can be found in Matsuyama [32]. One detail is that the model is normalised with labour in the production function (Eq. (4)) being unity ($L = 1$).

The model is autonomous and can be written (in state space form) as:

$$\dot{X} = f(X, U, \Theta), \quad X(0) = \xi \tag{11}$$

where

$X = [K, q, C, D, B]^T$ are the endogenous variables (states),
$U = [r, G, T]^T$ are the exogenous variables (controls), and
$\Theta = [p, \theta, \alpha, a, b]^T$ are the parameters.

For this illustration, the aim is to generate a linear model which is in perturbations around a steady state. Linearising the model around a steady state (X^*, U^*) generates:

$$\dot{x} = Ax + Bu \tag{12}$$

where

$$x = X - X^* \tag{13}$$

$$u = U - U^* \tag{14}$$

$$A = \left. \frac{\partial f(X,U)}{\partial x} \right|_{x=x^*, U=U*} \tag{15}$$

$$B = \left. \frac{\partial f(X,U)}{\partial x} \right|_{x=x^*, U=U*} \tag{16}$$

In this illustration, the aim is to find A and B with the modelling language doing the hard work. In MATLAB the variables are numeric by default, so firstly the symbolic variables must be declared. The declaration is:

syms K q D C B % states
syms p theta alpha a b % parameters
syms r G T % controls

Next the model is defined with the MATLAB statements:

$f = a * K$^alpha;
fk = simplify(diff(f,$'K'$)); % first derivative of f w.r.t. K
$L = (q-1)/(2*b*q)$; % Lambda
$f1 = K * L * (1 - b * L)$;
$f2 = (r - b * L * L) * q - fk$;
$f3 = (r -$ theta$) * C - p * (p +$ theta$) * (q * K - D + B)$;
$f4 = C - f + K * L + r * D + G$;
$f5 = G - T + r * B$;

Notice the similarity to the model as coded and as specified in Eqs (4) to (10). The statement diff(f', K') uses the symbolic differentiation diff() method[11] to follow the symbolic rules of differentiation to take the first derivative of the variable f, which is an expression of symbols, with respect the the symbol K. The simplify() method uses MAPLE's rules of simplification to create a simpler expression.

Now the model is coded, then generating the state form requires the setting up of the variables:

[11]The numeric differentiation method is overridden here. The rules of differentiation by symbols apply rather than the rules of numeric differentiation.

$X = [K, q, C, D, B]$; % the states
$P = [p$; theta;alpha; a; $b]$; % the parameters
$U = [r, G, T]$; % the controls
$F = [f1; f2; f3; f4; f5]$; % the function

Finding A and B is easy, using the package's method:

$A =$ jacobian(F, X);
$B =$ jacobian(F, U);

Now both the linear and nonlinear model are available in symbolic form. To illustrate the swapping between symbolic and numeric forms and to check the code, the model can be evaluated at the steady state. Assuming that numeric variables for the steady state (indicated by the 'star' suffix) exist, then they can be substituted for the symbolic variables by:

```
Fn = subs(F, ...
    {K,q,C,D,B,r,G,T,p,theta,alpha,a,b}, ...
    {Kstar,qstar,Cstar,Dstar,Bstar,rstar,Gstar,Tstar,pstar, ...
    thetastar,alphastar,astar,bstar});
```

The variable Fn will be close to zero. Displaying it can check this, and the command line response shows that the answer is close to zero.

```
>> Fn'
ans =
   1.0e-014 *
    0    0.0007    -0.0076    -0.3553    0
```

Like all the packages in modelling languages, the Symbolic Math Toolbox has a large number of methods. As a final illustration, I wanted to include the eigenvalues of the state equation driving matrix of the linear system, A, into this paper, so the statement:

latex(simplify(eig(A)))

generates the LaTeX [23] which produces:

$$\begin{bmatrix} r \\ r+p \\ -p+r-\theta \\ 1/4\frac{2rq^2bK+\sqrt{4r^2q^4b^2K^2-2q^2K^2-4rq^4bK^2+q^4K^2+4rq^2bK^2-8K^{(1+\alpha)}a\alpha bq}}{Kq^2b} \\ 1/4\frac{2rq^2bK+\sqrt{4r^2q^4b^2K^2-2q^2K^2-4rq^4bK^2+q^4K^2+4rq^2bK^2-8K^{(1+\alpha)}a\alpha bq}}{Kq^2b} \end{bmatrix}$$

2.3. Visual simulation

One source of the development of modelling languages has been from the early simulation languages, like CSMP, DYNAMO, SIMULA and SIMSCRIPT [15]. One path of evolution was into the visual simulation languages, where the aim is to make the construction of simulation programs easier by using visual software tools. Modelling languages incorporating these features include STELLA and ITHINK [20] in the systems dynamics area, and MODELER[12] and OPNET [34] in the computer network area.

The MATLAB modelling language includes a package for visual simulation of dynamic systems. The package is known as SIMULINK [29], and it is an add-on to the modelling language. The visual simulation capabilities add considerably to the power of the language. It adds visual modelling constructs, like the use of 'drag and drop' technology for objects, and lines to indicate the data flow, to the MATLAB language.

The MATLAB language has had considerable use in the control engineering community. Developments in the language reflect this background. For example using the standard control engineering model forms makes available a large body of model construction techniques and related MATLAB software methods.

In this illustration the use of transfer functions and standard state space form will be used. These forms are used in the control engineering community to represent a wide range of dynamic linear models.

For the illustration, consider the scalar, auto-regressive model with exogenous input given by

$$y_t = \alpha_1 y_{t-1} + \alpha_2 y_{t-2} + \beta_0 u_t \tag{17}$$

Let the initial conditions be $y_{t-1} = \gamma_1$ and $y_{t-2} = \gamma_2$. This is a single input, single output system with the exogenous input (u) being contemporaneous to the output endogenous variable.

The programming problem of simulating this model is not difficult. It can easily be simulated in a spreadsheet or, as shown above, in a few simple MATLAB statements. This illustration generates a visual simulation environment for it. For the illustration the model is calibrated with $\alpha_1 = 0.1, \alpha_1 = 0.2, \beta_0 = 0.5$ and $\gamma_1 = \gamma_2 = 0$. The input (u) is white gaussian noise with a variance of 0.1.

Taking z-transforms [5] as delay operators then the model can be written as

$$Y(z) = \alpha_1 z^{-1} Y(z) + \alpha_2 z^{-2} Y(z) + \beta_0 U(z) \tag{18}$$

In the form of a transfer function [5] from the input variable to the output variable, the model can be written as

$$\frac{y(Z)}{u(Z)} = \frac{\beta_0}{1 - \alpha_1 Z^{-1} - \alpha_2 Z^{-2}} \tag{19}$$

---

[12] Which has a similar name to the econometrics package MODLER [1,2].

The model may also be transformed [17] into state space form of

$$x_{t+1} = Ax_{t_t} + Bu_t \tag{20}$$

$$Y_t = Cx_t + Du_t \tag{21}$$

where

$$A = \begin{bmatrix} o & 1 \\ \alpha_2 & \alpha_1 \end{bmatrix} \quad B = \begin{bmatrix} 0 \\ \beta_0 \end{bmatrix}$$

$$C = [\alpha_2 \ \ \alpha_1] \quad D = \beta_0$$

with

$$x_t = \begin{bmatrix} y_{t-1} \\ y_{t-2} \end{bmatrix} \quad x_0 = \begin{bmatrix} \gamma_1 \\ \gamma_2 \end{bmatrix}$$

This illustration is concerned with simulation of the model in various forms. These forms have been chosen because MATLAB and SIMULINK have a wide variety of routines, and indeed special data structures, for manipulating such forms. It also illustrates how particular modelling languages have special features for particular application domains.

The illustration considers simulating the model's time response to a random sequence of inputs. To add detail to the illustration, the three forms of the model are each given the same input and the output from each is displayed at each time point and is plotted over time. The overall simulation environment or SIMULINK model is given in Fig. 2. The model consists of the four objects or blocks and lines indicating the flow of data between these objects. This figure shows the overall simulation environment, the actual details of the forms of the model are given in the Models object (or sub-system). In this simulation three outputs are produced with one for each form of the model. These form a vector (wide line) flowing into the Graph object, which generates a time plot, and Display object which displays the values of the vector at each time point. These objects automatically adjust to the dimensionality of their input, so that copying the Graph object and joining a data flow line from that from the output of the White Noise object into the new Graph object would generate a graph of a single line showing the input into the Models. Similarly, selecting the White Noise object and modifying its properties through a dialog box allows it to produce a vector of random numbers. Modifying the simulation environment in such a manner is done using the usual windowing 'drag and drop' technology.

Selecting the Models object opens another window that contains the details of the autoregressive model in its various forms. This is shown in Fig. 3. For the transfer function and state space forms SIMULINK has built in objects that are easily modifiable for this particular model. For the auto regression form the model is built

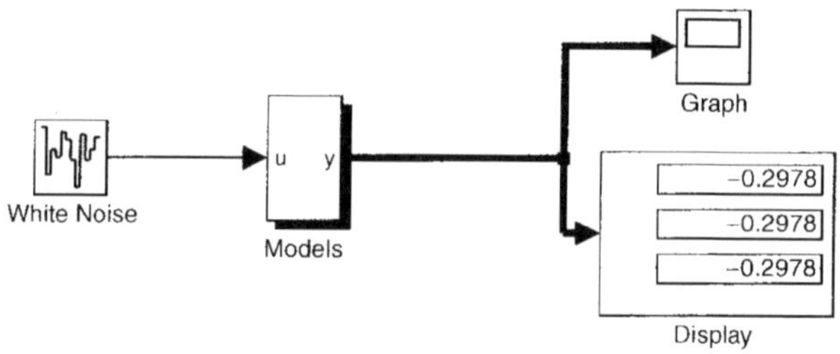

Fig. 2. Visual simulation environment for the linear model of equation 17.

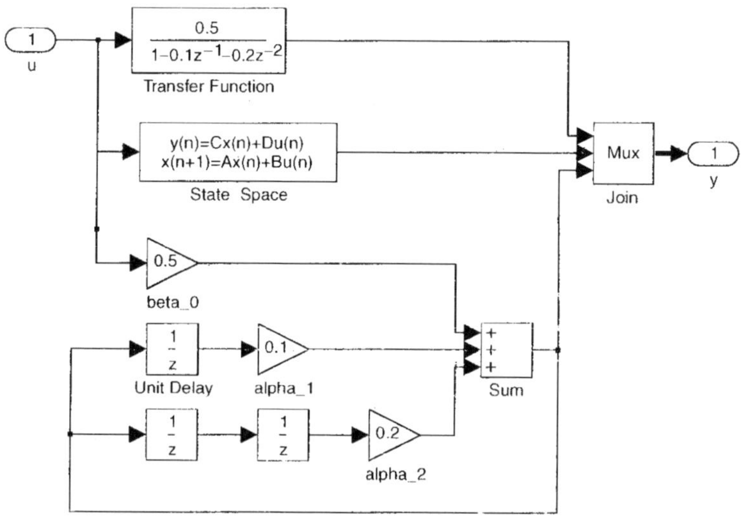

Fig. 3. Details of the Models subsystem.

up of lower level objects consisting of multiplication, summation and unit delays. The figure also uses the Join object to create the vector of output from the models.

Visual simulation adds to the power of modelling languages by aiding the programmer in rapidly developing simulation environments. It is possible to develop large complex simulations with being able to focus more on the model than on setting up and generating a simulation environment. This is the real power of visual simulation languages. But visual simulation languages are higher level languages and the cost of moving towards higher levels can be in flexibility and programmer control over the simulation. Most visual simulation languages overcome this by incorporating features which allow the programmer to create their own objects from lower level code. In SIMULINK this can be using MATLAB code or a conventional programming language (such as C/C++).

This illustration used a simple linear model. The software can be used to construct much larger, nonlinear and more complex models. For further applications to economic models see Herbert and Bell [19] and Herbert and Leeves [18].

3. Conclusion

In this paper I have tried to show the power of modelling languages for economic modellers by taking some specific and simple illustrations and using a single modelling language. I have highlighted its power and have shown that this power does not come without compromise. If your view of the first illustration is that it would have been a lot easier with a conventional econometrics package; of the second illustration that it would have been good practice at differentiation; and of the third that a spreadsheet would have been much easier; then modelling language may not be the software tool for you. But if you enjoy a little programming, really want to understand what is involved in generating, say, a test statistic, or want an interface to a wide range of modelling software methods, then they may be an appropriate tool.

There is a large number of modelling languages. How can one choose between them? This is a particular case of choosing between any similar software tools. One approach has been to define the choice as a function of the attributes of utility of the software tool and then to use econometric methods [3]. In that study the software attributes used were basic functions, advanced functions, training time, documentation, ease of use and vendor support. These attributes give some point of comparison, but exactly what attributes should be used and how they should be measured is a vexing question and one that has not been solved in the information systems arena. Some international standards (such as ISO/IEC 14598: Information Technology – Software Product Evaluation}) have been developed and the standardisation process is continuing [6], but these are often too broad for the economic modeller trying to decide on a modelling language.

My view is whether to use a modelling language and which modelling language to use depends upon the task at hand and the abilities and attributes of the modeller. The real skill is knowing which tool is the appropriate tool for a particular task. In some cases this will be a modelling language. I use a variety of software tools for modelling. I prototype in a modelling language; I use econometric packages for estimation; and when I want speed or control over my source code, I use a conventional programming language.

There has been a trend in economics (as in other disciplines) towards the use of modelling languages. Some argue that these languages will cause economists and econometricians to move away from traditional econometrics packages. I do not see this as necessarily the case. I see the languages as different tools serving different (though evolving) functions. Modelling languages are not new, and many (e.g., CSMP) proceed the development of traditional econometrics packages. Many of these languages are designed more for developing econometrics packages, than in replacing them.

This paper has shown that modelling languages can be powerful tools in the construction and analysis of economic models. They have several advantages. They are designed for modelling. They incorporate computational accuracy by using high precision storage of data, and by appropriate modelling data types. They aim to reduce round-off error. They also include libraries of routines of 'best practice' algorithms that may be used by the modeller. This is not only convenient, but provides routines that are designed to include computationally efficiency and accuracy. They are though programming languages and not simply end user packages. They are higher level languages than conventional commercial languages, and the cost (and advantage) of higher software tools is that details are hidden from the user. They can still allow a user to try some method simply because it is available and without understanding what the method is designed to do and what is actually occurring with the software.

Acknowledgements

The issues considered in this paper have been discussed with many people over a number of years. I would like to specifically acknowledge Rod Bell, David Kendrick, Charles Renfro.

References

[1] Alphametrics, *MODLER: User Guide 1995*, Alphametrics Corp, Bala Cynwyd, PA, 1995.
[2] Alphametrics, World Wide Web – Home Page. Alphametrics Corp, Bala Cynwyd, PA, 1999.
[3] E.E. Anderson and Y.-M. Chen, Microcomputer software evaluation: An econometric model, *Decision Support Systems* **19** (1997), 75–92.
[4] Aptec, World Wide Web – Home Page. Aptec Systems Inc., www.aptech.com, 1998.
[5] K.J. Åström and B. Wittenmark, *Computer Controlled Systems: Theory and Design,* Third Ed., Prentice-Hall, Englewood Cliffs, NJ, 1997.
[6] M. Azuma, Software products evaluation system: Quality models metrics and processes – international standards and japanese practice, *Information and Software Technology* **38** (1996), 145–154.
[7] CACI, World Wide Web – Home Page, CACI Products Company, www.caciasl.com/modsim.html, 1998.
[8] F. Cribari-Neto, Econometric programming environments: Gauss, Ox and S-Plus, *Journal of Applied Econometrics* **12** (1997), 77–89.
[9] J.B. Dabney and T.L. Harman, *The Student Edition of Simulink, Dynamic System Simulation for Matlab Version 2 – User's Guide,* Prentice-Hall International Inc., Englewood Cliffs, NJ, 1998.
[10] J.A. Doornik, World Wide Web – Home Page, www.nuff.ox.ac.uk/Users/Doornik.
[11] J.W. Eaton, GNU- Octave-, Free Software Foundation, Boston, MA, 1997.
[12] D. Eddelbüttel, Object-oriented econometrics: Matrix programming in C++ using GCC and Newmat, *Journal of Applied Econometrics* **11** (1996), 199–209.
[13] GAMS, World Wide Web – Home Page, GAMS Development Corp.gams.com.
[14] GNU, World Wide Web – Home Page, Free Software Foundation.www.gnu.org.
[15] G. Gordon, System Simulation, Prentice-Hall, Inc., Englewood Cliffs, NJ, 1969.
[16] D. Hanselman and B. Littlefield, *The Student Edition of Matlab, Version 5 – User's Guide,* Prentice-Hall International Inc., Englewood Cliffs, NJ, 1997.

[17] R.D. Herbert, *Observers and Macroeconomic Systems: Computation of Policy Trajectories with Seperate Model Based Control,* Advances in Computational Economics, Kluwer Academic Press, Dordrecht, 1998.
[18] R.D. Herbert and G.D. Leeves, Troubles in wonderland, *Complexity International* **6** (1999).
[19] R.D. Herbert and R.D. Bell, Visualisation in the simulation and control of economic models, *Computational Economics* **10**(2) (1997), 107–118.
[20] High Performance Systems, World Wide Web – Home Page, High Performance Systems Inc., www.hps-inc.com.
[21] D.A. Kendrick and H.M. Amman, *Programming languages in economics,* Working paper, University of Texas, Department of Economics, University of Texas, Austin, TX, 1995.
[22] U. Küsters and J.P. Steffen, Matrix programming languages for statistical computing: A detailed comparison of gauss, matlab and ox, Technical report, Catholic University of Eichstatt, Ingolstadt, Germany, 1996.
[23] L. Lamport, *LaTeX: A Document Preparation System,* Second Ed., Addison-Wesley Publishing Company, New York, 1996.
[24] R.W. Lucky, Moore's law redux, *IEEE Spectrum* **35**(9) (1998), 17–18.
[25] Maple, World Wide Web – Home Page, Waterloo Maple Inc., www.maplesoft.com.
[26] MathSoft, World Wide Web – Home Page, MathSoft Inc., www.mathsoft.com/splus.
[27] MathTools, World Wide Web – Home Page, MathTools Ltd., www.mathtools.com.
[28] Mathworks, *MATLAB Compiler: User's Guide*, The Mathworks Inc., Natick, MA, 1995.
[29] Mathworks, *Using SIMULINK Version 2,* The Mathworks Inc., Natick, MA, 1997.
[30] Mathworks, *Using MATLAB Version 5,* The Mathworks Inc., Natick, MA, 1998.
[31] Mathworks, World Wide Web – Home Page, The Math Works Inc., www.mathworks.com.
[32] K. Matsuyama, Current account dynamics in a finite horizon model, *Journal of International Economics* **23** (1987), 299–313.
[33] H. McGhan and M. O'Connor, Picojava: A direct execution engine for java bytecode, *IEEE Computer* **31**(10) (1998), 22–30.
[34] MIL 3, World Wide Web – Home Page, MIL 3 Inc., www.mil3.com.
[35] M.S. Mirotznik, Translating matlab programs into c code, *IEEE Spectrum* **34**(2), 63–64.
[36] M.S. Mirotznik, Matlab-to-c++ time-saver, *IEEE Spectrum* **35**(4) (1997), 22–30.
[37] C. Moler and P.J. Costa, *Symbolic Math Toolbox Version 2.0: User's Guide,* The Mathworks Inc. Natick, MA, 1997.
[38] J.K. Ousterhout, Scripting: Higher-level programming for the 21st centrury, *IEEE Computer* **31**(3) (1998), 23–30.
[39] W.T. Padget, Enhanced matlab, *IEEE Spectrum* **35**(8) (1998), 75.
[40] E.S. Raymond, *The New Hacker's Dictionary,* Third Ed., MIT-Press, Boston, 1996.
[41] C.G., Renfro, On the development of econometric modeling languages: MODLER and its first 25 years, *Journal of Economic and Social Measurement* **22** (1996), 241–331.
[42] C.G. Renfro, Normative considerations in the development of a software package for econometric estimation, *Journal of Economic and Social Measurement* **23** (1997), 277–330.
[43] Visual Solutions, World Wide Web – Home Page, Visual Solutions Inc., www.vissim.com.
[44] Wolfram, World Wide Web – Home Page, Wolfram Research Inc., www.wolfram.com.

Journal of Economic and Social Measurement 29 (2004) 339–358
IOS Press

TSX and TSE: A proposal for an extended time series data interchange and transfer format

Tim Harrison[a] and Charles G. Renfro[b]
[a] *1005 Fox Hollow Road, Stroudsburg, PA 18360, USA*
E-mail: timh@ptd.net
[b] *601 West 113th Street, #12G, New York, NY 10025, USA*
E-mail: cgrenfro@modler.com

This paper addresses the need for an efficient standard data exchange and transfer format for economic and social time series data that provides not only numeric observations but also sufficient documentation for users to be able easily to understand their properties. The paper proposes that the goal in the development of such a standard should be to permit these data to be downloaded into a user's environment in such a way as to be immediately usable without the need for local editing. It is argued that to achieve this goal will require that data producers and distributors, as well as developers of econometric and statistical software packages, honor and support such a standard. A candidate standard is identified, the TSD format, originally developed in 1984 and used since by a number of organizations and econometric software packages. However, the argument is made that to support future needs in the modern Internet-based world it will be necessary to extend this format, in the process developing evolving data exchange protocols for both downloaded byte stream data, based upon XML, and file transfers, based upon some extension of the TSD format.

1. Introduction

An aspect of the development of computing capabilities to support economic research during the past 50 years has been the ability to perform numeric calculations progressively more rapidly. This productivity increase can be considered specifically in terms of the calculation process, but more broadly it can also be considered in terms of the overall capacity to get the work done. Particularly with the recent development of the Internet, it makes sense to adopt this broader view and to consider not just local machine input-output, but also the optimal flow of data from the original source though the calculation process to ultimate disposition, asking the question, where are the bottlenecks presently? One of the more notable current bottlenecks is the physical acquisition of economic and social data, for although in principle it is now possible almost instantaneously to download to a given machine data originating anywhere in the world in such a way that these become immediately usable, in practice, this process remains highly inefficient. The stumbling block is not simple acquisition. once available on the Internet and once the distributing website has been identified, the data can now be downloaded rather easily. The problem specifically is that of making the downloaded data instantly usable.

The technical capability to solve this problem certainly exists today. The first step is the general adoption of an efficient data interchange and transfer protocol for these data by producers, distributors and users. A well-conceived common standard would immediately offer the benefit of a rapid data transfer from the original producer to the end user and, when necessary, between users. Ideally, this standard would be defined in such a way that not only could the observations be transferred more or less instantaneously, but at the same time all the relevant associated documenting information.

However, even this first step as stated essentially represents a goal that is likely to be attained only as the result of a progressive approach. There are a variety of data types, including cross-section, panel, and time series, each with their own particular characteristics. Therefore, it may be best to begin by considering a specific type, namely time series, with the focus essentially on macroeconomic time series data. Even for these commonly distributed data, there is today no standard data interchange format. The closest approximation to a standard is the TSD (Time Series Data) format, which was created in 1984 in order to permit the exchange of time series data and directly associated documentation between economic data base systems operated by the Alphametrics Corporation and Wharton Econometric Forecasting Associates, especially during the period 1984–1987. Created by the developers of AREMOS and MODLER, this format has since become supported by many organizations including initially not only Alphametrics and Wharton but also Data Resources and Haver Analytics. In 1987, the WEFA group, as the combination of Chase Econometrics and Wharton EFA, adopted it. Today it is supported by Global Insight, the present-day merger of Data Resources and the WEFA Group. Among econometric software packages, it is supported by a growing number including AREMOS, Eviews, MicroFit, MODLER, and RATS. The TSD data interchange format is described in detail in an appendix to a paper by Renfro in an earlier issue of this journal [4]; it is more briefly described in the first appendix to this paper.

The need for a standard data exchange and transfer format for documented time series data follows from the fact that an arbitrarily chosen time series, such as Gross Domestic Product (GDP), is by its nature more than simply a set of time-related numbers. For one thing, it will have, as a fundamental characteristic, a specific observation frequency, such as per week, per month, or per year, or else as in the case of financial time series particular, a tick-by-tick frequency definition. In addition, each series will be identified by a directly associated, more or less exact verbal description. The series will also be defined for a given time period of availability, a date range, over which its observations are available, although sometimes individual observations will be missing, for any of many reasons. The specified date range will vary depending on context: in a given case, this time period could be simply the range of availability of some transferred data or else the data as stored in a particular proprietary data base or file–or it alternatively could be the range of availability of the series as published by the original data source. Furthermore, a series always has a geo-political definition: for example, French Gross Domestic Product, or Japanese or US. More esoterically, but no less critical, the series has a revision dating: for instance, as of 1 March 2003, the quarterly frequency US GDP series, as published by the Bureau of Economic Analysis of the US Department of Commerce, contained observations that were last revised at the end of February 2003, and extended through the fourth quarter of 2002. The same series available on 1 February had the same published date range, but its observations were revised only through the end of January: same series, but to some degree different numbers, depending upon the specific date of publication.

We have described here only some of the characteristics of a time series. However, the remaining characteristics, while important, do not now need to be described in detail. It should be immediately obvious that, when you download a time series or otherwise acquire it, to know what you have "in hand," so to speak, you need both numbers and related information. However, to be able to use that data immediately, you need even more: in particular, you need to be able to read the file into whatever software package you happen to be using in such a way that the series it contains both constitutes a usable set of numbers and are in a format compatible with the protocols of that package. Ideally, you should be able to read the data file immediately upon receipt, without any subsequent editing, which would be possible if there were a universal data exchange standard, honored by both data producers or distributors and developers of econometric software packages.

In contrast, today, the way in which data are downloaded from the Internet and obtained from other sources varies widely. In practice, data are now often distributed in the context of an Excel workbook file, but in some cases they may come in a comma delimited file, or in a Lotus 123 Printfile format. Occasionally they are distributed using TSD or any of a number of other ACSII formats. In many cases, these time series are distributed simply as numbers with some sort of ad hoc descriptor attached, but the specific format of the individual series can also change, even within a given data file. For example, when distributed in the form of an Excel workbook file, in one instance a series might consist of a single spreadsheet row or column of numbers. In another, it might span two or more rows or columns. There may also be bits and pieces of information scattered about this file in a way that is to some degree informative, but often also constitutes a distinct nuisance for anyone trying to read the data into a particular software package without individual, sometimes rather tedious editing. In short, the present situation is far from optimal, requiring each user to waste even hours of his or her time, particularly as the number of series imported increases. Surely, there is a better way.

2. Nirvana at last? TSX and TSE

There is a better way, but even in this case absolute perfection will not necessarily be attained. In fact, perfection may be impossible to attain. To see this immediately, consider, for example, naming conventions: different data sources and different data users may wish to apply different names to a given data series. To use the earlier example of Gross Domestic Product, GDP as a mnemonic name is rather straightforward, and at first sight seemingly obvious; actually, it is hard to imagine an economist applying any other short name to this series. But, recognizing that the data actually apply to a particular economy, there is the immediate question of how to designate this in a context in which a user may be anywhere in the world. There is evidently a need to include some sort of geographic designator, but this immediately creates a problem of choice; for example, for the US, is it USGDP or is it GDPUS? That is, should the country code be applied as a prefix or as a suffix.

Some users or data producers may also wish to include in the name a code letter to designate observation frequency, such as Q or A. Or, alternatively, what about Durable Consumer Expenditures, excluding Automobiles; is it CEDXA, CEDEA, or what? Whichever interchange and transfer format might be established as a standard, individual software systems will need to be written in such a way that users are able to make a correspondence between their mnemonic name of choice and the name that is used during transfer or exchange. Similarly, series descriptions may be in Arabic, Chinese, English, French, German, Italian, Japanese, Spanish, or any of the remaining written languages.

Our proposed format takes account of language, but does not attempt to translate language. This limitation reflects that we are presently simply trying to introduce the subject of a standard data interchange format, not to dot every i and cross every t. Moreover, our proposed solution is restricted to simply the transmission of a given set of numeric observations and associated documentation, including given series mnemonics, not an attempt to define a standard that will allow anyone anywhere to understand immediately exactly what the numbers refer to in the language of his or her choice. It should be evident that, for a series to be immediately usable in a particular context by a given user, the developer of the software used, or perhaps the Internet data distributor will need to provide specific facilities to facilitate use.

The second area of difficulty is that our proposed format is actually two formats, as the format designator names in this paper's title imply. TSX is an XML schema and TSE is an extension of the present TSD format to allow a simple extension for existing code. In the case of each of these, the intention is to provide a framework that will improve the interoperability of statistical software packages, including econometric software packages, with minimal–ideally near zero–impact on the internal design of existing packages. But to succeed in this goal actually requires two formats. The reason is that in the foreseeable future, numeric date flows between software packages–or between the originating data sources and the software packages–will take one of two forms: they will take the form of Internet transmissions received as a downloaded byte stream, or else that of a data file transferred as a unit.

In the case of a transfer data file, the existing TSD format provides, either on its own or with slight editing to create TSE, a file transfer method that provides the user software package with more or less fully described time series in such a way that it is for the most part immaterial whether the number of series transferred is 2, 200, 2000, or more. This characteristic is significant, for although each package capable of reading such a data file needs to be written in such a way as to permit such flexibility, once done, this possibly never need be done again. Unlike an Excel workbook file, and most other file types commonly encountered, given that the software package used honors the TSD or TSE format, the user need not view the contents of the transfer file during or prior to the data import. So long as the software package also incorporates some means for the user to select the series to use, once the file's contents are imported, it is only at the immediate point of use that any choice among series needs to be made by the user.

One of the characteristics of both TSD and TSE is that there is no requirement that any receiving software package actually use all, or indeed any of the descriptive information; information not used can simply be discarded, although any discards will of course limit the re-transmission of the documented data from that package to any other. However, as will become clear, whereas the mnemonic, series description and other series-specific information will vary series to series, other specific, format-related information will be common to all the series in the transfer file, relating to such things as the way observations are represented (for example, the number of significant digits) and other aspects that are a declaration by the sending software how the receiving software should treat each series in the transmission. The point about the ability to discard information is simply that whenever information is present the user can choose to utilize it or not, as he or she wishes, but if it is lacking, there is generally no way to create it after the fact.

The specific discussion will begin with XML, as being the concept that is most likely to be new and unfamiliar. XML is a data representation standard that is being adopted quite generally for Internet transmissions of all "data," where in this context "data" refers not to the numeric observations on economic or social time series, but rather bits and bytes, and includes the transmission of anything involving these information flow measures from one point to another on the Internet. TSX, the family of formats proposed in this context, simply accepts the Internet world as it is and embodies in its protocols the XML standards. The logic of adopting these standards is simply that there is no need for economists to attempt to create an alternative particular to themselves. In fact, it makes sense for us to adopt this widely-supported standard and shape it to our specific data transmission requirements.

3. Why XML?

XML, or eXtensible Markup Language, is a "simple, very flexible text format derived from [an earlier mark up language protocol known as] SGML;" the definition of these terms and an historical description of their logic and origins can be found at http://www.w3.org/XML/. The protocol defining the properties of XML is an open standard maintained and controlled by the World Wide Web Consortium (W3C). As the X (for eXtensible) in its name implies, the XML "mark up" protocol originated

```
0         1         2         3         4         5         6         7         8
12345678901234567890123456789012345678901234567890123456789012345678901234567890


GDP             Gross Domestic Product: Billions of dollars (annual)
                Commerce Departm            19870101200201011
  4.73950000E+03  5.10380000E+03  5.48440000E+03  5.80310000E+03  5.99590000E+03
  6.33770000E+03  6.65740000E+03  7.07220000E+03  7.39770000E+03  7.81690000E+03
  8.30430000E+03  8.74700000E+03  9.26840000E+03  9.81700000E+03  1.01008000E+04
  1.04808000E+04
```

Fig. 1. TSD Format with Column Ruler Superimposed Above.

as a set of codes to describe the characteristics of documents and is similar in many respects to the HTML language used by much of the World Wide Web, the Internet, to describe documents for display in web browsers. The major difference is that XML describes data content separately from the way the data are or might be displayed, whereas HTML is specifically a text-display management protocol. In many contexts, XML is becoming the language of choice both for description of data and to specify the format of data-rich documents, including a wide variety of printed and onscreen forms.

If you do not already know about XML, you may at this point be wondering what the fuss is about and what the purpose is. The point very simply is that XML consists of a series of codes, as keywords, that are used to define the characteristics of documents so that these will be obvious to the processing computer as this processing occurs. In the case of a pure document, the words or text it contains may, for instance, be expressed in a particular font, such as Times Roman or Courier, and one or more typefaces, such as normal, bold, or italic. They otherwise may have various additional characteristics, such as type size and style. In order to process the document, a computer needs to be told these characteristics of the text during that processing. Moreover, it is easiest to provide this descriptive information in context, usually using bracketed keywords, which may be single letters that are placed before and after text, like <I>this example</I>, to designate not only that this example should be in italics, but also exactly where the italics should both begin and end, the specific character/indicating the ending delimiter. In a similar way, the various characteristics of a data series can be set out as a series of delimiting bracketed keywords to specify both the numbers that are the observations and the associated documentation. Because all the individual items are both delimited and identified by keywords, the computer can process the series and its descriptive information in an essentially free-format way. To be more precise, an XML file is made up of a nested sequence of elements which are individually of the form <element>data item</element>. A basic description of the language can be found in Castro [1] or Ray [3]. A more comprehensive and technical description is provided by Skonnard and Gudgin [7].

An example of the TSD format for a data series is shown in Fig. 1. In contrast to XML, which as just indicated attaches descriptor elements to both the observations

```
<series>
        <name>GDP</name>
        <source>Commerce Department - BEA</source>
        <description>Gross Domestic Product: Billions of dollars (annual)</description>
        <frequency>A</frequency>
        <first>1987</first>
        <last>2002</last>
        <obs>4739.5</obs><obs>5103.8</obs><obs>5484.4</obs><obs>5803.1</obs>
        <obs>5995.9</obs><obs>6337.7</obs><obs>6657.4</obs><obs>7072.2</obs>
        <obs>7397.7</obs><obs>7816.9</obs><obs>8304.3</obs><obs>8747</obs>
        <obs>9268.4</obs><obs>9817</obs><obs>10100.8</obs><obs>10480.8</obs>
<series>
```

Fig. 2. XML Format.

of a time series and the descriptive information associated with it, TSD relies on position. For example, the first 16 characters of a series record constitutes the name, or mnemonic, of the series. Each of the other components of the series' documentation and observations are required to be placed in a specific location. On the one hand, because the processing computer program properly "knows" where each of these is supposed to be, the consequence is that a TSD file can be relatively parsimonious, consisting of only the specific "data" to be transferred. However, the drawback of this parsimony is both that each element must be understood from its specific contextual location and that a requisite amount of space be allocated for each of those elements, irrespective of that element's pertinence in a particular instance. In contrast, if the series mnemonic or other descriptor element is bracketed by a code that identifies this item, one of the consequences is that the formatting can be much more flexible. In order to illustrate the difference, see Fig. 2, which provides comparably in XML the same series and its associated descriptive information as does the TSD code in Fig. 1.

In comparison with the TSD data file format, it is evident that XML has many advantages, some of which are:

i) *Self-Describing and (Human) Readable.* XML separates issues relating to the content of the data structure from the issues relating to its analysis. The use of the *element* format means that the file should be directly understandable by human eyes–as well as by a software package. This element-by-element formatting allows a software package to import only those fields that are relevant to its purpose. For example, a single equation parameter estimation package may not need to access even the full details of a series name including its geographic designator, if any. However, an econometric modeling language package will probably be written so as to import much more descriptive detail.
ii) *Consistent Extensibility* There will never be a complete definition of all the content fields relevant for time series data. The attraction of XML is precisely that, during processing, so long as a transfer file is well formed, the reader software will simply skip over information that it either does not understand or does not need. Furthermore, when a new version of the schema is released, both original and rewritten software will be compatible with files that enforce

the new schema: earlier releases will be able to read those fields that were used in the earlier release and will ignore the new fields. Similarly, individual users can extend the definition by adding their own fields; other users will, by design, simply ignore these fields automatically.

iii) *Verifiability and Transformability* Unlike HTML, XML is very strict about the formation of the document. Most importantly all of the elements must be properly closed; that is, there must be a trailing </element> for every <element>. An XML-based format can also have a corresponding schema definition (for details, see: http://www.w3.org/XML/Schema). The XML schema is the current definition of choice and is replacing the earlier–and still valid–Document Type Definition (DTD) format. The schema definition allows a new file to be verified to check that it conforms with the relevant schema and additionally allows XML data that conforms to one schema to be easily transformed to correspond to another. Tidwell [8] provides a comprehensive description of the XSLT language, the leading tool for XML transformation. Mangano [2] provides many useful examples of XSLT's use, including the process of transforming XML into Comma Delimited (CSV) format.

iv) *Ubiquity* The use of XML for the interchange of data between business entities has been growing rapidly; at the same time, government statistical agencies and commercial data vendors are adopting XML. The metadata issues that make XML attractive for international and national agencies are also highly relevant to regional and other sub-national geographic areas or even industry specific data. This growing ubiquity makes it important that econometric software developers, applied economists and other interested parties pay attention and participate to at least some degree in the setting of the evolving standards, or else risk having the research context be defined by others, particularly computer scientists, who possibly have no concept of economic research information needs.

As a general phenomenon, the adoption of XML as a data description protocol is occurring in many organizations around the world. However, this adoption has not been uniform. For example, in comparison with the domestic US, it seems as though the movement to XML by government statistical agencies is occurring more rapidly in Europe and on the part of international agencies, this movement being driven by their perceived greater need to share data between organizations. Some examples of XML initiatives on the part of these agencies are:

- *SDMX* (http://www.sdmx.org/) – is a "task force initiated by [such international organizations as] the BIS, ECB, IMF, OECD, EUROSTAT, and UN to address standardization of the exchange of statistical information." A white paper on their website entitled "Web services, XML, and reporting standards" is particularly relevant to the issue of data interchange standards.
- *GESMES* (http://www.gesmes.org/) – is a message format for the exchange of multi-dimensional data and time series, and related metadata. This website

contains information, success stories, technical documentation and access to software for the GESMES message. Although there is no official standard for GESMES/CB-related XML presently, there is a current proposals draft on the European Commission's website (http://www.forum.europa.eu.int/).
- *MDDL* (http://www.mddl.org/) – acronym for Market Data Definition Language is the XML specification to enable the interchange of information necessary to account, to analyze, and to trade financial instruments of the world's securities markets.

The formats discussed by all these groups generally share a common characteristic of being qualitatively more complex than is necessary for most econometric analysis. However, the definitions are sufficiently clear that abstracting the necessary subset of the data is practical and straightforward. Furthermore, it should be equally straightforward to construct the necessary dictionaries to allow XSLT-based converters to map different element names and to reformat and/or reorganize the corresponding data whenever necessary.

Notwithstanding these initiatives, we are not aware of much current use of XML in the context of econometric software packages. One notable exception is Gretl (http://gretl.sourceforge.net/), which package is described in the software compendium [5] found elsewhere in this volume. Gretl apparently uses XML as a basic data format. With this one exception, applied economists and econometricians, including software developers, otherwise generally appear to have taken the position, albeit implicitly, that such developments as XML are outside their subject area. However, it needs to be recognized by all economists that if computer scientists and other types of information technologists are left entirely to their own devices, it is unlikely that the result will be particularly suited to economic research needs: it bears mention that an ostrich does not protect itself by sticking its head in the sand, whatever it may think.

4. TSE – An extension of TSD

We have stated several reasons why XML is a good solution for the interchange of time series data in econometrics. However, there are also certain disadvantages and this section of the paper could be alternatively titled "Why not XML?". There are two immediately identifiable disadvantages to XML for time series economic and social data:

i) Implementation Almost all modern programming languages can incorporate infrastructure to support parsing and reading XML files very simply. This is particularly so in the case of Microsoft's .NET Framework (http://www.microsoft.com/net/) and Ximian's open source equivalent Mono project (http://www.go-mono.com/). However, many of the econometric software programs discussed by Renfro [5,6] have been existence for longer than

XML itself and could require significant re-engineering to incorporate XML directly.

ii) *Verbosity* The <element></element> basis of XML clearly makes an XML representation of a set of economic time series significantly larger than a matching TSD representation of the same data. This is true even if none of the facilities inherent in XML to add a richer description of the data are utilized. Even in a world of fast broadband communication and inexpensive storage media, XML's verbosity is clearly an issue. However, the use of compression of course reduces the size difference between a TSD-type representation and an XML representation of the data.

General compression techniques like the widely-used *zip* and *gzip* achieve very good compression of XML files. There are also some "schema aware" compression techniques designed specifically to compress XML files (see, for example, the discussion of XMill, originally developed by AT&T, at http://www.research.att.com/sw/tools/xmill/). This technology treats the *elements* of the XML separately from the actual content of the file to achieve better overall compression than other techniques.

Any such disadvantages may, in the end, not matter to the acceptance of XML, for this protocol appears to have reached the point of critical mass: it is our belief that inevitably XML will gain acceptance in Econometrics as it has and continues to do in other areas. In the worst case, this will occur because international and domestic governmental agencies adopt XML despite possible blissful ignorance of this development on the part of these agencies' own economists. In this event, economists in general will be forced to accept, after the fact, whatever implementations are made.

Such initiatives can of course be glacial in their momentum. We also believe that TSD will continue to play a useful part in allowing easy and accurate transfer of time series data. Unfortunately, the coverage of TSD cannot be easily extended further without creating interoperability issues between existing software packages. Our suggestions for the extended TSE format are summarized in Appendix 2. As noted earlier, for reference, the TSD format is originally published in Renfro [4], although informally specifications have passed from hand to hand for years.

The principal extension that the TSE format offers is to allow additional series characteristics to be specified. The proposed TSE format is also less restrictive as regards the amount of documentation per series and even the permitted length of the series mnemonics. To this end, we recommend a departure from the simplicity of the TSD format's use of identical groups of records for individual series, and propose adopting instead a format that employs a header record (record type zero) as a lead record for the file. This record would contain flags to indicate the presence or absence of individual metadata items. This record also allows the data layout of the actual observations to be either fixed or comma delimited. This approach conceptually replicates the flexibility characteristic of TSD, inasmuch as some of the fields (for example, those specifying number representation precision and default frequency conversion codes) can simply be omitted. If this flexibility characteristic is embodied properly, not only will it be possible for immediately irrelevant fields to be ignored in particular instances, but also the entirety of the TSE extensions, thus allowing the TSD format to be treated as a subset of TSE for the purpose of backward compatibility.

In addition to the flexibility afforded by the optional omission of some fields, the proposed format incorporates additional fields that enable a number of the characteristics of at least certain time series not identified in the TSD format to be taken into account–such as base year specification for indices, additional frequency conversion criteria, or fiscal year or crop year definitions of series. As proposed, and as noted earlier, compared to the TSD format, TSE also allocates additional space for series mnemonic, documentation and source fields.

5. Tools and facilities

In this paper, our overall aim is to suggest the possibility of simplifying the process of exchanging time series data between individual users and between organizations – at least in the sense of providing an efficient method that does not require much knowledge or effort on the part of the ultimate users. Unfortunately, the fact of the widespread introduction of XML-based data interchange protocols, combined with the possible more general adoption of TSD and its TSE extensions, will initially tend to make the situation more complex – at least in the short term. Moreover, inertia will also insure the continued common distribution of economic and social data sets in the form of Excel workbook files, Lotus PRN files, and a variety of other essentially flawed but historically sanctioned formats, making for a potentially confusing situation.

In order to provide a means for all interested parties – both econometric software developers and research economists, among others–to both learn and participate in this quest for greater applied research efficiency, we are now in the process of developing a website (http://www.timeseries.org) to serve as a clearing house for the sharing of tools to verify XML and TSD/TSE-based data files and also to provide support to those who wish to adopt and convert to the emerging data exchange formats. These tools will be made available as "open source" and they will make use (wherever possible) of industry-basic standard XML tools data. We already have developed or adopted Windows-based tools to enable conversions to and from TSX, TSD and TSE formats – and also to convert from any of these formats into Comma Separated Variable (CSV) formats. We are in addition starting to build a collection of converters to create TSX files from GESMES/TS-XML Internet messages. Our goal is to add as well Linux versions of all these tools. The website will furthermore serve as a home for the schema definition for TSX and updates to the TSE specification.

6. Summary and conclusions

The discussion here has focused specifically on the issues associated with data interchange and transfer formats. However, it is important to at least mention the larger context in which the adoption of common standards can serve to improve the research capabilities of economists. Anyone who has recently accessed journal articles on line, using for instance the facilities of the well-known JSTOR project (http://www.jstor.org/) – which makes the articles of a number of economics and other disciplinary journals not only available for downloading but also full-text searchable for as much as the past 100 years or more – will be aware of the power of the Internet and Internet-like tools to provide facilities today hardly imagined even 10 years ago. In a similar way, once it becomes possible to download sets of individual time series in an efficient manner, it will also become imaginable to make these data available in ways that will support a whole new level of economic research initiatives. For example, economists are used to obtaining National Income and Product Accounts data in the form of a particular set of standard tables, but in principle, as discussed in Renfro [4], there is no reason why these data could not be provided in such a way that would permit the individual economist to define, during the download or other data transfer process, alternative accounting combinations and cumulations if he or she wished, thus providing what is called there *accounts independence* (pp. 64–65). Paper-based data transfers are essentially limited to a single representational manifestation; Internet and other computer-based transfers need not be, except to the degree that imagination is lacking. The issue is not just how to move data efficiently but rather how to do this in such a way that these data become most useful to the researcher and other end users.

Data producers, especially governmental statistical agencies, as well as secondary data distributors, are no longer necessarily restricted by distribution costs or time in the determination of the compositional form in which they provide data, at least once the website facilities are put in place. The initial development of particular website facilities will obviously impose costs, as any transition does, but putting into place *efficient* and more content-rich distribution facilities, as opposed to alternative, inefficient facilities, might not involve significant additional marginal costs of operation, yet might at the same time provide users with the capability to obtain economic and social data in a way that makes these data immediately usable. At least ideally, the modern development of search engines, such as those that underlie Google and other services, combined with efficient data interchange standards and capabilities, will in time potentially provide facilities that are today generally unimagined. The question is our present ability to seize the moment.

However, to support the development of such facilities, it is first necessary to put into place appropriate underlying standards and for them to be adopted more or less universally by data producers, distributors, and econometric and other software developers. The essence of our proposal, as set out in this paper, is that there should initially be a more general adoption of the TSD format, as a first step. The TSD format has now been used quite successfully, if restrictedly, for 20 years. Those who use it regularly appear to be generally satisfied. However, it represents simply an approximation to a satisfactory data interchange and transfer file format, and it will not answer all future needs. Therefore, we have proposed that collectively, government statistical agencies, data distributors, and econometric software developers should move towards the gradual adoption of the TSX and TSE type standards that are presented tentatively in the appendices to this paper. We use the phrase "TSX and TSE type standards" in order to emphasize that these new standards are today being presented for consideration, not as a *fait accompli*. Our proposals are intended to be concrete, so as to be capable of adoption in the near future, however, we recognize the need for the widespread consideration of these proposals, as a means of beginning an iteration towards a more optimal final set of standards. We expect that it could take years for this iterative process to achieve this optional set, and therefore we stress in making our present proposals that every effort should be made at each step of this adoption process to insure backwards compatibility. There should neither be an attempt in the near future to establish some ideal final standard nor to adopt a standard that prohibits further evolution.

Appendix 1. – TSD Format

TSD has become a common transfer format for economic time series. This description is taken from Renfro [4]. There are three record types; the first two appear once for each series and the last type appears as many times as are necessary to define as many observations as are specified by the start and finish dates and the frequency of the series. The field formats are specified in Fortran notation, which reflects the context in which the format was originally defined.

Record Type	Char Position	Description	Data Format
1	1–16	Series Mnemonic	16A1
	17–80	Series Description	64A1
2	17–32	Source	16A1
	33–40	Date of last update	I2,A1,I2,A1,I2
	41–44	Time of last update	I4
	45–52	First available date	I4,I2,I2
	53–60	Last available date	I4,I2,I2
	61	Data Frequency	A1
	62	Observation precision	I1
	63	Observation representation	A1
	64	Frequency conversion code	I1
	65	Data quality check	A1
	74–80	Daily data switches	7I1 e.g. 0111110
3	1–80	Observation values	5E15.8

Record Type 1:

Series mnemonic: can be a maximum of 12 characters, left justified. Specific naming conventions are particular to organizations; some organizations support the use of ASCII characters not supported by others. Illegal characters generally include blanks and the "arithmetic characters" (+,−,/,*) Variable description: up to 64 characters, left justified

Record Type 2:

Data Source: up to 16 characters, left justified
Data of last update: 8 characters, in the form month/day/year
Time of last update: 4 digit integer, right justified. 24 hour clock
First available date: integer, left justified
Last available date: integer, left justified
Examples:

194701 = Annual data pertaining to 1948
196502 = Quarterly data: 2nd quarter of 1965
197805 = Monthly data: May of 1978
19940621 = Daily Data: 21 June 1994

Observation frequency: Single alphabetic character:

A = Annual
Q = Quarterly
M = Monthly
W = Weekly
D = Daily

All users support the above 5 frequencies, with Weekly defined as "true" weekly. Certain organizations support in addition:

S = Semi-annual
B = Bi-monthly
T = Ten Day (3 per month) Economic Data Base Systems

The Daily Data switches take the form of a set of 7 binary (zero/one) switches used to indicate the absence or presence of an observation for each day of the week. The usual maximum is 5 working days, inasmuch as few series exist that include observations for all days of the week.

The precision, representation, frequency conversion and quality codes are described in the original reference [4] and are not supported by all TSD consumer programs.

Record type 3:

For each series the records are kept together, and completely define that series and its set of observations. At least one observation on each series is expected, but the maximum number is unstated. Generally, all organizations offering software incorporating large scale data management facilities support a maximum of 1500 observations on any individual series. Individual software packages used simply for parameter estimation do not always permit the importation of this number of observations on each individual data series.

Appendix 2. – Suggested fields for TSX format

Clearly any format that is offered as an alternative to, and potential replacement for, the existing TSD format must include all the data fields present in the base TSD format. This appendix covers the general aspects of these choices as of 1 September 2003. The detailed, and possibly more up-to-date, schema for the TSX format is available on the web at http://www.timeseries.org/.

In addition to providing backwards compatibility insofar as possible, the design of a new data transfer file format must pay attention to the lengths of the various character string data items. It must also address international differences in data item specifications; for example, date/time fields and the default decimal point indicators for floating point numbers must take into account these are represented differently in different places in the world.

As we have indicated earlier, the TSX representation of time series may optionally be grouped into logical tables within the file. Many of the parameters for individual series can be defaulted to all series within a table. However, we have chosen not to base the format explicitly on a table because of our desire to allow information to be linked to individual series observations. This choice to some degree reflects our background as economists, rather than computer scientists, but we recognize that others approaching the question of the definition of the TSX format might prefer to adopt the table as a basis.

Lengths of mnemonic, description and source information

The specification of TSD format was heavily influenced by the software available 20 years ago and also by the constraints imposed by the existing transmission mechanisms, as well as the then common use of fixed field lengths.

- *Mnemonics*
  Most of the packages of which we are aware use relatively short mnemonics, usually in the range of 12–16 characters; however, some packages use as many as 32 characters. Most use a mnemonic syntax that is similar to the rules for TSD above. In contrast, data sources will sometimes use much longer series names that may contain embedded blanks, commas and other characters that are difficult to work with in the context of an econometric software package. Our suggestion is that as a maximum mnemonic length should be set at an arbitrary 32 characters and that the series table should include an optional parameter to specify the number of significant characters in series names. We also suggest, as

described below, the use of a user-supplied alias file, which will allow a particular user to specify local series names that can override the source mnemonics on input, either because of length limits on local names or simply because individual users may prefer to define the series names used locally.

- *Description and Source*
  As for the mnemonics, the description and source fields can be very long in some sources. Our proposal is that the TSX format should allow descriptions up to 80 characters while not requiring that the data user should read the entire field.
- *Date and Time Formats*
  XML has native support for much richer formats than the integers used in TSD. By default, these formats are used, but an optional parameter can specify the format of all date/time parameters, including control of the international aspects. This parameter, specified on the table element, affects all the series in the table.
- *Floating Point Formats*
  An optional second table option allows the choice of a point or comma as the decimal indicator for all floating point numbers in the file. A third related parameter specifies whether, in the case of the definition of a week, the daily indicator starts on Sunday or Monday.

Series complexity

A simple series is one with regular observations at a defined frequency. A complex series is one in which observations may occur at an irregular frequency; for example, tick-by-tick pricing data or where multiple values of the same observation exist in the file. Multiple values may exist because of revised values of the series, as in the case of revisions to most macro-economic data series, or where different values of the series exist at different times, as in the case of some financial instruments.

Fields in the table:

Date and Time Formats.
Floating point Format.

Fields in the series:

All fields marked with an asterisk can be set at the table level. If a field is set for the table then the setting may be overridden for any series. In some contexts, there may be fields that have defaults already supplied by the importing software.
Series mnemonic
Series Description

- Source: Original Source, responsible for the publication of the data
- Units: Units of measurement, such as thousands of people, dollars, etc.
- Complexity

```
<table>
       <tName>US_Macro</tName>
       <tDescription>U.S. Macro Data</tDescription>
       <tSource>Commerce Department - BEA</tSource>
       <tFrequency>A</tFrequency>
       <tFirst>1987</tFirst>
       <tLast>2002</tLast>

       <series>
              <name>GDP</name>
              <description>Gross Domestic Product: Billions of dollars</description>
              <obs.....</obs>
       </series>
       <series>
              <name>ConsExp</name>
              <description>Consumers Expenditure: Billions of dollars</description>
              <obs> ..... </obs>
       </series>
<table>
```

Fig. 3. Logical Table Format, Group of Series.

- First Date/Time of Availability.
- Last Date/Time of Availability.
- Frequency.
- Base Year for Index
- Frequency Transformation Criteria: To allow on-the-fly frequency conversion
  Higher to Lower: Average, Sum, first of period, last of period, etc.
  Lower to Higher: Recommended interpolation technique
- Number of significant digits..
- Calendar, Fiscal, or Agricultural Year designator..
  Formula: formula to reconstruct series
- Observation status – for each observation, indicates that the observation is an estimate, preliminary, or revised.
  Observation date of publication or revision of each observation – complex series only.
  Observation comment

Note in particular that the above protocol uses individual series as building blocks rather than employing a group of series that are logically grouped as a single object. Although this makes the proposed TSX schema somewhat more verbose than is strictly necessary, the beneficial result is that it allows comments and metadata to be added to individual observations. Furthermore, this approach also allows the inclusion of irregularly observed data, such as financial tick-by-tick market data, and, in addition, admits the possibility of including both preliminary and final values for the same observation within the same file. Figure 3 shows the series from Fig. 2 together with an additional series from the same source and with the same frequency; the series are included in a logical *table*. This table representation allows some of the series properties to be supplied for the table as a whole–although this restriction could be overridden for individual series within the table.

Appendix 3. – Suggested TSE format

The goal in the development of the TSE format is to provide a specification that incorporates the full set of variables of the TSX format, under the restriction that as many should be included as it is practical to include in a downloaded file. The specification below contains all the fields represented in the TSX format, except for those that apply to individual observations. The TSE format, like the TSD format, treats the observations on a series as a set, rather than as individually identified elements.

The restrictions on the character string length of mnemonics, descriptions and source are the same for TSE as for TSX, as defined above. The additional restriction is the maximum length of these fields; the limits defined below could be extended but presently these seem reasonable for all languages that we have considered. Note that these limits are proposed as tentative limits, subject to further consideration.

Record Type	Char Position	Description	Data Format
0	1-4	Flag	#TSE (a literal constant)
	5	Fixed or Delimited Data	"D" or "F"
	6	Format	Character String
	7	Record 2 Flag	"N" if record 2 omitted
	8	Record 3 Flag	"N" if record 3 omitted
	9	Record 4 Flag	"N" if record4 omitted
1	1–40	Variable Mnemonic	Character String
	41–48	First available date	I4,I2,I2
	49–56	Last available date	I4,I2,I2
	57	Data Frequency	A1
	58–64	Daily data switches	7I1
	65–68	Base Year for Index	I4
	69–70	Significant digits	I2
	71	Observation representation	A1
	72	Frequency conversion code	I1
	73	Data quality check	A1
2	1–80	Variable Description	Character String
3	1–40	Source	Character String
	41–48	Date of last update	I2,A1,I2,A1,I2
	49–52	Time of last update	I4
4	1–40	Source	Character String
	41	Year span	A1
9	1–80	Observation values	5E15.8

Record Type 1:

Variable mnemonic: can be a maximum of 12 characters, left justified. Specific naming conventions are particular to organizations; some organizations support the use of ASCII characters not supported by others. However, illegal characters usually include blanks and the "arithmetic characters" (+,−,/,*)

The remaining fields on this record are exactly as defined for TSD with the addition of a 4 digit integer to define the base year of the series if it is an index with a fixed base year.

Record Type 2:

Variable description: up to 80 characters, left justified.

Record Type 3:

Data Source: up to 40 characters, left justified
Data of last update: 8 characters, in the form month/day/year
Time of last update: 4 digit integer, right justified. 24 hour clock

Record type 9:

This record type is repeated until all observation values have been provided for each individual series. For each series, therefore, these records are kept together and completely define that series as a transferred set of observations. At least one observation on each series is expected, but the maximum number is unstated.
If the Fixed or Delimited Flag on Record 0 is set to "D" then the observations are read as comma delimited using as many records as is necessary. If the flag is set to "F" then the observations are read as Fortran-style fixed format using the format specified in the format field on Record 0. If "F" is specified but the format is left blank then the standard TSD "5E15.8" format is used.

Appendix 4. – Alias Dictionary

The maximum length of the variable mnemonics has been discussed earlier. This appendix considers the definition of an Alias File, one possible use for which is to manage the substitution of local (perhaps shorter mnemonic names) for the names provided by the original source or data distributor. As noted earlier, the need to substitute local names can also reflect a data source or distributor's use of characters in mnemonic names that are defined as illegal by the importing software.

The purpose in the use of an Alias file is generally to allow on-the-fly name translation as the input file is processed. We suggest two formats one in XML the other as a fixed format file with the same readability objectives as TSE.

More generally, the Alias file can be viewed as a particular representation of a data dictionary that matches the mnemonic names of the imported series to the names of series in a local data base. In a particular case, the default behavior is for mnemonics that do not already appear in this dictionary to be imported unchanged. Alternatively, series that have no explicit match may be discarded. Generally, the default behavior will be determined by the importing software package, but we have included the concepts of the Alias Dictionary and the Alias File as a data interchange construct, when considering the management of the data import process.

XML Alias Dictionary

The dictionary consists of local names and external names.

For example:

<aliasDictionary>
<alias>
<local>GDP</local> <external>Gross Domestic Product</external>
</alias>
<alias>
<local>Cons</local> <external>Consumers Expenditure</external>
</alias>
<aliasDictionary>

TSE Alias Dictionary

The TSE Alias Dictionary format specifies both local and external names, in common with the XML Alias Dictionary. But in the case of TSE, a simple fixed format is used, where the local name is in character positions 1 thru 32 and the external name starts in character position 33 and is terminated by a line break (carriage return line feed control character pair).

For the example above, the example lists GDP and Cons as the local names and *Gross Domestic Product and Consumer Expenditures* as the respective external names. Specifically:

GDP	Gross Domestic Product
Cons	Consumers Expenditure

References

[1] E. Castro, *XML for the World Wide Web*, Peachpit Press, Berkeley, CA, 2001.

[2] S. Mangano, *XSLT Cookbook*, O'Reilly & Associates, Sebastopol, CA, 2003.

[3] E.T. Ray, *Learning XML,* Second Ed., O'Reilly & Associates, Sebastopol, CA, 2003.

[4] C.G. Renfro, Economic Data Base Systems: Further reflections on the state of the art, *Journal of Economic and Social Measurement* **23**(1) (1997), 43–85.

[5] C.G. Renfro, ed., A compendium of existing econometric software packages, *Journal of Economic and Social Measurement* **29** (2003).

[6] C.G. Renfro, Econometric software: The first fifty years in perspective, *Journal of Economic and Social Measurement* **29** (2004), 9–107, this volume.

[7] A. Skonnard and M. Gudgin, *Essential XML Quick Reference: A Programmer's Reference to XML, XPath, XSLT, XML Schema, SOAP and More*, Addison Wesley, New York, 2002.

[8] D. Tidwell, *XSLT*, O'Reilly & Associates, Sebastopol, CA, 2001.

Journal of Economic and Social Measurement 29 (2004) 359–409
IOS Press

A compendium of existing econometric software packages

Edited by Charles G. Renfro
601 West 113th Street, #12G, New York, NY 10025, USA
E-mail: cgrenfro@modler.com

This compendium of existing econometric software packages is intended to be a full census of all existing packages of this type that are publicly available and used by economists today. It is intended to provide the developer's view of each package: in all but a few instances, the person providing each entry is the primary author or current principal developer of the package. These program descriptions generally provide both a development history and a statement of current capabilities. Most entries also include references to more detailed descriptions, including manuals and other publications, as well as providing a website URL.

1. Introduction

This document is a supplement to the introductory article of this volume, "Econometric Software: The first fifty years in perspective". As that article began to be written, it quickly became evident that it would not and could not provide a balanced and reasonably comprehensive description of each of the currently available econometric software packages, both because of its author's lack of direct knowledge of the history, features and capabilities of every package and because no ready reference existed that provided such documentation. Consequently, it seemed sensible to try to provide separately, in the form of this compendium, a document that could generally serve as a public reference and at the same time provide a statement of the state of the art in the year 2003.

The first step taken was to contact the authors or developers of each of the software packages currently listed on the American Economics Association's Resources for Economists on the Internet (www.rfe.org) asking first if the software they provided met the criterion of being econometric software and, if so, then asking them to provide a description. Subsequently, by word of mouth, as well as by recommendation, additional packages were discovered. In every case that a package was found that has subsequently been identified by its author or developer(s) as being an econometric software package, an entry has been provided and is included. It does not appear that any developer has refused to submit a package description.

For inclusion, the criterion applied has been that the package is primarily econometric in its features and capabilities. As a consequence, there are packages that are used by economists, but identify themselves as being primarily statistical software packages, or some other type of software package, and therefore are not included.

Of course, it is inevitable that one or more packages have been omitted that will subsequently be identified as econometric software packages, but the intention has always been to include every such publicly available package as of 1 June 2003. To this end, drafts of this compendium have been circulated widely during the past six months and more.

Each of the econometric software packages represented is described in some detail and in a roughly consistent style. As an editorial intention, each description identifies the principal author(s), provides brief historical information, and describes the program's salient characteristics. As a rule, the descriptions were provided by the principal, often original author(s) of the program or, in a few cases, the principal current developer, and have simply been edited for style. One of the purposes in the creation of this document is to provide both descriptions of packages and a clear statement of each package's development history, which may include the range of machines the software has been mounted on during its life, as well as operating systems under which the software runs or has run historically. In a few cases – particularly when a package is important historically, but is no longer supported – a description of it and its history has been independently provided, usually in cooperation with former and, in some cases, current users of the package.

The context in which each package is presented depends on its characteristics. Currently available packages are classified into four categories: Independent Econometric Software Packages, Econometric Programming Libraries, Econometric and Mathematical Programming Languages, and Applications of Econometric and Mathematical Programming Languages. A fifth category consists of packages that are of historical interest, but are no longer supported. This classification scheme is not ideal, but it is difficult to determine how else to proceed.

A qualification

As indicated earlier, the packages included here have not been, in any way, "vetted." Dates of original release and subsequent modification should be interpreted as representing developers' claims. Similarly, all claims that a particular package performs some particular operation should be regarded as no more than that. However, the issue here is not so much the ostensible inclusion or not of some technique or feature, but rather that of qualitative assessment: the degree to which each package reliably does what the developer represents that it does. The independent evaluation of econometric software, especially an assessment of the degree to which packages are numerically reliable, is quite recent in origin and still only rarely made. McCullough and Vinod, in their *Journal of Economic Literature* article (June 1999) on the numerical reliability of econometric software, have stated that they "surveyed five journals that regularly publish reviews of econometric software. For the years 1990–1997, over 120 reviews appeared. All but three paid no attention to numerical accuracy, and only two applied more than a single test of numerical accuracy"

(p. 633). What this finding indicates is that economists have not been at all rigorous in the evaluation of the software they use.

These qualifying statements are not made in order to call into question the skill or integrity of the econometricians who develop econometric software. There is no evidence that econometric software is any less reliable than software produced by Microsoft or any other major software developer; in fact, if anything, what evidence exists actually suggests just the opposite. Furthermore, there is no reason to believe that any of the developers of any of the packages described here have done less than their best to insure numerical reliability, nor that the statements about packages made here are not accurate. But it is important for all software users and developers to realize both that insuring numerical reliability is inherently difficult and that the economics profession numbering tens of thousands of people is currently depending upon the dedication of a literal handful of people to insure that numerical reliability. The difficulty in evaluating software reliability in part resides in the fact that, for a developer – representing the first stage of this evaluation, there are very few benchmark test results available in the literature against which packages can be measured. Yet the process of implementing algorithms so as to precisely represent the concepts described in the theoretical econometrics literature is subject to both direct implementation errors and errors of interpretation. Moreover, for a variety of reasons, some of them considered in the aforementioned article that this compendium supplements, independent assessment is a critical element in software validation, quite apart from any self-validation by developers. Econometric software development is not an activity that should be performed in isolation by the few on behalf of the many, for there is a general need for both developers and users of this software to participate in its ongoing evaluation. But until such time as the profession takes such verities to heart, users need to take care when they use this software. Even then, it will still be necessary for users to understand how to apply the software used, which includes an appreciation of the limitations and qualifications associated with the particular techniques that are employed.

2. Independent econometric software packages

The term "independent" refers to the degree to which a package operates as a standalone package: an independent software package requires a computer and a compatible operating system, as a minimum operating environment. For the purpose of this definition, what constitutes the operating system may include one or more "run time" modules of a standard development package such as Microsoft Visual Basic, but it certainly does not include any additional applications software package that the user must license or otherwise acquire separately in order to be able to run the econometric software package.

The software packages presented in this section of the compendium are econometric in orientation, which is to say that they provide the capability to perform operations that ostensibly implement the techniques that are described in the economics and econometrics literature as regards parameter estimation techniques, specification and other hypothesis tests, and the like. These packages range in characteristic from those that incorporate a command structure that permits the user to select specific econometric techniques to those that provide some degree of programming capability and therefore to some extent may allow the user to define the particular intrinsic properties of the operations performed.

In all cases, the packages described are written in a standard programming language (or languages) and operate using a standard computer operating system. Examples of the former are C/C+, FORTRAN, Pascal, and Visual Basic. Examples of the latter are DOS, Linux, Unix, and Windows.

AREMOS

URL: www.globalinsight.com

The precursors of AREMOS are the DEMOS and HASH software systems created by Tim Harrison as part of the University of Southampton's Econometric Model of the UK. The development of AREMOS in the period 1982–1986 was sponsored by CiSi – a French computing services group – both for its own modeling requirements and for use by its then subsidiary Wharton Econometric Forecasting Associates. The system was very heavily influenced by Lawrence Klein's modeling methodology as implemented at Wharton. The system was originally designed with the goal of using a common base for both PC DOS and IBM VM/CMS operating systems with its orientation becoming more heavily PC-oriented as the PC platform developed. Both PC and mainframe versions were extensively used internally at CiSi and Wharton Econometrics in the early '80s with the first public PC release for DOS in July 1985. A Windows version was developed during the period 1994–1995 and first released in September 1995.

AREMOS is designed as an integrated software system comprising data management, analysis and support for the construction and use of econometric models, as well as the production of sophisticated presentation graphics and reports. As a DOS package, AREMOS incorporated both interactive command line operation and an extensive macro language including prompt messages and default values, looping and flow control, Boolean logical operation, subroutines, functions, and a command-line interface. The Windows version of AREMOS preserves many of these features, but incorporates a graphical user interface. The program's report-generating features include a spreadsheet-like report design grid, a table generator, automatic updating of reports, and the use of calculations and functions instead of pre-calculated data.

AREMOS is capable of reading data provided in any of a number of different formats, including XLS and TSD. Output to XLS, RTF, and HTML is also supported.

AUTOBOX

URL: www.autobox.com

The principal author of AUTOBOX is David Reilly. The program began to be developed in 1966 at the University of Wisconsin Statistics Department under the direction of George Box under the title "The Pack Program" with David J. Pack as the principle statistician/programmer. Beginning in 1968, David Reilly, then at the University of Pennsylvania, developed a rule-based heuristics system that is today the Autobox approach to ARIMA modeling. The main thrust was to provide a mechanized or automated option to the Box-Jenkins (ARIMA) approach to modeling a time series process. SAS and BMDP were early source code customers in 1972 for the Pack Program.

The first release of AUTOBOX (then called AUTOBJ) occurred in November 1969 on an IBM 360 located at The American Stock Exchange. The Interactive Data Corporation and Chase Econometric Forecasting Associates provided AUTOBJ in the context of XSIM as a time sharing package. It was also provided in a time sharing environment by Compuserve and Computer Science. AUTOBJ was converted to the PC beginning in 1982, and first released as a DOS application later that year. It was converted to Windows beginning in 1990 and first released as a Windows application in 1991. The name was changed to AUTOBOX in January 1988. It is also available as both a DLL and an object library for Unix/Linux platforms. AUTOBOX has in addition been successfully integrated (OEM) into a number of more general software packages.

AUTOBOX is an interactive program with a Visual Basic wrapper that uses Access as its database. The program's objectives can be summarized under the term Generalized Least Squares inasmuch as it renders a noise process that has constant mean, constant variance and is free of both auto projective structure and dependence on lags of any known input series. The objectives of the Gaussian Assumptions are met and model statistics are then useable. FreeFore is the shareware version of Autobox, announced in 2003.

S. Armstrong (2001), *Principles of Forecasting*, Kluwer Academic Publishers, Boston.

R. Bewley (1988), Review of Autobox, *Journal of Applied Econometrics* **3**(3).

U. Kusters (1995), *Software Review: AUTOBOX 3.0 and SCA PC-EXPERT*, The Forum, International Institute of Forecasters.

K. Ord and S. Lowe (Feb. 1996), Automatic Forecasting, *The American Statistician* **50**(1), 88–94.

D.J. Pack (1971), *The Pack Program User Guide*, Automatic Forecasting Systems, Philadelphia, PA.

D.P. Reilly (1980), Experiences with an Automatic Box-Jenkins Modeling Algorithm, in: *Time Series Analysis*, O.D. Anderson, ed., North-Holland, Amsterdam, pp. 493–508.

D.P. Reilly (1987), Experiences with an Automatic Transfer Function Algorithm, in: *Computer Science and Statistics Interface*, R.M. Heiberger, ed., American Statatistical Association, Alexandria, VA, pp. 128–135.

D.J. Pack (1971), *The Pack Program User Guide*, Automatic Forecasting Systems, Philadelphia, PA.

B34S

URL: www.uic.edu/∼hhstokes

The principal author of B34S is Houston H. Stokes. The program began to be developed at the University of Chicago in 1964 by Hudson Thornber. The program's original name was B34T. It was written in Fortran II and ran on an IBM 7094. Stokes became the developer in 1972 and moved the program to the University of Illinois at Chicago. At that time the program name was changed to B34S, and the code converted to Fortran IV and ported to the IBM 360 MVS operating system. In the 1980's, it was converted to Fortran 77 and moved to an IBM 370 running under CMS at the University of Illinois at Chicago. In 1991, B34S was ported to the PC as a DOS program using the Lahey F77EM32 compiler. In the late 1990's it was ported to the RS/6000 and Sun platforms and in 2000 to Linux. B34S is currently written in Fortran 95.

B34S was originally a regression program that offered OLS and GLS regressions. It was later expanded to include time series modeling (Box Jenkins and VARMA) and a variety of general procedures (Stokes, 2003). B34S essentially has two aspects: it contains a number of procedures and in addition incorporates a programming language that permits matrix operations. Both of these modes are closely linked and the data are equally accessible in either. Both provide extensive links with other systems such as LIMDEP, MATLAB, RATS, SAS, and SPEAKEASY. The MATRIX command in fact allows a user to develop custom applications in a higher language or to link with Fortran programs. User-defined PROGRAMS, SUBROUTINES and FUNCTIONS are supported.

M. Aoki (1987), *State Space Modeling of Time Series*, Springer-Verlag, New York.

L. Breiman (May, 1991), The Π Method for Estimating Multivariate Functions From Noisy Data, *Technometrics* **33**(2), 125–143.

J. Dennis, D.Gay and R. Welsch (1981), An adaptive nonlinear least-squares algorithm, *ACM Trans. Math. Software* **7**(3), 348–368.

J. Friedman (1991), Multivariate Adaptive Regression Splines, *Annals of Statistics* **19**(1), 1–67.

D. Pack (1977), *A Computer Program for the Analysis of Time Series Models Using the Box-Jenkins Philosophy*, Department of Statistics, Ohio State University, Cleveland, Mimeo.

H.H. Stokes (1991, 1997), *Specifying and Diagnostically Testing Econometric Models*, Quorum Books, New York.

H.H. Stokes (2004), The evolution of econometric software design: A developer's View, *Journal of Economic and Social Measurement* **29** (2004), 205–259, this volume.

H. Thornber (1965), *The Autoregressive Model: Bayesian vs. Sampling Theory Analysis*, Technical report No. 6504, Center for Mathematical Studies in Business and Economics, University of Chicago Business School.

H. Thornber (1966), *Manual for B34T (8 MAR 66)-A Stepwise Regression Program*, University of Chicago Business School Technical Report 6603.

H. Thornber (15 September 1967), *BAYES Addendum to Technical Report 6603: Manual for B34T-A Stepwise Regression Program*, University of Chicago Business School.

H. Thornber (1 August 1968), *BLUS Addendum to Technical Report 6603: Manual for B34T-A Stepwise Regression Program*, University of Chicago Busienss School.

BETAHAT

URL: www.LFSoftware.com

The author of Betahat is Paul Calvert. Development began in 1991 and the first versions ran under DOS and OS/2. These were written in Basic PDS, the predecessor to Visual Basic for Windows. The first general release of Betahat (then called Beta) was in June 1995 as a Windows application. The interface was written in Visual Basic, but the core computations were generally done in FORTRAN DLL's. Starting with version 3.0, most computations were moved to Visual Basic except for the Census X-11 code and some library routines which remain in FORTRAN and Pascal DLL's.

The major single equation model types that can be estimated include OLS, AR-1, ARIMA, linear & nonlinear ARMAX, various types of exponential smoothing, Box-Cox, binomial and multinomial logit, probit, tobit, poisson, multivariate t with uncorrelated errors, multivariate t with independent errors, 2SLS and 2SNL with or without ARMA errors, LIML, linear and nonlinear GMM with options for 6 different lag patterns, and programmable nonlinear maximum likelihood. For pooled or panel data there are 7 different model types. AR-1 correction for each of the panel model types is available. The structural systems model types that can be estimated include SUR, 3SLS, GMM, and FIML. Other system estimators include VAR, vector ARIMAX, and multivariate stochastic variance. The algorithms included for estimation are Marquardt, Gauss-Newton, DFP, BFGS, Newton, and BHHH.

A wide variety of tests and options are incorporated including autocorrelations, Ljung-Box Q statistic, partial autocorrelations, influence measures, recursive residuals, autocorrelation and heteroskedastic consistent covariance matrices, imposition and testing of linear restrictions, and unit root tests. There are also many tests for heteroskedasticity.

Betahat can simulate all of the model types that it can estimate. Estimated, and unestimated equations with user supplied coefficients, can be saved in the database for later use or inclusion in a simulation. There are options for add factors and identities. Stochastic simulation is available for both single equations and systems. There is an automatic comparison of the values from a simulation to a base simulation so the user can easily compare the effect of a changed model. The output is also selectable, permitting display of only equations and identities that are of interest.

The features that are distinctive to the program include robust methods for reading data, and a dual mode interface. Supported file formats for input/output include Access®, dBase, FoxPro, Excel®, Lotus, text, and others. SQL statements can be used when reading most file formats. Betahat was originally developed with a Windows-based GUI interface by using standard interface devices such as spreadsheets, dialog boxes, and pull down menus. This interface works well for exploratory type work with datasets that have a fairly small number of series. Starting with version 2.0 a command/batch interface was added to the program. The command mode interface made larger scale macroeconometric models more feasible using Betahat, since they usually have a very large number of data series, equations, and identities, and they are commonly run as a large set of instructions.

CEF

URL: www.ms.ic.ac.uk/sghall/

The principal author is Stephen G. Hall. The CEF software was originally written in FORTRAN 77 for the IBM PC and compatibles. It developed from model solution software originally created by Richard Pierce at the National Institute of Economic and Social Research in the early 70's, also written in FORTRAN 77, but mainframe computer based. During the first half of the 1980s, CEF was extended to include a range of model analysis and solution techniques (Hall and Henry, 1988). In 1987, CEF was moved to the Bank of England. In 1991, it was installed at the London Business School Centre for Economic Forecasting and used for the LBS model. In the late 1990s, it was converted to Windows.

CEF is a model solution package that runs under Windows. It accesses large data bases. It incorporates a range of different model analysis and solution techniques, including optimal control, stochastic simulation, model inversion rational expectations solutions, and the well known stacked solution algorithm for rational expectations (Hall 1985a, 1985b).

S.G. Hall and S.G.B. Henry (1988), *Macroeconometric Modeling*, North-Holland, Amsterdam.

S.G. Hall (May, 1985a), An Improved Solution Technique for Large Economic Models with Consistent Expectations, *System and Control Letters* **5**.

S.G. Hall (May, 1985b), On the Solution of Large Economic Models with Consistent Expectations, *Bulletin of Economic Research*.

EasyReg International

URL: econ.la.psu.edu/~hbierens/EASYREG.HTM

The author of EasyReg (Easy Regression) is Herman Bierens. EasyReg is called International because it accepts dots and/or commas as decimal delimiters, regardless of the local number setting of Windows. Development as a Windows program began in 1995. EasyReg was initially written in Visual Basic 3, and is now further developed in Visual Basic 5. EasyReg is unusual among econometrics program in being genuine freeware. It can be downloaded and distributed freely without restrictions.

EasyReg offers a wide range of estimators of single and multiple equation models, comparable with commercial econometric software. The single equation models supported are: linear regression models, which in the time series case can be extended to models with ARMA errors and/or GARCH errors, discrete dependent variables models (Logit and Probit, multinomial Logit, Poison regression, binomial, negative binomial, and ordered Logit and Probit), Tobit, Heckman's sample selection model, quantile regression, 2SLS, nonparametric kernel regression, and ARIMA models. The multiple equation models that are suported are: linear GMM (with SUR and panel data models as special cases), structural and nonstructural VAR, and Johansen's VECM. Although EasyReg is mainly a point-and-click program, it is possible to program and estimate user-defined nonlinear regression, maximum likelihood and GMM models. The programming itself is still done by point-and-click, though. Moreover, EasyReg contains various data analysis tools, such as unit root and stationarity tests, kernel density estimation, time series plotting, and scatter diagrams.

Two types of data files are supported, namely Excel files in CSV format, and particular space delimited text files containing the number of variables, missing value code, variable names, and the data matrix. EasyReg also comes with its own database which contains data samples.

S.P. Sephton (1998), EasyReg: Version 1.12, *Journal of Applied Econometrics* **13**, 203–207.

EVIEWS

URL: www.eviews.com

EViews is a product of the staff of Quantitative Micro Software. The immediate predecesor of EViews, MicroTSP, was developed by David Lilien, and first released in 1981 for the Apple II personal computer. MicroTSP was subsequently rewritten for IBM compatible PCs, taking direct advantage of the latter platform's increased memory and superior graphical support. All development of MicroTSP ended in 1990 and work began on an all new program for the Windows operating system. The result of this project, EViews, was released in early 1994. Written in C++ and designed from the ground-up to use modern GUI interfaces, EViews provides an integrated environment for estimation and forecasting, large-scale model construction and solution, database management, and presentation of results. Currently available for systems running 32-bit versions of Windows, EViews features an innovative, Windows-based, object-oriented user-interface, as well as traditional command line and programming interfaces.

EViews provides extensive support for estimation and forecasting of linear and nonlinear single and multiple equation econometric models. While the original emphasis of the program was on standard econometric and time series methods such as OLS, TSLS, ARMAX, GMM, VARs, ARCH and Kalman filtering, EViews also supports a wide range of limited dependent variable and panel data estimators, as well as the ability to estimate user-specified maximum likelihood models. In addition, EViews includes a variety of tools for general statistical analysis.

Sophisticated model analysis and simulation tools allow for the construction of and solution of linear and nonlinear models with virtually no limits on the number of equations (save those imposed by Windows' 2GB limit on a single application). These models may be solved using dynamic or static methods, and optionally, stochastic simulation and forward solution. All of EViews' estimation and simulation tools are tied into presentation quality graphics and table construction tools which allow users to quickly and easily summarize results and to exchange them with other Windows programs.

EViews reads and writes ASCII, MDB (Access), TSD, XLS and WKx files, as well as the native files of many econometrics and statistics packages, including PC-Give, RATS, SAS, SPSS, STATA and TSP. EViews also provides access to FAME, Haver Analytics, and DRI-Pro databases. ODBC support is available in EViews 5.

FP

URL: Fairmodel.Econ.Yale.Edu

The authors of FP (The Fair-Parke Program for the Estimation and Analysis of NonlinearEconometric Models) are Ray C. Fair and William R. Parke. The program is written in FORTRAN, and source code is distributed for use on any machine with a FORTRAN compiler. An executable version is also distributed for use on PCs. The program runs in DOS on PCs. The original release date is 1980 for the mainframe version; the PC version was first released in 1990. The current version can be obtained free of charge from the website.

The FP program allows one to estimate and analyze dynamic, nonlinear, simultaneous equations models. The models can include 1) nonlinearity in variables, 2) nonlinearity in coefficients, 3) autoregressive and moving average errors of any order, and 4) rational expectations. The estimation techniques include OLS, 2SLS, 3SLS, FIML, LAD, 2SLAD, and some versions of Hansen's method of moments estimator. Many single equation tests can be performed. Other options include 1) running forecasts, 2) calculation RMSEs, 3) calculating multipliers, 4) solving optimal control problems, and 5) performing stochastic simulation and bootstrapping. One of the advantages of the program is that it allows one to move easily from the estimation of the individual equations to the solution and analysis of the entire model. The Parke algorithm is used for 3SLS and FIML estimation. The extended path method is used for the solution of models with rational expectations. For stochastic simulations the draws can either be from estimated distributions or from estimated residuals. The data can be read in free or fixed format. Each technique in the program is discussed in at least one of the three references below, and all of the techniques used in the three references are in the program. Appendix C in Fair (1984) is a discussion of the logic of the program.

R.C. Fair (1984), *Specification, Estimation, and Analysis of Macroeconometric Models*, Harvard University Press.
R.C. Fair (1994), *Testing Macroeconometric Models*, Harvard University Press.
R.C. Fair (2004), *Estimating How the MacroeconomyWorks*, Harvard University Press, forthcoming.

GRETL

URL: Gretl.sourceforge.net

The principal author of gretl is Allin Cottrell. Gretl inherited an initial code base from Ramu Ramanathan, in the form of Ramanathan's ESL (Econometrics Software Library), the DOS program that accompanied his textbook *Introductory Econometrics*. ESL was originally written in Fortran, and then converted to C. gretl extends ESL into a cross-platform package supporting both graphical and command-line user interfaces. Although C is the language used, some extensions ("plugins") use the fortran-based Lapack library. gretl is unusual among econometrics programs in being open-source and free, in the specific sense of the Free Software Foundation. Binary packages are available for Windows and various Linux versions; the source, which uses the GNU autoconf apparatus, should compile on any unix variant that supports GTK.

gretl offers a reasonably full range of single-equation least-squares estimators (OLS plus several autocorrelation- and heteroskedasticity-corrected variants), Two-stage Least Squares, SUR systems, Least Absolute Deviations regression, and ML estimation of binomial logit and probit. It also offers VARs, unit-root tests and cointegration tests. For users who wish to carry out further analyses not available within gretl itself, the program offers several links to other software, allowing data to be saved in GNU Octave (closely related to Matlab) and GNU R (closely related to the "S" statistical system); there are also gretl plugins that can exchange data with X-12-arima and TRAMO/SEATS, for analysis of seasonality and ARIMA modeling. In batch mode, gretl permits Monte Carlo analysis and iterative estimation of non-linear specifications.

The program will read Excel and Gnumeric worksheets, BOX1 data (from the Bureau of the Census), comma- and space-separated plain text data files, and RATS 4 databases.

IDIOM

URL: www.camecon.com

The principal current developer of IDIOM is Terry Barker; earlier authors are given in the references below. It is a FORTRAN90 program designed for the specification and solution of large-scale econometric non-linear simulation models incorporating a wide range of relationships, including input-output equations. IDIOM was originally written by the Cambridge Growth Project, Department of Applied Economics, University of Cambridge, the original package being funded by UNIDO to help provide software tools for industrial development. Since 1987, the use and development of IDIOM was taken over by Cambridge Econometrics Ltd, following the closure of the Project in that year. IDIOM has been revised and extended by Cambridge Econometrics as the software platform for a number of econometric models covering economic, energy and environmental models for countries and regions, namely, the UK models MDM-E3 and LEFM, the Europe regional E3 model E3ME, and the global model E3MG. In 1989, IDIOM was re-written for compilation and solution using the Salford FORTRAN compiler FTN77 and the operating system DBOS, so that it could run models unconstrained by the 640k limitations of the IBM-PC-compatible 386 and 486 PCs. In 1997 the software was further developed so that it could be used as part of a user-friendly system for solving models under Windows 95. The latest version uses the Salford compiler FTN95.

The purpose of IDIOM is to provide a means of organizing the historical data, the assumptions and the relationships of large econometric models, including those for inter-relating economies and regions of one economy, then solving the models over a number of periods and finally storing and presenting the results.

Various features of IDIOM are common across the models built and solved using the package (the housekeeping routines) and are described in the model manual. Other features have to be provided by the model builder as specific to the model. Builders of models should prepare a separate manual for model users; and users of the models should consult the appropriate model manual for details of a particular model.

IDIOM differs from other economic model solving packages, such as AREMOS, EViews, MODLER, or TROLL, in two respects. Firstly the organising concept and principle of IDIOM is that of matrix algebra. In this it is more like the GAUSS or Ox packages than MODLER and others. The specification of equations can be in terms of industries or regions or both, so that one line of commands can replace many lines required by a package organised around scalar variables and equations for each such variable. This is particularly useful for cross-section, time-series econometric modelling involving large datasets. Secondly, IDIOM does not provide facilities for estimating equations or managing associated databanks. These tasks must be done using the MREG software package or the Ox applications developed by Cambridge Econometrics.

The main benefits from such specialisation are time-saving in computer calculations and ease of managing large models by organising solutions about matrix variables. IDIOM can solve and store large-scale E3 models (e.g. involving about 10,000 estimated equations and over a million variables) taking a few seconds for each year of solution on a year on a PC with Pentium 3, 1Ghz processor and 192 MB RAM. IDIOM operates by interpreting directives from the model-builder defining the specification of the model required and the computations to be performed. Since these directives are interpreted rather than compiled, substantial changes in the model structure can be made without knowledge of the internal program structure. In addition, the provision of facilities for the conditional or repeated execution of directives provides the model-builder with much of the control over the models normally obtained by writing in a conventional high-level computer language.

T. Barker, W. Peterson and A. Winters (1984), An international dynamic input-output model, *Proceedings of the Seventh International Conference on Input-Output Techniques*, UNIDO, ed., United Nations, New York, pp. 183–192.

Cambridge Econometrics (2002), *IDIOM User's Manual*, at www.camecon.com.

W. Peterson (1987), Computer software for a large econometric model, in: *The Cambridge Multisectoral Dynamic Model of the British Economy*, T. Barker and W. Peterson, eds, Cambridge University Press.

LIMDEP

URL: www.limdep.com

The author of LIMDEP is William H. Greene. Development of the program began in 1974 on a Univac 1108 at the University of Wisconsin, based upon a Fortran implementation of Nerlove and Press's multinomial logit model (1973). Development of what ultimately became program modules continued at Cornell University in 1976–1980, primarily the probit, tobit, and sample selection model estimators. Wide usage began in 1981 after it was ported to a VAX at New York University, where the parts were integrated and gathered under a common interface and distribution to other mainframe installations began. In 1986 LIMDEP was converted for use on the PC. In 1997, it was converted to Windows. The Windows version is a mixed language package, with roughly equal amounts of Fortran and C++ code and heavy implementation of the API in the Microsoft Foundation Class library in C++. The numeric code includes low level implementation of most algorithms and methods as well as integration of numerous IMSL routines.

The first version of LIMDEP was created to implement Ray Fair's (1977) EM algorithm for the tobit model, hence the name LIM(ited) DEP(endent) variable modeling. An obvious extension was to incorporate truncation and discrete choice (probit, ordered probit, logit) models. The second major extension was to Heckman's sample selection model in 1980; see Heckman (1979) and Greene (1980). The third major development was estimators for McFadden's conditional logit model, and a very early limited information maximum likelihood estimator for the nested logit model. Subsequent development has included the automation of a large number of related limited and discrete dependent variable models, as well as a constellation of nonlinear econometric techniques such as survival, count, and other types of applications. The most recent developments have extended many models for use with panel data, the present primary focus of the package, as well as the estimation of stochastic frontier models. LIMDEP and Tim Coelli's FRONTIER are unique in containing any variety of estimators for this model. LIMDEP is currently an integrated program for the estimation of linear and nonlinear single equations model, using any of three types of data: cross section, time series and panel. LIMDEP provides a wealth of estimators. The discrete choice (multinomial logit and probit) estimation component was embodied in NLOGIT in 1995 and in 2002 (with version 8.0 of LIMDEP) NLOGIT was made available as a separate package and is described elsewhere in this compendium.

R. Fair (1977), A Note on Computation of the Tobit Estimator, *Econometrica* **45**, 1723–1727.

W. Greene (1981), Sample Selection Bias as a Specification Error: Comment, *Econometrica* **49**, 795–798.

W.H. Greene (2003), *Econometric Analysis*, 5th Ed., Prentice-Hall, Englewood.

J. Heckman (1979), Sample Selection Bias as a Specification Error, *Econometrica* **47**, 153–161.

M. Nerlove and S. Press (1973), *Univariate and Multivariate Log-Linear and Logistic Models*, RAND – R1306-EDA/NIH, Santa Monica.

MICROFIT

The authors of MicroFit are Hashem and Bahram Pesaran. Originally called DataFit, as a program for the microcomputer, MicroFit was originally implemented under DOS in 1986. It was converted to Windows in 1999.

MicroFit is an interactive econometric software package designed specifically for the econometric modeling of time series data. It incorporates some data file management capabilities and graphics display facilities, but primary focuses on providing a range of parameter estimation techniques for estimation, hypothesis testing, and forecasting under a variety of univariate and multivariate model specification. It provides a large variety of diagnostic and non-nested specification tests, based upon the work of L.G. Godfrey, Hashem Pesaran and others.

MicroFit accepts ASCII, binary data files, Excel worksheets, and other data files with a variety of formats, including CSV, PRN, and TSD. Data can be exported in CSV and TSD formats.

L.G. Godfrey (1988), *Misspecification Tests in Econometrics. The Lagrange Multiplier Principle and Other Approaches*, Cambridge University Press, Cambridge.

L.G. Godfrey, ed. (1992), *The Implementation and Constructive Use of Misspecification Tests in Econometrics*, Manchester University Press, Manchester.

M.H. Pesaran and L.J. Slater (1980), *Drynamic Regression. Theory and Algorithms*, Elim Horwood, Chichester.

M.H. Pesaran and B. Pesaran, *Working with MicroFit 4.0*, Oxford University Press, Oxford.

Modeleasy+

URL: www.modeleasy.com

The program was originally written in Fortran IV at the U.S. Federal Reserve Board of Governors (FRB), Washington, D.C., under the direction of Jim Condie.

The first release of Modeleasy was in the mid-1970's on an IBM 360 system located at the FRB. The Bank of Italy also had a copy on an IBM 360 system. The program has since been further developed and expanded by Giuseppe Bruno, Andrea Cividini, and William Teeters. Today, the principle authors of Modeleasy+ are the staffs of the Research Department of the Bank of Italy and Econometric Modeling & Computing Corporation (EMCC). A substantial rewrite of the code during the mid-1990's allowed a port of the program (renamed Modeleasy+) to other systems; its first general release was in 1997. The program is written in Fortran 95 and runs mainly on AIX, Solaris, Linux, and Windows platforms.

The initial purpose of Modeleasy was to allow users easy access to estimation and simulation tools. Modeleasy+ is today an econometric computing environment incorporating array, matrix, and time series manipulation capabilities as well as graphical and reporting tools. User written programs, subroutines and functions are supported. The command-line/GUI interface allows users access to a wide variety of econometric analysis tools. Interfaces to databases such as FAME are supported. Models written in a model description language can be estimated and simulated with simple commands. Tools for VAR analysis, coefficient sensitivity analysis, and computation of elasticities and multipliers are included.

Econometric Modeling & Computing Corporation (2003) *The Modeleasy+ Reference Manual*, Palm Harbor, FL.

Econometric Modeling & Computing Corporation (2003) *The Speakeasy Reference Manual*, Palm Harbor, FL.

C. Bianchi, G. Bruno and A. Cividini (1992), Analysis of Large-Scale Econometric Models Using Supercomputer Techniques, *Computer Science in Economics and Management* **5**, 271–281.

G. Bodo, G. Bruno, G. Parigi and S. Siviero (1994), Diagnostic Checking of Large-Size Econometric Models: an application to the Models of the Bank of Italy, *Economic Notes by Monte dei Paschi di Siena* **23**(1), 26–52.

MODLER

URL: www.modler.com

The principal author of MODLER is Charles G. Renfro; co-authors are identified in the references below. MODLER began to be developed in 1968/69 on an IBM 7040, to support the estimation of a version of the Brookings Quarterly Econometric Model of the United States. In 1969–1970 it was ported to a Digital Equipment Corporation PDP 10, and there first developed as an interactive, network-resident program. During the period 1970-1981, it was mounted on a series of IBM mainframe computers, in certain cases providing the core networked facilities of a publicly-available, time-sharing economic data base and econometric modeling system.

Beginning in October 1981, MODLER was ported to the IBM PC. It was first released in October 1983 as a DOS-based program (Dun & Bradstreet Corporation being the first licensee), versions of which still operate: the oldest version still in daily use dates to 1987 and runs as a DOS application under Windows. In September 1984, PC-Mark7/MODLER, incorporating a 250+ equation Wharton Quarterly Econometric Model of the United States, was inaugurated by Wharton Econometric Forecasting Associates as the central element of the first microcomputer-based forecasting service. In early 1985, the full 600+ equation Wharton Mark7 model was both estimated and solved in MODLER. Beginning in 1985, the Economist Workstation, developed jointly with Data Resources, Inc, was created with MODLER as its core software. Other companies that have made their models available to their clients in MODLER include Chase Econometrics, Merrill Lynch Economics and UBS bank, among many consulting companies and organizations worldwide. In 1996, the first Windows version was released. Significantly, the current Windows version of MODLER is sufficiently backwardly-compatible functionally that data banks and models from 1984 can still be used; customarily, as each new Intel processor is released, PC-Mark7 – first solved on the original PC – is once again solved with the latest MODLER version: a 12-quarter solution that took approximately 4 minutes on the original PC takes less than 1 second on a 2-gigahertz Pentium IV or later machine. A Unix version was also developed during the 1980s for a Pyramid super-mini computer, originally for Townsend-Greenspan & Company.

MODLER is designed as a comprehensive time series economic data base management and econometric modeling package that permits its users to construct, maintain, and solve essentially structural econometric models, generally ranging in size from 1 to 1000 equations, although models of as much as 3000 equations have been solved with it. These models can be linear or nonlinear, dynamic or static, and simultaneous or recursive. Input-output structures and various types of objective functions can also be embedded. MODLER's estimation facilities are characteristically those normally used to estimate equations of a large-scale macroeconometric model. Its model construction and solution facilities are similarly oriented, including those that aid in the evaluation and debugging of a model during its construction. The presentation facilities are extensive and can be closely integrated with Microsoft Office and other such combination suites. MODLER can be tightly connected to the Internet via a standard browser.

The program reads TSD, PRT, XLS, and WKx files, as well as a (configurable) range of ASCII text files. It writes TSD, PRT, and XLS files. Historically, links have been made by MODLER users to virtually all the major economic data vendors of the past 20 years, as well as to data formats supported by organizations such as the European Commission, the IMF, OECD, the UN, and the World Bank, as well as European and North American government statistical agencies.

A. Drud (1983), A survey of model representations and simulation algorithms in some existing modeling systems, *Journal of Economic Dynamics & Control* **5**, 5–35.

M.O. Adams (1986), The Kentucky Economic Information System, in: *Exemplary Systems in Government Awards '85-'86: the State of the Art*, Urban and Regional Information Systems Association, pp. 144–158.

Data Resources (1985), *Economist Workstation User Guide*, DRI/McGraw-Hill, Lexington, MA.

Data Resources (1986), *Economist Workstation User Guide, Version 2.0*, DRI/McGraw- Hill, Lexington, MA.

F. Cooper, C.G. Renfro and R.W. Wescott (1987), *Merrill Lynch Economics US Model User Guide*, Merrill Lynch Economics, New York.

C.G. Renfro (1970), *An Interactive Regression Program for the PDP-10, Description and User Manual*, Brookings Quarterly Model Project, Brookings Institution, Washington, DC.

C.G. Renfro (1980), Economic data base systems: some reflections on the state of the art, *Review of Public Data Use* **8**, 121–140.

C.G. Renfro (1981), The computer as a factor of production in economic data provision and research, A paper presented at the *Annual Meeting of the American Economic Association*, Washington, DC, 30 December 1981.

C.G. Renfro (1982), Syntactical Considerations in the Development of an Econometric Modeling Language, A paper presented at the *1982 Conference on Economic Dynamics and Control*, Washington, DC, 9–11 June 1982.

C.G. Renfro (1996), On the development of econometric modeling languages: MODLER and its first twenty-five years, *Journal of Economic and Social Measurement* **22**, 241–311.

C.G. Renfro (1997), Normative considerations in the development of a software package for econometric estimation, *Journal of Economic and Social Measurement* **23**, 315–368, [Paper originally presented at the *Society for Computational Economics Third International Conference on Computing in Economics and Finance*, Stanford University, 30 June–2 July 1997.]

C.G. Renfro (1998), Multidimensional data for regional analysis: a consideration of software requirements, a paper presented at the *Regional Economic Indicator Models Workshop*, Universidade do Minho, Braga, Portugal, 8–10 June 1998.

A.E. Scowcroft (1988), The mechanics of joint cross sectional time series modelling, Paper presented to the *1988 MODLER Users Conference*, Philadelphia, PA, 15–16 November 1988.

Wharton Econometric Forecasting Associates (1984), *PC-Mark7/MODLER User Guide*, Wharton Econometric Forecasting Associates, Philadelphia.

Wharton Econometric Forecasting Associates (1986), *PC-Mark8/MODLER User Guide*, Wharton Econometric Forecasting Associates, Philadelphia.

R.F. Wescott and M.V. Yates (January 1989), The PC Corner: desktop publishing is for economists, *Business Economics* **24**, 51–53.

MODLER BLUE

URL: www.modler.com

MODLER BLUE was originally created in 1986 as a separate DOS PC application by Charles G. Renfro and Paul A. Coomes. It is a MODLER "spin off" and its creation reflected the RAM space constraints then existing under DOS, which made it difficult to progressively add facilities to a program without either exceeding the 640 KB RAM limit, or using program overlays. Functionally, MODLER BLUE makes available the subset of MODLER facilities related to parameter estimation and model construction, including all the data bank maintenance facilities and the capability to create models of up to 1000 equations, but excludes the model compilation and solution routines, as well as certain model-related table display facilities. In their stead, MODLER BLUE provides support for system estimators, in particular Seeming Unrelated Regression Equations (SURE), Three Stage Least Squares, and related variants, implementing these in such a way as to maximize the number of simultaneously estimated equations and parameters. The reference below (Renfro, 1997) considers in detail the whys and wherefores of the development of MODLER BLUE and its characteristics. The first Windows version was released in 1996, although the DOS version also continues to be used and, to some degree, supported.

C.G. Renfro (1997), Normative considerations in the development of a software package for econometric estimation, *Journal of Economic and Social Measurement* **23**, 315–368, [Paper originally presented at the *Society for Computational Economics Third International Conference on Computing in Economics and Finance, Stanford University*, 30 June-2 July 1997.]

MOSAIC

URL: www.informetrica.com

MOSAIC is a direct decendant of the DATABANK system first created by Michael McCracken on a CDC 1604 at Southern Methodist University in 1964–1965, and then transferred to the Economic Council of Canada. The MASSAGER component was added in 1968 and the SIMSYS component in 1970/71. In an evolutionary process, MOSAIC was developed by Michael McCracken and Keith May at Informetrica from DATABANK/MASSAGER/SIMSYS, beginning in the late 1970s, and as MOSAIC/SIMSYS was field tested by using it for the construction of Informetrica's first macroeconometric model in 1978. MOSAIC was publicly released in 1979 through several IBM OS/360 service bureaus. It was subsequently ported to VAX/VMS in 1984 and to the IBM PC in 2002.

MOSAIC is designed to support the development, use and maintenance of large econometric models, ranging in size to more than 10,000 equations and with the added capability to embed Input-Output and other types of submodels. Its facilities include those for data base management, parameter estimation, model construction and use, and presentation quality report generation. Using a command interface, it can be operated interactively or in batch mode. The modeling language of MOSAIC is effectively a superset of Fortran, which allows users to integrate arbitrary modules/code. Equations are translated into Fortran and thus models run "natively." The Informetrica T1 model of over 10,000 equations, and with an embedded I-O module runs a 25 year annual solution on a 1 GHz PC in under 10 seconds.

Issues arising from model size include equation coding errors, run-time performance, and the analysis of solution results. Coding errors are addressed through an algebraic coding language and an explicit solution mode to verify that model equations replicate estimation results and database identities. Model solutions are analyzed and models debugged using an interactive solutions browser. Solutions can be viewed and compared, results traced through equations via cross-references. "Impact" lists can be generated to display "significant" differences.

The PC version permits the creation of a DLL containing the model, using a standard interface for model control. This permits management and control of models using third party software, such as VBA in Excel. The Informetrica T1 model has been integrated with the Canadian version of the NEMS energy model being developed at Natural Resources Canadian in this way. MOSAIC/SIMSYS functionality is being exposed through the use of Microsoft's Component Object Model (COM). COM objects are well suited for use in Visual Basic/VBA applications.

NLOGIT

URL: www.nlogit.com

The primary author of NLOGIT is William H. Greene. David Hensher and Kenneth Train have also participated in the development of the package. NLOGIT is an extension (superset) of the LIMDEP package described elswhere in this compendium. The specific content of NLOGIT is a collection of estimators and analysis tools for discrete choice models such as McFadden's conditional logit (multinomial logit) model and the multinomial probit model. Prior to the release of Version 8.0 of LIMDEP in 2002, NLOGIT was one of the model commands in LIMDEP. (Please see the description of LIMDEP for technical details on the program's development.)

The first module in what ultimately became LIMDEP was a Fortran program for estimating Nerlove and Press's (1973) multinomial logit model. The more familiar form pioneered by McFadden (1973) was added to LIMDEP soon after the package was integrated in 1983. A limited information (two step) estimator for a two level nested logit model, with correction for the asymptotic covariance matrix along the lines of Murphy and Topel (1985) was added in 1986. Various minor extensions of this model constituted this part of LIMDEP until 1992-1994 when a major development effort began for full information maximum likelihood estimation of the nested logit model. The multinomial probit model, and several other variants were also added to the package at this time. NLOGIT took form at this time as a distinct package of routines within the LIMDEP program. Version 7.0 of LIMDEP was released in 1997, with these new developments embedded in the package as the NLOGIT extension. NLOGIT as an option was marketed with Version 7.0 of LIMDEP. Concurrent with the development of Version 8.0 of LIMDEP, a number of major extensions to NLOGIT were produced, including a latent class model, an implementation of the mixed logit (random parameters) model and various devices for simulation of discrete choice models. NLOGIT Version 3.0 (which includes all of LIMDEP as well as the suite of discrete choice models) was released in 2002 concurrently with the release of LIMDEP Version 8.0. NLOGIT is now marketed as a separate product by Econometric Software, Inc.

D. McFadden (1973), Conditional Logit Analysis of Qualitative Choice Behavior, in: *Frontiers in Econometrics*, P. Zarembka, ed., Academic Press, New York.

K. Murphy and R. Topel (1985), Estimation and Inference in Two Step Econometric Models, *Journal of Business and Economic Statistics* **3**, 370–379.

M. Nerlove and S. Press (1973), *Univariate and Multivariate Log-Linear and Logistic Models*, RAND – R1306-EDA/NIH, Santa Monica.

PcGets

URL: www.pcgive.com/pcgets and www.oxmetrics.net

PcGets is an automatic econometric model selection program written by David F. Hendry and Hans-Martin Krolzig that combines the user friendliness, powerful graphics and flexible data management of GiveWin with the latest methods for model selection, presently in a regression context. PcGets is an Ox Package (see Doornik, 2001), and is part of the OxMetrics family, so is a fully-interactive and menu-driven program as described in Hendry and Krolzig (2001).

An initial general model – designed to embed all the relevant information – is first tested for congruence with the evidence. The theory of reduction delineates what information losses accrue during simplifications, and how they can be evaluated empirically: see Hendry (1995). Then by implementing a general-to-specific (Gets) approach to econometric modelling, PcGets automatically selects an undominated, congruent model even though the precise formulation of the econometric relationship is not known a priori. PcGets currently focuses on linear, dynamic, regression models, so can also be applied to equations within (e.g.) vector autoregressive representations (VARs), or cross-section models.

Following Hoover and Perez (1999), PcGets adopts a multi-path search strategy, exploring the consequences of all initially feasible paths, and collecting the 'terminal' models resulting from each search. If many 'terminal' models are found, these are tested for parsimoniously encompassing their union, namely the smallest model that nests all the contenders. Multi-path searches re-commence from the latest union as needed, until either a unique congruent 'final' model emerges, or no further elimination is possible, in which case, model selection is made using an information criterion.

Monte Carlo experiments demonstrate that PcGets recovers the correct specification from a general model with size and power close to commencing from the data-generating process (DGP) itself. Moreover, the reported standard errors provide essentially unbiased estimates of the uncertainty from estimating the DGP parameters; and bias-corrected parameter estimates can be obtained despite having selected the model from the data: see Hendry (2000), Hendry and Krolzig (2003a,b), Krolzig (2000), and Krolzig and Hendry (2001).

J.A. Doornik (2001), *Object-Oriented Matrix Programming using Ox*, 4th Ed., Timberlake Consultants Press, London.

D.F. Hendry (1995), *Dynamic Econometrics*, Oxford University Press, Oxford.

D.F. Hendry (2000), Epilogue: The success of general-to-specific model selection, in: *Econometrics: Alchemy or Science?* New Edition, Oxford University Press, Oxford, pp. 467–490,

D.F. Hendry and H.-M. Krolzig (2001), *Automatic Econometric Model Selection*, Timberlake Consultants Press, London.

D.F. Hendry and H.-M. Krolzig (2003a), New developments in automatic general-to-specific modelling, in: *Econometrics and the Philosophy of Economics*, B.P. Stigum, ed., Princeton University Press, Princeton, pp 379–419.

D.F. Hendry and H.-M. Krolzig (2003b), *The properties of automatic Gets modelling*, Unpublished paper, Economics Department, Oxford University.

K.D. Hoover and S.J. Perez (1999), Data mining reconsidered: Encompassing and the general-to-specific approach to specification search, *Econometrics Journal* **2**, 167–191.

H.-M. Krolzig (2000), *General-to-specific reductions in vector autoregressive processes*, Economics discussion paper, 2000-w34, Nuffield College, Oxford.

H.-M. Krolzig and D.F. Hendry (2001), Computer automation of general-to-specific model selection procedures, *Journal of Economic Dynamics and Control* **25**, 831–866.

PcGive

URL: www.pcgive.com and www.oxmetrics.net

PcGive is an interactive econometric modelling package, emphasizing ease-of-use and extensive graphics to complement the statistical diagnostic procedures. PcGive provides advanced econometric techniques, from least-squares and instrumental variables single equation methods, for linear and non-linear specifications; system cointegration with any form of restriction; volatility models (GARCH, EGARCH and many variations of these models); static and dynamic panel-data models; time-series models such as ARFIMA(p,d,q); discrete choice and count-data models; and X-12-ARIMA for seasonal adjustment and ARIMA modelling. The focus, however, is more on modelling than estimation, so many evaluation procedures are also implemented, including recursive graphics.

PcGive is distributed with 4 books: Doornik and Hendry (2001a,b,c) and Hendry and Doornik (2001). The econometric volumes can be used as stand-alone textbooks, as well as providing a comprehensive reference for the PcGive system.

PcGive, as it is now called, began life in the late 1960s as a mainframe FORTRAN package, on punched cards, with complex job control commands that took some expertise to master (Hendry, 1970, 1974). The original aim was simply to make available the latest econometric estimators and tests: the rest, specifically how to apply such methods, was up to users. However, the ever-increasing demand for the suite led to a major effort to document and explain it, leading to the analysis of the role of computer software in implementing implicit methodologies in Hendry and Srba (1980).

The mainframe FORTRAN version was ported to the PC in 1983–1984, just after Hendry had moved to Nuffield College, University of Oxford. The first PC-GIVE release, version 2 in 1984, had only character-based plots, but was followed a year later by the next release with graphics and menus with defaults and colours. This was highly limited by the available hardware. The PC vintages of the program explicitly acknowledged the formal methodology of econometric modelling: see Hendry (1986, 1988). Version 6.01 (Hendry, 1989) was the last of the FORTRAN generation; up to that point development of PC-GIVE had been done largely by David Hendry, with assistance from Frank Srba and Adrian Neale.

In 1990, Jurgen Doornik started rewriting PcGive in C, resulting in a first release of version 7 (Doornik and Hendry, 1992). Also, the program was renamed from PC-GIVE to PcGive. Because the methodological innovations were starting to become mainstream, and adopted by other software packages, the rigid enforcement of the modelling methodology was dropped. With version 8, in 1994, PcFiml was finally translated into C. Version 7 and 8 had an MS-DOS based windowing system. This did not allow for text and graphics to be shown simultaneously on screen. Next, the Windows development was started, and the assembly graphics library, written by Doornik, could be dropped.

Starting from version 9 (1996), the front-end of PcGive was separated into a stand-alone 'desk-top' for econometric modules, called GiveWin. This front-end for graphics, text and data is now used by many modules, collectively denoted by 'OxMetrics'. Version 10 (2001) saw yet another rewrite of PcGive, this time in Ox, extended by some left-over C code via a dynamic link library. Versions 9 and 10 use the Microsoft Foundation Class (a C++ library) for the graphical user interface.

J.A. Doornik and D.F. Hendry (1992), *PcGive 7: An Interactive Econometric Modelling System*, Institute of Economics and Statistics, University of Oxford, Oxford.

J.A. Doornik and D.F. Hendry (2001a), *GiveWin: An Interface to Empirical Modelling*, 3rd Ed., Timberlake Consultants Press, London.

J.A. Doornik and D.F. Hendry (2001b), *Modelling Dynamic Systems using PcGive: Volume II*, 2nd Ed., Timberlake Consultants Press, London.

J.A. Doornik and D.F. Hendry (2001c), *Econometric Modelling using PcGive: Volume III*, Timberlake Consultants Press, London.

D.F. Hendry (1970), *The estimation of economic models with autoregressive errors*, Unpublished Ph.D. thesis, London University.

D.F. Hendry (1974), Stochastic specification in an aggregate demand model of the United Kingdom, *Econometrica* **42**, 559–578.

D.F. Hendry (1986), Using PC-GIVE in econometrics teaching, *Oxford Bulletin of Economics and Statistics* **48**, 87–98.

D.F. Hendry (1988), Econometrics in action, *Empirica* **2/87**, 135–156.

D.F. Hendry (1989), *PC-GIVE: An Interactive Econometric Modelling System*, Oxford Institute of Economics and Statistics, Oxford.

D.F. Hendry and J.A. Doornik (1996), A window on econometrics, *Cyprus Journal of Economics* **8**, 77–104.

D.F. Hendry and J.A. Doornik (1999), The Impact of Computational Tools on Time-series Econometrics, in: *Information Technology and Scholarship*, Oxford University Press, Oxford, pp. 257–269.

D.F. Hendry and J.A. Doornik (2001), *Empirical Econometric Modelling using PcGive: Volume I*, 3rd Ed., Timberlake Consultants Press, London.

D.F. Hendry and F. Srba (1980), AUTOREG: A computer program library for dynamic econometric models with autoregressive errors, *Journal of Econometrics* **12**, 85–102.

PcNaive

URL: www.oxmetrics.net

The authors of PcNaive are Jurgen A. Doornik and David F. Hendry. Versions of the software have been in use since mainframe days (see Hendry and Harrison, 1974) and the first menu-driven version dates to 1990 (Hendry, Neale and Ericsson, 1991). The present release appeared in 2001.

PcNaive is an interactive menu-driven Monte Carlo program, operating under Windows, for simulating on artificial data the range of estimators, tests, and modelling methods provided in PcGive for econometric modelling. Such experiments allow the finite-sample properties of these econometric methods to be evaluated in relevant settings. PcNaive formulates experiments in a design menu, then writes Ox code, which is executed by OxRun. Particular features of the program are its ease in designing complicated Monte Carlo experiments, and its focus on recursive methods, supported by powerful graphics through GiveWin. Screen editors make experimental design simple yet flexible for experiments involving linear stochastic dynamic systems: a vast range of correct and mis-specified models can be investigated, for both stationary and non-stationary data processes. The output includes live automatic graphing of recursive estimates and distributions. Ox code from PcNaive also can be edited prior to implementation.

The general artificial data generation process (DGP) covers a wide range of dynamic processes, density functions, and other data features of relevance to empirical econometrics. The baseline DGP is a multi-equation, stochastic, dynamic, linear, simultaneous system, allowing between- and within-equation contemporaneous and lagged feedbacks; constants; trends; unit roots, where sets of variables may or may not be cointegrated; structural breaks in conditional or marginal processes; scalar or vector autoregressive-moving average errors; autoregressive conditional heteroscedasticity; measurement errors; and many different forms of error (or data) distributions. Many model formulations and statistics of interest are available to study the consequences of mis-specifications, changes in data properties, and alternative estimators and tests.

J.A. Doornik and D.F. Hendry (2001), *Interactive Monte Carlo Experimentation in Econometrics using PcNaive*, Timberlake Consultants Press, London.

J.A. Doornik, D.F. Hendry and B. Nielsen (1998), Inference in cointegrated models: UK M1 revisited, *Journal of Economic Surveys* **12**, 533–572.

D.F. Hendry (1990), Using PC-NAIVE in teaching econometrics, *Oxford Bulletin of Economics and Statistics* **53**, 199–223.

D.F. Hendry (2000), On detectable and non-detectable structural change, *Structural Change and Economic Dynamics* **11**, 45–65.

D.F. Hendry and R.W. Harrison (1974), Monte Carlo methodology and the small sample behaviour of ordinary and two-stage least squares, *Journal of Econometrics* **2**, 151–174.

D.F. Hendry, A.J. Neale and N.R. Ericsson (1991), *PC-NAIVE, An Interactive Program for Monte Carlo Experimentation in Econometrics, Version 6.0*, Institute of Economics and Statistics, University of Oxford.

D.F. Hendry and F. Srba (1980), AUTOREG: A computer program library for dynamic econometric models with autoregressive errors, *Journal of Econometrics* **12**, 85–102.

RATS

URL: www.estima.com

The principal author of RATS is Tom Doan. The program began as an extension of the program SPECTRE written by Christopher Sims, initially at the University of Minnesota and the Federal Reserve Bank of Minneapolis in 1979. It was written in FORTRAN for a CDC. In 1979–1980, it was ported to a VM-CMS machine at Harvard and a Prime minicomputer at MIT. In 1980, the company VAR Econometrics was formed to market the program more broadly, and it was ported to many mainframe and minicomputer platforms during the next four years. The initial PC release was in 1984. It was made available for the Macintosh in 1989, and the first Windows release was in 1995. The programming language was switched from FORTRAN to C in 1991. It is available today for Windows, Macintosh, DOS, and (in a non-GUI form) for UNIX.

RATS is largely a command-driven program with some interactive features for the GUI platforms. Its econometric emphasis is on time series, including VAR's, ARIMA models and spectral analysis. One of its strong points is a very extensive programming language which includes not only loops, procedures and matrix calculations, but user-programmable interactive features such as menus and dialog boxes. This allows the development of very complex menu and dialog-driven procedures within the RATS language, such as CATS, a co-integration program written by Katarina Juselius, Henrik Hansen and Soren Johansen from the University of Copenhagen.

RATS can handle its own native format and in addition TSD, Excel, WKS, DBF, DIF, and data describable using Fortran formats. It can also link to both FAME and Haver Analytics.

REG-X

URL: www.ms.ic.ac.uk/sghall/

The principal author of REG-X is Stephen G. Hall. It was first developed in the late 1970s at the National Institute of Economic and Social Research in London as a direct clone of David Hendry's Give, which was not widely available at the time. The program was originally developed using FORTRAN on a Tandy microcomputer. Early development continued on a small minicomputer, which ran 6 terminals and had 20 MB of hard disk space. In this context, the program was run using card image files. With the introduction of the PC in the early 1980s, REG-X was converted to the PC again running from card image files. As PC's came in during the early 80's a proper interactive version was developed and it began extending well away from the basic GIVE structure. It is freely available for download from the above website.

REG-X is a general econometric estimation package. Extensions from the original basic GIVE structure include Kalman filter options for stochastic trend models and time varying parameter estimation, GARCH estimation, a general Kalman filter option for state space modelling and various other specialized options. In the second half of the 80's, cointegration techniques were added. In particular it was the first software available to apply the Johansen reduced rank regression (Hall, 1989)

S.G. Hall (1989), *Maximum Likelihood Estimation of Cointegrating Vectors: An Example of the Johansen Procedure*, Oxford Bulletin of Economics and Statistics.

SHAZAM

URL: www.econometrics.com

The principal authors are Ken White, Diana Whistler, David Bates, and Donna Wong. SHAZAM is a comprehensive computer program for econometrics and is available for Windows, DOS, Unix, and Macintosh operating systems. The primary strength of SHAZAM is for the estimation and testing of many types of regression models. The SHAZAM command language has great flexibility and provides capabilities for programming procedures. SHAZAM has an interface to the GNUPLOT package for high quality graphics.

SHAZAM includes features for:

- data transformations, handling missing observations, matrix manipulation, evaluation of derivatives and integrals, data sorting, computation of cumulative distribution functions for a variety of probability distributions;
- descriptive statistics, calculation of price indexes, moving averages, exponential smoothing, seasonal adjustment, financial time series, ARIMA (Box-Jenkins) time series models, Dickey-Fuller and Phillips-Perron unit root tests, tests for cointegration, nonparametric density estimation;
- OLS estimation, restricted least squares, weighted least squares, ridge regression, distributed lag models, generalized least squares, estimation with autoregressive or moving average errors, estimation with heteroskedastic errors, ARCH and GARCH models, Box-Cox regressions, probit models, logit models, tobit models, estimation using regression quantiles (including MAD estimation), regression with non-normal errors (including exponential regression, beta regression and poisson regression), regression with time varying coefficients, nonparametric methods, generalized entropy methods, fuzzy set models;

- linear and nonlinear hypothesis testing, calculation of confidence intervals and ellipse plots, computation of the Newey-West autocorrelation consistent covariance matrix, regression diagnostic tests (including tests for heteroskedasticity, CUSUM tests, RESET specification error tests), computation of p-values for many test statistics (including the p-value for the Durbin-Watson test), forecasting;
- nonlinear least squares, estimation of systems of linear and nonlinear equations by SURE, 2SLS and 3SLS, generalized method of moments (GMM) estimation, pooled time-series cross-section methods;
- principal components and factor analysis, principal components regression, linear programming, minimizing and maximizing nonlinear functions, solving nonlinear simultaneous equations.

D. Chotikapanich and W.E. Griffiths (1993), *Learning SHAZAM?: A Computer Handbook for Econometrics*, Griffiths-Hill-Judge Handbook, Wiley.

T.J. Coelli and W.E. Griffiths (1989), *Computer and Exercise Solutions Manual*, Judge 85 Handbook, Wiley.

T.T. Nguyen (1993), *Statistics with SHAZAM*, Narada Press.

Northwest Econometrics (2001), *SHAZAM User's Reference Manual Version 9.*

K.J. White, J.A.J. Boyd, S.D. Wong and D. Whistler (1993), *SHAZY: The SHAZAM Student Version*, McGraw-Hill.

K.J. White and L.T.M. Bui (1988), *Basic Econometrics: A Computer Handbook Using SHAZAM*, Gujarati (2nd Ed.) Handbook, McGraw-Hill.

K.J. White and L.T.M. Bui (1991), *The Practice of Econometrics: A Computer Handbook Using SHAZAM*, Berndt Handbook, Addison-Wesley.

K.J. White, S.A. Haun and D.J. Gow (1988), *Introduction to the Theory and Practice of Econometrics: A Computer Handbook Using SHAZAM and SAS*, Judge Handbook, Wiley.

K.J. White and S.A. Theobald (1995), *Basic Econometrics: A Computer Handbook Using SHAZAM*, Gujarati (3rd Ed.) Handbook, McGraw-Hill.

K.J. White, S.D. Wong, D. Whistler, R.Q. Grafton and M. Scantlen (1991), *Econometric Models & Economic Forecasts: A Computer Handbook Using SHAZAM*, Pindyck-Rubinfeld Handbook, McGraw-Hill.

SORITEC

URL: www.fisisoft.com

The principal author of SORITEC is John Sneed. Initial development was begun in 1977, for access over the Control Data Corporation CYBERNET time-sharing service. This original version was derived from ANALYZE, written at the University of Minnesota by John Sneed; NSTOK, another system written for the IBM 1130, also by John Sneed; and several public domain versions of TSP, notably the University of Maryland version compiled by Elizabeth Chase MacRae, and the San Francisco Fed version. George Hill was instrumental in the early development of SORITEC, contributing the first version of the databanking facility, which is essentially the same as that supported by the system today. The first release of the system was in early 1979, and in the next four years, SORITEC was implemented on several other time-sharing systems in the US and the UK, including the ICL 2900. It has since been ported to about 35 mainframe, minicomputer and microcomputer systems, including MVS/TSO, CMS, Univac, HP, DEC, DG, Cray, Convex, Burroughs, Honeywell, Sun, Nord, Prime, and most of the Unix workstations available up to the time of release of the IBM PC. The British Treasury was an early user, and SORITEC was used in many UK government departments in the 1980's.

In 1983, SORITEC was released on the PC with all the features of the mainframe product. Starting about 1984, SORITEC was sold by Data Resources, Inc., as its PC econometrics solution while EPS was being converted to the PC. In 1983, the SORITEC SAMPLER was also released on the PC, which made small-scale econometrics a free good for the first time.

In 1995, SORITEC was released with a full Windows interface. Most of its techniques are selectable from point-and-click windows (all techniques are also available from the command line, as before). The principal author of the Windows version is James Streets. SORITEC is currently distributed by Full Information Software, Inc. It is also incorporated into the TESLA electric load forecasting system, sold by TESLA, Inc.

SORITEC combines a large array of estimation techniques with a databanking facility, a report writer, a broad array of statistical commands, time-series estimation/forecasting, an algebraic command language (with integrated matrix algebra expressions), and a large-scale multi-equation simulation facility. The nonlinear estimation routines, including 3SLS, SUR and FIML, were likely the first to effectively utilize advanced Newton's method techniques (secant methods, esp. BFGS), which gave very fast convergence and accurate standard errors for the coefficients. Other methods supported include regression with ARMA errors, exponential smoothing, Shiller and Almon lags with AR corrections, rational distributed lags, logit, probit, and principal components. From the outset, SORITEC combined batch and interactive (command-line) availability with an econometric 4GL. Do loops and procedures can be opened in the interactive version, and closed on a subsequent line even in interactive mode. Procedures and macros can be stored on SORITEC databases.

STAMP

URL: www.stamp-software.com and www.oxmetrics.net

The authors of STAMP are Siem Jan Koopman, Andrew C. Harvey, Jurgen A. Doornik and Neil Shephard. It is a package designed to model and forecast time series, based on structural time series models. These models use advanced techniques, such as Kalman filtering, but are set up so as to be easy to use – at the most basic level all that is required is some appreciation of the concepts of trend, seasonal and irregular. The hard work is done by the program, leaving the user free to concentrate on formulating models, then using them to make forecasts.

Structural time series modelling can be applied to a variety of problems in time series. Macro-economic time series like gross national production, inflation and consumption can be handled effectively, but also financial time series, like interest rates and stock market volatility, can be modeled using STAMP. STAMP is also used for modelling and forecasting time series in medicine, biology, engineering, marketing and in many other areas.

A.C. Harvey (1989), *Forecasting, Structural Time Series Models and the Kalman Filter*, Cambridge University Press, Cambridge.

J. Durbin and S.J. Koopman (2001), *Time Series Analysis by State Space Methods*, Oxford University Press, Oxford.

S.J. Koopman, A.C. Harvey, J.A. Doornik and N. Shephard (1999), *Structural Time Series Analysis, Modelling, and Prediction using STAMP*, 2nd Ed., Timberlake Consultants Press, London.

STATA

URL: www.stata.com

Stata was developed in C and first released in 1985. Originally designed by William Gould, it is now developed by a team of people. Originally implemented as a DOS program, Stata is now available for Windows, Macintosh, and Unix, including Linux on a variety of hardware platforms. The first Unix port was to Interactive 386/ix in 1989 with 32 and 64-bit Unix ports to Sun, HP, DEC, Iris, Convex, and Linux following. Stata was ported to Macintosh in 1992 and to MS Windows in 1994.

Stata was designed as a complete system for data management, graphics, statistics. In 1985 that meant file management facilities, match-merging, variable management, summary statistics, OLS, 2SLS, and graphics, with modern publication-quality graphics added later. By the end of 1986, the first limited dependent variable estimators had been added – logit and probit – along with ANOVA and factor analysis. Limited dependent variables continued to be a focus with multinomial and conditional logit, Heckman selection models for continuous and binary data, choice models, Poisson regression, tobit, zero-inflated inflated count models, bivariate probit, and other models added later. Some of the first commercially available survival models, including Cox proportional hazards and parametric models, were implemented in 1988. Survival analysis expanded to include many nonparametric methods, more parametric families, individual and group frailty (random effects), censoring, and truncation. During 1991 and 1992 bootstrapping was introduced along with quantile regression, and proper treatment of survey sampling weights. Later developments added stratification and clustering and extended survey coverage to most estimators, including survival analysis and limited dependent variables. Additions in 1993 and 1994 included maximum-likelihood estimation of user-programmed likelihoods, nonlinear least squares, linear constraints, matrix programming facilities, generalized linear models (GLM), and importantly fixed- and random-effects estimators for linear panel-data models. Panel-data methods expanded to include Generalized Estimating Equations (GEE), Hausman-Taylor, random-effects frontier models, fixed- and random-effects with endogenous regressors or autocorrelated disturbances, fixed- and random-effects binary and count-data models, random-effects interval regression (including tobit), and the Arellano-Bond estimator for dynamic panel data. Recently time-series features were expanded to include time-series operators, ARIMA and ARMAX, GARCH (with many variants), a complete toolkit for estimating and analyzing VARS and SVARS and their IRFs, several smoothers, and a host of tests. Other features recently added include nested logit, marginal effects and elasticities for virtually all models, and HAC variance estimates for many models.

Possibly the most important addition occurred in April 1986 when programming features were expanded to include the ability for users to add new commands whose syntax and behavior appeared as though they were inbuilt commands. This spurred formation of an active community of Stata users and contributors who have extended Stata's capabilities by writing and sharing program files. To provide a forum for sharing programs, the Stata Technical Bulletin (STB) began publication in April 1991. The Bulletin later transformed into the Stata Journal, a refereed quarterly publication "about statistics, data analysis, teaching methods, and the use of Stata's language." In the Fall of 1994 an independent mail list, Statalist, began operation out of Harvard and has since grown to over 1,500 users who share Stata and statistics questions, answers and programs through the list. The "open system" capability was further enhanced in the Fall of 1998 when Stata became web aware, meaning it could locate, download, and install user written commands or datasets from either shared program archives or individual author websites.

C.F. Baum, M.E. Schaffer and S. Stillman (2003), Instrumental variables and GMM: Estimation and testing, *Stata Journal* **3**(1), 1–31.

S.O. Becker and A. Ichino (2002), Estimation of average treatment effects based on propensity scores, *Stata Journal* **2**(4), 358–377.

M. Cleves, W. Gould and R. Gutierrez (2002), *An Introduction to Survival Analysis Using Stata*, Stata Press, College Station, TX.

S.B. Cohen (1997), An evaluation of alternative PC-based software packages developed for the analysis of complex survey data, *The American Statistician* **51**(3), 285–293.

A. Deaton (1998), *The Analysis of Household Surveys*, Johns Hopkins University Press.

W.W. Gould (2001), Statistical software certification, *Stata Journal* **1**(1), 29–50.

W. Gould and W. Sribney (1999), *Maximum Likelihood Estimation with Stata*, Stata Press, College Station, TX.

L.C. Hamilton (2002), *Statistics with Stata*, Duxbury Press, New York.

J.W. Hardin (2002), Robust Murphy-Topel, *Stata Journal* **2**(3), 253–266.

J.W. Hardin and J.M. Hilbe (2003), *Generalized Estimating Equations*, Chapman and Hall/CRC, New York.

J.W. Hardin and J.M. Hilbe (2001), *Generalized Linear Models and Extensions*, Stata Press, College Station, TX.

F.E. Harrell and R. Goldstein (1997), A survey of microcomputer survival analysis software: the need for an integrated framework, *The American Statistician* **51**(4), 360–373.

J.H. Horton and S.R. Lipsitz (1999), Review of software to fit generalized estimating equation regression models, *The American Statistician* **53**(2), 160–169.

S. Kolenikov (2001), Review of Stata 7, *Journal of Applied Econometrics* **16**(5), 637–646.

J.S. Long and J. Freese (2001), *Regression Models for Categorical Dependent Variables using Stata*, Stata Press, College Station, Texas.

J.S. Long and L.H. Ervin (2000), Using heteroscedasticity consistent standard errors in the linear regression model, *The American Statistician* **54**(3), 217–224.

M.J. Moreira and B.P. Poi (2003), Implementing tests with correct size in the simultaneous equations model, *Stata Journal* **3**(1), 57–70.

R.A. Oster (2002), An examination of statistical software packages for categorical data analysis using exact methods, *The American Statistician* **56**(3), 235–246.

S. Rabe-Heskith and B. Everitt (2000), *A Handbook of Statistical Analyses using Stata*, second Ed., Chapman & Hall/CRC, New York.

StataCorp (2003), *Stata Reference Manuals: Release 8* **1-4**, Stata Press, College Station, TX.

StataCorp (2003), *Getting Started with Stata for Windows (for Macintosh) (for Unix): Release 8*, Stata Press, College Station, TX.

StataCorp (2003), *Stata Cross Sectional Time-Series Reference Manual: Release 8*, Stata Press, College Station, TX.

StataCorp (2003), *Stata Cluster Analysis Reference Manual: Release 8*, Stata Press, College Station, TX.

StataCorp (2003), *Stata Graphics Reference Manual: Release 8*, Stata Press, College Station, TX.

StataCorp (2003), *Stata Programming Reference Manual: Release 8*, Stata Press, College Station, TX.

StataCorp (2003), *Stata Survey Data Reference Manual: Release 8*, Stata Press, College Station, TX.

StataCorp (2003), *Stata Survival Analysis and Epidemiological Tables Reference Manual: Release 8*, Stata Press, College Station, TX.

StataCorp (2003), *Stata Time-Series Reference Manual: Release 8*, Stata Press, College Station, TX.

StataCorp (2003), *Stata User's Guide: Release 8*, Stata Press, College Station, TX.

TROLL

URL: www.intex.com/troll (in Europe: www.hendyplan.com)

TROLL (Timeshared Reactive OnLine Laboratory) exists in two versions: Mainframe and Portable. Development of Mainframe TROLL began at MIT in 1966 under the guidance of Edwin Kuh, with Mark Eisner as principle designer; the first version was finished in 1971. The system was written in AED, with portions in assembler language and FORTRAN. It was designed as an interactive system with an algebraic modeling language, free-format English-like commands with prompts, online help, email, and a hierarchical filesystem for online storage of numeric data (timeseries, constants, vectors), models, and "macro" programs. Symbolic differentiation improved performance on nonlinear problems. In 1971, TROLL was running on an IBM System 360 Model 67 under CP-67 (precursor to VM); address space was 24-bit (16 MB), and a typical user allocation was 440K. TROLL ran on many generations of IBM mainframes, and in the mid-1970's Mark Gelfand ported it to other mainframe operating systems such as CMS (under VM), MVS/TSO and MTS. TROLL was hosted by the National Bureau of Economic Research from 1972 through 1977, at which point it returned to MIT. TROLL served as a testbed for new algorithms, including the GREMLIN system-estimation package, the NL2SOL nonlinear least-squares optimizer, Belsley-Kuh-Welsch regression diagnostics, and LIMO eigenanalysis to study the dynamics of simulation models. Large model solution capabilities were provided using Newton-Raphson and sparse-matrix technology.

Peter Hollinger has been chief developer since 1979. In 1987, MIT licensed to Intex Solutions the exclusive right to develop and distribute TROLL. Intex released the final update to Mainframe TROLL, Version 14.1, in 1991. At that time a totally new "Portable" TROLL began to be developed in order to provide the capabilities of Mainframe TROLL in a more flexible package with no size limitations. Portable TROLL is written in 'C' and supports a variety of datatypes (numeric, string, date, boolean) and shapes (scalar, timeseries, multi-dimensional arrays, and timeseries-of-arrays); time dimensions may have calendar-based periodicities such as hourly, daily, business-daily or weekly. It has been ported to: PCs running DOS, OS/2, SCO UNIX, Windows (3.x, 95, 98, ME, NT, 2000, XP) and Linux; Cray X-MP running UNICOS; IBM RS/6000 running AIX; PA-RISC running HP-UX; Sun Sparc running Solaris 1.x and 2.x; and DEC Alpha running Tru64. A GUI front-end is available, developed by Hendyplan.

A particular feature of TROLL is its ability to simulate large macroeconometric models, including forward-looking "rational expectations" models with simultaneity over time; maximum model size ranges upwards of 3000 equations times 200 periods, using a Stacked-Time Newton algorithm. Simulations can be fully simultaneous or equation-by-equation, dynamic, static or periodically constrained. Estimation methods include linear and nonlinear least-squares, distributed lags, ARMA corrections, two-stage least squares, and principle components. TROLL also provides optimization (including user-written functions), and a variety of time series methods (Kalman filtering with maximum likelihood estimation of hyperparameters; estimation, testing and forecasting of cointegrated systems; estimation, testing, and forecasting of VAR systems).

D.A. Belsley (1974), Estimation of systems of simultaneous equations, and computational specification of GREMLIN, *Annals of Economic and Social Measurement* **3**, 551–614.

D.A. Belsley and E. Kuh, eds (1986), *Model Reliability*, MIT Press, Cambridge, MA.

D.A. Belsley, E. Kuh and R.E. Welsch (1980), *Regression Diagnostics*, Wiley-Interscience, New York.

D.A. Belsley (1991), *Conditioning Diagnostics*, Wiley, New York.

J.E.J. Dennis, D.M. Gay and R.E. Welsch (1981), An Adaptive Nonlinear Least-Squares Algorithm, *ACM Transactions on Mathematical Software* **7**, 348–368.

M. Eisner (1972), TROLL/1 - an interactive computer system for econometric research, *Annals of Economic and Social Measurement* **1**, 95–96.

M. Eisner and R.S. Pindyck (1973), A generalized approach to estimation as implemented in the TROLL/1 system, *Annals of Economic and Social Measurement* **2**, 29–51.

A. Harless (2003), *Portable TROLL User's Guide for Release 1.2*, Intex Solutions, Inc., Needham, MA.

P. Hollinger (1996), The Stacked-Time Simulator in TROLL: A Robust Algorithm for Solving Forward-Looking Models, presented at the *Second International Conference on Computing in Economics and Finance, Geneva, Switzerland, 26–28 June 1996*, Intex Solutions, Inc., Needham, MA.

P. Hollinger (2000), Beyond Newton: Robust Methods for Large Nonlinear Models in TROLL, presented at the *Sixth International Conference on Computing in Economics and Finance, Barcelona, Catalonia, Spain, 6–8 July 2000*, Intex Solutions, Inc., Needham, MA.

P. Hollinger and L. Spivakovsky (1996), *Portable TROLL Reference Manual for Release 1.0*, Intex Solutions, Inc., Needham, MA.

M. Juillard, D. Laxton, P. McAdam and H. Pioro (1998), An Algorithm Competition: First-Order Iterations Versus Newton-Based Techniques, *Journal of Economic Dynamics and Control* **22**(8-9), 1291–1318.

E. Kuh (1972), Some Notes on the Research Program at the NBER Computer Research Center for Economics and Management Science, *Annals of Economic and Social Measurement* **1**(2), 233–236.

E. Kuh, J. Neese and P. Hollinger (1985), *Structural Sensitivity in Econometric Models*, John Wiley & Sons, New York.

J. Kirsch and W. Zafft (1972), *TROLL/1 User's Guide*, National Bureau of Economic Research, New York.

J. Kirsch, ed. (1983), *TROLL Reference Manual 3rd Edition*, Massachusetts Institute of Technology, Cambridge, MA.

T. Lane, ed. (1979), *TROLL Reference Manual* (*Standard System*), 2nd Ed., MIT Center for Computational Research in Economics and Management Science, MIT Information Processing Services, Cambridge, MA.

D. Laxton, P. Isard, H. Faruqee, E. Prasad and B. Turtelboom (1998), *MULTIMOD Mark III: The Core Dynamic and Steady-State Models,* Occasional Paper 164, International Monetary Fund, Washington, DC. (http://www.imf.org/external/pubs/ft/op/op164/index.htm).

W. Zafft, G. Solomon and R. Perron (1973–1976), *TROLL Reference Manual, in installments*, National Bureau of Economic Research, New York.

TSP

URL: www.tspintl.com

TSP's development was begun at MIT in 1965–1966 and at UC Berkeley in 1967–1969 by Robert E. Hall, in association with Robert Gordon, Charles Bischoff, and Richard Sutch, and later at Princeton with Ray Fair and J. Phillip Cooper. The early versions featured essentially linear, single equation techniques, but in the late 1960s nonlinear single equation techniques were added by Hall based upon an analytic derivative algorithm that is still the basis of all the nonlinear estimation in the program. Beginning in 1970, at Harvard and continuing during 1977-1985 in Palo Alto, Bronwyn Hall became the principal developer, assisted by Rebecca Schnake, Sean Becketti, and Clint Cummins. During this period TSP took its present form. Bronwyn Hall added the non-linear estimators for two and three stage least squares, SURE, and FIML. Sean Becketti programmed the Box-Jenkins routines and incorporated the Beech-MacKinnon AR(1) algorithm. Rebecca Schnake created the first interactive version of the program for IBM 370 series computers. Post 1977, TSP was ported to a variety of mainframe and minicomputers, including those of Honeywell, Univac, DEC, ICL, Burroughs, and Siemens. In 1985, TSP began to be ported to the IBM PC. In 1985, Clint Cummins became the principal developer and has been responsible for the incorporation of a wide variety of procedures, including GMM, Probit, Logit, Poisson, Negbin, and the general purpose maximum likelihood routine, MaxLik. Most recently, TSP has been ported to the Apple Macintosh and a native version for MAC OS version X, is expected to be released in June 2003.

TSP is operated using free-format commands and offers all the standard econometric estimation methods, including ordinary least squares, two and three stage least squares, GMM, LIML, FIML, ARIMA, Kalman filter, ARCH and other time series techniques. It also provides a "roll-your-own" maximum likelihood estimator, where the likelihood function can be evaluated either by a single equation or using a user-programmed procedure. It provides variety of diagnostic and testing facilities, including a procedure to test nonlinear hypotheses. Recently TSP has joined the Ox-metrics family of packages, using GiveWin as an interactive Windows shell; in this implementation it can be run either as a traditional batch program or interactively. TSP also incorporates programming features, including support for matrix algebra and user-written procedures, that permit users to use it for the development of new econometric techniques.

E.R. Berndt, B.H. Hall, R.E. Hall and J.A. Hausman (1974), Estimation and Inference in Nonlinear Structural Models, *Annals of Economic and Social Measurement* **3**, 653–665.

C. Calzolari and L. Panattoni (1988), Alternate Estimators of FIML Covariance Matrix: A Monte Carlo Study, *Econometrica* **56**, 701–714.

C. Cummins and B.H. Hall (1986), *Time Series Processor Version 4.0/4.1 Programmer's Manual*, TSP International, Stanford, CA.

B.H. Hall (1987), The Relationship between Firm Size and Firm Growth in the U.S. Manufacturing Sector, *Journal of Industrial Economics* **36**, 583–606.

B.H. Hall and C. Cummins (2000), *TSP Version 4.5 Reference Manual*, TSP International, Palo Alto, CA.

B.H. Hall and C. Cummins (2000), *TSP Version 4.5 User's Manual*, TSP International, Palo Alto, CA.

R.E. Hall (July, 1967), Polynomial Distributed Lags, *Econometrics Working Paper, No. 7*, Department of Economics, MIT.

J.A. Hausman, B.H. Hall and Z. Griliches (1984), Econometric Models for Count Data with an Application to the Patents-R&D Relationship, *Econometrica* **52**, 909–938.

D.W. Jorgenson and J.-J. Laffont (1974), Efficient Estimation of Nonlinear Simultaneous Equations with Additive Disturbances, *Annals of Economic and Social Measurement* **4**, 615–640.

WinSolve

URL: www.econ.surrey.ac.uk/winsolve/

The principal author is Richard G. Pierse. WinSolve arose from a 1994 commission from the UK Economic and Social Research Council to create a modern model solution program to replace existing software such as the author's own NIMODEL. It was written in C++ for the IBM PC although a version for Unix systems also exists.

WinSolve is a model solution package for Windows that accepts models defined in a simple algebraic language. It can read and write data in a wide variety of formats including those of the major econometrics packages. It offers a range of solution methods for both backward-looking and rational-expectations models, including traditional first order methods such as Gauss-Seidel, (stacked-) Newton methods (using automatic analytic derivatives) and other specialised methods such as parameterised expectations. In addition, it offers the facility for the user to define new solution methods using a flexible language. WinSolve has flexible facilities for stochastic simulation and optimal control as well as for model linearisation. Blanchard-Kahn solution methods are also available for linear models.

R.G. Pierse (2000), WinSolve Version 3: An Introductory Guide, available at URL: http://www.econ.surrey.ac.uk/winsolve/.

WYSEA

The author of Wysea is Clifford R. Wymer. Wysea is a set of programs for the estimation, dynamic analysis, forecasting and simulation of difference or differential equation systems. Development began in 1965 at the London School of Economics using the Atlas computer of the UK Atomic Energy Research Establishment, Harwell. This Atlas was one of only three ever built, the other two being installed in the University of London and University of Manchester. The programs were initially written in Hartran (Harwell's version of Fortran, in some ways closer to Fortran 95 than earlier versions) but were later modified to standard Fortran. The programs were installed on an ICL computer which replaced the Atlas, IBM 360, 370, 3090 and VAX computers at a number of universities and other organizations, and other mainframes such as a CDC Cyber of CSIRO, Canberra, and a Burroughs B7800 at the International Monetary Fund. Development on mainframes continued until about 1985 but then was switched to PCs and IBM workstations such as RS6000. The current versions are written in Fujitsu-Lahey Fortran 95 for PC's and IBM Fortran 95 for workstations such as IBM 43P. String handling procedures are written in C and an interface for all programs is in Java; the suite of programs runs on Windows, AIX and Linux platforms.

The aim of the programs throughout was to allow, as directly as possible, the estimation of models derived from economic theory, hypothesis testing within these models, and their use for dynamic analysis, simulation and forecasting. In general, such models will be heavily over-identified. The earliest program, Simul, was developed at the London School of Economics in 1965/66 for 2SLS, 3SLS and FIML estimation of linear difference equation models but with special features to allow estimation of differential equation systems. In 1967/68 Resimul provided FIML estimates of linear models with non-linear within and across equation constraints on the parameters and Discon provided similar estimates for the exact discrete model equivalent to a differential equation system. A feature introduced in Resimul but then used in all programs is an algorithm which allows the true partial derivative (not a numerical approximation) to be calculated from function specifications without the need for symbolic partial differentiation. Subsequent programs such as Contines

(1968) calculated the eigenvalues (with asymptotic standard errors) of discrete or continuous systems systems, together with a sensitivity analysis of the eigenvalues, and Predic for forecasting, again with (dynamic or static) asymptotic standard errors. Programs for the estimation, simulation and forecasting of non-linear difference and differential equation systems (Asimul and Apredic) were developed in 1973/74 and Escona in 1990. The non-linear differential equation programs allow the estimation, simulation or forecasting of models subject to boundary point conditions and, if required, inequality constraints on control variables and thus can handle systems which incorporate targeting, present value, rational expectations, optimal control and game theory specifications.

Throughout development of the programs in Wysea, particular attention has been given to numerical precision within the whole system; thus some algorithms are used for precision rather than speed. Most real number calculations are in real(8) but in order to maintain precision at this level some crucial operations are in real(16). In general, modified second order Newton or Generic algorithms are used for maximisation and this is aided by the partial differentiation procedure mentioned above.

C.R. Wymer (1972), Econometric estimation of stochastic differential equation systems, *Econometrica* **40**, 565–578, [Reprinted in *Statistical Inference in Continuous Time Economic Models*, A.R. Bergstrom, ed., North-Holland, 1975.]

C.R. Wymer (1987), Sensitivity analysis of economic policy presented at a *Seminar on The Application of Sensitivity Analysis to the Evaluation of Financial Policies, World Bank, Washington, DC., 1982*; published in: *Essays in Memory of Vittorio Marrama*, Giancarlo Gandolfo and Ferraccio Marzano, eds, Guiffre, pp. 953–965.

C.R. Wymer (1993), Continuous time models in macro-economics - specification and estimation, presented at the *SSRC – Ford Foundation Conference on Macro-economic Policy and Adjustment in Open Economies, Ware, England, 1976*; published with an additional Section, in: *Continuous Time Econometrics: Theory and Application*, Giancarlo Gandolfo, ed., Chapman and Hall, London, pp. 35–79.

C.R. Wymer (1993), Estimation of Non-Linear Differential Equation Systems presented at the *International Symposium on Economic Modelling, University of Urbino, Italy, 23–25 July*; published in: *Models, Methods and Applications of Econometrics*, P.C.B. Phillips, ed., Blackwell, Oxford, pp. 91–114.

A.R. Bergstrom, K.B. Nowman and C.R. Wymer (1992), Gaussian estimation of a second order continuous time macroeconometric model of the United Kingdom, *Economic Modelling*, 313–351.

C.R. Wymer (1996), The role of continuous time disequilibrium models in macro-economics presented at the *SEMECON Conference on Dynamic Disequilibrium Modelling, University of Munich, Germany, 30 August–3 September 1993*; published in: *Dynamic Disequilibrium Modelling*, W.A. Barnett, G. Gandolfo and C. Hillinger, eds, Cambridge University Press, Cambridge, pp. 67–123.

C.R. Wymer (1997), Structural non-linear continuous time models in econometrics, *Macro-Economic Dynamics* **1**, Cambridge University Press, 518–548.

C.R. Wymer, *WYSEA User Guide and Reference.*

3. Econometric programming libraries

The software packages described in this section of the Compendium are essentially library tools that can be used in conjunction with computer programming languages in order to produce an executable econometric software package. They generally require the use of one of the standard programming languages, such as C/C+, Visual Basic, or some other similar development language.

The concept of a "library" of routines actually originates in the 1950s, at the beginning of the era of stored program computers. Those who began programming for the EDSAC, EDVAC, and other early machines of this type at the Universities of Cambridge, Pennsylvania and elsewhere quickly realized that once a certain set of fundamental operations had been programmed that could be utilized as components of some other package, it made sense to document these routines and make them generally available. Originally, such libraries took the form of decks of punched cards, or rolls of paper tape, but as online storage facilities came into being, these collections of standard routines, "libraries" that is, began to be made available online at individual computing centers. Over time, many have become generally distributed and widely used and a number are quite well known to programmers generally, as described in the papers by Nerlove and Stokes in this volume.

The libraries described here are of course specifically econometric in orientation and, if anything, represent a new development in econometric software. In past years, program libraries were "statically" linked, indicating that the included routines were linked into, or combined with, an overall program at the time of its original production. Today, in the context of Windows and other operating systems, "dynamic" linking has become common: routines that are dynamically linked are linked with a given program at the time that one or more users actually execute that program. Among the implications of this process is that a modern computer could have a number of dynamically linkable routines available, ready for selection at a moment's notice. Such routines could perform standard operations, or operations that might be performed only occasionally.

BACC

URL: www.cirano.qc.ca/bacc

The principal authors of BACC (Bayesian Analysis, Computation, and Communication) are John Geweke and William McCausland. A continuing goal of the BACC project is to make tools for Bayesian econometrics as accessible to practitioners as are tools for classical econometrics. BACC orginated in 1996 as stand-alone software for Unix and DOS, developed by John Geweke and Siddharta Chib. Users executed commands for posterior simulation and related tasks at the Unix or DOS command line. These commands operated on special input and control files provided by the user, and generated output files, including posterior simulation files. By 1998, BACC supported univariate regression (where residuals are normal, autoregressive or finite mixtures of normals), seemingly unrelated regressions, probit regression and finite state Markov chains. In 1999, BACC was reworked as a dynamically linked (or shared object) library, enabling the use of the software within Gauss for Unix. Since then, BACC has expanded its support to several new mathematical applications (Matlab, SPlus, and R) and the Windows and Linux operating systems. Several models have been added, and further model development is a priority.

The BACC software provides its users with tools for Bayesian Analysis, Computation and Communications. It implements these tools as extensions to popular mathematical applications such as Matlab, S-PLUS, R, and Gauss, running under Windows, Linux or Unix. From the user's perspective, there is a seamless integration of special-purpose BACC commands for posterior simulation and related tasks with powerful built-in commands for matrix computation, graphics, program ow control, and I/O. Nineteen models are currently available, and many others are planned. BACC is designed to be extendible, not only by the developers of BACC, but also by others who wish to implement their own models and thus make them available to BACC users.

J. Geweke (1999), Using Simulation Methods for Bayesian Econometric Models: Inference, *Development, and Communication, Econometric Reviews* **18**, 1–126.

J. Geweke and W. McCausland (2000), Embedding Bayesian Tools in Mathematical Software, *Proceedings of the International Society for Bayesian Analysis (ISBA): 165–173*, 1.

G. Koop (1999), Bayesian Analysis, Computation and Communication Software, *Journal of Applied Econometrics* **14**, 677–689.

W. McCausland (forthcoming) Using the BACC Software for Bayesian Inference, *Journal of Computational Economics* **2**.

MLE++

URL: www.magma.ca/~cahill/

MLE++ is a C++ class library for maximum likelihood estimation developed by Ian Cahill. To be used it requires a specific C++ compiler. The first version was completed in 1997 for the Borland C++ Builder product, which was supplied with each unit purchased. The library was ported to be compatible with the Microsoft Visual C++ 6.0 compiler in 2001, and the Borland version was discontinued. A new version is currently being developed, and should be released within a year. It will run on Microsoft Visual C++ Net.

MLE++ is designed as a tool for general maximum likelihood estimation, and can be applied to the estimation of many nonlinear models. As a class library it extends the C++ language by providing vectors and matrices as data types, and classes that manage data files and support the use of named variables in estimation routines. To develop a new model estimation routine, the user derives a class from an abstract base called Model. A number of algorithms for maximization without constraints are provided as part of the class Model. These can be called to maximize the log-likelihood function, as specified by a user for a particular model. Algorithms for numerical gradients are also provided, and will be called if the user does not specify the analytical gradients. There are a number of choices for methods to calculate the covariance matrix.

MLE++ also includes 25 packaged nonlinear models used on cross-sectional data. The models are implemented using the general maximum likelihood estimation tools in order to serve a dual purpose: they are practical model estimation routines for popular models, and they are also documented examples showing how to implement new models. The packaged models include binary logit and probit, Tobit models and their generalizations, truncated regression, sample selection, treatment effects, endogenous switching regression, bivariate probit, multinomial logit, conditional logit, poisson regression, Weibull and exponential survival models (including heterogeneity and time-varying covariates), the lognormal survival model, the loglogistic survival model (including time-varying covariates), and Meyer's semiparametric survival model (including time-varying covariates and heterogeneity).

Data can be imported from ASCII files in various forms, and written to an ASCII file with space delimiters.

I.G. Cahill (2001), *MLE++™ Maximum Likelihood Estimation in C++ User's Manual, Version 2.0*, Cahill Software.

I.G. Cahill (2001), *MLE++™ Maximum Likelihood Estimation in C++ With Microsoft Visual C++ 6.0, Version 2.0*, Cahill Software.

B.D. Meyer (1990). Unemployment Insurance and Unemployment Spells, *Econometrica* **58**, 757–782.

MODLER

URL: www.modler.com

MODLER is described in the section on Independent Econometric Software Packages and references are given there. However, in addition to the package itself, related library routines have been made available since the 1980s that permit access to MODLER facilities in the form of callable subroutines and functions. The original set of library routines was written in 1987 in C and Fortran by Len Schmirl, then at Townsend Greenspan and Company, for the purpose of linking other Townsend Greenspan software to MODLER data banks. Subsequently, these routines were collected into libraries that have since been made available generally to MODLER users and others, including Haver Analytics, Data Resources and other data vendors, who have used the Fortran library in particular to create and maintain MODLER data banks that they have distributed. Another example is the use of the Fortran library by economists at United Bank of Switzerland (UBS) in London (then Phillips and Drew) to create small programs, called FITOUT and FITIN, to permit data to be transferred between MODLER and MicroFit. A variety of such applications have been developed during the past 20 years.

This facility was extended in 1996, with the first release of the Windows version of MODLER. By design, most MODLER facilities are contained in a Dynamic Link Library (DLL) that is called from a Visual Basic "front end." As a consequence, these facilities can also be accessed from other Windows programs resident on the same machine – or, in principle, another machine connected via a network. To date, MODLER users who have taken advantage of this capability have tended to make use of it simply to read and write MODLER data banks. In the future, much more could be done.

4. Econometric and mathematical programming languages

The software packages described in this section of the Compendium provide the user with the capability to program mathematical and statistical operations that are econometric in nature. Some of these packages have been created specifically for use by economists and econometricians. Others have a more general application that includes use by economists and econometricians. These programming languages and their use are also described, as a type, in the articles by Herbert, Nerlove, and Stokes elsewhere in this volume.

Econometric programming languages can be used in order to create specific econometric software packages that perform particular operations or types of operations. The next section of this compendium provides a number of examples of such packages, created using the software described in this section. These languages can also be used individually by economists and econometricians to create locally developed packages used only by the author of that package, or perhaps also by colleagues.

In all cases, the packages described in this section are themselves written in a standard programming language (or languages) and operate using a standard computer operating system. Examples of the former are C/C+, FORTRAN, Pascal, and Visual Basic. Examples of the latter are Linux, Windows, and Unix.

GAUSS

URL: www.aptech.com

Lee Edlefsen and Sam Jones designed the GAUSS matrix programming language in the early to mid 1980's. GAUSS became generally available in June 1985. Currently GAUSS is available on Windows, Linux, Solaris, HPUX and AIX. The power of GAUSS can also be added to applications written in C, C++, Java or other development environments that support the C language API through the GAUSS Engine, a dynamically linked library for compiling and executing GAUSS programs from another application. Data can be passed back and forth between the GAUSS Engine workspace and the application.

GAUSS is a full featured matrix programming language with emphasis on statistical and mathematical applications. In addition to the language, Aptech Systems distributes applications written in GAUSS. The most popular applications are MAXLIK (Maximum Likelihood) and CML (Constrained Maximum Likelihood) for the estimation and inference of statistical models.

LINDO/LINGO

URL: www.lindo.com

The principal authors of LINDO/LINGO are Kevin Cunningham and Linus Schrage. LINDO was originally written in FORTRAN for the DEC 20 computer in 1977. When a Fortran compiler became available on the IBM PC in 1982, LINDO was ported to the IBM PC. The extensive matrix and set handling capabilities of LINGO were added in 1987. The latest versions are written in C/C++ and run mainly on Windows, Linux, and Solaris operating systems.

LINGO is essentially a linear, quadratic, integer, and global solver for large scale optimization problems. It consists of a modeling language front end that is sometimes used for solving econometric and statistical problems with nonstandard objectives. These include problems with minimum average absolute deviation regression, maximum absolute regression, and constrained regression. Some special features of LINGO include: a) a recently added global optimization capability that is of particular interest when the criterion is nonconvex in the parameters, for example, as in some maximum likelihood estimation problems; b) a quasi-random number generation feature for generating low discrepancy multi-dimensional uniform random numbers. Many of the features of LINGO are also available in spreadsheet add-in solver called What'sBest. The underlying solver engine is callable directly from programs written in C/C++, Visual Basic, Fortran, Matlab, Delphi/Pascal, Ox, and Java.

L. Schrage (2003), *Optimization Modeling with LINGO*, LINDO Systems Press, Chicago.

OX

URL: www.nuff.ox.ac.uk/Users/Doornik/ and www.oxmetrics.net

Ox is written by Jurgen Doornik. Development of Ox started in April 1994, based on an earlier failed attempt called ECL. The first release was in 1996, when it was available on its own, but also given as a add-on to PcGive. The object-oriented features of Ox were modelled on C++. A major design aim for Ox was to avoid the complexity of C++, see Doornik (2002). As a consequence, several aspects are more like Java and C#, which both did not exist yet at the time (although the Java project had already started).

Ox is an object-oriented matrix programming system. At its core is a powerful matrix language, which is complemented by a comprehensive statistical library. Among the special features of Ox are its speed, well-designed syntax and editor, and graphical facilities. Ox can read and write many data formats, including spreadsheets and GiveWin files; Ox can run many Gauss? programs directly; if necessary, existing C or FORTRAN code can be added to Ox in the form of dynamic link libraries (see, e.g. SsfPack, Koopman, Shephard and Doornik, 1999); there is sufficient flexibility in the Ox system to allow it to be fully integrated in applications requiring an econometric or statistical engine; Ox is available on Windows, Linux, and several Unix platforms.

There are many functions integral to Ox, including numerical optimization (unconstrained, quadratic programming and constrained maximization) and differentiation, solving non-linear equations, probability (density, quantile, cumulative density and random generation of many probability functions), ARMA, econometrics (e.g. VAR and cointegration), and Monte Carlo simulation. Many additional packages are available for downloading. Some of these are comprehensive econometric systems, which can also be used interactively.

Ox comes in two versions: Ox Professional and Ox Console. Ox Professional interfaces with GiveWin for its graphical output, and allows for several packages to be run interactively via GiveWin through the OxPack module. Ox Console lacks the interfaces of GiveWin, and instead is supplied with the freely available OxEdit text-editor. Ox Console is freely available for academic research and teaching.

F. Cribari-Neto and S.G. Zarkos (2003), Econometric and statistical computing using Ox, *Computational Economics* **21**, 277–295.

J.A. Doornik (2001), *Object-Oriented Matrix Programming using Ox*, 4th Ed., Timberlake Consultants Press, London.

J.A. Doornik (2002), Object-oriented programming in econometrics and statistics using Ox: A comparison with C++, Java and C#, in: *Programming Languages and Systems in Computational Economics and Finance*, S.S. Nielsen, ed., Kluwer Academic Publishers, Dordrecht.

J.A. Doornik, D.F. Hendry and N. Shephard (2002), Computationally-intensive econometrics using a distributed matrix-programming language, *Philosophical Transactions of the Royal Society of London* **Series A 360**, 1245–1266.

J.A. Doornik and M. Ooms (2001), *Introduction to Ox*, Timberlake Consultants Press, London.

5. Applications of econometric and mathematical programming languages

The software packages described in this section of the Compendium are each created as applications of and using a high level econometric or mathematical-statistical programming language of the type represented in the previous section of this compendium. Some of the applications packages described here have been created specifically for use by economists and econometricians. Others have a more general application that includes use by economists and econometricians. The programming languages these applications use are Gauss, Mathematica, or Ox.

Because the packages described are themselves written in the proprietary econometric and mathematical programming language of which they are applications, in each case they require either the developers' prior use of one of these programming languages or that the user's computer have a resident copy of one of these languages, or that both of these requirements are met.

ARFIMA package for Ox

URL: www.nuff.ox.ac.uk/Users/Doornik/ and www.oxmetrics.net

The Arfima package, developed by Jurgen Doornik and Marius Ooms, provides an Ox class for estimation and forecasting of ARFIMA(p,d,q) and ARMA(p,q) models. The available estimation methods are exact maximum likelihood (EML), modified profile likelihood (MPL), and nonlinear least squares (NLS). The mean of the process the ARFIMA process can be a (nonlinear) function of regressors. This makes it straightforward to model (nonlinear) deterministic trends and additive outliers. Missing observations can easily be estimated. Regressors can also be used to model the innovations of the process. This allows ARFIMA distributed lag modelling, an extension of autoregressive distributed lag (ARDL) modelling. Innovative outliers can be estimated. A simulation class is also provided.

J.A. Doornik and M. Ooms (1999), *A Package for Estimating, Forecasting and Simulating ARFIMA Models*, Mimeo, Nuffield College, Oxford.

J.A. Doornik and M. Ooms (2003), Computational Aspects of Maximum Likelihood Estimation of Autoregressive Fractionally Integrated Moving Average Models, *Computational Statistics and Data Analysis* **42**, 333–348.

M. Ooms and J.A. Doornik (1999), *Inference and Forecasting for Fractional Autoregressive Integrated Moving Average Models, with an application to US and UK*, inflation Econometric Institute Report EI-9947/A, Erasmus University Rotterdam.

CML – Constrained maximum likelihood

URL: www.aptech.com

CML was developed in 1995 in the GAUSS programming language by Ron Schoenberg at Aptech Systems. It implements the sequential quadratic programming method to solve the maximum likelihood problem with general constraints on parameters, linear and nonlinear equality, and linear and nonlinear inequality (Han, 1977; Jamshidian and Bentler, 1993).

Its features include the calculation of the approximate covariance matrix of the parameters for models with constraints on parameters (Hartmann and Hartwig, 1995), Bayesian weighted likelihood bootstrap (Newton and Raftery, 1994), likelihood profile and profile t trace (Bates and Watts, 1988), bootstrap, confidence limits by inversion of the Wald statistic, and confidence limits by inversion of the likelihood ratio statistic and quasi-maximum likelihood (QML) inference.

D.M. Bates and D.G. Watts (1988), *Nonlinear Regression Analysis and Its Applications*, John Wiley & Sons, New York.

S.P. Han (1977), A globally convergent method for nonlinear programming, *Journal of Optimization Theory and Applications* **22**, 297–309.

W.M. Hartmann and R.E. Hartwig (1995), *Computing the Moore-Penrose Inverse for the Covariance Matrix in Constrained Nonlinear Estimation*, SAS Institute, Inc., Cary, NC.

M. Jamshidian and P.M. Bentler (1993), A modified Newton method for constrained estimation in covariance structure analysis, *Computational Statistics & Data Analysis* **15**, 133–146.

M.A. Newton and A.E. Raftery (1994), Approximate Bayesian inference with the weighted likelihood bootstrap, *J.R. Statist. Soc. B* **56**, 3–48.

DPD for Ox

URL: www.nuff.ox.ac.uk/Users/Doornik/ and www.oxmetrics.net

The DPD (Dynamic Panel Data) package for Ox is developed by Manuel Arellano, Stephen Bond and Jurgen Doornik. DPD98, an earlier GAUSS package by Arellano and Bond, is still available at www.ifs.org.uk/econometindex.shtml .

DPD is for estimating dynamic panel data models, but also implements some of the static panel data estimators. DPD is designed to handle unbalanced panels. DPD is a class written in Ox, and is used by writing small Ox programs which create and use an object of the DPD class. The package can also be used interactively, which requires Ox Professional, together with GiveWin 2.00 or newer.

G@RCH

URL: www.core.ucl.ac.be/~laurent/ and www.nuff.ox.ac.uk/Users/Doornik/

G@RCH, by Sebastien Laurent and Jean-Philipe Peters, is an Ox package dedicated to the estimation and forecast of various univariate ARCH-type models in the conditional variance and an AR(FI)MA specification in the conditional mean. These ARCH processes include ARCH, GARCH, EGARCH, GJR, APARCH, IGARCH, FIGARCH, FIEGARCH, FIAPARCH and HYGARCH. These models can be estimated by Approximate (Quasi-) Maximum Likelihood under four assumptions:

normal, Student-t, GED or skewed Student-t errors. Moreover, "in-mean" ARCH-type models are available and explanatory variables can enter the mean and/or the variance equations. One-step-ahead (density) forecasts of both the conditional mean and variance are available as well as some miss-specification tests and several graphical features.

Two versions of G@RCH are available. The 'Light' version requires some experience with the program, its structure and the Ox language. The light version is aimed at advanced users, and those who only have access to Ox Console. The 'Full' version provides the same features as the light version, but also offers a user-friendly interface and some graphical features. This version needs to be launched from OxPack, and requires Ox Professional.

S. Laurent and J.P. Peters (2002), G@RCH 2.2: an Ox Package for Estimating and Forecasting Various ARCH Models, *Journal of Economic Surveys* **16**, 447–485.

GaussX

URL: www.econotron.com

The principal author of Gaussx is Jon Breslaw. The program, which began as an extension of TSP, was ported to the newly released matrix programming language Gauss in 1988. The interactive menu component was written first in Gauss, but then replaced with a C interface in 1994. The initial PC release was for DOS, and the first Windows release was in 1994. The programming language has always been open source, written in Gauss. It is currently available for Windows, Unix and Linux.

Gaussx incorporates a full featured set of professional, state of the art, econometric routines that run under Gauss. These tools can be used within Gaussx, both in research and in teaching. Alternatively, since the Gauss source is included, individual econometric routines can be extracted and integrated in stand-alone Gauss programs.

Gaussx is a command file driven program, where a command file is executed, the results displayed, and an output file created. This replicates the classic edit/execute/view sequence. It is an open source program, and thus allows the user to include her own code, written in Gauss, where necessary. The concept is similar to Latex: Latex lets you get stuff done in TEX, without knowing TEX; Gaussx lets you get stuff done in Gauss, without knowing Gauss. Both allow you to use the underlying language, when required. The concept provides a very shallow learning curve to leading edge econometric techniques. Thus, a wide range of estimation techniques, tests and models are available as preprogrammed modules, which can first be used either as is, or adapted and used as a template. The most recent developments include fractionally integrated GARCH, cluster analysis, robust estimation, Bayesian estimation, stochastic volatility model estimation, constrained optimization, trust regions, genetic algorithms, EM estimation, DBDC models, Markov switching models, feasible MNP, Gibbs sampling, wavelet denoising and Census X12 smoothing.

Since the entire Gauss language can be used within the Gaussx command files, the program provides a vehicle for econometricians to have a full range of econometric methods at their disposal, with the potential to customize any part of the program or models. Gaussx is used by academics, students and companies in over 40 countries. It is current (last revision 5.0)., and is distributed by Aptech Systems, Inc., who also distribute Gauss.

J. Breslaw (1991), Gaussx: An Integrated Environment for Gauss, *Computer Science in Economics and Management* **4**, 65–74.

D. Nitzsche (1993), Gaussx, *The Economic Journal* **103**(420), 1342–1345.

R.G. Pierse (1996), Gaussx: Version 3.4, *Journal of Applied Econometrics* **11**(6), 687–693.

J. Breslaw (2003), *Gaussx, Version 5.0*, Aptech Systems, Inc, WA.

mathStatica

URL: www.mathStatica.com

The principal authors of mathStatica are Colin Rose and Murray D. Smith. mathStatica is a software package – and add-on to Mathematica – that provides a sophisticated toolset specially designed for doing mathematical statistics. After more than 6 years in development, version 1.0 was released in March 2002, while version 1.2 was released in April 2003.

mathStatica was designed to solve the algebraic/symbolic problems that are of primary interest in mathematical statistics. It does so by building upon the symbolic computational power of Mathematica to create a sophisticated toolset specially designed for doing mathematical statistics. By contrast, packages like SPSS, Systat, SAS, Gauss, JMP and S-Plus provide a numerical/graphical toolset. They can illustrate, they can simulate, and they can find approximate numerical solutions to numerical problems, but they generally cannot find exact symbolic solutions to statistical problems. Features include: a complete suite of functions for manipulating PDFs, automated expectations, probability, density plotting, automated transformations (functions of RVs), symbolic MLE, numerical MLE, automated Pearson curve fitting, Johnson curve fitting, Gram-Charlier expansions, nonparametric kernel density estimation, moment conversion formulae, component-mix and parameter-mix distributions, stable distributions, copulae, random number generation, asymptotics, sufficient statistics, decision theory, order statistics, Fisher Information, h-statistics, k-statistics, polykays, and much more.

It runs on Mac (Classic and OS X), Windows, Linux, SPARC, Solaris, SGI, IBM RISC, DEC Alpha and HP-UX. It requires Mathematica 4 or later.

B.D. McCullough (December, 2002), A Review of Mathematical Statistics with Mathematica, *Journal of the American Statistical Association*, 1202–1203.

M. Quine (2003), Review: Mathematical Statistics with Mathematica, Economic Record, forthcoming

C. Rose and M.D. Smith (2002), mathStatica: Mathematical Statistics with Mathematica, in: *COMPSTAT 2002: Proceedings in Computational Statistics*, E. Härdle and B. Rönz, eds, Physica-Verlag, Heidelberg, pp. 437–442.

C. Rose and M.D. Smith (2002), *Mathematical Statistics with Mathematica*, Springer-Verlag, New York.

C. Rose and M.D. Smith (2003), *mathStatica, Proceedings of the American Statistical Association 2002*, Statistical Computing Section.

H.D. Vinod (2003), Review of MATHSTATICA, *Journal of Applied Econometrics* (August), 485–491.

MSVAR

URL: www.economics.ox.ac.uk/research/hendry/krolzig

MSVAR (Markov-Switching Vector Autoregressions) is an Ox package written by Hans-Martin Krolzig. MSVAR is designed for the econometric modelling of univariate and multiple time series subject to shifts in regime. It provides the statistical tools for the maximum likelihood estimation (EM algorithm) and evaluation of Markov-Switching Vector Autoregressions and Markov-Switching Vector Equilibrium Correction models as discussed in Krolzig (1997). A variety of model specifications regarding the type of regime switching (including Treshold models and Switching Regressions), the number of regimes, regime-dependence versus invariance of parameters etc. provides the necessary flexibility for empirical research. MSVAR will be of use to econometricians intending to construct and use models of the business cycle and other regime-switching phenomena.

MSVAR can be used by writing a small Ox program. As MSVAR derives from the Modelbase class, it allows the easy use and exchange with other Ox classes such as PcFiml. In conjunction with Ox professional, MSVAR can be used interactively via the user-friendly interface OxPack in combination with GiveWin 2 for data input and graphical and text output.

M.P. Clements and H.-M. Krolzig (2003), Business Cycle Asymmetries: Characterisation and Testing based on Markov-Switching Autoregressions, *Journal of Business and Economic Statistics* **21**, 196–211.

H.-M. Krolzig (1997), Markov-Switching Vector Autoregressions. Modelling, Statistical Inference and Application to Business Cycle Analysis, *Lecture Notes in Economics and Mathematical Systems* **454**, Springer, Berlin.

Time series modelling 3.2 (TSMod32)

URL: http://www.cf.ac.uk/carbs/econ/davidsonje/

Econometric software should ideally combine ease of use and an intuitive interface, with flexibility and user extendibility – requirements that can appear mutually incompatible. TSMod by James Davidson (earlier versions were known as LMMod for Long Memory Modelling) represents one attempt to get the best of both worlds. While TSMod is an Ox program, it runs as a stand-alone GUI application, started from an icon on the desktop and controlled entirely by menus and dialogs, with Ox running transparently in the background.

The program is platform-independent, running under Windows and Linux. In addition to Ox 3.3 Console, the software components needed are the Java Runtime Environment (JRE) and OxJapi, a port to Ox, by Christine Choirat and Rafaello Seri, of the Java Application Programming Interface due to Merten Joost. Graphics capabilities are supplied by GnuPlot, interfaced with Ox using GnuDraw, an extension of the OxDraw package by Charles Bos. All the required components are freeware, as is TSMod – to academic users.

TSMod32 estimates a range of time series models including ARIMA, ARFIMA, several ARCH/GARCH variants, and Markov-switching models. It offers full graphics capabilities, data manipulation, routine diagnostics, forecasting, and the ability to impose and test parameter restrictions. However, its star feature is the facility to code the equation to be estimated (including general dynamic specifications) as an Ox function. This allows nonlinear time series models such as bilinear, SETAR, ESTAR, etc. etc., to be handled very easily. The programming skills and effort called for are far less than would be required to write a free-standing Ox application from scratch. The user-defined equation can be combined with the built-in model features (e.g., have ARCH residuals, or exhibit Markov switching) to provide almost limitless flexibility in model specification.

Estimators include OLS, GMM, time domain MLE for Gaussian, Student-t and skewed-student disturbances, and Whittle estimation for ARFIMA models. Available formats for data input and output including text files, spreadsheets (.xls and .wks) and GiveWin format (.in7). Formats for graphics output include Postscript (.eps, .epc), bitmaps (.png) and GiveWin format (.gwg). The estimation module can also be run without the Java front end, and called from another Ox program. This provides both a straightforward command line operating mode, if preferred, and the ability to (for example) incorporate the code in Monte Carlo simulations.

TSMod is a new project, still very much under development. Planned extensions include more ARCH variants, VAR models with cointegration and fractional cointegration, bootstrap tests, and more self-coding features including test statistics.

J. Davidson (2003), Moment and memory properties of linear conditional heteroscedasticity models, and a new model, *Journal of Business and Economics Statistics*, forthcoming.

6. No longer supported econometric software programs

The packages described in this section are historically significant, but are now no longer supported. In one case, the package has been absorbed into a sibling package,

In other cases, particularly that of EPS and XSIM, the packages have become victims of the merger and acquisition process.

DAMSEL

The original author of DAMSEL is Douglas Bracy. This software is an extension of the PLANETS software, originally created at the Brookings Institution by Bracy during the period 1968–1971, becoming operational on a Digital Equipment Corporation PDP-10 there in 1971. As DAMSEL, the software was adopted by Wharton Econometric Forecasting Associates in 1974 and implemented on a series of IBM 360/370 computers between then and 1985, when it began to be replaced by AREMOS, although it continued to be used to some degree even as late as 1988 or possibly later.

DAMSEL provided support for the maintenance of Wharton's large scale data bases and general analytic facilities, including in particular parameter estimation and single equation model simulations and forecasts, but stopped short of incorporating multi-equation model solution capabilities, which were provided by the SIMPLE model solution software beginning in the early 1980s, and by Brian Brown's "WEFA Batch Solution Program" and other programs prior to that. During the mid 1970s, on a quarterly basis, the Wharton US quarterly model was made available to WEFA clients in the context of Brown's program. Once mounted on the client's mainframe computer, this software could be used either to replicate the Wharton quarterly model forecasts, or to develop alternative forecasts on the basis of and as extensions of these. In principle, of course, independent forecasts could also have been made, but there is no known instance of this. In the late 1970s, online model building and solution support for client and WEFA models was provided in the form of four programs: USER MODELS, SETUP, SOLUTION and TABLES, used respectively to code, edit and maintain models; create, edit, and maintain solution files; solve models; and to create and print tables.

D.B. Bracy (1972), *PLANETS: Programming Language for the Analysis of Economic Time Series*, Washinton, DC: Social Science Computing Center, Brookings Institution.

D.B. Bracy, B.W. Brown, J.M. Golderer, M.O. Procter, D.M. Rowe, G.R. Schink and W. Serad (1975), *Computer Programs Available for Distribution*, Wharton Econometric Forecasting Associates, Philadelphia, PA.

B. Brown (1975), WEFA batch solution program, WEFA Program Usage Guide #2, in: *Computer Programs Available for Distribution*, D.B. Bracy, B.W. Brown, J.M. Golderer, M.O. Procter, D.M. Rowe, G.R. Schink and W. Serad, eds, Wharton Econometric Forecasting Associates, Philadelphia, PA.

G.R. Green and I. Green, eds (1973), *The Wharton Short Term Forecasting System Computer Programs* **3**, Wharton Econometric Forecasting Associates, Philadelphia, PA.

C.G. Renfro (1980), Economic Database Systems: Some Reflections on the State of the Art, *Review of Public Data Use* **8**, 121–140.

D. Sheinson (1973), SOLVEM model solution program, in: *The Wharton Short Term Forecasting System Computer Programs*, G.R. Green and I. Green, eds, Vol. 3, Wharton Econometric Forecasting Associates, Philadelphia, PA.

Wharton Econometric Forecasting Associates (1979), *WEFA User Guide: DAMSEL. WEFATS Data Management System and Econometric Language*, Wharton Econometric Forecasting Associates, Philadelphia, PA.

EPS

The original principal author and designer of EPS is Robert Lacey, with important design contributions by Robert Hall and Edward Green. It was introduced by Data Resources Inc. (DRI) in 1977–1978 and replaced the EPL software originally developed by Robert Hall during the period 1968–1977, which was in turn based on TSP. By the early 1980s, the responsibility for maintaining and updating EPS became a corporate activity. The original installation was on a Burroughs B6700 and then a B7700. EPS was ported to the IBM mainframe environment in the mid-1980s as EPS/VM. A version for the PC, implemented as a DOS package, became operational in or about 1990. With the merger of the WEFA Group and DRI, to form Global Insight in late 2002 or early 2003, EPS has apparently ceased to be a supported product and is currently in a winding down phase.

A fundamental characteristic of EPS was its design to be used in conjunction with large scale multi-frequency databases, both created by DRI and licensed from other organizations worldwide. During the 1970s, DRI data banks in the aggregate grew to contain literally millions of time series pertaining to a number of national economies, as well as sub-national regions and certain super-national aggregates. EPS began its life as software designed to be used in-house by DRI economists and by DRI clients as a mainframe time-sharing package, accessible from a remote telecommunications terminal; for many years it was used in this form (Renfro, 1980).

Generally characterized by a free-format, if slightly stylized, command language, EPS permits its users to access and query data retrieved from data banks and, beyond that, to select series by mnemonic name in the context of a variety of commands, including both display (PRINT, plotting, table-making) and regression commands. The software supports a wide variety of data transformations, incorporating both arithmetic symbols and an array of implicit functions. It also supports such operations as seasonal adjustment, as well as a number of financial functions and operations.

However, if the general sense of the package from a user's perspective has always been its noticeably user-friendly, command-oriented facility to be used interactively for general analytic work, it is nevertheless true that EPS provides broad support for data base management, parameter estimation, and the construction and use of econometric models, albeit mainly small models. Since the late 1970s/early 1980s, EPS has always generically included econometric model solution capabilities, but for large DRI models, such as the US quarterly model, several standalone packages, considered to be more efficient, were successively used by DRI economists. By name, the PC solution packages used include e*model, PC*model, and model 386.

Data Resources (1978), *EPS Reference Manual*, Data Resources, Lexington, MA.

Data Resources (1979), *EPS On-line: An Example Session*, fourth printing, Data Resources, Lexington, MA.
A. Drud (1983), A survey of model representations and simulation algorithms in some existing modeling systems, *Journal of Economic Dynamics & Control* **5**, 5–36.
W. Raduchel and O. Eckstein (1983), Economic Modeling Languages: the DRI Experience, *Journal of Economic Dynamics and Control* **5**, 59–74.
C.G. Renfro (1980), Economic Database Systems: Some Reflections on the State of the Art, *Review of Public Data Use* **8**, 121–140.

PcFiml

PcFiml was the multiple-equation counterpart of PcGive. Technical and methodological limitations forced the initial PC-implementation to be a separate program. The first version was PC-FIML 5 (1987, released with PC-GIVE 5), see Hendry, Neale and Srba, 1988. PcGive version numbering was followed subsequently, except for version 7 which never existed. Version 6.01 was the last of the FORTRAN generation, and already incorporated the Johansen (1988) cointegration procedure. Version 8 extended much of the single-equation testing methodology of PcGive to the multiple-equation setting. As of PcGive 10, however, PcFiml is a fully integrated part of PcGive, and ceased to exist as a stand-alone program.

J.A. Doornik (1995), *Econometric Computing. Oxford: University of Oxford*, Unpublished Ph.D Thesis.
J.A. Doornik and D.F. Hendry (1994), *PcFiml 8: An Interactive Program for Modelling Econometric Systems*, International Thomson Publishing, London.
S. Johansen (1988), Statistical analysis of cointegration vectors, *Journal of Economic Dynamics and Control* **12**, 231–254.
D.F. Hendry, A.J. Neale and F. Srba (1988), Econometric analysis of small linear systems using PC-FIML, *Journal of Econometrics* **38**, 203–226.

XSIM

The original principal author of XSIM is Mark Eisner. It originated as a commercial extension of the TROLL package and was developed in the late 1970s, organizationally, by Dynamics Associates for Interactive Data Corporation/Chase Econometric Associates (IDC/CEA); Dynamics Associates subsequently became part of IDC, which in turn was owned by Chase Manhattan Bank. XSIM was designed to operate in a time sharing environment, supporting both economists and other employees of Chase Econometrics and the Interactive Data Corporation and clients of these firms. It was also licensed by IDC/CEA clients during the 1980s for inhouse corporate use on their own IBM and IBM-compatible mainframe computers. When used as a time shared system, it could be accessed from a remote telecommunications terminal using either a voice grade or dedicated line (Renfro, 1980).

Seen as econometric modeling language software, the program was designed as a broadly based system incorporating data base management, parameter estimation, model solution, tabular report generation, and graphics displays. The parameter estimation facilities offered included the standard time-oriented techniques commonly used at the beginning of the 1980s. However, it also included a relatively comprehensive high level programming language that provided support for the development of both macro command facilities and XSIM applications that were capable of creating an intermediate command interface. Such applications, developed in an XSIM framework, included a broad range of both economic and financial applications, each as a type of expert system. For example, one such application was &FORECAST (Fay, 1981), which was intended to provide access to XSIM's model solution facilities without requiring the user to learn the full set of XSIM commands.

XSIM was developed to be used with large scale economic and financial data bases, both those created and maintained by IDC/CEA and those licensed from other organizations worldwide.

A. Drud (1983), A survey of model representations and simulation algorithms in some existing modeling systems, *Journal of Economic Dynamics & Control* **5**, 5–36.

Dynamics Associates (1979), *Economic Forecasting in XSIM User's Guide*, Interactive Data Corporation, Waltham, MA.

D. Fay (1981), *&FORECAST: General Model Simulator User's Manual and Reference Manual*, Chase Econometric Forecasting Associates, Bala Cynwyd, PA.

C.G. Renfro (1980), Economic Database Systems: Some Reflections on the State of the Art, *Review of Public Data Use* **8**, 121–140.